Brief Review in United States History and Government

Bonnie-Anne Briggs
Catherine Fish Petersen

72-77
Review 25-29

P 196-199
1 DBQ
P 240-243
DBQ
P 420-435
1-50

ORDER INFORMATION

Send orders to:
PRENTICE HALL
CUSTOMER SERVICE CENTER
P.O. Box 2500
Lebanon, IN 46052

or
CALL TOLL-FREE: 1-800-848-9500
(8:00 A.M.–4:30 P.M.)

- Orders are processed when you call.
- Your price includes all shipping and handling.

Also available from Prentice Hall to help you meet the requirements of the Regents:

Brief Review in Global History and Geography

PEARSON
Prentice
Hall

Boston, Massachusetts
Upper Saddle River, New Jersey

ISBN 0-13-133587-1
1 2 3 4 5 6 7 8 9 10   10 09 08 07 06

Contents

About This Book

This book has been written to help you, the student, review your United States history and government courses in order to take the New York State Regents Examination. The purpose of this book is to:

- Help you focus on the key facts, themes, and concepts tested on the Regents Examination.
- Familiarize you with the format of the Regents Examination.
- Provide you with the test-taking skills you need to succeed on the Regents Examination.

Content Review Just like the New York State Core Curriculum, this book is organized into seven units.

- The concepts and content that are consistently tested are emphasized in this text.
- Special emphasis has been given to the second unit on United States government and constitutional history to 1865.
- The charts, maps, cartoons, timelines, and graphic organizers in this text will help reinforce your understanding of the content.
- *The Big Idea* notes at the beginning of each section organize the section content at a glance.
- *Key Themes and Concepts* notes summarize important content and link it to the key themes and concepts of United States history and government.

Test-Taking Skills You can practice your test-taking skills on a variety of Regents Examination questions throughout the book.

- Every multiple-choice question has been on a New York State Regents Examination.
- Document-based essay questions, thematic essay questions, and multiple-choice questions are provided in each history and government unit of the book.
- **Six** sample Regents Examinations are provided for additional practice.
- For online test-taking practice, multiple-choice questions and document-based essay questions are available at the Prentice Hall Web site at **www.phschool.com.**
- An extensive Test-Taking Strategies section teaches you the skills and strategies you need for the exam.
- *Preparing for the Exam* notes in the margins help reinforce test-taking skills and strategies.

ABOUT THE AUTHORS

Bonnie-Anne Briggs is a graduate of Nazareth College of Rochester and the State University of New York at Brockport. She retired in June 2002 from her position as teacher and Teacher-in-Charge of Social Studies (department head) at Gates Chili High School in suburban Rochester. She continues to be an adjunct professor in social studies education at the State University of New York at Brockport. Miss Briggs is currently treasurer of the Rochester Area Council for the Social Studies and is a past president of that organization. She is also a past officer of both the New York State Social Studies Supervisory Association and the New York State Council for the Social Studies. Miss Briggs is a recipient of the Rochester Area Council Distinguished Educator Award, the New York State Social Studies Supervisory Association Supervisor of the Year Award, the New York State Council for the Social Studies Distinguished Educator Award, and the Outstanding Alumni Award from Nazareth College of Rochester. She has been inducted into the Gates Chili High School Alumni Hall of Fame, and in 1993, she was a semi-finalist for the New York State Teacher of the Year Award.

Catherine Fish Petersen is a graduate of Wellesley College, Harvard University, and the State University of New York at Stony Brook. Ms. Petersen was the consultant to the New York State Education Department on the *Social Studies Curriculum Resource Guide* and is their social studies consultant for the New York State Academy for Teaching and Learning. In addition to her position with the state education department, she currently serves as an educational consultant on social studies curriculum to BOCES as well as school districts.

Before retirement, she chaired the Department of Humanities (Social Studies and English) in the East Islip School District on Long Island. She served two terms as the president of the New York State Social Studies Supervisory Association. Currently, she is the executive secretary/treasurer of the Long Island Council for the Social Studies and is a past president of that organization. She has served on the Board of Directors of the New York State Council for the Social Studies. The Long Island Council for the Social Studies has awarded Ms. Petersen the Presidential Award for Outstanding Leadership in Social Studies Education. She is also a recipient of the New York State Social Studies Supervisory Association Supervisor of the Year Award as well as that organization's Special Service Award. The New York State Council for the Social Studies named her its 1998 recipient of the Distinguished Social Studies Service Award.

Test-Taking Strategies

HOW TO SUCCEED ON THE REGENTS EXAM IN SOCIAL STUDIES

This section of the book is intended to help you prepare to take the Regents Examination itself. Other parts of the book review the contents of the course you have studied. This section includes hints about preparing for and actually taking the examination based on test-taking skills you have probably been developing for years in social studies classes. Read and think carefully about all parts of this section as you prepare for the examination.

PREPARING TO TAKE THE REGENTS EXAMINATION

1. **Attend review sessions.** If review sessions are offered by your teacher or school, attend them. You will probably be reminded of something you studied earlier in the year and have not thought of since then. Review sessions also help you bring together the main ideas of the whole course.
2. **Find a study partner.** Two heads can be better than one. Try to review with a friend or a family member who can give you the chance to explain various parts of this course. You will have a better chance of remembering details if you have already explained them correctly to someone else. It has been said that the best way to learn something is to teach it to someone else.
3. **Do not "over-study."** As important as it is to review carefully and over a period of time for your exams, do not make the mistake of "over-studying" or cramming at the last minute. This could leave you exhausted and unable to think clearly during the exam itself. This exam is important enough for you to ask your employer for time off right before the test.
4. **Eat a good meal.** Eat something before the exam so your energy level stays high.
5. **Know the exam site.** Be sure you know the correct time and place of the examination. Arriving half an hour late can make the difference between passing and failing. Be sure someone else at your house has a schedule of your exams.
6. **Be prepared.** Bring several dark ink pens and pencils.
7. **Wear a watch, if possible.** You will need to pay close attention to the time during the exam, and you might be seated where you cannot see a clock.

8. **Stay for the full allotted time.** Come to the exam prepared to stay for the full three-hour examination period. Do not tell someone to pick you up in two hours—you will need all the time allowed. Don't sacrifice a year's worth of work to get outside faster on a nice day.

TAKING THE REGENTS EXAMINATION

1. **Arrive on time.** Use a reliable method of getting to school so you can arrive early in the exam room. This will allow you to get your mind on the task at hand.
2. **Select a seat.** If you are allowed to select your own seat, be sure to choose one with the least distraction. Choose one away from doors or windows.
3. **Dress comfortably.** You will be sitting in one place for a long period of time, so be sure you are comfortably dressed.
4. **Listen to instructions.** Pay full attention to all instructions given by the proctor(s).
5. **Read directions carefully.** Read all directions written on the test booklet as you take the exam. If you have reviewed well, you will be familiar with the terms *discuss, explain, show,* and *describe.* Nonetheless, take the time to read carefully the instructions given to you on the test.
6. **Be an active test-taker.** Become a participant in the exam, not a spectator. You may write on the exam. Underline key ideas. You may write in the margins as you think about the questions. The idea is for you to interact with the exam. Other hints are given as you review the multiple-choice questions from the practice examination.
7. **DON'T leave blanks.** No credit can be given for a blank on either multiple-choice or essay questions. Write something. Write anything, but never leave an answer blank.

THE MULTIPLE-CHOICE SECTION

Part I of the Regents Examination is made up of 50 multiple-choice questions. These questions tend to fall into certain categories that you can identify as you take an examination. The following is about identifying these categories and improving your ability to answer certain types of questions. Samples of these questions come from the June 2000 sample exam.

Data-Based Questions

Data-based questions provide specific information to be used in answering a question or questions. You will probably not be able to answer the question(s) without this information, and you will also need to know some social studies background to help interpret the information. There are several types of data-based questions.

READING PASSAGES Some questions on the practice exam are based on a selected reading passage. These questions often require an ability to recognize opinions expressed in a passage.

If there are words you are unsure of in the selection, try to find a root word you know. Be sure to look for dates or other historical references to help you. You may write notes in the margin near the selection.

EXAMPLE:

"To take a single step beyond these specific [Constitutional] limits to the powers of Congress is to grasp unlimited power.

"The power to create a [national] bank has not, in my opinion, been delegated to Congress by the Constitution. Supporters of the Bank Bill argue that a [national] bank would be a great convenience in collecting taxes. Even if this argument were true, the Constitution allows only for laws which are 'necessary,' not those which are merely 'convenient' for carrying out delegated powers."

The speaker is basing his argument mainly on a strict interpretation of which provision of the federal Constitution?
1 Preamble
2 elastic clause
3 judicial review
4 apportionment of representatives

Answer: The correct answer is 2. The phrase "laws which are 'necessary'" near the end of the reading passage should help you make an association with the elastic clause or "*necessary* and proper" clause. As you read this book, you will find key vocabulary and social studies phrases highlighted throughout.

SPEAKER QUESTIONS Speaker questions present different reading passages by different people on the same topic. When answering speaker questions, follow these steps:
- Determine the theme or topic that all of the speakers are addressing.
- Read the questions before you study the speakers' statements too closely; often you do not have to read each speaker's viewpoint to answer a question.
- Be sure you are reading the correct speaker when answering each question.
- Take your time when answering speaker questions. You will probably need to go back and forth among the readings as you analyze the difference between speakers.

EXAMPLE:

Speaker A: "We cannot make the same mistakes that led to the sinking of the *Lusitania*. Freedom of the seas is important, but we must keep our ships away from possible danger."

Speaker B: "We should encourage Great Britain and France to follow a policy of appeasement."

Speaker C: "Continued isolation is the only alternative. Whichever way we turn in this conflict, we find an alien ideology."

Speaker D: "The future of the free world depends now on the United States and Great Britain. We must not only help win this war, but also ensure that no others occur in the future."

The speakers are most likely discussing the situation facing the United States just before
1 the American Revolution
2 the Spanish-American War
3 World War II
4 the Korean War

Answer: The correct answer is 3, World War II. Underline all hints such as the phrases *mistake of the* Lusitania, *freedom of the seas, Great Britain and France, appeasement, continued isolation,* and *future of the free world.* The correct answer cannot be the American Revolution or the Spanish-American War, because the sinking of the *Lusitania* occurred after both of those wars. The correct answer cannot be the Korean War, because the United States had abandoned its isolationist policy before the Korean War. All of the hints together indicate that these speakers are discussing the situation facing the United States just before World War II.

GRAPHS Graphs may appear in several forms—bar graphs, line graphs, or pie graphs. Some graphs may provide all of the information that you need to answer the question. Others may require you to draw upon your knowledge of social studies to interpret the graph.

EXAMPLE:

Source: *Statistical Abstract of the United States*

The trend shown in the graph was mainly the result of
1 increases in immigration
2 demands for more schoolteachers
3 a buildup in the defense industry
4 new social attitudes

Answer: The correct answer is 4. The graph indicates a steady increase in the number of women working outside the home between 1955 and 1990. You must draw upon your knowledge of U.S. history to provide the reason for this trend.

TABLES Some questions require you to draw conclusions from information provided in tables. Be *very* careful to base your conclusions only on the information in the table unless the question specifically asks you to do otherwise. Be sure to note the source and date of the information given in the table.

EXAMPLE:

Rural and Urban Populations in the United States		
Year	Rural (thousands)	Urban (thousands)
1860	25,227	6,217
1870	28,656	9,902
1880	36,026	14,130
1890	40,841	22,106
1900	45,835	30,160
1910	49,973	41,999
1920	51,553	54,158

Source: Bureau of the Census

Which statement is best supported by the chart?
1 In the early 1900s, there was an increase in the number of immigrants who became farmers.
2 In the early 1900s, people who lived in cities were more likely to vote than those who lived in rural areas.
3 In 1920, more people lived in cities than on farms.
4 In 1920, there were fewer women working in factories than on farms.

Answer: The correct answer is 3. This question tests your ability to read the table, as well as your understanding of the words *urban* and *rural*. To answer a question such as this, eliminate all possible answers that do not have information given in the chart. For example, answer 1 mentions immigrants, but the table provides no information about immigrants.

POLITICAL CARTOONS Some questions ask you to analyze and interpret a political cartoon. When analyzing a political cartoon, follow these steps:
• Study the caption.
• Look for a date.
• Read all words in the cartoon. Look closely for any small print written on figures or objects in the cartoon.
• Identify the symbolism used by a cartoonist.

EXAMPLE:

According to the cartoon, what was a major contributing factor that led to the collapse of communism in Eastern Europe in the early 1990s?
1 overpopulation   3 democratic elections
2 military force   4 high tax rates

Answer: The correct answer is 3, democratic elections. When analyzing this cartoon, be sure to look very carefully at all parts of the cartoon: the title of the cartoon, the writing on the people's clothing, the symbols used on their clothing, and the words they are saying. The question itself also gives you a good hint about the downfall of communism.

OUTLINES Some questions ask you to complete a hypothetical outline.

EXAMPLE:
In an outline, one of these entries is a main topic and three are subtopics. Which is the main topic?
1 Alexander Hamilton's Economic Program
2 The Rise of National Political Parties
3 The Constitution's First Tests
4 John Adams's Stormy Presidency

Answer: In this question, you are simply asked to determine the main topic. Look for the most general answer. Recognize that the other choices would be subheads on the outline under the main topic. The right choice is 3 because 1, 2, and 4 are examples of the Constitution's first tests.

QUOTATION INTERPRETATION This type of question asks you to explain the idea of a given quotation. Sometimes the date and speaker of the quotation are identified and sometimes not.

EXAMPLE:

"(Sec. 4.) Every person presenting himself for registration shall be able to read and write any section of the Constitution in the English language, and before he shall be entitled to vote, he shall have paid on or before the first day of March of the year in which he proposes to vote his poll tax as prescribed by law for the previous year."

—Public Laws of North Carolina, 1899, chapter 218

The principle purpose of this law was to
1 assure equality of voting rights for all peoples
2 encourage literacy for former slaves
3 prevent African Americans from using their suffrage rights
4 promote the racial integration of southern society

Answer: The correct answer is 3. The date and place of origin of this quotation are important clues, which should remind you that Jim Crow laws were legal in much of the South at the end of the 1800s.

MAPS When maps are given, be sure to look for the following:
• A key explaining any symbols used
• Dates
• Specific place locations
• Compass point for directions

TIMELINES A timeline is a graphic way of showing relationships among events over time. Questions dealing with timelines often ask you to draw a conclusion about a series of events. When answering timeline questions, be careful to focus on the time period shown; do not jump to a different era to answer the question.

Other Multiple-Choice Questions
Many other types of multiple-choice questions appear on the Regents Examination.

"HEADLINE" QUESTIONS In this type of question, you are given a few sample headlines that usually have to do with a common event. Your goal is to determine the connection between the headlines.

EXAMPLE:

"Raise Tariffs!"
"Buy American!"
"Impose Import Quotas!"

Which policy do these slogans reflect?
1 militarism   3 isolationism
2 protectionism   4 détente

Answer: The correct answer is 2. The subject of all three headlines is economics and trade. The words and phrases *tariffs, buy American,* and *import quotas* suggest foreign trade. The only possible answer that deals with foreign trade is protectionism.

RECALL QUESTIONS These questions require you to know specific information about people, events, topics, concepts, and vocabulary studied in the course. Throughout this review book, you will find many suggestions about test-taking strategies, as well as references to the many important people and events covered in this course. There is also a glossary at the end of this book to help you with vocabulary.

EXAMPLE:

At the Constitutional Convention of 1787, a bicameral legislature was proposed as the solution to the disagreement over
1 taxation within each state
2 control of interstate commerce
3 limits on the treaty-making power of a President
4 state representation in the national government

Answer: The correct answer is 4. The key to answering this question correctly is understanding the meaning of the term *bicameral legislature* and the reason for its proposal.

CAUSE-AND-EFFECT QUESTIONS These questions test your understanding of the concepts of cause and effect. A cause is an event or action that brings about another event or action—an effect. Your study of history will have revealed that almost everything is either the cause or result of some event.

EXAMPLE:

Which factor contributed most directly to the settlement and development of the Great Plains after the Civil War?
1 freeing of the slaves in Southern states
2 construction of railroads west of the Mississippi River
3 influx of immigrants from eastern and southern Europe
4 hospitality of the Indian tribes inhabiting the region

Answer: The correct answer is 2. The use of the newly developed railroad as transportation was key to the western development (choice 2). Choice 1 is wrong because the freed slaves did not move west, and 3 is wrong because those immigrants generally stayed in urban areas to work in factories. Note the word *hospitality* in choice 4. Few of the Indian tribes welcomed the arrival of the settlers on the plains.

TIME REFERENCE OR CHRONOLOGY QUESTIONS These are questions that make reference to a particular time period. You rarely need to identify specific dates on Regents exams. However, you often do need to know the time sequence or order of events.

EXAMPLE:

In the period between World War I and World War II, which group made the greatest gains in political rights?
1 African Americans
2 women
3 new immigrants
4 Native Americans

Answer: The correct answer is 2. With a question like this, it is a good idea to write the dates of the period above the question so that you can focus on that specific time. Remember, a condition that was true in one time period may cease to exist in another time period. When answering this question, you should remember that the Nineteenth Amendment granting women the right to vote was passed in 1920 (between the wars). Not until well *after* World War II did the other groups make great gains in their political rights.

GENERALIZATIONS These questions require you to make a general statement about a particular event, time period, or body of information. You are really being asked to draw a conclusion.

EXAMPLE:

A primary aim of the writers of the United States Constitution was to
1 strengthen the power of the central government
2 change from a government based on division of powers to one based on a single power
3 develop a governmental system based on the principle of supremacy of the states
4 weaken the power of the executive

Answer: The correct answer is 1. This question asks you to explain why the Constitution was written. To do so, you need to recall the problems of the Articles of Confederation. Choice 1 is correct because the Constitution does establish a strong central government.

FACT AND OPINION These questions require you to find a statement that is clearly either fact or opinion. If you keep in mind that certain words such as *most important, most significant,* and *greatest contribution* signal opinions, you should have no trouble with this type of question. It is difficult to make true statements that include the words *always, never, all,* or *none.*

SOURCES AND REFERENCES Some questions test your ability to identify a valid source of information. A primary source is one written or told by someone who was present at an event. These sources can be biased, but they can also give a special insight into an event. Secondary sources, such as textbooks, are those that are written after an event.

QUESTIONS ABOUT SOCAL SCIENTISTS Some questions ask about the jobs of certain types of social scientists. These might include the following:

Historian: a person who studies the past and makes judgments about why events happened and how they affected other events

Economist: a person who studies the monetary systems of countries or cultures. The work of economists is important to our understanding of events such as the Great Depression.

Political scientist: a person who studies the workings of government and politics. For example, political scientists analyze the results of elections to determine trends in voting patterns.

THE THEMATIC ESSAY

There will be one thematic essay on your examination. The score on the thematic essay ranges from 0 to 5 points, using a generic scoring rubric. You should become familiar with this rubric as you prepare for the exam, because it will help you learn how to write the most effective essay possible.

You will not have a choice of theme or topic, but you will have many choices within the provided list of suggested examples you may draw upon in writing your essay. You may choose examples that are not on the list of suggestions, but that approach may not be a good idea. The most frequently studied examples are the ones that are usually given in the suggestions.

Blocking Essay Answers

Blocking an essay will help you organize your ideas before you write your answer. Organizing your thoughts before writing will help you earn more points on the essay and avoid leaving out parts of the essay. Experts in helping students prepare for tests know that the more involved you become with a test, the better you will do on it.

STEPS IN BLOCKING AN ESSAY

1. Underline the words that tell you what you need to do: *discuss, describe, explain,* etc.
2. Study the directions next to each bulleted point (•).
3. Use those directions to form headings for your block.
4. Under each section of your block, write facts to help you answer that part of the question.
5. Review to see if you have completed all parts of the *Task.*
6. Check to see that your introduction and conclusion show thought and are not just a repetition of the ones you are given in the question.
7. When you have arranged all your facts in the section of the block, check to be sure you have not left any blocks empty.

SAMPLE BLOCK

This chart blocks the thematic essay that is part of the June 2004 sample Regents examination at the back of this book.

	Two actions	Discuss historical circumstances that resulted in government actions	Discuss influence of a geographic factor (location, physical environment, actions, movement of people, climate resources)	Impact of action on U. S.
Sample answer	Louisiana Purchase	France wanted and needed to sell area much cheaper than U. S. expected to buy; President Jefferson decided the government could purchase the land	U. S. could expand to the west and end French presence on U. S. western border	Gave U. S. chance to double size of territory to allow for future growth and exploration for new resources. U. S. set precedent that it could add additional territory

THEMATIC ESSAY SCORING RUBRIC

SCORE OF 5:
- Thoroughly develops all aspects of the task evenly and in depth
- Is more analytical than descriptive (analyzes, evaluates, and/or creates* information)
- Richly supports the theme with many relevant facts, examples, and details
- Demonstrates a logical and clear plan of organization; includes an introduction and a conclusion that are beyond a restatement of the theme

SCORE OF 4:
- Develops all aspects of the task but may do so somewhat unevenly
- Is both descriptive and analytical (applies, analyzes, evaluates, and/or creates information)
- Supports the theme with relevant facts, examples, and details
- Demonstrates a logical and clear plan of organization; includes an introduction and a conclusion that are beyond a restatement of the theme

SCORE OF 3:
- Develops all aspects of the task with little depth or develops most aspects of the task in some depth
- Is more descriptive than analytical (applies, may analyze, and/or evaluate information)
- Includes some relevant facts, examples, and details; may include some minor inaccuracies
- Demonstrates a satisfactory plan of organization; includes an introduction and a conclusion that may be a restatement of the theme

SCORE OF 2:
- Minimally develops all aspects of the task or develops some aspects of the task in some depth
- Is primarily descriptive; may include faulty, weak, or isolated application or analysis
- Includes few relevant facts, examples, and details; may include some inaccuracies
- Demonstrates a general plan of organization; may lack focus; may contain digressions; may not clearly identify which aspect of the task is being addressed; may lack an introduction and/or a conclusion

SCORE OF 1:
- Minimally develops some aspects of the task
- Is descriptive; may lack understanding, application, or analysis
- Includes few relevant facts, examples, or details; may include inaccuracies
- May demonstrate a weakness in organization; may lack focus; may contain digressions; may not clearly identify which aspect of the task is being addressed; may lack an introduction and/or a conclusion

SCORE OF 0:
Fails to develop the task or may only refer to the theme in a general way; *OR* includes no relevant facts, examples, or details; *OR* includes only the theme, task, or suggestions as copied from the test booklet; *OR* is illegible; *OR* is a blank paper

DOCUMENT-BASED ESSAY QUESTION

There will be one document-based essay question (DBQ) on the examination. The score on the document-based essay question ranges from 0 to 5 points, using a generic scoring rubric. You should become familiar with this rubric as you prepare for the exam, because it will help you learn how to write the most effective essay possible.

The DBQ has two important parts. Part A includes the scaffolding questions in which you examine documents individually and complete short-answer questions. Part B is the essay question in which you draw upon your analysis of the documents and your knowledge of United States history and government to write the essay. You must complete all sections of both parts. There are several steps you should take to ensure success in answering the DBQ:

- **Read the *Historical Context* section carefully.** This sets the time frame in which all parts of the question are set. It also limits the time period that you can write about in your answer. Remember to highlight or underline important data.
- **Read and understand the *Task*.** Read this part carefully to be sure that you complete all parts. Underline any parts of the test that you do not want to forget or overlook.
- **Do not leave any blanks on the scaffolding question section.** Any blanks you leave will cause you to lose points automatically.
- **Keep track of main ideas/block your essay.** As you work through the scaffolding questions, write down the main idea or ideas of each document on your scrap paper. Briefly listing the main ideas of each document will help you organize your thoughts so that you can successfully support your viewpoint in the essay. You may choose to organize the main ideas by creating a simple chart.

Sample Block or Prewriting Outline

The chart on the next page blocks the document-based essay question that is part of the June 2004 sample Regents examination at the back of this book.

Writing the Document-Based Essay Question

Use the list you created while answering the scaffolding questions to help guide the writing of your essay. Using the question from the June 2004 Regents, you should have a list of social, political and economic changes from the given documents. Be sure to note that not all of the changes have to be positive and that some changes definitely had a negative impact on the Untied States.

In your essay, you should take care to draw as much information out of the documents as you can. However, you should also include other information from your knowledge of United States history if that information helps support your viewpoint. In the document-based essay question from the sample Regents examination, for example, you could also include information about other changes that occured such as the work of Martin Luther King, Jr., Rosa Parks, Civil Rights legislation of the 1960's, etc.

Be sure to study carefully the *Guidelines* that are provided in the instructions on writing the document-based essay question. These *Guidelines* will remind you of what you must include in order to score the full five points for the essay.

Document (number and source)	Type of Change (social, political, economic)	Specific Application
1 14th Amendment	political	gave persons natural born or naturalized citizenship
2 F. Douglass	economic	freed slaves that were not given land, money or other assistance to help them get stared as free citizens
3 Senate document	social, political	KKK depriving freed slaves basic human rights, i.e. life, liberty as well as new political right to vote
4 Plantation map	economic	slaves had a right to be tenant farmers, big plantations had been subdivided, therefore change for the old "elite" or Master too
5 Harper's Magazine	economic and social	multiple examples of new types businesses in the south in 1887, iron foundries, cotton mills, train car production
6 separate drinking fountain	social	illustrates separate AND unequal public facilities as recent as the 1950's and 60's
7 Afro-American Council	political	changes did not always happen when they should have, some Southern states made their own laws to deprive African Americans of voting rights
8 NAACP Parade	social, political, economic	shows that in 1917 African Americans were using parades and demonstrations to protest their lack of right to be truly equal (note formal, business dress on marchers)

DOCUMENT-BASED QUESTION ESSAY SCORING RUBRIC

SCORE OF 5:
- Thoroughly develops all aspects of the task evenly and in depth
- Is more analytical than descriptive (analyzes, evaluates, and/or creates information)
- Incorporates relevant information from *at least* **xxx** documents
- Incorporates substantial relevant outside information
- Richly supports the theme with many relevant facts, examples, and details
- Demonstrates a logical and clear plan of organization; includes an introduction and a conclusion that are beyond a restatement of the theme

SCORE OF 4:
- Develops all aspects of the task but may do so somewhat unevenly
- Is both descriptive and analytical (applies, analyzes, evaluates, and/or creates information)
- Incorporates relevant information from *at least* **xxx** documents
- Incorporates relevant outside information
- Supports the theme with relevant facts, examples, and details
- Demonstrates a logical and clear plan of organization; includes an introduction and a conclusion that are beyond a restatement of the theme

SCORE OF 3:
- Develops all aspects of the task with little depth *or* develops most aspects of the task in some depth
- Is more descriptive than analytical (applies, may analyze, and/or evaluate information)
- Incorporates some relevant information from some of the documents
- Incorporates limited relevant outside information
- Includes some relevant facts, examples, and details; may include some minor inaccuracies
- Demonstrates a satisfactory plan of organization; includes an introduction and a conclusion that may be a restatement of the theme

SCORE OF 2:
- Minimally develops all aspects of the task *or* develops some aspects of the task in some depth
- Is primarily descriptive; may include faulty, weak, or isolated application or analysis
- Incorporates limited relevant information from the documents or consists primarily of relevant information copied from the documents
- Presents little or no relevant outside information
- Includes few relevant facts, examples, and details; may include some inaccuracies
- Demonstrates a general plan of organization; may lack focus; may contain digressions; may not clearly identify which aspect of the task is being addressed; may lack an introduction and/or a conclusion

SCORE OF 1:
- Minimally develops some aspects of the task
- Is descriptive; may lack understanding, application, or analysis
- Makes vague, unclear references to the documents or consists primarily of relevant and irrelevant information copied from the documents
- Presents no relevant outside information
- Includes few relevant facts, examples, or details; may include inaccuracies
- May demonstrate a weakness in organization; may lack focus; may contain digressions; may not clearly identify which aspect of the task is being addressed; may lack an introduction and/or a conclusion

SCORE OF 1:
Fails to develop the task or may only refer to the theme in a general way; *OR* includes no relevant facts, examples, or details; includes only the historical context and/or task as copies from the test booklet; *OR* includes only entire documents copied from the test booklet; *OR* is illegible; *OR* is a blank paper

UNIT 1

Geography and the Development of the United States

UNIT OVERVIEW

This unit provides a general review of the physical and cultural geography of the United States. It also reviews some of the ways in which geography has influenced the history of the country. Geographers use five themes to study an area. The five themes are location, place, movement, regions, and human-environment interaction.

These are some of the key questions relating to the nation's geography. Each question relates to one of the five geographic themes:

- Where is the United States located, both absolutely and relatively? How has the country's relative location changed over time?
- What are the physical and human characteristics of the United States?
- How have people, goods, and ideas moved between places?
- How are places within the United States similar to and different from other places?
- How have people in the United States interacted with the natural environment?

KEY THEMES AND CONCEPTS

As you review this unit, take special note of the following key themes and concepts:

Physical Systems How have the nation's systems of mountains and waterways influenced the development of the United States?

Immigration and Migration What have been the major patterns of immigration and movement of people over the course of the country's history?

Places and Regions What different types of regions exist within the United States?

LOCATION

Geographers describe the location of an area in both absolute and relative terms.

Absolute Location

In terms of its absolute location, the United States is located in the Northern and Western hemispheres. With the exception of Hawaii, the country is located on the continent of North America. The country is bordered by the Atlantic Ocean on the east and the Pacific Ocean on the west.

Relative Location

Geographers also consider an area's relative location, or where it is located in relation to other places. For example, the United States is located south of Canada and north of Mexico. California is west of New York.

The relative location of a place can also change over time. For much of the country's history, Americans felt relatively isolated from Europe and Asia. Likewise, people in the West felt relatively isolated from the East.

Changes in transportation and communication technologies changed these perceptions. For example, the number of post offices in the nation leaped from 75 in 1790 to 8,450 in 1830. Regular mail delivery made it easier for people in distant places to communicate with one another. Improved communication and transportation helped tie together different parts of the country as it grew in both size and population.

ANALYZING DOCUMENTS

This map shows the 50 states of the United States.

- Where is New York located in relation to Florida?

- What types of regions are shown on this map?

The United States: Political

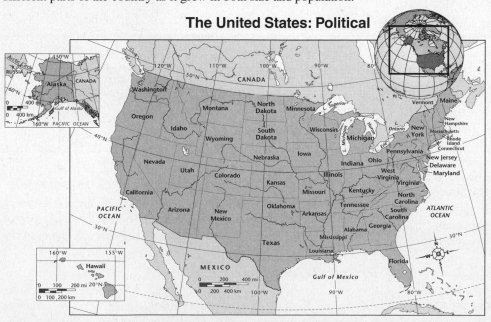

The United States and Canada: Physical

KEY

Elevation

Feet		Meters
Over 13,000		Over 3,960
6,500–13,000		1,980–3,960
1,600–6,500		480–1,980
650–1,600		200–480
0–650		0–200
Below sea level		Below sea level

Lambert Azimuthal Equal-Area Projection

ANALYZING DOCUMENTS

Study the map on this page; then answer the following questions.

- What major landform occupies the central region of the United States?

- Which mountain range is higher, the Appalachians or the Rocky Mountains?

PLACE

Geographers study both the physical and human characteristics of places. Both physical and human characteristics of the geography of the United States have had a huge impact on the development of the country.

Physical Characteristics

Physical characteristics include landforms, water bodies, vegetation, and climate. Because of its size, the United States has a wide variety of landforms. As the map on this page shows, the **Great Plains** and the

Central Plains occupy the central regions of the country, also known as the Midwest. The rich soils and climate of the Midwest encouraged Americans to move to these regions, where they could acquire inexpensive farmland. The **Mississippi River** cuts through the Central Plains as it flows south to the Gulf of Mexico. Boats traveling along the Mississippi allowed farmers and traders to transport their goods to markets throughout the country.

Two mountain ranges run from north to south on either side of the central plains regions. In the east are the lower, older **Appalachian Mountains.** In the west are the **Rocky Mountains.** The Rockies are a cordillera, or a related set of mountain ranges, that stretches from northern Alaska to Mexico, forming the longest mountain chain in North America.

Human Characteristics

Several waves of immigration have created a unique cultural mix of people in the United States. People from every region of the world have settled in the United States. As a result, the region's human characteristics, such as a language, religion, and customs, are varied. About half of all African Americans live in the South. About 9 percent of southern residents are of Latino origin.

In general, population density is greater in the eastern half of the country. The most densely settled region of the country is the Northeast Corridor, which stretches along the east coast from Washington, D.C., to Boston, Massachusetts.

Compared with those in many nations of the world, people in the United States have long life expectancies, high per capita incomes, and high literacy rates.

MOVEMENT

Geographers study the movement of people, goods, and ideas within an area. The movement of people into and within the United States over the course of the region's history can be broken into the following large patterns.

Bering Strait Land Bridge

Geographers believe that during the Ice Ages—between about 20,000 and 12,000 years ago—much of the earth's water was frozen into glaciers and ice sheets. As a result, ocean levels dropped, exposing a flat bridge of land between Alaska and eastern Asia where the Bering Strait is today. Over thousands of years, hunters from East Asia crossed the land bridge and gradually spread out over North and South America. These Paleo-Indians were the first humans in the Americas, ancestors of all the Native American peoples.

ANALYZING DOCUMENTS

The movement of people from east to west put pressure on the government to expand the territory of the United States. Study the map below; then answer the following questions.

- What was the date of the Louisiana Purchase?

- When were the lands of the present-day states of Washington and Oregon added to the country's territory?

- Using the information on this map, describe the acquisition of present-day California.

European Exploration and Slavery

By the 1500s, better ships and navigation methods allowed European explorers to find their way to North America. The first European newcomers, mainly from Spain, settled in what are now Florida, the Southwest, and Mexico. About a century later, people from France and Great Britain set up colonies on the eastern coast of North America. In addition, millions of Africans were enslaved and brought unwillingly to North America.

Migration from East to West

During the 1800s, the promise of land and gold led many Americans of European descent to move westward. Native Americans were forced from their lands to locations even further west. Rivers, wagons, canals, and railroads all played a part in the movement of people to the frontiers of the west. **Manifest destiny** was the concept that expressed the American belief that the United States was destined to expand across North America.

African American Migration

African Americans moved from the South to the Northeast and Midwest in search of economic opportunities from about 1890 to 1920 and again during the 1940s.

The Rise of the Sun Belt

Beginning around 1950, many Americans moved from the industrial cities of the North and Midwest to the so-called **Sun Belt**—the southern states stretching from Florida to California. Newcomers were attracted by job opportunities and warmer climates.

United States Territorial Expansion, 1783–1853

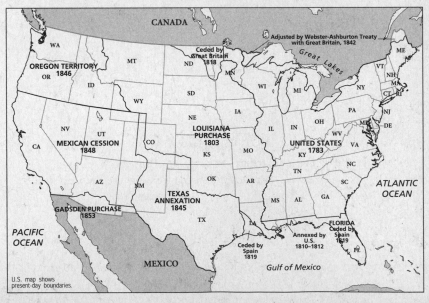

This population shift, along with its corresponding reapportionment of congressional seats, has given the South greater influence in American politics. Once a stronghold for Democrats, the South has become more strongly Republican and conservative.

REGIONS

The continental United States from east to west covers a distance of over three thousand miles. The states of Hawaii in the Pacific Ocean and Alaska in the north Pacific expand the country's geographic dimensions. Given this huge size it is not surprising that geographers can identify hundreds of regions within the country.

Different Types of Regions

Geographers describe regions as places having at least one common characteristic. Regions can be defined by physical characteristics, such as landforms or climate. They can also be defined by cultural characteristics, such as the economy of the area or the political organization of the area. The map on the next page shows regions that share similar economies or land use patterns. Political regions include towns, counties, cities, states, and the United States as a whole.

In the United States, geographers use terms like the Midwest to describe a group of states (Ohio, Indiana, Illinois), or the Northwest (Oregon and Washington) or the Rocky Mountain area. Climatic conditions can cause a region to be identified for its frequency of tornadoes, hurricanes, or snowstorms. The cultural characteristics of people might also designate a region, such as the region around Lancaster, Pennsylvania, where many Amish people live. As you study the history and development of the United States, think about how various immigrant groups gave certain regions distinctive names, for example, New York City's Chinatown.

Regions within New York State

In New York State, some examples of regions include the **Great Lakes** region, the Adirondack Mountains, Long Island, the Finger Lakes, Manhattan, and the Capital District around Albany.

HUMAN-ENVIRONMENT INTERACTION

When studying an area, geographers also examine how people use the environment and how they have changed it. What are the consequences of those changes?

Early Land Use Patterns

From the earliest days of settlement, Americans have been interacting with their environment to survive. When the Europeans began to settle along the Atlantic coast, they faced a range of climatic and geographic

Land Use in the United States

Pacific
Northwest

Northwest

Midwest

West

KEY

☐ Forestry
▨ Livestock Raising
☐ Commercial Farming
■ Manufacturing and Trade
▨ Commercial Fishing

South

Southeast

ANALYZING
DOCUMENTS

Study the land use map on this page; then answer the following questions.

• What is the major land use activity in the Midwest?

• How do the economic activities of the Pacific Northwest compare with those of the Northeast?

• Where are the most concentrated areas of manufacturing and trade located?

conditions. At various points in this nation's history, these conditions both encouraged and discouraged settlement. In some places, Native Americans assisted the Europeans in adapting to their unfamiliar surroundings.

The great Atlantic coastal plain fostered agricultural development in the Mid-Atlantic region, while further to the south, the long, hot summers gave rise to the tobacco and cotton industries. Settlers of coastal South Carolina drained swamps to create thriving rice plantations. The rocky soil of New England discouraged extensive farming, but the rich coastal waters encouraged the development of fishing and shipbuilding. The waterfalls in the area and elsewhere in the Middle Atlantic states encouraged the development of factories that could benefit from water power. These factories produced goods that were then traded all over the world. Port cities, such as Boston, New York, Charleston, Savannah, and New Orleans developed as centers of this trade.

Tourism and Conservation

In addition to the land use patterns shown on the map above, tourism is another form of land use. The national parks are an example of human-environment interaction in which the landscape and natural resources are preserved for the enjoyment of future generations. Niagara Falls, New York, leads a double life as a tourist attraction for its natural beauty and as a major source of hydroelectric power.

It was only in the late twentieth century that many people began to realize the need to protect and preserve the environment for future generations. Today, geographic issues include waste disposal, air and water pollution, energy sources, energy use, and topics related to demographics, such as the changing composition of the population, the "graying" of America, and the effects of the baby boom generation.

LOOKING AHEAD

As you continue through this review book, you will have many opportunities to utilize the concepts of location, place, movement, regions, and human-environment interaction. Use the maps located in this unit and elsewhere in this text to help you draw conclusions about the impact geography has had and continues to have on the development of the United States.

ANALYZING DOCUMENTS

Study the climate map on this page; then answer the following questions.

- Much of the southwestern United States has a hot, dry, arid climate and receives less than 10 inches of rainfall each year. Many people have been moving to this region in recent decades. How do you think climate affects the human-environment interaction in this region?

- Describe the climate of the southeastern half of the United States.

The United States and Canada: Climate Regions

KEY

- Tropical wet
- Tropical wet and dry
- Semiarid
- Arid
- Mediterranean
- Humid subtropical
- Marine west coast
- Humid continental
- Subarctic
- Tundra
- Highlands

Lambert Azimuthal Equal-Area Projection

2 **Constitutional Foundations for the United States Democratic Republic**

Section 1 The Constitution: The Foundation of American Society

Section 2 The Constitution Tested: Nationalism and Sectionalism

UNIT OVERVIEW

Unit 2 covers the period from the first English settlement in 1607 through the end of the Civil War in 1865. The focus of the unit is the Constitution of the United States—its historical and constitutional foundations, including the ways in which the nation's government, based on the Constitution, developed and was then tested.

Some of the key questions about the United States government and constitutional history through 1865 include:

- What was the influence of the colonial settlement pattern, colonists' experience living in the American colonies, colonial slavery, and Enlightenment thought on the development of the United States Constitution?
- What opinions about government were discussed and debated by the Framers? What compromises did they reach in order to create the Constitution and ensure approval by the states?
- What is the structure of the United States Constitution, and how does the government it describes function?
- What are the basic constitutional principles of American democracy? Why were they important when the Constitution was written? Why have they remained critical principles throughout United States history?
- How did the new nation go about putting its constitution into effect? What helped to build nationalism? What conflicting opinions about government were discussed and debated in those early years?
- How did sectionalism and slavery bring on a constitutional crisis that led the nation to civil war?

The Constitution: The Foundation of American Society

SECTION OVERVIEW

For centuries, the only inhabitants of North American were Native Americans. In the 1600s, English settlers arrived to found colonies and were soon joined by other Europeans, as well as Africans brought as slaves. By the mid-1700s, tensions between the colonies and Great Britain increased sharply. The colonies declared independence and won the American Revolution. They established a weak central government under the Articles of Confederation, but in 1787 replaced that with the United States Constitution that is still the guiding document of this nation today.

KEY THEMES AND CONCEPTS

Take special note of the following key themes and concepts:

Diversity In what ways did the Native Americans, Europeans, and Africans who met in North America differ?

Citizenship What led the colonists to rebel against the British government?

Foreign Policy Why did France forge an alliance with the colonists during the American Revolution?

Constitutional Principles How does the Constitution ensure that no single part of the government can gain too much power?

KEY PEOPLE

Be sure you understand the significance of these key people:

John Adams
Samuel Adams
Benjamin Franklin
Alexander Hamilton
Patrick Henry
Thomas Jefferson
John Locke
James Madison

John Marshall
James Monroe
Baron de Montesquieu
Jean-Jacques Rousseau
Voltaire
George Washington
John Peter Zenger

★ **THE BIG IDEA**
The Constitution is the foundation of American society. The United States

- developed from 13 English colonies.

- developed its political system based on British traditions, Enlightenment thought, and American experience.

- won independence in the American Revolution.

- bases its government around the 1787 U.S. Constitution.

KEY TERMS

French and Indian War
indentured servants
triangular trade
Middle Passage
republic
Enlightenment
natural rights
charter
House of Burgesses
Albany Plan of Union
salutary neglect
Proclamation of 1763
mercantilism
Stamp Act
First Continental Congress
Second Continental Congress
Declaration of Independence
Articles of Confederation

23

GEOGRAPHY IN HISTORY

How did the environment influence the culture of Native Americans?

 PREPARING FOR THE EXAM

On the examination, you will need to have a thorough understanding of important United States historical and governmental terms.

- What is a confederacy?
- What are two examples of confederacies in United States history?

PART 1 THE HISTORICAL FOUNDATIONS OF AMERICAN SOCIETY AND GOVERNMENT

Before examining the Constitution of the United States and the features that make it unique, it is important to understand the roots of the ideas in that document. To do that, we must start with the historical origins of the United States of America.

THE PEOPLES AND PEOPLING OF THE COLONIES

In North America, three different cultures came together—Native Americans (the original inhabitants), Europeans, and Africans brought as slaves.

NATIVE AMERICANS

Native Americans were the first people to occupy the Western Hemisphere. In the late 1400s, they numbered as many as 15 million in North America alone. The way of life of Native Americans was heavily influenced by the environment. The eastern Native American lifestyle was based on agriculture, hunting, and fishing. Trade was an important part of this economic system.

Native American religious beliefs were closely linked to nature. Another feature of their way of life was their strong social organizations based on ties between extended families, with women in positions of some power in some tribes.

The Iroquois Confederacy

The most powerful government of the eastern woodlands' Indians was that of the Iroquois. The Iroquois Confederacy, formed in 1570, was made up of first five and then six Iroquois nations located in central and western New York. At the peak of its power between 1644 and 1700, the Confederacy made it possible for the Iroquois to hold onto its lands against European pressure for almost two centuries.

Trade and Alliances

Relations between colonists and Native Americans often centered around trade and exchange, alliances, or warfare. The survival of the English settlers depended on Indian crops, such as corn and squash. Native Americans' interactions with the settlers led to outbreaks of deadly diseases, such as measles and smallpox.

Patterns of trade developed that influenced later relations between the settlers and Native Americans. For example, the Iroquois wanted control of the fur trade between the Great Lakes region and New York.

In the 1640s and 1650s, the Iroquois fought the Huron and Erie tribes, which threatened French dominance in that region. Wars with France ended only in 1701 when the Iroquois adopted a neutrality policy toward France and England.

The survival of Jamestown, founded in 1607 as the first permanent English settlement in North America, must be credited in part to the food supplied by the many Algonquin tribes that made up the Powhatan Confederacy. Powhatan was motivated by the possibility of the Europeans allying with him in his wars with other tribes.

Different Views and Values

Land control was the central conflict between Native Americans and colonists. Native Americans held land in common and believed it should be used for the good of all. It could not be bought or sold, although the rights to the use of land could be transferred. The English valued individual ownership and had a tradition of buying and selling land.

Secondly, there were cultural and technological differences. The European colonists believed in the superiority of their way of life and acted accordingly. They attempted to convert the Native Americans to Christianity and assumed that they would adopt an English lifestyle.

Warfare

Profitable tobacco farming led settlers to move into Native American

KEY THEMES AND CONCEPTS

Interdependence

Contact between Native Americans and English colonists was not always hostile. The Powhatan Confederacy, for example, provided food to the Jamestown settlers to help them survive. What was their motivation for helping the colonists?

ANALYZING DOCUMENTS

Examine the cartoon, then answer the following questions.

- Which groups do the speakers in this cartoon represent?

- What point is the cartoonist making about immigration to the United States?

ANALYZING DOCUMENTS

"I am now grown old , and must soon die; . . . Why should you take by force that from us which you can have by love? Why should you destroy us, who have provided you with food? . . . What is the cause of your jealousy? You see us unarmed, and willing to supply your wants, if you come in a friendly manner, not with swords and guns, as to invade an enemy."

—King Powhatan, 1609

• What is the answer to Powhatan's question, "What is the cause of your jealousy?"

ANALYZING DOCUMENTS

Examine the timeline below, then answer this question.

• Which event occurred first: the election of representatives to the Virginia House of Burgesses or the signing of the Mayflower Compact?

lands in the Chesapeake area. In 1622, Powhatan's brother attacked, killing about one fourth of the colony's population. Fighting continued for over 20 years, but eventually, the Powhatan Confederacy was destroyed.

In the mid-1670s, an alliance of New England tribes launched King Philip's War. Native Americans were threatened by the growing number of English settlements. Two years of fighting resulted in victory for the settlers. Numerous Indian survivors were sold into slavery in the West Indies. By the mid-1700s, settlers were moving into the interior of the continent.

The **French and Indian War** (1754–1763) was one of many wars between France and England in the 1700s. France and England were great rivals, and when they battled over issues in Europe, their colonists often fought in America. The French and Indian War erupted when the English challenged the French for control of the land that is now Ohio and western Pennsylvania.

The war pitted the English against the French and their Indian allies. (Native Americans tended to support the French because as fur traders, they built forts rather than settlements, as English colonists did.) The Iroquois, influenced by their earlier trade conflict with the French, supported the English toward the end of the war.

THE COLONISTS

The oldest settlement in what is now the United States is Saint Augustine, in Florida (1565). Founded by the Spanish, it did not become part of the United States until the 1800s. What was to become the United States began with the settlement of Virginia in 1607. By 1732, with the charter of Georgia, there were a total of 13 English colonies.

The Colonial Experience, 1607–1732

| 1619 Virginia landowners elect representatives to House of Burgesses | 1664 New Netherland taken by English, renamed New York | 1689 William and Mary sign English Bill of Rights |

| 1600 | 1625 | 1650 | 1675 | 1700 | 1725 | 1750 |

| 1607 Virginia founded | 1620 Mayflower Compact signed | 1660s Parliament passes Navigation Acts | 1688 Glorious Revolution in England | 1732 Georgia founded |

Who Came to the Colonies

The settlers were a diverse group. They included Africans brought against their will, Scotch-Irish from northern Ireland, Germans, Portuguese, Jews, Swedes, Dutch, French, Welsh, Irish, Scots, Belgians, and Swiss. In the colonial period, a large number of European immigrants came as **indentured servants** who contracted to work as many as seven years to repay the cost of their passage.

Most of each colony's population, however, was English. This fact would greatly affect the nature of the government that developed in the United States.

Why They Came

Just as the colonists represented many ethnic backgrounds, so did their motivations for coming to the colonies vary.

RELIGIOUS REASONS Some colonies were founded for religious reasons, but the colonists represented different religions and had different motivations. Massachusetts, for example, was founded by Pilgrims, or Separatists, who had left the Church of England, and Puritans who wanted to reform it. Colonies controlled by the Puritans allowed no religious freedom. Rhode Island, on the other hand, permitted all religions including Judaism. Pennsylvania was founded as a refuge for Quakers; Maryland for Roman Catholics.

ECONOMIC REASONS Economic motives were a major factor in the founding of Virginia, Delaware, and New Netherlands (later New York), as well as North and South Carolina. Georgia, the last of the colonies to be founded, was settled by debtors.

POLITICAL REASONS Separatists and Puritans came to North America after having fallen into political disfavor because of their objections to the established Church of England and the king who headed it. Quakers, Catholics, French Huguenots, and Jews came to escape religious intolerance and even governmental persecution.

What Influenced Their Experiences

Geography was a primary influence on the colonial way of life. So were the practices colonists brought from their homelands. Ethnic groups tended to settle together. Large distances and difficult transportation encouraged continuing family patterns, gender roles, and farming methods brought from Europe although these were sometimes modified by the new environment. Native American and African cultures also influenced changes in colonial lifestyles.

READING STRATEGY

Organizing Information Europeans came to the colonies for three major reasons. In the space below, name these reasons and provide examples of each.

1.

2.

3.

GEOGRAPHY IN HISTORY

Examine the map at right, then answer the following questions.

- How did geography influence colonists' decisions about where to settle and build colonies?

- By 1776, two thirds of the population of the English colonies lived no more than 50 miles from the ocean. Why?

- Which ethnic groups had the largest settlements in 1770? Which had the smallest settlements?

Colonial Settlement by Ethnic Group in 1770

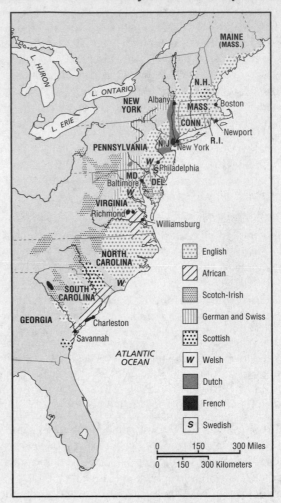

Legend:
- English
- African
- Scotch-Irish
- German and Swiss
- Scottish
- **W** Welsh
- Dutch
- French
- **S** Swedish

0   150   300 Miles
0   150   300 Kilometers

New England

Every aspect of New England life was influenced by religion in the early colonial period. Church membership was a requirement for participation in government. Strict moral codes were enforced.

The cold climate and poor soil of New England challenged Puritan farmers, who grew crops mostly for their own families' consumption. Only when they reached the Connecticut River valley with its richer soil were they successful at commercial farming.

New England developed a diversified economy. Although farming was the most common occupation, New England also became the center of colonial shipping, with major ports at Boston and Salem. Fishing and ship building were among the related industries. Merchants and professionals made up the wealthiest social class.

The Middle Colonies

The middle colonies had a diverse population, including Dutch, Germans, and Scotch-Irish. These colonies, especially New York and Pennsylvania, benefited from more fertile soil. They exported wheat and corn, and this trade helped build New York and Philadelphia. Large numbers of tenant farmers—who rented rather than owned the land—lived in the Hudson River valley of New York and in New Jersey.

The Southern Colonies

Agriculture flourished in the southern colonies, which had a warmer climate and rich soil. The southern economy was based on crops grown for export, such as tobacco, rice, and indigo. They were cultivated first by indentured servants and then by enslaved Africans.

The wealthiest social class included Chesapeake tobacco planters and the owners of the Carolina rice plantations. The labor of servants and slaves contributed to their growing wealth. By 1775, South Carolina and Georgia had the highest average wealth per free landholder in the colonies.

THE AFRICANS

By 1700, the institution of slavery—involving Africans primarily—already served to highlight the regional differences in the colonies.

Origins of the Atlantic Slave Trade

The first enslaved people in the Americas were Native Americans. In the 1500s, the Spanish and Portuguese forced them to work in mines and on sugar plantations. After the Native American population declined as a result of European diseases, the Spanish, Portuguese, and French began enslaving West Africans. With the growth of tobacco, indigo, and rice plantations, the British colonies also began to participate in the slave trade. By the early 1700s, England controlled the Atlantic slave trade.

For some goods, there was a two-way trade between England and the colonies: grains, fish, fur, wood products, tobacco, indigo, and rice from the colonies were exchanged for English manufactured goods. The slave trade, however, was a **triangular trade.** New England merchants traded rum for slaves in West Africa. The slaves were sold in the West Indies for molasses or sugar, which was shipped to New England to make more rum.

Development of Slavery in the Colonies

The first Africans in the colonies were brought to Virginia in 1619. At this time, most were considered indentured servants and were considered free when their contracts ended.

KEY THEMES AND CONCEPTS

Environment

The types of economic activities that took place in the different colonies were greatly affected by the environment. The New England colonies had poor, rocky soil, which made agriculture difficult. However, good harbors at Boston and Salem led to the development of thriving shipping and fishing industries.

In the southern colonies, agriculture flourished, and the economy did not diversify as much as in New England. The central role of agriculture in the southern economy led to a growing dependence on slavery.

How did the environment affect the middle colonies?

⚲ KEY THEMES AND CONCEPTS

Places and Regions
Slavery was more common in the southern colonies than in New England. Why?

READING STRATEGY

Organizing Information
Many enslaved Africans found both peaceful and violent ways to resist their enslavement. What are two peaceful ways that slaves resisted?

1.

2.

What are two violent ways that they resisted?

1.

2.

By the middle of the 1600s, large numbers of Africans began to be brought to the colonies as slaves. As the tobacco market grew, planters sought enslaved Africans to work the fields because of a shortage of workers. Free workers were reluctant to suffer the difficult working conditions on tobacco plantations, and indentured servants were now scarce. Soon, a system of permanent slavery was in place.

Slavery

By 1700, a race-based definition of a slave was written into law. Slavery became central to the southern economy. In South Carolina and Georgia, slavery was based on the Caribbean plantation system. The Africans were slaves from the time of their arrival and worked on huge rice plantations. The slave code was the strictest in the colonies.

By the early 1800s, the lower Mississippi Valley contained the greatest number of large plantations—those with 100 or more slaves. Cotton was increasingly important, and profits related directly to the amount of land cultivated. This encouraged the slave system to grow.

In contrast, slavery in the middle and New England colonies was less common, because the diverse economy and smaller farms made the region less dependent upon agriculture. At the end of the colonial period, seven out of every eight enslaved Africans lived in the South. In the North, most slaves worked in agriculture, but in northern cities some slaves worked as skilled tradesmen, domestic workers, and other laborers. The slave codes were also milder in the North.

Slave Resistance

Throughout the period in which slavery was legal, Africans and African Americans resisted their enslavement. On the slave ships during the voyage (called the **Middle Passage**) from Africa to the Americas, some staged revolts. Others chose starvation or drowning over enslavement.

Even in the face of severe punishment, some enslaved Africans attempted escape. Small communities of escaped slaves formed in Spanish Florida, South Carolina, Georgia, and Virginia. Other slaves offered more subtle resistance, such as slowing down at work, pretending illness, or damaging tools and crops.

In colonial America, open rebellion was not very common. Two notable colonial revolts took place in New York City in 1712 and at the Stono River near Charleston, South Carolina, in 1739. Both rebellions were put down by local militia. Most of those slaves who survived were later executed.

The Influence of Africa and African American Culture on Colonial Cultures

The blending of West African cultural traditions with European culture became the basis of a new African American culture. Some African words found their way into the English language, as did certain farming methods, foods, folk literature, and folk art. African building traditions of multiple small dwellings, front porches, and decorative iron work influenced southern colonial architecture. Some African musical styles and instruments, such as the banjo, continued to be incorporated into religious music and work songs. African musical traditions later influenced many forms of American music.

MAJOR HISTORICAL INFLUENCES ON AMERICAN GOVERNMENT

The government of each of the 13 colonies reflected ideas that came from the heritage of Western civilization. Those ideas were then modified by centuries of English thought and practice and by the American colonial experience.

Ideas from Ancient Greece

The concept of democracy, or government by the people, began in the city-state of Athens (in what is now Greece) between 750 B.C. and 550 B.C. Athens had a direct democracy, one in which all eligible citizens participated in government.

Ideas from Ancient Rome

The concept of republican government was established by the ancient Romans. In a **republic,** voters elect representatives who speak and act for other citizens in the business of government. These representatives

KEY THEMES AND CONCEPTS

Civic Values

American political rights and governmental institutions had three major sources:

1. British constitutional, political, and historical traditions

2. 17th- and 18th-century Enlightenment ideas

3. American colonial experience

What is an example of how each source influenced the political rights and governmental institutions in the United States?

Foundations of American Rights

	Sources of Rights			
Rights	**Magna Carta (1215)**	**English Bill of Rights (1689)**	**Virginia Declaration of Rights (1776)**	**Bill of Rights (1791)**
Trial by jury	✔	✔		✔
Due process	✔	✔		✔
Private property	✔			✔
No unreasonable searches or seizures			✔	✔
No cruel punishment		✔	✔	✔
No excessive bail or fines		✔		✔
Right to bear arms		✔		✔
Right to petition		✔		✔
Freedom of speech			✔	✔
Freedom of the press			✔	✔
Freedom of religion			✔	✔

PREPARING FOR THE EXAM

Common law is law that developed from traditional and court decisions in England. It became the basis of English and then United States law.

• Why do you think that the colonists used English common law as the basis for United States law?

READING STRATEGY

Problem Solving
Why is the writ of *habeas corpus* called the "Great Writ of Liberty"?

READING STRATEGY

Reinforcing Main Ideas
Which two rights guaranteed in the U.S. Constitution can be traced directly to the English Bill of Rights?

are supposed to work for the common good. This form of government is sometimes called representative democracy.

Influence of English Events and Documents
Other basic concepts of government and law were established in England before or during the colonial period in America.

MAGNA CARTA In 1215, English noblemen forced King John of England to agree to the Magna Carta, or Great Charter, a document that placed limits on his power to rule. For example, this document established the right to a jury trial—but only for nobles.

PETITION OF RIGHT In 1628, King Charles I signed the Petition of Right. It put in writing certain basic rights and legal traditions, such as a writ of *habeas corpus,* which prevented people from being imprisoned without a trial.

THE ENGLISH BILL OF RIGHTS In 1689, the Glorious Revolution ended a decades-long power struggle between the English Parliament and the monarchy. Parliament overthrew James II and replaced him with William and Mary, who were required to agree to the English Bill of Rights. This established that representative government and the rule of law outweighed the power of any monarch.

17th- and 18th-Century Enlightenment Thought
The framers of the Constitution were also strongly influenced by the ideas of the philosophers of the **Enlightenment.** This intellectual movement held that reliance on reason and experience would lead to social progress.

JOHN LOCKE John Locke believed that people are born free with certain **natural rights,** including the rights to life, liberty, and property. Such rights predate any government and exist in the "state of nature." Locke also wrote about the social contract theory. This theory holds that to protect their natural rights, people agree to form a state and grant to its government the powers necessary to protect those rights. When a government fails to do so, the contract has been broken and the people are free to change or replace that government. This means that governments exist with the consent of the governed.

THE BARON DE MONTESQUIEU The French philosopher Baron de Montesquieu believed that the British political system was successful because the power to govern was divided among the monarch and the two houses of Parliament. This division helped balance political power among the branches, so that no one branch had too much power.

JEAN-JACQUES ROUSSEAU Another French philosopher, Jean-Jacques Rousseau, developed further the idea of a social contract. His arguments in support of government by the consent of the governed influenced our Declaration of Independence.

VOLTAIRE A third important French philosopher, Voltaire, wrote *Philosophical Letters,* praising British institutions and rights. He wrote against religious intolerance and persecution.

THE COLONIAL EXPERIENCE: POLITICAL RIGHTS AND MERCANTILE RELATIONSHIPS

During the colonial period, two important forces helped shape a uniquely American way of life: (1) political ideas based on the English experience and on Enlightenment thinking and (2) the colonists' experience thousands of miles from their home country.

Colonial Charters and Self-Government

Twelve of the 13 original colonies were founded based on charters issued by the British government. A **charter** provided legal authority to companies or individuals to start a colony. Most of the colonies were originally self-governing private enterprises, but by 1730, most became royal colonies. Even after England later centralized control, the colonies remained largely self-governing and independent.

Colonial Principles and Practices of Government

The beliefs that colonists held about the proper role of government had a strong influence over the way they structured their governments.

LIMITS ON GOVERNMENT The colonists believed that the power of government should be limited, in accordance with English laws and traditions. The colonists wrote laws based on the principle that government existed to protect people's natural rights. The rights to life, liberty, and protection of property were most often mentioned. As early as 1641 in Massachusetts, the right to own property and protect it from being illegally seized by the government was written into law. The right to vote helped to protect property rights.

ENFORCEABLE CONTRACTS Colonists believed in the right to enter into contracts. Enforceable contracts between parties can be traced to the idea of a political compact, or contract. After the United States won independence, decisions of the Marshall Court protected individuals' right to enter into contracts.

FREEDOM OF THE PRESS Colonists believed there should be legal limits on government attempts to control what is written. In 1735, John Peter Zenger, a German immigrant to New York, was tried for seditious libel for accusing the governor of the colony of wrongdoing. Zenger's lawyer argued that no crime was committed when what Zenger had printed was true, and the jury found Zenger not guilty. Later, this case helped establish the principle of freedom of the press in the United States.

ANALYZING DOCUMENTS

"I may detest what you say, but will defend to the death your right to say it."
                                    —Voltaire

• What basic civil liberty is Voltaire defending?

KEY THEMES AND CONCEPTS

Constitutional Principles
The following two cases deal with property rights and economic policy:

Fletcher v. *Peck* (1810) established that a state cannot interfere with constitutionally protected contract rights.

Dartmouth College v. *Woodward* (1819) extended constitutional protection of contracts to corporate charters.

Why are *Fletcher* v. *Peck* and *Dartmouth College* v. *Woodward* important to economic freedom?

READING STRATEGY

Formulating Questions
From the context of the paragraph about the Zenger case, define what is meant by *seditious libel.*

ANALYZING DOCUMENTS

"We whose names are underwritten . . . covenant and combine ourselves together into a civil body politic, for our better ordering and preservation and furtherance of the ends aforesaid; and by virtue hereof to enact, constitute, and frame such just and equal laws, ordinances, acts, constitutions, offices from time to time as shall be thought most meet and convenient for the general good of the colony; unto which we promise all due submission and obedience."

—Mayflower Compact

- What words indicate that this is a contract or compact?

- Is this to be a limited government?

MAYFLOWER COMPACT In 1620, before landing at Plymouth in present-day Massachusetts, the Pilgrims signed the Mayflower Compact. This was a contract in which the colonists consented to be governed by a government that they created—**self government**.

Colonial Assemblies and Local Governments

The importance of self-government is seen in the colonial assemblies established in each colony. As early as 1619, Virginia colonists took the first step toward republican government when they instituted the colonies' first representative lawmaking body, the **House of Burgesses.** Most colonies established a bicameral, or two-house, legislature modeled after the two-house English Parliament.

Colonists also recognized the need for local governments. The county was the center of local government in most of the colonies. In New England, local government was at the town level, where the town meeting allowed citizens to govern themselves through direct democracy.

THE CAUSES OF THE AMERICAN REVOLUTION

For almost a century before the outbreak of the American Revolution in 1775, Britain and France were involved in a rivalry for power, not only in Europe, but wherever the two nations had colonies. In 1754, Benjamin Franklin tried to get the colonies to agree to the **Albany Plan of Union** as protection against the French. The colonies rejected the plan because they feared the loss of self-government.

Events Leading to the American Revolution

1754 French and Indian War begins; Albany Plan of Union	1763 France and Britain sign Treaty of Paris	1765 Parliament passes Stamp Act	1773 Tea Act; Boston Tea Party

1750   1755   1760   1765   1770   1775

1759 British capture Quebec	1764 Sugar Act	1766 Parliament repeals Stamp Act	1774 Intolerable Acts; First Continental Congress

Preoccupied with France, Britain governed the colonies until 1763 under a policy known as **salutary neglect,** or a healthy ignoring of the colonies. Thus, the colonies had many years in which to practice self-government. The British government controlled foreign affairs and foreign trade, while the colonists governed local matters.

The Treaty of Paris of 1763 marked Britain's victory over France in the Seven Years' (or French and Indian) War. It also shifted the way power was distributed in North America. With the French defeated, Native Americans could no longer benefit from balancing the French and British against one another.

Land Claims After the French and Indian War, 1763

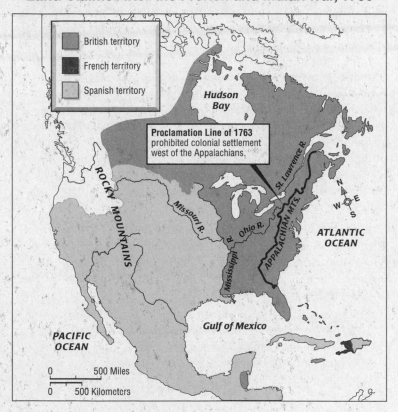

TURNING POINT

Why is the Treaty of Paris of 1763 considered a turning point in history?

ANALYZING DOCUMENTS

In May 1765, Patrick Henry voiced his opposition to the Stamp Act with a speech to the Virginia House of Burgesses. In that speech, he said:

"Caesar had his Brutus; Charles the First, his Cromwell; and George the Third . . . may profit by their example. If <u>this</u> be treason, make the most of it."

Brutus assassinated Caesar, and Cromwell defeated Charles I and had him beheaded.

- What is Patrick Henry's message?
- What might Patrick Henry have been implying but would not say?

KEY THEMES AND CONCEPTS

Economic Systems
The 16th to 18th century economic system called mercantilism was based on the belief that a strong national state was built by accumulating precious metals through increasing exports, establishing colonies to supply raw materials and markets, limiting colonies' trade with other nations, and protecting industries.

With the French defeat, the colonists felt free to move west and resented the **Proclamation of 1763,** which prohibited movement into the lands gained from France.

Economic Causes of the Revolution

After winning the French and Indian War, Britain was left with a large debt. The British government believed that the colonies should pay for their own defense. Parliament began to enforce the policy of **mercantilism,** which held that colonies existed to provide raw materials and markets for the economic benefit of the home country.

Parliament passed several new tax laws, such as the Sugar Act (1764), which taxed foreign imports and the **Stamp Act** (1765), which required a tax stamp on printed materials. The colonists resented these

READING STRATEGY

Organizing Information
The American Revolution had economic, political, and social and ideological causes. List them, then identify those you consider the most significant.

1. Economic

2. Political

3. Social and Ideological

acts and forced their repeal. Parliament then passed the Townshend Acts, which taxed imported goods. Colonists saw the Townshend Acts as a serious economic threat.

Political Causes of the Revolution

Some colonists also saw the Townshend Acts as a political threat. The money raised by the acts would be used to pay some of the English officials in the colonies. Colonial legislatures believed this undermined their power to exert control over officials by withholding their salaries. The colonists reacted to the new taxes with petitions, boycotts, and other more violent protests.

In the Virginia House of Burgesses, for example, Patrick Henry introduced resolutions opposing the Stamp Act. Samuel Adams, a Boston political organizer and journalist, helped create the Sons of Liberty and the Massachusetts Committee of Correspondence.

Colonists viewed these new taxes as a threat to their liberties, including the right to property. They charged that Britain had violated their natural rights as British citizens. Because they had no representation in Parliament, colonists reasoned that taxation could only come from the colonial legislatures. Britain insisted that Parliament represented all of its subjects.

Social and Ideological Causes of the Revolution

The British government failed to understand the colonists' fears of its power. It also failed to recognize that the colonists had developed an independent political life and thought. The following factors helped lay the foundation for revolution:

- The colonists' firm belief in their natural rights, combined with factors in the colonial experience, produced a greater sense of equality among colonists than among British citizens in general.
- Because of abundance of available land, as much as 90 percent of the white male population held enough land to qualify them for the right to vote.
- In the decades before the Revolution, the colonial population grew rapidly, while increased numbers of immigrants came from nations other than England. Appeals had to be made to all peoples.
- The Great Awakening, a religious movement, encouraged people to question authority and enjoy a sense of equality with others.

THE AMERICAN REVOLUTION AND THE DECLARATION OF INDEPENDENCE

In 1773, the issue of taxation without representation rose again when Parliament passed the Tea Act, which made British tea less expensive than tea imported by colonial tea merchants. Colonists protested by destroying three shiploads of British tea in the Boston Tea Party. The British government reacted with the "Intolerable Acts" of 1774. These acts punished Massachusetts by closing the port of Boston, forbidding town meetings, and reducing the powers of the legislature. More British troops were sent to occupy the colony and enforce the acts.

ANALYZING DOCUMENTS

Use the timeline to answer the following questions.

- How long did the American Revolution last?

- Was the Declaration of Independence issued before or after fighting began in the American Revolution?

The American Revolution and the Declaration of Independence, 1775–1783

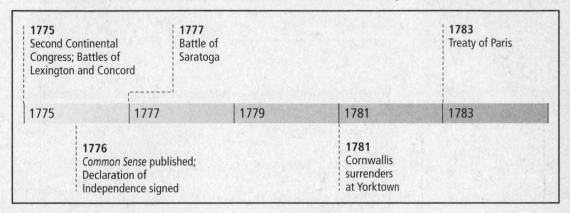

1775
Second Continental Congress; Battles of Lexington and Concord

1777
Battle of Saratoga

1783
Treaty of Paris

| 1775 | 1777 | 1779 | 1781 | 1783 |

1776
Common Sense published; Declaration of Independence signed

1781
Cornwallis surrenders at Yorktown

Colonial Efforts at Union

In the late summer of 1774, twelve of the colonies sent representatives to Philadelphia to plan a response to these British actions. This meeting became known as the **First Continental Congress.** After the start of the American Revolution in 1775, a **Second Continental Congress** met and took charge of the war effort.

Decision for Independence

In June 1776, Richard Henry Lee of Virginia presented a resolution to the Second Continental Congress calling for independence from Great Britain. The Congress appointed a committee (including Thomas Jefferson, Benjamin Franklin, and John Adams) to draft a formal declaration. The resulting **Declaration of Independence** was almost entirely the work of Thomas Jefferson. The delegates adopted the Declaration of Independence on July 4, which marks the birth of the United States of America. The key facts about this important document are listed on the next page:

JOIN, or DIE.

The Declaration of Independence

The PURPOSE of the Declaration:	The Declaration's KEY IDEAS OF GOVERNMENT:
• To announce to the world that the colonies were now a new, independent nation • To explain and justify the reasons that the united colonies had decided to become the United States of America	• People have natural rights, including the rights to "Life, Liberty, and the pursuit of Happiness." • Governments receive their power to govern "from the consent of the governed" by social contract or compact in which the government agrees to protect the people's natural rights.
The THREE PARTS of the Declaration:	• When a government fails to protect and respect those rights, it is the "Right of the People to alter or to abolish" that government.
• A theory of government • A list of grievances against the King • A formal resolution declaring independence	

READING STRATEGY

Reading for Evidence
"We have boasted the protection of Great Britain, without considering, that her motive was *interest* not *attachment;* and that she did not protect us from *our enemies* on *our account;* but from *her enemies* on *her own account.* . . . A government of our own is our natural right: and . . . it is infinitely wiser and safer, to form a constitution of our own in a cool deliberate manner, while we have it in our power, than to trust such an interesting event to time and chance."
　　　　—Thomas Paine, *Common Sense,* 1776

• What is common sense to Paine?

The Ideals of the Declaration of Independence

The ideals of the Declaration of Independence are still goals for the nation. They have also served to inspire others—during the French Revolution of the late 1700s, the South American independence movement in the early 1800s, and even twentieth-century independence movements in Africa and Asia.

Although few people noted it at the time, there was a fundamental contradiction between the Declaration's ideals of freedom and the institution of slavery. The colonists had looked to John Locke's compact theory (which stated that no person may rule another without the consent of the other person) as justification for choosing freedom. Few, however, advocated such freedom for slaves.

Fighting the War for Independence

The American Revolution began in 1775 and ended with the British surrender at Yorktown, Virginia, in 1781. A peace treaty, the Treaty of Paris, was negotiated by John Adams, John Jay, and Benjamin Franklin and was signed in 1783.

Throughout the American Revolution, the Second Continental Congress served as the national government. The Congress had no constitutional basis but was created in a crisis and supported by popular opinion. It remained in place until 1781.

The British army was larger in number, better trained, and aided by the Creek, Cherokee, and Shawnee in the South and most Iroquois in the North. It was disadvantaged by its use of European military techniques in America and by the behavior of its troops, which alienated many colonists in the territories it occupied.

The continental army (the colonists' army) was the achievement of George Washington, the colonial commander in chief. The continental army was reinforced as it moved from region to region by an untrained militia or home guard defending their homes.

The colonists were aided by an alliance with France, negotiated by Benjamin Franklin. Motivated by its ongoing rivalry with Great Britain, France supplied the colonists with military arms, troops, and naval support and engaged Britain in war elsewhere in the world.

The American victory at Saratoga helped bring the French into the war. They saw that the colonists might possibly win the war. The victory also prevented the British from isolating New England from the rest of the colonies by taking control of the Hudson River valley and the area north of it to Canada.

Slavery, African Americans, and the Outcome of the American Revolution

Although African Americans fought on both sides during the American Revolution, more fought on the British side because of British promises of freedom from slavery. After first hesitating, Washington and the Continental Congress eventually recruited African Americans, as did state militias.

During the Revolution, some African slaves in the South successfully escaped. Others were freed in return for military service. Some left the country with the British army, while others settled in northern cities and became part of a growing free black population.

TURNING POINT

Why is the Battle of Saratoga considered a turning point in the war?

ANALYZING DOCUMENTS

Reading for Evidence
"We have in common with all other men a natural and unalienable right to that freedom which the Great Parent of the Universe hath bestowed equally on all mankind, and which they have never forfeited by any compact or agreement whatsoever."
—From a petition of a group of slaves to the Massachusetts legislature, 1777

• What evidence is there that the writers knew about Enlightenment ideas and the Declaration of Independence?

Some Effects of the American Revolution

States draft new constitutions emphasizing limitations on governmental power.

Britain recognizes the United States as an independent nation.

Ideals of the revolution influence events in other parts of the world.

The American Revolution

The Iroquois League is destroyed, and Native Americans are pushed farther west.

Some begin to reexamine traditional ideas about women's roles in society.

Ideas of freedom and natural rights inspire some people to begin opposing slavery.

The Revolution had important consequences for many groups of people.

An antislavery movement led by Quakers started in the North before the Revolution. After the war, northern states passed laws that immediately or gradually abolished slavery. Although free, African Americans in the North still faced discrimination. Many were not allowed to vote, except in New England. There was segregation in public places, housing, and transportation.

THE ARTICLES OF CONFEDERATION, 1781–1789

The first constitution of the United States was the **Articles of Confederation.** This constitution, proposed by the Second Continental Congress in 1777, went into effect in 1781 after all 13 states had ratified, or approved, it. The Articles of Confederation reflected the colonists' fear of a strong central government and the desire of the individual states to protect their powers. As a result, the Articles created a weak national government.

An Alliance of Independent States

The Articles set up a confederation among the 13 states. A confederation is an alliance of independent states in which the states give as much power as they choose to the central government, while keeping the greater part of the power and remaining sovereign. The Articles were more like a treaty among the states than a plan of centralized government.

Achievements of the Confederation Government

The government under the Articles of Confederation had the power to make treaties, declare war, and receive ambassadors. The Confederation also made some notable achievements:

The Articles of Confederation, 1781–1789

1777 Articles of Confederation; first New York State Constitution		1783 Treaty of Paris	1786 Shays' Rebellion	1788 Constitution ratified
1775	1780	1785		1790
	1781 Articles of Confederation approved	1785 Land Ordinance of 1785 passed	1787 Northwest Ordinance passed	

1. Successful conclusion of the American Revolution
2. Negotiation of the Treaty of Paris of 1783, ending the war and setting the United States border at the Mississippi River
3. Passage of the Land Ordinance of 1785 and the Northwest Ordinance of 1787, which (a) set the pattern by which new states could join the nation, and (b) prohibited slavery in the Northwest Territory

Weaknesses of the Confederation Government

The Confederation government proved too weak to deal with the problems during the critical period of the 1780s. There was no single national currency, because the states could also coin money. The Congress could not tax the people directly but had to ask the states for funds. The government lacked a president to direct operations. The Congress did not have the money to raise an army without the consent of the states.

The new nation soon suffered severe economic problems, while its government was unable to command respect at home or abroad. However, all 13 states had to agree before the Articles could be changed, so it was nearly impossible to change this constitution.

STATE GOVERNMENTS BASED ON REPUBLICAN PRINCIPLES

Between 1776 and 1787, 11 of the 13 states adopted new constitutions. State constitutions were based on republican principles creating a government grounded in representation of the people, the consent of the governed. Special state conventions were called so that the constitutions could be written by the people. When complete, they were ratified or approved by the voters.

Fears of a strong executive led the framers of the first state constitutions to emphasize limitations on power. The New York Constitution of 1777, which even included the text of the Declaration of Independence, gave most of the power to the legislature, rather than to a single person such as a governor. In New York as in most states, the legislature remained bicameral, rather than unicameral.

Some states granted more people the right to vote by lowering property qualifications. Some states gave the right to vote to property-owning African Americans and Native Americans. State constitutions, including the New York state constitution, protected some individual rights, such as the right to religious freedom. In addition, the state government could not give money to any religion. This was part of a national movement to disestablish churches, which meant the end of government endorsement and financial support of any single religious group.

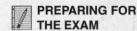

KEY THEMES AND CONCEPTS

Government

The purpose of the Constitutional Convention was to create a government which did not have the weaknesses of the Articles of Confederation while avoiding a national government so strong that it threatened the liberties of its citizens.

- How did the U.S. Constitution create a stronger national government than that of the Articles of Confederation?

PART 2 WRITING AND RATIFYING THE CONSTITUTION, 1787–1789

By the late 1780s, it was clear that the national government created by the Articles of Confederation was too weak. The government faced increasing difficulty in regulating trade and dealing with the nation's debt.

The problems plaguing the national government led to a call for a Constitutional Convention in Philadelphia in May 1787 for "the sole and express purpose of amending the Articles of Confederation." The chart below shows how the delegates tried to correct the weaknesses of the Articles of Confederation.

THE CONSTITUTIONAL CONVENTION

Fifty-five delegates, representing all the states except Rhode Island, met in the Pennsylvania State House (now known as Independence Hall) in Philadelphia in May 1787 at the Constitutional Convention. The delegates were prominent lawyers, planters, and merchants at a time when most of the population were small farmers.

Governments of the United States: 1781 and 1789

How the Weaknesses of the Articles of Confederation Were Corrected by the Constitution	
Articles of Confederation	**Constitution of the United States**
• States have most of the power. The national government has little.	• States have some power, but most power is given to the national government.
• No executive officer to carry out the laws of Congress.	• A President heads the executive branch of the government.
• No national courts. Only state courts exist.	• Both national and state courts exist.
• Congress is responsible to the states.	• Congress is responsible to the people.
• Nine out of 13 states have to approve a law before it can go into effect.	• Laws may be passed by a majority vote of both houses of Congress.
• Congress has no power to tax.	• Congress given the power to tax.
• Congress can not regulate trade among the states.	• Congress given the power to regulate interstate and foreign trade.
• Each state coins its own money. There is no national currency.	• Only the national government has the power to coin money.

The most famous delegate was George Washington, who was elected president of the Constitutional Convention. Another well-known figure was James Madison, whom some consider to have had the most influence on the Constitution. Also attending were Benjamin Franklin and Alexander Hamilton, a strong nationalist from New York.

Some famous Americans from the Revolution were noticeably absent. Thomas Jefferson and John Adams were serving the country as diplomats in Europe. A few patriots, such as Patrick Henry, refused to attend because they suspected that the convention would try to create a strong national government, which they opposed. Still others were not selected by their states.

In addition, no women, Native Americans, African Americans, or poorer white men attended the Constitutional Convention. At that time, these groups had limited political and legal rights.

KEY COMPROMISES AT THE CONVENTION

The delegates agreed that discussions would be kept secret in order to debate freely without outside pressure. They also decided not to revise the Articles of Confederation, but to write a new constitution instead.

Most of what we know about the Convention comes to us from Madison's notes. The delegates' task was to create a government with enough authority to govern effectively while protecting individual liberties. The debates involved much conflict and much compromise. In fact, the United States Constitution has been called a "bundle of compromises." Three key compromises made the Constitution possible.

KEY THEMES AND CONCEPTS

Diversity

Certain groups of people were not represented at the Constitutional Convention. How does their absence explain some sections of the Constitution? Why were these groups absent?

READING STRATEGY

Organizing Information

- Which groups stood in opposition to each other on the major issues at the Constitutional Convention?

- Why did they take their particular positions?

Major Compromises of the Constitutional Convention

Compromise	Issue	Solution
Connecticut	Representation in Congress	Bicameral legislature: States have equal representation in Senate; representation in the House depends on State's population.
Three-Fifths	Counting slaves within population to determine representation	Slaves were counted as if 3/5 of one person, both for representation and taxation.
Commerce and Slave Trade	Granting Congress the power to regulate foreign and interstate trade	Congress was forbidden to tax a State's exports or take action against the slave trade for 20 years.

KEY THEMES AND CONCEPTS

Individuals, Groups, Institutions
At the Constitutional Convention, three major compromises were achieved.

- For each issue, how did the compromise satisfy each side?

- Why were the compromises necessary?

READING STRATEGY

Problem Solving
Only nine states needed to ratify the U.S. Constitution to put it into effect.

- Why was it essential that Virginia and New York be among those states that ratified it?

KEY THEMES AND CONCEPTS

Government
In which states was there strong division of opinion about ratification?

The Great Compromise, or Connecticut Plan

The first issue to be resolved was that of representation. The delegates from Virginia proposed the Virginia Plan, which called for a bicameral legislature. A state's representation in each house would be based on its population. Larger states supported this plan. The smaller states favored the New Jersey Plan. This plan called for a unicameral legislature in which each state had equal representation.

The Virginia Plan served as the basis for much of the new Constitution. However, the matter of representation had to be settled by what is known as the **Great Compromise** or the Connecticut Plan, which gave something to both large and small states. The compromise created the Congress, a bicameral legislature. The states had equal representation in the upper house, or the Senate. In the lower house, or the House of Representatives, representation was based on population. In addition, all bills dealing with money would have to start in the House, but would need the approval of the Senate.

The Three-Fifths Compromise

Meanwhile, a bitter debate continued over slavery and power. Southerners wanted slaves to be counted for purposes of deciding representation in the House, but not for purposes of determining taxes. The compromise reached was that three fifths of the enslaved African Americans in a state were counted for both representation and taxation purposes.

The Commerce Compromise

Northerners wanted a government that could regulate trade. Southerners, however, feared that the importing of African slaves would be prohibited and that their agricultural exports would be taxed. The delegates agreed that no export duties could be passed by Congress and that Congress could not prohibit the slave trade for 20 years.

RATIFICATION OF THE CONSTITUTION

After months of debate in Philadelphia, delegates approved the Constitution of the United States. On September 17, 1787, thirty-nine of the delegates remaining in Philadelphia signed the Constitution. The fact that three, including George Mason, author of the Virginia Declaration of Rights, refused to sign gave an indication of the coming debate. The Framers had written that 9 of the 13 states must approve the Constitution for it to go into effect. Approval would be done through special conventions called in each state rather than through the state legislatures.

The Great Debate and Ratification

Two groups formed in each state: the **Federalists,** who favored ratification, and the **Anti-Federalists,** who opposed it.

The Great Debate

The Federalist Arguments:	The Anti-Federalist Arguments:
• Wanted a strong national government to provide order and protect rights of people.	• Wanted a weak national government so that it would not threaten the rights of the people or the powers of the states.
• Claimed that a bill of rights was unnecessary because the new government's powers were limited by the Constitution.	• Wanted to add a bill of rights to protect the people against abuses of power.

The first five states ratified the Constitution within a few months. By June 1788, nine states had given their approval—enough for ratification. But these did not include the states of Virginia and New York. The success of the new government depended upon acceptance of the Constitution by these two key states.

In Virginia, James Madison led the fight for ratification against the opposition of George Mason and Patrick Henry. Virginia approved the Constitution by 10 votes but with amendments suggested. New York was the next battleground. Here, *The Federalist*—a series of pro-ratification essays by Alexander Hamilton, John Jay, and James Madison—helped turn the tide against the Anti-Federalists, led by Governor George Clinton. Ratification was by a margin of three votes. *The Federalist* remains one of the finest statements on government and the Constitution ever written.

PART 3 WHAT YOU NEED TO KNOW ABOUT THE U.S. CONSTITUTION AND GOVERNMENT

The Constitution of the United States includes a number of important basic principles, which are listed below.

Popular Sovereignty

The Constitution is based on the idea of popular sovereignty— that the source of all power or authority to govern is the people. This type of government is considered a democracy.

Limited Government

Governmental powers are defined by the Constitution. In this way, our government is limited by law. The Constitution places limits on state and national governments and government officials as well.

Separation of Powers

The Constitution establishes the **separation of powers,** meaning that power to govern is divided among the legislative, executive, and

ANALYZING DOCUMENTS

"Ambition must be made to counteract ambition . . . If men were angels, no government would be necessary. If angels were to govern men, neither external nor internal controls on government would be necessary. In framing a government which is to be administered by men over men, the great difficulty lies in this: you must first enable the government to control the governed; and in the next place oblige it to control itself."

—James Madison,
The Federalist No. 51

• Based on this quote, what is James Madison's view of the relationship between human nature and good government?

Three Branches of U.S. Government

Legislative	Executive	Judicial
Senate **House of Representatives**	**President** **Vice President**	**Supreme Court** **Federal Courts**
Makes laws	Enforces laws and treaties	Explains and interprets laws
• Overrides presidential vetoes • Approves presidential appointments • Approves treaties • Taxes to provide services • Provides for defense, declares war • Regulates money and trade • Impeaches officials	• Can veto laws • Appoints high officials • Conducts foreign policy • Enforces laws and treaties • Commander in chief of the military • Recommends bills to Congress • Reports the state of the Union to Congress	• Settles legal disputes between states • Settles State and federal disputes • Settles disputes between States and foreign countries • Hears cases with ambassadors of foreign governments • Settles disputes between individuals and Federal Government

Source: U.S. Department of Justice

ANALYZING DOCUMENTS

"We the People of the United States . . . do ordain and establish this Constitution for the United States."

— Preamble to the U.S. Constitution

• According to the Preamble, who is creating this Constitution?

• In what other documents have we seen a concept that is restated here?

judiciary branches to ensure that no single branch can dominate the government. Each branch takes its power directly from the Constitution, not from another branch.

Checks and Balances

The system of **checks and balances** gives each branch of the national government ways to check, or control, the other branches. This prevents too much power from falling into the hands of any one part of the government.

Flexibility

The Constitution is a flexible document that can meet changing conditions over time.

THE ELASTIC CLAUSE Article I, Section 8, Clause 18, states that Congress can make all laws "necessary and proper" for carrying out the tasks listed in the Constitution.

THE AMENDMENT PROCESS Article V describes how the Constitution may be formally amended. Both Congress and the states must agree to such changes.

JUDICIAL INTERPRETATION The Supreme Court and lower federal courts review cases which involve possible conflicts with the Constitution and federal laws. This involves interpreting local, state, and federal laws, as well as executive actions.

The Checks and Balances System

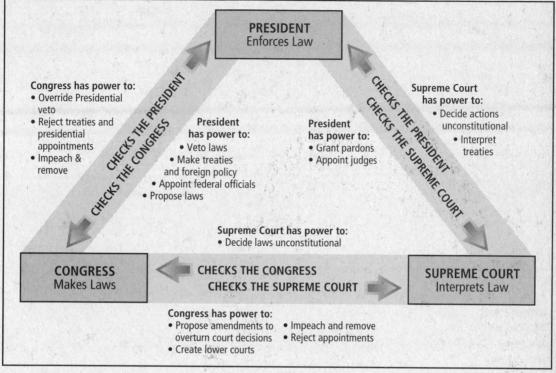

PRESIDENT
Enforces Law

CHECKS THE PRESIDENT

CHECKS THE CONGRESS

CHECKS THE PRESIDENT

CHECKS THE SUPREME COURT

Congress has power to:
• Override Presidential veto
• Reject treaties and presidential appointments
• Impeach & remove

President has power to:
• Veto laws
• Make treaties and foreign policy
• Appoint federal officials
• Propose laws

President has power to:
• Grant pardons
• Appoint judges

Supreme Court has power to:
• Decide actions unconstitutional
• Interpret treaties

Supreme Court has power to:
• Decide laws unconstitutional

CONGRESS
Makes Laws

CHECKS THE CONGRESS
CHECKS THE SUPREME COURT

SUPREME COURT
Interprets Law

Congress has power to:
• Propose amendments to overturn court decisions
• Create lower courts
• Impeach and remove
• Reject appointments

FEDERALISM IN THE CONSTITUTION

The Constitution divides the power to govern between the national and the state governments. Disputes between the national and state governments are settled by the courts, but the Supremacy Clause of Article VI of the Constitution makes the Constitution, federal laws, and treaties superior to state laws.

DELEGATED POWERS Certain powers of the national government are spelled out in the Constitution. Most of these delegated powers are listed in Article I, Section 8. One example is the power of the national government to declare war.

IMPLIED POWERS Certain powers of the national government are not stated in writing. Their existence is implied by the Elastic Clause. One example of an implied power is the regulation of child labor; this power is implied by the delegated power to regulate interstate commerce.

DENIED POWERS Certain powers are denied to the national government, for example, the power to pass an export tax. Other powers

The Supremacy Clause

U.S. Constitution
• Acts of Congress
• Treaties
• State Constitutions
• State Statutes
• City and County Charters and Ordinances

System of Federalism

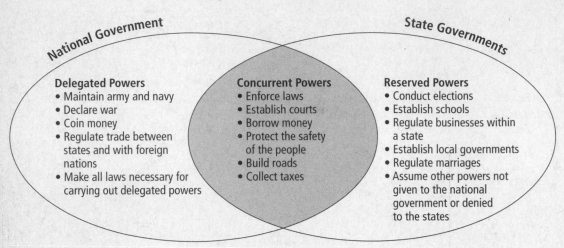

National Government

State Governments

Delegated Powers
- Maintain army and navy
- Declare war
- Coin money
- Regulate trade between states and with foreign nations
- Make all laws necessary for carrying out delegated powers

Concurrent Powers
- Enforce laws
- Establish courts
- Borrow money
- Protect the safety of the people
- Build roads
- Collect taxes

Reserved Powers
- Conduct elections
- Establish schools
- Regulate businesses within a state
- Establish local governments
- Regulate marriages
- Assume other powers not given to the national government or denied to the states

KEY THEMES AND CONCEPTS

Government

What do you call a power that is shared by both national and state governments?

Name two examples:

1.

2.

What do you call a power that is held only by the national government?

Name two examples:

1.

2.

What do you call a power that is held only by the states?

Name two examples:

1.

2.

are denied to the states, for example, the power to print money. Still other powers are denied to both national and state governments, for example, the power to deny the right to vote because of sex or race.

CONCURRENT POWER Certain powers belong to both national and state governments. One example of such a concurrent power is the power to tax.

RESERVED POWERS The reserved powers are neither delegated to the national government nor denied to the states. One example is the power to make divorce laws.

Article IV of the Constitution describes relations among the states and lists guarantees that the national government makes to the states. Article VII, which describes ratification of the Constitution, serves as a reminder that the new national government had to be approved by the individual states.

THE BASIC ORGANIZATION AND FUNCTIONS OF GOVERNMENT UNDER THE CONSTITUTION

The first three articles of the Constitution describe and define the powers of the legislative, executive, and judicial branches of the national government. These articles detail the separation of powers, while showing how each branch can check and balance the others.

Federal Officeholders

Office	Number	Term	Selection	Requirements
Representative	at least 1 per state; based on state population	2 years	Elected by voters of congressional district	• Age 25 or over • Citizen for 7 years • Resident of state in which elected
Senator	2 per state	6 years	Original Constitution-elected by state legislature Amendment 17-elected by voters	• Age 30 or over • Citizen for 9 years • Resident of state in which elected
President and Vice-President	1	4 years	Elected by electoral college	• Age 35 or over • Natural-born citizen • Resident of U.S. for 14 years
Supreme Court justice	9	Life	Appointed by President with approval of the Senate	• No requirements in Constitution

ARTICLE I: THE LEGISLATIVE BRANCH

Article I establishes the United States Congress with its two houses—the Senate and the House of Representatives. Congress is the legislative branch of government. Article I gives the qualifications for election to Congress, the rights and privileges of members of Congress, and some basic operating procedures of both houses. The article also lists the powers delegated to Congress. Each house of Congress also has special duties that it alone can perform.

Article I briefly outlines how a bill becomes a federal law. This process requires the approval of each house and of the President. A presidential veto, or rejection, of a bill can be overridden by a two-thirds vote of each house. As the diagram on page 57 shows, the process today is quite complex, and a bill must pass through numerous committees before becoming a law.

 PREPARING FOR THE EXAM

Some examination questions require you to read and interpret charts. Study the chart above and answer this question.

• How does the term of a Supreme Court justice differ from those of other federal officeholders?

The Powers of Congress as Stated (by Clause) in Article I, Section 8 of the United States Constitution

Expressed Powers

Peace Powers

1. To lay taxes
   a. Direct (not used since the War Between the States, except income tax)
   b. Indirect (customs [tariffs], excise for internal revenue)
2. To borrow money
3. To regulate foreign and interstate commerce
4. To establish naturalization and bankruptcy laws
5. To coin money and regulate its value; to regulate weights and measures
6. To punish counterfeiters of federal money and securities
7. To establish post offices and post roads
8. To grant patents and copyrights
9. To create courts inferior to the Supreme Court
10. To define and punish piracies and felonies on the high seas; to define and punish offenses against the law of nations
17. To exercise exclusive jurisdiction over the District of Columbia; to exercise exclusive jurisdiction over forts, dockyards, national parks, federal buildings, and the like

War Powers

11. To declare war; to grant letters of marque and reprisal; to make rules concerning captures on land and water
12. To raise and support armies
13. To provide and maintain a navy
14. To make laws governing land and naval forces
15. To provide for calling forth the militia to execute federal laws, suppress insurrections, and repel invasions
16. To provide for organizing, arming, and disciplining the militia, and for its governing when in the service of the Union

Implied Powers

18. To make all laws necessary and proper for carrying into execution the foregoing powers, such as:
    To define and provide punishment for federal crimes
    To establish the Federal Reserve System
    To improve rivers, canals, harbors, and other waterways
    To fix minimum wages, maximum hours of work

Special Powers of the House and Senate

House	Senate
• To select the President if no candidate receives a majority of the electoral vote	• To select the Vice President if no candidate has a majority of the electoral vote
• To bring impeachment charges	• To act as jury in cases of impeachment
• To originate all revenue (money) bills	• To ratify treaties (by a two-thirds vote)
	• To approve presidential appointments (by a majority vote)

How Bills Become Laws

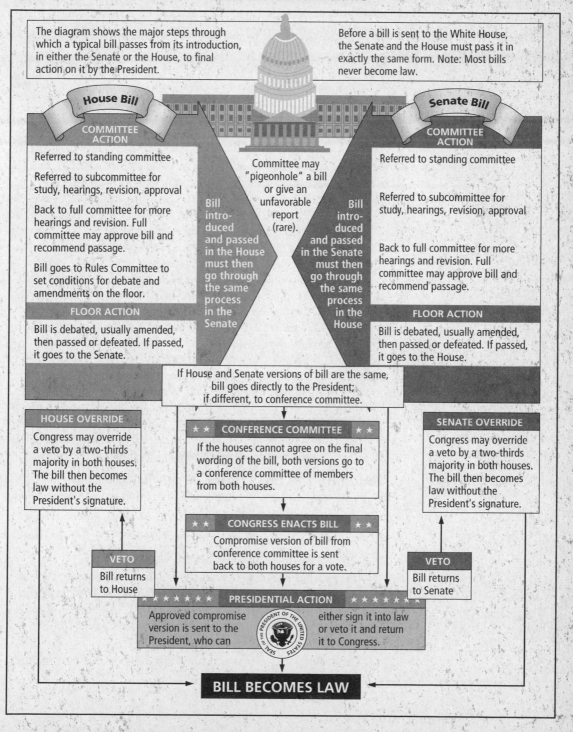

The diagram shows the major steps through which a typical bill passes from its introduction, in either the Senate or the House, to final action on it by the President.

Before a bill is sent to the White House, the Senate and the House must pass it in exactly the same form. Note: Most bills never become law.

House Bill

COMMITTEE ACTION

Referred to standing committee

Referred to subcommittee for study, hearings, revision, approval

Back to full committee for more hearings and revision. Full committee may approve bill and recommend passage.

Bill goes to Rules Committee to set conditions for debate and amendments on the floor.

FLOOR ACTION

Bill is debated, usually amended, then passed or defeated. If passed, it goes to the Senate.

Bill introduced and passed in the House must then go through the same process in the Senate

Committee may "pigeonhole" a bill or give an unfavorable report (rare).

Bill introduced and passed in the Senate must then go through the same process in the House

Senate Bill

COMMITTEE ACTION

Referred to standing committee

Referred to subcommittee for study, hearings, revision, approval

Back to full committee for more hearings and revision. Full committee may approve bill and recommend passage.

FLOOR ACTION

Bill is debated, usually amended, then passed or defeated. If passed, it goes to the House.

If House and Senate versions of bill are the same, bill goes directly to the President; if different, to conference committee.

HOUSE OVERRIDE

Congress may override a veto by a two-thirds majority in both houses. The bill then becomes law without the President's signature.

★ ★ **CONFERENCE COMMITTEE** ★ ★

If the houses cannot agree on the final wording of the bill, both versions go to a conference committee of members from both houses.

SENATE OVERRIDE

Congress may override a veto by a two-thirds majority in both houses. The bill then becomes law without the President's signature.

★ ★ **CONGRESS ENACTS BILL** ★ ★

Compromise version of bill from conference committee is sent back to both houses for a vote.

VETO

Bill returns to House

VETO

Bill returns to Senate

★ ★ ★ ★ ★ ★ **PRESIDENTIAL ACTION** ★ ★ ★ ★ ★ ★

Approved compromise version is sent to the President, who can either sign it into law or veto it and return it to Congress.

BILL BECOMES LAW

READING STRATEGY

Analyzing Cause and Effect

The U.S. Constitution requires that a census of the population be taken every 10 years. The census is used to determine how many representatives each state will send to the House.

- What impact does the census have on the electoral college?

KEY THEMES AND CONCEPTS

Government

A precedent is an action or decision which serves as a basis for later actions or decisions. For example, George Washington set a precedent when he decided not to run for President after completing two terms. No President served for more than two terms until Franklin D. Roosevelt was elected to a third and fourth term in 1940 and 1944.

ARTICLE II: THE EXECUTIVE BRANCH

Article II outlines the workings of the executive branch, including the method of electing the President as well as the powers and duties of the office.

Electing the President

Article II describes the process by which the president is elected. Amendments 12, 20, 22, and 25 have changed this process.

A key compromise of the Constitutional Convention involved the method of electing the President. Under the resulting **electoral college** system, voters cast their ballots for electors. Those electors cast the actual votes for President and Vice President. Each state was granted as many presidential electors as it had senators plus representatives.

The Constitution requires that a census, or counting of the population, be taken every 10 years. Changes to reflect shifts in population are then made in the number of representatives per state, which in turn affects the electoral vote. Today, data from the census is also used to make decisions about other national needs.

Customs and precedents influenced how the President is elected. After Washington's two terms, the formation of political parties forced changes in the election process. No longer did electors exercise their own judgments. Rather, they pledged in advance to vote for the presidential candidate of their party. Today, while the names of the presidential candidates appear on the ballot, voters are actually casting their ballots for electors chosen by each candidate's party.

By 1832, national conventions had become the method of selecting party candidates. Today more than half the delegates to such national conventions are selected through party presidential primaries. Such primaries are only one step in today's complex path to the presidency. The chart on the next page summarizes key steps along that path.

Debating the Electoral College System

From the days of the Constitutional Convention, people have argued over the method of selecting the president.

REASONS TO CHANGE THE SYSTEM There are two major arguments against the electoral college system.

1. It is a "winner-take-all" system. A winning candidate gets all the electoral votes in a state, no matter how close the popular vote is. Four times—in 1824, 1876, 1888, and 2000—the winner of the popular vote has lost the presidency because he failed to win a majority of the electoral vote.

2. Generally, electors are not required by law to vote for the candidate who wins in their state.

The Path to the Presidency

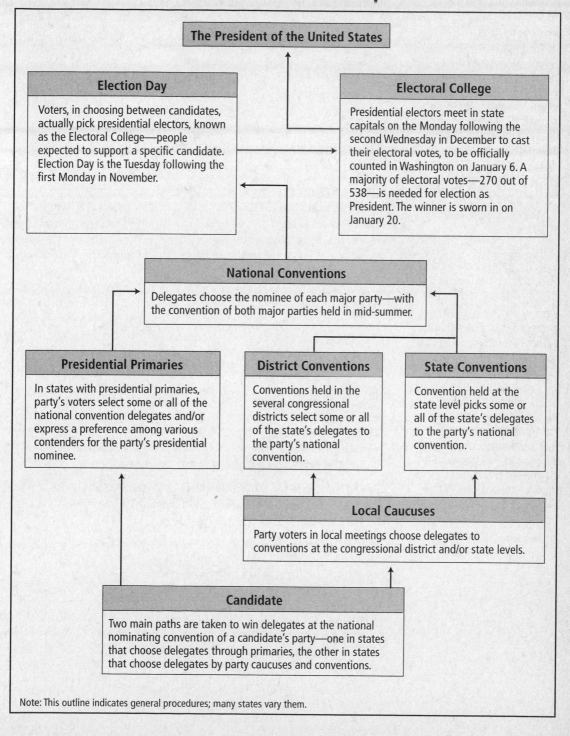

The President of the United States

Election Day

Voters, in choosing between candidates, actually pick presidential electors, known as the Electoral College—people expected to support a specific candidate. Election Day is the Tuesday following the first Monday in November.

Electoral College

Presidential electors meet in state capitals on the Monday following the second Wednesday in December to cast their electoral votes, to be officially counted in Washington on January 6. A majority of electoral votes—270 out of 538—is needed for election as President. The winner is sworn in on January 20.

National Conventions

Delegates choose the nominee of each major party—with the convention of both major parties held in mid-summer.

Presidential Primaries

In states with presidential primaries, party's voters select some or all of the national convention delegates and/or express a preference among various contenders for the party's presidential nominee.

District Conventions

Conventions held in the several congressional districts select some or all of the state's delegates to the party's national convention.

State Conventions

Convention held at the state level picks some or all of the state's delegates to the party's national convention.

Local Caucuses

Party voters in local meetings choose delegates to conventions at the congressional district and/or state levels.

Candidate

Two main paths are taken to win delegates at the national nominating convention of a candidate's party—one in states that choose delegates through primaries, the other in states that choose delegates by party caucuses and conventions.

Note: This outline indicates general procedures; many states vary them.

KEY THEMES AND CONCEPTS

Government

In the presidential election of 2000, George W. Bush became the fourth President to win the electoral college without winning the popular vote. The other Presidents were John Quincy Adams, elected in 1824; Rutherford B. Hayes, who ran in 1876; and Benjamin Harrison, elected in 1888.

PREPARING FOR THE EXAM

A flowchart is a diagram that shows the different steps in a process. Study the flowchart of the route to the presidency on the previous page, then answer the question below:

What are three sources of delegates to a political parties national convention?

1.

2.

3.

REASONS TO KEEP THE SYSTEM Despite such criticisms, the electoral college system remains in use for three key reasons:

1. It is very difficult to amend the Constitution.

2. Small states would lose the advantage they now have of being over-represented in the electoral college; they would, therefore, oppose any change.

3. Changes in the electoral college system might threaten the two-party political system. The fact that a presidential candidate needs a majority of the electoral college vote, critics believe, prevents many small political parties from springing up.

Presidential Roles and Powers

Article II describes the powers and duties of the President of the United States. Since power in the executive branch centers in one individual, a president can act swiftly in time of war and national crisis. In carrying out the duties of office, the president fills several different roles.

CHIEF EXECUTIVE In this role, the President has the power to
- enforce or put the laws into effect
- act as administrator of the huge federal bureaucracy
- issue executive orders that have the effect of laws
- appoint judges, diplomats, and other high government officials— some with Senate approval and others without
- remove appointed government officials within the executive branch

CHIEF DIPLOMAT In this role, the President has the power to
- make treaties
- make executive agreements with nations without Senate approval
- extend or withdraw diplomatic recognition to a nation

COMMANDER IN CHIEF In this role, the President has broad military powers that are shared with Congress. In times of war, these powers are even stronger.

CHIEF LEGISLATOR In this role of lawmaker, the President has the power to
- recommend legislation to Congress
- veto potential laws

CHIEF OF STATE In addition to being head of the government, the President is also chief of state, the ceremonial head of government, and the symbol of all the people of the nation. He fills this role in such ceremonies as the laying of a wreath on the Tomb of the Unknowns.

JUDICIAL POWERS The President can grant reprieves, pardons, and amnesties, or pardons extended to groups rather than individuals.

HEAD OF THE PARTY The President is also the leader of the political party in power. The duties of this role are not mentioned in the Constitution because the party system developed through custom.

The Federal Bureaucracy

The federal bureaucracy consists of the administrative agencies and staff that put the decisions or policies of the government into effect. Such a bureaucracy has developed through legislation, executive action, and custom.

Most of the bureaucracy is part of the executive branch and includes the White House staff, 14 executive departments, and more than 200 independent agencies. This bureaucracy is explained in more detail in the chart on the next page.

ARTICLE III: THE JUDICIAL BRANCH

Article III of the Constitution creates the Supreme Court and gives Congress the power to create lower federal courts. The role of this judicial branch is to interpret the law. In addition to this national court system, each of the 50 states has its own court system.

Jurisdiction

With two court systems—federal and state—the Constitution had to define the jurisdiction, or authority, of the federal courts in order to make clear which cases go to federal courts and which to state courts. The court that has the authority to hear a case is determined by two factors:

SUBJECT MATTER Federal courts hear cases involving federal laws, treaties, maritime law, and interpretation of the Constitution.

PARTIES Federal courts are directed to have jurisdiction if cases involve certain parties, or participants in a case. For example, cases involving representatives of foreign governments or states suing other states are tried in federal courts.

The Constitution states that in some types of cases, the Supreme Court will have original jurisdiction. This means the Supreme Court will hear the case first and make a decision. In most cases, the Supreme Court has appellate jurisdiction. This means that, in a lower court, if the losing side believes a judge made a mistake in applying the law in a case, that case may be appealed to a higher court. The Supreme Court hears only about 150 cases of the nearly 5,000 appealed to it each year.

KEY THEMES AND CONCEPTS

Government
The executive branch is the largest branch of the government, as shown in the chart on the next page.

- Why is the executive branch so large?

- How were the departments and agencies shown created?

The United States Government

Legislative	Executive	Judicial
THE CONGRESS Senate House	**THE PRESIDENT** **Executive Office of the President**	**SUPREME COURT OF THE UNITED STATES**
• Architect of the Capitol • General Accounting Office • Government Printing Office • Library of Congress • United States Botanic Garden • Office of Technology Assessment • Congressional Budget Office • United States Tax Court	• White House Office • Office of Management and Budget • Council of Economic Advisers • National Security Council • Office of National Drug Control Policy • Office of the United States Trade Representative • Council on Environmental Quality • Office of Science and Technology Policy • Office of Administration **The Vice President**	• Courts of Appeals • District Courts • Federal Claims Court • Court of Appeals for the Federal Circuit • Court of International Trade • Territorial Courts • Court of Appeals for the Armed Forces • Court of Veterans Appeals • Administrative Office of the United States Courts • Federal Judicial Center

Executive Departments

State	Treasury	Defense	Justice	Interior	Agriculture	Commerce
Labor	Health and Human Services	Housing and Urban Development	Transportation	Energy	Education	Veterans Affairs

Major Independent Agencies*

• Central Intelligence Agency
• Commission on Civil Rights
• Consumer Product Safety Commission
• Corporation for National and Community Service
• Defense Nuclear Facilities Safety Board
• Environmental Protection Agency
• Equal Employment Opportunity Commission
• Export-Import Bank of the U.S.
• Farm Credit Administration
• Federal Communications Commission

• Federal Deposit Insurance Corporation
• Federal Election Commission
• Federal Housing Finance Board
• Federal Maritime Commission
• Federal Mediation and Conciliation Service
• Federal Reserve System
• Federal Trade Commission
• General Services Administration
• Merit Systems Protection Board
• National Aeronautics and Space Administration

• National Labor Relations Board
• National Transportation Safety Board
• Nuclear Regulatory Commission
• Office of Government Ethics
• Securities and Exchange Commission
• Selective Service System
• Small Business Administration
• Social Security Administration
• Tennessee Valley Authority
• U.S. Arms Control and Disarmament Agency
• U.S. Postal Service

*There are more than 200 independent agencies in the executive branch.

Judicial Review

The most important power of the federal courts is the right to **judicial review.** This power enables the courts to hear cases involving the application and interpretation of law. Laws that are judged not in keeping with the Constitution's intent are declared unconstitutional and void.

The Supreme Court is the final voice in interpreting the Constitution. The right of judicial review strengthened the power of the judiciary against the other two branches of government. Chief Justice John Marshall first stated the right of judicial review in the 1803 case of *Marbury* v. *Madison.*

READING STRATEGY

Problem Solving
The process of amending the Constitution is an excellent example of federalism in practice. Why?

AMENDING THE CONSTITUTION

Article V describes methods of amending, or formally changing, the Constitution. In the most common method of amendment, Congress approves a proposed amendment by a two-thirds vote in each house. The amendment then goes to the state legislatures. If three quarters of them ratify it, the amendment becomes part of the Constitution. Twenty-six amendments have been adopted by this method. To date, only the Twenty-first Amendment has been ratified by special conventions called in the states.

The Formal Amendment Process (Four Methods)

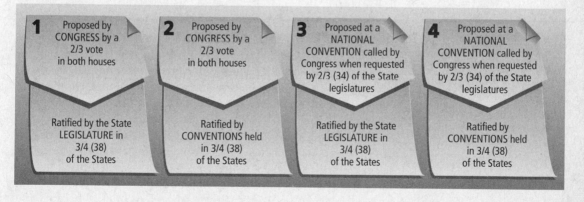

1 Proposed by CONGRESS by a 2/3 vote in both houses → Ratified by the State LEGISLATURE in 3/4 (38) of the States

2 Proposed by CONGRESS by a 2/3 vote in both houses → Ratified by CONVENTIONS held in 3/4 (38) of the States

3 Proposed at a NATIONAL CONVENTION called by Congress when requested by 2/3 (34) of the State legislatures → Ratified by the State LEGISLATURE in 3/4 (38) of the States

4 Proposed at a NATIONAL CONVENTION called by Congress when requested by 2/3 (34) of the State legislatures → Ratified by CONVENTIONS held in 3/4 (38) of the States

The Bill of Rights

The Bill of Rights is the name given to the first 10 amendments to the Constitution adopted in 1791. These amendments guarantee certain basic or fundamental rights of the people against the power of the federal government.

The Bill of Rights

Amendment	Subject
1st	Guarantees freedom of religion, of speech, and of the press; the right to assemble peacefully; and the right to petition the government.
2nd	Protects the right to possess firearms.
3rd	Declares that the government may not require people to house soldiers during peacetime.
4th	Protects people from unreasonable searches and seizures.
5th	Guarantees that no one may be deprived of life, liberty, or property without due process of law.
6th	Guarantees the right to a trial by jury in criminal cases.
7th	Guarantees the right to trial by jury in most civil cases.
8th	Prohibits excessive bail, fines, and punishments.
9th	Declares that rights not mentioned in the Constitution belong to the people.
10th	Declares that powers not given to the national government belong to the states or to the people.

Extending Constitutional Protections

In the 200 years since the Bill of Rights was added to the Constitution, the rights of the people have been expanded by court decisions and by other amendments. The Fourteenth Amendment contains the equal protection clause. Court interpretations have held that the Fourteenth Amendment extends the protections of most of the Bill of Rights against the states as well as the national government.

The courts have held that civil rights (as defined in the Bill of Rights and other amendments) are relative, not absolute. The courts have thus tried to balance an individual's rights against the rights of society and other individuals. Sometimes basic civil rights conflict with each other. For example, the Fifth Amendment right of the accused to confront witnesses might clash with a reporter's First Amendment, freedom-of-the-press right to protect news sources. In such conflicts, the courts must decide the issue.

Additional Constitutional Amendments

Between 1795 and 1992, an additional 17 amendments have been
added to the Constitution. Note that the Thirteenth, Fourteenth, and
Fifteenth Amendments were passed after the Civil War to make citizens of
former slaves, and to give them the right to vote.

Amendments 11–27

Amendment	Year Ratified	Subject
11th	1795	Lawsuits against the states
12th	1804	Separate voting for President and Vice President
13th	1865	Abolition of slavery
14th	1868	Citizenship and civil rights
15th	1870	Voting rights for African American men
16th	1913	Income tax
17th	1913	Direct election of senators
18th	1919	Prohibition of alcoholic beverages
19th	1920	Voting rights for Women
20th	1933	Terms of the President, Vice President and Congress
21st	1933	Repeal of Eighteenth Amendment
22nd	1951	President limited to two terms
23rd	1961	Electoral votes for the District of Columbia
24th	1964	Abolition of poll taxes
25th	1967	Presidential disability and succession
26th	1971	Voting age lowered to eighteen
27th	1992	Changing congressional salaries

The Right to Vote

Year	People Allowed to Vote
1789	White men over age 21 who meet property requirements (state laws)
Early 1800s–1850s	All white men over age 21 (state laws)
1870	Black men (15th Amendment)
1920	Women (19th Amendment)
1961	People in the District of Columbia in presidential elections (23rd Amendment)
1971	People age 18 or over (26th Amendment)

ANALYZING DOCUMENTS

Based on the chart at left, what has been the most common way of extending the right to vote to more people?

NEW YORK STATE GOVERNMENT COMPARED TO THE FEDERAL GOVERNMENT

The government of New York has many similarities to the federal government. New York has a constitution and a Bill of Rights. The New York government has three branches. The executive branch is headed by the governor. The bicameral legislature has a Senate and an Assembly. The highest court in the judicial branch is the Court of Appeals.

PART 4 THE THIRTEEN BASIC CONSTITUTIONAL PRINCIPLES

Thirteen basic constitutional principles have endured since the ratification of the Constitution. These principles continue to be important to the development of American government and society.

Constitutional Principle 1
National Power—Limits and Potential

The powers of the federal government are limited. The Constitution states the powers held by each branch of government. The powers that are not delegated to the national government are reserved to the states or to the people (Tenth Amendment). The Bill of Rights also limits the government's inter-ference with basic rights.

However, the powers of all three branches of the federal government have grown.
• Has the national government become too powerful?
• Do the limits placed on the national government make it incapable of dealing with the problems of the modern age?

Examples of This Principle as a Recurring Theme in U.S. History

Need for a strong central government: debate over ratification
Loose vs. strict interpretation of the Constitution: Hamilton's financial plan, Louisiana Purchase
Conflict over slavery: 1820–1860
Civil War: establishing federal supremacy over the states
Imperialism: Spanish-American War, acquiring an overseas empire

Progressive movement: Theodore Roosevelt and Woodrow Wilson
Elastic clause: Pure Food and Drug Act, Social Security
Commerce clause: expanding powers of government
New Deal: expanding role of government
Great Society: demand for reform
New Federalism: less government involvement

Constitutional Principle 2
Federalism—Balance Between Nation and State

The Constitution created a new federal government that divided power between the states and the national government. The Constitution reserved certain powers to the states and to the people, but the Constitution and the laws and treaties of the United States are supreme to state laws.

• Is the power still balanced, or has it tilted to the federal government?
• Has the shift of power to the federal government become greater since the New Deal, or did Reagan's New Federalism reverse this trend?

Examples of This Principle as a Recurring Theme in U.S. History

Marshall Supreme Court cases: *McCulloch* v. *Maryland, Gibbons* v. *Ogden*
John C. Calhoun: nullification, states' rights
Conflict over slavery: 1820–1860
Civil War: establishing federal supremacy over the states
Reconstruction: greater federal supremacy; 13th, 14th, and 15th Amendments

Populists and Progressive reform
New Deal legislation
Rights of minorities: *Brown* v. *Board of Education*
Fourteenth Amendment: use to extend Bill of Rights protections to states
Great Society, mid-1960s
New Federalism, 1980s

Constitutional Principle 3
The Judiciary—Interpreter of the Constitution or Shaper of Public Policy

The Judiciary interprets the law (Article III) and has the power to declare laws unconstitutional. This power of judicial review dates from Marshall's decision in *Marbury* v. *Madison,* which was based on Article III, and the supremacy clause in Article VI, which states that the Constitution is the "supreme law of the land."

- By acting when Congress has not acted, or by reversing congressional actions to favor the states, have the courts become lawmakers instead of law interpreters?
- If the courts did not have the power to shape public policy, would the Bill of Rights and democracy itself be endangered?

Examples of This Principle as a Recurring Theme in U.S. History

Marbury v. *Madison:* judicial review strengthened judiciary, government, and national unity

Federal vs. state powers: *McCulloch* v. *Maryland, Gibbons* v. *Ogden*

Limiting protections and rights: *Dred Scott* v. *Sandford, Civil Rights Cases*

Reversals of decisions: *Plessy* v. *Ferguson, Brown* v. *Board of Education*

State vs. federal powers: *United States* v. *E.C. Knight Co., Lochner* v. *New York, Schechter Poultry* v. *United States*

Rights of accused: *Miranda* v. *Arizona, Gideon* v. *Wainwright*

First Amendment cases (freedom of speech, press, religion, assembly): *Engel* v. *Vitale, Schenck* v. *United States, New York Times Co.* v. *United States, Tinker* v. *Des Moines Independent Community School District*

Ninth Amendment privacy cases: *Roe* v. *Wade; Cruzan* v. *Director, Missouri Department of Health*

Checks and balances: *Watkins* v. *United States, United States* v. *Nixon*

Constitutional Principle 4
Civil Liberties—Protecting Individual Liberties from Government Abuses; the Balance Between Government and the Individual

A problem unique to a democratic government is how to balance the rights of the individual and the needs of society. The Constitution's Bill of Rights and Fourteenth Amendment guarantee certain basic rights, rights which predate any government. But these rights are not unlimited.

- What are the rights of the individual?
- Should government protect and/or extend the rights of the individual?
- Should government decide where the balance should be between individual and societal rights?

Examples of This Principle as a Recurring Theme in U.S. History

Equal protection clause: Fourteenth Amendment—*Civil Rights Cases, Heart of Atlanta Motel* v. *United States*

Freedom of speech vs. "clear and present danger": *Schenck* v. *United States*

Relocation of Japanese Americans: *Korematsu* v. *United States*

Red Scare, McCarthyism: fear of subversion, the erosion of liberties

Testing for drug use: *Vernonia School District* v. *Acton*

Rights of individuals: effects of technology

Constitutional Principle 5
Criminal Procedures—The Balance Between the Rights of the Accused and the Protection of the Community and Victims

This is a question of balancing the rights of individuals accused of crimes and those of citizens to be safe and secure.
- Why does an individual accused of a crime have rights?

- Are those rights easily defined?
- What are the rights of a victim of a crime?
- When do the rights of the accused interfere with society's ability to maintain law and order?

Examples of This Principle as a Recurring Theme in U.S. History

Free press vs. the rights of the accused

Death penalty: individual rights vs. rights of society

Writ of *habeas corpus:* purpose

Due process of law, search and seizure: *Mapp* v. *Ohio*

Students' rights and search and seizure: *New Jersey* v. *T.L.O.; Vernonia School District* v. *Acton*

Rights of the accused: *Miranda* v. *Arizona, Gideon* v. *Wainwright*

Constitutional Principle 6
Equality—Its Historic and Present Meaning as a Constitutional Value

This issue involves questions of who is equal and in what ways. When Jefferson wrote that "all men are created equal," he referred to the equality before the law of white, property-owning males. The equal protection clause of the Fourteenth Amendment and the due process clause of the Fifth Amendment were later interpreted to make equal justice more of a reality for all Americans.

- According to the Constitution, who is equal: men and women? All races? Rich and poor? Young and old?
- How has the Constitution expanded equality?
- Has equality been achieved?
- How are people equal: equal in opportunity? Before the law? In entitlements?

Examples of This Principle as a Recurring Theme in U.S. History

Conflict over slavery: Constitutional Convention; 1820–1860
Passage of 13th, 14th, and 15th Amendments
Equal protection clause: 14th Amendment
Jim Crow laws: legal basis for segregation
Plessy v. *Ferguson*
Brown v. *Board of Education*
Martin Luther King, Jr.: civil rights movement

19th-century women's rights movement
19th Amendment
1960s women's rights movement
Treatment of Native Americans: *Worcester* v. *Georgia*
Native American movement
New Deal: relief of human suffering
Great Society: help for less fortunate
Affirmative action: court decisions

Constitutional Principle 7
The Rights of Women Under the Constitution

Women are not mentioned in the Constitution except in the Nineteenth Amendment, which protects their right to vote.
- What is the historic and present meaning of equality for women as a constitutional value?

- How were these changes achieved?
- Are federal laws and court rulings sufficiently protective of the rights of women?
- Was there a need for the defeated Equal Rights Amendment?

Examples of This Principle as a Recurring Theme in U.S. History

Elizabeth Cady Stanton and Susan B. Anthony: Women's suffrage movement
Seneca Falls: Women's rights movement
Effects of industrialization on the role of women

1960s women's rights movement
Roe v. *Wade:* Ninth amendment, right to privacy, abortion
Affirmative action and women

Constitutional Principle 8
The Rights of Ethnic and Racial Minority Groups Under the Constitution

The Constitution has not always protected ethnic, racial, and other minority groups. When first ratified, in fact, the Constitution contained clauses that protected slavery and the rights of slaveholders.
- Has the Constitution protected the rights of ethnic and racial minority groups?

- Has the Constitution protected the rights of economically powerful groups better than those of minority groups?
- Are the gains that minorities have made secure, or do such groups need more protection of their rights?
- How do we balance minority rights and rule by a majority?

Examples of This Principle as a Recurring Theme in U.S. History

Conflict over slavery: Constitutional Convention; 1820–1860
Frederick Douglass: abolition movement
Dred Scott v. *Sandford*
Civil War: Emancipation Proclamation
Reconstruction: 13th, 14th, and 15th Amendments
Jim Crow laws, *Plessy* v. *Ferguson:* legal basis for segregation
Equal protection clause: 14th Amendment

Brown v. *Board of Education*
Martin Luther King, Jr.: civil rights movement of 1960s
Restrictions on immigration: quota system, exclusion of Chinese and Japanese
Relocation of Japanese Americans: *Korematsu* v. *United States*
Native Americans: treaty rights, *Worcester* v. *Georgia,* Dawes Act, citizenship in 1924
Native American movement

Constitutional Principle 9
Presidential Power in Wartime and in Foreign Affairs

The Constitution gives the President the power to make treaties, as well as other major foreign-policy responsibilities. The President is also the commander in chief of the armed forces. The powers of the President have grown since the early days of the United States government, and they are even greater in wartime.
- Does the President have too much power, particularly since the Civil War?
- Are broad presidential powers necessary to conduct war and foreign affairs?

Examples of This Principle as a Recurring Theme in U.S. History

George Washington: expanded governmental powers, Proclamation of Neutrality

Increase of presidential power during wartime by Lincoln, Wilson, and FDR.: *Schenck* v. *United States, Korematsu* v. *United States*

T. Roosevelt: increase of presidential power because of U.S. involvement in world affairs

T. Roosevelt: Roosevelt Corollary to Monroe Doctrine

Truman: decision to drop atomic bomb

Korean and Vietnam Wars: expanded presidential wartime powers

Kennedy: Cuban missile crisis

War Powers Act: a check on presidential power

Carter: Camp David Accords

Sandinistas and Contras

Persian Gulf Crisis

Intervention in Somalia, Bosnia, Haiti, Yugoslavia

Clinton: Israeli-PLO Agreement

Constitutional Principle 10
The Separation of Powers and the Effectiveness of Government

The Constitution established three branches of government with separate powers, as well as a system of checks and balances among them.
- Has the system of separation of powers and of checks and balances been effective in preventing dominance by one branch?
- Is this system necessary, or has it resulted in a badly-run government that is slow to respond to the needs of the people and the nation?

Examples of This Principle as a Recurring Theme in U.S. History

Checks and balances: presidential veto

Judicial review: *Marbury* v. *Madison*

Reconstruction: period of legislative power

Checks and balances: Treaty of Versailles

Checks and balances: FDR and Supreme Court reorganization

Checks and balances: Vietnam War

Checks and balances: *Watkins* v. *United States, United States* v. *Nixon*

War Powers Act: check on presidential power

Watergate: government based on laws and not on an individual

Clinton: impeachment and acquittal

Constitutional Principle 11
Avenues of Representation

Since the Constitution was ratified, there has been a continuing expansion of the right to vote. However, while the system has become more democratic and more reflective of majority rule, the power of political parties and special interest groups has grown.
- Has the federal government become more or less representative of "we the people"?

Examples of This Principle as a Recurring Theme in U.S. History

Great Compromise: representation in Congress

Electoral college system

Direct election of senators

Passage of 15th, 19th, 24th, and 26th Amendments

19th-century and Progressive reform movements

Populist and Grange movements

Women's suffrage movement

Third parties' effect on the political process

"One man, one vote": effect on representative government

Campaign funding: individual rights vs. influence of special interests

Politics: effects of technology

Constitutional Principle 12
Property Rights and Economic Policy

The Constitution gives the government responsibility for promoting the general welfare and Congress the power to regulate commerce and taxes.

- Has government balanced its two roles as the promoter of capitalism and free enterprise and as the protector of the public from the abuses of business?

Examples of This Principle as a Recurring Theme in U.S. History

Hamilton: government encouragement of business, national bank
Andrew Jackson: second national bank
Expanded interstate commerce clause: *Gibbons* v. *Ogden; Wabash, St. Louis & Pacific R.R.* v. *Illinois*
Weakened interstate commerce clause: *United States* v. *E.C. Knight Co., Lochner* v. *New York, Schechter Poultry* v. *United States*
Interstate commerce clause used against labor: *In Re Debs*

Antitrust activities: Sherman Antitrust Act, T. Roosevelt and W. Wilson, *Northern Securities Co.* v. *United States,* Clayton Antitrust Act
Federal Reserve: regulating monetary system
Government action for environmental and consumer protection
New Deal: government farm price supports
New Deal: collective bargaining, Wagner Act
Reagan: supply side economics, budget deficits

Constitutional Principle 13
Constitutional Change and Flexibility

The Constitution has adapted to changing circumstances over the years because of certain provisions built into it, such as the necessary and proper clause and the interstate commerce clause.
- Has the Constitution proven adaptable to changing times?

- Should the Constitution be easier to change?
- Has the amendment process, combined with judicial interpretation and the implied powers of the executive and legislative branches, kept the Constitution able to meet the challenges of the modern world?

Examples of This Principle as a Recurring Theme in United States History

Washington: the unwritten constitution
Hamilton's bank plan: implied powers
Commerce clause: expansion of government authority, regulation of business, Federal Reserve System

Amendments and court decisions used to expand rights
Cabinet and congressional committees: custom and precedent
Role of political parties

PART 5 PUTTING THE CONSTITUTION INTO EFFECT

From the time of our first Presidents, an unwritten constitution developed in response to changing times and circumstances. This unwritten constitution resulted from a combination of (1) executive interpretations and actions, (2) congressional interpretations and actions, (3) court decisions, especially judicial review, (4) customs and traditions, and (5) the actions of political parties.

EXECUTIVE INTERPRETATION, ACTION, AND CUSTOM

Starting with George Washington, presidents sought advice from the heads of the executive departments, who were called the President's **cabinet,** when developing policy. Today, the White House staff also plays a major role in this advisory process. The President appoints cabinet members with Senate approval but can dismiss a cabinet member without Senate approval.

The early Presidents also consulted with congressional leaders when developing policies. Such consultation is an informal procedure. Today, the Senate's official role often seems more "to consent" than "to advise" on presidential decisions. This method of advising the President has become custom.

Developing a Financial Plan

With Washington's support, Alexander Hamilton, the first secretary of the treasury, set out to put the government on a sound economic footing. He proposed a plan that included four key elements:

**♀ KEY THEMES AND
ⱳ CONCEPTS**

Government
In the early years of the new nation, the United States government grew from the basic framework of the Constitution to a functioning governmental system. Provide an example of how interpretation, action, and custom each contributed to this process.

Interpretation:

Action:

Custom:

First Years of the New Government, 1789–1820

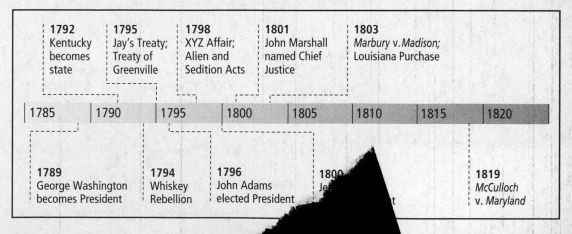

| 1792 Kentucky becomes state | 1795 Jay's Treaty; Treaty of Greenville | 1798 XYZ Affair; Alien and Sedition Acts | 1801 John Marshall named Chief Justice | 1803 *Marbury* v. *Madison*; Louisiana Purchase |

| 1785 | 1790 | 1795 | 1800 | 1805 | 1810 | 1815 | 1820 |

| 1789 George Washington becomes President | 1794 Whiskey Rebellion | 1796 John Adams elected President | 1800 Je... ...t | 1819 *McCulloch* v. *Maryland* |

ASSUMPTION Hamilton wanted the national government to pay off American Revolution war debts run up by the Continental Congress as well as the wartime debts of the states. Hamilton believed that this would establish the credit of the nation. Congress approved this plan.

A NATIONAL BANK Hamilton wanted Congress to create a national bank, which he believed would win the government the support of the business community. Such a bank would also help the government in all of its financial dealings. Congress chartered a national bank in 1791.

AN EXCISE TAX Hamilton proposed that the government raise operating revenues through an excise tax on whiskey.

A PROTECTIVE TARIFF Hamilton called for a protective tariff to shield products of the nation's infant industries from foreign competition. Congress rejected the protective tariff but passed other tariffs to generate income for the government.

The Hamilton plan raised some controversy, but it put the new nation on a sound financial footing. It also encouraged the wealthy to support the government and built a solid foundation for the nation's future as an industrial power.

The Whiskey Rebellion

In 1794, western Pennsylvania farmers protested and refused to pay excise tax on the whiskey they made from grain. Washington called out state militias and put down this "Whiskey Rebellion." There is debate today over how serious a threat this rebellion really was, but Washington's actions demonstrated that the new government intended to enforce federal law.

Foreign Policy in the Federalist Era

From 1789 to 1815, the French Revolution and the European wars that grew out of it put many pressures on the new nation. Washington and the other early Presidents tried to protect the nation from such pressures. Washington, for example, supported the unpopular **Jay's Treaty,** an agreement designed to resolve conflicts with Great Britain and keep the United States from going to war. With his Proclamation of Neutrality in 1793 and his Farewell Address in 1796, Washington set the tone for United States foreign policy by warning of the danger of political alliances. Instead he urged the nation to take independent action in foreign affairs.

John Adams, the first Vice President and second President, also ___ood the importance of keeping the new nation out of war. ___ather than expand an undeclared naval war with France ___is actions divided his own Federalist Party, which ___ilure to win a second term. But Adams, in resisting internal and external pressures for war and ending the 1778 alliance with France, made possible a peaceful and independent entry into the new century.

Reacting to Dissent: The Alien and Sedition Acts

Taking advantage of the emotions stirred up by the French Revolution, the Federalists passed the Alien and Sedition Acts (1798), which were designed to strengthen the Federalist party and weaken the Republican opposition. The Alien Acts made it more difficult to become a citizen and easier to arrest and deport any noncitizens thought to endanger national security. The Sedition Act made it easier to arrest a person for criticizing the government. Protests were made against these acts for challenging the freedom of speech and of the press. Madison and Jefferson in the Virginia and Kentucky Resolutions declared the acts dangerous to civil liberties and representative government.

The Two-Term Presidency

After serving two terms, Washington rejected a third term as president. In doing so, he established a tradition that was not broken until 1940 and 1944, when Franklin D. Roosevelt won a third and then a fourth term. Unhappiness over Roosevelt's break with tradition led to passage of the Twenty-second Amendment that limited a President to two terms in office.

CONGRESSIONAL INTERPRETATION, ACTION, AND CUSTOM

The Constitution supplied few details of how the machinery of government would operate, so early congressional actions helped set up that machinery. For example, Congress also created the first five executive departments—Treasury, State, War (Defense), Attorney General (Justice), and Postmaster General. Today, there are 14 departments and more than 200 independent agencies.

In 1789, Congress began the custom of assigning bills to committees. This developed into today's committee system, in which standing committees review all bills before sending them on to the full House or Senate. Congressional committees can also operate as investigative committees, gathering information in order to determine the need for new laws or to examine how current laws are working.

Lobbying

Custom has also led to the development of lobbying, or actions by people representing special-interest groups for the purpose of influencing legislation. Such lobbying is protected by the First Amendment's right to petition but also regulated by federal law.

⚷ **KEY THEMES AND CONCEPTS**

Presidential Decisions and Actions
What impact did Franklin D. Roosevelt's decision to run for a third and fourth term eventually have on the U.S. Constitution?

⚷ **KEY THEMES AND CONCEPTS**

Constitutional Principles
The practice of lobbying is protected by the First Amendment's right to petition, but it is also regulated by federal law.

- Why should the government limit lobbyists' First Amendment right to petition?

Strict vs. Loose Construction

Hamilton's proposal for a national bank started the first national debate between "strict" and "loose" constructionists. Strict constructionists favor a narrow interpretation of the Constitution, holding that government can do only those things the document specifically spells out. Loose constructionists favor a freer reading of the Constitution that gives government more room to act.

In 1803, Jefferson had the chance to double the size of the nation through the Louisiana Purchase. However, supporting the purchase meant adopting a loose interpretation of the Constitution. Jefferson overcame his reluctance to spend public money and backed the purchase. In addition to adding new lands, the Louisiana Purchase also gave the United States control of the vital Mississippi River.

The Louisiana Purchase, 1803

Legend:
- United States, 1803
- Louisiana Purchase

JUDICIAL INTERPRETATION OF THE CONSTITUTION

The power of the judicial branch was greatly strengthened during the period in which John Marshall served as the nation's fourth chief justice (1801–1835).

The Marshall Court

The decision of the Supreme Court in *McCulloch* v. *Maryland* (1819) upheld the congressional creation of the Second Bank of the United States. Supporting loose interpretation, this decision strengthened federal supremacy and national economic interests.

Similarly, in 1824, the verdict in *Gibbons* v. *Ogden* expanded the powers of the national government over commerce through a broad interpretation of the congressional power to regulate interstate commerce (Article I, Section 8, Clause 3).

Perhaps most critically, Marshall led the Court in the 1803 decision in *Marbury* v. *Madison*. This decision established the court's right of judicial review, its power to rule on the constitutionality of a law.

Activism versus Restraint

Those favoring judicial activism believe the Court should use this power to help make public policy, particularly when Congress has failed to act on pressing social problems. Those favoring judicial restraint believe that this power should be used only when there is an obvious violation of the Constitution. They feel that policy-making should be left to the other two branches.

ACTIONS OF POLITICAL PARTIES

Political parties developed through custom and tradition. The debate between Federalists and Anti-Federalists over ratification revealed the existence of differences of opinion on government. These differences led to the formation of the first two political parties—the Federalists and the Democratic-Republicans.

The formation of political parties led to constitutional changes in the method of electing the president. Party politics also gave rise to nominating conventions and the pledging of electoral votes to a candidate. Today, due to the growth of primaries and party caucuses, the presidential candidate has usually been selected before the delegates attend the nominating convention.

The First Political Parties

Federalists	Republicans
1. Led by Alexander Hamilton, John Adams	1. Led by Thomas Jefferson, James Madison
2. Wealthy and well-educated should lead nation	2. People should have political power
3. Strong central government	3. Strong state governments
4. Emphasis on manufacturing, shipping, and trade	4. Emphasis on agriculture
5. Loose interpretation of Constitution	5. Strict interpretation of Constitution
6. Pro-British	6. Pro-French
7. Favored national bank	7. Opposed national bank
8. Favored protective tariff	8. Opposed protective tariff

KEY THEMES AND CONCEPTS

Government

Supreme Court decisions have affected the separation of powers in the federal system. How did *Marbury* v. *Madison* affect the separation of powers?

KEY THEMES AND CONCEPTS

Government

The peaceful transfer of political power from one party to another is an important feature of the democratic system in the United States.

ANALYZING DOCUMENTS

Jefferson left instructions that his gravestone be inscribed:

"Author of the Declaration of Independence, the Statute of Virginia for Religious Freedom, and father of the University of Virginia."

• What does this tell you about a man who was both President and Vice President of the United States, governor of Virginia, the first secretary of state, and the second minister to France?

READING STRATEGY

Reading for Evidence

Is the War of 1812 best described as

- a second war for independence?

- a war of expansion?

- a war for rights on the seas?

Explain your answer.

In the first half of the 1800s, many more men had the right to vote, and the campaign techniques and organization of political parties changed to appeal to this broader electorate.

While major political parties have changed infrequently, the nation has seen many influential "third parties." Such parties have offered criticisms and suggested reforms later adopted by the major parties when in power.

FOREIGN POLICY: 1800–1823

Events in Europe from 1789 to 1815 influenced domestic and foreign policies of the United States. Presidents maintained American neutrality, staying out of European wars while insisting on the rights of the United States as a nation. The distance from Europe made it easier to keep out of European affairs. However, the right to trade with European nations remained a major concern because America's economic well-being depended on such trade.

War of 1812

Meanwhile, Britain and France remained at war, and Britain outraged Americans by seizing American merchant ships trying to reach France. Congress passed the Embargo Act of 1807—which prohibited trade with other nations—in an attempt to punish Britain. American exports fell, but Britain was largely unaffected. Protests led to the repeal of the act in 1809.

ANALYZING DOCUMENTS

Examine the table. What effect did the War of 1812 have on U.S exports? Why?

United States Exports, 1800–1820

Source: *Historical Statistics of the United States, Colonial Times to 1970*

Britain continued to violate American freedom of the seas, seizing American ships and forcing American sailors to serve in the British navy. Meanwhile, western and southern "War Hawks"—interested in expanding into British Canada and Spanish Florida—urged war. In 1812, Congress declared war on Britain. The war, however, was not supported by all Americans and provoked disputes among different sections of the nation.

Although the war ended in a draw in 1814, it produced some significant long-term results.

- The war reinforced the American belief that a policy of neutrality regarding European affairs was justified.
- Native American tribes in the West lost their ally, Britain, and were much less able to stand up to American expansion.
- American manufacturing began to grow, particularly in New England, when the United States was cut off from European imports.
- Opposing the war weakened the Federalist Party, which soon ceased to be a major factor in national politics.
- In Andrew Jackson and William Henry Harrison, the nation gained new war heroes. "The Star Spangled Banner" was inspired by the bombarding of Fort McHenry.

Foreign Policy After the War of 1812

The new national self-confidence also revealed itself in the field of diplomacy. John Quincy Adams, secretary of state for President James Monroe, settled the border between the United States and Canada. He also acquired Florida from Spain and reached agreement with that nation on the southern boundary of the Louisiana Purchase.

Monroe Doctrine

Adams was the chief adviser on the 1823 Monroe Doctrine, which became the foundation of the United States' foreign policy in the Western Hemisphere. The Monroe Doctrine called for

- an end to European colonization in the Western Hemisphere
- no intervention by Europe in existing nations in this hemisphere
- a declaration that European interference was "dangerous to our peace and safety"
- a promise of noninterference by the United States in European affairs and European colonies

In 1823, the United States lacked the military might to enforce this doctrine. However, Great Britain agreed to support the United States if this policy were challenged. By the end of the 1800s, the United States was actively enforcing the policy on its own.

Questions for Regents Practice

For online Questions for Regents Practice,
visit the Prentice Hall Web site at www.phschool.com.

MULTIPLE CHOICE

Directions

Review the Test-Taking Strategies section of this book. Then answer the following questions, drawn from actual Regents examinations. Each question is followed by four choices. Read each question carefully. Decide which choice is the correct answer. Then on a separate piece of paper, mark your answer for each question.

1 "We hold these truths to be self-evident, that all men are created equal, that they are endowed by their Creator with certain unalienable rights, that among these are life, liberty, and the pursuit of happiness."

This quotation reflects beliefs mainly derived from
1 the Magna Carta
2 the divine right monarchs of Europe
3 John Locke's theory of natural rights
4 Marxist philosophy

Base your answers to questions 2 and 3 on the quotation below and on your knowledge of social studies.

"That to secure these rights, governments are instituted among men, deriving their just powers from the consent of the governed; that whenever any form of government becomes destructive of those ends, it is the right of the people to alter or abolish it, and to institute new government. . . ."

2 This quotation presents a justification for
1 anarchy
2 revolution
3 despotism
4 laissez faire

3 According to the quotation, governments get their authority from
1 the people
2 powerful leaders
3 the justice system
4 political parties

4 "The individual can be free *only* when the power of one governmental branch is balanced by the other two."

—Baron de Montesquieu, 1735 (adapted)

The idea expressed in this quotation is best illustrated by which aspect of the United States government?
1 existence of a Cabinet
2 separation of powers
3 elastic clause
4 executive privilege

5 In the colonial era, developments such as the New England town meetings and the establishment of the Virginia House of Burgesses represented
1 colonial attempts to build a strong national government
2 efforts by the British to strengthen their control over the colonies
3 steps in the growth of representative democracy
4 early social reform movements

6   "The only representatives of the people of these colonies are persons chosen therein by themselves; and that no taxes ever have been, or can be constitutionally imposed on them but by their respective legislatures."

—Statement by the Stamp Act Congress, 1765

What is a valid conclusion that can be drawn from this quotation?
1 The colonial legislatures should be appointed by the English King with the consent of Parliament.
2 Only the colonists' elected representatives should have the power to levy taxes.
3 The English King should have the right to tax the colonists.
4 The colonists should be opposed to all taxation.

7   One way in which the United States Constitution differed from the Articles of Confederation was that the Constitution
1 created a national government having three branches
2 provided for the direct election of the President by the voters
3 made the amendment process more difficult
4 increased the powers of the states

Base your answers to questions 8 and 9 on the discussion below and on your knowledge of social studies.

Speaker A: States must be represented in the national government solely on the basis of population. It is indeed the only fair situation.

Speaker B: The national legislature must be based on equal representation of the states to protect the interests of the small states.

Speaker C: States must accept the supremacy of the national government on all issues; otherwise, the system will fail.

Speaker D: The national Congress should

consist of two houses: one in which representation is based on population, and one in which states are equally represented.

8   Which document was being written when this discussion most likely occurred?
1 Declaration of Independence
2 United States Constitution
3 Covenant of the League of Nations
4 Charter of the United Nations

9   Which speaker's idea about representation was actually included in the document that was written?
1 A
2 B
3 C
4 D

10   "We should consider we are providing a constitution for future generations of Americans, and not merely for the particular circumstances of the moment."

—Delegate at the Constitutional Convention of 1787

The writers of the Constitution best reflected this idea when they provided that
1 Senators should be elected directly by the people
2 Three-fifths of the slaves should be counted as part of the total population
3 Congress shall make all laws necessary and proper to carry out its constitutional powers
4 Political parties should be established to represent various viewpoints

11   During the debates over the ratification of the United States Constitution, Federalists and Anti-Federalists disagreed most strongly over the
1 division of powers between the national and state governments
2 provision for admitting new states to the Union
3 distribution of powers between the Senate and the House of Representatives
4 method of amending the Constitution

12 The main purpose of the Bill of Rights is to
1 prevent governmental abuse of power
2 increase the power of the Federal judiciary
3 provide for separation of powers
4 create a bicameral legislature

13 The fact that the United States Constitution provided for federalism and a system of checks and balances suggests that
1 the original thirteen states sought to dominate the national government
2 its writers desired the national government to rule over the states
3 its writers feared a concentration of political power
4 the American people of that time supported a military government

limited gov

14 The United States Supreme Court is sometimes said to fulfill a legislative function because
1 its members are appointed by the President
2 its judgments may determine the effect of the law
3 its members serve only so long as Congress approves
4 it meets regularly with Congress to advise on the appropriateness of proposed laws

15 Which quotation taken from the United States Constitution provides for limiting the power of government?
1 "All persons born or naturalized in the United States . . . are citizens of the United States . . ."
2 "This Constitution . . . shall be the supreme law of the land . . ."
3 "The President shall be commander in chief of the army and navy . . ."
4 "Congress shall make no law respecting an establishment of religion . . . or abridging the freedom of speech, or of the press . . ."

16 Which action is an example of lobbying by a special interest group?
1 labor union members threatening to strike if their company opens a factory in a foreign nation
2 members of Congress introducing a bill that will provide for low-interest college loans
3 a congressional committee investigating the activities of organized crime
4 several lumber companies asking Senators to allow logging on Federal lands

17 If the President has vetoed a bill, the United States Constitution provides that the bill will become a law when the bill is
1 declared constitutional by the Supreme Court
2 passed again by two-thirds of both houses of Congress
3 approved by three-fourths of the State legislatures
4 approved by a joint committee of Congress

18 In the United States, the electoral college system affects the campaigns of major-party presidential candidates by influencing candidates to
1 concentrate upon the states with large populations
2 place more emphasis on controversial issues than on personality
3 focus upon the states where winning by a large plurality is likely
4 appeal to the electoral college members rather than to the general public

# of electoral vote = # of people in cong

19 The decision of President George Washington to use the state militia to put down the Whiskey Rebellion in 1794 demonstrated that the
1 states were still the dominant power in the new nation
2 President was becoming a military dictator
3 Federal Government had no authority to impose an excise tax
4 new National Government intended to enforce Federal laws

20 In United States history, which statement best represents the political ideology of Alexander Hamilton and the Federalists?
1 Only the wealthy will survive in the economic system.
2 A strong central government is essential for the economic growth of the nation.
3 No one should have to pay taxes to the National Government.
4 Elected officials should give public jobs to those who helped them into office.

21 The major role of political parties in the United States is to
1 protect the American public from corrupt public officials
2 insure that free and honest elections are held
3 nominate candidates for public office and conduct campaigns
4 meet constitutional requirements for choosing the President

22 The term "judicial review" refers to the power of the ~~Marbury vs. Madison~~
1 Supreme Court to determine the constitutionality of laws
2 Congress to pass laws over the veto of the President
3 states to approve amendments to the Constitution
4 President to veto bills passed by Congress

23 In deciding to purchase the Louisiana Territory, President Thomas Jefferson had to overcome the problem of
1 obtaining the support of Western settlers
2 passing the constitutional amendment necessary to authorize the purchase
3 avoiding a possible war with England over the purchase
4 contradicting his belief in a strict interpretation of the Constitution

24 "The great rule of conduct for us in regard to foreign nations is, in extending our commercial relations to have with them as little *political* connection as possible."

—George Washington, Farewell Address, 1796

This statement helped establish the United States foreign policy called
1 containment
2 internationalism
3 imperialism
4 neutrality

25 The Monroe Doctrine declared that the United States would
1 prevent the establishment of new European colonies anywhere in the world
2 help colonies in North and South America adopt a democratic form of government
3 view European interference in the Americas as a threat to the national interest of the United States
4 prevent other nations from trading with South American nations

1 or 3

26   "Many, if not most, of our Indian wars have had their origin in broken promises and acts of injustice on our part."

The author of this statement would most likely agree that the history of United States treatment of Native Americans was primarily the result of
1   prejudice toward Native American religions
2   the desire for territorial expansion
3   a refusal of Native Americans to negotiate treaties
4   opposing economic and political systems

27   Which was the most important reason for the social mobility that existed in the English colonies of North America during the 18th century?
1   absence of racial prejudice among the colonists
2   existence of a strong cultural heritage
3   early emphasis on rapid industrialization
4   availability of land

28   Under mercantilism, the thirteen American colonies were expected to provide Great Britain with
1   finished American-manufactured goods
2   raw materials and markets for British products
3   officials to represent colonial interests in Parliament
4   laborers to work in British factories

29   Which feature of the United States government is based upon principles found in the Magna Carta and the Petition of Right?
1   the levying of a personal income tax
2   the power of Congress to declare war
3   the power of the House of Representatives to originate all revenue bills
4   Presidential veto power

30   In the 18th century, the British colonies in North America were most similar to Great Britain in their
1   common law legal system
2   countrywide established church
3   opportunities for social mobility
4   dependence upon manufacturing as the economic base

31   Which was most influential in making the idea of separation of church and state a part of the United States political tradition?
1   the democratic heritage of ancient Athens
2   the Roman Republic's principles of religious freedom
3   practices of European colonial governments
4   the diversity of the new nation's population

32   Which idea had a major influence on the authors of the Articles of Confederation?
1   A strong central government threatens the rights of the people and the states.
2   All of the people must be granted the right to vote.
3   Three branches of government are needed to protect liberty.
4   The central government must have the power to levy taxes and to control trade.

33   At the Constitutional Convention of 1787, the Three-fifths Compromise and the Great Compromise dealt with the issue of
1   amendments to the Constitution
2   women's rights
3   representation in Congress
4   the rights of the accused

34 In the 1780s, the publication of *The Federalist* papers was intended to
1 justify the American Revolution to the colonists
2 provide a plan of operation for the delegates to the Constitutional Convention
3 encourage ratification of the United States Constitution
4 express support for the election of George Washington to the Presidency

35 Under the United States Constitution, those powers not delegated to the federal government are
1 exercised only by state governors
2 concerned only with issues of taxation
3 reserved to the states or to the people
4 divided equally between the states and the national government

36 "The accumulation of all powers, legislative, executive, and judicial, in the same hands . . . may justly be pronounced the very definition of tyranny."

The writers of the United States Constitution intended to prevent the situation described in this quotation by
1 developing a system of checks and balances
2 relying on an electoral college
3 establishing political parties
4 including the implies powers clause

37 Only a small number of amendments have been added to the United States Constitution mainly because the
1 executive branch has feared a loss of power
2 Constitution has been broadly interpreted and applied
3 public has not objected to the government's use of its power
4 Constitution is clear in its original intent and seldom needs amending

38 "The privilege of the writ of *habeas corpus* shall not be suspended, unless when in cases of rebellion or invasion the public safety may require it."

This provision is evidence that the writers of the United States Constitution
1 wanted the President to have unlimited power during wartime
2 wanted to balance individual liberty with the needs of the nation
3 did not trust the common people to obey the laws
4 expected the American people to oppose most government policies

Four statements dealing with the formation of a new government are given below. Base your answers to questions 39 and 40 on these statements and on your knowledge of social studies.

Statement A: Each person must be able to voice his or her concerns on all issues that involve this new nation and bear the responsibility for the decisions made.

Statement B: The power of this new nation must rest in a strong, stable group that makes important decisions with the approval, but not the participation, of all.

Statement C: There must be several governments within one nation to ensure adequate voice and responsibility to all.

Statement D: Individuals must not allow their freedoms to be swallowed by an all-powerful government.

39 Which statement best shows the desire for safeguards such as those in the Bill of Rights?
1 A   3 C
2 B   4 D

40 Which statement best represents the ideas of federalism?
1 A   3 C
2 B   4 D

THEMATIC ESSAY 1

In developing your answers to the essay, be sure to keep these general definitions in mind:

(a) <u>discuss</u> means "to make observations about something using facts, reasoning, and argument; to present in some detail"

(b) <u>describe</u> means "to illustrate something in words or to tell about it"

(c) <u>evaluate</u> means "to examine and judge the significance, worth, or condition of; to determine the value of"

Directions

Write a well-organized essay that includes an introduction, several paragraphs addressing the task below, and a conclusion.

Theme: Government—Separation of Powers

The Constitution of the United States provides for three branches of government— legislative, executive, and judicial—with separate powers as well as a system of checks and balances among them. Issues in United States history have sometimes led to disagreements between government branches.

Task

From your study of United States history, identify two important issues which involved disagreements between branches of the government.

   For each issue identified:

- Describe the disagreement between two branches of the federal government over the issue
- Discuss the historical circumstances surrounding the disagreement
- Discuss how the disagreement was resolved
- Discuss one immediate or one long-term effect of the disagreement on United States history

Suggestions

You may use any important issue in United States history which involved disagreement between branches of the government. Some suggestions you might wish to consider include: *Marbury* v. *Madison* (1803); Andrew Jackson's Indian removal policy (1830s); extension of slavery (1850s); impeachment of President Andrew Johnson (1868); ratification of the Treaty of Versailles (1919); Franklin D. Roosevelt's New Deal legislation (1930s); War Powers Act (1973); impeachment of President Bill Clinton (1998–1999)

You are *not* limited to these suggestions.

Guidelines

In your essay be sure to:

- Address all aspects of the *Task*
- Analyze, evaluate, or compare and/or contrast issues and events whenever possible
- Fully support the theme of the essay with relevant facts, examples, and details
- Write a well-developed essay that consistently demonstrates a logical and clear plan of organization
- Introduce the theme by establishing a framework that is beyond a simple restatement of the *Task*
- Conclude your essay with a strong summation of the theme

THEMATIC ESSAY 2

In developing your answers to the essay, be sure to keep these general definitions in mind:

(a) <u>discuss</u> means "to make observations about something using facts, reasoning, and argument; to present in some detail"

(b) <u>describe</u> means "to illustrate something in words or to tell about it"

(c) <u>evaluate</u> means "to examine and judge the significance, worth, or condition of; to determine the value of"

Directions

Write a well-organized essay that includes an introduction, several paragraphs addressing the task below, and a conclusion.

Theme: Constitutional Principles and the Supreme Court

Throughout United States history, Supreme Court decisions concerning conflicts over constitutional issues have had a long-term effect on the nation.

Task

From your study of United States history, identify two Supreme Court decisions concerning conflicts over constitutional issues which have had a long-term effect on the nation.

For each Supreme Court decision identified:

- State the conflict over a constitutional issue which the Supreme Court decision addressed.
- Discuss the historical circumstances surrounding the Supreme Court decision.
- Discuss the extent to which the Supreme Court decision resolved the conflict over the constitutional issue.
- Discuss the long term impact of the Supreme Court decision.

Suggestions

You may use any Supreme Court decision concerning conflicts over constitutional issues which has had a long-term effect on the nation. Some suggestions you might wish to consider include: *McCulloch* v. *Maryland* (federalism); *Marbury* v. *Madison* (role of the judiciary); *Gibbons* v. *Ogden* (commerce); *Scott* v. *Sandford* (separation of powers); *Schenck* v. *United States* (freedom of expression); *Gideon* v. *Wainwright* (right to legal counsel); *Heart of Atlanta Motel* v. *United States* (equal protection under the law).

You are *not* limited to these suggestions.

Guidelines

In your essay be sure to:

- Address all aspects of the *Task*
- Analyze, evaluate, or compare and/or contrast issues and events whenever possible
- Fully support the theme of the essay with relevant facts, examples, and details
- Write a well-developed essay that consistently demonstrates a logical and clear plan of organization
- Introduce the theme by establishing a framework that is beyond a simple restatement of the *Task*
- Conclude your essay with a strong summation of the theme

2 The Constitution Tested: Nationalism and Sectionalism

★ THE BIG IDEA
In the early to mid-19th century,

- the North and South developed different patterns of life and philosophies of government.

- immigration and territorial expansion produced growth and change.

- reform movements attempted to correct many of the injustices of American society.

- sectional differences increased and led to war.

⚷ KEY TERMS

Industrial Revolution
potato famine
spoils system
Tariff of 1828
Indian Removal
Trail of Tears
abolition
Underground Railroad
Seneca Falls Convention
manifest destiny
Compromise of 1850
popular sovereignty
secede
Confederate States of
  America
Battle of Antietam
Battle of Gettysburg
Emancipation Proclamation

SECTION OVERVIEW

In the first half of the 1800s, the United States grew in size and population. The North, blessed with natural resources and a growing population, began industrializing. In the agricultural South, cotton became the dominant crop, and slavery became more firmly rooted in place.

As a new age of mass politics and reform dominated the 1830s and 1840s, tensions grew among the regions, pulling North and South apart. The southern states began to see their power and influence decreasing, and soon after the election of 1860, 11 southern states seceded from the Union. The Civil War that followed tested whether the nation and its Constitution would survive.

KEY THEMES AND CONCEPTS

Places and Regions How did the sectional differences between North and South lead to civil war?

Individuals, Groups, Institutions How did territorial expansion affect the lives of Native Americans, African Americans, and white Americans?

Constitutional Principles How did the United States become more democratic from 1820 to 1865?

Reform Movements What major reform movements were organized, and how successful were they?

KEY PEOPLE

Meriwether Lewis and William Clark

Andrew Jackson

Martin Van Buren

Abraham Lincoln

Ulysses S. Grant

Robert E. Lee

KEY SUPREME COURT CASES

Worcester v. *Georgia*

Scott v. *Sandford*

PART 1 TESTING THE CONSTITUTION: STRESS AND CRISIS

In the decades before the Civil War, some forces contributed to national unity, while others began splitting the nation apart.

FACTORS UNIFYING THE UNITED STATES

The factors that unified the United States include the first and second two-party systems, the market economy and interstate commerce, and decisions of the Marshall Court.

The first two-party system consisted of the Federalists and the Democratic-Republicans, parties that offered different political philosophies and proposals for action. The second two-party system developed in 1834, when the new Whig party opposed Andrew Jackson's party, now called the Democrats. Both parties ran campaigns that attracted interest and voters.

The development of a market economy and increased interstate commerce helped to stimulate economic growth nationwide. In the 1800s, revolutions in transportation and technology led to industrialization and urbanization. Specialization was possible because people could now purchase what they did not make or grow. Banks expanded to provide the capital for investment and the funds needed for exchange of goods and services. Southern and western crops were exchanged for northern manufactured goods.

Decisions of the Marshall Court also promoted national unity. These decisions helped to encourage a national economy by expanding interstate commerce and protecting the validity of contracts.

READING STRATEGY

Organizing Information
List three factors which unified the United States between 1789 and 1861.

1.

2.

3.

Nationalism and Sectionalism, 1820–1865

| **1820** Missouri Compromise | **1832** *Worcester v. Georgia* | **1852** *Uncle Tom's Cabin* published | **1857** *Scott v. Sandford* | **1861** Confederacy founded; fall of Fort Sumter | **1865** Civil War ends; Lincoln assassinated |

| 1820 | 1830 | 1840 | 1850 | 1860 |

| **1828** Andrew Jackson elected President | **1850** Compromise of 1850 | **1854** Kansas-Nebraska Act | **1858** Lincoln-Douglas debates | **1863** Emancipation Proclamation |

Comparing Household and Market Economies

	Household Economy	Market Economy
Producers	Household	Industries
Labor	Members of the household produce a variety of goods at home	Workers specialize in producing a certain product outside the home. They exchange their labor for cash.
Goods	Goods are made primarily to be used by the household	Goods are sold on the open market for a profit.

ANALYZING DOCUMENTS

Based on the table above and your knowledge of American history, answer the following questions.

- How were workers affected by the change to a market economy?

- How did the shift to a market economy promote nationalism?

⚷ KEY THEMES AND CONCEPTS

Factors of Production
The first successful textile mill was built in Rhode Island in 1793. By 1814, there were about 240 mills in the United States, most of them in New England, Pennsylvania, and New York.

The American System Supports a National Economy

Senator Henry Clay, supported by John Quincy Adams, designed a legislative program called the "American System." The program benefited the North, South, and West, and unified the nation by

- Establishing a better national transportation system to aid trade and national defense
- Setting the first protective tariff to encourage manufacturing and provide funds for improved transportation networks
- Creating a second national bank to promote the financial support necessary

URBAN AND INDUSTRIAL PATTERNS IN THE NORTH

The use of new technologies in manufacturing—particularly steam engines and machines to spin thread and weave cloth—gave rise to the **Industrial Revolution** in Great Britain during the 1700s. By the early 1800s, these new technologies reached the United States. Factory builders flocked to the North, particularly New England, because of its abundant supplies of iron, coal, and swiftly flowing rivers used for water power.

By 1860, northern factories had entered a worldwide competition for markets. The North began to take on a new identity as an urban manufacturing and commercial area. About 70 percent of national manufacturing was located in the North.

The Transportation Revolution

New technologies also stimulated the development of transportation systems to connect northern markets to western farmlands. Railroads and canals, such as the Erie Canal in New York State, encouraged the growth of industry. The Erie Canal connected the Atlantic Ocean (at New York City) through the Great Lakes to the vast interior of the United States. New York became a major port. Railroads later

The Transportation Revolution

Steam Power
- In 1807, Robert Fulton's *Clermont* steams up the Hudson River.
- Steamships help farmers ship their goods to markets around the world.

Canals
- Erie Canal connects Lake Erie to New York City in 1825.
- By 1840, 3,000 miles of canals are in use.

Changes in Transportation

Roads
- By 1833, the Cumberland Road runs from Maryland to Ohio.
- New roads of stone and gravel help Americans move west.

Railroads
- In 1828, the B & O railroad line becomes nation's first railroad.
- By 1840, U.S. has more miles of railroad track than any other country in the world.

connected New York to other major cities and to the West. In the 19th century New York became the financial and industrial center of the nation.

The Factory System

By 1850, most American manufacturing was no longer done in homes and small shops, but instead in factories by workers using machines. This was called the factory system. The first mills were in New England, with the "model" Lowell mill the most well known. It employed white, teenage farm girls as its labor force, offering them an opportunity for financial independence. The girls lived at the mill in a highly regulated environment. Most planned to stay only a few years. Here the first work protests and strikes were organized against wage cuts.

By the 1840s and 1850s, the mills acquired a more permanent work force—Irish immigrant women who needed to work to help support their families. Working conditions were dictated by a strict routine. Twelve-hour days and six-day weeks were the routine. Gains made by the first union movements often were lost when demand for goods dropped in the fluctuating business cycle.

Urban Problems

By 1860, nine of the ten largest cities in the nation were in the North. After 1840, immigrants made up the majority of the population in some cities. The gap between rich and poor widened, as a distinctive rich upper class and poor working class developed in the cities. Private companies provided sanitation and water only to those who could afford to pay for these services. Cities were unsafe, and police forces did not begin to appear until the mid-1830s.

GEOGRAPHY IN HISTORY

Between 1800 and 1850, a substantial migration of people from the South to northern cities began.

- What caused this shift in population?
- What were the benefits of this migration? What problems were created?
- What was the impact on sectionalism?

KEY THEMES AND CONCEPTS

Change

Cities grew tremendously during the first half of the 19th century. The population of New York City (Manhattan only), for example, soared from about 33,000 in 1790 to 124,000 in 1820, and about 516,000 by 1850.

Urban and Rural Populations, 1800–1850

Source: *Historical Statistics of the United States, Colonial Times to 1970*

Both urban and rural populations grew rapidly in the early 1800s. By 1850, 12 percent of the total population lived in urban areas.

Middle-Class and Working-Class Life in the North

Industrialization changed family life and gender roles. Previously, families worked together at home and on the farm, taking on different tasks according to gender. After industrialization, both working-class men and women worked, and their jobs also differed depending on their gender. More women worked as servants, more men in factories. The lives of middle-class men were often centered in the new business world, while middle-class women found their lives defined by the home. One of the few jobs considered proper for a single middle-class woman was teaching.

Working-class children usually had to make economic contributions to the family, but middle-class children did not. Childhood, as a specific stage in one's life, received new attention. Middle-class parents supported the growing movement for public schools.

Free African Americans in the North continued to face racism and legal restrictions. Public places remained segregated. African Americans also faced discrimination in hiring. Women were more likely than men to find permanent work, most often as household helpers.

Immigration

Until about 1850, most immigrants came from northern and western Europe, particularly Ireland and Germany. The Germans included many who were Jewish. Scandinavians, Dutch, Swiss, and English also immigrated. They generally settled in the North and West because of greater economic opportunities there.

REASONS FOR IMMIGRATION Between 1845 and 1850, millions of Irish people came to the United States because of the **potato famine,** a period of mass starvation caused by failure of the potato crop. Many Germans came seeking peace and stability after the failed 1848 Revolution in Germany. Most immigrants arrived in search of better economic opportunity.

AREAS OF SETTLEMENT The Irish tended to settle in northeastern cities. Some Germans also stayed in cities, but many moved west to start farms, as did many Scandinavian immigrants.

DIFFICULTIES THEY FACED Irish and German Catholic immigrants often faced hostility from native-born Americans, some of whom feared economic competition from the newcomers. Others resented the Catholic or Jewish immigrants at a time when the nation was mostly Protestant. Anti-immigrant feelings were so strong that a political party called the Know-Nothings was formed to ensure that native-born Americans received better treatment than immigrants. The party did very well in local elections in northern states.

CONTRIBUTIONS Immigrants made significant contributions to the growth of this nation. Irish workers helped build railroads and labored in factories. Germans and Scandinavians brought advanced farming techniques and new ideas on education, such as kindergarten.

KEY THEMES AND CONCEPTS

Immigration and Migration

- Where did the immigrants of the first half of the 19th century come from?

- Why did they come to the United States?

- How did their reasons for coming differ from those of earlier immigrants? How were they the same?

- What reaction did these new immigrants face from native-born Americans?

PATTERNS OF SOUTHERN DEVELOPMENT

In contrast to the North, the South remained agricultural. Its wealth remained invested in land and slaves, and its economy was dependent chiefly on its cotton crop grown with slave labor. The southern population grew slowly because it failed to attract immigrants.

Growth of a Cotton Economy

Most southern farms were small and were worked without slaves. Eli Whitney's 1793 invention of the cotton gin, which removed the seeds from cotton, transformed cotton into a successful commercial crop.

The profitability of cotton growing stimulated the growth of slavery. It also spurred westward migration of planters with their slaves, looking for new land on which to grow cotton. Planters moved first into the Old Southwest (Alabama and Mississippi), and later into Louisiana, Arkansas, and Texas.

In time, cotton made up half of all exports from the United States. However, the South's agricultural base kept it economically dependent on the North, both as a market for cotton and as a source of manufactured goods.

The Growth of "King Cotton"

```
┌─────────────────────┐          ┌─────────────────────┐
│  South has good     │   ───▶   │ South develops      │
│  conditions for     │          │ economy based on    │
│  farming.           │          │ farming and slavery.│
└─────────────────────┘          └─────────────────────┘
                                            │
                                            ▼
┌─────────────────────┐          ┌─────────────────────┐
│ Rich landowners     │          │ Invention of cotton │
│ create huge         │          │ gin makes cotton    │
│ plantations, relying│          │ manufacturing       │
│ on slave labor to   │          │ more profitable.    │
│ grow cotton.        │          └─────────────────────┘
└─────────────────────┘                     │
       ▲                                     ▼
┌─────────────────────┐          ┌─────────────────────┐
│ Cotton becomes the  │   ◀───   │ Industrial Revolution│
│ most valuable       │          │ leads to growing    │
│ product in the South.│         │ textile industry    │
└─────────────────────┘          │ which needs cotton  │
                                 │ to make cloth.      │
                                 └─────────────────────┘
```

In the early 1800s, cotton became the South's most important crop.

ANALYZING DOCUMENTS

Examine the graphic organizer above. What caused the increased dependence on slavery in the first half of the 19th century?

READING STRATEGY

Reinforcing Main Ideas
What were some results of the expansion of slavery?

Men and Women on Plantations

Slaveholding men dominated political, economic, and social life in the South. Planters' wives and daughters were responsible for the domestic sphere. They managed the care, feeding, and clothing of their families and the slave families as well.

Life Under Slavery

Daily life for most slaves was very difficult. They had no control over their own lives or their children's lives, and they were at the mercy of the slaveholders or overseers. Slaves who worked as field hands often worked from dawn to sunset, while those who were house servants often worked long past sunset.

Slaves generally ate inexpensive food and wore rough clothing. Cabins housed one or two families. However, slaves were also a financial investment, and this affected their treatment. After the importing of slaves ended, the economic value of slaves increased, and their health care improved.

Slaves could not legally marry, but families remained central to the African American community. Parents instilled the importance of family in their children, while preparing them to cope with a life of slavery. Children were not educated and began work as young as eight years old. As planters moved westward in search of new lands for growing cotton, slave families were often tragically broken up.

The religious practices of slaves were a mixture of Protestant Christian and African elements. Music was an important part of worship services. Religion provided slaves with comfort and hope for salvation.

Resistance

Resistance against slavery took many forms. Most protests took the forms of escape, self-mutilation, sabotage, or work slowdowns. Although open rebellions were rare, they instilled fear within the white slaveholding society. There were several notable slave revolts.

- 1800: Gabriel Prosser's Conspiracy in Virginia led by urban skilled workers is discovered.
- 1822: Denmark Vesey's plans to lead a South Carolina revolt are uncovered.
- 1831: Nat Turner leads a revolt in Virginia.

Rebellions led southern lawmakers to pass increasingly strict laws to maintain slavery. Freeing slaves became more difficult, and teaching a slave to read became illegal.

THE AGE OF JACKSON

The rise of Andrew Jackson to the presidency in 1829 signaled a change in American politics. Born in Tennessee, Jackson was the first President from the West. He was also the first President elected on a wave of popular support, rather than through party politics.

The Rise of Mass Politics

By the mid-1820s, most states had dropped their property qualifications for voting. In 1828, the number of voters was three times larger than it had been in 1824. Andrew Jackson, a popular hero of the War of 1812, appealed to these new voters and won the popular vote.

Selecting a presidential candidate became more democratic in 1832. Candidates were chosen for the first time by a national nominating convention, rather than a few party leaders.

Rallies, slogans, and often vicious written attacks marked the advent of mass politics. "Secret" ballots became popular, but parties printed them in colors so it was easy to tell for whom a person voted. Only after the Civil War did the truly secret ballot come into general use.

The Spoils System and Civil Service Reform

During Jackson's presidency, a system developed in which government jobs were given to loyal supporters of the political party that won the election. This was called the **spoils system.**

By the 1880s, people began to demand that people should be given government jobs based on merit, rather than on party loyalty. During Chester Arthur's presidency, the Pendleton Act of 1883 was passed, marking the beginning of civil service reform. The act required that competitive exams be used to hire certain government workers, and it set up a commission to administer the tests. It also banned the common practice of forcing government employees to give money to political parties.

ANALYZING DOCUMENTS

"This Fourth of July is yours, not mine. You may rejoice, I must mourn. . . . What, to the American slave, is your 4th of July? I answer; a day that reveals to him, more than any other days in the year, the gross injustice and cruelty to which he is the constant victim."

—Frederick Douglass, Rochester, New York, 1852

- Why does Douglass find it impossible to celebrate the Fourth of July?

- How did slavery contradict the civic values expressed in the Declaration of Independence?

PREPARING FOR THE EXAM

On the exam, you will need to understand how national elections work. Be sure you know the answers to the following questions.

- What is the difference between a popular and electoral vote?

- What happens when a candidate fails to win a majority of the electoral college?

The Presidency of Andrew Jackson

President Andrew Jackson

Fires over 2,000 government workers and replaces them with his own supporters

Vetoes more acts of Congress than all six previous Presidents combined

Closes Bank of the United States

Threatens to send huge army to South Carolina to force the state to obey tariff laws

Uses Indian Removal Act to force 100,000 Native Americans from their homelands

Jackson's forceful actions earned him both strong support and angry opposition throughout the country.

 KEY THEMES AND CONCEPTS

Economic Systems

- Why did the South believe that the North benefited from a protective tariff?

- How did this debate increase sectional conflict?

PREPARING FOR THE EXAM

After John C. Calhoun resigned the vice presidency, he was replaced by a New Yorker, Martin Van Buren, who later succeeded Jackson to the presidency.

- How is a President or Vice President replaced when one resigns? Review the case of Richard Nixon and Spiro Agnew.

GROWING SECTIONALISM

In the first half of the 1800s, growing feelings of sectionalism developed, pulling the sections of the nation apart.

States' Rights versus Federal Supremacy

Debate raged over how the balance of power between the states and the federal government should be achieved. One part of this debate focused on protective tariffs.

THE TARIFF ISSUE Southern states opposed protective tariffs, which resulted in higher prices paid for imported manufactured goods. The agricultural South saw northern industries as the chief beneficiaries of such tariffs.

John C. Calhoun of South Carolina, Jackson's first Vice President, protested the **Tariff of 1828.** Calhoun argued that a state had the right to nullify, or declare void, any federal law that the state considered unconstitutional. This argument had first been advanced by Madison and Jefferson in the Virginia and Kentucky Resolutions.

In 1832 a new, lower tariff was passed, but South Carolina and Calhoun still protested. Calhoun resigned the vice presidency and led his state in nullifying the new tariff. President Andrew Jackson declared South Carolina's action treasonous.

The crisis resolved after Congress agreed to a gradual lowering of the tariff and passed a Force Bill authorizing the use of federal troops in South Carolina to collect the tariff. South Carolina withdrew its nullification of the tariff. However, South Carolina then nullified the Force Bill, indicating that the issue was not permanently settled.

The National Bank Issue—The Bank War

The Second Bank of the United States also provoked sectional differences. Most opposition to the bank came from southerners and westerners, who wanted a greater supply of money in circulation. They also resented the national bank's control over state banking.

In 1832, President Jackson vetoed a bill to recharter the bank. He then withdrew federal money from the bank, effectively killing it. To Jackson and many of his followers, the Second Bank of the United States had symbolized privilege and the power of special northern interests.

RELATIONS WITH NATIVE AMERICANS

As American settlers moved ever westward in the 1800s, conflict continued with the Native Americans who lived in these territories.

Native American Cultural Survival Strategies

Native Americans tried a variety of strategies to cope and retain their land and culture. In the early 1800s, two Shawnee brothers, Prophet and Tecumseh, tried to build a Pan-Indian Movement in the Old Northwest, but this movement died with Tecumseh in the War of 1812. Meanwhile, a Seneca named Handsome Lake urged the Iroquois to adopt a lifestyle based on temperance, education, farming, and peace. This lifestyle became known as cultural revitalization.

In 1813, Creeks attacked settlers in Georgia and Alabama in a series of raids, but in 1814, they were defeated at Horseshoe Bend, Alabama. The Southwest was now open to settlement.

The Cherokee attempted to survive and retain their culture through cultural adaptation, combining elements of Native American and European culture including a written constitution. This strategy, however, did not save them.

The Removal Policy

The federal government used a combination of treaties and force to move Indians westward. The treaties were worthless, because Native Americans were forced repeatedly to give up their land that had been guaranteed by treaty.

In the 1830s, President Andrew Jackson began his policy of **Indian removal**—forcing all Native Americans to move west of the Mississippi. In 1832, the Cherokee went to court to prevent Georgia from taking their land. In *Worcester* v. *Georgia*, Chief Justice John Marshall ruled that Georgia had no authority over Cherokee territory, but Georgia simply ignored the ruling. In 1838, the U.S. Army forced the Cherokee to leave in a forced march known as the **Trail of Tears.**

The Seminole of Florida were also faced with removal. A group fought the effort in the Second Seminole War. Many remained in Florida. By the 1840s, however, only scattered groups of Native Americans still lived in the East.

ANALYZING DOCUMENTS

"The consequences of a speedy removal will be important. . . . It will separate the Indians from immediate contact with settlements of whites; . . . and perhaps cause them . . . to cast off their savage habits and become an interesting, civilized, and Christian community."

—President Andrew Jackson, 1830

- What does this quote reveal about Jackson's attitude toward Native Americans?

ANALYZING DOCUMENTS

"We wish to remain on the land of our fathers. We have a perfect and original right to remain without interruption."

—Cherokee public appeal, July 17, 1830

- What does this quote reveal about how the Cherokee viewed their possession of the land?

Native American Land Transfer Before 1850

Native American land cessions

- [dotted] Land ceded before 1784
- [light gray] Land ceded 1784–1819
- [medium gray] Land ceded 1820–1834
- [dark gray] Land ceded 1835–1850
- [hatched] Reservations established by 1850
- *Iroquois* Native American culture group

ANALYZING DOCUMENTS

Compare the map above with the map on page 92.

- How does the map above relate to the territorial expansion of the United States?

THE AMERICAN REFORM TRADITION

In the early 1800s, great changes affected the way people lived and interacted with each other. The Industrial Revolution, urbanization, growth in immigration, westward expansion, and the cotton-based southern economy created opportunities as well as serious problems.

The Second Great Awakening, a religious revival movement, motivated reform with its emphasis on self-reliance, on one's ability to affect one's future and to improve the world. The movement called for self-improvement and for joining to fight forces of evil. The religious feelings that drove reform were reinforced by the republican political belief in civic virtue—that a good citizen acts for the common good.

Reform Movements

Many areas of American life inspired reform movements, including education and care of the mentally ill.

PUBLIC SCHOOLS Reformers recognized that if the people were to govern, they needed to be educated. Under the leadership of Horace Mann, Massachusetts led the 19th-century drive for public education. Mann believed that every human being had the right to an education, and he developed an educational system with grade levels and teacher training. His ideas spread rapidly. By 1860, most people had at least an elementary education in all regions but the South. Educational opportunities for girls and young women also expanded.

CARE OF THE MENTALLY ILL In the early 1800s, most mentally ill people were kept locked up in prisons. In the 1840s, a Massachusetts reformer named Dorothea Dix studied the poor treatment of the mentally ill and reported her findings to the state legislature, which authorized funds for state mental hospitals. Dix later worked with several other states that followed the example of Massachusetts.

OTHER REFORMS Reformers also pushed for the creation of prisons, hospitals, orphanages, and institutions to care for physically disabled people. In addition, a strong temperance movement organized to eliminate alcohol consumption.

Abolition

In the 1820s, the **abolition** (or antislavery) movement grew as cotton production became more profitable and slavery spread. The abolition movement attracted a wide variety of activists, including African Americans such as Frederick Douglass, Harriet Tubman, and Sojourner Truth, and white activists such as Angelina and Sarah Grimké and William Lloyd Garrison.

Abolitionists organized the **Underground Railroad,** a series of safe houses where escaping slaves could rest safely as they made their way north and into Canada. Harriet Tubman, who made 19 trips to escort runaways, was a famous leader of the Underground Railroad.

Although the abolition movement was stronger in the North than in the South, not all northerners supported it. Some northern merchants feared that the abolition movement would further sour relations between North and South and harm trade. White workers feared the competition from escaped or freed slaves willing to work for lower wages.

Women's Rights

By the 1830s, reform-minded women recognized that they faced discrimination, even within their own organizations. For example, the women delegates attending the 1840 World Anti-Slavery Convention were not allowed, after much debate, to participate in the convention.

The women's rights movement began officially in 1848, when Elizabeth Cady Stanton and Lucretia Mott organized the **Seneca Falls Convention** in Seneca Falls, New York. The first goal of this chiefly middle-class movement was to end legal inequalities faced by married women. At this time, a husband had the legal right to control all of his wife's property, earnings, and children.

In 1853, Susan B. Anthony joined Stanton in the drive for women's rights. By the 1850s, the women's rights movement began focusing on winning the vote for women. Women's right to vote in national elections was not won until 1920.

ANALYZING DOCUMENTS

"On this subject, I do not wish to think, or speak, or write, with moderation. No!, no! Tell a man whose house is on fire, to give a moderate alarm; . . . tell the mother to gradually extricate [pull out] her babe from the fire into which it has fallen;—but urge me not to use moderation in a cause like the present. I am in earnest . . .—I will not retreat a single inch—AND I WILL BE HEARD."
—William Lloyd Garrison, *The Liberator,* 1831

- Based on this quote, how would you characterize Garrison's view of how slavery should be abolished?

ANALYZING DOCUMENTS

"We hold these truths to be self-evident: that all men and women are created equal. . . . The history of mankind is a history of repeated injuries and usurpations [seizure of power] on the part of man toward woman, . . . [to establish] absolute tyranny over her. . . ."
— Declaration of Sentiments, 1848

This document was written by Elizabeth Cady Stanton at the Seneca Falls Convention.

- Which phrase did Stanton borrow from the Declaration of Independence? Why?

Study the map below and review the physical geography of the United States from Unit 1. Then answer the following questions.

- What was the effect of the Appalachian and the Rocky Mountains on settlement?

- Why were the Great Plains the last region to be settled?

- How did the arid conditions affect settlement of parts of the Mexican Cession?

TERRITORIAL EXPANSION

From 1803 to 1853, the United States expanded to its present continental boundaries.

Manifest Destiny

Many Americans believed in **manifest destiny,** the conviction that the United States had a divine mission to expand in order to spread the ideals of freedom and democracy. What Americans saw as manifest destiny was viewed quite differently by the Native American and Mexican peoples, who were in possession of these western lands. Expansion increased national pride, but by raising serious questions about slavery, also contributed to growing sectional tensions.

People Moving Westward

The first Americans to move westward were explorers, naturalists, trappers, traders, and missionaries. These were followed by trailblazers and settlers who traveled westward along routes such as the Santa Fe and the Oregon Trails. Mormons, led by Brigham Young, settled at the Great Salt Lake in 1846. In order to escape religious persecution, they selected a spot which placed them far from others. Most settlers chose

Territorial Expansion of the United States and Other Acquisitions

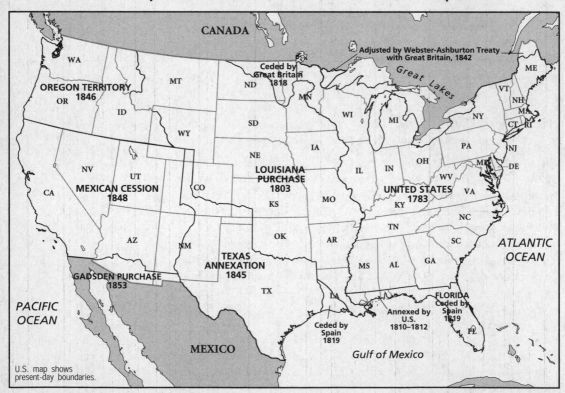

more prosperous lands in the far West, leaving the Great Plains to be settled only after the 1860s.

Lands Acquired Between 1783–1853

By 1853, the continental United States had expanded to its present boundaries. This expansion took place in several stages.

LOUISIANA PURCHASE (1803) This huge territory was acquired from France for $15 million. President Jefferson sent Meriwether Lewis and William Clark to explore this land in 1803. The information and maps they brought back contributed to expansion into this territory.

FLORIDA (1819) This territory was acquired by treaty from Spain, satisfying southern expansionists. In the Adams-Onís Treaty, Spain also gave up its claims to the Pacific Northwest in return for the United States giving up its claims to Texas.

TEXAS (1845) The United States acquired Texas and what is now parts of New Mexico, Oklahoma, Colorado, Wyoming, and Kansas from Mexico by annexation. The Spanish had long established missions and settlements in Texas. After Mexico declared its independence from Spain in 1821, southern slaveholders and other American settlers moved into Texas. In 1836, the settlers declared independence from Mexico and created the Republic of Texas. Soon, Texas requested admission to the Union, and in 1845, Texas joined as a slave state.

OREGON COUNTRY (1846) What is now Oregon, Washington, Idaho, and parts of Montana and Wyoming, was gained from Great Britain in a compromise that continued the northern border set at the 49th parallel all the way to the coast.

MEXICAN CESSION (1848) What is now California, Nevada, Utah, Arizona, and parts of New Mexico, Colorado, and Wyoming became part of the United States by the Treaty of Guadalupe Hidalgo, which ended the Mexican War (1846–1848). The Mexican War erupted in part because of Mexican objections to the Texas annexation and a dispute over the border between Texas and Mexico. President James Polk's outspoken desires to acquire California and the Southwest made it difficult to ease tensions with Mexico. After war broke out, national opinion was divided. Expansionists welcomed an opportunity to acquire more land. Northerners feared the future addition of more slave states. Some, such as Abraham Lincoln, saw it as a "war of conquest."

GADSDEN PURCHASE (1853) This piece of land in southern Arizona and New Mexico was purchased from Mexico as a possible railroad route.

Organizing Information
Below are eight events
that led to the Civil War.
Place them in order of
occurrence.

- Compromise of 1850
- Confederacy formed
- *Dred Scott* decision
- John Brown's raid
- Kansas-Nebraska Act
- Lincoln elected President
- Missouri Compromise
- South Carolina secedes

**⚷ KEY THEMES AND
CONCEPTS**

Government
Compromise is essential
to democratic government.

- How did the Missouri
  Compromise postpone
  the clash between North
  and South?

**⚷ KEY THEMES AND
CONCEPTS**

Constitutional Principles
In 1836, southern members
of Congress succeeded in
passing the so-called gag
rule, which prohibited the
reading of any antislavery
petitions in the House. The
gag rule stayed in place for
eight years.

- Why might abolitionists
  point to the gag rule as
  an example of how slav-
  ery threatened the rights
  of all Americans?

PART 2 THE CONSTITUTION IN JEOPARDY: THE AMERICAN CIVIL WAR

Differences between the North and the South finally threatened the existence of the nation. The debate that followed on how slavery should be treated in new lands centered on constitutional issues.

GREAT CONSTITUTIONAL DEBATES: THE SLAVERY ISSUE

Until the Civil War, the Constitution had recognized and protected slavery in three ways: the Three-Fifths Compromise, the provision that Congress could not end the importing of slaves before 1808, and the fugitive slave clause. These compromises had been made in order to encourage southern states to ratify the Constitution. With the expansion of American territory in the West, controversy brewed over whether these new territories should allow slavery or not.

Northern Views

Northerners who sought to stop the spread of slavery argued that the Congress had power over the territories. The Northwest Ordinance had banned slavery in the territory north of the Ohio River, while the **Missouri Compromise** of 1820 had banned slavery in the part of the Louisiana Purchase north of 36°30' N latitude. These precedents (or previous acts), they argued, showed that Congress had the power to ban slavery in new territories.

Southern Views

Southerners argued that the Constitutional recognition and protection of slavery meant that Congress did not have the authority to prevent the extension of slavery into the territories. They also argued that Congress had a constitutional duty to protect slavery where it already existed in the South.

Differences between North and South

	Northern States	Southern States
Population	21.5 million	9 million
Number of Factories	110,100	20,600
Miles of Railroad	21,700	9,000
Bank Deposits	$207 million	$47 million
Cotton Production	4 thousand bales	5 million bales

During the 1850s, differences between the North and South
continued to grow.

The Compromise of 1850

Until 1850, there were an equal number of slave and free states in the Union. The South thus maintained a balance of power in the Senate. The admission of California as a free state in 1850 threatened to upset this balance.

The issue of slavery in the new territories was settled for a brief time by the **Compromise of 1850,** which included three key provisions:

1. California entered the Union as a free state.
2. The Fugitive Slave Act required that escaped slaves be returned to their owners.
3. **Popular sovereignty,** or a vote of the people living in the territory, would determine whether a territory in the Mexican Cession was to be slave or free.

The Compromise of 1850 pleased almost no one. Northerners ignored the Fugitive Slave Act. The popular sovereignty provision was unclear. Would the vote to make a territory slave or free be held at the time the territory was settled or when it applied to become a state? This uncertainty almost certainly ensured future conflict.

The Kansas-Nebraska Act

In 1820, the **Missouri Compromise** had prohibited slavery in the lands that made up Kansas and Nebraska. The Kansas-Nebraska Act of 1854 overturned the Missouri Compromise by allowing those territories to decide the question of slavery by popular sovereignty.

When pro- and antislavery people rushed into Kansas to vote on the issue, violence erupted, known as **Bleeding Kansas**. A pro-slavery mob destroyed homes, stores, and an antislavery newspaper office in Lawrence, Kansas. John Brown and an antislavery group killed pro-slavery settlers at Pottawatomie Creek. Violence even erupted in the U.S. Senate, where the southern congressman Preston Brooks beat abolitionist Senator Charles Sumner because of remarks made in a Sumner speech.

Rise of the Republican Party

Reactions to the Kansas-Nebraska Act led to changes in the political party system. One major party, the Whigs, split into Northern and Southern wings and soon died out. The Democrats were seriously weakened in the North. A new party, the Republicans, was founded to oppose the spread of slavery. It was a sectional rather than a national party and proclaimed a platform of "Free Soil, Free Labor, Free Men."

The Dred Scott Case

In 1857 the Supreme Court gave its ruling on the question of slavery in the territories in *Dred Scott* v. *Sandford*. The ruling held that no African Americans, slave or free, were citizens, and therefore, they were not entitled to constitutional protection. The ruling also held that the

READING STRATEGY

Reinforcing Main Ideas
Why did the Compromise of 1850 satisfy neither side?

ANALYZING DOCUMENTS

"It is the opinion of the Court that the Act of Congress which prohibited a citizen from holding and owning property of this kind in the territory of the United States north of the line . . ., is not warranted by the Constitution, and is therefore void. . . ."
—*Dred Scott* v. *Sandford*, 1857

- What is meant by "property of this kind"?

- What act of Congress did this decision declare unconstitutional?

- Did the decision accelerate the march toward Civil War? Did it make the war inevitable? Why or why not?

Missouri Compromise was unconstitutional because Congress could not deprive people of their right to property—slaves—by banning slavery in any territory.

The Lincoln-Douglas Debates

In Illinois in 1858, Abraham Lincoln, a Republican, challenged the well-known senator Stephen A. Douglas, author of the Kansas-Nebraska Act, in the campaign for U.S. Senate. A series of debates were held, then the Illinois legislature reelected Douglas to the Senate. The Lincoln-Douglas debates weakened Douglas in the South while making Lincoln a national political figure unacceptable to the South because of his position against the extension of slavery.

John Brown's Raid at Harper's Ferry

In 1859, John Brown led a small group in a raid against a federal arsenal in what is now West Virginia. His plan was to seize weapons and lead a slave uprising. Although he was unsuccessful and was later executed for treason, he became a Northern hero. The incident increased Southern distrust of the North.

The Election of 1860

The election of 1860 showed clearly how divided the United States had become. The only remaining national party, the Democratic party, split between North and South with each wing running a candidate. Abraham Lincoln, the first Republican to be elected President, received only 39 percent of the popular vote.

The election of a Northerner who opposed the extension of slavery drove some Southerners to threaten secession. To prevent secession, Senator John Crittenden of Kentucky proposed the Crittenden Compromise, which would have divided the nation, slave versus free territory, all the way to California, along the Missouri Compromise line. The compromise was defeated because congressional Republicans would not support it. Some did not believe that the South would go through with their threats to leave the Union.

The Secession Crisis

In December 1860, South Carolina decided to **secede** from, or leave, the Union. By February 1861, six more southern states seceded and with South Carolina formed the **Confederate States of America.**

President James Buchanan took no action to stop them. He stated that neither he nor Congress had the power to preserve the Union because it "rests upon public opinion and can never be cemented by the blood of its citizens shed in war." Lincoln disagreed and denied that states could secede. In his First Inaugural Address in March 1861, Lincoln stated that "in view of the Constitution and the law, the Union is unbroken."

PREPARING FOR THE EXAM

On the exam, you will need to understand how legislators are elected and how that has changed over time. Why did the Illinois legislature, not the people of Illinois, vote in this Senate election? Check your constitutional amendments!

TURNING POINT

The Election of 1860 can be considered a turning point in United States history. Examine the chart below and answer the question that follows.

Election of 1860

Popular Vote

Candidate	Popular Vote	% of Popular Vote
Lincoln	1,865,593	39.5
Douglas	1,382,713	29.5
Breckinridge	848,356	18
Bell	592,906	13

Electoral Vote

Candidate	Electoral Vote	% of Electoral Vote
Lincoln	180	59
Douglas	12	4
Breckinridge	72	24
Bell	39	13

Why did southern states respond to the election of 1860 by seceding from the Union?

The Union and the Confederacy, 1861

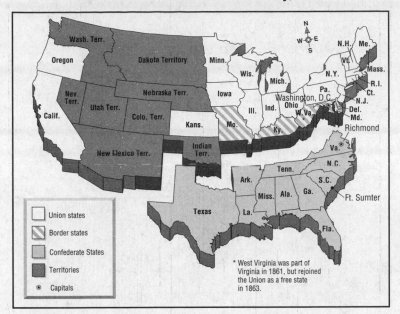

Union states

Border states

Confederate States

Territories

⊛ Capitals

* West Virginia was part of
Virginia in 1861, but rejoined
the Union as a free state
in 1863.

ANALYZING DOCUMENTS

Review the chart on page 96 and the map on this page to analyze the relative positions of the North and South at the start of the Civil War.

- What advantages did the South have at the beginning of the Civil War? What advantages did the North have?

- From your review and this data, how can the differences in the two areas best be explained?

- What advantages did each side have that are not seen on either the chart or the map?

- Why does the map show the border states differently? With which side did these states align?

THE CIVIL WAR

Lincoln's policy was to oppose secession but to take no military action until the South started fighting. In April 1861, the South seized Fort Sumter in Charleston Harbor, South Carolina. Lincoln called for troops to put down the rebellion. Four more southern states, including Virginia, seceded. The Civil War had begun.

Great Constitutional Debates: Preservation of the Union

Once a state had entered the United States, did it have the right to leave? From the Southern view, the South had the right to secede because the United States had not protected Southern rights. (In this case, only the rights of the white population were being considered.) Lincoln took the position that states could not leave the Union. No minority could act to destroy the nation and its government.

Lincoln's Aims and Actions

From the beginning of the secession crisis, Lincoln's goal was to preserve the Union. He took bold executive action to achieve this aim. He called out state militias, increased the size of the Navy, ordered a naval blockade of the South, and approved funds for military expenses while Congress was not in session. Congress later gave its approval of these actions.

Lincoln also ordered the arrest of Southern sympathizers in Maryland and Delaware to prevent secession of those states. Lincoln suspended the writ of *habeas corpus* in areas not in rebellion. He later won congressional approval for this step. He also declared martial law, which led to the arrests of thousands for suspected disloyalty.

Constitutional Questions

Lincoln's actions broadened the power of the executive. They also raised troubling questions: Were such actions constitutional? Did they fall within the scope of the President's war powers, or were they dictatorial? Did the fact that some Northerners sympathized with the rebelling South justify the limiting of their civil rights? Did Lincoln set precedents for expanded executive action that later Presidents might use in more questionable circumstances?

Other Government Policies During the War

In order to help to finance the Civil War, a new federal banking system was created, establishing a national currency. The currency was backed by government bonds and issued by the new federal banks.

In 1862, the Congress passed three major acts to facilitate economic growth after the war ended. The Homestead Act provided for the settlement of western lands. The Morrill Land Grant Act gave public lands to states and territories to found agriculture, mechanical arts, and military science colleges. Congress also authorized the building of the transcontinental railroad, financed with public land grants and cash loans.

Military Strategy

The Confederate war strategy was to attack the Union army repeatedly, inflicting casualties and wearing it down until it lost the will to fight. The Confederacy hoped to gain aid and diplomatic recognition from Great Britain and France, two nations that relied on southern cotton. Neither strategy was successful.

The Union relied on its superior resources and technology. Union ships blockaded southern ports, preventing the Confederacy from importing food and military supplies. In 1863, General Ulysses S. Grant led the victorious Union forces at Vicksburg, Mississippi, giving the North control of the Mississippi and dividing the South. In 1864, Lincoln appointed Grant to head the Union forces. As the new commander, Grant's strategy was to destroy not only the Confederate army but also all southern resources that supported the war effort.

The Human Cost

The Civil War was the bloodiest war the United States has ever known. Some 600,000 Americans lost their lives as new military technologies and old diseases struck down soldiers and civilians. Families along the border between the Union and the Confederacy were particularly devastated, as family members fought on opposite sides.

The worst single day of the war occurred in 1862 at the **Battle of Antietam** in Maryland, where the Southern commander

General Robert E. Lee attempted to invade Maryland. Some 5,000 people died and more than 17,000 were wounded. In 1863, the three-day **Battle of Gettysburg** in Pennsylvania was the most costly battle of the war, leaving more than 50,000 dead and wounded on both sides.

The Emancipation Proclamation

In 1863, Lincoln's **Emancipation Proclamation** freed all slaves in those areas still in rebellion against the Union. The Proclamation had largely a symbolic value. The Union could not enforce it, because it freed slaves only in areas under Confederate control.

Although African Americans had fought for the Union since the start of the war, after the Proclamation, their numbers in the Union military swelled. In all, more than 185,000 enlisted.

The Proclamation drew both criticism and praise. Some attacked it for freeing slaves only where the government could not enforce the decree, while permitting slavery where it could act. On the other hand, the Proclamation lessened the chances of European aid to the South. Most of all, it added a new humanitarian objective to the war.

The Gettysburg Address

In November 1863, Lincoln dedicated the Union military cemetery at Gettsyburg, just a few months after the battle there. His short speech summarized the meaning of the Civil War.

The End of the War

The Battle of Gettysburg was the last time that the South attempted to invade the North. From then on, Lee fought a defensive war. The war ended in 1865 with Lee's surrender at Appomattox Court House.

The Civil War on the Home Front

In the North, production in factories and on farms increased during the Civil War. Women and African Americans took more factory jobs to replace the white men who had gone to war. Women also ran the farms and raised money to help the wounded soldiers.

On both sides, women served as nurses, even in field hospitals. However, medicine was seen as a male profession, and even Clara Barton, founder of the American Red Cross, met with resistance.

The South lacked industrial support and a good transportation network. Furthermore, the Confederate government, led by Jefferson Davis, met opposition when calling for a military draft or attempting to collect food for the army.

In the South, the Northern blockade of southern ports led to food shortages. Inflation soared. As in the North, women took over the work on the farms. On the plantations, they supervised the slaves. They also worked as government clerks and as teachers.

By the end of the Civil War, the South was devastated. The war left a legacy of bitterness and new problems. The dead on both sides included Lincoln himself, assassinated within days of the war's end.

ANALYZING DOCUMENTS

"Four score and seven years ago our fathers brought forth on this continent, a new nation, conceived in Liberty, and dedicated to the proposition that all men are created equal.

"Now we are engaged in a great civil war, testing whether that nation, or any nation so conceived and so dedicated, can long endure. We are met on a great battle-field of that war. We have come to dedicate a portion of that field, as a final resting place for those who here gave their lives that the nation might live. . . .

"It is . . . for us to be here dedicated to the great task remaining before us— . . . that we here highly resolve that these dead shall not have died in vain—that this nation, under God, shall have a new birth of freedom—and that government of the people, by the people, for the people, shall not perish from the earth."

—Abraham Lincoln,
The Gettysburg Address

- For what event did Lincoln make the Gettysburg Address?

- Why did Lincoln refer back to the founding of the United States?

- In Lincoln's view, what was the purpose of the Civil War?

Questions for Regents Practice

For online Questions for Regents Practice,
visit the Prentice Hall Web site at www.phschool.com.

MULTIPLE CHOICE

Directions

Review the Test-Taking Strategies section of this book. Then answer the following questions, drawn from actual Regents examinations. Each question is followed by four choices. Read each question carefully. Decide which choice is the correct answer. Then on a separate piece of paper, mark your answer for each question.

1 Base your answer to question 1 on the cartoon below and on your knowledge of social studies.

"King Andrew the First"

The cartoonist is most clearly accusing President Jackson of which behavior?
1 involving the United States in European wars
2 exceeding the constitutional limits of his authority
3 using government funds to support an extravagant lifestyle
4 violating the Federal Constitution by granting titles of nobility

2 Which was most characteristic of the early factory systems in the United States?
1 Factories provided workers with a voice in management and employment conditions.
2 Women and children were not allowed to work in factories.
3 Unsafe working conditions were common.
4 Many workers had the opportunity to move up in social class.

Base your answers to questions 3 and 4 on the quotation below and on your knowledge of social studies.

"How can an industrialized Northeast, a plantation South, and a small farms West peacefully share the same nation?"

3 This quotation best describes the United States during which time period?
  1 Federal Era (1789–1800)
  2 Pre-Civil War (1820–1860)
  3 Era of Overseas Expansion (1898–1914)
  4 Great Depression of the 1930s

4 Which term can be most accurately applied to the situation in the quotation?
  1 sectionalism
  2 protectionism
  3 liberalism
  4 militarism

5 Which was most responsible for the rapid economic growth of New York City during the 19th century?
  1 presence of the New York Stock Exchange
  2 rise of domestic and foreign commerce
  3 rise of urban mass transportation
  4 migration of blacks from the rural South

6 In the United States, the belief in manifest destiny was most similar to later demands for
  1 restrictions on immigration
  2 a laissez-faire economic policy
  3 regulation of interstate commerce
  4 imperialistic expansion

7 In United States history, which characteristic was common to the War of 1812, the Mexican War, and the Spanish-American War?
  1 They were fought to promote democratic principles.
  2 Their aim was expansion of United States self-interest.
  3 They reflected conditions in Western Europe.
  4 They were necessary to protect national security.

Base your answers to questions 8 and 9 on your knowledge of social studies and on the quotation below, from a speech made by a United States Senator in 1847.

"What is the territory, Mr. President, which you propose to wrest from Mexico? It is consecrated to the heart of the Mexican by many a well-fought battle with his old Castilian master. His Bunker Hills, and Saratogas, and Yorktowns are there and shall he surrender that consecrated home of his affection to the Anglo-Saxon invaders? What do we want with it? The Senator from Michigan says he must have this. Why, my Christian brother, on what principle of justice?"

8 The parallel between the United States and Mexico which the Senator indicated in his speech was that both
  1 claimed Oregon
  2 disliked England
  3 had a revolutionary heritage
  4 were overcrowded

9 With which position would the speaker most likely have agreed?
  1 The United States should pressure Britain out of Oregon.
  2 The pursuit of a policy of manifest destiny is unfair.
  3 The annexation of Texas is justified because most of its population are settlers from the United States.
  4 The extension of United States democracy to parts of Mexico is divinely intended.

10 Laws requiring individuals to pass civil service examinations to obtain government jobs were enacted to
  1 eliminate patronage and corruption in government hiring
  2 allow the government to compete with private industry for employees
  3 support the development of public employee labor unions
  4 encourage the growth of local political parties

11 During the 19th century, the expansion of the population of the United States affected the lives of the Native Americans in that most Indians
1 moved to urban areas in large numbers
2 sought to form alliances with other minority groups
③ were forced to move westward
4 chose to adopt the culture of the settlers

12 The reason for ending the importation of enslaved persons in the United States after 1807 was the
1 success of the American colonial revolution against Britain
2 rapid industrialization of the South
3 replacement of slave labor by immigrant workers from eastern Europe
④ passage of legislation that forbid the practice

13 The activities of Nat Turner and Denmark Vesey in the United States indicated that
① slave revolts occurred in the South
2 cotton was a profitable crop
3 political rivalries existed in the North
4 slavery could be extended into the territories

14 A similarity between the pre-Civil War abolitionist movement and the Progressive movement is that both
1 were mainly concerned with improving the status of African Americans
2 worked to reduce income taxes
3 contributed directly to the start of a major war
④ sought to improve the conditions of poor or oppressed peoples

15 The main goal of the Seneca Falls Convention (1848) was to
① obtain equal rights for women
2 make the public aware of environmental problems
3 correct the abuses of big business
4 organize the first labor union in the United States

16 "To the Honorable Senate and House of Representatives in Congress Assembled: We the undersigned, citizens of the United States, but deprived of some of the privileges and immunities of citizens, among which is the right to vote, beg leave to submit the following Resolution: . . ."

—Susan B. Anthony, Elizabeth Cady Stanton (1873)

This statement is an example of a citizen's constitutional right to
1 petition for a redress of grievances
2 seek election to public office
3 receive a speedy, public trial
4 assemble peacefully

Base your answers to questions 17 and 18 on this excerpt from a resolution adopted at the Seneca Falls Convention in 1848 and on your knowledge of social studies.

"We hold these truths to be self-evident: that all men and women are created equal; that they are endowed by their Creator with certain inalienable rights; that among these are life, liberty, and the pursuit of happiness. . . ."

17 Which document served as the most direct model for this resolution?
1 Articles of Confederation
2 Emancipation Proclamation
3 United States Constitution
4 Declaration of Independence

18 The philosophy stated in this resolution was based on the
1 idea of rugged individualism
2 natural rights theory
3 theory of separation of powers
4 "necessary and proper" clause of the United States Constitution

19 **"Compromise Enables Maine and Missouri to Enter Union" (1820)**

"California Admitted to Union as Free State" (1850)

"Kansas-Nebraska Act Sets Up Popular Sovereignty" (1854)

Which issue is reflected in these headlines?
1 enactment of protective tariffs
2 extension of slavery
3 voting rights for minorities
4 universal public education

20 "By the 1850s, the Constitution, originally framed as an instrument of national unity, had become a source of national discord."

This quotation suggests that
1 vast differences of opinion existed over the issue of States rights
2 the federal government had become more interested in foreign affairs than in domestic problems
3 the Constitution had no provisions for governing new territories
4 the southern States continued to import slaves

21 Which event was the immediate cause of the secession of several southern states from the Union in 1860?
1 the Dred Scott decision, which declared that all prior compromises on the extension of slavery into territories were unconstitutional
2 the Missouri Compromise, which kept an even balance between the number of free and slave states
3 the raid on the federal arsenal at Harper's Ferry, which was led by the militant abolitionist John Brown
4 the election of President Abraham Lincoln, who opposed the spread of slavery into the territories

22 "You have no oath registered in heaven to destroy the government, while I shall have the most solemn one to 'preserve, protect, and defend' it."

—Abraham Lincoln, Inaugural Address, 1861

When President Abraham Lincoln made this statement, he indicated his commitment to
1 allow the southern states to leave the Union
2 defend the institution of slavery throughout the United States
3 take strong action to maintain the Union
4 make fundamental changes in the United States government

23 "Restriction of free thought and free speech is the most dangerous of all subversions. It is the one un-American act that could easily defeat us."

In the United States, the danger identified in this statement was the greatest during the
1 Age of Jackson
2 Civil War
3 Spanish-American War
4 New Deal Era in the 1930s

24 A major result of the Civil War was that the
1 economic system of the South came to dominate the United States economy
2 federal government's power over the states was strengthened
3 members of Congress from southern states gained control of the legislative branch
4 nation's industrial development came to a standstill

25 In the United States during the 1800s, the growth of industrialization resulted in
1 the end of rural life and values
2 a decline in the influence of big business
3 a decrease in child labor
4 the rising influence of the middle class

26 Which statement best explains why candidates for President of the United States are nominated during national nominating conventions?
1 It is mandated by the U.S. Constitution.
2 It is mandated by state constitutions.
3 It is part of the United States political tradition.
4 It was instituted by an act of Congress.

27 During the period from 1800 to 1865, the issues of states rights, tariffs, and slavery led most directly to the growth of
1 imperialism
2 sectionalism
3 national unity
4 industrialization

28 The United States Supreme Court decision in *Scott* v. *Sandford* (1857) was important because it
1 strengthened the determination of abolitionists to achieve their goals
2 caused the immediate outbreak of the Civil War
3 ended the importation of slaves into the United States
4 increased the power of Congress to exclude slavery from the territories

29 Which argument did President Abraham Lincoln use against the secession of the southern states?
1 Slavery was not profitable.
2 The government was a union of people and not of states.
3 The southern states did not permit their people to vote on secessions.
4 As the Commander in Chief, he had the duty to defend the United States against foreign invasion.

30 Which situation was an immediate result of the United States Civil War?
1 Women gained the right to vote as an acknowledgment of their role in the conflict.
2 Secession was no longer regarded as an option to be exercised by states.
3 Sectionalism disappeared as a force in American economic and political life.
4 The South retained its pre-Civil War economic and social structure.

Base your answer to questions 31 and 32 on the speakers' statements below and on your knowledge of social studies.

Speaker A: "Secession from the Union caused this war, and all those who supported it must now be punished."

Speaker B: "The nation's wounds will heal most quickly if we forgive the southerners and welcome them back into the Union."

Speaker C: "The freedmen must be given economic assistance and guaranteed the constitutional right to protect themselves."

Speaker D: "The war may have ended, but the fight must continue to preserve the system of white supremacy in the South."

31 Which speakers best represent the attitudes of the Radical Republicans who controlled Congress during Reconstruction?
1 A and D
2 A and C
3 B and C
4 B and D

32 The position taken by *Speaker B* is closest to the beliefs expressed by
1 Abraham Lincoln
2 Thaddeus Stevens
3 the carpetbaggers
4 the Ku Klux Klan

THEMATIC ESSAY

In developing your answers to the essay, be sure to keep these general definitions in mind:
(a) <u>discuss</u> means "to make observations about something using facts, reasoning, and argument; to present in some detail"
(b) <u>describe</u> means "to illustrate something in words or to tell about it"
(c) <u>evaluate</u> means "to examine and judge the significance, worth, or condition of; to determine the value of"

Directions
Write a well-organized essay that includes an introduction, several paragraphs addressing the task below, and a conclusion.

Theme: Government: Federalism
The United States Constitution created a new type of government—federalism—which divided power between the states and the national government. The proper balance of power under federalism has been debated throughout the history of the United States.

Task
From your study of United States history, identify two time periods in which there was an important debate about federalism.
   For each era or time period identified:
- Identify a specific disagreement that occurred concerning the principle of federalism.
- Discuss the historical circumstances surrounding the disagreement over federalism.
- Describe the actions taken by each side during the disagreement over federalism.
- Discuss the extent to which these actions were successful in resolving the disagreement.

Suggestions
You may use any time period in United States history in which there was an important debate about federalism. Some suggestions you might wish to consider include: the Supreme Court under John Marshall (1801–1835); the extension of slavery (1820–1860); Civil War (1861–1865); Reconstruction (1865–1876); Populist and Progressive reform movements (1890–1920); Franklin D. Roosevelt's New Deal (1933–1945); civil rights movement (1950–1970); Ronald Reagan's New Federalism (1981–1989).

You are *not* limited to these suggestions.

Guidelines
In your essay be sure to:
- Address all aspects of the *Task*
- Analyze, evaluate, or compare and/or contrast issues and events whenever possible
- Fully support the theme of the essay with relevant facts, examples, and details
- Write a well-developed essay that consistently demonstrates a logical and clear plan of organization
- Introduce the theme by establishing a framework that is beyond a simple restatement of the *Task*
- Conclude your essay with a strong summation of the theme

DOCUMENT-BASED ESSAY

This task is designed to test your ability to work with historical documents and is based on the accompanying documents (1–6). Some of the documents have been edited for the purposes of this question. As you analyze the documents, take into account both the source of each document and any point of view that may be presented in the document.

Directions

This document-based question consists of two parts: Part A and Part B. In Part A, you are to read each document and answer the question or questions that follow the document. In Part B, you are to write an essay based on the information in the documents and your knowledge of United States history.

Historical Context

In May 1787, 55 delegates came together in Philadelphia to amend the Articles of Confederation. What they did was create a new Constitution, a plan of government designed to solve the governmental problems experienced under the Articles of Confederation. The Constitution they created has remained a flexible, living document that continues to guide this nation today.

Task

Using information from the documents and your knowledge of United States history and government, answer the questions that follow each document in Part A. Your answers to the questions will help you write the Part B essay in which you be asked to:

Discuss how the Constitution was both (a) a product of its time, and (b) a document that has had enough flexibility to meet the challenges of the future.

PART A: SHORT ANSWER

DOCUMENT #1

> *"The United States in Congress assembled shall never engage in a war, . . . nor enter into any treaties or alliances, nor coin money, nor regulate the value thereof, . . . nor borrow money on the credit of the United States, nor appropriate money, . . . nor appoint a commander in chief of the army or navy, unless nine States assent [agree]."*
>
> **—The Articles of Confederation**

1   Why might it be difficult for the government under the Articles of Confederation to be effective?

_____

_____

_____

_____

_____

_____

_____

_____

_____

DOCUMENT #2

Year Ratified	Amendment Number	Excerpt from the Amendment
1870	15	"The right of the citizens of the United States to vote shall not be denied or abridged . . . on account of race, color, or previous condition of servitude."
1920	19	"The right of citizens of the United States to vote shall not be denied or abridged . . . on account of sex"
1971	26	"The right of citizens of the United States, who are eighteen years of age or older, to vote, shall not be denied or abridged . . ."

2 How do these amendments demonstrate the ability of the Constitution to adapt to a change in attitude about who should have the right vote?

_____

_____

_____

_____

_____

_____

_____

_____

_____

_____

DOCUMENT #3

"Representatives . . . shall be determined by adding to the . . . number of free persons . . . three fifths of all other persons [slaves]."

—**U.S. Constitution, Article I, Section 2**

3 How was the debate over the counting of slaves for representation resolved in the Constitution?

_____

_____

_____

_____

_____

_____

_____

_____

_____

_____

DOCUMENT #4

> *"The accumulation of all powers, legislative, executive, and judiciary, in the same hands, whether one, a few, or many . . . may justly be pronounced the very definition of tyranny [cruel or unjust use of power]."*
>
> —**James Madison, *The Federalist*, No. 47**

4 How might the system of checks and balances address the fears expressed in the quote by James Madison?

_____

_____

_____

_____

_____

_____

_____

_____

_____

DOCUMENT #5

> *"So if a law be in opposition to the Constitution, if both the law and the Constitution apply to a particular case . . . the court must decide that case conformably [in agreement] to the law, disregarding the Constitution or conformably to the Constitution, disregarding the law, the court must determine which of these conflicting rules governs the case. This is the very essence of judicial duty. If, then, the courts are to regard the Constitution, and the Constitution is superior to any ordinary act, the Constitution and not such ordinary act, must govern the case to which both apply."*
>
> —*Marbury v. Madison* (1803)

5   How did the ruling in *Marbury* v. *Madison* expand the power of the Supreme Court?

_____

_____

_____

_____

_____

_____

_____

_____

_____

DOCUMENT #6

6 How does the map above demonstrate the ability of Congress to make laws to deal with the extension of slavery?

_____

_____

_____

_____

_____

_____

_____

_____

_____

_____

PART B: ESSAY

Directions
Using information from the documents provided, and your knowledge of United States history, write a well-organized essay that includes an introduction, several paragraphs, and a conclusion.

Historical Context
In May 1787, 55 delegates came together in Philadelphia to amend the Articles of Confederation. What they did was create a new Constitution, a plan of government designed to solve the governmental problems experienced under the Articles of Confederation. The Constitution they created has remained a flexible, living document that continues to guide this nation today.

Task
Using information from the documents and your knowledge of United States history and government, write an essay in which you

Discuss how the Constitution was both (a) a product of its time, and (b) a document that has had enough flexibility to meet the challenges of the future.

Guidelines
When writing your essay, be sure to
- Address all aspects of the *Task* by accurately analyzing and interpreting at least four documents
- Incorporate information from the documents in the body of the essay
- Incorporate relevant outside information throughout the essay
- Richly support the theme with relevant facts, examples, and details
- Write a well-developed essay that consistently demonstrates a logical and clean plan of organization
- Introduce the theme by establishing a framework that is beyond a simple restatement of the *Task* or *Historical Context* and conclude the essay with a summation of the theme.

UNIT 3

Industrialization of the United States

Section 1 The Reconstructed Nation

Section 2 The Rise of American Business, Industry, and Labor—1865–1920

Section 3 American Society Adjusts to Industrialization

UNIT OVERVIEW

The Civil War had torn the United States apart. With Union victory came the task of putting the nation back together. Yet the rebuilt nation would be a very different one. This unit reviews those changes that the Civil War brought to the United States. It also highlights how the shift from an agrarian to an industrial economy changed the United States and its people.

Some key questions to help you focus on the industrialization of the United States include

- What social, political, and economic changes occurred as the nation sought to rebuild after the Civil War?
- What factors in the United States led to the shift from an agrarian to an industrial society, and what were the results of this shift?
- How did patterns of immigration to the United States change in the 19th and early 20th centuries, and what did those changes mean for American society?

114

SECTION 1
The Reconstructed Nation

SECTION OVERVIEW

After the Civil War, the nation faced the immense task of restoring the Union. Conflicting plans for Reconstruction produced bitter political battles that led to the impeachment of a President. Enormous resources were poured into rebuilding the shattered Southern economy. Meanwhile, new political gains for African Americans were gradually rolled back in the South as whites regained power.

KEY THEMES AND CONCEPTS

As you review this section, take special note of the following key themes and concepts:

Change How did the nation rebuild and reunify after the Civil War?

Citizenship How did African Americans win political rights in the South?

Places and Regions How did white southerners react to the terms of Reconstruction?

KEY PEOPLE

As you review this section, be sure you understand the significance of these key people:

Andrew Johnson	Samuel Tilden	Thomas Nast
Ulysses S. Grant	Rutherford B. Hayes	W.E.B. Du Bois
William "Boss" Tweed	Booker T. Washington	

KEY SUPREME COURT CASES

As you review this section, be sure you understand the significance of these key Supreme Court cases:

The *Civil Rights Cases* (1883)
Plessy v. *Ferguson* (1896)
Brown v. *Board of Education of Topeka, Kansas* (1954)

★ THE BIG IDEA
Reconstruction followed the Civil War in the South. During this period

- President Abraham Lincoln was assassinated.
- President Andrew Johnson was impeached.
- African Americans won voting and political rights.
- Southern whites regained political control.

⚷ KEY TERMS

Reconstruction
Radical Republicans
Radical Reconstruction
scalawags
carpetbaggers
Thirteenth Amendment
Fourteenth Amendment
Fifteenth Amendment
solid South
Compromise of 1877
black codes
Ku Klux Klan
poll taxes
literacy tests
Freedmen's Bureau
grandfather clauses
segregation
Jim Crow laws

The effort to rebuild the southern states and restore the Union was known as **Reconstruction,** a period that lasted from 1865 to 1877. Reconstruction required the rebuilding of the nation's economy as well as its government. With so much at stake, rival political factions—with competing plans for the future—waged bitter battles in Washington.

The Reconstructed Nation, 1865–1876

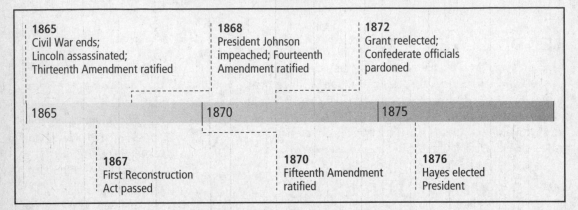

1865	1868	1872
Civil War ends; Lincoln assassinated; Thirteenth Amendment ratified	President Johnson impeached; Fourteenth Amendment ratified	Grant reelected; Confederate officials pardoned

1865 — 1870 — 1875

1867	1870	1876
First Reconstruction Act passed	Fifteenth Amendment ratified	Hayes elected President

ANALYZING DOCUMENTS

Examine the timeline above, then answer these questions.

- How many years passed between the end of the Civil War and the states' ratification of the Fifteenth Amendment?

- Which event occurred first: the impeachment of President Johnson or the election of President Hayes?

TURNING POINT

Why is President Lincoln's assassination considered a turning point in history?

PLANS OF RECONSTRUCTION

Several different plans for Reconstruction emerged during and after the war. Much debate about differing plans centered on who would control Reconstruction—the President or Congress.

Lincoln's Plan

President Lincoln had begun planning for the restoration of the South long before the end of the war. His plan of Reconstruction was based on the idea that the southern states had never left the Union. It featured the following elements:

- Pardons to southerners who swore oaths of loyalty to the United States
- Recognition of new southern state governments when 10 percent of those who had voted in the 1860 election took these oaths and when the states adopted new constitutions abolishing slavery.

Lincoln was open to suggestions from Congress for changes in his plan, but his assassination in April 1865 meant he would never carry out his program.

Johnson's Plan

Vice President Andrew Johnson became President after Lincoln's death. He intended to follow the broad outlines of Lincoln's plan. Johnson recognized four southern state governments and prepared to readmit the others.

Radical Republicans, however, controlled Congress, and they wanted harsher terms for Reconstruction. Johnson's failure to consider congressional views on Reconstruction and his efforts to block radical plans finally led Republicans in Congress to attempt to impeach him. In 1868, the House charged the President with "high crimes and misdemeanors"—specifically, for violating the Tenure of Office Act. The Senate fell one vote short of the two-thirds vote required by the Constitution to remove a President from office. Although Johnson was acquitted, his political power was gone.

Radical Reconstruction

Now the Republican-controlled Congress dictated the terms of Reconstruction. The chief features of this so-called **Radical Reconstruction** included

- The division of the South into five military districts controlled by the U.S. Army, while new state constitutions and governments were being set up
- The requirement of the new state governments to grant African American males the right to vote
- The requirement of southern states to ratify the Fourteenth Amendment. In addition to addressing several fundamental civil rights issues, the amendment prohibited many former Confederate government officials from holding office.

State Governments During Reconstruction

Immediately after the Civil War ended, white southerners who had served in leadership positions before and during the Civil War tried to reassert their control of state and local governments. They were especially concerned with limiting the freedom and movement of the former slaves.

When the radical plan of Reconstruction took effect, most of the former Confederate leaders—largely Democrats—were barred from holding office and voting. Republicans headed the new state governments that emerged and they were overwhelmingly supported by African Americans, who had recently won the right to vote. In many cases, African Americans themselves won election to office.

Many white southerners deeply resented the federal government's imposition of Radical Reconstruction. They also resented the new Reconstruction governments and the role of African Americans in them. They branded the few white southerners active in those governments as **scalawags** and the Republican northerners who came South to take part in Reconstruction as **carpetbaggers.** White southerners sometimes used terror and violence in efforts to keep African Americans from taking part in government.

READING STRATEGY

Reinforcing Main Ideas
Why did Congress impeach President Johnson?

READING STRATEGY

Organizing Information
During Radical Reconstruction, some groups of people exerted great power over the terms of Reconstruction, while others had very little power.

- Which groups had the largest roles in the Radical Reconstruction?

- Which had the smallest roles?

⚷ KEY THEMES AND CONCEPTS

Government
Which amendment to the Constitution limited the voting rights of former Confederate officers?

Government

During Reconstruction, three new amendments to the Constitution were ratified. In the space below, name these three amendments and provide the major provisions of each.

1.

2.

3.

READING STRATEGY

Analyzing Cause and Effect

Why were scandals common during President Grant's administration?

New Constitutional Amendments

During the Reconstruction period, the states ratified three amendments to the Constitution:

- **Thirteenth Amendment** (1865)—abolished slavery in the United States
- **Fourteenth Amendment** (1868)—(1) declared that all native-born or naturalized people, including African Americans, were citizens; (2) forbade states to make laws that "abridge the privileges . . . of citizens" or that "deprive any person of life, liberty, or property, without due process of law" or that "deny to any person . . . the equal protection of the laws"; (3) limited the rights of former Confederate officers and government officials; and (4) promised to pay Civil War debts owed by the federal government, but declared Confederate debts to be void
- **Fifteenth Amendment** (1870)—declared that states could not keep citizens from voting because of "race, color, or previous condition of servitude" (slavery)

President Grant

The first presidential election after the end of the Civil War took place in 1868. Union war hero General Ulysses S. Grant ran as a Republican and won. Grant's strengths, however, were those of a military leader, not those of a politician or government leader. Scandals and corruption damaged Grant's administration, as business owners in the booming postwar economy offered bribes to politicians who would do favors for them. Among the most notorious scandals were:

- *Crédit Mobilier Scandal:* Railroad officials impoverished the railroad, then bribed members of Congress to block any investigation.
- *"Salary Grab":* Congress voted itself a 50 percent pay raise and added two years of "back pay." Public outcry forced repeal of this act.
- *"Whiskey Ring":* Whiskey distillers paid graft to federal tax collectors rather than pay tax on their liquor.

Political corruption was also common at state and local levels. Perhaps the most notorious figure was William "Boss" Tweed, who ran the Tammany Hall political machine in New York City in the 1860s and 1870s. The artist Thomas Nast attacked Tweed's behavior in a series of stinging cartoons that helped turn public opinion against Tweed.

THE END OF RECONSTRUCTION

Corruption in the Grant administration weakened the political strength of the Republican party. In addition, by the early 1870s, all but a handful of former Confederates could vote again. Most of these white southern males now voted Democratic in reaction to Radical Republican Reconstruction. For most of the next century, the Democratic party would dominate voting in the South, giving rise to the term **solid South**.

While nearly dying out in the South, the Republican party remained strong in the North and Midwest. It focused on issues of interest to businessmen and farmers, such as keeping the money supply tight and tariffs on imports high.

The Election of 1876

The emergence of the solid South gave the Democrats greater power in politics at the national level. In 1876, Democrats nominated Samuel Tilden, the governor of New York, to run for President against Republican Rutherford B. Hayes, the governor of Ohio.

Tilden clearly won the popular vote, but the electoral vote was contested. Four states sent in disputed election returns. Which votes were counted would determine the outcome of the election.

A special electoral commission was named to count the votes. The Republican majority on the commission gave all the electoral votes in question to Hayes, thus guaranteeing his victory.

In the **Compromise of 1877,** Democrats agreed to go along with the commission's decision in return for promises by Hayes to

- Withdraw remaining federal troops from the South, thus ending Reconstruction
- Name a southerner to his cabinet
- Support federal spending on internal improvements in the South

The Compromise of 1877 effectively weakened the North's political victory in the Civil War, restoring to power many of the southern families who, 16 years before, had formed the Confederacy and led it into war.

White Control in the South

The withdrawal of federal troops enabled white southerners to eliminate any political advances African Americans had made during Reconstruction. Various methods were used to curb the rights of African Americans, and by 1900, their civil rights had been sharply limited.

BLACK CODES These measures, passed in most southern states immediately after the Civil War, were based on old slave codes and aimed at keeping blacks in conditions close to slavery. The **black codes** produced an angry reaction in the North that helped passage of

GEOGRAPHY IN HISTORY

How did voting patterns in the South affect the presidential election of 1876?

 PREPARING FOR THE EXAM

On the examination, you will need to understand the influences that brought Reconstruction to an end.

- Why do you think the Democrats agreed to support the Compromise of 1877?

the Radical Reconstruction program. Reconstruction governments in the South overturned these codes.

KEY THEMES AND CONCEPTS
Individuals, Groups, Institutions
Why did some white southerners form secret societies such as the Ku Klux Klan?

SECRET SOCIETIES White southerners originally formed groups like the **Ku Klux Klan** to try to frighten African Americans and their supporters out of taking part in Reconstruction governments. The lawlessness and brutality demonstrated by these groups led the federal government to use the army against the societies. With the end of Reconstruction and the growth of white political power, the Klan and other similar groups played a less active role in the South. Such organizations, however, remain in existence to this day.

POLL TAXES Southern states imposed a tax on every voter. Those who were too poor to pay **poll taxes**—including many African Americans—could not vote.

LITERACY TESTS Some states required citizens to demonstrate that they could read and write before they voted. Often **literacy tests** involved interpreting a difficult part of the Constitution. Few African Americans could pass these tests because they had received little schooling. While the **Freedmen's Bureau,** created by Congress in 1865 to aid former slaves, established many schools for young African Americans, the bureau lasted only a few years. Thereafter, state laws forced African American children to attend separate schools that were poorly equipped and funded.

READING STRATEGY
Reading for Evidence
Reread the section entitled "White Control in the South." What were five major ways in which white southerners reasserted their control in the South after Reconstruction?

GRANDFATHER CLAUSES Poll taxes and literacy tests might have also kept poor and uneducated whites from voting. To prevent this, southern states added **grandfather clauses** to their constitutions. These clauses allowed the son or grandson of a man eligible to vote in 1866 or 1867 to vote himself even if he could neither pay the tax nor pass the test. Since few African Americans could vote in 1867, the clause benefited whites almost exclusively.

Jim Crow Laws

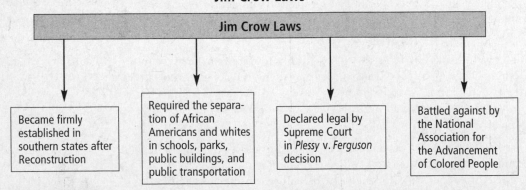

Jim Crow Laws

| Became firmly established in southern states after Reconstruction | Required the separation of African Americans and whites in schools, parks, public buildings, and public transportation | Declared legal by Supreme Court in *Plessy* v. *Ferguson* decision | Battled against by the National Association for the Advancement of Colored People |

Jim Crow laws were a part of everyday life in the South after Reconstruction.

JIM CROW LAWS Southern states also passed laws establishing social **segregation,** or the separation of people on the basis of race. Such **Jim Crow laws** forbade African Americans from sharing facilities with whites, such as railroad cars or water fountains.

The Supreme Court's Response

The Supreme Court did not interfere with efforts to restore white control in the South. In the 1883 *Civil Rights Cases,* the Court ruled that the Thirteenth Amendment abolished slavery but did not prohibit discrimination and that the Fourteenth Amendment prohibited discrimination by government but not by individuals. Later, in the landmark case of *Plessy* v. *Ferguson* (1896), the Court ruled that segregation was legal as long as African Americans had access to "equal but separate" facilities.

The Court's ruling in the *Plessy* case set a precedent that justified segregation in all public facilities—schools, hospitals, passenger terminals, and more—until the 1950s. It was not until the pivotal case of *Brown* v. *Board of Education of Topeka, Kansas* (1954) that the Supreme Court reversed the finding in *Plessy* v. *Ferguson.* The *Brown* decision stated that educational facilities separated solely on the basis of race were by their nature unequal.

African Americans Debate Their Future

Two prominent leaders offered contrasting strategies to improve the lives of African Americans. Booker T. Washington argued that African Americans should temporarily put aside their desire for political equality and instead focus on building economic security by gaining useful vocational skills. W.E.B. Du Bois called for the brightest African Americans to gain an advanced liberal arts education (rather than a vocational education) and then demand social and political equality. However, widespread discrimination against African Americans made either strategy difficult to follow.

⚷ KEY THEMES AND CONCEPTS

Constitutional Principles

The following three cases deal with segregation and Jim Crow laws:

- *Civil Rights Cases* (1883) ruled that slavery was abolished but that discrimination by individuals was not prohibited by the Constitution.

- *Plessy* v. *Ferguson* (1896) established segregation to be legal as long as "equal but separate" facilities were available to African Americans.

- *Brown* v. *Board of Education of Topeka, Kansas* (1954) established that facilities separated by race were unequal.

How did these three cases influence laws concerning segregation?

SECTION 2

The Rise of American Business, Industry, and Labor—1865–1920

⭐ **THE BIG IDEA**
The United States developed a prosperous new economy based on the mass production of goods. During this period

- economic development expanded in the North, but weakened in the South.

- entrepreneurs became wealthy and powerful.

- government began to regulate business.

- labor unions formed to improve working conditions.

🔑 **KEY TERMS**

transcontinental railroad
New South
sharecroppers
tenant farmers
capital
corporations
monopoly
merger
trust
entrepreneurs
assembly line
laissez-faire
free enterprise system
robber barons
Sherman Antitrust Act
collective bargaining
Haymarket Riot

SECTION OVERVIEW

From Reconstruction through World War I, the United States developed a prosperous industrial economy that revolutionized American society. New machines made possible the mass production of goods. Industrial growth led to a new type of business, the corporation, headed by a rising class of enterprising industrialists such as Henry Ford. With little government interference, these corporate giants created new business structures, some legal and some not, that brought them fabulous wealth. They used their riches both to benefit society and to increase their power. Industries attracted a new type of laborer, the factory worker, who often worked long hours in hazardous conditions. These conditions spurred the growth of labor unions, which gradually gained the right to bargain with employers.

KEY THEMES AND CONCEPTS

As you review this section, take special note of the following key themes and concepts:

Science and Technology How did technological developments lead to the growth of industrialization?

Government How did the government respond to the growth of powerful industries and to complaints about business practices?

Factors of Production What factors led to the growth of the labor movement, and what strategies did unions pursue?

KEY PEOPLE

As you review this section, be sure you understand the significance of these key people:

Andrew Carnegie	Henry Ford	Charles Darwin
John D. Rockefeller	Horatio Alger	Terence Powderly
J. Pierpont Morgan	Adam Smith	Samuel Gompers

122

KEY SUPREME COURT CASES

As you review this section, be sure you understand the significance of these key Supreme Court cases:

Munn v. *Illinois* (1877)
Wabash, St. Louis & Pacific Railway v. *Illinois* (1886)
United States v. *E. C. Knight Company* (1895)
In re Debs (1895)

The Civil War changed the economies of the northern and southern regions of the United States. The Civil War stimulated economic growth in the North. Meanwhile, the South struggled to recover from the devastation of the war.

Economic Developments in the North

The industrialization that had started before the war accelerated as northern factories rushed to keep up with the Union's demand for guns, ammunition, uniforms, and other necessary products. Improvements in railroad systems helped speed troop movements. Since so many northern farm workers entered the army, farms became more heavily mechanized, using fewer workers to produce more crops. Little of the fighting took place in the North, and the region was spared much physical destruction from the war.

After the war, the growing northern factories looked to overseas markets for their goods. Meanwhile, completion of the **transcontinental railroad** opened new markets in the West and brought products of western farms and mines east.

Economic growth attracted new waves of immigrants to the United States. Some sought farms in the West, but many found employment in the booming industries of the North.

Economic Developments in the South

The Civil War ruined the South's economy. It ended slavery, thus killing the plantation system on which southern wealth was based. During the fighting, plantations had been burned, railroads ripped up, and the region's few factories destroyed.

After the war, many farmers and planters had to sell off parts of their land to pay off debts or to start over. These land owners often found themselves in debt to banks or merchants. Yet despite such hardships, southern farmers again began to produce cotton and tobacco.

Some southern leaders, however, believed that the South's economy should not rest simply on agriculture. They began to create a **New South,** with rebuilt railroads, new textile and steel mills, and, later, new industries, such as oil and coal production.

Despite these changes, the South lagged behind the North in economic growth. Agriculture still offered the most jobs, and many southerners had to farm land owned by others. These landless farmers

GEOGRAPHY IN HISTORY

What factors contributed to the development of factories in the North?

 PREPARING FOR THE EXAM

On the examination, you will need to have a thorough understanding of important United States economic developments.

- What is the transcontinental railroad?

- How did it contribute to economic growth?

KEY THEMES AND CONCEPTS

Places and Regions
New manufacturing technologies were less commonly used in the South than in the North. Why?

KEY THEMES AND CONCEPTS

Individuals, Groups, Institutions
As the southern economy began to grow in the decades after the Civil War, some groups still lagged behind others.

- Who were the sharecroppers?

- How did they differ from tenant farmers?

KEY THEMES AND CONCEPTS

Economic Systems
What do you call a business in which many investors own shares?

Name two kinds of businesses that speeded the growth of American industry:

1.

2.

What do you call a company that has complete control over a particular kind of business?

Name two examples:

1.

2.

What do you call the merger of a group of unrelated companies?

Name an example:

1.

included **sharecroppers,** who gave part of each year's crop to the landowner and received the rest as payment, and **tenant farmers,** who paid cash to rent land.

Beginning in the 1880s, African Americans began a migration to the North in search of better jobs. This migration accelerated during and after World War I.

BUSINESS DEVELOPMENTS

Before the Civil War, sole proprietors, or single owners, and partnerships had controlled most American businesses. The mills and factories that came with industrialization, however, usually required greater **capital,** or money for investment, than one person or a few partners could raise.

The Growth of Corporations

To raise capital for expansion, many businesses became **corporations.** A corporation is a business in which many investors own shares, usually called stocks. In exchange for their investment, each stockholder receives a dividend, or part of the corporation's profits.

Besides paying dividends, the corporations also limited investor losses. If a corporation failed, an investor lost only his or her investment and was not responsible for the corporation's debts.

The money raised by corporations speeded the growth of American industry. Among the fastest growing industries were transportation (railroads, urban transportation, and, later, automobiles), building materials (steel), energy (coal, oil, and electricity), and communications (telegraph and telephone).

Other Forms of Business Organization

As the nation's economy boomed and industries grew larger in the late 1800s, other ways of organizing business appeared. Often the aim of such business organizations was to eliminate competition and dominate a particular area of the economy.

MONOPOLY A company or small group of companies that has complete control over a particular field of business is a **monopoly.** One example of a monopoly in the late 1800s was the E. C. Knight Sugar Company. Having a monopoly in a field often allowed a company to raise prices to almost any level it desired. Such abuses led to federal legislation aimed at curbing monopolies.

Some monopolies are permitted today. Public utility companies that provide gas, water, and electricity are examples of private companies that often have monopolies in their fields. Government agencies closely monitor the operations of such utilities.

CONGLOMERATE A corporation that owns a group of unrelated companies is a conglomerate. Such conglomerates are usually formed by **merger,** the process by which one company acquires legal control over another. Mergers and conglomerates are both legal and common today. General Electric, for example, is a conglomerate that has acquired many different divisions through mergers.

POOL Sometimes competing companies in one field entered into agreements to fix prices and divide business. Such an agreement was a pool. Railroad companies in the late 1800s formed such pools, which were later outlawed.

TRUST A group of corporations in the same or related fields sometimes agreed to combine under a single board of trustees that controlled the actions of all the member corporations. This was a **trust.** Shareholders in the corporations received dividends from the trust but lost any say in its operation. The Standard Oil Trust was one example of such a combination. Trusts were later made illegal.

HOLDING COMPANY To get around the outlawing of trusts, corporations formed holding companies. The holding company bought controlling amounts of stock in different corporations rather than take operations over directly as a trust did.

Innovation

While these new forms of business organization helped young industries to get started and to maximize profits, other innovations enabled businesses to market their products more effectively. In urban areas, new department stores offered customers a wide variety of goods under one roof. For rural areas, retailers developed mail-order catalogs that saved customers a trip to faraway stores. The items offered in these stores and catalogs expanded as well, thanks to new inventions such as the vacuum cleaner, the telephone, the electric light bulb, the electric iron, and the safety razor.

ANALYZING DOCUMENTS

Examine the timeline below, then answer these questions.

- How many years passed between the formation of Standard Oil Trust and the formation of Carnegie Steel?

- Which event occurred first: the invention of the telephone or the introduction of the assembly line?

Innovations and Business Developments, 1868–1913

1868 Sholes improves typewriter

1882 Standard Oil Trust formed

1894 Pullman strike

1913 Ford introduces assembly line

1865 1870 1875 1880 1885 1890 1895 1900 1905 1910 1915

1876 Bell invents telephone

1892 Carnegie Steel formed

1900 ILGWU formed

Entrepreneurs

These new forms of business organization and innovative ideas from inventors helped American industry grow in the late 1800s and early 1900s. Yet without the business knowledge and daring of certain individuals, that growth would have been much slower.

These individuals were **entrepreneurs,** people who take responsibility for the organization and operation of a new business venture. Entrepreneurs often risk large sums of venture capital in hopes of making enormous profits. The business decisions made by turn-of-the-century entrepreneurs had great impact on the lives of most Americans. Some of the key entrepreneurs of the late 1800s and early 1900s are listed below.

READING STRATEGY

Organizing Information
In the space below, name four key entrepreneurs of the late 1800s and early 1900s and the industries each operated.

1.

2

3.

4.

ANDREW CARNEGIE An immigrant from Scotland, Andrew Carnegie started work in a textile factory at age 12. He worked his way up through a variety of jobs and invested his money shrewdly. At age 38, Carnegie entered the steel industry, which was booming because of the growth of railroads. Carnegie sought to control all aspects of steel-making and built his company into the world's largest steelmaker.

Carnegie sold his company in 1901 for a quarter billion dollars. He believed the wealthy had a duty to society and gave hundreds of millions to charities. He also underwrote the founding of free public libraries all across the country.

JOHN D. ROCKEFELLER Industrialist John D. Rockefeller entered the oil-refining business during the Civil War. He believed competition was wasteful and used ruthless methods to eliminate competitors. By 1882, his Standard Oil Company controlled over 90 percent of American oil refining. In 1882, he formed the Standard Oil Trust to control more aspects of oil production. Rockefeller also gave away hundreds of millions to charity.

J. PIERPONT MORGAN Trained as a banker, J. Pierpont Morgan profited by making loans to growing businesses. He took control of many bankrupt railroads in the late 1800s, reorganized them, and made a profit. He also controlled electrical, insurance, and shipping companies. Morgan bought Carnegie Steel in 1901, merged it with other companies, and created the United States Steel Corporation, the world's largest.

HENRY FORD Entrepreneur Henry Ford revolutionized auto making in 1913 by using a moving **assembly line** that permitted the mass production of cars, significantly lowering the cost of production. Ford also paid workers higher wages and set a standard that enabled laborers to afford such purchases.

Attitudes Toward Business

Industrialization and the changes associated with it caused American attitudes toward business to alter in the late 1800s. Traditional attitudes, of course, still existed. They could be found in books by the popular writer Horatio Alger. Alger's novels describe poor boys who become rich through hard work and luck.

Alger's novels illustrate what is known as the Puritan work ethic. This is the belief, brought with the Puritans to colonial New England and embodied in the preaching of Puritan minister Cotton Mather, that hard work builds character and is its own reward.

The tremendous wealth some entrepreneurs gained during the late 1800s, as well as the cut-throat business methods they used, led some Americans to rethink their ideas on the meaning of business success. New philosophies tried to explain and justify both the accumulation of wealth and the practices used to achieve it.

LAISSEZ-FAIRE Many supporters of late 1800s business growth restated the older principle of **laissez-faire,** or noninterference. Economist Adam Smith, in his 1776 book, *The Wealth of Nations,* and many other writers had supported this principle, which holds that government should not interfere in the economic workings of a nation. They believed that a **free enterprise system,** in which private individuals make the economic decisions, is most efficient.

During the late 1800s, economists restated the importance of laissez-faire policies to economic growth. Government interference with business was minimal for much of this period, and entrepreneurs expanded their businesses and earned great wealth.

SOCIAL DARWINISM Laissez-faire capitalists found justification for their beliefs in new scientific theories being developed at that time. Naturalist Charles Darwin had developed a theory of evolution that described how animal species live or die by a process of natural selection. Other writers simplified Darwin's theories and created a philosophy called Social Darwinism.

Social Darwinists held that life was a struggle for the "survival of the fittest." Unregulated business competition would see weak businesses fail and healthy businesses thrive. Government action regulating business practices would interfere with the process of natural selection. Likewise, any government programs to aid the poor or workers would also violate natural "laws."

ROBBER BARONS OR PHILANTHROPISTS? The philosophies described above and the growing gulf between rich and poor led some Americans to criticize laissez-faire policies and those who profited from them. Instead of viewing wealthy entrepreneurs as Horatio Alger heroes, critics condemned them as **robber barons,** those who gained their riches at the expense of the poor and the working class. The

PREPARING FOR THE EXAM

What system was based on the principle that private individuals should make economic decisions?

KEY THEMES AND CONCEPTS

Human Systems
Charles Darwin's theory of natural selection was simplified by philosophers and turned into a philosophy called Social Darwinism.

- How was Social Darwinism applied to business competition?

lavish lifestyles of the wealthy at this time fed such criticism. During this so-called Gilded Age, the rich spent freely to show off their wealth, a practice known as conspicuous consumption.

Public criticism and a sense of social responsibility led entrepreneurs to use a part of their wealth to aid society. People like Carnegie and Rockefeller became philanthropists, donating vast sums of money to charities and institutions such as schools, museums, libraries, and orchestras.

GOVERNMENT POLICIES TOWARD BUSINESS

The federal government generally held a laissez-faire attitude toward business for much of this period. Expanding industries and growing foreign trade seemed to justify such an attitude. In addition, many business leaders made financial contributions, legal and illegal, to the politicians who set federal policies.

A number of government policies were designed to aid the growth of business. These included loans and land grants to large railroad companies, high tariffs that discouraged competition from foreign manufacturers, tight limits on the amount of money in circulation, and few limits on immigration.

Steps Toward Government Regulation

Several factors led the government to take the first steps in the late 1800s toward regulating business:

- Periodic downturns in the national economy
- Growing criticism of practices that saw big business profit at the expense of the poor and working class
- Increasing grassroots political pressure for change

Although government intervention at this time had limited impact, it did set the course for more federal actions in years to come.

SUPREME COURT DECISIONS During the late 1800s, railroads developed a number of policies that discriminated against farmers and small shippers. These groups pressured some states to pass laws regulating railroad practices. The railroads sued to have such laws overturned.

In the 1877 case *Munn* v. *Illinois,* the Supreme Court upheld an Illinois law controlling grain elevator rates. The Court ruled that the Constitution recognized a state's right to a "police power" that permitted regulation of private property "affected with a public interest."

In the 1886 case *Wabash, St. Louis & Pacific Railway Co.* v. *Illinois,* however, the Court ruled that states could not regulate railroad rates on portions of interstate routes that lay within their borders. Under the Constitution, only the federal government can regulate interstate trade. This decision meant that states could do little to regulate the railroads.

READING STRATEGY

Reinforcing Main Ideas
What factors led the government toward regulating business in the late 1800s?

♀ **KEY THEMES AND** ⚷ **CONCEPTS**

Constitutional Principles
Two landmark Supreme Court cases dealt with railroad regulation: *Munn* v. *Illinois* (1877) and *Wabash, St. Louis and Pacific Railway* v. *Illinois* (1886).

- How did these two cases influence railroad regulation?

INTERSTATE COMMERCE COMMISSION In 1887, public pressure for reform of railroad policies led Congress to pass the Interstate Commerce Act. The act set up the Interstate Commerce Commission, an agency charged with ending such railroad abuses as pools and rebates, discounts only available to special customers. Although court decisions kept the commission ineffective for several years, its establishment set a precedent for federal regulation of interstate commerce.

SHERMAN ANTITRUST ACT By the late 1800s, some large corporations and trusts had eliminated most competition and won almost total monopolies in their fields. Politicians heeded the public protests over the ensuing abuses. One result was the **Sherman Antitrust Act** of 1890. The act prohibited monopolies by declaring illegal any business combination or trust "in restraint of trade or commerce."

Yet when the federal government tried to enforce the act, the Supreme Court, in *United States* v. *E.C. Knight Company,* 1895, ruled that many businesses were exempt from the new law. In addition, some other corporations circumvented the act by forming holding companies rather than trusts. Once again, the precedent set by the act proved more important than the act itself.

LABOR ORGANIZATIONS

Business growth in the late 1800s brought generally higher wages to American workers. Yet periodic unemployment and poor working conditions remained a fact of life for workers. In addition, employers held enormous power over the lives of their workers and could lower wages and fire employees at will.

The Growth of Unions

To improve conditions, increasing numbers of American workers formed labor unions beginning in the 1820s. As working conditions changed with industrialization, many more workers became interested in unions.

Americans had long understood the values of cooperation and association, and labor unions provided a means to put these values into action. In **collective bargaining,** union members representing workers negotiated labor issues with management. Instead of each worker trying to achieve individual aims, a united group would put pressure on management. Several early unions helped advance the cause of labor.

KNIGHTS OF LABOR Under the direction of Terence Powderly, the Knights of Labor, formed in 1869, welcomed skilled and unskilled workers as well as women and African Americans. The Knights fought for broad social reforms such as an eight-hour day for workers, an end to child labor, and equal opportunities and wages for women. As a rule, the union opposed strikes, but a successful strike against railroads in 1885 brought many new members. However, antilabor feeling swept

READING STRATEGY

Organizing Information
American workers began to form a number of labor unions in the 1800s. In the space below, name three different labor unions and describe the workers who joined each of them.

1.

2.

3.

KEY THEMES AND CONCEPTS

Interdependence
What do you call the process through which union members represent workers in labor negotiations with management?

the nation after the **Haymarket Riot** in late 1886. The Knights declined in influence due to a series of unsuccessful strikes and competition from the American Federation of Labor.

AMERICAN FEDERATION OF LABOR   In 1886, Samuel Gompers formed the American Federation of Labor (AFL). The AFL was a collection of many different craft unions, unions of skilled workers in similar trades. In contrast to the Knights of Labor, the AFL fought for immediate goals such as better wages, hours, and working conditions. The policy that the AFL followed is known as *bread-and-butter unionism*. It so appealed to workers that AFL membership reached about a million by 1900, making the AFL the most powerful union in the nation. Nevertheless, groups such as women, immigrants, and African Americans generally were not welcome in the AFL.

INTERNATIONAL LADIES' GARMENT WORKERS UNION Women made up the majority of workers in the garment industries. In 1900, the International Ladies' Garment Workers Union (ILGWU) was formed to represent the laborers who toiled in sweatshops. After a successful strike in 1910, the ILGWU soon became an important part of the AFL.

Labor Conflict

If collective bargaining failed, labor unions often used strikes, or work stoppages, to achieve their aims. Strikes sometimes ended in union victories; often, however, they led to violence as business owners sought state and even federal support to end walkouts. The strikes and labor-associated violence described below sometimes advanced the cause of labor and sometimes set it back.

GREAT RAILWAY STRIKE   In 1877, a series of pay cuts for railroad workers led to a strike that spread across several states. At the request of state governors, President Rutherford B. Hayes sent federal troops to help end the strike. The workers gained little benefit from the strike, and owners took a harder position against unions.

HAYMARKET RIOT   A labor rally called by Chicago anarchists in 1886 ended with a bomb blast and riot that left many people dead, including 7 police officers. Although the Knights of Labor had no responsibility for the violence, some public opinion blamed them.

HOMESTEAD STRIKE   In 1892, union members at the Carnegie steel plant in Homestead, Pennsylvania, went on strike to protest a wage cut. Management brought in security guards to protect the plant. In the violence that followed, 16 people were killed. The National Guard finally ended the fighting and the strike. Fewer than 25 percent of the striking workers got their jobs back. The strike halted the union movement in the steel industry for 20 years.

PREPARING FOR THE EXAM

For the examination, you will need to understand the history of labor conflict in the United States.

Identify the outcome of each of the following strikes:

1. Great Railway Strike (1877)

2. Haymarket Riot (1886)

3. Homestead Strike (1892)

4. Pullman Strike (1894)

5. Lawrence Textile Strike (1912)

An Era of Strikes, Late 1800s

Increasing tensions between workers and employers led to large, often violent strikes.

PULLMAN STRIKE In 1894, a strike by railway-car makers in Illinois spread and tied up other rail lines. President Grover Cleveland sent in federal troops to end the strike. (The Supreme Court, in the 1895 case *In re Debs,* ruled that the President had the right to deploy the troops, even over the objection of the governor of Illinois.) Cleveland's action confirmed the belief of many that government favored the interests of business over those of labor.

LAWRENCE TEXTILE STRIKE The Industrial Workers of the World (IWW), a radical union of skilled and unskilled laborers, led a huge strike against the textile mills in Lawrence, Massachusetts, in 1912. The strike proved one of the greatest successes of that era, and workers won most of their demands.

PREPARING FOR THE EXAM

A flow chart is a diagram that shows the different steps in a process. Based on the text and the flow chart above, answer the question.

What were three reasons that tensions increased between workers and business owners?

1.

2.

3.

3 American Society Adjusts to Industrialization

★ THE BIG IDEA
Immigration and urbanization changed the United States dramatically. During the late 1800s

- a prosperous middle class developed.

- cities became crowded and workers lived in unhealthful conditions.

- immigrants arrived from eastern Europe and Asia.

- women and other workers became a larger part of the workforce.

- settlers continued to move westward.

⚷ KEY TERMS
tenements
political machines
settlement house
  movement
company towns
suffrage
ghettos
nativism
reservations
Dawes Act
Grange
Populist party
free silver

SECTION OVERVIEW

Industrialization and new building technologies triggered an explosion of urban growth that brought social changes, both good and bad. A prosperous middle class emerged, while urban crowding and disease took a heavy toll on the working poor, many of whom were immigrants. New arrivals came in waves, first from western Europe and Africa, then from eastern Europe and Asia. Despite widespread discrimination, many immigrants prospered. A growing United States population and a demand for new lands and resources lured Americans westward, reducing the Native American population and forcing them into ever-shrinking parcels of land. Western land was gobbled up by miners, ranchers, and a growing political force: farmers.

KEY THEMES AND CONCEPTS

As you review this section, take special note of the following key themes and concepts:

Change What effects did industrialization and urbanization have on American culture, work life, and family life?

Immigration and Migration How did patterns of immigration change from colonial times through the early 1900s?

Places and Regions What types of land, resources, and economic opportunities caused Americans to move farther and farther westward?

KEY PEOPLE

As you review this section, be sure you understand the significance of these key people:

John Dewey
Jane Addams
Frederick Jackson Turner

William Jennings Bryan
William McKinley

Cities offered the best and the worst of life for newcomers from the countryside and from abroad. The dazzling skyscrapers and bustling streets were symbols of the new opportunities for prosperity in America. Yet behind the dazzle grew a darker side of city life.

INDUSTRIALIZATION AND URBANIZATION

Industrialization and the growth of cities went hand in hand. Cities offered large numbers of workers for new factories. Cities provided transportation for raw materials and finished goods. As more plants were built, more workers moved to cities seeking jobs. In 1880, about a quarter of Americans lived in cities. By 1900, roughly 40 percent did. By 1920, more than half of all Americans lived in cities. This shift from rural to urban life had both positive and negative effects.

Negative Effects of City Growth

Some of the negative effects of urbanization included crowded, unsanitary living conditions for workers, as well as corrupt city politics.

HOUSING Construction of decent housing often lagged behind the growth of city populations. Much city housing consisted of multifamily buildings called **tenements.** Immigrant and working-class families, who could pay little for rent, crowded into such buildings. These poorly maintained tenements deteriorated, and whole neighborhoods became slums. Crime flourished in such poor, congested neighborhoods.

HEALTH Urban crowding helped spread disease. Water and sanitation facilities were often inadequate. Poor families could not afford proper diets and lacked knowledge of basic health procedures.

POLITICS **Political machines** took control of many city governments, partly by providing help to the growing number of poor immigrant voters and thereby gaining their support. Corruption increased, and money that could have been spent on public works often ended up in private pockets.

Positive Effects of City Growth

Urbanization was aided and improved by new technologies in transportation, architecture, utilities, and sanitation. In addition, cities offered new cultural opportunities.

NEW TECHNOLOGIES Builders turned to new technologies to meet the challenge posed by huge numbers of people living together. Subways, elevated trains, and streetcars provided mass transportation. Steel girders and elevators made possible high-rise skyscrapers. Gas and electric lights brightened city streets and made them safer.

READING STRATEGY

Analyzing Cause And Effect

- How was industrialization related to urbanization?

- Did one process lead to the other, or were these processes interdependent?

READING STRATEGY

Predicting Content
The growth of cities had both positive and negative effects. Some of the negative effects included crowded and unsanitary living conditions for workers.

- How might these conditions change over time?

- How might they stay the same?

Growing health problems forced officials to design and build new water and sewage systems.

CULTURAL ADVANCES Public and private money funded new museums, concert halls, theaters, and parks. New printing presses turned out mass-circulation newspapers, magazines, and popular novels by authors such as Mark Twain and Horatio Alger. Public schools educated more students than ever before. Reformers, including the philosopher and educator John Dewey, improved the quality of teaching.

COMMUNITY IMPROVEMENT Other reformers founded groups intended to correct the problems of society. In Chicago, Jane Addams started Hull House, a model project that led a **settlement house movement** to provide education and services to the poor. Political reformers sought to unseat corrupt political machines and see that public money was spent on improved services such as police and fire departments and new hospitals, rather than on graft.

PREPARING FOR THE EXAM

Some examination questions require you to read and interpret charts. Study the chart and answer these questions.

- Approximately how much did the urban (city) population in the United States grow between 1860 and 1900?

- Did the rural population increase or decrease between 1870 and 1890?

Urban and Rural Population, 1850–1900

Source: *Historical Statistics of the United States*

READING STRATEGY

Organizing Information

- Into which three groups can the urban population of the late 1800s be divided into?

- Which group was the largest?

- Which group was the smallest?

The Urban Mixture

The people of these growing cities generally could be divided into three broad groups.

WORKERS AND THE POOR The largest group contained the workers and the poor. Most immigrants belonged to this group, whose members lived in slums and poorer neighborhoods. (Living conditions generally were better in the **company towns,** which were built and owned by a single employer, but workers in these towns were dependent on their employer for everything from housing to food to police protection.) Often workers lacked the time and money to go to theaters or museums or use other resources that cities provided.

THE MIDDLE CLASS Doctors, lawyers, office workers, and skilled laborers made up a growing middle class. Middle-class neighborhoods offered more spacious, better maintained housing. The middle-class people had both money and leisure time. Their homes contained the new consumer goods becoming available, such as sewing machines and phonographs. They could afford to go to concerts, attend increasingly popular football, basketball, or baseball games, and save money for their children's higher education.

THE WEALTHY Entrepreneurs and wealthy business people usually made the city their chief residence, although they often had summer estates outside it. The rich made up the smallest segment of urban society. They lived in large mansions or elegant apartment buildings. They often contributed to charities and cultural institutions such as opera companies and libraries. They could enjoy the broadest range of benefits of city life.

Changes for Women, Families, and Work

Industrialization and urbanization brought changes to the lives of women in all the classes. Many Americans had long held the view that the ideal woman devoted herself to home and family, instilling in her husband and children high moral values. In fact, usually only wealthy women could dedicate themselves full-time to such tasks.

In the late 1800s, more women began taking jobs outside the home, some out of economic necessity and others out of a desire for a larger role in society. These jobs provided added income and personal fulfillment but sometimes produced added stress for family members. For example, women who worked outside the home also were expected to continue performing most of the jobs in the home, and children often had to be cared for by relatives or neighbors during the day.

NEW EMPLOYMENT OPPORTUNITIES FOR WOMEN

Working-class women often had to hold jobs outside the home. In addition to jobs women had traditionally filled, such as household service, sewing, or laundering, women took some new jobs created by recent inventions such as the typewriter and telephone.

Middle- and upper-class women also sought jobs. Many of these women had long been active in reform movements, including abolition and temperance, and had attended college in increasing numbers through the 1800s. They sought to apply their educations and social concerns in the job market. Women took jobs as teachers, social workers, doctors, and lawyers, often struggling against public disapproval.

Women thus became an ever-larger part of the workforce. Between 1880 and 1910, the number of working women grew from 2.6 million to more than 7 million. Conditions they met in the workplace—hostility, laws that barred women from certain jobs, unequal pay—led more women to seek legal remedies. To gain the political power to force change, however,

KEY THEMES AND CONCEPTS

Change

In the late 1800s, more women began to seek paid employment outside the home.

- What reasons led to this change?
- What kinds of new jobs did women seek outside the home?

READING STRATEGY

Problem Solving

- How much did the number of working women grow between 1880 and 1910?
- What challenges did women face in the workplace?
- How did some women address those challenges?

women first needed to win the right to vote, called **suffrage.** The women's suffrage movement grew more active.

**♀ KEY THEMES AND
⌐ CONCEPTS**
**Individuals, Groups,
Institutions**
What other groups of
workers also began
working in the late 1800s?
What kinds of conditions
did they face?

OTHER GROUPS OF WORKERS Groups besides women faced problems in the workplace. Employers regularly discriminated against African American workers and workers who were older or disabled, refusing to hire them or keeping them in low-paying jobs.

Nor did laws protect children from dangerous and unhealthful work, such as in mines and factories. Nevertheless, many families were forced to send their children to work rather than school in order to help make ends meet.

IMMIGRATION

The United States has always been a nation of immigrants. After the Civil War, however, industrialization drew an even greater flood of immigrants. From 1865 to 1900, some 13.5 million people arrived from abroad. Not until the 1920s would the numbers begin to dwindle. Immigration to the United States can be divided into three stages.

**♀ KEY THEMES AND
⌐ CONCEPTS**
**Immigration and
Migration**
During the colonial
period, a huge number of
immigrants arrived in the
United States. People from
England, Germany, and
Sweden, for example, made
up a large number of these
immigrants, but people
from other countries came
as well.

• What motivated immi-
  grants in the colonial
  period to come to the
  United States?

Colonial Immigration

This period lasted from the arrival of the first people from England through the Declaration of Independence. The following features characterize this period of immigration.

COLONIAL IMMIGRANTS People from England made up the largest part of these immigrants. However, Scotch-Irish, German, Swedish, and Dutch also came in significant numbers. Large numbers of Africans were also part of the colonial immigration.

REASONS FOR IMMIGRATION Some came seeking political and religious freedom. Others sought to improve their economic standing and their way of life. The Africans came unwillingly, as slaves.

**GEOGRAPHY
IN HISTORY**
Organizing Information
During the colonial period,
in what areas did most
English immigrants settle?
List two other examples of
immigrant groups and the
areas in which they settled.

1.

2.

AREAS OF SETTLEMENT English settlement spread along the Atlantic Coast from Maine to Georgia and inland to the Appalachians. Within this area, other ethnic groups became concentrated in certain regions. For example, many Dutch settled in New York and New Jersey, many Germans in Pennsylvania, and many Scotch-Irish in the backcountry areas of the Carolinas. Most Africans came at first to the Chesapeake region, then spread through the South.

DIFFICULTIES THEY FACED Immigrants came into conflict with the Native Americans. They also had to overcome the challenge of building homes, farms, and a new way of life in an unfamiliar region.

CONTRIBUTIONS The immigrants succeeded in establishing a culture much like the one they had left in Europe, yet heavily influenced by the geographic factors encountered in North America.

In addition to their language, people coming from England brought forms of government, religions, family and cultural traditions, and economic patterns from their home country. Other groups contributed customs from their home countries. All worked to build a successful economy in North America.

Old Immigration

The old immigration covered the years from the establishment of the United States until around 1850. Most immigrants came from northern and western Europe, especially Ireland, Germany, and Scandinavia.

REASONS FOR IMMIGRATION Massive famine caused by failure of the potato crop drove millions of Irish immigrants to seek opportunity in the United States. Revolution in Germany caused many immigrants to seek peace and stability in America. Many people continued to arrive in search of better economic opportunity.

AREAS OF SETTLEMENT The Irish largely settled in cities in the Northeast. Some Germans also stayed in cities, but many moved west to start farms, as did a large number of Scandinavian immigrants.

DIFFICULTIES THEY FACED Irish and German Catholic immigrants often faced hostility on their arrival in the United States. Some Americans feared economic competition from the newcomers. Since at this time the nation was predominantly Protestant, resentment toward Catholics and Jews was also strong.

CONTRIBUTIONS Irish workers helped build railroads and canals and labored in factories. Germans and Scandinavians brought, among other things, advanced farming techniques and new ideas on education such as kindergarten.

New Immigration

The new immigration covered the time from roughly 1850 to 1924. This period was marked by a shift in sources of immigration to southern and eastern Europe, especially the nations of Italy, Poland, and Russia. In addition, substantial numbers of Japanese and Chinese arrived.

REASONS FOR IMMIGRATION Hope of greater economic opportunity prompted many of these immigrants to come to America. Some also came seeking political freedom. Other groups, such as Russian Jews, sought religious freedom.

AREAS OF SETTLEMENT Most of the new immigrants settled in cities, especially industrial centers and ports, and often were concentrated in **ghettos,** or urban areas (usually poor) that are dominated by a single ethnic group. Asian immigrants tended to settle on the west coast, usually in California.

⚷ KEY THEMES AND CONCEPTS

Immigration and Migration

"Old immigration" took place during the first half of the 19th century. People from northern and western Europe, Ireland, and Scandinavia for example, made up a large number of these immigrants, but people came from other countries as well.

- What motivated immigrants in the period before 1850 to come to the United States?

GEOGRAPHY IN HISTORY

Organizing Information

- Where did most Irish and German immigrants settle?

- What difficulties did these immigrant groups face?

Immigrants

Where they came from 1840–1860

93%
3%
2%
1.5%
.5%

Where they came from 1880–1900

33%
59%
6%
1%
1%

- ▢ Northern and Western Europe
- ▢ Eastern and Southern Europe
- ▢ Americas
- ▢ Asia
- ▢ All others

Source: *Historical Statistics of the United States*

ANALYZING DOCUMENTS

Examine the pie charts above, then answer the following questions.

- What percentage of immigrants between 1840 and 1860 came from northern and western Europe?

- How much did the percentage of immigrants from eastern and southern Europe increase from the period 1840–1860 to the period 1880–1900?

DIFFICULTIES THEY FACED Adjusting to life in the United States could cause strains in immigrant families. At school, immigrant children learned not only English but American tastes and customs. Immigrant parents often feared that their children were losing their religious and cultural heritage.

In addition, the growing numbers of new immigrants produced reactions of fear and hostility among many native-born Americans whose ancestors had come from very different backgrounds. Newcomers faced discrimination in jobs and housing. (As low-wage workers, they also competed against other minority groups, such as African Americans.) Popular pressure to limit immigration increased.

CONTRIBUTIONS The new immigrants found an abundance of jobs in the nation's expanding industries. Yet the steady stream of incoming workers to fill such jobs kept wages low. Young Italian and Jewish girls worked in the sweatshops of the garment industry. Poles and Slavs labored in the coal mines and steel mills of Pennsylvania and the Midwest. Chinese workers helped build the transcontinental railroad. These immigrants aided America's economic expansion and contributed to the nation's rich cultural diversity.

Reaction Against Immigration

The flood of immigration in the late 1800s brought with it a new wave of **nativism.** This was the belief that native-born Americans and their ways of life were superior to immigrants and their ways of life. In the late 1800s, descendants of the old immigrants were often among the nativists protesting the arrival of new immigrants.

Nativists believed that immigrant languages, religions, and traditions would have a negative impact on American society. Nativist workers believed that the many new immigrants competing for jobs kept wages low. A series of downturns in the economy added to fears that immigrants would take jobs from native-born Americans.

Immigrants thus often met with prejudice and discrimination. Jokes and stereotypes about the newcomers were common. Nativists also tried to influence legislation against immigrants. Key developments in this area are included in the chart on the following page.

Immigrants and American Society

Over the years, sociologists and others who studied immigration developed different theories on how immigrants were absorbed into the larger society.

"MELTING POT" THEORY According to this theory, people from various cultures have met in the United States to form a new American. The contributions of individual groups are not easily distinguished. The resulting culture is more important than its parts.

Reaction Against Immigration

- **Know-Nothing Party:** The party's members worked during the 1850s to limit the voting strength of immigrants, keep Catholics out of public office, and require a lengthy residence before citizenship. Also known as the American party, the Know-Nothing party achieved none of these goals and died out by the late 1850s.

- **Chinese Exclusion Act of 1882:** Some native-born Americans labelled immigration from Asia a "yellow peril." Under pressure from California, which had already barred Chinese from owning property or working at certain jobs, Congress passed this law sharply limiting Chinese immigration.

- **"Gentlemen's Agreement":** In 1907 President Roosevelt reached an informal agreement with Japan under which that nation nearly halted the emigration of its people to the United States.

- **Literacy Tests:** In 1917 Congress enacted a law barring any immigrant who could not read or write.

- **Emergency Quota Act of 1921:** This law sharply limited the number of immigrants to the United States each year to about 350,000.

- **National Origins Act of 1924:** This law further reduced immigration and biased it in favor of those from northern and western Europe.

ASSIMILATION According to this theory, immigrants disappeared into an already established American culture. They gave up older languages and customs and became Americanized, adopting the appearances and attitudes of the larger society in order to be accepted. Immigrants from Africa and Asia, who looked least like nativist Americans, had the hardest time becoming assimilated.

PLURALISM This theory recognizes that groups do not always lose their distinctive characters. They can live side by side, with each group contributing in different ways to society. This approach is sometimes called the salad bowl theory, since groups, like different vegetables in a salad, remain identifiable but create a new, larger whole.

THE AMERICAN WEST IN THE LATE 1800s

In 1893, Frederick Jackson Turner wrote in his paper "The Significance of the Frontier in American History" that the frontier "and the advance of American settlement westward, explain American development." Turner claimed life in the West had given rise to inventiveness, independence, and unique American customs. (While other historians would argue instead that other factors, such as the nation's European heritage or economic abundance, were the key influences, Turner's thesis has had lasting influence.) In 1890, the government had announced that the West was closed. Industrialization had aided the settling of the West.

ANALYZING DOCUMENTS

Examine the chart above, then answering the following questions.

- How influential was the Know-Nothing party?

- What prompted Congress to pass the Chinese Exclusion Act of 1882?

- Which laws restricted the number of immigrants to the United States each year?

 PREPARING FOR THE EXAM

Which sociological theory argues that different immigrant groups can live side-by-side without losing their distinctive characters?

The American West, 1862–1896

1862 Homestead Act	**1887** Dawes Act		**1896** McKinley defeats Bryan

1860	1865	1870	1875	1880	1885	1890	1895	1900

1876 Sioux War; Battle of the Little Bighorn

1890 Battle of Wounded Knee

ANALYZING DOCUMENTS

Examine the timeline above, then answer the following questions.

- How many years passed between the Homestead Act and the Battle of Wounded Knee?

- Which event occurred first: the Battle of Little Bighorn or passage of the Dawes Act?

KEY THEMES AND CONCEPTS

Government
The Dawes Act was aimed at breaking up Native American tribes and reservations. It offered Native Americans who gave up tribal ways the deeds to their land and United States citizenship after 25 years.

- Was the Dawes Act fair to Native Americans?

- Did Native Americans support it?

Native Americans and Westward Expansion

The westward expansion of the late 1800s continued to create problems for the Native Americans who stood in its path. By the 1840s, only scattered groups of Native Americans still lived in the East. Most lived west of the Mississippi on lands that few whites wanted. The California gold rush, the building of the transcontinental railroad, and the discovery of rich farmland in the Great Plains changed this situation. Now white people began to move onto Native American lands in the West.

INDIAN WARS The Native Americans fought back. From the 1850s to 1890, a series of wars raged in the West. Gradually the Native Americans were forced to accept treaties that crowded them into smaller and smaller areas of land called **reservations.** Native American resistance was weakened by the greater numbers of whites with superior technology, and divisions among Native American peoples that did not permit a unified resistance. The defeat of the Sioux at Wounded Knee, South Dakota, in 1890 is usually considered the end of the Indian wars.

CHANGING GOVERNMENT POLICIES In victory, the federal government continued to display little understanding or respect for Native American cultures and values. Native Americans were given reservation land that rarely could produce adequate crops or support game for the people living on it. Further, in 1887, Congress passed the **Dawes Act,** aimed at Americanizing the Native Americans. It proposed to break up tribes and reservations and to grant land directly to Native Americans as individuals and families. Native Americans who abandoned tribal ways would be granted deeds to their land and United States citizenship. Relatively few Native Americans accepted the terms

The Sioux Wars

1865	Federal government decides to build a road through Sioux territory. Sioux warriors resist violently, sparking Red Cloud's War.
1867	Red Cloud's War ends. Sioux agree to live on reservation in Dakota Territory.
1875	Federal government allows miners to search for gold on Sioux reservation. Second Sioux War begins. Chief Sitting Bull leads many Sioux off the reservation.
1876	At the Battle of the Little Bighorn, Sitting Bull's warriors destroy General Custer's army. In response, federal government sends more troops to the region. Most Sioux agree to move to reservations.
1890	At the Massacre of Wounded Knee, American soldiers open fire on unarmed Sioux, killing 200.

ANALYZING DOCUMENTS

American expansion onto Native American lands led to many wars and the near destruction of western Native American nations. The table at left outlines the struggle experienced by one tribe, the Sioux. Examine the chart, then answer the following questions.

• What caused the first Sioux War in 1865?

• How did the federal government respond to Sitting Bull's defeat of General Custer?

• How many Sioux were killed by American soldiers at the Massacre of Wounded Knee?

of the Dawes Act. By the turn of the twentieth century, the effect of the government policies had greatly reduced the size of the Native American population and had made them among the poorest Americans.

The Economy of the West

New technologies helped people who moved onto Native American lands exploit the wealth of the West. Railroads brought people and carried western crops and products to eastern markets. Barbed wire aided the growth of both farming and ranching. Steel plows cut tough prairie soil. Windmills pulled water to the surface of dry western lands. Mechanical reapers and farm tools allowed a smaller number of workers to plant and harvest larger crops.

The riches of the West, like the land itself, took many forms. In the Rocky Mountains, miners dug millions of dollars in gold, silver, copper, lead, and zinc ore. In the Great Plains, ranchers turned cattle raising into big business, as cowhands moved huge herds across the open ranges to rail lines. Farmers, too, were attracted to the Great Plains because of its rich topsoil and overcame heat, blizzards, droughts, insects, and occasional conflicts with ranchers to raise crops. Many settled lands claimed under the Homestead Act and later built huge farms. (Through the Homestead Act, as well as government land grants and other aid to large railroad companies, the federal government played a significant role in encouraging development of the resources of the West.) By the late 1800s, American farmers were raising enough to feed the nation and still export wheat and other crops.

Spurred by the expansion of mining, ranching, and farming, cities like Omaha, Denver, and San Francisco became some of the fastest-growing in the nation.

KEY THEMES AND CONCEPTS
Economic Systems
Did the economy of the West rely on the same kinds of businesses as the economy of the North? Why or why not?

GEOGRAPHY IN HISTORY

How was the economy of the West influenced by each of the following?

• Rocky Mountains
• Great Plains
• Railroads
• Homestead Act

Farmers, Populists, and Politics

Farmers gained more influence and power through two organizations:
the Grange and the Populist party.

THE GRANGE Many farmers facing the hardships and isolation
of rural life joined the **Grange.** This organization, founded in 1867,
was originally meant to develop social ties. However, poor economic
conditions made farmers aware that railroad companies, which often
stored farmers' crops and carried them to market, had great control
over their livelihoods. To win back some of this control, the Grange
began to press for political changes to limit the power of the railroads.
Pressure from the Grange and other groups led to the state laws
regulating railroads that were upheld in *Munn* v. *Illinois* and to the
federal law creating the Interstate Commerce Commission.

THE POPULIST PARTY Farmers realized that the best hope of
winning more reforms was the formation of a new political party. In
1891, they founded the **Populist party,** which had among its goals a
graduated income tax, direct election of United States senators, and
government ownership of railroads, telegraphs, and telephones. The
new party had strong grassroots support—support directly from the
people rather than established political figures. Populist candidates
soon made strong showings in elections for state legislatures and for
the United States Congress.

THE ELECTION OF 1896 The Populists made their strongest showing
in the election of 1896, the first election to follow an economic
depression that had begun in 1893. The chief Populist issue in the campaign was **free silver.** The free coinage of silver would produce cheap
money, or currency inflated in value that would make it easier for
farmers to pay off debts. William Jennings Bryan, who ran on both the
Populist and Democratic tickets, argued tirelessly for this idea.
Republican candidate William McKinley had the support of big business, which contributed heavily to his campaign. McKinley claimed
the nation's economy was sound and opposed free silver.

McKinley won the election by a fair margin. The nation's economy
meanwhile improved, and the Populists disappeared as a political
party. Yet, as has happened with other minor parties in American
history, some of the Populists' ideas were later adopted by the other
political parties.

The defeat of the Populists symbolized the great changes that had
swept the nation since the Civil War. The economy had changed from
agrarian to industrial. The United States was becoming a nation
of cities rather than farms and villages. The West was closing and
its influence coming to end. New immigrants were creating a new,
complex, pluralistic culture in America. By 1900, the United States
was entering both a new century and a modern age.

Questions for Regents Practice

For online Questions for Regents Practice,
visit the Prentice Hall Web site at www.phschool.com.

MULTIPLE CHOICE

Directions

Review the Test-Taking Strategies section of this book. Then answer the following questions, drawn from actual Regents examinations. Each question is followed by four choices. Read each question carefully. Decide which choice is the correct answer. Then on a separate piece of paper, mark your answer for each question.

1 Which problem in American society is dealt with in this poem?

Merry-Go-Round
Where is the Jim Crow section
On this merry-go-round,
Mister, 'cause I want to ride?
Down South where I come from
White and colored
Can't sit side by side,
Down South on the train
There's a Jim Crow car
On the bus we're put in the back-
But there ain't no back
To a merry-go-round!
Where's the horse
For a kid that's black?

—Langston Hughes

1 nationalism
2 migration
3 sectionalism
4 discrimination

2 The literacy tests and poll taxes used in the southern states after 1870 were designed to
1 ensure that only well-informed people voted
2 prevent African Americans from voting
3 provide an alternative to citizenship tests
4 promote advances in public education

3 President Abraham Lincoln's post-Civil War plan for reconstruction of the South was based on the theory that the former Confederate States
1 should be treated as conquered territories
2 could be readmitted to the Union only by Congress
3 had never actually left the Union
4 must grant full equality to all people

4 During Reconstruction, what was a belief of the Radical Republicans?
1 The former Confederate States should be brought back into the Union as quickly as possible.
2 Reconstruction should be used to force political and social reform in the southern states.
3 The North and South should take equal responsibility for causing the Civil War.
4 The freedmen should be denied equal civil rights.

5 One similarity between the Know-Nothings and the Ku Klux Klan is that both
 1 opposed the spread of communism
 2 exposed abuses in big business and government
 3 believed the problems of society were caused by the growth of labor unions
 ④ fostered resentment against minority groups in American society

6 The most long-lasting victory for civil rights achieved during Reconstruction was the
 ① ratification of the 13th, 14th, and 15th amendments to the United States Constitution
 2 establishment of a strong two-party political system in the South
 3 increased prominence given to the Office of the President
 4 passage of Black Codes throughout the South

7 The Solid South refers to the political situation in the post-Reconstruction South where
 1 most eligible voters supported the Prohibition party
 2 freedmen held most government posts
 ③ the Democratic party was dominant
 4 civil rights issues were strongly supported

8 Which statement best describes a major economic trend in the United States during the period from 1865 to 1900?
 ① Many business practices were developed to eliminate competition.
 2 Workers determined working conditions and factory output.
 3 The gross national product decreased steadily.
 4 Basic industries were taken over by the government.

9 An important result of industrialization in the United States was a growth in the
 1 influence of small family-owned businesses
 2 idea of socialism as the main political philosophy
 ③ power of large corporations
 4 political power of small farmers

10 The Interstate Commerce Act, Sherman Antitrust Act, and Clayton Antitrust Act were attempts to limit
 1 business competition
 2 labor unions
 ③ monopolies
 4 tariffs

11 Which factor that contributed to the economic growth of the United States in the period from 1865 to 1920 aroused the most opposition?
 1 growth of rapid transportation
 2 existence of democratic government
 3 mechanization of agriculture
 ④ liberal immigration policies

12 Between 1865 and 1900, an issue that dominated national politics in the United States was
 1 slavery
 ② the rise of big business
 3 sectionalism
 4 environmental protection

13 During the second half of the 19th century, a major goal of new types of business organizations was to
 1 introduce safer and less expensive products to consumers
 ② consolidate the manufacture and distribution of products
 3 support the large number of government regulations
 4 compete successfully with Japanese imports.

Base your answers to questions 14 and 15 on the chart below and on your knowledge of social studies.

American Territorial Growth
(As a percentage of present United States territory)

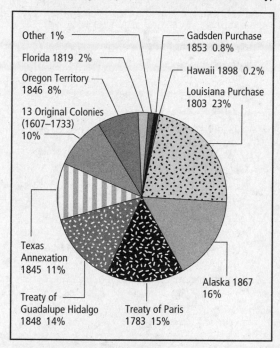

16 "[Buffalo hunters] have done more in the last two years, and will do more in the next year, to settle the . . . Indian question than the entire regular army has done in the last thirty years. . . . For the sake of peace let them kill, skin, and sell until the buffalo are destroyed."

—General Philip Sheridan

What was the result of the process described in this quotation?

1 Native Americans were granted farmland under the Homestead Act.

2 The disappearance of their economic base helped drive Native Americans onto reservations.

3 Many Native Americans moved to eastern cities to work in factories.

4 Most Native Americans migrated to Canada to find new ways to earn a living.

Base your answer to question 17 on the graph below and on your knowledge of social studies.

Farm and Nonfarm Workers 1860–1900

14 Which territorial gain accounted for the largest increase in United States land growth?

1 Treaty of Guadalupe Hidalgo

2 Texas Annexation

3 Louisiana Purchase

4 purchase of Alaska

15 Which policy is best illustrated by the chart?

1 isolationism

2 manifest destiny

3 containment

4 globalization

17 Which development contributed most to the trends shown in this graph?
① industrialization
2 westward migration
3 commercial revolution
4 trade restrictions

18 A pioneer wanting to settle in the West in the 1870s would have benefited most from the
① Homestead Act
2 Sherman Antitrust Act
3 Interstate Commerce Act
4 Agricultural Adjustment Act

19 Unlike other minorities in the United States, Native Americans have some of their rights guaranteed by
1 the Emancipation Proclamation
② treaties with the federal government
3 the Declaration of Independence
4 black codes

20 In which pair of events did the first event most directly influence the second?
1 discovery of gold in California / Louisiana Purchase
2 building of the transcontinental railroad / disappearance of the frontier
③ settling of the Oregon Territory / passage of the Homestead Act
4 assimilation of Native Americans into American society / passage of the Dawes Act

21 A belief in manifest destiny, the passage of the Dawes Act, and the completion of the transcontinental railroad are most closely associated with the
1 rise of big business
2 growth of the labor movement
3 abolitionist movement
④ expansion and settlement of the West

22 "I am tired of fighting. . . . Hear me, my chiefs. I am tired. My heart is sick and sad. From where the sun now stands, I shall fight no more forever!"

—Chief Joseph, 1877

In this statement, Chief Joseph of the Nez Percé expressed his reluctant acceptance of a government policy of
① placing Native American tribes on reservations
② requiring Native Americans to settle west of the Mississippi River
3 granting immediate citizenship to Native Americans
④ forcing Native Americans to assimilate into American culture

23 Which factor was most critical to the building of the transcontinental railroads after the Civil War?
1 government ownership of the railroads
2 capital investments by labor unions
③ land and money provided by the federal government
4 willingness of Native Americans to leave tribal lands

24 During the late 1800s, the growing of cash crops by an increasingly large number of farmers resulted in
1 greater isolation of farmers from American economic life
② a shift from self-sufficiency to commercial farming
3 less food available for export
4 general economic prosperity for all farmers

25 In the late 1800s, the desire for new markets for manufactured goods and coaling stations led the United States to pursue a policy of
1 isolationism
2 containment
3 collective security
④ imperialism

26 A primary source for information on the Spanish-American War would be
  1 a historical novel about the war
  2 a movie called *Theodore Roosevelt: The Rough Rider*
  ③ the diary of a soldier who fought in the war
  4 a chapter on wars in an American history textbook

27 As the United States became industrialized, an important effect of mechanization and the division of labor was that
  ① smaller industries had difficulty maintaining their competitiveness
  2 the price of most manufactured goods increased
  3 the demand to improve transportation systems decreased
  4 pools and trusts became less efficient forms of business organization

28 In the late 1800s, most strikes by unions were unsuccessful mainly because
  1 unions were generally considered to be unconstitutional
  ② government usually supported business instead of workers
  3 strikes had never been used before in labor disputes
  4 strikers failed to use militant tactics

29 The poll tax, the literacy test, and the actions of the Ku Klux Klan were all attempts to limit the effectiveness of
  ① the 14th and 15th amendments
  2 the Supreme Court's decision in *Brown* v. *Board of Education*
  3 civil rights legislation passed in all states after the Civil War
  4 immigration laws such as the Gentleman's Agreement and the Chinese Exclusion Act

30 The Rockefeller Foundation, Carnegie Hall, and the Morgan Library illustrate various ways that entrepreneurs and their descendants have
  1 suppressed the growth of labor unions
  ② supported philanthropic activities to benefit society
  3 applied scientific discoveries to industry
  4 attempted to undermine the United States economic system

31 The major reason the United States placed few restrictions on immigration during the 1800s was that
  1 few Europeans wished to give up their economic security
  2 little opposition to immigration existed
  ③ the growing economy needed a steady supply of cheap labor
  4 most immigrants spoke English and thus needed little or no education

32 From 1865 to 1900, how did the growth of industry affect American society?
  1 The United States experienced the disappearance of the traditional "family farm."
  2 Population centers shifted from the Northeast to the South.
  3 Restrictions on immigration created a more homogenous culture.
  ④ The percentage of Americans living in urban areas increased.

33 Many wealthy American industrialists of the late 19th century used the theory of social Darwinism to
  1 support the labor union movement
  ② justify monopolistic actions
  3 promote legislation establishing a minimum wage
  4 encourage charitable organizations to help the poor

34 A main goal of the Grange movement of the 1870s and 1880s was to
  ① force the railroads to lower freight rates
  2 reduce the rate of inflation
  3 strengthen labor unions
  4 improve living conditions in urban slums

THEMATIC ESSAY
In developing your answers to the essay, be sure to keep these general definitions in mind:
(a) <u>discuss</u> means "to make observations about something using facts, reasoning, and argument; to present in some detail"
(b) <u>describe</u> means "to illustrate something in words or to tell about it"
(c) <u>evaluate</u> means "to examine and judge the significance, worth, or condition of; to determine the value of"

Directions
Write a well-organized essay that includes an introduction, several paragraphs addressing the task below, and a conclusion.

Theme: Industrialization
The growth of industry in the 19th century had a major impact on many aspects of American society.

Task
Identify any three aspects of American society. Using specific examples, discuss how the growth of industry had an impact on that aspect of society. Evaluate whether the role of industrialization had a positive or a negative effect and explain your reasoning using specific historic examples.

Suggestions
You may use any examples from your study of industrialization in the United States. Some suggestions you might wish to consider include: rise of organized labor, government involvement in the economy, status of the farmer, urbanization, or the role of women.

You are *not* limited to these suggestions.

Guidelines
In your essay be sure to:
- Address all aspects of the *Task*
- Analyze, evaluate, or compare and/or contrast issues and events whenever possible
- Fully support the theme of the essay with relevant facts, examples, and details
- Write a well-developed essay that consistently demonstrates a logical and clear plan of organization
- Introduce the theme by establishing a framework that is beyond a simple restatement of the *Task*
- Conclude your essay with a strong summation of the theme

DOCUMENT-BASED ESSAY

> For online Document-Based Essays,
> visit the Prentice Hall Web site at www.phschool.com.

This task is designed to test your ability to work with historical documents and is based on the accompanying documents (1–8). Some of the documents have been edited for the purposes of this question. As you analyze the documents, take into account both the source of each document and any point of view that may be presented in the document.

Directions

This document-based question consists of two parts: Part A and Part B. In Part A, you are to read each document and answer the question or questions that follow the document. In Part B, you are to write an essay based on the information in the documents and your knowledge of United States history.

Historical Context

After the Civil War, America faced new challenges including the rebuilding of the South and the rise of big business. These events changed American society.

Task

Using information from the documents and your knowledge of United States history and government, answer the questions that follow each document in Part A. Your answers to the questions will help you write the Part B essay in which you be asked to:

  Discuss whether or not the changes that occurred after the Civil War created a more democratic America with greater opportunities for all.

PART A: SHORT ANSWER

DOCUMENT #1

> *"This case turns upon the constitutionality of an act of the General Assembly of the State of Louisiana, passed in 1890, providing for separate railway carriages for the white and colored races. . . .*
>
> *"We consider the underlying fallacy [error in reasoning] of the plaintiff's argument to consist in the assumption that the enforced separation of the two races stamps the colored race with a badge of inferiority. If this be so, it is . . . solely because the colored race chooses to put that construction upon it. . . . The argument also assumes that social prejudices may be overcome by legislation, and that equal rights cannot be secured . . . except by an enforced commingling [mixing] of the two races. We cannot accept this proposition. . . . If the civil and political rights of both races be equal, one cannot be inferior to the other civilly or politically. If one race be inferior to the other socially, the Constitution of the United States cannot put them upon the same plane. . . ."*
>
> —*Plessy v. Ferguson* **(1896)**

1 State one reason why the Supreme Court ruled in 1896 that separate railroad cars for African Americans and white Americans were constitutional.

_____

_____

_____

_____

_____

_____

DOCUMENT #2

"In piecework they would reduce the time, requiring the same work in a shorter time, and paying the same wages. . . . They would start work every morning at seven, and eat their dinners at noon, and then work until ten or eleven at night without another mouthful of food."

—Upton Sinclair, ***The Jungle***

2   What conditions would a labor union leader want to change in the factory described?

_____

_____

_____

DOCUMENT #3

THE VULTURES' ROOST

3   How does this cartoon portray the relationship between the trusts and the United States Senate?

_____

_____

_____

DOCUMENT #4

> *"Every contract, combination in the form of trust or otherwise, or conspiracy, in restraint of trade or commerce among the several States, or with foreign nations, is declared to be illegal. Every person who shall make any contract or engage in any combination or conspiracy hereby declared to be illegal shall be deemed guilty of a felony, and, on conviction thereof, shall be punished by fine not exceeding $10,000,000 if a corporation, or, if any other person, $350,000, or by imprisonment not exceeding three years . . ."*
>
> **—Sherman Antitrust Act (1890)**

4   How did the Sherman Antitrust Act restrict monopolies?

_____

_____

_____

_____

DOCUMENT #5

Source: *Historical Statistics of the United States, Colonial Times to 1970*

5   What effect did the Chinese Exclusion Act (1882) have on immigration?

_____

_____

_____

_____

DOCUMENT #6
Major Reconstruction Legislation

Date	Legislation	Purpose
1865	13th Amendment	• Abolished slavery
1865, 1866	Freedmen's Bureau	• Provided services for newly freed people
1867	Reconstruction Acts	• Established Republican Reconstruction program
1868	14th Amendment	• Defined citizenship to include African Americans • Guaranteed equal protection under the law
1870	15th Amendment	• Guaranteed voting rights
1875	Civil Rights Act	• Protected the rights of African Americans in public places

6 Based on the chart, what are two rights that were given to African Americans during Reconstruction?

_____

_____

_____

_____

_____

_____

DOCUMENT #7

> *"American social development has been continually beginning over again on the frontier. This perennial [lasting for a long time] rebirth, this fluidity of American life, this expansion westward with its new opportunities, . . . furnished the forces dominating American character. The true point of view in the history of this nation is not the Atlantic Coast, it is the Great West. The frontier is the line of most rapid and effective Americanization. The wilderness masters the colonists."*
>
> **—Frederick Jackson Turner,**
> **"The Significance of the Frontier in American History" (1893)**

7 According to Frederick Jackson Turner, why was the frontier significant in the development of America?

_____

_____

_____

DOCUMENT #8
A Squelcher for Woman Suffrage

HOW CAN SHE VOTE,
WHEN THE FASHIONS ARE
SO WIDE, AND THE VOTING
BOOTHS ARE SO NARROW?

8 According to the cartoonist, what is one problem associated with granting women the vote?

_____

_____

9 What does this cartoon suggest about the cartoonist's opinion of woman suffrage?

_____

_____

PART B: ESSAY

Directions
Using information from the documents provided, and your knowledge of United States history, write a well-organized essay that includes an introduction, several paragraphs, and a conclusion.

Historical Context
After the Civil War, America faced new challenges including the rebuilding of the South and the rise of big business. These events changed American society.

Task
Using information from the documents and your knowledge of United States history and government, write an essay in which you
   Discuss whether or not the changes that occurred after the Civil War created a more democratic America with greater opportunities for all.

Guidelines
When writing your essay, be sure to
- Address all aspects of the *Task* by accurately analyzing and interpreting at least four documents
- Incorporate information from the documents in the body of the essay
- Incorporate relevant outside information throughout the essay
- Richly support the theme with relevant facts, examples, and details
- Write a well-developed essay that consistently demonstrates a logical and clean plan of organization
- Introduce the theme by establishing a framework that is beyond a simple restatement of the *Task* or *Historical Context* and conclude the essay with a summation of the theme.

UNIT 4

The Progressive Movement: Responses to the Challenges Brought About by Industrialization and Urbanization

UNIT OVERVIEW

Between the end of the Civil War and the turn of the twentieth century, the United States became a more industrialized and urbanized nation. These changes brought many benefits to society, but they created problems as well. In this unit, you will review how Americans responded to change, both at home and overseas, in the years from 1900 to 1920. This period is called the Progressive Era. The term comes from the word "progress" and indicates that Americans were reacting to problems by working for reform.

Some key questions to help you focus on the Progressive Era include:

- What were the pressures for reform that led to the Progressive movement?
- Who were the Progressives?
- How successful were the Progressives in meeting their goals?
- What were the causes of increased international involvement of the United States from 1890 to 1920?
- What were the effects of this involvement on the United States and other peoples around the world?

SECTION 1 Reform in America

SECTION OVERVIEW

The process of industrialization and urbanization in the United States had both positive and negative effects. From the 1890s to 1920, a reform movement swept the nation as many people began focusing their energies on correcting those negative effects. These reformers were known as Progressives, and their movement was so strong that this period has become known as the **Progressive Era.** Progressive reformers had a variety of motivations, used different methods, and had different degrees of success in achieving reform. Progressives supported the use of government power to bring about reform. Two strong Progressive Presidents—Theodore Roosevelt and Woodrow Wilson—implemented bold domestic programs to take Progressive reform to the national level.

KEY THEMES AND CONCEPTS

As you review this section, take special note of the following key themes and concepts:

Reform Movements What conditions stirred Progressive reformers to action?

Diversity How did women and African Americans work for their own rights during the Progressive era, and how successful were they?

Environment How did Progressive reform result in certain environmental protections?

Government What role did the government play in Progressive reform?

★ THE BIG IDEA
The Progressive Era was a period of great reform movements, including

- political reforms at the city, state, and federal levels.
- social welfare reforms.
- economic reforms.

These reforms affected some groups differently and had varying degrees of success.

⚲ KEY TERMS
Progressive Era
muckrakers
secret ballot
initiative
referendum
recall
direct primary
New Nationalism
New Freedom
Federal Reserve system
Clayton Antitrust Act

KEY PEOPLE

As you review this section, be sure you understand the significance of these key people:

ANALYZING DOCUMENTS

Using the information in this section and the timeline below, answer the following questions.

- During whose presidency was the Supreme Court case *Lochner* v. *New York* decided?

- Which event on the time-line involved the creation of an organization that worked for the rights of African Americans?

- How did Sinclair's *The Jungle* lead to reform?

Upton Sinclair

Jane Addams

Jeannette Rankin

Carrie Chapman Catt

Alice Paul

Margaret Sanger

Booker T. Washington

W.E.B. Du Bois

Marcus Garvey

Ida B. Wells-Barnett

Robert M. La Follette

Theodore Roosevelt

Gifford Pinchot

John Muir

William Howard Taft

Woodrow Wilson

KEY SUPREME COURT CASES

As you review this section, be sure you understand the significance of these key Supreme Court cases:

Lochner v. *New York* (1905)

Muller v. *Oregon* (1908)

Northern Securities Co. v. *United States* (1904)

Reform During the Progressive Era, 1901–1916

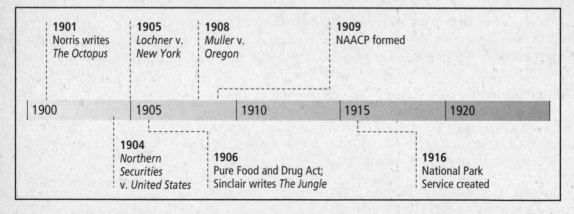

| 1901 | 1905 | 1908 | 1909 |
| Norris writes *The Octopus* | *Lochner* v. *New York* | *Muller* v. *Oregon* | NAACP formed |

1900   1905   1910   1915   1920

| 1904 | 1906 | 1916 |
| *Northern Securities* v. *United States* | Pure Food and Drug Act; Sinclair writes *The Jungle* | National Park Service created |

PRESSURES FOR PROGRESSIVE REFORM

By 1900, the United States was a rich and powerful nation. Industrialization, urbanization, and immigration had transformed the United States into a major world economy. The changes in American life, however, also brought problems. The negative effects of these changes led many Americans to call for reform.

Effects of Business Practices

In technology-driven fields such as railroads, steel production, and electric utilities, powerful monopolies restricted competition, often by using unfair methods. Without competition, monopolies could raise prices as much as they wished. Abuse of the nation's natural resources was accepted practice.

The corporate world grew increasingly wealthy and more powerful. Industrial leaders justified their actions by using the philosophy of social Darwinism—the concept that in society as in nature, the strong would survive and the weak would not. Those who succeeded earned their position, and those who failed deserved their failure. Social Darwinists believed that the government should not intervene in this process.

Conditions for Industrial Workers

Working conditions for factory workers continued to be harsh. Many laborers worked 60-hour weeks on machinery, often in unsafe, unhealthy conditions. Getting hurt on the job often resulted in the worker being fired. Workers earned low wages, and women and children were paid even less than male workers. Workers had little security, because their employers could fire them at any time.

Soon, workers grew less tolerant of these terrible working conditions. Some tried to organize labor unions, but employers often fired those who did. Strikes were met with armed attacks from factory security guards and sometimes even federal troops.

Life for the Urban Poor

The gap between living standards of the rich and the poor increased widely during this period. This gap was most apparent in the cities. As the rich grew richer, building lavish townhouses in relatively safe and clean neighborhoods, the poor grew even poorer. They lived in urban slums characterized by poverty, crime, congestion, and poor sanitation. Housing in the cities was segregated by social and economic status, by race, and often by ethnic background.

Mixed Response of Government at All Levels

Government at all levels remained relatively unresponsive to the impact of industrialization and urbanization. Industries were unrestrained by federal and many state governments; the courts most

PREPARING FOR THE EXAM

Movements can be traced through history. In Unit Two you reviewed the birth of the American reform tradition. For the exam, you may need to be able to identify and understand the different periods of reform in United States history.

- The Populists preceded the Progressives in the 19th and early 20th century reform movements.

- Reform continued under the New Deal of the 1930s and the period of reform in the 1960s.

KEY THEMES AND CONCEPTS

Government

Two landmark Supreme Court cases dealt with state laws limiting the number of working hours.

"There is no reasonable ground for interfering with the liberty of a person or the right of free contract by determining the hours of labor . . . Clean and wholesome bread does not depend upon whether the baker works but ten hours per day or only sixty hours per week. . . ."

—*Lochner* v. *New York* (1905)

- What seems to be the position of the Court on Progressive reform?

- How does the Court's action compare with the Supreme Court's decisions during the New Deal?

often failed to support fair standards of business. The laissez-faire philosophy prevailed, and so did political corruption at all levels of government. The public received little help from its elected representatives.

Several United States Supreme Court rulings provide examples of the mixed response of the federal government in the struggle for improved working conditions:

• In *Lochner* v. *New York* (1905), the Supreme Court ruled that a New York law limiting bakers' hours was unconstitutional because it interfered with the contract between employer and employee.
• In *Muller* v. *Oregon* (1908), the Court let stand an Oregon law limiting women to a ten-hour work day, ruling that the law was justified because it protected women's health. The effect of laws like this, however, was to keep women out of better paying jobs.

WHO WERE THE PROGRESSIVES?

The Progressives set out to tackle the problems of their era. They did not form one single group. The Progressive movement was made up of many different movements, and the Progressives were many different kinds of Americans. Their commitment and their success varied from person to person and from cause to cause. They did have some things in common, however.

Characteristics

The Progressives were influenced by the Populists but differed from them. While the Populists lived in the country or in small towns, the Progressives were largely city dwellers. Most of the Populists were farmers, who focused on farm problems. The Progressives tended to be educated professionals—doctors, lawyers, social workers, clergy, and teachers—with a wide range of concerns. The Progressive movement demonstrated the rising power and influence of America's middle class.

Beliefs and Goals

Like all reformers, the Progressives were optimists. They believed that abuses of power by government and business could be ended. They believed that new developments in technology and science could be used to improve the basic institutions of American society—business, government, education, and family life. Progressives believed in capitalism and were concerned about the growth of socialism as a more radical reaction to the effects of industrialization. Progressives wanted to bypass party politics, which they saw as corrupt, but they had faith that a strong government could and should correct abuses and protect rights.

Not all Americans were Progressives or agreed with Progressive goals. Many business and political leaders opposed business regulation. They accepted the social Darwinists' view that the vast differences in wealth and power in American society were the result of scientific forces that could not be changed. Many workers and farmers did not benefit from Progressive reform, nor did most African Americans, Asian immigrants, and Native Americans.

Factors Aiding the Movement
Many Progressives worked with national voluntary organizations, which grew rapidly in the 1890s. The movement was centered in cities at a time when more of the population was living in cities. This helped communication among Progressives, as did the expanding telephone and telegraph systems. The availability of inexpensive mass-circulation magazines and newspapers also helped spread Progressive ideas. Finally, the Progressives were aided by an improved economy. The first decade of the twentieth century brought prosperity. Industrial profits, wages, and employment all rose; farmers thrived. The result was an optimistic climate and the financial resources to support reform.

PROGRESS TOWARD SOCIAL AND ECONOMIC REFORM AND CONSUMER PROTECTION
A wide variety of reform movements developed from the 1890s to the 1920s.

The Muckrakers and Reform
Muckrakers helped bring reform issues to the attention of the public. Most were journalists and writers, but others were artists and photographers. Muckrakers investigated and exposed corruption and injustice through articles in mass-circulation magazines. They also wrote novels dramatizing situations that demanded reform.

In 1906, the work of the muckrakers resulted in the passage of the Pure Food and Drug Act and the Meat Inspection Act—the first two acts of consumer protection legislation. The federal government passed these laws after it became clear that the unsanitary conditions exposed by Upton Sinclair's novel *The Jungle* were based on fact.

As time passed, the muckrakers' influence declined, partly because readers tired of their sensationalism. Nevertheless, their tradition has continued to the present day.

Other Areas of Concern
Other people and groups also worked to bring Progressive reforms to American society.

PROBLEMS OF POVERTY Attempts to end the poverty, crowding, and disease in American cities began before 1900. Once the germ theory of disease was accepted, cities put more effort into improving water and sewage systems. A well-known urban reformer was Jacob Riis,

KEY THEMES AND CONCEPTS
Culture and Intellectual Life
Media has played an investigative role at various times in United States history. Newspaper, radio, and television journalists provide a different view in order to balance that of governments, corporations, and other sources of power.

The muckraking tradition continued long after the Progressive Era. The publication by *The New York Times* of the Pentagon Papers and the reporting of the Watergate scandal by Bob Woodward and Carl Bernstein in *The Washington Post* are two later examples of the muckraking tradition.

- What are some current examples of investigative media using television and other new media forms?
- What is the difference between investigative reporting and sensationalism in the media?

Progressive Era Muckrakers

Muckraker	Book/Article	Subject of Exposé
Frank Norris	*The Octopus* (1901)	monopolistic railroad practices in California
Ida Tarbell	*History of the Standard Oil Company* (1904)	ruthless practices of Standard Oil
Lincoln Steffens	*The Shame of the Cities* (1906)	urban political corruption
Jacob Riis	*How the Other Half Lives* (1890)	life in New York's tenements
Upton Sinclair	*The Jungle* (1906)	dangerous conditions in meatpacking industry

READING STRATEGY

Analyzing Cause and Effect

Examine the chart above. What effect did the work of each muckraker have on Progressive reform? Use the text and the chart on page 169 to answer this question.

GEOGRAPHY IN HISTORY

Some urban problems persist over time, while others change. When answering the following questions, consider issues of concern in urban areas, such as waste disposal, water and air pollution, energy usage, and congestion.

• Which urban problems at the beginning of the 20th century continue to be urban problems today?

• What new problems exist today?

who used writings and photographs to show the need for better housing for the poor. Some Protestant church leaders became part of the Social Gospel movement, which worked to help poor city dwellers. One goal of urban reformers was building codes that would require safer, better-lighted, better-ventilated, and more sanitary tenements.

SOCIAL SETTLEMENT MOVEMENT One early group of Progressive urban reformers was the settlement-house workers. Settlement houses, located in working-class slums, offered people—especially immigrants—education, child care, social activities, and help in finding jobs. Well-known settlement houses included Hull House in Chicago, founded by Jane Addams, and the Henry Street Settlement in New York City, founded by Lillian Wald.

THE PEACE MOVEMENT Addams and Wald were among the Americans who led peace groups, such as the Woman's Peace Party, in the period before and during World War I. Support of pacifism—the policy of opposition to war and fighting—weakened with America's entry into World War I in 1917 but was later revived. Pacifist Jeannette Rankin, the first woman elected to Congress (1916), voted against the United States entry into World War I (and World War II as well). For her pacifist efforts, Jane Addams won the Nobel Peace Prize in 1931.

TEMPERANCE AND PROHIBITION The temperance movement, which opposed the use of alcoholic beverages, began in the 1820s. Over the years, its chief goal became prohibition—outlawing the manufacture and sale of alcoholic beverages. Under the leadership of Frances Willard, the Woman's Christian Temperance Union (WCTU), founded in 1874, was a strong advocate of prohibition. Its members included many Populists and Progressives. It joined with the Anti-Saloon League, and the two groups sought moral reform through prohibition. They believed that through prohibition, problems of poverty and disease could be eased, family life improved, and the national economy made more productive. The temperance crusade led to national prohibition with the adoption of the Eighteenth Amendment, which banned the manufacture, sale, and transportation of alcoholic beverages in the United States as of 1920.

Women's Rights

Women were involved in all aspects of social reform, but suffrage for women continued to be the main goal of the women's rights movement in the Progressive Era. Women who had experienced success in other reform activities wanted to be able to vote. Furthermore, many suffragists thought that the women's vote would serve to correct various social problems.

WOMEN'S SUFFRAGE MOVEMENT The women's suffrage movement began as part of a larger drive for women's rights in 1848 at Seneca Falls, New York. The intellectual leader was Elizabeth Cady Stanton, author of the Declaration of Sentiments. She was joined in the 1850s by Susan B. Anthony, who provided the driving leadership of the movement. In the 1860s, the women's suffrage movement split over the best way to achieve its goals. The more radical organization was led by Stanton and Anthony; the more moderate organization was headed by Lucy Stone and her husband Henry Blackwell. In 1890, the groups merged to form the National American Woman Suffrage Association (NAWSA).

Stanton died in 1902, and Anthony died in 1906, without achieving the objective of their life work. However, the Progressive spirit gave the movement a new surge. In the early 1900s, leadership of NAWSA and the campaign passed to Carrie Chapman Catt, who devised the strategy that was to win women the vote. She abandoned the state-by-state efforts for women's suffrage, which had given women the vote in only nine states by 1912. Now, the movement would concentrate on achieving women's suffrage through a constitutional amendment. NAWSA swelled to two million members.

Alice Paul led the more militant Congressional Union until she was expelled from NAWSA. She then formed the National Woman's Party. Paul alienated many women by her use of militant tactics and her campaigning against Woodrow Wilson for reelection in 1916. In the end, it was the highly visible activity of women during World War I that brought them the final public support needed. In 1920, the Nineteenth Amendment was ratified, giving women the right to vote.

EDUCATION FOR WOMEN Another sign of women's progress was the growth of educational opportunities. Among women's colleges founded in the late 1800s were Vassar (1861), Wellesley (1870), and Smith (1871). State universities set up under the Morrill Act of 1862 were coeducational. By the early 1900s, more than 100,000 women were attending college.

THE FIGHT FOR BIRTH CONTROL The women's movement also included a campaign for family planning through birth control. This

READING STRATEGY

Reading for Evidence
Reread the section entitled "Women's Suffrage Movement." Based on the information in that section, answer the following questions.

- How many years passed between the beginning of the women's rights movement and the passage of the Nineteenth Amendment?

- How did suffragists change their tactics over time?

- What finally resulted in women winning the right to vote?

KEY THEMES AND CONCEPTS

Civic Values
"The right of citizens of the United States to vote shall not be denied or abridged by the United States or by any state on account of sex."
—Section 1, Nineteenth Amendment

- Whose rights does this amendment protect?

- What are the other important steps in U.S. history in the extension of the right to vote?

Women's Suffrage Before 1920

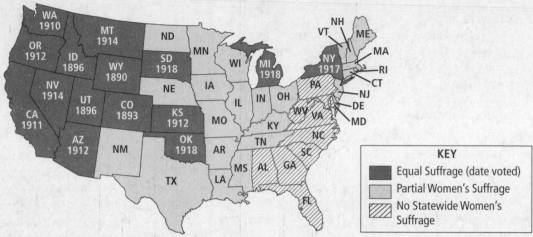

By the time the Nineteenth Amendment became law, many western states had already given women the right to vote.

campaign was led by Margaret Sanger, who began her work as a nurse caring for poor immigrant women in New York City. The American Birth Control League founded by Sanger later became the Planned Parenthood Federation. Sanger's movement was very controversial. She was arrested several times for sending information about contraception through the mail.

The Rights of African Americans

The decades after the Civil War were a difficult time for African Americans. Laws prevented them from exercising their right to vote. In *Plessy* v. *Ferguson* (1896), the Supreme Court upheld the Jim Crow laws, which required segregated—"separate but equal"—public facilities for African Americans and whites.

Lynchings by white mobs took the lives of hundreds of African Americans. Key African American leaders who worked to secure their people's rights are described below.

- Booker T. Washington, a former slave and founder of Tuskegee Institute, urged African Americans to get vocational training in order to establish themselves economically. This strategy, he believed, would increase their own self-esteem and earn them respect from white society. Washington's policy, called accommodation, was expressed in an 1895 speech known as the Atlanta Compromise.

- W.E.B. Du Bois, a Harvard-educated professor, shared Washington's view of the importance of education but rejected accommodation. He felt that African Americans should protest unfair treatment and receive a broad, liberal education, rather than a vocational one. In 1905, Du Bois founded the Niagara Movement to work for equal rights. More successful was the National Association for the Advancement of Colored People (NAACP), started in 1909 by a group of reformers that included Du Bois and Jane Addams. The NAACP successfully used lawsuits as a weapon on behalf of civil rights.

- In 1914, Marcus Garvey founded the Universal Negro Improvement Association, an African American nationalist and separatist group. The group wanted a separate black economy and urged African Americans to emigrate to Africa. Many of Garvey's ideas influenced the Black Power movement of the 1960s.
- Ida B. Wells-Barnett was a journalist who launched a national crusade against lynching in the 1890s. She was also a suffragist and one of the founders of the NAACP.

Rights of Jewish Americans

In 1913, a group of American Jews established the Anti-Defamation League, an agency of the Jewish service organization B'nai B'rith ("Sons of the Covenant") which had been founded in 1843. The Anti-Defamation League worked mainly to combat defamation, or libel and slander, directed against Jews. Later, its program was broadened to aim at securing the civil liberties of all Americans.

PROGRESSIVISM AND GOVERNMENT ACTION

During the Progressive Era, political reform took place at all levels of government—city, state, and national.

Reform of City Government

Given the Progressives' urban, middle-class roots, it is not surprising that they first concentrated their efforts on the governments of the cities in which they lived and in which they were influential citizens. In the 1890s, Americans interested in good government worked to elect reformist mayors. Success in doing so, however, did not always insure permanent improvement. Progressives had to change not only the leader, but also the way city government worked.

Two new types of city government are associated with the Progressive movement. They were popular in small and medium-sized cities. In the city commissioner plan, the city is run by a group of commissioners, rather than by a mayor and city council. In the city manager plan, the city council hires a professional city manager to run the various municipal departments.

KEY THEMES AND CONCEPTS

Reform Movements
One significant urban reform was the regulation of utilities, such as water, gas, and electricity. In many cities, utilities were controlled by monopolies. Beginning in the 1890s, cities began to extend control over utilities, and by 1915, two out of every three cities had some form of city-controlled utilities. This provided residents with more affordable services.

READING STRATEGY

Organizing Information
To help you understand the various reforms made at the city, state, and federal level, create a chart that outlines the major reforms made at each level.

Cities Respond to Urban Problems

Some Progressives concentrated not only on making city governments more efficient and less corrupt, but on improving city services. They worked to regulate services such as transportation systems, water, sanitation, and other utilities. They also tried to improve the appearance of cities by constructing large, elaborate libraries, museums, and other public buildings.

Reform of State Government

Progressives also acted to limit the power of boss-controlled political machines and powerful business interests at the state level. Progressives recognized that states exercised control over many of their cities. Extension of reform to the state, even the national level, was necessary to protect any gains made at the municipal level.

Progressive reforms often proved difficult to enforce, meeting opposition from business interests and the courts. Thus, changes in the way state governments worked were also part of the Progressive program. These changes, aimed at increasing citizen participation in government, included the following:

- The **secret ballot** prevents party bosses (and anyone else) from knowing how people vote.
- The **initiative** is a system that allows voters to petition the legislature to consider a proposed law.
- In a **referendum,** voters decide whether a given bill or constitutional amendment should be passed.
- **Recall** is the method used to force elected officials from office.
- A **direct primary** allows voters, rather than party leaders, to select candidates to run for office.

In 1913, Progressive reform resulted in ratification of the Seventeenth Amendment, which provided for the direct election—election by the people—of United States senators. Up to this time senators had been elected by state legislatures, which were often controlled by corporations or political bosses.

Remember that the secret ballot, initiative, referendum, and direct election of senators were all parts of the Populist party program. Adoption of these reforms offers an example of how third parties can influence major parties.

State Social, Economic, and Environmental Reforms

Wisconsin, under Governor Robert M. La Follette, was the model for Progressive reform. The state passed laws to regulate railroads, lobbying, and banking. It also started civil service reforms, shifted more of the tax burden to the wealthy and to corporations, required employers to compensate workers injured on the job, and provided for factory inspections.

Several other states passed laws like those of Wisconsin. Leading Progressive governors included Hiram Johnson of California, who reformed the railroad industry, and Theodore Roosevelt of New York. As governor of New York (1899–1900), Roosevelt, a friend of Jacob Riis and other Progressives, was concerned about social and economic reform. He supported the creation of the New York State Tenement Commission to investigate New York City tenements. He also worked to eliminate sweatshop factory conditions which forced women and children to work long hours for very low pay in dangerous conditions.

THEODORE ROOSEVELT AND THE SQUARE DEAL

The first three Presidents of this century—Theodore Roosevelt, William Howard Taft, and Woodrow Wilson—are known as the Progressive Presidents. Roosevelt, elected Vice President in 1900, became President when President William McKinley was assassinated in 1901. He was elected in his own right in 1904.

Roosevelt saw his job as one of stewardship—leading the nation in the public interest, like a manager or supervisor. He believed that the President had any powers not specifically denied to the executive in the Constitution. Roosevelt's administration is often known as the Square Deal because of the many reforms made during his presidency.

Consumer Protection

Although basically conservative, Roosevelt did not hesitate to use the power of the presidency to deal directly with social and economic problems. On the national level, he recognized the need for consumer protection, influencing passage in 1906 of the Pure Food and Drug Act and the Meat Inspection Act.

PREPARING FOR THE EXAM

- What did Theodore Roosevelt mean by the Square Deal?

- What was meant by the stewardship theory of government?

- What did Wilson mean by the New Freedom?

- How did Theodore Roosevelt use the Presidency?

- What was the effect on the powers of that office?

KEY THEMES AND CONCEPTS

Government
The three Progressive Presidents were Theodore Roosevelt, Taft, and Wilson. Based on the information in the text, what would you consider the most significant reform made during each President's administration? Why?

The Presidents of the Progressive Era

| 1900 | 1903 | 1906 | 1909 | 1912 | 1915 | 1918 |

1901 McKinley shot; Theodore Roosevelt succeeded as President

1906 Square Deal

1908 William Howard Taft elected President

1913 16th, 17th Amendments ratified

1915 New Freedom

1904 Roosevelt elected

1906 Meat Inspection Act passed

1912 Progressive Party formed; Wilson elected President

1916 Child Labor passed; Wilson reelected President

Regulating Business

Roosevelt's reforms in business focused on strengthening regulations and breaking up trusts.

STRENGTHENING RAILROAD REGULATION In 1906, Congress passed the Hepburn Act, strengthening the Interstate Commerce Commission (ICC) and allowing it to regulate railroad shipping rates. Also, the ICC's powers were expanded to include regulation of pipelines, ferries, bridges, and terminals. Some complained because the act allowed railroads to appeal to the courts. However, Roosevelt was often willing to compromise on details to make a larger point—in this case the right of government to regulate business.

TRUST-BUSTING Roosevelt saw a difference between "good trusts," which were to be subject only to regulation, and "bad trusts," which were to be dissolved. The actions he took against big business earned him a reputation as a trust buster.

In 1903, Roosevelt convinced Congress to form the Bureau of Corporations within the Department of Commerce and Labor. He used the bureau to pressure corporations through investigations and publicity about their activities.

THE NORTHERN SECURITIES CASE By the end of the 1800s, the Northern Securities Company controlled the railroad system in the Pacific Northwest. In 1901, the Justice Department began prosecution of Northern Securities under the Sherman Antitrust Act. The case was eventually appealed to the Supreme Court. In its 1904 ruling

ANALYZING DOCUMENTS

Examine the cartoon, then answer the following questions.

- Who are the men at the desks?
- What place is pictured?
- Who do the large figures represent?
- Which constitutional amendment was the result of concern over the problem that is the subject of this cartoon?

in *Northern Securities Co.* v. *United States,* the Supreme Court upheld the judgment against the company and ordered the company to be dissolved.

THE "BEEF TRUST" Another government antitrust action was directed against a group of meatpackers known as the "beef trust." This prosecution, too, was upheld by the Supreme Court in its 1905 ruling in *Swift & Co.* v. *United States.* This decision reversed one the Court had made in 1895.

Labor Conditions

Roosevelt also achieved important reforms in working conditions.

THE ANTHRACITE COAL STRIKE In 1902, when Pennsylvania coal mine owners refused to negotiate with striking workers, Roosevelt threatened to send the army to take over the mines. The mine owners then agreed to arbitration, and the United Mine Workers, under John Mitchell, won shorter hours and higher wages.

Progressive Era Legislation

Date	Legislation	Purpose
1890	Sherman Antitrust Act	Outlawed monopolies and practices that result in restraint of trade, such as price fixing
1902	National Reclamation Act	Created to plan and develop irrigation projects
1905	United States Forest Service	Created to manage the nation's water and timber resources
1906	Hepburn Act	Required railroads to obtain permission from the Interstate Commerce Commission before raising rates
1906	Pure Food and Drug Act	Outlawed interstate transportation of impure or diluted foods and the deliberate mislabeling of foods and drugs
1906	Meat Inspection Act	Required federal inspection of meat processing to ensure sanitary conditions
1913	Department of Labor	Cabinet department created to protect and promote the welfare and employment of working people. Began with four existing bureaus, including the Children's Bureau
1913	16th Amendment	Gave Congress the power to levy an income tax
1913	17th Amendment	Provided for the direct election of senators
1916	National Park Service	Created to take over the administration of the nation's parks
1919	18th Amendment	Prohibited the manufacture and sale of liquor (repealed in 1933)
1920	Women's Bureau	Created within the Department of Labor to promote the status of working women

EMPLOYERS' LIABILITY One Progressive goal was to make employers assume more liability, or responsibility, for their workers. The Employers Liability Act of 1906 provided accident insurance for workers on interstate railroads and in Washington, D.C.

WORKING HOURS Another Progressive goal was to limit workers' hours on the job. As you read above, in *Lochner* v. *New York* (1905) and *Muller* v. *Oregon* (1908), there were inconsistent results in conflicts between the rights of individuals and the rights of businesses.

Conservation

As a naturalist, Theodore Roosevelt was interested in protecting the nation's environment and its wilderness lands. His policies were influenced by the conservationists Gifford Pinchot and John Muir.

Before Roosevelt, the government's land policy put land in the private hands of homesteaders, railroads, and colleges. Roosevelt shifted this policy and kept some land under federal government protection. This was the philosophy of John Muir, a founder of the Sierra Club, who was also instrumental in the creation of Yosemite National Park.

- Roosevelt used the Forest Reserve Act of 1891 to place national forests under the control of the U.S. Forest Service, headed by conservationist Gifford Pinchot. A total of about 150 million acres of public lands were placed under the protection of the federal government. When Roosevelt left office, he had tripled the amount of land set aside for the public as national forests, national parks, wildlife refuges, and national monuments.
- The National (Newlands) Reclamation Act of 1902 set aside money from the sale of public lands to build dams and irrigation systems in the West.
- In 1908, Roosevelt called a national Conservation Congress, attended by hundreds of naturalists and conservationists as well as by 44 governors.

PROGRESSIVISM UNDER TAFT

After Roosevelt declined to run for a third term, William Howard Taft succeeded him in 1909. Taft began his presidency with the support of Roosevelt and the Progressive wing of the Republican party.

Reforms Under Taft

Under Taft, the Justice Department brought twice as many suits against big business as it had under Roosevelt. One of the most important cases involved the Standard Oil Company. The Supreme Court's ruling in *Standard Oil Co. of New Jersey* v. *United States* (1911) held that the monopoly should be dissolved. But it also applied the so-called "rule of reason" to the Sherman Antitrust Act. There was

KEY THEMES AND CONCEPTS
Environment
- How did Roosevelt's land policy differ from that of earlier Presidents?
- What was the end result of Roosevelt's land policy by the time he left office?

KEY THEMES AND CONCEPTS
Economic Systems
By the late 1800s, Standard Oil controlled most of the nation's oil-refining capacity through a new kind of monopoly called a trust. Standard Oil and some 40 other companies allied with it turned over their assets to a board of nine trustees (controlled by Standard Oil's founder, John D. Rockefeller) in exchange for a share of the profits of the new organization. The Sherman Antitrust Act of 1890 made trusts illegal, but the federal government rarely enforced it. The 1911 decision in *Standard Oil Co. of New Jersey* v. *United States* finally dissolved the Standard Oil trust.

a difference, said the Court, between "reasonable" and "unreasonable" business combinations. Size alone did not mean that a company was "unreasonable."

The Taft era witnessed other reforms, too. The Mann-Elkins Act of 1910 gave the ICC the power to regulate communication by telephone and telegraph. In 1913, the Sixteenth Amendment was ratified, authorizing Congress to impose an income tax.

Problems for Taft

Taft, who not as politically able as Roosevelt, soon ran into problems that split the Republican Party into a Taft faction and a Progressive faction. Like other Progressives, Taft wanted to lower tariffs, but he was unable to stand up to the Republican Congress that raised them with the Payne-Aldrich Act of 1909. Taft angered Progressives by calling the law "the best bill that the Republican party ever passed."

Taft ran into more trouble the following year when he dismissed Forest Service head Gifford Pinchot—a favorite of Progressive conservationists. Taft's secretary of the interior, Richard A. Ballinger, had allowed a group of business people to obtain several million acres of Alaskan public lands. Pinchot protested the action, and Taft fired him. Ballinger was identified with mining, lumbering, and ranching interests who wanted to develop the land for personal profit. They were supported by many senators from western states.

WOODROW WILSON AND THE NEW FREEDOM

In 1912, Theodore Roosevelt challenged Taft for the Republican presidential nomination. When the nomination went to Taft, Roosevelt ran as the candidate of a third party, the Progressive Party. Woodrow Wilson was the Democratic candidate, and Eugene Debs ran on the Socialist ticket.

Roosevelt offered what he called the **New Nationalism,** while Wilson called his program the **New Freedom.** Both were Progressive philosophies. Roosevelt, however, accepted social legislation and business regulation. The more traditional Wilson aimed for a return to competition in the marketplace with enforcement of antitrust laws. Wilson won the election of 1912 by a landslide of electoral votes, although he received only 41 percent of the popular vote. In 1916, he was reelected into office in an even closer race.

Financial Reforms

Wilson accomplished two major financial reforms while in office. In 1913, he pressured Congress to pass the Underwood Tariff Act, which lowered tariffs for the first time since the Civil War. The law also provided for a graduated income tax—one that taxed larger

READING STRATEGY

Formulating Questions
Taft, a Progressive President, wanted to keep tariffs low, but when Congress raised tariffs with the Payne-Aldrich Act of 1909, he praised the bill. What might have prompted him to do this?

KEY THEMES AND CONCEPTS

Government
What was the central theme of Wilson's New Freedom philosophy?

PREPARING FOR THE EXAM

Established in 1913, the Federal Reserve system created the first central banking system since the Second Bank of the United States. Twelve banks, rather than just one, exercised monetary controls.

- Who proposed the first national bank of the United States?

- Why was the Second Bank of the United States terminated?

- What is the primary role of the Federal Reserve system?

incomes at a higher rate (6 percent) than it did lower ones (1 percent). This kind of tax, which takes a bigger share of higher incomes, is known as a progressive tax.

Also in 1913, the **Federal Reserve system** was created. This national banking system is divided into 12 districts, each with a Federal Reserve bank. The federal government could now (1) issue a new, sound currency—Federal Reserve notes; (2) control the amount of money in circulation and interest rates; and (3) shift money from one bank to another as needed.

Business Regulation

Wilson also achieved two important business regulations. The Federal Trade Commission Act of 1914 aimed to prevent unfair competition. It created a commission to investigate such practices as false advertising and mislabeling.

The **Clayton Antitrust Act** of 1914 strengthened the government's power to control business practices that threatened competition. Among other things, the act prohibited companies from price fixing and from buying stocks in competing firms. The Clayton Act tried to end the practice of using antitrust laws against unions, but later Supreme Court decisions undercut this provision.

Other Reforms Under Wilson

- The Adamson Act (1916) set an eight-hour day for workers on railroads in interstate commerce.
- The Federal Farm Loan Act (1916) made low-interest loans available to farmers.
- The Keating-Owen Child Labor Act (1916) tried to outlaw child labor, but the Supreme Court ruled the law unconstitutional in the case of *Hammer* v. *Dagenhart* (1918).
- Ratification of the Nineteenth Amendment in 1920 gave women the right to vote.

END OF THE PROGRESSIVE ERA

The Progressive Era came to an end when the United States entered World War I. During the war, American priorities shifted to the war effort, and in the 1920s, the trend shifted away from reform and toward acceptance of society as it was.

2 The Rise of American Power

SECTION OVERVIEW

This section deals with American foreign policy during the Progressive Era, after reviewing the background of American expansion since 1865. From 1865 until 1920, the United States moved beyond the borders of North America to become an imperialist power on a global scale. Presidential power is the central issue. You will review the reasons for these actions and the national debate caused by them. Again, Theodore Roosevelt and Woodrow Wilson dominate foreign policy in the first two decades of the twentieth century. Their motivations, their policies, and the effects on people at home and abroad are all important understandings.

KEY THEMES AND CONCEPTS

As you review this section, take special note of the following key themes and concepts:

Places and Regions How did America's industrialization increase pressures for overseas expansion?

Constitutional Principles How did reactions to the Russian Revolution and World War I result in the restriction of some people's civil rights in the United States?

Change How did World War I change the role of the United States in the world?

KEY PEOPLE

As you review this section, be sure you understand the significance of these key people:

Frederick Jackson Turner   Theodore Roosevelt
Henry Cabot Lodge   William Howard Taft
Matthew Perry   Woodrow Wilson

★ **THE BIG IDEA**
From 1865 until 1920, the United States emerged from isolation to become an imperial power. The United States gained power and territory through

- victory in war.
- annexation.
- purchase.
- economic influence.

🔑 **KEY TERMS**
Open Door Policy
jingoism
imperialism
Roosevelt Corollary
dollar diplomacy
Central Powers
Allies
U-boats
Zimmermann note
Russian Revolution
Selective Service Act
Fourteen Points
self-determination
Treaty of Versailles
League of Nations
reparations

173

KEY SUPREME COURT CASES

As you review this section, be sure you understand the significance of this key Supreme Court case:

Schenck v. *United States* (1919)

EMERGING GLOBAL INVOLVEMENT

In the late 1800s and early 1900s, American expansion was in many ways a resumption of the expansionist drive that had been halted by the Civil War. A number of factors led the United States into greater global involvement in the late 1800s.

New Technology

Improvements in transportation and communication technology shortened distances around the world. At the same time, other inventions accelerated industrial growth. Railroads connected factories and farms to Atlantic and Pacific ports, from which steamships carried goods to Europe, Latin America, and Asia. Communication was faster and easier thanks to the telegraph, telephone, and transatlantic cable. Communications technology quickly provided information on international markets and on events in other nations that might affect the United States. The world was becoming more interdependent.

Drive for Markets and Raw Materials

Economics linked the domestic and foreign policy goals of the United States. Business leaders wanted raw materials from abroad. Both business leaders and farmers also wanted overseas markets. Overseas markets could provide economic stability, especially when, as in the 1890s, domestic consumption could not absorb the nation's output. At the same time, international competition increased as European nations, Japan, and the United States sought raw materials and

KEY THEMES AND CONCEPTS

Change

Using the chart below and the text, answer the following questions.

- How did U.S. foreign policy between 1890 and 1919 change from previous policy directions?

- In what ways was it a continuation of existing foreign policy directions?

- How did the motives for expansion differ between the period 1803–1867 and 1890–1914?

United States Expansion, 1803–1867

Date	Territory	How Acquired
1803	Louisiana Purchase	purchased from France
1819	Florida	occupation, followed by treaty with Spain
1845	Texas	annexation
1846	Oregon Country	agreement with Great Britain
1848	Mexican Cession	Mexican War/treaty with Mexico
1853	Gadsden Purchase	purchase from Mexico
1867	Alaska	purchase from Russia
1867	Midway	annexation

Value of United States Exports, 1870–1920

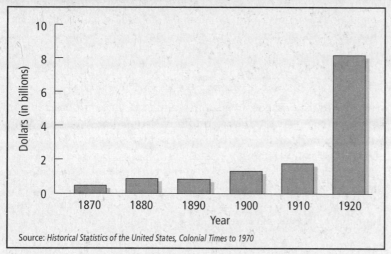

Source: *Historical Statistics of the United States, Colonial Times to 1970*

ANALYZING DOCUMENTS

Bar graphs help you to compare quantities over a period of time. Based on the graph at left, answer the following question.

What was the value of United States foreign trade

- in 1865?
- in 1900?
- in 1915?

markets. Foreign trade increased dramatically. High U.S. tariffs played a role in revolutions in Hawaii and in Cuba.

Growth of Naval Power

The U.S. Navy began to expand in the 1880s, building steel-hulled warships with steam engines and the latest in weapons. Behind this growth was the urging of expansionists like Alfred T. Mahan, who argued that as foreign trade grew, a nation needed a strong navy to protect shipping routes. The navy, in turn, needed bases at which to refuel and restock supplies.

Manifest Destiny and the Closing of the Frontier

As you will recall, the idea of manifest destiny took hold in the United States in the mid-1800s. Manifest destiny is the idea that the United States had a divine mission to expand in order to spread the ideals of freedom and democracy.

This belief was fueled by historian Frederick Jackson Turner's frontier thesis. In a famous 1893 essay, Turner argued that the existence of a frontier throughout our history had been vital in shaping the American character. By 1893, Turner noted, that frontier no longer existed, an argument supported by the 1890 census. Some people interpreted this development to mean that Americans needed new frontiers beyond the current borders.

Social Darwinism

Closely tied to manifest destiny was the idea that the American way of life was so superior that the United States was obliged to carry its benefits to other peoples. Few wondered whether these peoples wanted American "benefits," or recognized that this notion implied that other peoples and their ways of life were inferior. The belief in American

 PREPARING FOR THE EXAM

The history of United States foreign policy can be viewed as a sequence of stages listed below.

1776–1823
Protecting national independence

1824–1897
Fulfilling manifest destiny

1898–1918
Emerging global involvement

1919–1940
Limiting international involvement

1941 to the present
Accepting world leadership

superiority was a form of social Darwinism. According to social Darwinists, the law of nature resulted in the survival of superior people. Similarly, the same law led to the survival of superior nations, which are meant to dominate inferior nations. Few questioned the fact that no scientific evidence supported this theory.

The Missionary Spirit

Another motive for expansion was the missionary spirit. It lay behind attempts to introduce Christianity and "civilization" to others, particularly in China, where the movement was strongest. The missionary impulse did result in certain improvements, such as the building of schools and hospitals. However, it also fostered a paternalistic view—one that saw the United States as a parent supervising weaker, less "developed" peoples. Underlying manifest destiny, social Darwinism, and the missionary movement were nationalism, racism, and a strong sense of cultural superiority.

THE UNITED STATES AS A WORLD POWER: ASIA AND THE PACIFIC

The United States role in Asia expanded because of the establishment of trade with China and Japan and the acquisition of Hawaii, Pacific bases, and the Philippines.

China

American trade with China began in the 1780s through the port of Canton. By the late 1800s, however, Americans were afraid that their economic opportunities in China might be limited. Throughout the nineteenth century, China had been subjected to imperialistic demands by Japan, Germany, Russia, Britain, and France. Each nation gained a sphere of influence—a region in which it had exclusive trade, mining, or other economic rights.

American Imperialism, 1867–1914

1867 Alaska purchased	**1889** Samoa agreement signed	**1900** "Big stick diplomacy"	**1906** U.S. troops restore order in Cuba	**1914** Panama Canal opens

1860   1870   1880   1890   1900   1910   1920

1880s U.S. trade abroad increases

1898 Spanish-American War; Hawaii annexed

1904 Roosevelt Corollary established

1910 "Dollar diplomacy"

Open Door Policy

In 1899, Secretary of State John Hay tried to assure economic opportunity for the United States. He asked the European powers to keep an "open door" to China. He wanted to ensure through his **Open Door Policy** that the United States would have fair access to the Chinese market. The European powers, however, met his request with a cool response.

The Boxer Rebellion

In 1900, a secret patriotic Chinese society called the Boxers attacked missionaries, diplomats, and other foreigners in China in what is known as the Boxer Rebellion. The Boxers were revolting against the Manchu Dynasty and against the intervention of Western powers in China. The Western powers, including the United States, sent troops to restore order. Fearing that rival nations would take even more Chinese land, Hay expanded the Open Door Policy to mean that the current boundaries of China should be preserved.

Japan

Japan had developed into a major economic power after 1854, the year Commodore Matthew Perry ended Japan's isolation by negotiating a treaty opening two Japanese ports to ships from the United States. Unlike China, Japan carried out a far-reaching modernization program making it a major economic power by 1900.

From 1900 to 1941, a key aim of American foreign policy in Asia became providing the balance of power to restrict Japanese expansion. Japan displayed its growing strength by defeating Russia in the Russo-Japanese War of 1904–1905. In an effort to protect American interests in Asia, President Theodore Roosevelt mediated the peace treaty that ended the war. It was understood that Japan could remain in Manchuria and annex Korea. The agreement of the United States to the Japanese takeover of Korea was formalized in the 1905 Taft-Katsura Agreement. In return, Japan would not threaten the Philippines.

Relations between Japan and the United States experienced a setback when the San Francisco schools placed Japanese children in separate classes in the early 1900s. The Japanese government condemned this segregation. President Theodore Roosevelt achieved a compromise with Japanese officials called the Gentlemen's Agreement of 1907. This agreement ended school segregation in San Francisco but also restricted Japanese immigration to the United States.

In 1908, the two nations also entered into the Root-Takahira Agreement, in which both countries agreed to uphold the Open Door Policy and support China's independence and integrity. It also meant each nation would not attempt to seize the other's possessions.

ANALYZING DOCUMENTS

"The policy of the United States is to seek a solution which may bring about permanent safety and peace to China, preserve Chinese territorial and administrative entity, protect all rights guaranteed to friendly powers by treaty and international law, and safeguard for the world the principle of equal and impartial trade with all parts of the Chinese Empire."
—Open Door Policy, 1899

- Is this policy different from the principles of the Monroe Doctrine? If so, how?

- Why was it in American self-interest to call for the preservation of Chinese territorial and administrative integrity?

ANALYZING DOCUMENTS

The power that rules the Pacific . . . is the power that rules the world. And, with the Philippines, that power is and will forever be the American Republic."
—Congressional Record, 1900

Which policy is supported by this quotation?

1. Imperialism

2. Self-determination

3. Isolationism

4. Humanitarianism

**GEOGRAPHY
IN HISTORY**

Locate China, Japan, Korea, and the Philippines on a world map.

- How did geography affect United States policies in this part of Asia?

- Why were the strategic locations of Hawaii, the Philippines, Panama, and Samoa important to the United States?

**φ KEY THEMES AND
ι̇ CONCEPTS**

Economic Systems
The acquisition of Hawaii was motivated in part by Americans living there wanting to avoid U.S. protective tariffs.

Backers of free trade oppose protective tariffs. When tariffs rise, nations that are hurt economically raise their own tariffs in retaliation. Free trade, its supporters say, increases world trade in an era of economic interdependence. It also forces a nation's less competitive industries to improve.

Hawaii

Until the 1890s, Hawaii was an independent country ruled by a monarch. The United States had important business interests there, namely, sugar plantations. In 1890, the United States placed a protective tariff on imported sugar, including that from Hawaii, in order to protect sugar producers in the United States. This meant that Americans would be more likely to buy domestic sugar rather than Hawaiian sugar, and American planters in Hawaii would lose money.

In addition to being hurt economically by this protective tariff, American planters in Hawaii also feared the growth of Hawaiian nationalism and resentment toward the power of American interests.

In 1893, American planters, aided by the chief U.S. diplomat to Hawaii and by marines, carried out a successful revolution against the Hawaiian ruler. Against the wishes of the Hawaiian people, the American sugar growers asked that the United States annex Hawaii, but President Grover Cleveland opposed expansion by force. Hawaii remained in the hands of the American sugar interests as the independent Republic of Hawaii. Now American planters in Hawaii could get as much for their sugar as growers on the mainland.

Not until 1898 during the Spanish-American War did Hawaii become a United States possession. Then it became important as a military and commercial link to the Philippines and the rest of East Asia. Annexation was accomplished by a joint resolution of Congress rather than a treaty.

Samoa

In 1878, the United States gained the rights to a naval station at Pago Pago in the Samoan Islands. The port was also used by Germany and Great Britain. Samoa was situated in the Pacific on the trade route to Australia. Conflicts arose among the three nations. In 1899, Germany and the United States divided Samoa.

IMPERIALISM:
THE SPANISH-AMERICAN WAR

In 1898, the United States began to acquire new territories, making it an imperial power. Most of these territorial gains resulted from the Spanish-American War.

Underlying Causes of the Spanish-American War

There were several underlying causes of the war between Spain and the United States.

ECONOMIC In Spanish-controlled Cuba, economic chaos led to revolution and a demand for U.S. intervention. In the 1890s, Spain had imposed increased taxes on Cuba. In addition, the United States placed a protective tariff on Cuban sugar, which had previously entered the nation duty-free. The effect of these taxes was economic collapse. Resentment toward Spain fueled Cuban anger, and soon revolution erupted. Cubans provoked U.S. involvement by destroying American sugar plantations and mills in Cuba.

HUMANITARIAN Many Americans sympathized with the Cuban revolution and were appalled by the tactics of the Spanish military commander, Valeriano Weyler. He imprisoned hundreds of thousands of Cuban civilians in camps, where about 30 percent of them died from disease and starvation.

EXPANSIONIST American expansionists—including Theodore Roosevelt, Senator Henry Cabot Lodge, and Secretary of State John Hay—recognized that war offered an opportunity to seize territory from Spain, a weak nation.

Immediate Causes of the Spanish-American War

In addition to the underlying causes of the Spanish-American War, several immediate events aroused Americans' emotions. These fed a growing **jingoism**—a super patriotism and demand for aggressive actions—that created a warlike mood.

YELLOW JOURNALISM In the late 1890s, two of the most famous American publishers, William Randolph Hearst of the *New York Morning Journal* and Joseph Pulitzer of the *New York World,* were battling for readers in a circulation war. Both newspapers printed the most sensational stories and pictures they could find about the horrors of the Cuban revolution. The stories often exaggerated and distorted events for emotional effect. This kind of sensationalism is called "yellow journalism."

THE DE LÔME LETTER A personal letter written by the Spanish minister to the United States, Enrique Dupuy de Lôme, was printed in the *New York Journal* in February 1898. De Lôme's unfavorable comments—he called McKinley "weak and catering to the rabble"—made it hard for the President and other political leaders to withstand demands for war.

SINKING OF THE MAINE Less than a week after publication of the de Lôme letter, the United States battleship *Maine* exploded and sank in the harbor of Havana, Cuba, killing 266 Americans. The public blamed Spain, although a later investigation was never able to determine the cause of the explosion nor assign responsibility.

Fighting the Spanish-American War

In April 1898, despite Spain's agreement to an armistice with Cuba, McKinley asked Congress to declare war. Congress complied. It also approved the Teller Amendment, which promised that the United States would not annex Cuba.

The Spanish-American War

Causes

- United States wants to expand in Latin America and Pacific.
- In Cuba and Philippines, people rebel against Spanish rule.
- Demands for involvement from American expansionists and newspapers.
- Explosion sinks American battleship U.S.S. *Maine* in Cuban harbor. Cause of the explosion is unknown, but angry Americans blame Spain.

The Spanish-American War

Effects

- United States defeats Spain in less than four months.
- Spain recognizes Cuba's independence. United States begins to control Cuban politics and economy.
- Puerto Rico, Philippines, and Guam become United States territories.
- United States is recognized as a world power.

With a quick victory in the Spanish-American War, the United States established itself as a new world power.

ANALYZING DOCUMENTS

Examine the graphic organizer above, then answer the following questions.

- Which are the *basic* causes of the war?
- Which are the *immediate* causes of the war?
- Which effects were long term?

ANALYZING DOCUMENTS

"It has been a splendid little war; begun with the highest motives, carried out with magnificent intelligence and spirit."

—Secretary of State John Hay, 1898

- How is this description of a war unusual?
- Why would anti-imperialists and pacifists object to this description?

The war lasted four months, with fighting in both the Caribbean Sea and the Pacific Ocean. Of the 2,446 Americans who lost their lives, fewer than 400 were killed in combat; the rest died from infection and disease.

The Results of the Spanish-American War

In December 1898, the Treaty of Paris, negotiated with Spain granted Cuba its independence, gave the United States the Philippines, in return for $20 million, and ceded Puerto Rico and Guam to the United States.

The Treaty of Paris of 1898 led to the acquisition of many former Spanish territories that formed the basis of an American empire. This set off a national debate among imperialists and anti-imperialists. It also led to increased American involvement in Latin America and Asia as the nation sought to protect its new lands.

IMPERIALISM: THE GREAT DEBATE

Ratification of the Treaty of Paris set off a great debate in the United States. As with all treaties, it had to be approved by a two-thirds vote of the Senate. The fundamental question was whether the United States should pursue **imperialism**—the policy of expanding a nation's power by foreign acquisitions.

Debating Imperialism

Americans in both political parties, in all regions, and from all social classes could be found on either side of the debate. Progressives were also divided. Imperialists included Theodore Roosevelt, Senator Henry

The American Empire During the Progressive Era, 1898–1917

Date	Territory	How Acquired
1898	Hawaii	annexation after 1893 revolution
1898	Puerto Rico	gained from Spain after war
1898	Guam	gained from Spain after war
1898	Philippines	gained from Spain after war
1899	Samoa	treaty with Great Britain
1899	Wake Island	annexation
1903	Panama Canal Zone	treaty with Panama
1917	Virgin Islands	purchased from Denmark

Cabot Lodge, and Alfred T. Mahan. Among the anti-imperialists were Andrew Carnegie, Mark Twain, Jane Addams, William Jennings Bryan, Booker T. Washington, and former Presidents Grover Cleveland and Benjamin Harrison. The chart summarizes the arguments of the two groups.

Acquiring the Philippines
In February 1899, the Senate approved the Treaty of Paris by a small margin. That January, Emilio Aguinaldo, who had been fighting the Spanish for Philippine independence, declared the Philippines a republic. The bitter war ended in 1902. More 4,000 Americans and some 16,000 Filipinos were killed in the Philippine insurrection. An additional 200,000 Filipinos died from starvation and disease. Atrocities were committed by both sides. At the end of the insurrection, the Philippines were under American control.

TURNING POINT

It what ways was the Spanish-American War a turning point in United States history?

Imperialists' Point of View	Anti-Imperialists' Point of View
The United States needs colonies to compete economically.	Supporting an empire would be a financial burden.
To be a true world power, the United States needs colonies and naval bases.	The United States should concentrate its energies on solving problems at home.
It is the American destiny to expand, and its duty to care for poor, weak peoples.	Nonwhite people cannot be assimilated into American society.
To abandon territories makes the United States appear cowardly before the world.	An empire would involve the United States in more wars.
It is only honorable to keep land that Americans lost their lives to obtain.	It is a violation of democratic principles to annex land and not offer its people the same rights as those of U.S. citizens.

The Constitution and the Territories

Imperialism was supported by the Supreme Court from 1901 to 1904, with decisions in the Insular Cases. The Court ruled that the Constitution only applied in those territories that Congress decided would be incorporated into the United States. The Court also held that people in annexed territories did not automatically have the rights of United States citizens. Congress would make that decision, based on the status given to a territorial possession.

Governing the Territories

The United States set up different means of governing its new territories.

- Hawaii was made a territory in 1900, its first step on the way to statehood.
- In 1916, the Jones Act promised the Philippines independence, but the law did not name a date. In 1934, the Philippines was promised independence in 10 years. This promise was delayed because of World War II but was honored in 1946.
- The Foraker Act of 1900 provided for a Puerto Rican legislature elected by the people with a governor and council appointed by the American President. Puerto Ricans received United States citizenship in 1917. In 1952, the island became a commonwealth. This status gives Puerto Rico many rights of a state excluding sending representatives to Congress.

GEOGRAPHY IN HISTORY

Based on the map below and the text, answer the following questions.

- Which United States acquisition was closest to Japan?
- Under what circumstances did the United States acquire the Philippines?
- What was particularly controversial about these circumstances?

United States Expansion, 1857–1903

- U.S. troops remained in Cuba until 1902. American troops were sent to Cuba twice between 1902 and 1922. Cuban independence was limited by the Platt Amendment (1901), which remained part of the Cuban constitution until 1934. The amendment (1) required that the United States approve treaties between Cuba and other nations, (2) gave the United States the right to lease naval bases in Cuba, and (3) allowed the United States to intervene in Cuba to preserve order or peace.

AMERICA AS A WORLD POWER: LATIN AMERICA

Having acquired an empire, the United States found itself increasingly involved around the globe as it protected its new territories and interests. Of particular interest to the United States was Latin America.

Expanding the Monroe Doctrine

The Monroe Doctrine of 1823 warned foreign powers to stay out of the Western Hemisphere. For several decades, the relatively weak United States seldom referred to the doctrine. It was used, however, to support the American annexation of Texas as well as the Mexican War. It was used again, at the end of the Civil War, against France, which had set up a puppet government in Mexico and refused to give in to American demands to withdraw. France withdrew only after the United States massed troops along the Mexican border.

THE VENEZUELAN BORDER DISPUTE In 1895, the United States had an opportunity to restate and expand the Monroe Doctrine. Great Britain and Venezuela were involved in a quarrel over the boundary between Venezuela and British Guiana (now Guyana). The United States offered to arbitrate, or help settle the dispute. When Britain refused arbitration, the United States claimed that the British were violating the Monroe Doctrine and forced them to negotiate by threatening war. Secretary of State Richard Olney, in the Olney Interpretation of the Monroe Doctrine, claimed, "Today, the United States is practically sovereign of this continent."

THE ROOSEVELT COROLLARY President Theodore Roosevelt, further reinforced, even reinterpreted, the Monroe Doctrine. Economic problems in Venezuela and the Dominican Republic led to threats of European intervention. In both cases, the United States stepped in to restore order. Roosevelt explained American policy in a 1904 message to Congress. If a nation in the Western Hemisphere is guilty of consistently behaving wrongly, he said, the Monroe Doctrine requires that the United States step in and act "as an international police power." This policy is known as the **Roosevelt Corollary** to the Monroe Doctrine.

READING STRATEGY

Organizing Information

- For each of the following Presidents, summarize U.S. foreign policy in Latin America in the first half of the 20th century.

Theodore Roosevelt:

William Howard Taft:

Woodrow Wilson:

Franklin D. Roosevelt:

- Which presidents in the second half of the 20th century should be added to this list because they made important Latin American foreign policy decisions?

ANALYZING DOCUMENTS

Theodore Roosevelt was famous for the statement, "Speak softly and carry a big stick." Examine the cartoon, then answer the questions that follow.

- What does the big stick in the cartoon represent?

- What evidence is there that in recent decades the Roosevelt Corollary was used in Latin America?

- The Roosevelt Corollary to the Monroe Doctrine stated that "Chronic wrongdoing . . . may force the United States, however, reluctantly . . . to the exercise of an international police power. "How is his attitude expressed in the cartoon?

THE "BIG STICK" POLICY With the Monroe Doctrine as its justification, the United States intervened often in Latin American affairs, usually to protect American economic interests. President Theodore Roosevelt was famous for the motto "Speak softly and carry a big stick." This meant that the United States would use peaceful methods to protect its interests whenever possible, but that it would use military force if necessary.

The United States occupied Nicaragua with troops from 1912 until 1933. It also maintained a military occupation of Haiti (1915–1934) and the Dominican Republic (1916–1924).

The Dominican Republic had trouble paying its debts to European nations. When the Europeans threatened force, the United States took over Dominican finances, supervising them between 1905 and 1941. Haiti was supervised between 1916 and 1941 as was Nicaragua from 1911 until 1924.

DOLLAR DIPLOMACY President Taft's foreign policy approach was known as **dollar diplomacy.** This meant that the United States could help maintain orderly societies in other countries by increasing American investment in foreign economies. These investments tended to increase American intervention in foreign affairs.

INTERVENTION IN MEXICO During the Mexican Revolution, President Wilson intervened in Mexico's affairs in order to protect huge U.S. investments there. He also believed in moral diplomacy—conducting foreign affairs in terms of judgments about right and wrong. In 1913, after Victoriano Huerta overthrew the Mexican president and had him murdered, Wilson refused to recognize Huerta's government. The next year, the U.S. Navy seized the port of Vera Cruz to prevent a German shis from landing its cargo of arms for Huerta. Wilson also sent a force into northern Mexico in 1916 in an attempt to capture Pancho Villa, a Mexican rebel whose border raid into New Mexico in 1916 led to American deaths.

THE GOOD NEIGHBOR POLICY Only under Presidents Herbert Hoover (1929–1933) and Franklin D. Roosevelt (1933–1945) did the United States try to improve its relations with Latin America. Roosevelt backed what came to be called the "good neighbor policy." This meant less emphasis on intervention and more on cooperation. However, American economic dominance of the region continued.

THE PANAMA CANAL Since the mid-1850s, the advantages of a canal linking the Atlantic and Pacific Oceans were well recognized. With a canal, navy and merchant ships could move more quickly between the two oceans. Interest in a canal increased when the United States aquired colonies in the Pacific. In 1901 the United States, through negotiations, gained the sole right to build and control such a canal as long as it would be open to all nations.

Under Theodore Roosevelt, the United States settled on a route across Panama, which was part of Colombia. When Colombia seemed reluctant to agree to financial terms, Roosevelt encouraged Panamanians to revolt and declare their independence. The United States quickly negotiated a treaty with the new nation of Panama, which gave the United States a 99-year renewable lease on a 10-mile-wide strip of land across Panama. Panama remained a United States protectorate from 1903 to 1939.

Building the canal was a mammoth task, begun in 1904. Yellow fever and malaria caused delays as did the difficulty of moving more than 250 million cubic yards of soil. However, workers made the remarkable achievement of completing the canal ahead of schedule and under budget. The canal opened to traffic in 1914.

Responding to Panamanian demonstrations, the United States agreed in a 1977 treaty to return the canal to Panamanian control. Panama took over the canal on December 31, 1999.

THE UNITED STATES AND WORLD WAR I

World War I began in Europe in 1914 and lasted until 1918. The United States did not enter the war until 1917. The financial and human costs of this devastating conflict were enormous.

Causes of World War I

There were several factors that led to the outbreak of war in Europe.

NATIONALISM Strong nationalistic competition had developed among France, Britain, Russia, Austria-Hungary, and Germany, espe-

 PREPARING FOR THE EXAM

Before understanding how the United States became involved in World War I, it is important to review the basic causes of that war which began in 1914.

For each cause listed, give an example.

Nationalism:

Industrialism:

Imperialism:

Alliances:

Militarism:

Analyzing Cause and Effect

Use the text and these three quotes to summarize the steps by which the United States entered World War I. Note the dates on each quote.

" . . . impartial in thought as well as in action."
—Woodrow Wilson, 1914

"He kept us out of war."
—Wilson campaign slogan, 1916

"The world must be made safe for democracy."
—Wilson request for declaration of war, April 2, 1917

- Did United States policy contradict Wilson's earlier statements and therefore involve the U.S. in the war, OR
- Did circumstances beyond the United States' control lead the nation to break its policy of neutrality?

cially after the unification of Germany in 1871. There was also national unrest within nations. For instance, the Czechs and Slovaks wanted to free themselves from Austro-Hungarian control.

IMPERIALISM Several nations were involved in keen competition for markets and colonies throughout the world.

THE ALLIANCE SYSTEM As national and imperial goals conflicted, two groups of nations organized against each other in an effort to maintain a balance of power. The Triple Alliance consisted of Germany, Austria-Hungary, and Italy. The Triple Entente was made up of France, Russia, and Great Britain. If fighting were to break out, members of either alliance were pledged to help each other.

MILITARISM The early 1900s witnessed a continual buildup of armies and navies. Germany, for instance, tripled naval construction in order to challenge Britain's control of the seas.

Causes of United States Entry into World War I

War broke out in Europe in July 1914, after the heir to the Austro-Hungarian throne was assassinated. Because of the alliance system, most major European nations soon joined the conflict. The United States was officially neutral. In 1917, however, the United States was drawn into the war. There were several reasons for this.

CULTURAL LINKS Few Americans were truly neutral. Some sympathized with the **Central Powers,** dominated by Germany and Austria-Hungary. These included German-Americans because of ties to Germany and Irish-Americans because of anti-British feeling. The majority of Americans, however, favored the **Allies,** or the Triple Entente nations. Americans had long-standing cultural ties with Britain. Many also felt loyalty to their first ally, France.

ECONOMIC TIES United States links to the Allies were economic as well as cultural. A British blockade of the North Sea effectively

The United States and World War I

			1913 Civil war erupts in Mexico		1915 Germans sink *Lusitania*		1917 U.S. enters war; Espionage Act passed		1919 Senate rejects Treaty of Versailles
1910	1911	1912	1913	1914	1915	1916	1917	1918	1919	1920
				1914 War begins in Europe		1916 Germany suspends submarine attacks		1918 Fourteen Points announced; Germany surrenders	

Europe During the War

Europe During the War

0 200 400 Miles
0 200 400 Kilometers

ATLANTIC OCEAN

NORWAY   SWEDEN   FINLAND

North Sea   DENMARK

Baltic Sea

RUSSIA

GREAT BRITAIN

NETH.   GERMANY

BELG.

LUX.

AUSTRIA-HUNGARY

FRANCE   SWITZ.

ROMANIA   Black Sea

ITALY   SERBIA

MONTENEGRO   BULGARIA

Corsica (Fr.)   ALBANIA   OTTOMAN EMPIRE (TURKEY)

SPAIN   Sardinia (It.)   GREECE

PORTUGAL   Sicily (It.)

Mediterranean   Sea   Cyprus (Br.)

Crete (Gr.)

SP. MOROCCO

MOROCCO (Fr.)   ALGERIA (Fr.)   TUNISIA (Fr.)   LIBYA (It.)   EGYPT (Br.)

Legend:
- Allied Powers
- Central Powers
- Neutral nations

ANALYZING DOCUMENTS

Examine the map at left, then answer the following questions.

- Which nations were the Allied Powers?
- Which were the Central Powers?
- Which nations remained neutral?

ended American exports to Germany, which dropped in value from about $345 million in 1914 to $29 million in 1916. Meanwhile, the value of trade with the Allies increased fourfold. American business and agriculture benefited from this trade, much of it financed by U.S. government loans to the Allies, totaling more than $2 billion by 1917.

Most Americans did not believe that trade with or loans to the Allies violated the nation's neutrality. In fact, President Wilson and his closest advisers were in favor of the Allies. However, even in the 1916 election for President, Wilson continued to proclaim American neutrality, campaigning on the slogan "He kept us out of war."

PROPAGANDA Aided by their control of the transatlantic cable, the Allies conducted an effective propaganda campaign in the United States. They pictured the war as one of civilized, democratic nations against the barbaric monarchy of Germany.

GERMAN SUBMARINE WARFARE The Germans made frequent use of submarines in World War I. Because a submarine was very vulnerable when surfaced, Germany announced a policy of unrestricted submarine warfare, ignoring international law that required a warship to stop and identify itself before its crew boarded the enemy vessel and to remove the ship's crew before sinking it. Germany's attempt to destroy the British blockade by attacking Allied ships was the single most important reason for American entrance into the war. Wilson still insisted that America as a neutral nation had the right to trade with the nations at war and to send its civilians on ships into war zones.

READING STRATEGY

Organizing Information

Suppose you were a member of Congress in 1917. You must decide whether the United States should go to war against Germany and the other Central Powers.

- Based on the information from this section, which events would influence your decision?

ANALYZING
DOCUMENTS

American public opinion was extremely critical of Germany and its use of U-boats. Germany, however, did warn travelers—including passengers of the *Lusitania*—to stay out of the war zone.

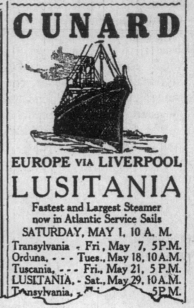

NOTICE!

TRAVELLERS intending to embark on the Atlantic voyage are reminded that a state of war exists between Germany and her allies and GreatBritian and her allies; that the zone of war includes the waters adjacent to the British Isles; that, in accordance with formal notice given by the Imperial German Government, vessels flying the flag of Great Britian, or of any of her allies, are liable to destruction in those waters and that travellers sailing in the war zone on ships cf Great Britian or her allies do so at their own risk.

IMPERIAL GERMAN EMBASSY,
WASHINGTON, D. C., APRIL 22, 1915.

CUNARD

EUROPE VIA LIVERPOOL

LUSITANIA
Fastest and Largest Steamer now in Atlantic Service Sails
SATURDAY, MAY 1, 10 A. M.
Transylvania - Fri , May 7, 5P.M.
Orduna, - - - Tues., May 18, 10A.M.
Tuscania, - - - Fri., May 21, 5 P.M.
LUSITANIA, - Sat., May 29, 10 A.M.
Transylvania, - - - - - 5P.M.

ANALYZING
DOCUMENTS

"We shall endeavor to keep the United States neutral. In the event of this not succeeding, we make Mexico a proposal of alliance. . . : Make war together, make peace together, . . . and . . . Mexico is to reconquer the lost territory in Texas, New Mexico, and Arizona."
—German foreign secretary Arthur Zimmermann

- What was Germany's first plan concerning the United States?

- If that plan failed, what did Germany propose to do in alliance with Mexico?

- What reaction would this note have had in the United States?

When a German submarine sank the British passenger liner *Lusitania* in 1915, almost 1,200 persons lost their lives, including 128 Americans. Even though the ship was carrying ammunition and Germany had posted warnings, the United States was outraged by the attack on civilians. In 1916, the Germans torpedoed a French steamer, the *Sussex,* with injury to Americans. Wilson threatened to break diplomatic relations with Germany, which then agreed to the Sussex Pledge. This stated that Germany would no longer sink passenger or merchant ships without warning and that the Allies would no longer violate international law with their blockade. Wilson accepted the first part of the pledge but ignored the second.

EVENTS OF 1917 A series of events early in 1917 finally led to America's entry into World War 1.

- On February 1, Germany announced a policy of unrestricted submarine warfare. It warned it would attack without warning all vessels headed for Allied ports. The main reason for Germany's decision was that the war was at a stalemate. Germany knew that its move would probably bring the United States into the war. However, Germany believed its **U-boats,** or submarines, could break the blockade and defeat the Allies before the United States could get troops to the battlefields.

- Two days later, the United States broke diplomatic relations with Germany. Tension and suspicion increased with the **Zimmermann note** of March 1. This was a message from the German foreign secretary, Arthur Zimmermann, to the German minister in Mexico. It urged a German military alliance with the Mexicans, promising them support in regaining their "lost territories" in the southwestern United States. When the message was made public, Americans reacted angrily.

• Four U.S. merchant ships were sunk by the Germans in March.
• Also in March, the **Russian Revolution** overthrew the czar. It appeared that more democratic forces would take control in Russia, so that if the United States went to war, it would be joining an alliance of democratic nations.

Role of the United States in the War
The United States entered World War I on the side of the Allies in April 1917. But earlier, in 1916, passage of the National Defense Act and the Navy Act, began the expansion of the armed forces. The 1916 Revenue Act was also passed to pay for military expansion.

THE DRAFT ISSUE Even before the entrance of the United States into World War I, the question of how to raise an army was being debated. Those favoring the draft saw it as being fair and democratic, with all Americans serving together. Those opposed to the draft—who preferred that military service be voluntary—viewed the draft as an example of the rich and educated exercising power over the poor, the working class, and immigrants. In May 1917, Congress passed the **Selective Service Act,** which established a draft. Eventually all males between the ages of 18 and 45 had to register. The constitutionality of the draft was challenged but upheld by the Supreme Court.

AMERICAN EXPEDITIONARY FORCE By the end of the war, 4.8 million Americans had served in the armed forces, 2.8 million of them draftees. Eventually, over 2 million Americans served in France in a separate command, the American Expeditionary Force, led by General John J. Pershing.

The United States supplied fresh troops to a war in which both sides were exhausted by years of trench warfare. Neither side had moved more than a few miles, but casualties were in the millions. The entry of the United States tipped the scale in favor of the Allies. The United States lost about 51,000 men, far fewer than the millions lost by other nations.

MOBILIZING THE ECONOMY To get the nation's economy geared up for war, certain economic operations were centralized and concentrated through a series of government agencies. Relying on the broad wartime powers of the President, Wilson used the Council of National Defense to oversee these agencies. Government control over the American economy increased vastly during World War I. For the first time, the government entered fields such as housing and labor relations. It also supervised various public utilities, including the telephone and

**♀ KEY THEMES AND
CONCEPTS
Diversity**
Discrimination in the armed forces denied African Americans the opportunity to serve in combat. Many volunteered to fight with the French as the 369th Infantry Regiment. Though facing combat for the first time, they performed with such skill and bravery that they were awarded the French Croix de Guerre.

ANALYZING DOCUMENTS

Examine the graphs, then answer the questions that follow.

- Approximately how many casualties did Russia suffer in the war?

- Approximately, how much money did the United States spend on the war?

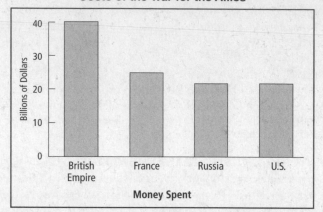

Costs of the War for the Allies

Money Spent

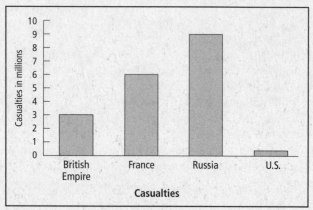

Casualties

Source: V.J. Esposito, *A Concise History of World War I*

KEY THEMES AND CONCEPTS

Diversity

The entry of the United States into World War I led to a general hostility toward Germans and German Americans. German composers and musicians were banned from symphony concerts. German measles became "liberty measles," and a hamburger (named after the German city of Hamburg) became a "liberty sandwich."

telegraph. About 16 percent of male workers went into the military, and their jobs were filled by women, African Americans, and retirees.

PATRIOTISM To Wilson, World War I was a crusade. He believed that the Allies were fighting the war to end all wars, a war to make the world "safe for democracy." These idealistic goals helped make Wilson the Allies' moral leader. They also helped mobilize the American people to support the first conflict the United States had ever fought outside the Western Hemisphere. The nation geared up for the war with patriotic enthusiasm.

A propaganda campaign organized by the Committee on Public Information encouraged patriotism. Songs, posters, and pamphlets attacked Germany, urged the purchase of Liberty Bonds, and encouraged the conservation of resources. Patriotism was accompanied by an outbreak of anti-German and anti-immigrant hysteria. Americans burned German books, banned the teaching of German in some schools, and renamed sauerkraut "liberty cabbage." Nativism was expressed in a 1917 law, passed over Wilson's veto, that required a literacy test for immigrants.

Wartime Constitutional Issues

This social climate of patriotism and nativism led to actions that restricted some people's civil rights, usually in the name of national security. Not only were German Americans and other immigrants suspected of being possible traitors, but so were socialists, pacifists, and others who questioned the war.

THE ESPIONAGE AND SEDITION ACTS Two broadly worded acts served to control and punish those who opposed the war effort. The Espionage Act of 1917 made it a crime to interfere with the draft and allowed the postmaster general to bar "treasonous" materials from the mail. The Sedition Act of 1918 made it a crime to speak or publish anything "disloyal, profane . . . or abusive" about the government, Constitution, flag, or military services of the United States.

Under these acts, the government prosecuted more than 2,000 Americans and sent 1,500 of them to jail. Pacifists, socialists, and others seen as extremists suffered the most. A special target was the Industrial Workers of the World (IWW), a radical union active in the West. Its leaders were arrested, its strikes broken up, and many of its members interned.

SCHENCK V. UNITED STATES In 1919, the Supreme Court ruled that free speech could be restricted during wartime in the landmark case *Schenck* v. *United States*. In a unanimous decision, Justice Oliver Wendell Holmes wrote, "Free speech would not protect a man falsely shouting *fire* in a theater and causing a panic." Holmes went on to say that Congress has the right to prevent words that would cause "a clear and present danger." That same year, the Court upheld the Sedition Act, but in that decision the minority expressed concern that freedom of expression was endangered.

THE RED SCARE 1918–1919 In 1917, the Russian Revolution resulted in the communist overthrow of the czar. The communist system was openly hostile to American values and beliefs, such as capitalism, private ownership of property, and certain freedoms. By 1918, an intense fear of communism swept the United States, and many Americans began to call for the imprisonment or exile of communists in the United States, even though the number of American

ANALYZING DOCUMENTS

In wartime (particularly during the Civil War, World War I, and World War II), civil liberties were restricted. The Red Scare and McCarthyism that followed each of the world wars also led to violations of certain civil liberties.

"Words can be weapons. . . . The question . . . is whether the words used are used in such circumstances and are of such nature as to create a clear and present danger that will bring about the substantial evils that Congress has a right to prevent."
—*Schenck* v. *United States* (1919)

- According to this Supreme Court ruling, under what circumstances was it constitutional to restrict freedom of speech?

communistswas very small. This fear led some Americans to target others as well, including socialists, anarchists, labor leaders, and immigrants.

THE SEARCH FOR PEACE AND ARMS CONTROL

World War I ended in November 1918 with an Allied victory. The United States, particularly President Wilson, played a major role in the peacemaking process.

KEY THEMES AND CONCEPTS

Government

- Were Wilson's Fourteen Points a realistic basis for the peace treaty written at Versailles?

- Why did the Senate refuse to ratify the Treaty of Versailles?

- Was the failure to approve the Treaty of Versailles a turning back or a temporary halt in United States foreign policy?

The Fourteen Points

Wilson had first suggested his own peace proposals in January 1918. His **Fourteen Points** included the following:

- Open, not secret, diplomacy
- Freedom of the seas
- Removal of trade barriers
- Arms reduction
- **Self-determination** of peoples—that is, letting various national groups make their own political decisions
- An "association of nations" to guarantee political independence and territorial integrity

Wilson and the Treaty of Versailles

The Fourteen Points became the basis for the peace negotiations held at Versailles, France, beginning in January 1919. Wilson led the American delegation, thus becoming the first President of the United States to leave American soil while in office. Other Allied leaders included Georges Clemenceau of France, David Lloyd George of Britain, and Vittorio Orlando of Italy.

European nations, who had suffered far more than the United States, were cool to Wilson's plans. They wanted to be repaid for some of their losses, and some had made secret wartime deals involving territorial changes and money settlements that contradicted provisions of the Fourteen Points.

The most important agreement reached at Versailles was the treaty with Germany, the **Treaty of Versailles.** According to its provisions, Germany had to do the following:

- Accept complete responsibility for causing the war
- Pay huge reparations to the Allies
- Give up its military forces
- Cede lands to the new nations of Poland and Czechoslovakia
- Give up its overseas colonies

Wilson opposed many of the settlements of the Versailles Treaty and treaties with the other Central Powers. However, he was willing to

THE CHILD WHO WANTED TO PLAY BY HIMSELF.
President Wilson: "Now come along and enjoy
yourself with the other nice children. I promised
that you'd be the life and soul of the party."

ANALYZING
DOCUMENTS

Examine the cartoon,
then answer the following
questions.

• Who is the man in the
cartoon?

• What does the child
represent?

• Who does the man want
the "child" to play with?

• Why does the "child" want
to play by himself?

compromise because the treaties provided for a new world organization, the League of Nations. The League, Wilson believed, would correct any problems caused by the peace treaties.

The League of Nations

The United States Senate had to approve the Versailles Treaty, and
there Wilson ran into a great deal of opposition. Wilson had angered
Republicans by excluding them from the American delegation to the
Versailles Conference. Yet Republicans had a majority of seats in the
Senate. The chairman of its foreign relations committee, Henry Cabot
Lodge, distrusted and disliked Wilson. The feeling was mutual.

Some features of the League of Nations worried Americans. They
feared, for instance, that the United States might be obligated to
furnish troops to defend member nations.

Wilson stubbornly refused to allow any but the most minor changes
in the Treaty of Versailles. He became increasingly moralistic and
uncompromising.

When Wilson went on a speaking tour to gain popular support for
the treaty, he collapsed and then suffered a stroke. His illness thereafter
prevented him from playing an active role in the treaty debate.

The Senate voted several times on the Treaty of Versailles, but always defeated it. The United States made a separate peace with Germany, and never did join the League. Fundamentally, the nation had voted to retain its traditional foreign policy of preferring nonintervention and of acting alone when it did choose to play a role.

The Peace Movement: Women's International League for Peace and Freedom

Although the United States failed to join the League of Nations, there was still great concern in the United States about keeping the peace. During the Paris Peace Conference, for example, many American women met with others from around the world to form the Women's International League for Peace and Freedom. Jeannette Rankin, a prominent American pacifist, and reformer Jane Addams were among this group, and Addams was voted the first president of the league.

The Women's International League opposed peace terms that would create additional anger and hostility among nations. The organization opposed the Treaty of Versailles for that reason, suggesting that its legacy would only be more war. Peace organizations wanted disarmament, arms control, and neutrality.

Reparations and War Debts

Postwar Loans and Debts

In 1914, the United States had been a debtor nation, meaning that it owed more money to foreign nations than they owed to the United States. After World War I, the United States became the world's leading creditor nation, meaning that other countries owed more to the United States than it owed them. The nation was also the world's leading industrial producer, exporter, and financier. These changes were due in large part to money from the payment of war debts owed this nation by the former Allies.

During World War I, the European Allies borrowed a great deal of money from the United States in order to buy war supplies from American manufacturers. After the war, these debts became a source of conflict. European nations argued that their debts should be canceled because, while the United States had contributed money, Europe had paid a heavy price in lives. Nevertheless, the United States insisted on repayment.

A factor that made repayment difficult was U.S. protectionist policy. High American tariffs limited European trade with the United States and thus reduced earnings that might have been used to pay off war debts. These tariffs also led to retaliation by 26 nations, which raised their own tariff rates.

One step aimed at making repayment easier was the Dawes Plan, adopted in 1924. Under this plan, the United States lent funds to Germany so that it could make war **reparations**—money it owed to the European Allies as payment for economic losses during the war. The Allies would, in turn, use the funds to make payments on the war debts they owed the United States.

Steps Toward Peace and Arms Control

In 1921, President Warren G. Harding hosted the Washington Naval Conference. The United States, Britain, France, Italy, and Japan agreed to set limits on the number of warships each nation could build. They also pledged to keep the peace in Asia and to protect the independence of China. The conference, however, failed to establish any means of enforcement.

In 1928, 15 nations met in Paris to sign the Kellogg-Briand Pact, which outlawed war except in self-defense. Enforcement provisions were missing from the pact, which 60 nations eventually signed.

Although the United States never joined the League of Nations or the World Court, it did send observers to League meetings. American judges also served on the World Court, which was based in Geneva, Switzerland.

Questions for Regents Practice

For online Questions for Regents Practice,
visit the Prentice Hall Web site at www.phschool.com.

MULTIPLE CHOICE

Directions

Review the Test-Taking Strategies section of this book. Then answer the following questions, drawn from actual Regents examinations. Each question is followed by four choices. Read each question carefully. Decide which choice is the correct answer. Then on a separate piece of paper, mark your answer for each question.

1   In the late 1800s, which reason led the United States to give greater attention to the world beyond its borders?
   1   fear of revolution in Latin America
   2   fear of Russian expansion in Alaska
   3   interest in finding places to settle surplus population
   4   interest in obtaining markets for surplus goods

2   The United States government economic policy shifted away from laissez-faire in the early 1900s. The main reason for this shift was the desire to
   1   increase government ownership of major industries
   2   make the United States more competitive with foreign economies
   3   coordinate the economy for a war effort
   4   reduce the abuses of big business

3   "Third parties in the United States are not . . . especially important in their own right, but only in terms of their influence on the major parties." Which is the most valid conclusion to be drawn from this quotation?
   1   The contribution of third parties has been insignificant in American history.
   2   The ideas of third parties have often been adopted by the two major parties.
   3   Third-party leaders have often become the candidates of the major parties.
   4   Third parties have failed to become important because they have been unable to develop new ideas.

4   Which is the most valid conclusion to be drawn from a study of the role of the Populist, Progressive, and Prohibition parties in United States history?
   1   Coalition government is a practical idea for United States society.
   2   Improvements for racial minorities are often initiated by third parties.
   3   Third-party platforms are often important in helping to bring about change.
   4   Voters are most greatly influenced by the religious beliefs they hold.

5   In the United States, the term "muckraker"
    has been used to describe authors whose
    writings deal mainly with
    1 criticizing the government's social
       welfare policies
    2 publicizing constitutional issues relating
       to minorities' rights
    3 advancing the cause of socialism
    4 exposing social conditions in need of
       reform

6   Which event of the early 1900s is evidence
    that Upton Sinclair's novel *The Jungle* had
    an important impact on the United States?
    1 adoption of reform in public education
    2 passage of legislation limiting immigration
    3 adoption of the 18th amendment estab-
       lishing Prohibition
    4 passage of legislation requiring federal
       inspection of meat

7   "All forms of life developed from earlier
    forms. In every case the fittest survived and
    the weak died out. It is the same for people
    and nations." This passage expresses a view
    most often found in
    1 fundamentalism
    2 social Darwinism
    3 liberalism
    4 utopian socialism

8   Jacob Riis's photographs and the settlement
    house movement led by Jane Addams drew
    attention to the needs of the
    1 former slaves immediately after the
       Civil War
    2 farmers in the 1880s and 1890s
    3 urban poor in the late 19th and early
       20th centuries
    4 Japanese and Chinese laborers in the
       late 1800s

9   "In the period between the Civil War and
    World War I, often the first American to
    greet the sea-weary immigrants when they
    walked down the gangplank into the United
    States was a member of the local political
    machine. This considerate politician helped
    the immigrant through customs, got him a
    job, and lent him a few dollars until payday."

    The process described in the quotation was
    a major benefit to the immigrant and to the
    nation because political machines
    1 encouraged new citizens to vote accord-
       ing to issues, not party labels
    2 helped provide a supply of cheap and
       willing labor for industry
    3 assisted the social, economic, and politi-
       cal assimilation of immigrants into the
       community
    4 helped to assure honest government

10 Western territories were among the first to
    adopt laws granting political rights to
    women because the
    1 Native American heritage of matriarchy
       served as an example to territorial
       governors
    2 strongest women's rights movements
       began in the West
    3 settlers brought a tradition of women's
       suffrage to American homesteads
    4 hardships of pioneer life encouraged men
       and women to share responsibilities

11 A major purpose of the Federal Reserve
    System is to
    1 deal with the trade deficit through tariffs
       and quotas
    2 control the minimum wage
    3 establish the federal budget
    4 regulate interest rates and the money
       supply

12 The views of W.E.B. Du Bois clashed with those of Booker T. Washington, because Du Bois insisted that African Americans should
1 seek immediate equality of all types and resist any form of second-class citizenship
2 pursue a policy of gradual integration
(3) accept racial segregation laws because they were constitutional
4 learn a trade before pursuing political equality

13 Theodore Roosevelt's New Nationalism and Woodrow Wilson's New Freedom were designed primarily to
1 increase the power and influence of the United States in foreign affairs
2 reduce the role of government in the economy
(3) help the United States solve problems caused by industrialization
4 protect the constitutional rights of religious and racial minorities

14 Which statement reflects a foreign policy view held by both President James Monroe and President Theodore Roosevelt?
1 Revolutionary movements in western Europe must be stopped.
2 Close economic ties with Asia must be maintained.
3 Noninvolvement in world affairs is the wisest policy for the United States.
(4) United States influence in Latin America must by accepted by other countries.

Base your answers to questions 15 and 16 on the excerpt from the Progressive party platform of 1912 below and on your knowledge of United States history.

"We of the Progressive party here dedicate ourselves to the fulfillment of the duty laid upon us by our fathers to maintain the government of the people, by the people, and for the people whose foundations they laid. . . .

"To destroy this invisible government, to dissolve the unholy alliance between corrupt business and corrupt politics is the first task of statesmanship of the day."

15 The phrase "invisible government" refers to the power exerted by
1 the President's cabinet
2 the Supreme Court
(3) pressure groups
4 minority parties in Congress

16 The phrase "government of the people, by the people, and for the people" has been previously stated in the
1 Declaration of Independence
2 Bill of Rights
(3) Preamble to the Constitution
4 Gettysburg Address

17 Which pair of terms represent two major causes of imperialism in the 19th century?
1 industrialism and communism
2 communism and fascism
3 nationalism and industrialism
4 collectivism and missionary zeal

18 "The Constitution rides behind
And the Big Stick rides before
(Which is the rule of precedent
In the reign of Theodore)."

This rhyme from the early 1900s suggests that President Theodore Roosevelt
1 relied heavily on the advice of his cabinet and Congress
2 failed to make adequate use of executive power
(3) developed strong foreign policies but neglected domestic needs
4 ignored democratic principles in carrying our foreign policy

19 During the late 19th century, some United States newspapers printed exaggerated accounts of Spanish cruelty in Cuba. These reports helped to bring about the Spanish-American War primarily by
1 arousing public anger against Spain
2 provoking the anger of the business community
3 alienating the Spanish government
4 encouraging the formation of Spanish revolutionary groups

20 In the late 19th and early 20th centuries, United States intervention in Latin America was motivated mainly by the United States desire to
1 suppress Latin American movements for national independence
2 reduce the influence of communism
3 ensure the safety of its growing investments in the area
4 counteract Spain's economic dominance of the area

21 The main reason the United States developed the Open Door Policy was to
1 allow the United States to expand its trade with China
2 demonstrate the positive features of democracy to Chinese leaders
3 aid the Chinese Nationalists in their struggle with the Chinese Communists
4 encourage Chinese workers to come to the United States

22 The "clear and present danger" ruling in the Supreme Court case *Schenck* v. *United States* (1919) confirmed the idea that
1 prayer in public schools is unconstitutional
2 racism in the United States is illegal
3 interstate commerce can be regulated by state governments
4 constitutional rights are not absolute

23 The main objective of President Woodrow Wilson's Fourteen Points was to
1 establish a military alliance with European nations
2 punish Germany for causing World War I
3 provide for a just and lasting peace
4 encourage open immigration in industrial nations

24 "Why, by interweaving our destiny with that of any part of Europe, entangle our peace and prosperity in the toils of European ambition, rivalship, interest, humor, or caprice?"

Which action by the United States best reflects the philosophy expressed in this quotation?
1 passage of legislation restricting immigration
2 rejection of the Treaty of Versailles
3 enactment of the Lend-Lease Act
4 approval of the United Nations Charter

25 "The chief opponents of the Versailles Treaty were dead men: Washington, Jefferson, and Madison."

This statement suggests that opposition in the United States to the Versailles Treaty was based on the
1 rejection of Woodrow Wilson's Fourteen Points
2 fear that the treaty would violate the tradition of noninvolvement
3 belief that the treaty was too harsh on the Central Powers
4 unhappiness of citizens with United States participation in World War I

26 The greatest contribution of the United States to world peace during the period between World War I and World War II was
1 support of the League of Nations
2 support of the disarmament movement
3 membership in the World Court
4 adoption of free trade

THEMATIC ESSAY

In developing your answers to the essay, be sure to keep these general definitions in mind:

(a) <u>discuss</u> means "to make observations about something using facts, reasoning, and argument; to present in some detail"

(b) <u>describe</u> means "to illustrate something in words or to tell about it"

(c) <u>evaluate</u> means "to examine and judge the significance, worth, or condition of; to determine the value of"

Directions

Write a well-organized essay that includes an introduction, several paragraphs addressing the task below, and a conclusion.

Theme: Foreign Policy

The primary aim of a nation's foreign policy is the self-interest of that nation. Throughout United States history, certain foreign policy actions have led to debate over whether they were in the national interest.

Task

From your study of United States history, identify two foreign policy actions that have led to debate over whether they were in the national interest.

   For each foreign policy action identified:

- Discuss the historical circumstances that led the United States to take a specific foreign policy action.
- Describe the foreign policy action that was taken.
- Describe the opposing viewpoints about the role of national self-interest in that action.
- Evaluate whether the action taken succeeded in promoting the national self-interest.

Suggestions

You may use any major controversial foreign policy action from your study of United States history. Some suggestions you might wish to consider include: War of 1812; Mexican War (1846–1848); acquisition of the Philippines(1898–1902); Roosevelt Corollary to the Monroe Doctrine (1904); Treaty of Versailles (1919); Lend Lease Act (1941); Vietnam War; Persian Gulf Crisis (1990–1991).

You are *not* limited to these suggestions.

Guidelines

In your essay be sure to:

- Address all aspects of the *Task*
- Analyze, evaluate, or compare and/or contrast issues and events whenever possible
- Fully support the theme of the essay with relevant facts, examples, and details
- Write a well-developed essay that consistently demonstrates a logical and clear plan of organization
- Introduce the theme by establishing a framework that is beyond a simple restatement of the *Task*
- Conclude your essay with a strong summation of the theme

DOCUMENT-BASED ESSAY

For online Document-Based Essays,
visit the Prentice Hall Web site at www.phschool.com.

This task is designed to test your ability to work with historical documents and is based on the accompanying documents (1–5). Some of the documents have been edited for the purposes of this question. As you analyze the documents, take into account both the source of each document and any point of view that may be presented in the document.

Directions
This document-based question consists of two parts: Part A and Part B. In Part A, you are to read each document and answer the question or questions that follow the document. In Part B, you are to write an essay based on the information in the documents and your knowledge of United States history.

Historical Context
As the United States transformed into an industrialized nation, the effects of this massive change were felt at all levels of society. Industrialization had long-term social, economic, and political effects on American society.

Task
Using information from the documents and your knowledge of United States history and government, answer the questions that follow each document in Part A. Your answers to the questions will help you write the Part B essay in which you be asked to:

Discuss the social, economic, and political reactions to industrialization and urbanization in the United States from 1890 to 1920.

PART A: SHORT ANSWER

DOCUMENT #1

> *"Today three-fourths of [New York's] people live in tenements. . . . The gang is the ripe fruit of tenement-house growth. It was born there, endowed with a heritage of instinctive hostility to restraint by a generation that sacrificed home to freedom, or left its country for its country's good. . . . New York's tough represents the essence of reaction against the old and the new oppression, nursed in the rank soil of its slums."*
>
> **—Jacob Riis, *How the Other Half Lives*, 1890**

1 According to Jacob Riis, what problems developed as a result of urbanization?

_____

_____

_____

DOCUMENT #2

> *"I insist that the true object of all true education is not to make men carpenters, it is to make carpenters men. . . . The Talented Tenth of the Negro race must be made leaders of thought and missionaries of culture among their people. No others can do this work and Negro colleges must train men for it."*
>
> **—W.E.B. Du Bois**

2 According to Du Bois, what should be the role of well-educated African Americans in society?

_____

_____

_____

DOCUMENT #3

political

Reform	Before the Reform	After the Reform
Primary	Party leaders pick candidates for state and local offices	Voters select party's candidates
Initiative	Only members of state legislatures can introduce bills	Votes can put bills before state legislatures
Referendum	Only legislators pass laws	Voters can vote on bills directly
Recall	Only courts or legislatures can remove corrupt officials	Voters can remove elected officials from office

3 State one way in which Progressive legislation granted citizens greater participation in state governments.

_____

_____

_____

DOCUMENT #4

political

"It shall be unlawful for any person engaged in commerce . . . to discriminate in price between different purchasers of commodities of like grade and quality . . . where the effect of such discrimination may be substantially to lessen competition or tend to create a monopoly. . . .

"No person engaged in commerce . . . shall acquire . . . the whole or any part of the stock . . . where in any line of commerce or in any activity affecting commerce in any section of the country, the effect of such acquisition may be substantially to lessen competition, or to tend to create a monopoly."

—**Clayton Antitrust Act**

4 What effect did the Clayton Antitrust Act have on monopolies such as Standard Oil?

_____

_____

_____

DOCUMENT #5
Value of United States Exports, 1870–1920

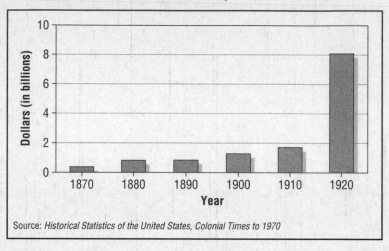

economy

Source: *Historical Statistics of the United States, Colonial Times to 1970*

5 Based on this graph and your knowledge of United States history, how did industrialization affect the activity of American businesses in international markets?

_____

_____

_____

PART B: ESSAY

Directions

Using information from the documents provided, and your knowledge of United States history, write a well-organized essay that includes an introduction, several paragraphs, and a conclusion.

Historical Context

As the United States transformed into an industrialized nation, the effects of this massive change were felt at all levels of society. Industrialization had long-term social, economic, and political effects on American society.

Task

Using information from the documents and your knowledge of United States history and government, write an essay in which you

Discuss the social, economic, and political reactions to industrialization and urbanization in the United States from 1890 to 1920.

Guidelines

When writing your essay, be sure to
- Address all aspects of the *Task* by accurately analyzing and interpreting at least <u>four</u> documents
- Incorporate information from the documents in the body of the essay
- Incorporate relevant outside information throughout the essay
- Richly support the theme with relevant facts, examples, and details
- Write a well-developed essay that consistently demonstrates a logical and clean plan of organization
- Introduce the theme by establishing a framework that is beyond a simple restatement of the *Task* or *Historical Context* and conclude the essay with a summation of the theme.

At Home and Abroad: Prosperity and Depression, 1917–1940

Section 1   War and Prosperity: 1917–1929

Section 2   The Great Depression

UNIT OVERVIEW

During the decades of the 1920s and 1930s, the United States completed the transition to a modern, urban, industrial nation. In the 1920s, the United States experienced sharp differences in income levels and shifts in cultural values, which created tensions in society and raised issues of civil liberties. At the end of that decade, the nation and the world plunged into a severe economic depression. President Franklin D. Roosevelt's New Deal programs in the 1930s attempted to overcome the effects of the Great Depression in the United States.

Some key questions to help you focus on America between the wars include:

- What tensions developed between the people who were a part of the traditional rural culture and those who were members of the new, urban-based society in the 1920s?
- What were the causes of the Great Depression, and how did that event affect the American people and their institutions?

SECTION 1

War and Prosperity: 1917–1929

SECTION OVERVIEW

The 1920s were a time of many changes in the economic and social aspects of life in the United States. Following World War I, the United States struggled to return to what President Harding called "normalcy." However, the impact of the war, the new age of consumerism, the automobile, and the growth of the suburbs contributed to the creation of a different and new national lifestyle.

While transportation and communications technology served to unite the nation, a clash of values between the new urban-centered life and the legacy of the traditional rural life caused uneasiness and conflict. In addition, all Americans did not share in the good times. Beneath the surface was an economy with structural flaws that brought the Roaring Twenties to an abrupt end with the stock market crash in October 1929.

KEY THEMES AND CONCEPTS

As you review this section, take special note of the following key themes and concepts:

Diversity What effects did World War I have on women and minorities?

Economic Systems Who benefited, and who was left out of economic growth in the 1920s?

Factors of Production What caused the increase in mass consumption in the 1920s?

Culture and Intellectual Life What social changes caused a clash of values during the twenties?

Government What major constitutional and legal issues emerged during the twenties, and how were these issues resolved?

★ THE BIG IDEA
In the 1920s and 1930s:

- American society was unsettled by social and cultural change.

- The boom economy of the 1920s was not shared by all, and it came to an end with the 1929 stock market crash.

- The Great Depression dominated American life in the 1930s.

- FDR's New Deal helped relieve some of the suffering, but did not end the Great Depression.

⚷ KEY TERMS

Coolidge prosperity
on margin
flapper
Harlem Renaissance
Jazz Age
Red Scare
quotas
Scopes Trial

KEY PEOPLE

As you review this section, take special note of the following key people:

Warren G. Harding	Zora Neale Hurston
Calvin Coolidge	Alain Locke
Charles Evans Hughes	Duke Ellington
Albert Fall	Bessie Smith
Andrew Mellon	A. Mitchell Palmer
Sigmund Freud	Nicola Sacco
Charlie Chaplin	Bartolomeo Vanzetti
F. Scott Fitzgerald	Clarence Darrow
Ernest Hemingway	William Jennings Bryan
Langston Hughes	

THE IMPACT AND AFTERMATH OF WAR

World War I triggered a number of important changes in American society, most notably for some women and for many immigrants and African Americans. Some changes were subtle and gradual, while others were immediate and dramatic.

The Twenties

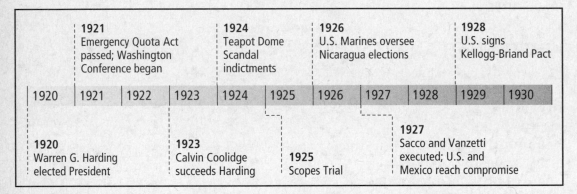

1921 Emergency Quota Act passed; Washington Conference began

1924 Teapot Dome Scandal indictments

1926 U.S. Marines oversee Nicaragua elections

1928 U.S. signs Kellogg-Briand Pact

1920 | 1921 | 1922 | 1923 | 1924 | 1925 | 1926 | 1927 | 1928 | 1929 | 1930

1920 Warren G. Harding elected President

1923 Calvin Coolidge succeeds Harding

1925 Scopes Trial

1927 Sacco and Vanzetti executed; U.S. and Mexico reach compromise

ANALYZING DOCUMENTS

Based on the timeline above, how many years did Warren G. Harding serve as President?

Effects on Women and Minorities

As many men went off to fight in Europe, the roles and responsibilities of women were affected in limited ways. Some women went to work in male-dominated fields, such as weapons factories. Many women served overseas with the Red Cross and the Salvation Army. Most, however, worked in traditionally female jobs, for which there was an increased demand. Only about five percent of the women entering the wartime workforce were new to work outside the home. At war's end, with the return of male workers, women were expected to quit their jobs. Between 1910 and 1920, only 500,000 more women were added to the workforce.

The war had harsh consequences for immigrant families. Further immigration to the United States was halted. Many immigrant families already in the country faced fierce social and job discrimination in an antiforeign climate whipped up by the war.

Most African American civil rights leaders supported World War I, and some 400,000 African American troops served in it. Black soldiers were assigned to segregated units and often worked as laborers. Discrimination was common.

Where they saw combat, African American soldiers served with distinction. Several black regiments fighting alongside of French troops were honored by that nation. Many returning black soldiers questioned why the liberties and freedoms they had fought to preserve in Europe were denied them in their own country. Civil rights leader W.E.B. Du Bois expressed resentment at the continuing racism.

> We return.
>
> We return from fighting.
>
> We return fighting.
>
> *—W.E.B. Du Bois*

 PREPARING FOR THE EXAM

Examine the graphic below and use your knowledge of social studies to answer the following questions.

- What is the cause of the effects of World War I shown in the graphic?

- Did any of these conditions exist after World War II? If so, what actions were taken in the late 1940s and 1950s?

READING STRATEGY

Formulating Questions
Read the quote in the text by W.E.B. Du Bois again.

- What question does it raise?

- What message is Du Bois sending?

- To whom is he speaking?

After World War I

United States after the war

- American economy slows as war-time production ends.

- Returning troops face difficult adjustment to civilian society.

- Many women and minority workers faced with loss of jobs as men return to workforce.

- Despite contribution to war effort, returning African American troops continue to face discrimination and segregation.

- Death and destruction of war leads to feelings of gloom among many Americans.

After World War I, many Americans faced a difficult adjustment to peacetime life.

Election of 1920

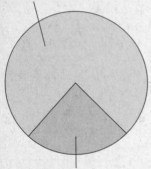

Republican Warren G. Harding
76% of electoral vote

Democrat James M. Cox
24% of electoral vote

Migration to the North

World War I accelerated the migration of African Americans to northern cities. This migration began after the Civil War. From about 1910 to 1920, southern agricultural jobs were lost to floods and to crop damage. About 500,000 African Americans moved from the South to jobs in the industrial North. Meanwhile in the North, workers were needed to meet war production goals. The wartime immigration ban produced an additional need for workers to replace those in uniform.

After the war, this northward migration continued. Between 1910 and the 1940s, almost 2 million African Americans left the South. Although they were usually able to improve their economic situation, they still faced discrimination, segregation, and sometimes even race riots.

The "Return to Normalcy," 1918–1921

After World War I, disillusioned Americans wanted to return to the traditional foreign policy of isolationism. The 1920 landslide election of Republican President Warren G. Harding and Vice President Calvin Coolidge represented the desire of many Americans to remove themselves from the pressures of world politics. Progressivism continued, but at a slower pace, and reforms took place largely at the state and local levels.

THE 1920s: BUSINESS BOOM OR FALSE PROSPERITY?

For many Americans, postwar life did return to "normalcy." Yet beneath the surface, troubling political and economic problems had begun to develop.

Greed and Scandal Under Harding

Harding was an Ohio newspaper publisher with little experience in politics. Historians credit him for pardoning socialist Eugene V. Debs (who had been jailed for opposing the war) and for supporting antilynching legislation. Harding appointed some dedicated people to office, including Charles Evans Hughes as secretary of state.

However, the President also gave political jobs to members of the so-called Ohio Gang, corrupt associates who took advantage of him. After Harding's death in 1923, the public learned of several scandals during his administration.

- *Theft:* The head of the Veterans Bureau was convicted of selling hospital supplies for his own profit. He was imprisoned and fined.
- *Fraud:* The Alien Property Custodian was imprisoned for selling former German property for private profit.
- *The Teapot Dome Scandal:* Secretary of the Interior Albert Fall was convicted of accepting bribes from two oil executives in exchange for allowing them to lease government-owned petroleum reserves. One of the oil fields was at Teapot Dome, Wyoming.

Under Coolidge, Prosperity for Some

Calvin Coolidge became President when Harding died in office in 1923. In the 1924 election, Coolidge was returned to office. Coolidge is best known for his laissez-faire approach to the economy and his strong commitment to business interests. Coolidge retained financier Andrew Mellon as secretary of the treasury. Mellon acted on the philosophy that government's role was to serve business.

RECESSION The end of World War I was followed by a recession caused by the shift from a wartime to a peacetime economy. Production, farm income, and exports fell. Unemployment rose, reaching 12 percent in 1921. For farmers, in particular, hardship continued throughout the decade.

RECOVERY In other sectors of the economy, however, a period of economic recovery had begun by 1923, when Coolidge became President. The years between 1923 and 1929 were seen as a time of booming business. The Gross National Product (GNP) rose 40 percent. Per capita income went up 30 percent. With little inflation, actual purchasing power—and therefore the standard of living—increased. At the time, few people questioned this **Coolidge prosperity.**

PRO-BUSINESS POLICIES Some groups, especially big corporations and the wealthy, benefited greatly from Coolidge prosperity. For example:

- Businesses and the most wealthy were helped by tax laws that reduced personal income tax rates, particularly for upper income groups, removed most excise taxes, and lowered corporate income taxes.
- The government reduced the national debt and balanced the budget by raising tariffs and demanding repayment of war debts.
- Tariff rates were raised in a return to protectionism. Republicans argued that higher tariffs would limit foreign imports, thus helping both industry and agriculture. However, the actual effect was to weaken the world economy.
- Regulatory agencies such as the Federal Reserve Board, the Federal Trade Commission, and the Interstate Commerce Commission saw their role as assisting business rather than regulating it.
- A relaxed attitude toward corporate mergers was supported by the executive branch and by the Supreme Court. By 1929, about 1,300 corporations produced three fourths of all American manufactured goods, and 200 companies owned half the nation's wealth.

Economic Boom Bypasses Others

Coolidge prosperity was not for everyone. Key segments of the population failed to share in the general rise in living standards.

Election of 1924

Republican Calvin Coolidge
72% of electoral vote

Democrat
John W. Davis
26% of electoral vote

Progressive Party
Robert M. La Follette
2% of electoral vote

☑ PREPARING FOR THE EXAM

You will need to understand certain important economic terms on the exam.

The **Gross National Product** (GNP) is the total value of all goods and services produced in one year.

Per Capita Income means income per individual; it is based on the national income divided by the population.

**READING
STRATEGY**

Reading for Evidence
What evidence is presented in the text to support the following statement?

"Important segments of the population failed to share in the general rise in living standards."

**⚷ KEY THEMES AND
  CONCEPTS**

Factors of Production
The term used to describe the resources used to make all goods and services is the *factors of production.* The three factors of production are land, labor, and capital.

- *Land* refers to all natural resources needed to produce goods and services. Land includes coal, water, or farmland.

- *Labor* is the paid effort that a person devotes to a task. Labor can include the medical aid provided by a doctor as well as the tasks performed by an assembly-line worker.

- *Capital* is any human-made resource used to produce other goods and services. Physical capital includes factory buildings and tools, while human capital includes workers' knowledge and experience.

LABOR Strikes had dropped sharply during World War I, mainly because the Wilson government supported collective bargaining in return for a no-strike pledge. Membership in the American Federation of Labor grew, and wages for war industry employees rose sharply. However, inflation wiped out any real gains in buying power.

The 1920s saw a reversal of any union gains. Strikes in the steel, mining, and railroad industries failed, in part because the government used not only troops to end the strikes but also injunctions, which are court orders that prohibit specified actions. The Supreme Court also ruled against child labor laws and against minimum wages for women and children. In addition, some companies began to offer health and life insurance in hopes of lessening workers' interest in unions. The strategy often worked. Membership in labor unions fell from a high of about 5 million in 1921 to under 3.5 million in 1929.

Unemployment remained between 1 and 11 percent throughout the 1920s. In general, however, real wages for workers increased only slightly during this period, boosted primarily by wages of workers in the new industries, such as communications and automobile manufacturing. Therefore, even though workers' wages increased 26 percent and their productivity increased 40 percent, they could not afford to buy many of the new consumer goods.

FARMERS The only farmers to benefit from Coolidge prosperity were those involved in large commercial operations. Small farmers were hurt by a combination of factors.

- Farmers expanded production during World War I in response to rising prices and the demand for food. They added to their acreage and bought more farm machinery.
- New machinery and new farm techniques increased farmers' crop yield per acre.
- After the war, when European farms began producing again, American farmers were growing too much. The prices of both farm products and farmland decreased dramatically.
- Net farm income fell 50 percent during the 1920s. As a result, the number of farmers declined, too. By 1930, only about 20 percent of the labor force made a living by farming.

NATIVE AMERICANS During the 1920s, Native Americans had the highest unemployment rate of any group and the shortest average life span. Most lived on reservations, without the basics of heat and running water.

AFRICAN AMERICANS African Americans who migrated to the North enjoyed a higher standard of living than in the South. However, they still earned less than white workers and experienced a higher rate of unemployment.

Stock Market Speculation

The economic recovery helped produce a surge of investment in the stock market. Optimistic business and government leaders saw no end to the boom. They encouraged everyone to play the bull market—that is, the rising stock market. Some families invested their life savings. The profits rolled in—for a while.

Yet the new wealth flowed from a stock market with a deeply flawed structure. Many stocks were traded **on margin.** This meant that buyers could purchase stocks by making only small down payments in cash— sometimes as low as 5 percent of the value of the stocks. They borrowed the rest from brokers and counted on their profits to repay the loans. The system worked as long as the profits continued.

MASS CONSUMPTION

The 1920s were a time of mass consumption—huge quantities of manufactured goods were available, and many people had more money to spend on them.

The Effects of New Industries on American Life

Automobile Industry:
1. stimulated steel, rubber, paint, glass, and oil industries
2. set off a real-estate boom in suburbs
3. led to an increase in highways and a decline in railroad construction and use
4. caused tractors to replace horses on farms
5. increased social equality as low prices made cars available to Americans at almost all income levels
6. stimulate installment buying
7. contributed to growing sophistication of advertising techniques

The Electrical Industry:
1. changed homes, businesses, and cities through electric lights
2. helped double business productivity through electric power
3. transformed life and leisure with electric-powered durable goods such as washing machines, stoves, vacuum cleaners, refrigerators, and irons
4. stimulated installment buying

Radio and Motion Pictures:
1. helped erase regional differences and homogenize American culture
2. increased people's expectations, often unrealistically
3. helped end rural isolation
4. helped popularize ragtime and jazz
5. provided an outlet for advertising
6. increased interest in politics and spectator sports

KEY THEMES AND CONCEPTS

Science and Technology
Homogenization is a process used to keep the cream in milk distributed throughout the container rather than rising to the top. The term can also be applied to cultures. Radio, movies, and telephones helped produce a more homogenized national culture in which regional differences became less distinct.

- What technology since the 1920s has resulted in further national and even international homogenization?

- According to the chart, in what ways did the automobile, electrical industry, radio, and motion pictures influence the lifestyle of the 1920s?

READING STRATEGY

Formulating Questions
Consider that in the 1920s:

- 15 million cars were sold.

- 80 percent were bought on credit.

- A Model T Ford cost $290 in 1920.

- 20% of U.S. homes had electricity by the end of the decade.

- 10 million families owned radios by 1929.

In addition to these facts, what information do you need in order to have a more complete picture of the effect of new technologies in the 1920s?

Role of Technology

Technology, combined with new marketing strategies, best explains the transformation of American society in the 1920s. Led by Henry Ford and the automobile industry, mass production and the moving assembly line resulted in uniform products produced at lower costs. It made possible a consumer-oriented economy, one in which more goods were available to more Americans. Often these goods were purchased over time through installment buying.

Growing Cultural Homogenization

The new technology also made American culture more homogeneous, or uniform. Americans from one coast to the other tended to use the same products, wear the same styles, see the same movies, and listen to the same music. Regional and class differences were blurred, and individualism became less important than conformity.

Suburban Growth

With over half the population living in places with populations of more than 2,500 people, the United States in the 1920s was an urban rather than a rural nation for the first time in its history. Only the Great Depression ended the building boom that was part of this growth. Suburbs grew even faster than cities. These new suburbs drew people from the cities. The ultimate result was the present-day conflict between urban and suburban needs, priorities, and values.

SHIFTING CULTURAL VALUES

During the 1920s, American society experienced a struggle with social change as it became an urban, industrial nation. Changes in lifestyle, values, morals, and manners increased tension and conflict. Wealth, possessions, having fun, and sexual freedom—ideas influenced by the psychology of Sigmund Freud—were the new values.

LEISURE With a shorter work week and with more paid vacation, Americans had more leisure time. Movies such as *The Ten Commandments* and the first movie with sound, *The Jazz Singer,* drew millions of people a week to theaters during the 1920s. Americans idolized Charlie Chaplin and other movie stars. They also admired sports figures, such as Babe Ruth. Games such as bridge, crossword puzzles, and the board game of mah-jongg swept the country.

The popular image of young women of the 1920s was the **flapper,** a young, pretty woman with bobbed hair and raised hemlines. She drank alcohol, she smoked, she thought for herself, and she took advantage of women's new freedoms. However, the flapper lived more in the media than in reality. The flapper figured in movies, magazines, advertising, and novels, such as those of F. Scott Fitzgerald.

LITERATURE The conflict and concern created by changing American values also saw expression in literature. American writers of the 1920s protested the effects of technology and mass consumption. They criti-

Passenger Car Sales, 1920–1929

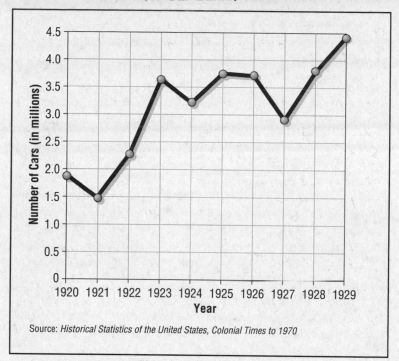

Source: *Historical Statistics of the United States, Colonial Times to 1970*

ANALYZING DOCUMENTS

What information from the graph at left helps you to gain a more complete picture of the effect of the automobile industry in the 1920s?

cized the business mentality, the conformity of the times, and the preoccupation with material things. Some writers, such as Ernest Hemingway, became expatriates, leaving the United States to settle in Europe.

HARLEM RENAISSANCE One of the most important cultural movements of the 1920s was the **Harlem Renaissance,** led by a group of African American writers in the New York City neighborhood of Harlem. These creative intellectual figures—mainly well-educated members of the middle class—felt alienated from the society of the 1920s. In their works they called for action against bigotry and expressed pride in African American culture and identity. Outstanding literary figures of the Harlem Renaissance include W.E.B. Du Bois, Langston Hughes, Zora Neale Hurston, and Alain Locke.

The Great Depression of the 1930s ended the Harlem Renaissance, cutting the sales of books and literary magazines. However, during the civil rights movement of the 1960s, the writers of the Harlem Renaissance and their works attracted renewed interest.

African American artists, musicians, and dancers also participated in the Harlem Renaissance. Black musicians in the South blended elements of African, European, and American music to create the distinctive sounds of jazz and the blues. This music was carried all over the country and abroad.

ANALYZING DOCUMENTS

"We build our temples for tomorrow, strong as we know how, and we stand on the top of the mountain, free within ourselves."
—Langston Hughes, on the Harlem Renaissance in *The Big Sea*

- What ideas of the Harlem Renaissance are expressed in this quote?

KEY THEMES AND CONCEPTS

Culture and Intellectual Life

The culture and intellectual life of a time period reflects the era's social, economic and political mood.

- How did the work of each writer in the chart at right reflect the 1920s?

- How did the Harlem Renaissance express the feelings of its participants?

- How did it have an influence beyond its time?

Leading Writers of the Twenties

Willa Cather	novelist	My Antonia
F. Scott Fitzgerald	novelist	The Great Gatsby
Ernest Hemingway	novelist	A Farewell to Arms
Langston Hughes	poet, novelist	The Weary Blues
Sinclair Lewis	novelist	Main Street, Babbitt
Eugene O'Neill	playwright	Desire Under the Elms
Edith Wharton	novelist	The Age of Innocence

Edward K. "Duke" Ellington is one of the towering figures in jazz. Ellington recorded and composed music, performed on the piano, and conducted his own orchestra until his death in 1974. Bessie Smith, known as the "Empress of the Blues," was one of the most popular singers of the 1920s. This new music, to which people danced such daring new steps as the Charleston, became so popular that the period of the 1920s is often called the **Jazz Age.**

Women's Changing Roles

The conflict between modern and traditional values in the 1920s also found expression in the contradictory roles of women.

WOMEN IN THE WORKFORCE Throughout the 1920s, the number of women in the workforce increased. By 1930, 10.5 million women were working outside the home, making up 22 percent of the workforce. This figure, however, represented an increase of only 1.4 percent of the total workforce. Most working women were single, widowed, or divorced. Most Americans still believed that married women belonged at home, where 90 percent of them were to be found. When working women married, they usually quit or were fired from their jobs.

Most women who worked outside the home continued to hold jobs in traditionally female—and traditionally low-paying and low-status—occupations, such as teaching, clerical work, and retail sales. Fewer than 20 percent worked in better-paying factory jobs. The number of female doctors and scientists actually decreased.

One important gain for working women was the creation in 1920 of the Women's Bureau, part of the federal Department of Labor. It tried to improve working conditions for women from inside the government and provided data about working women.

INVOLVEMENT IN POLITICS In 1920, women voted in a national election for the first time. However, their vote did not have a distinctive effect on the outcome. Women did not vote in large numbers, nor did they vote as a bloc. To encourage women to play a greater part in politics, the National American Woman Suffrage Association reorganized itself as the nonpartisan League of Women Voters.

HEALTH, RIGHTS, AND WORKING CONDITIONS The divisions of the 1920s were reflected in the fate of two pieces of legislation. Encouraged by women reformers, Congress passed the Sheppard-Towner Act in 1921. With the aim of reducing infant mortality, the law provided for public health centers where women could learn about nutrition and health care. The program came to an end in 1929, largely because of opposition from physicians.

An equal rights amendment to the Constitution, proposed by Alice Paul in 1923, led to bitter disagreement among women. Many feminists supported it, but others opposed it because they believed it would do away with special laws protecting women workers.

DAILY LIFE Contrary to the image of the flapper, women were still restricted by economic, political, and social limits. The image of the flapper meant little to most women.

In some ways, technology made life easier in the 1920s. With electric washing machines, vacuum cleaners, stoves, and refrigerators, household chores did not require so much time, and there was less need for servants. On the other hand, the typical homemaker now was expected to handle almost all the household tasks herself and to meet higher standards of cleanliness.

EMPHASIS ON WIFE RATHER THAN MOTHER The role of the woman as wife received increased importance. Women did have more choices in life. Families changed during this period, and divorce and family planning became more acceptable. However, divorce laws continued to favor men, and wives were expected to stay at home rather than work outside the home. Family size decreased; only 20 percent of women who married during the 1920s had five or more children. The family, which in earlier times had been a producing unit, growing and processing much of its food, was now a consuming unit. Marketing and advertising appeals flooded the media, encouraging consumers to buy more goods.

CONSTITUTIONAL AND LEGAL ISSUES

Major constitutional and legal issues divided Americans in the 1920s. Many issues reflected the struggle between modern and traditional values and showed how international affairs affected domestic policies and attitudes.

Threats to Civil Liberties

In the 1920s, the Red Scare and the Ku Klux Klan threatened the civil liberties of some Americans.

THE RED SCARE 1918–1919 The imposition of stern measures to suppress dissent after World War I in a crusade against internal enemies was known as the **Red Scare.** It was fueled by the October 1917

PREPARING FOR THE EXAM

Remember that fear of foreigners and of foreign ideas has been an issue that has arisen many times throughout United States history.

- 1790s: Alien and Sedition Acts
- 1840s: nativism and Know-Nothings
- 1917–1918: suppression of dissent during World War I
- 1920s: Ku Klux Klan, Sacco and Vanzetti case, National Origins Quota Acts
- 1940s: internment of Japanese Americans during World War II
- 1950s: McCarthyism

Bolshevik Revolution, an uprising of Communists in Russia. In the United States, Communists made up only one half of 1 percent of the population, but many of them were targeted by the crackdown, as were various other groups viewed as un-American. Among them were socialists, anarchists, labor leaders, and foreigners.

The Red Scare was led by Attorney General A. Mitchell Palmer. It was sparked by several events that took place after the war ended. Frustration over discrimination led to race riots in more than 25 cities. In Boston, a series of labor strikes climaxed with a walkout by the police. Several unexplained bombings added to the hysteria. All these events were seen as part of a Communist conspiracy.

The attorney general ordered the first so-called Palmer raids late in 1919. In 33 cities, police without warrants raided the headquarters of Communists and other organizations. Eventually they arrested 4,000 people, holding them without charges and denying them legal counsel. Some 560 aliens were deported. Palmer's extreme actions and statements soon turned the public against him. However, the Red Scare had lingering effects, discouraging many Americans from speaking their minds freely in open debate, thus squelching their constitutional right to freedom of speech.

SACCO AND VANZETTI   Closely linked to the Red Scare was the case of Nicola Sacco and Bartolomeo Vanzetti. These two Italian immigrants—admitted anarchists—were convicted of murder in 1921 in connection with a Massachusetts robbery. Many people questioned the evidence against Sacco and Vanzetti, concluding that the two men were convicted more for their beliefs and their Italian origin than for a crime. In spite of mass demonstrations and appeals, the two men were executed in 1927. The governor of Massachusetts eventually cleared the two men in 1977, some 50 years later.

THE KU KLUX KLAN   Antiforeign attitudes encouraged a revival of the Ku Klux Klan. The first organization, active during Reconstruction, had died out in the late 1800s. A reorganized Klan, formed in 1915, grew slowly until 1920. In that year, it added 100,000 members. The Klan of the 1920s targeted not only African American but also Catholics, Jews, and immigrants. To the Klan, the only true Americans were white, Protestant, and American-born.

Restrictions on Immigration

The nativism expressed in the Red Scare, the Sacco-Vanzetti case, and the new Klan was also evident in 1920s immigration legislation. Immigrants were seen by many as somehow threatening to American values. The nativist climate led to the Immigration Act of 1924. This act established a system of national **quotas,** which limited the number of immigrants from each country. These quotas deliberately kept the totals for eastern and southern Europe low and excluded all immigration from Asia.

Immigration to the United States, 1921 and 1926

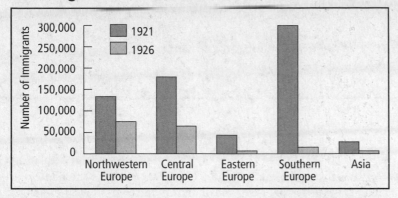

Prohibition

Both the rebirth of the Klan and the movement to restrict immigration reflected the struggle in the 1920s between what some saw as old, rural American values and the new values of a changing urban, industrialized culture. However, the clash between these two sets of values did not divide on the basis of where one lived.

For example, the movement for Prohibition, a ban on the sale and consumption of alcoholic beverages, was not confined to rural America, though it received much support there. The Eighteenth Amendment, allowing Prohibition, became part of the Constitution in 1919. Congress passed the Volstead Act to implement Prohibition, but the law turned out to be unenforceable. Most Americans were simply unwilling to accept a total ban on alcohol. Furthermore, it stimulated crime, encouraging smuggling and **bootlegging,** the illegal manufacture and sale of alcoholic beverages. In 1933, the Twenty-first Amendment ending Prohibition was ratified.

The Scopes Trial

The 1925 **Scopes Trial,** held in Dayton, Tennessee, received nationwide attention because it pitted the scientific ideas of Darwinian evolution against the Protestant fundamentalist view of biblical creationism. John Scopes, a biology teacher, had deliberately violated a state law forbidding anyone to teach the theory of evolution. Scopes was represented by a famous trial lawyer, Clarence Darrow. The prosecution relied on the assistance of William Jennings Bryan, three-time presidential candidate and a firm believer in fundamentalist Christianity. Although Scopes was convicted and fined $100, Bryan's confused testimony weakened fundamentalist arguments.

 KEY THEMES AND CONCEPTS

Immigration and Migration

During the 1920s, immigration from the western hemisphere was not limited. Large numbers of Mexicans moved into southwestern cities and Puerto Ricans into New York City, most in search of economic opportunities.

- What are the most dramatic changes pictured on the chart at left?

- What changes were made in immigration laws in the 1920s? Why?

PREPARING FOR THE EXAM

Prohibition turned out to be unenforceable because too many Americans were unwilling to accept it. The massive evasion of this law is often compared to the reaction to the 1850 Fugitive Slave Law. In 1933, the 21st Amendment repealed the 18th Amendment.

SECTION 2 The Great Depression

⭐ THE BIG IDEA
In the 1930s:

- The world economy collapsed after the 1929 crash of the stock market started the Great Depression.

- President Hoover's efforts toward economic recovery did not succeed.

- President Franklin Roosevelt's New Deal provided relief, but did not end the Great Depression.

🔑 KEY TERMS
Great Crash
Great Depression
Bonus Army
Hoovervilles
Dust Bowl
New Deal

SECTION OVERVIEW

The 1930s were dominated by the Great Depression, which affected virtually every aspect of American life and caused ripple effects throughout the worldwide economy. With roots in unregulated stock market speculation, a flawed banking system, and the overproduction of goods, the Great Depression was triggered by the stock market crash in 1929. Banks failed, and many people lost their life savings. The losses shut down businesses, producing widespread unemployment, homelessness, and hunger.

President Franklin D. Roosevelt's New Deal launched ambitious programs to speed economic recovery. The New Deal dramatically increased the role of government in American life and strengthened the power of the presidency. The entry of the United States into World War II in 1941 finally put an end to the nation's worst economic collapse.

KEY THEMES AND CONCEPTS

As you review this section, take special note of the following key themes and concepts:

Economic Systems What were the main causes of the Great Depression?

Government How did Hoover respond to the depression, and why did people disapprove of his actions?

Culture and Intellectual Life How did the depression affect daily life and culture in America?

Government What were some of the key programs of the New Deal?

Diversity How did the New Deal affect organized labor, minorities, and women?

KEY PEOPLE

As you review this section, take special note of the following key people:

Herbert Hoover	Eleanor Roosevelt
John Steinbeck	John L. Lewis
Walker Evans	Mary McLeod Bethune
Margaret Bourke-White	John Maynard Keynes
William Faulkner	Al Smith
Louis Armstrong	Norman Thomas
Franklin Delano Roosevelt	Francis E. Townsend
Frances Perkins	Father Charles E. Coughlin
Harry Hopkins	Huey Long

KEY SUPREME COURT CASES

As you review this section, take special note of the following key Supreme Court case:

Schechter Poultry Corporation v. *United States* (1935)

The Great Depression

1929 Stock market crash; Great Depression begins

1933 New Deal begins; drought on Great Plains

1935 Wagner Act; Social Security Act

1939 *The Wizard of Oz* becomes popular movie

1929 | 1931 | 1933 | 1935 | 1937 | 1939 | 1941

1932 Jobless veterans march on Washington; Roosevelt elected President

1934 Indian Reorganization Act passed

1938 *War of the Worlds* broadcast

In the 1920s, the science of economics was still fairly young. Few scholars—and even fewer business leaders or politicians—recognized the many warning signs of a looming crisis in the economy. In 1929 and the years to follow, the nation would wake up to the terrible reality that the economic freewheeling of the 1920s came at a price.

ANALYZING DOCUMENTS

According to the timeline above, who was President when the New Deal began?

THE GREAT CRASH

The end of the prosperity of the 1920s was marked by a series of plunges in the U.S. stock market in 1929 known as the **Great Crash.**

Throughout the 1920s, the stock market had grown on speculation by people who bought on margin and, in fact, owned only a small portion of their stocks. Many could not meet margin calls, demands to put up the money to cover their loans. The result was panic selling. On October 29 (Black Tuesday) alone, stock values fell $14 billion. They dropped lower and lower in the weeks that followed.

The Great Crash triggered the start of the **Great Depression.** It broke the national sense of optimism and confidence of the 1920s. The Great Crash dramatically exposed the fact that the national economy had serious weaknesses.

ANALYZING DOCUMENTS

Based on the graph at right and your knowledge of social studies, answer the following questions.

- When did the stock market crash occur?

- In what year did stock prices reach their lowest point?

- What role did speculation play in the crash?

- What is the relationship of the stock market crash to the Great Depression?

The Stock Market Crash

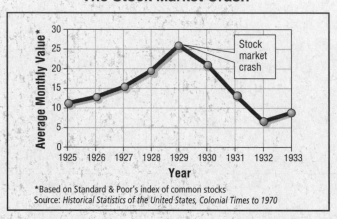

*Based on Standard & Poor's index of common stocks
Source: *Historical Statistics of the United States, Colonial Times to 1970*

CAUSES OF THE GREAT DEPRESSION

The Great Depression was caused by weaknesses in the economy—overproduction and underconsumption, overexpansion of credit, and fragile corporate structures—combined with ineffective government action. The growing interdependence of international trade and banking made the effects even more damaging.

Weaknesses in the Overall Economy

Weaknesses in the economy had existed before 1929 and were expanding.

- The agricultural sector had been depressed throughout the 1920s, with a worldwide drop in prices.
- Unemployment plagued the railroad, coal, and textile industries well before 1929.
- Speculation in real estate and the resulting building boom had declined.
- Automobile sales had slowed.
- As early as the summer of 1929, the economy showed signs of underconsumption. Inventories of unsold goods began to accumulate in warehouses as consumer demand slowed.

PREPARING FOR THE EXAM

Underconsumption or overproduction means that people buy fewer goods than are produced. In other words, supply is greater than demand.

Some Economic Changes Between 1928 and 1932
(Figures in millions unless otherwise noted)

	1928	1929	1930	1931	1932
A. United States exports (merchandise)	$5,030	$5,157	$3,781	$2,378	$1,576
B. Spending for new housing	$4,195	$3,040	$1,570	$1,320	$485
C. Farm spending for lime and fertilizer	$318	$300	$297	$202	$118
D. Federal spending	$2,933	$3,127	$3,320	$3,578	$4,659
E. Cash receipts from farming	$10,991	$11,312	$9,055	$6,331	$4,748
F. Lumber production (billions of board ft.)	36.8	38.7	29.4	20	13.5
G. Unemployment (in thousands)	2,080	1,550	4,340	8,020	12,060
H. Average weekly earnings of production works in manufacturing (actual dollars)	$24.97	$25.03	$23.25	$20.87	$17.05

Unequal Distribution of Income
Contributing to underconsumption and to the weakness of the economy was an unequal distribution of wealth.

- In the 1920s, some 40 percent of all families had an income of less than $1,500, which put them below the poverty line. At the same time, the 24,000 richest families in the nation had a total income *three times as large* as the total income of the 6 million poorest families. In short, while 1 percent of the population owned 59 percent of the nation's wealth, 87 percent of the population owned only 10 percent of the wealth.
- As a result, the economy was dependent on the spending of a very small portion of the population. These wealthy people spent their money on luxury goods and on investments. This type of spending was greatly affected by the stock market crash.
- The wealthy, not the great mass of the population, had benefited from increased output per worker in the face of stable salaries. With the increased output, production costs had dropped and profits had risen, but the workers could not buy what they produced. As a result, demand dropped. As the economy weakened, this non-purchasing group grew in size and became less and less able to buy even the necessities of life.

Excessive Buying on Credit
Excessive buying on credit resulted from these low and unequally distributed wages. Under consumption grew as workers could no longer make installment payments.

Weak Corporate Structure
The Great Crash set off the collapse of the nation's business structure. Business consolidations of the 1920s resulted in a few large companies

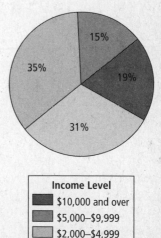

Income Distribution, 1929

15%

19%

31%

35%

Income Level
- $10,000 and over
- $5,000–$9,999
- $2,000–$4,999
- $1,999 and under

The prosperity of the 1920s did not bring great wealth to most Americans.

ANALYZING
DOCUMENTS

Examine the chart on the
previous page entitled
"Some Economic Changes
Between 1928 and 1932,"
then answer the following
questions.

- How much did spending
  for new housing change
  between 1928 and 1932?

- What does the drop in
  U.S. exports indicate
  about the nature of the
  depression?

- How much did unemploy-
  ment increase between
  1928 and 1932?

- Based on this chart,
  which year was the
  economy in its most
  serious state?

in each industry. Holding companies controlled the stock of many different corporations and depended on the earnings of the various companies they held. This was a very fragile system, because when one company collapsed, it affected—in a domino fashion—the rest of the holding company.

Weak Banking Structure

Some 6,000 banks failed in the 1920s. This showed clearly that there were serious weaknesses in the banking industry.

Inadequate Government Policies

Actions by the federal government contributed to the depression.

- Stock market speculation was unregulated by the government.
- Tax policies that favored the wealthy resulted in further uneven distribution of income.
- The consolidation of corporations was not challenged under antitrust laws.
- The Federal Reserve Board allowed a low discount rate—the interest charged to member banks. This policy led to stock speculation. The board then raised interest rates in 1931, discouraging spending at just the time when spending would have helped the economy.

Weak International Economy

The world's economies were affected by the collapse triggered by the crash of the U.S. stock market. Many European economies had never fully recovered from World War I, and the international economy depended heavily on the economy of the United States.

Foreign nations owed the United States money that they could repay only after the United States bought their goods and made foreign investments and loans. However, high American tariffs kept out goods from overseas and led to high foreign tariffs. Meanwhile, Americans invested at home in businesses or in the stock market rather than abroad.

When the U.S. economy slowed, the United States made fewer foreign investments and had less money to lend. This meant that foreign nations had less money to buy American goods and often defaulted on loans. The international nature of the banking system can be seen by the fact that banks in both Europe and the United States failed as a result of defaults on loans.

HOOVER'S RESPONSE TO THE GREAT DEPRESSION, 1929–1933

Herbert Hoover was the President who first had to deal with the deepening depression. Hoover had taken office in 1929, after having served as Coolidge's secretary of commerce. An engineer by training, Hoover was a good businessman, a self-made millionaire, and a humanitarian. During and after World War I, he had an international reputation as leader of a successful relief effort to aid starving Europeans and to help Europe recover economically.

Hoover's Economic Plan

In order to improve economic conditions, Hoover took the following actions:

- Tried to restore confidence in the American economy with such statements as "Prosperity is just around the corner."
- Altered his view that government should not become directly involved in the economy. He promoted programs that aided businesses, on the theory that as businesses recovered, economic benefits would trickle down to the workers and consumers.
- Allowed the organization of the Reconstruction Finance Corporation (1932) to lend money to railroads, mortgage and insurance companies, and banks on the verge of bankruptcy.
- Set a precedent for Franklin Roosevelt's New Deal with his use of federal works projects to create jobs and stimulate the economy.
- Obtained voluntary agreements from businesses not to lower wages or prices. However, as companies increasingly faced collapse, they often could not honor these promises.
- Halted the payment of war debts by European nations.

Failure of Hoover's Program

Despite these efforts, Hoover's refusal to provide direct relief damaged his image as the nation's leader. Also damaging was his insistence, in the face of worsening conditions, that the economy was actually improving.

In the summer of 1932, thousands of unemployed World War I veterans and their families set up camps in Washington, D.C., to demand early payment of the bonus due to them for their war service. When the bill was defeated by Congress, most of **Bonus Army,** as they were called, refused to leave town. Hoover insisted that the veterans were influenced by Communists and other agitators. He called out the army to break up the Bonus Army's camps and disperse the veterans. The news photographs showing tanks and tear gas being used against war veterans destroyed what little popularity Hoover had left.

Herbert Hoover took many steps to use the power of the federal government to stop the growing depression. In the end, his efforts were too little. Historians still debate whether he should be praised for the efforts he did make or condemned for not going far enough. Hoover's ability to act was limited by his beliefs. For example:

- He had great faith in the American economic system, insisting that the forces of the market would eventually set the economy right again.
- He stood for the Puritan work ethic—the idea that hard work earns its own rewards.
- He believed in voluntary rather than governmental action to solve problems of society.

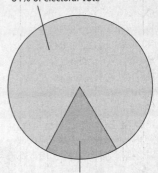

Election of 1928

Republican Herbert C. Hoover 84% of electoral vote

Democrat Alfred E. Smith 16% of electoral vote

ANALYZING DOCUMENTS

"Our Republican leaders tell us economic laws . . . cause panics which no one could prevent. But while they prate of [chatter about] economic laws, men and women are starving . . . I pledge you, I pledge myself, to a new deal for the American people.
— F. D. Roosevelt, 1932

"The urgent question today is the prompt balancing of the budget. When that is accomplished, I propose to support adequate measures for relief of distress and unemployment."
— Herbert Hoover, 1932

Both of these quotes were made during the 1932 presidential campaign.

- What is the clearest difference between Roosevelt's and Hoover's approaches to the Great Depression?

• He believed in self-help and opposed direct relief on the grounds that it would destroy people's "rugged individualism."

THE HUMAN IMPACT OF THE GREAT DEPRESSION

The Great Depression had a profound effect on all Americans.

Unemployment

By 1932, some 12 million people—25 percent of the American labor force—were unemployed. The human toll was seen in long "bread lines" at soup kitchens. Relief efforts by organizations such as the Red Cross were limited, because voluntary contributions slowed down. As banks failed, people lost their savings; as companies failed, people lost their jobs as well.

African Americans and unskilled workers were the first to experience unemployment. In 1931, African American unemployment was estimated as 30 to 60 percent greater than white unemployment. Women were criticized for working while men could not find jobs. In truth, female occupations, usually in service sectors such as nursing and clerical work, were less affected than positions in manufacturing that were usually given to men. Family life was disrupted as parents looked for ways to stretch what money the family had. Families moved in with relatives. Marriages were postponed. The birth rate dropped, as did college enrollment.

READING STRATEGY

Reading for Evidence
Unemployment affected more than just those people who lost their jobs. After individuals became unemployed, what other people or organizations were affected?

ANALYZING DOCUMENTS

Based on the graph below, what relationship was there between the unemployment rate and Hoover's defeat in the election of 1932?

Unemployment, 1929–1940 (in millions)

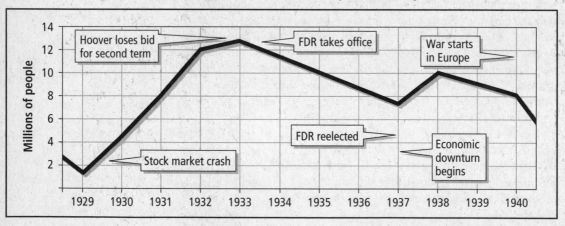

Urban Life

In many cities, families who had lost their homes lived in unheated shacks they had built of cardboard, tin, or crates. These communities became known as **Hoovervilles.** Some people slept under old newspapers called "Hoover blankets." Others slept in city parks.

People selling apples and shoelaces on the street became a common sight. Cases of malnutrition, tuberculosis, and typhoid increased, as did deaths from starvation and suicide. Parents often went hungry to give what food they had to their children.

Rural Life

With more people unable even to buy food, farmers found that their already depressed income dropped by one half. Farm foreclosure sales grew in number. The farmers' desperate situation only worsened in the 1930s with a prolonged drought in parts of Texas, Oklahoma, Kansas, Colorado, and New Mexico, a region that became known as the **Dust Bowl.** The drought, combined with poor farming methods, resulted in the loss of the topsoil, which was whipped into giant dust storms that swept across the Great Plains. Devastation in the Dust Bowl created a group of migrant farmers called "Okies" who moved to California in search of work. Their sufferings were made famous in John Steinbeck's novel *The Grapes of Wrath.*

The Culture of the Great Depression

The sufferings of people during the Great Depression changed the popular culture of the 1930s, as people sought inexpensive and escapist leisure activities.

Spectator sports, especially baseball, remained popular, but fewer people could afford to attend. Instead, they played miniature golf, softball, pinball machines, the new board game Monopoly, or they read comic books. Dick Tracy was one of the most popular comic strips of the decade.

About one third of the nation's movie theaters closed during the depression, but each week as many as 90 million people turned out to see Hollywood films. Movies of the 1930s often dealt with issues other than the grim realities of depression life. Depression-era movies included *King Kong, Gone With the Wind,* and *The Wizard of Oz,* as well as cowboy adventures, serials, musicals, comedies, and Walt Disney cartoons starring characters such as Mickey Mouse.

Radio, which was free, offered the comedy of George Burns and Gracie Allen or Jack Benny, as well as soap operas, news, sports, serials, and music. Radio was to the 1930s what television is today—an influential, unifying means of communication.

Literature, photography, and paintings of the 1930s reflected the concerns of the times. The photographs of Walker Evans and Margaret Bourke-White revealed the suffering of the people. Bourke-White's work appeared in *Life* magazine, which for decades depicted American life in pictures. Government programs provided work for artists, writers, and actors through theater and art projects. Artists painted murals on public buildings. Writers wrote histories and guide books about various regions. Actors appeared in plays funded by the Federal Theater Project. Dancers performed, and orchestras played.

GEOGRAPHY IN HISTORY

Starting in the late 1800s, farmers using steel plows cut through the thick grasses that covered the Great Plains. They grew wheat in areas too dry to grow corn. After World War I, when farm prices dropped, farmers responded by clearing more land and growing more wheat. The 1930s were a decade of drought. For seven years, winds blew the top soil, no longer protected by the grass cover, east from New Mexico, Texas, Oklahoma, Colorado, and Kansas to the Atlantic and beyond. Sixty percent lost their farms.

READING STRATEGY

Formulating Questions
Reread the section about the culture of the Great Depression, then answer the following questions.

- What forms of entertainment were most popular during the Great Depression?

- Why were these forms of entertainment so popular?

- How did the tone of popular entertainment (such as movies and radio) differ from that of art and literature?

Some novels, such as those of John Dos Passos or John Steinbeck, protested the life of the 1930s. Other works, such as those of William Faulkner, were less political. Langston Hughes continued to write about African Americans, especially the poor and working class. He also wrote a novel about life in Chicago, which succeeded Harlem in the 1930s and 1940s as the center of African American culture.

Music of the 1930s continued to be dominated by jazz created by Louis Armstrong, Duke Ellington, and other musicians. It was also the age of big swing bands, such as those of Glenn Miller and Benny Goodman. The musical became a popular form of theater, with music by greats such as George Gershwin, Irving Berlin, Cole Porter, and Jerome Kern.

FRANKLIN DELANO ROOSEVELT

"I pledge you, I pledge myself, to a new deal

for the American people."

—*Franklin Delano Roosevelt*

In 1932, Franklin Delano Roosevelt was elected the thirty-second President. He was educated at Harvard University and the School of Law at Columbia University. He served as a Democrat in the New York State legislature, as assistant secretary of the navy under Woodrow Wilson, and as governor of New York before being elected President. He served as President throughout the rest of the depression and most of World War II, until his death in 1945.

Restoring Public Confidence

Franklin Roosevelt is ranked by historians as one of the greatest Presidents in American history. He inspired support and confidence in people. He was a master politician—intelligent, energetic, self-confident, charming, and optimistic. He had been tested by polio, which had left him in a wheelchair but made him tougher, more patient, and more compassionate.

Roosevelt, popularly called FDR, was also a master communicator. He held press conferences and effectively used the radio for "fireside chats" with the American public. He involved the public emotionally in his explanations of what he was doing to solve the nation's economic problems. He was able to convince people that he had confidence in himself and in our nation as well as genuine concern for the people.

FDR was controversial. While many respected and even loved him, others saw him as taking on almost dictatorial powers for himself and for the government. His attempt to make major changes in the Supreme Court is one example of controversy in his administration.

Election of 1932

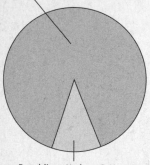

Democrat Franklin D. Roosevelt 89% of electoral vote

Republican Herbert C. Hoover 11% of electoral vote

Another is his decision to break the so-called unwritten Constitution and run for a third term in 1940. Roosevelt ran for and was elected to a fourth term in 1944. He died in office in 1945. In 1951, the Twenty-second Amendment was added to the Constitution, limiting a President to two terms in office. Some saw it as a reaction against Roosevelt.

Preparing to Lead the Nation

In the months between his election and his inauguration, Roosevelt surrounded himself with a group of formal and informal advisers. His cabinet members included Postmaster James Farley, Secretary of State Cordell Hull, and the first woman to hold a Cabinet post, Frances Perkins, as secretary of labor. FDR's informal advisers, known as the "brain trust," were a group of intellectuals and lawyers, several of whom were Columbia University professors. They favored reform and strongly influenced Roosevelt's New Deal administration. The most well-known brain trust member was social worker Harry Hopkins.

FDR's Eyes and Ears: Eleanor Roosevelt

Another major influence on Roosevelt and his New Deal was his wife, Eleanor Roosevelt. She was a humanitarian, active on behalf of women and minorities, especially African Americans. As First Lady, she became an important political figure in the nation. Through her travels, she served as the President's eyes and ears, but what he heard and saw was filtered through her progressive views and sensitivity to the plight of others. She helped to mold New Deal policy in several ways: through intervention with her husband on behalf of social reform; through her syndicated newspaper column; and through her travels and speeches around the nation. After Franklin Roosevelt's death in 1945, Eleanor Roosevelt became a leader in the issue of human rights, playing a key role in the creation of the 1948 Universal Declaration of Human Rights.

Old Reliable

Source: Berryman, Graft Collection Apr 12, 1938

ANALYZING DOCUMENTS

Note that cartoons can convey a great amount of information quickly. Examine the cartoon above. Does the cartoonist support or oppose FDR's policies?

THE NEW DEAL IN ACTION: RELIEF, RECOVERY, REFORM

Roosevelt's program to combat the problems caused by the depression was called the New Deal. The programs of the New Deal had the following goals:

- Relief for those people who were suffering
- Recovery for the economy, so it could grow again
- Reform measures to avoid future depressions

Relief Legislation of the New Deal

Congress passed a wide range of relief legislation as part of the New Deal.

READING STRATEGY

Organizing Information

Organize the information on the chart to categorize those programs that provided for:

1. Relief
2. Recovery
3. Reform

EMERGENCY BANKING ACT, 1933 Roosevelt's first act as President was to close the nation's banks by declaring a bank holiday in order to stop the collapse of the national banking system. The time was used to assure the public that it could have confidence in the banks once they reopened. The law required the examination of banks to ensure that only financially sound banks were operating.

FEDERAL EMERGENCY RELIEF ACT (FERA), 1933 Between 1933 and 1935, some $500,000 was provided for distribution by states and cities for direct relief and work projects for hungry, homeless, and unemployed people.

PUBLIC WORKS ADMINISTRATION (PWA), 1933 Operating from 1933 until 1939, the PWA provided jobs through construction projects, such as bridges, housing, hospitals, schools, and aircraft

New Deal Programs

Program	Initials	Begun	Purpose
Civilian Conservation Corps	CCC	1933	Provided jobs to young men to plant trees, build bridges and parks, and set up flood control projects
Tennessee Valley Authority	TVA	1933	Built dams to provide cheap electric power to seven southern states; set up schools and health centers
Federal Emergency Relief Administration	FERA	1933	Gave relief to unemployed and needy
Agricultural Adjustment Administration	AAA	1933	Paid farmers not to grow certain crops
National Recovery Administration	NRA	1933	Enforced codes that regulated wages, prices, and working conditions
Public Works Administration	PWA	1933	Built ports, schools, and aircraft carriers
Federal Deposit Insurance Corporation	FDIC	1933	Insured savings accounts in banks approved by government
Rural Electrification Administration	REA	1935	Loaned money to extend electricity to rural farmers
Works Progress Administration	WPA	1935	Employed men and women to build hospitals, schools, parks, and airports; employed artists, writers, and musicians
Social Security Act	SSA	1935	Set up a system of pensions for elderly, unemployed, and handicapped

carriers. The PWA also moved government money into the economy. It was hoped that this "pump priming" would create jobs, revive production, and lead to more consumer spending.

CIVILIAN CONSERVATION CORPS (CCC), 1933 Between 1933 and 1941, the CCC provided work for 2.5 million young men ages 18 to 25 conserving natural resources. Only 8,000 young women joined the CCC.

WORKS PROGRESS ADMINISTRATION (WPA), 1935 From 1935 until 1943, the WPA provided temporary jobs for 25 percent of adult Americans. The agency was created to replace direct relief with public works projects. The WPA spent more government money than any other program. While WPA workers built roads, bridges, airports, public buildings, playgrounds, and golf courses, the program also offered work to writers, artists, musicians, scholars, and actors. Critics attacked the cultural work projects in particular. Others criticized the WPA for being inequitable. With WPA employment limited to one member of a family, only women who were heads of households were eligible for WPA jobs.

TENNESSEE VALLEY AUTHORITY (TVA), 1933 The federally funded TVA provided jobs, cheap electricity, and flood control to poor rural areas of seven states through dam construction on the Tennessee River and its tributaries. The TVA was made possible through the efforts of Republican Senator George Norris of Nebraska. The TVA was praised as a bold experiment in government intervention to meet regional needs. It was attacked as "creeping socialism."

Recovery Legislation of the New Deal

Congress also passed a wide range of recovery legislation as part of the New Deal.

NATIONAL INDUSTRIAL RECOVERY ACT, 1933 The National Recovery Administration (NRA) had the authority to work with businesses to help them recover. The NRA set "codes of fair competition" within industries to maintain prices, minimum wages, and maximum hours. The public was encouraged to buy from companies that followed the NRA codes. The NRA was not popular, however. Some consumers complained that the NRA plan raised prices. Companies opposed the provisions giving unions the right to organize. Small companies felt at a disadvantage compared to larger companies. The NIRA was declared unconstitutional in 1935.

HOME OWNERS LOAN CORPORATION (HOLC), 1933 This agency was created to help homeowners save their houses from foreclosure. It provided funds to pay off mortgages and provided new long-term mortgages at lower, fixed-interest rates.

READING STRATEGY

Organizing Information
A timeline can help you understand how the New Deal progressed. Create a timeline of the most significant legislation of the New Deal. Be sure to include all three categories of New Deal legislation (relief, recovery, and reform).

The purpose of agricultural price supports is to keep the prices of farm products at a reasonable and stable level. By paying farmers to reduce the number of acres they plant, the government helps reduce the supply of farm products. When demand stays the same for the reduced supply, prices will rise.

- Does this type of a program still exist today?
- If so, in what form?

KEY THEMES AND CONCEPTS

Government

"Every qualified person shall be entitled to receive, with respect to the period beginning on the date he attains the age of sixty-five . . . an old-age benefit. . . ."
—Social Security Act, 1935

- What was the reason for the Social Security Act?
- How was it funded?
- What are current concerns and proposals regarding social security?

FEDERAL HOUSING ADMINISTRATION (FHA), 1934 The FHA was created by the National Housing Act to insure bank mortgages. These mortgages were often for 20 to 30 years and at down payments of only 10 percent.

FIRST AGRICULTURAL ADJUSTMENT ACT (AAA), 1933 The aim of the AAA was to raise farmers' income by cutting the amount of surplus crops and livestock. In that way, farmers would be able to sell their crops at the same prices of the years 1909–1914, a time when farm prices were high. The government paid farmers for reducing the number of acres they planted. The plan was financed through a processing tax on companies that made the wheat, corn, cotton, hogs, milk, and tobacco into consumer products. Large farmers, rather than small farmers and tenant farmers, benefited from the AAA. The public was outraged at the destruction of crops and animals in order to keep production down. However, farm prices did increase. Although the AAA was declared unconstitutional in 1936, the principle of farm price supports had been established. The AAA was replaced with a law that encouraged using soil conservation methods.

SECOND AGRICULTURAL ADJUSTMENT ACT (AAA), 1938 The second AAA was passed in response to a drop in farm prices in 1938. The government paid farmers to store portions of overproduced crops until the price reached the level of 1909–1914 prices. In spite of New Deal efforts, America's farmers did not regain prosperity until the 1940s, when World War II brought increased demand for food.

Reform Legislation of the New Deal

Congress also passed a wide range of reform legislation as part of the New Deal.

GLASS-STEAGALL ACT, 1933 This law created the Federal Deposit Insurance Corporation (FDIC), which guaranteed individual bank deposits up to $5,000. The law also increased the powers of the Federal Reserve Board so that it had more control over speculation on credit.

SECURITIES EXCHANGE ACT, 1934 This act created the Securities and Exchange Commission (SEC), which had the authority to regulate stock exchanges and investment advisers. SEC powers included the right to bring action against those found practicing fraud. The SEC could require financial information about stocks and bonds before they were sold.

SOCIAL SECURITY ACT, 1935 The 1935 Social Security Act was a combination of public assistance and insurance. The law had three main parts: (1) It provided old-age insurance, paid by a tax on both the employer and employee while the employee was working. The worker and employer, not the government funded this part of social security.

(2) It provided unemployment insurance for workers, paid by employers. (3) It gave assistance to dependent children and to the elderly, ill, and handicapped.

NATIONAL LABOR RELATIONS ACT (WAGNER ACT), 1935
The Wagner Act, named for its author, New York Senator Robert Wagner, guaranteed labor the right to form unions and to practice collective bargaining. It created the National Labor Relations Board (NLRB) to ensure that elections to select unions were conducted fairly.

FAIR LABOR STANDARDS ACT, 1938 This law set a minimum wage (originally 25 cents per hour) and a maximum work week (originally 44 hours) for workers in industries involved in interstate commerce. The law also banned child labor in interstate commerce. It is one of many examples of New Deal legislation passed using the power given to Congress to regulate interstate commerce.

THE NEW DEAL AND ORGANIZED LABOR

Roosevelt was interested in helping workers primarily through social legislation, such as social security. He also wanted to work cooperatively with business, as seen in the NRA legislation. When the NRA was ruled unconstitutional and with it the part that ensured labor the right to form unions, Roosevelt turned to the Wagner Act as a means of aiding labor. By 1935, he had turned away from business and saw organized labor unions as a force in society that would balance the power of big business.

This pro-labor attitude of the New Deal resulted in an increase in union membership of more than 1.5 million members between 1933 and 1935. After the Wagner Act became law in 1935, membership grew another 3 million. By 1938, it had reached 7 million organized workers. These gains took place during a split within organized labor over how to unionize workers.

The American Federation of Labor (AFL), whose craft unions of skilled workers had dominated the labor movement since 1886, was challenged for control by a new union organized by industry. These new unions organized all workers, skilled and unskilled, in a given industry, such as textiles, coal, steel, and automobiles, much like the old Knights of Labor. But unlike the Knights, the industrial unions concentrated on "bread and butter" issues of wages, hours, and working conditions. Led by John L. Lewis, head of the United Mine Workers, the new industrial unions formed the Committee for Industrial Organization (CIO) within the AFL. In 1937 the CIO became a separate union, the Congress of Industrial Organizations (CIO).

In addition to the way it organized workers, the CIO differed from the AFL because its members included women, African Americans, and immigrants from southern and eastern Europe. These groups made

ANALYZING DOCUMENTS

"Employees shall have the right of self-organization, to form, join, or assist labor organizations, to bargain collectively through representatives of their own choosing. . . ."
—National Labor Relations Act (Wagner Act) July 5, 1935

• Why can this act be called the "Magna Carta of Labor"?

**ANALYZING
DOCUMENTS**

"They picked me up about
eight different times and
threw me on my back on
the concrete. While I was
on the ground they kicked
me in the face, head, and
other parts of my body . . .
I never raised a hand."
—Walter Reuther, 1937
Ford Motor Company strike

• Did the Wagner Act re-
solve problems between
management and labor?
What is your evidence?

up a large percentage of the unskilled work force that comprised the
CIO unions. Despite their differences, the two organizations merged in
1955 to form the powerful AFL-CIO.

The 1930s were marked by a series of bitter strikes as the CIO
attempted to unionize large industries, including the steel and automobile industries. Union workers demanded that companies enter into
collective bargaining. Often police and company-paid guards used
force against strikers. The workers made effective use of the **sit down
strike,** a tactic in which they remained in the plant but refused to work
until their demands were met.

THE NEW DEAL'S EFFECTS ON MINORITIES AND WOMEN

The New Deal legislation affected Native Americans, African
Americans, Latinos, and women in a variety of ways.

Native Americans and the New Deal

In 1924, Native Americans were finally granted citizenship by
Congress. However, Native Americans continued to suffer under the
government policy of forced assimilation enacted in 1887 by the
Dawes Act. It aimed at breaking up the tribal structure of Native
American life and forcing Indians to become landowning farmers. The
Native Americans lost an additional 90 million acres of land between
1887 and 1934.

Under Roosevelt and the New Deal, government policy changed to
one of tribal restoration. The 1934 Indian Reorganization Act, also
called the Wheeler-Howard Act, was passed largely through the efforts
of Roosevelt's commissioner of Indian affairs, John Collier. The bill's
aim was restore tribal self-government as well as Native American
languages, customs, and religious freedom. Another New Deal
program provided for the education of Native American children under
the Bureau of Indian Affairs.

African Americans and the New Deal

African Americans were not a well-organized interest group in the
1930s. Therefore, they benefited less from the New Deal than did other
groups. Roosevelt was not a strong advocate of civil rights, in part
because he did not want to alienate southern Democrats in Congress,
whose votes he needed to pass New Deal legislation. He did not
support African American efforts to abolish the poll tax or to pass an
antilynching law. Lynchings, in fact, increased during the 1930s.

However, within the New Deal programs, Eleanor Roosevelt and
Harry Hopkins gave strong support to African Americans. As many as
50 African Americans were appointed to posts in various New Deal
agencies. The most influential among them was Mary McLeod
Bethune, who served in the National Youth Administration. While

African Americans protested discrimination within New Deal programs, some 40 percent of the nation's African Americans received help through a New Deal program. Many moved from the Republican party to the Democratic party during the New Deal.

Latinos and the New Deal

Many Latinos worked in agriculture and were particularly hard hit by the depression. "Okies" fleeing the Dust Bowl competed with Mexicans and Mexican Americans for migrant farm work in California. While the New Deal provided relief for these workers, the government's policy was to stop immigration and return to Mexico any unemployed noncitizens.

Women and the New Deal

Like African Americans, women were not an organized group during the 1930s. As you have read, women experienced less unemployment during this period, because they worked in low-paying jobs less affected by the depression. Single women and female heads of families made up a large portion of the female work force. Women earned about 50 cents for every dollar a man was paid, and they were often expected to give up jobs to male heads of families. The belief that the proper work for women was that of a wife and mother remained strong. Many New Deal programs simply would not hire women.

While women made little progress in the workplace, the New Deal did help women in government. Eleanor Roosevelt, Frances Perkins, and Mary McLeod Bethune were only a few of the women visibly active in the New Deal administration. More women also ran for and won political office although they were still far outnumbered by men.

The 1936 Election Mandate

In his first term, Roosevelt won the support of large numbers of Americans. Popular belief in him and in his New Deal program that seemed to offer something to everyone translated into votes. Roosevelt carefully built what is known as the New Deal coalition, a voting bloc that embraced the solid Democratic South, new immigrant workers, the big cities, African Americans who had previously voted Republican, organized labor, the elderly, and farmers who usually voted Republican.

This coalition emerged in the 1936 election, when Roosevelt was reelected to a second term. Roosevelt received a mandate, or a clear endorsement, from the electorate, carrying all but two states. This change in the two-party system was to dominate American politics over the next generation.

READING STRATEGY

Organizing Information
The New Deal affected various groups in different ways. To help you understand how different people were affected by the New Deal, create a chart showing the impact of the New Deal on:

- African Americans
- Latinos
- Women

ANALYZING DOCUMENTS

Examine the chart at right, then answer the following questions.

- What was the significance of the "First Hundred Days"?

- What is meant by the term *Second New Deal*, and what did it accomplish?

- Why did the economy weaken in 1937 and 1938?

- What ultimately caused the unemployment rate to improve?

PREPARING FOR THE EXAM

Compare the New Deal to other reform movements, such as Progressivism and the Great Society.

- Do they too appear to have stages?

Stages of the New Deal

1. **1933–early 1935:** New Deal legislation dealt with relief and recovery. Much of this legislation was passed in the "First Hundred Days" after FDR took office in March 1933. The 1934 Congressional elections increased the size of the Democratic majority in each house, which helped the New Deal legislative effort.

2. **1935 and early 1936:** Often called the "Second Hundred Days" or the "Second New Deal," this period's legislation focused more on social reform.

3. **1936 election:** This year is considered the high point of the New Deal.

4. **1937–1938:** A recession led to a new collapse in the weak economy that had just been starting to improve. The recession was due in part to New Deal cutbacks in spending after the 1936 election.

5. **1938:** By 1938 the New Deal had ended due to increased opposition in Congress and preoccupation with the danger of world war. Unemployment did not improve significantly until World War II created jobs in the production of war goods.

NEW DEAL GENERATES CONTROVERSY

Roosevelt and his New Deal mobilized the government and the nation to fight the effects of the Great Depression. His program for relief, recovery, and reform provoked controversy. Criticisms came from those who it felt that it was too radical or went too far as well as from those who felt its programs were too conservative or did not go far enough.

FDR's Policy Strategies

Roosevelt was a pragmatist. That means he did not come to office committed to a single theory or set of beliefs but rather was a man of action, interested in whatever worked to solve a problem. In short, he was an experimenter. The New Deal showed his willingness to make choices based on trial and error in order to solve problems.

FDR was influenced by Populist and Progressive philosophies of using the government to solve social and economic problems. He also used ideas of the Hoover administration and lessons learned in mobilizing the nation to fight World War I. The strategies used by the New Deal included:

- Passing relief measures that involved the federal government in the nation's economy to a greater degree than ever before. This direct governmental action was justified by using the commerce and elastic clauses of the Constitution.

- Taking fiscal action to stimulate the economy and lower unemployment by lowering taxes and increasing government spending.

- Assuming responsibility for the general welfare by protecting people against risks that they could not handle on their own.

- Increasing the regulatory role of the federal government over banks, businesses, and the stock exchange.
- Adopting deficit spending as an economic means of reviving the economy. This policy was based on the theories of economist John Maynard Keynes, who argued that the government must spend huge amounts of money to encourage production levels and purchasing power to increase. This policy, Keynes argued, would result in economic recovery.

Federal Income and Spending, 1928–1940

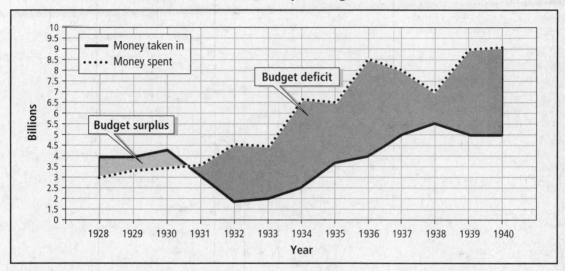

Supreme Court Reaction

Throughout the New Deal, the Supreme Court majority practiced judicial restraint, narrowly interpreting the interstate commerce clause and striking down many of FDR's programs, which were based on a broad interpretation of that part of the Constitution. In a series of decisions, the Court ruled that several key New Deal laws were unconstitutional.

SUPREME COURT AND THE NRA The National Recovery Act (NRA) was declared unconstitutional in *Schechter Poultry Corporation v. United States* (1935). The Court ruled that the law illegally gave Congress power to regulate intrastate commerce (or commerce within a single state) and violated the separation of powers by giving the legislative powers to the executive branch.

SUPREME COURT AND THE AAA In *United States* v. *Butler* (1936), the Supreme Court struck down the Agricultural Adjustment Act (AAA) on the grounds that agriculture was a local, not an interstate, matter under the provisions of the Tenth Amendment.

ANALYZING DOCUMENTS

Use the chart above and your knowledge of social studies to answer the following questions.

- What is the definition of a *budget deficit?*
- In what year was the budget deficit the largest?
- What caused this increase in the budget deficit?

Review the New Deal programs to determine on what these funds were spent.

FDR's Court-Packing Plan

Supreme Court opposition to FDR's programs continued with the Court consistently vetoing New Deal legislation. Franklin Roosevelt asked Congress to approve a law that would permit the President to increase the number of judges from nine to fifteen if the judges refused to retire at the age of 70.

The Judicial Reorganization Bill—or the "court-packing" plan, as its opponents called it—was intended to make the Supreme Court approve the New Deal laws. It never became law because it was a threat to the separation of powers.

THE INGENIOUS QUARTERBACK!

Political Opposition

In his first two terms, Roosevelt's strongest opposition was from big business. In 1934, a group of conservative Democratic and Republican business owners and politicians, including former presidential candidate Al Smith, formed the American Liberty League. It claimed that Roosevelt was exercising too much power as President. It attacked the New Deal because its programs were being financed through deficit spending. The group expressed fear that the American free enterprise system was being destroyed.

Radical groups such as the Communist party also offered alternatives to the New Deal but failed to gain any major public support. At its peak in 1938, the Communist party of the United States of America had only 55,000 members, and its 1936 presidential candidate won only 80,000 votes. Meanwhile, the pro-Nazi German-American Bund became active, as did the **Black Shirts,** fascists who supported the views of Italian dictator Benito Mussolini.

The Socialist party in America drew some rising support, although some members began to vote for Roosevelt. The party was led by Eugene Debs and by Norman Thomas, the party's presidential candidate. Unlike the Communist party, the Socialists believed in the use of democratic means to make changes in the American economic structure.

As frustration grew in the face of the prolonged depression, various individuals entered the political scene, each criticizing the New Deal and offering often simplistic solutions to the economic crisis. These men were called "homegrown demagogues" because their philosophies did not come from a foreign nation and because they appealed to people's emotions and prejudice. These demagogues included:

- Francis E. Townsend, who created a financially impossible plan to provide government pensions for the elderly.
- Father Charles E. Coughlin, a Catholic priest who blamed business owners, especially Jewish ones, for the economic crisis.
- Huey Long, a powerful United States senator from Louisiana, who proposed that income and inheritance taxes on the wealthy be used to give each American a $2,500 income, a car, and a college education. Long was assassinated in 1935.

ANALYZING DOCUMENTS

Using the table below and the text, answer the following questions.

- Who are some specific people who voiced the criticisms shown in the graphic summary?
- What evidence is there to support each of these positions?

Critics of the New Deal

Women and African Americans	Progressives and Socialists	Republicans and other political opponents
New Deal programs offer more opportunities to white men than to women and minorities. Women and African Americans are paid less for the same work.	New Deal programs are not doing enough to solve the nation's problems. More should be done to distribute the nation's wealth among all Americans.	Government is taking on too much responsibility and becoming too powerful. FDR is like a dictator. New Deal taxes on the wealthy are unfair. New Deal programs are too much like socialism.

While FDR remained popular, his programs drew criticism from a wide variety of opponents.

EVALUATING THE NEW DEAL

Most historians agree on the following assessment of the New Deal:

- World War II was largely responsible for ending the Great Depression. The New Deal did not solve unemployment, the farm crisis, or underconsumption.
- Nevertheless, the New Deal did help people cope with the effects of the Great Depression.
- The New Deal brought more power to the presidency and to the federal government. The government now had a role and a responsibility in more aspects of the nation's economic and social life.
- The New Deal preserved the free-enterprise system.

ANALYZING DOCUMENTS

"Roosevelt is the only President we ever had that thought the Constitution belonged to the poor man too."

—George Dobbin, mill worker, 1939

- How would a worker such as George Dobbin evaluate the New Deal?

Questions for Regents Practice

For online Questions for Regents Practice,
visit the Prentice Hall Web site at www.phschool.com.

MULTIPLE CHOICE

Directions

Review the Test-Taking Strategies section of this book. Then answer the following questions, drawn from actual Regents examinations. Each question is followed by four choices. Read each question carefully. Decide which choice is the correct answer. Then on a separate piece of paper, mark your answer for each question.

1 Which was a major problem faced by United States farmers in both the 1890s and 1920s?
   1 lagging technology
   2 lack of tariff protection
   3 overproduction of basic staples
   4 inflationary currency

2 In which respect were the decades of the 1920s and the 1960s in the United States most similar?
   1 organized militancy by ethnic minorities
   2 public concern with pollution of the environment
   3 widespread government activity dealing with social issues
   4 significant changes in manners and morals

3 What was the one similarity between the Red Scare following World War I and the Cold War following World War II?
   1 Fear of communism led to the suppression of the civil liberties of some Americans.
   2 Large numbers of Russian revolutionaries settled in the United States.
   3 Congressional investigations proved that the federal government was heavily infiltrated by Communist spies.
   4 Renewed fighting between wartime enemies was a constant threat.

4 Which is most commonly associated with the presidencies of Ulysses S. Grant and Warren G. Harding?
   1 depression in business
   2 corruption of public officials
   3 humanitarian reforms
   4 territorial expansion

5 In the United States, the widespread disregard of the fugitive slave laws and of Prohibition laws most clearly indicated that
   1 strongly held values are difficult to regulate
   2 the federal government is generally unable to enforce its own laws
   3 little respect is given to the legal system
   4 the judicial system is too lenient in its treatment of offenders

6 A major reason for the isolationist trend in the United States following World War I was
   1 a desire to continue the reforms of the Progressives
   2 the public's desire to end most trade with other nations
   3 the failure of the United States to gain new territory
   4 a disillusionment over the failure to achieve United States goals in the post-war world

7 The "boom" years of the 1920s were characterized by
1 decreases in both agricultural surpluses and farm foreclosures
2 limited investment capital and declining numbers of workers in the labor force
3 widespread use of the automobile and an increase in buying
4 increased regulation of the marketplace by both federal and state governments

8 The racial segregation and poverty experienced by African Americans in the South during the 1920s led them to
1 move to the North in great numbers to find factory jobs
2 join with whites in strong national movements to protest unjust laws
3 evolve their own strong labor movement
4 support federal programs that gave them their own farmland

9 The Harlem Renaissance of the 1920s was a period when African Americans
1 left the United States in large numbers to settle in Nigeria
2 created noteworthy works of art and literature
3 migrated to the West in search of land and jobs
4 used civil disobedience to fight segregation in the armed forces

10 In the 1920s, the Sacco and Vanzetti case, the Red Scare, and the activities of the Ku Klux Klan all represented
1 threats to civil liberties
2 victories over discrimination and persecution
3 support for the Prohibition movement
4 greater social freedom for Americans

11 The conviction of John Scopes in 1925 for teaching about evolution supported the ideas of those Americans who
1 believed in religious freedom and the separation of church and state
2 hoped to lessen the differences between rural and urban lifestyles
3 wanted to promote traditional fundamentalist values
4 favored the changes resulting from the new technology of the 1920s

12 One important cause of the Great Depression in the United States was that by the end of the 1920s
1 the government controlled almost every aspect of the economy
2 tariffs were so low that foreign products had forced many United States companies out of business
3 investors were too cautious and put their money only into government bonds
4 factories and farms were able to produce far more than buyers could afford to purchase

13 President Herbert Hoover's refusal to provide funds for the unemployed during the Depression was based on his belief that
1 the unemployment problem was not serious
2 workers would not accept government assistance
3 labor unions should provide for the unemployed
4 federal relief programs would destroy individual initiative

14 Which is a valid conclusion based on a study of the presidencies of Thomas Jefferson and Franklin D. Roosevelt?
1 Strong third parties develop when the two major parties ignore popular demands.
2 Presidential success depends mainly on a sympathetic Supreme Court.
3 Economic crisis can force a President to suspend basic civil liberties.
4 A President's political program may change in the face of current needs.

15 The rapid, worldwide spread of the Great Depression of the 1930s was evidence of
1 the failure of government job programs
2 global financial interdependence
3 a shortage of American factories making consumer goods
4 the negative effects of unrestricted immigration

16 Which New Deal reforms most directly targeted the basic problem of the victims of the Dust Bowl?
1 guaranteeing workers the right to organize and bargain collectively
2 regulating the sale of stocks and bonds
3 providing farmers low-cost loans and parity payments
4 raising individual and corporate income tax rates

17 Deficit spending by the federal government as a means of reviving the economy is based on the idea that
1 purchasing power will increase and economic growth will be stimulated
2 only the national government can operate businesses efficiently
3 the national government should turn its revenue over to the states
4 lower interest rates will encourage investment

18 The main purpose of the New Deal measures such as the Securities and Exchange Commission (SEC) and the Federal Deposit Insurance Corporation (FDIC) was to
1 provide immediate employment opportunities
2 develop rules to limit speculation and safeguard savings
3 enable the federal government to take over failing industries
4 assure a guaranteed income for American families

19 During President Franklin D. Roosevelt's administration, which situation was viewed by critics as a threat to the principle of separation of powers?
1 changing the date of the Presidential inauguration
2 congressional support of banking legislation
3 proposing the expansion of Supreme Court membership
4 passage of Social Security legislation

20 "Section 202. (a) Every qualified individual shall be entitled to receive . . . on the date he attains the age of sixty-five . . . and ending on the date of his death, an old-age benefit. . . ."

A major purpose of this section of federal legislation was to
1 guarantee an annual income to experienced employees
2 assure adequate medical care for the elderly
3 reward workers for their support of the union movement
4 provide economic assistance to retired workers

21 The popularity of escapist novels and movies during the Great Depression is evidence that
1 the Great Depression was not really a time of economic distress
2 popular culture is shaped by economic and social conditions
3 American society did not try to solve the problems of the Great Depression
4 the greatest employment opportunities for the average person in the 1930s were in the field of entertainment

22 A major effect of the National Labor Relations Act (Wagner Act, 1935) was that labor unions
1 were soon controlled by large corporations
2 experienced increasing difficulty in gaining new members
3 obtained the right to bargain collectively
4 lost the right to strike

23 The effectiveness of the New Deal in ending the Great Depression is difficult to measure because
1 President Franklin D. Roosevelt died during his fourth term
2 United States involvement in World War II rapidly accelerated economic growth
3 the Supreme Court declared most New Deal laws unconstitutional
4 later Presidents failed to support most New Deal reforms

24 Many opponents of New Deal programs claimed that these programs violated the American tradition of
1 welfare capitalism
2 governmental regulation of business
3 collective bargaining
4 individual responsibility

25 A lasting result of the New Deal in the United States has been the
1 reduction of the national debt
2 control of stock prices by the federal government
3 joint effort of business and labor to strengthen the Presidency
4 assumption by the federal government of greater responsibility for the nation's well-being

26 The process of collective bargaining is best described as
1 meetings of joint congressional committees to achieve compromise on different versions of a proposed law
2 diplomatic strategies used to make treaties between two nations
3 discussions between labor union leaders and management to agree on a contract for workers
4 negotiations between a multinational company and a nation with which the company wishes to do business

27 Which generalization most accurately describes the literary work of Langston Hughes, Sinclair Lewis, and John Steinbeck?
1 Politics and art seldom mix well.
2 The best literature concerns the lives of the wealthy.
3 Literature often reflects the times in which it is created.
4 Traditional American themes are the most popular.

28 An immediate result of the Supreme Court decision in *Schechter Poultry* v. *United States* was that
1 some aspects of the New Deal were declared unconstitutional
2 state governments took over relief agencies
3 Congress was forced to abandon efforts to improve the economy
4 the constitutional authority of the President was greatly expanded

THEMATIC ESSAY

In developing your answers to the essay, be sure to keep these general definitions in mind:

(a) <u>discuss</u> means "to make observations about something using facts, reasoning, and argument; to present in some detail"

(b) <u>describe</u> means "to illustrate something in words or to tell about it"

(c) <u>evaluate</u> means "to examine and judge the significance, worth, or condition of; to determine the value of"

Directions

Write a well-organized essay that includes an introduction, several paragraphs addressing the task below, and a conclusion.

Theme: Reform Movements

Throughout United States history, there have been times when movements or programs have developed in response to demands for political, economic, or social reform.

Task

From your study of United States history, identify two movements or programs which developed in response to demands for reform.

   For each movement or program identified:

• State one problem that led to the movement or program.

• Describe a specific reform advocated by the movement or program to deal with the problem.

• Describe the tactics or means used by supporters of the movement or program to achieve the specific reform.

• Discuss the extent to which the movement or program reform was successful in achieving the specific reform.

Suggestions

You may use any major reform movement or program from your study of United States history. Some suggestions you might wish to consider include: abolitionist movement (1830–1865); temperance movement (1830–1933); women's movement (1848–1920); Progressivism (1900–1920); New Deal (1933–1945); Great Society (1960s); American Indian movement (1960–present).

You are *not* limited to these suggestions.

Guidelines

In your essay be sure to:

• Address all aspects of the *Task*

• Analyze, evaluate, or compare and/or contrast issues and events whenever possible

• Fully support the theme of the essay with relevant facts, examples, and details

• Write a well-developed essay that consistently demonstrates a logical and clear plan of organization

• Introduce the theme by establishing a framework that is beyond a simple restatement of the *Task*

• Conclude your essay with a strong summation of the theme

DOCUMENT-BASED ESSAY

For online Document-Based Essays,
visit the Prentice Hall Web site at www.phschool.com.

This task is designed to test your ability to work with historical documents and is based on the accompanying documents (1–5). Some of the documents have been edited for the purposes of this question. As you analyze the documents, take into account both the source of each document and any point of view that may be presented in the document.

Directions

This document-based question consists of two parts: Part A and Part B. In Part A, you are to read each document and answer the question or questions that follow the document. In Part B, you are to write an essay based on the information in the documents and your knowledge of United States history.

Historical Context:

The federal government responded quite differently to the prosperity of the 1920s and the Great Depression that followed. Roosevelt's New Deal was not only a decisive plan to combat the Depression, but it also marked a new direction in the role of government in managing the economy—a role that is still being debated today.

Task:

Using information from the documents and your knowledge of United States history and government, answer the questions that follow each document in Part A. Your answers to the questions will help you write the Part B essay in which you be asked to:

   Discuss the response of the United States government to the Great Depression. In your essay, include a discussion of how this response can be considered a turning point in the role of the federal government in managing the economy.

PART A: SHORT ANSWER

DOCUMENT #1

> " . . . *we must have tax reform. The method of raising tax revenue ought not to impede the transaction of business; it ought to encourage it. I am opposed to extremely high taxes, . . . because they are bad for the country, and because they are wrong. We cannot finance the country through any system of injustice, even if we attempt to inflict it on the rich. . . . The wise and judicious course to follow in taxation and economic legislation is not to destroy those already who have secured success, but to create conditions under which everyone will have a better chance to be successful.*
>
> —**Calvin Coolidge,** *Inaugural Address,* **March 4, 1925**

1 According to this quote, how did Calvin Coolidge feel about the role of government in managing business?

_____

_____

DOCUMENT #2
Economic Impact of the Great Depression

Source: *Historical Statistics of the United States, Colonial Times to 1970*

2 Based on the chart above, what effect did the stock market crash of 1929 have on the overall economy of the United States?

_____

_____

_____

DOCUMENT #3

> "*I have recounted to you in other speeches, and it is a matter of general information, that for at least two years after the crash, the only efforts by the [Hoover] administration to cope with the distress of unemployment were to deny its existence.*"
>
> **—Franklin D. Roosevelt, 1932**

3 Based on this quote that Roosevelt made during the 1932 presidential campaign, how did Roosevelt evaluate the efforts made by the Hoover administration to resolve the nation's economic problems?

_____

_____

_____

DOCUMENT #4

> "*So, first of all, let me assert my firm belief that the only thing we have to fear is fear itself-nameless, unreasoning, unjustified terror which paralyzes needed efforts to convert retreat into advance. In every dark hour of our national life a leadership of frankness and vigor has met with that understanding and support of the people themselves which is essential to victory. I am convinced that you will again give that support to leadership in these critical days.*
>
> *In such a spirit on my part and on yours we face our common difficulties. They concern, thank God, only material things. Values have shrunken to fantastic levels; taxes have risen; our ability to pay has fallen; government of all kinds is faced by serious curtailment of income; the means of exchange are frozen in the currents of trade; the withered leaves of industrial enterprise lie on every side; farmers find no markets for their produce; the savings of many years in thousands of families are gone.*
>
> *More important, a host of unemployed citizens face the grim problem of existence, and an equally great number toil with little return. Only a foolish optimist can deny the dark realities of the moment.*"
>
> **—Franklin D. Roosevelt, *First Inaugural Address*, March 4, 1933**

4 In this excerpt from FDR's first inaugural speech, how did he attempt to win the support of the American people for his leadership during the economic crisis of the Great Depression?

_____

_____

_____

DOCUMENT #5

5 According to the above cartoon, how did some Americans view the New Deal?

_____

_____

_____

PART B: ESSAY

Directions: Using information from the documents provided, and your knowledge of United States history, write a well-organized essay that includes an introduction, several paragraphs, and a conclusion.

Historical Context

The federal government responded quite differently to the prosperity of the 1920s and the Great Depression that followed. Roosevelt's New Deal was not only a decisive plan to combat the Depression, but it also marked a new direction in the role of government in managing the economy-a role that is still being debated today.

Task

Using information from the documents and your knowledge of United States history and government, write an essay in which you

Discuss the response of the United States government to the Great Depression. In your essay, include a discussion of how this response can be considered a turning point in the role of the federal government in managing the economy.

Guidelines

When writing your essay, be sure to

- Address all aspects of the *Task* by accurately analyzing and interpreting at least four documents
- Incorporate information from the documents in the body of the essay
- Incorporate relevant outside information throughout the essay
- Richly support the theme with relevant facts, examples, and details
- Write a well-developed essay that consistently demonstrates a logical and clean plan of organization
- Introduce the theme by establishing a framework that is beyond a simple restatement of the *Task* or *Historical Context* and conclude the essay with a summation of the theme.

UNIT OVERVIEW

This unit covers the time period from 1933 to 1960, a period that included the Great Depression, World War II, and the Cold War. This unit focuses on American foreign policy and how it affected life in the United States during those years.

Some of the key questions about the United States history during this period include:

- What caused the United States to change its foreign policy from isolationism and neutrality to a growing commitment to global involvement?

- Why did the world go to war from 1939 until 1945? How and when did the United States become involved in the conflict? How did the Allies strategize to end the war? How did World War II affect the lives of Americans on the home front?

- Why did the United States and the Soviet Union change from being allies in World War II to enemies during the Cold War?

- How did the United States try to stop the spread of communism in Europe and Asia? How did the desire to halt the spread of communism lead the United States into war in Korea? What effects did the fear of communism have within the United States?

SECTION 1 Peace in Peril, 1933–1950

SECTION OVERVIEW

In the 1930s, great changes were happening in Europe and Asia. Totalitarian regimes rose to power in Germany, Italy, and Japan, threatening the freedom of nations on their borders. In 1939, the German invasion of Poland launched World War II, which quickly engulfed Europe and much of Asia. The United States, still embracing isolationism, tried to maintain neutrality, but the 1941 Japanese bombing of Pearl Harbor drew the nation into the conflict. Four more years of bloody fighting in Europe and Asia left millions of soldiers and civilians dead and hundreds of cities damaged or destroyed. The United States suffered relatively light losses in comparison to other nations, and it emerged as a world leader with a growing commitment to international involvement.

KEY THEMES AND CONCEPTS

As you review this section, take special note of the following key themes and concepts:

Presidential Decisions and Actions How did Presidents Roosevelt and Truman influence the events and outcomes of World War II?

Foreign Policy How did world events change American foreign policy from one of isolationism to a growing commitment to global involvement?

Diversity How did World War II change the lives of women, African Americans, and Japanese Americans?

KEY PEOPLE

Adolf Hitler	Franklin D. Roosevelt	Robert Oppenheimer
Benito Mussolini	Winston Churchill	Harry S Truman
Francisco Franco	Joseph Stalin	

⭐ **THE BIG IDEA**
The United States fought on the side of the Allies in World War II. The United States

- entered the war in 1941 when the Japanese bombed Pearl Harbor in Hawaii.
- fought in Europe and defeated the Germans.
- fought in Asia and defeated the Japanese.
- emerged from the war as a world leader.

🔑 **KEY TERMS**
totalitarian
fascism
appeasement
Lend-Lease Act
Allies
Axis Powers
Manhattan Project
Holocaust
Rosie the Riveter
Nisei
WRA camps

In the 1920s and 1930s, the United States pursued a policy of neutrality and isolationism. In order to understand the reasons for this policy, we must examine the lingering impact of World War I.

GEOGRAPHY IN HISTORY

How did the United States' location relative to Europe and Asia contribute to isolationist sentiment before and after World War I?

ISOLATIONIST SENTIMENT AFTER WORLD WAR I

The United States had been reluctant to enter World War I. Fighting had begun in Europe in 1914, and the United States stayed out of the war until 1917. Between April 1917, when the United States formally declared war, and Germany's surrender in November 1918, some 48,000 American soldiers were killed in battle, 2,900 were declared missing in action, and 56,000 soldiers died of disease. These losses were far less than those of the European nations, some of which had lost millions of soldiers and civilians. Nevertheless, the American losses were great enough to cause Americans to take a close look at the reasons for the entry of the United States into the war and at the nation's foreign policy.

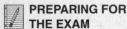 **PREPARING FOR THE EXAM**

Many questions on the exam will require you to distinguish between similar concepts and terms.

• What is the difference between isolationism and neutrality?

Isolation and Neutrality

Isolationism and neutrality are similar foreign policies, but an important difference exists between them. Isolationism is a national foreign policy of remaining apart from political or economic entanglements with other countries. Strict isolationists do not support any type of contact with other countries, including economic ties or trade activities.

When a country chooses a policy of neutrality, it deliberately takes no side in a dispute or controversy. Countries following this path are often referred to as being nonaligned or noninvolved. Neutral nations do not limit their trading activities with other nations, unless a trading partnership would limit that country's ability to stay politically noninvolved.

Events Preceding American Involvement in World War II

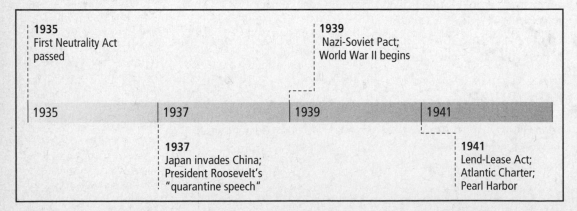

1935	1937	1939	1941
1935 First Neutrality Act passed		**1939** Nazi-Soviet Pact; World War II begins	
	1937 Japan invades China; President Roosevelt's "quarantine speech"		**1941** Lend-Lease Act; Atlantic Charter; Pearl Harbor

Historical Roots of Isolationism and Neutrality

The roots of isolationist and neutralistic sentiments in the United States can be traced to the late eighteenth and early nineteenth centuries.

PRECEDENTS SET BY GEORGE WASHINGTON In his years as President, George Washington set the important precedent of an American foreign policy of neutrality—but not isolationism. He knew that trade was necessary for the new nation to prosper, but that foreign alliances might force it into war.

In 1793, Washington issued his Proclamation of Neutrality, making it clear that the United States would not respond to requests for aid during the French Revolution. In his farewell address of 1796, Washington warned the United States to steer clear of "entangling alliances," or political commitments to other nations, although he supported economic ties to foreign countries. These basic ideas guided American foreign policy into the twentieth century.

MONROE DOCTRINE The policy that became known as the Monroe Doctrine reinforced the neutral position of the United States toward Europe. In 1823, President Monroe proclaimed that the United States would not interfere in European affairs. He also warned European powers to remain out of the affairs of nations in the Western Hemisphere. This doctrine formed the backbone of American foreign policy for many years.

Isolationism in the 1930s

In 1934, when the United States was trying to recover from the worst economic depression in its history, Senator Gerald Nye led an investigation into the reasons the United States entered World War I. The committee concluded that the United States had gone to war at the encouragement of financiers and armament makers, eager for profits. As a result of this investigation, many Americans supported a return to isolationism. They believed that the country would be secure without worrying about the actions of the rest of the world.

The refusal of the United States to join the League of Nations was reinforced by the Senate's move in 1935 to forbid the United States to join the World Court. That same year, Congress also passed the first of a series of neutrality acts, intended to prevent Americans from making loans to nations at war. Any sales of goods to such nations were to be strictly on a "cash and carry" basis. In 1937, President Roosevelt made his famous quarantine speech, in which he likened the spreading world lawlessness to a disease. He stated that the United States would attempt to quarantine the "patients" in order to protect the rest of the community of nations.

READING STRATEGY

Reinforcing Main Ideas
How did the Monroe Doctrine contribute to isolationist and neutralist sentiments in the United States prior to World War II?

KEY THEMES AND CONCEPTS

Foreign Policy
The Neutrality Acts passed in 1935, 1936, and 1937 declared that the United States would withhold weapons and loans of money from all nations at war and that U.S. citizens who traveled on ships belonging to nations at war did so at their own risk. The acts also required that non-military goods sold to nations at war be paid for in cash and transported by the purchaser.

• What events in the nation's history caused the government to be wary of Americans' involvement in ocean trade and travel?

EVENTS LEADING TO WORLD WAR II

The rise of totalitarian governments in Germany and Italy in the 1930s set the stage for World War II.

The Rise of Totalitarian Governments

In **totalitarian** governments, one political party has complete control over the government and bans all other parties. Totalitarian governments rely on terror to suppress individual rights and silence opposition. In other words, totalitarian governments are the opposite of all that the United States considers its tradition of political freedom and liberty.

In Germany and Italy, totalitarian governments were established based on the philosophy of **fascism.** Fascism places the importance of the nation above all else, and individual rights and freedoms are lost as everyone works for the benefit of the nation. Nazi Germany (led by Adolf Hitler) and Fascist Italy (led by Benito Mussolini) were two fascist governments characterized by extreme nationalism, racism, and militarism (desire to go to war).

Hitler and Mussolini provided military assistance to Francisco Franco, a Fascist leader in Spain who was attempting to overthrow the republican government there and establish a totalitarian one. The devastating Spanish civil war that erupted in 1936 would become a "dress rehearsal" for World War II. The war in Spain was a testing ground for new weapons and military strategies that would later be used in World War II.

In the United States, opinions about support for the Spanish civil war were divided. Some Americans traveled to Spain to fight for the republican cause. The United States government, however, continued to pursue a policy of neutrality. Congress passed a resolution forbidding the export of arms to either side in 1937. Franco won the Spanish civil war in 1939, established a fascist government, and remained leader of Spain until his death in 1975.

Major World Events, 1919–1941

The chart on the next page summarizes the major events between the end of World War I and the entry of the United States into World War II. During this time, peace failed, and aggressors achieved their goals, even though their success did not last long. As you review the chart, look for relationships between events in order to understand how certain events caused others that occurred later.

Some events in the chart on the next page are so significant that they require further discussion.

1938 MUNICH AGREEMENT With this agreement, Great Britain and France allowed Germany to annex the Sudetenland, a region of Czechoslovakia with a large German-speaking population. Hitler convinced the British prime minister Neville Chamberlain and the French premier Édouard Daladier that Germany would make no further terri-

PREPARING FOR THE EXAM

One way to remember the meaning of the term *totalitarianism* is from the word *total*: totalitarian governments have total control over every aspect of life. They suppress all individual rights and silence all opposition with threats. Fascism places the importance of the nation above individual rights.

- What is the relationship between totalitarianism and fascism?

ANALYZING DOCUMENTS

Examine the chart on the next page, then answer these questions.

- How might dissatisfaction with the outcome of World War I and economic depression have contributed to the rise of dictators in Italy and Germany?

- Which events described in the chart represent actions of appeasement on the part of France and Britain?

Major World Events, 1918–1941

• **1918** Germany surrenders. World War I is concluded.	• **1935** Italy invades Ethiopia. The United States passes the first Neutrality Act.
• **1919** Germany signs the Treaty of Versailles. The United States refuses to approve the Treaty of Versailles.	• **1936** Hitler reoccupies the Rhineland. The German/Italian Axis is formed. The Spanish Civil War begins (ending in 1939). The United States passes the second Neutrality Act. The United States votes for nonintervention at the Pan-American Conference.
• **1921** Great Britain, France, and Japan attend the Washington Naval Conference on limiting arms. The conference produces the Four Power and Nine Power treaties.	
	• **1937** Japan invades China. Japan sinks an American gunboat in Chinese waters. The United States passes the third Neutrality Act, including a "cash and carry" plan.
• **1922** Benito Mussolini becomes Italy's Fascist dictator. The USSR is officially formed, following the Communist victory in the Russian Revolution.	
	• **1938** Germany annexes Austria (the *Anschluss*). Hitler demands the Sudetenland of Czechoslovakia. Great Britain, France, and Germany sign the Munich Pact, giving in to Hitler's demands.
• **1923** Adolf Hitler writes *Mein Kampf* in prison.	
• **1924** In the USSR, Lenin dies. Stalin continues his rise to power.	• **1939** A German/Soviet nonaggression pact is signed. Japanese and American relations are deadlocked. The United States Senate refuses to grant aid to Great Britain or France. Hitler invades Poland, marking the beginning of World War II.
• **1928** The Kellogg-Briand Pact outlawing war is signed by 62 nations. The pact contains no method of enforcement.	
• **1929** The most serious economic depression in history begins, continuing through the 1930s.	• **1940** Germany occupies Norway, Denmark, the Netherlands, Belgium, Luxembourg, and France. Germany attacks Great Britain. Japan joins the Axis powers. President Roosevelt arranges to supply destroyers to Great Britain. Congress passes the Selective Training and Service Act, the first peacetime draft in United States history.
• **1930** Japan occupies Manchuria.	
• **1932** Japan seizes Shanghai. The United States issues the Stimson Doctrine, condemning Japanese aggression against Manchuria.	
• **1933** Hitler assumes power in Germany. Japan announces its withdrawal from the League of Nations. President Roosevelt announces the Good Neighbor Policy in Latin America. The USSR is formally recognized by the United States. Nazi Germany begins operation of the first concentration camp at Dachau, near Munich.	• **1941** Germany invades the USSR. The United States passes the Lend-Lease Act, granting aid to countries whose defense was seen as critical to the defense of the United States. President Roosevelt and Prime Minister Churchill agree to the Atlantic Charter. Japan attacks the United States at Pearl Harbor. The United States enters World War II.

torial demands in Czechoslovakia after annexing the Sudetenland. When Chamberlain returned to Britain with this agreement, he told the world that he had achieved "peace for our time." Six months later, however, Hitler seized the rest of Czechoslovakia.

Great Britain and France had resorted to the policy of **appeasement,** which means to agree to the demands of a potential enemy in

KEY THEMES AND CONCEPTS

Foreign Policy
President Roosevelt explained the Lend-Lease policy to the American people though the use of a simple comparison:

If your neighbor's house is on fire, you don't sell him a hose. You lend it to him and take it back after the fire is out.

- How did the Lend-Lease policy lead to greater U.S. involvement in the war?

KEY THEMES AND CONCEPTS

Science and Technology
How did advances in aviation technology contribute to changes in American isolationist sentiments?

READING STRATEGY

Organizing Information
Who were the three major Allied powers?

1.

2.

3.

Who were the three major Axis powers?

1.

2.

3.

order to keep the peace. Hitler demonstrated by his action that he could not be permanently appeased, and the world learned a costly lesson.

LEND-LEASE ACT Although the United States was officially committed to a policy of neutrality, President Roosevelt soon found a way around the Neutrality Acts to provide aid, including warships in the Destroyer Deal, to Great Britain. In 1941, Roosevelt convinced Congress to pass the **Lend-Lease Act,** which allowed the United States to sell or lend war materials to "any country whose defense the President deems vital to the defense of the United States." Roosevelt intended to keep the United States out of the war, but he said that the nation would become the "arsenal of democracy," supplying arms to those who were fighting for freedom.

JAPAN'S ATTACK ON PEARL HARBOR The United States did not enter World War II until 1941. President Franklin D. Roosevelt had promised that the United States would not fight in a war in which the country was not directly involved. However, on December 7, 1941, Japanese war planes attacked the U.S. Navy fleet at Pearl Harbor, Hawaii. Roosevelt called the attack a day that would "live in infamy," a day that Americans would never forget. This surprise attack shattered the American belief that the Atlantic and Pacific Oceans would safely isolate the United States from fighting in Europe and Asia. The attack on Pearl Harbor fueled American nationalism and patriotism. Suddenly the war was no longer oceans away. The day after the attack, Congress agreed to President Roosevelt's request to declare war on Japan.

WORLD WAR II IN REVIEW

World War II began in 1939, when German forces invaded Poland. The United States entered the war two years later, after the Japanese attacked Pearl Harbor. War in Europe ended in May 1945, and fighting in the Pacific ended on August 14, 1945, when the Japanese surrender brought World War II to a conclusion.

Major Powers

The war pitted 26 nations united together as the **Allies** against eight **Axis Powers.** The major powers among the Allies were Great Britain, the Soviet Union, and the United States. Germany, Italy, and Japan were the major Axis nations. Leaders of the major powers are listed on the next page.

Major Events

World War II was fought primarily in two major regions: Europe and North Africa, and in the Pacific. Major military engagements and turning points in World War II are presented on the next page.

Europe During World War II

Legend:
- Axis powers
- Areas under Axis control, 1941
- Allies and areas under Allied control, 1941
- Neutral nations

Leaders During World War II

Allies	
• Great Britain	Winston Churchill, Prime Minister
• USSR	Joseph Stalin, Communist dictator
• United States	Franklin D. Roosevelt, President until his death in April 1945
	Harry S Truman, President following Roosevelt's death
	Dwight D. Eisenhower, Supreme Commander of Allied troops in Europe
	Douglas MacArthur, Commander of the Allied troops in the Pacific
• France	Charles de Gaulle, leader of the Free French during the Nazi occupation

Axis Powers	
• Germany	Adolf Hitler, leader of the National Socialist German Workers' Party (Nazis), known as "Der Führer" ("The Leader")
• Italy	Benito Mussolini, Fascist dictator known as "Il Duce" ("The Leader")
• Japan	Emperor Hirohito
	Tojo Hideki, General and Prime Minister

Major Events of World War II

- **1939** Germany invades Poland with a rapid attack by armored vehicles supported by airplanes that is called **blitzkrieg**, or "lightning war."

- **1940** Denmark, Norway, Belgium, the Netherlands, and much of northern France fall to Nazi invasion. Battle of Britain—months of terrifying air raids by Germany against Britain known as the **blitz**.

- **1941** Germany invades the Soviet Union. The siege of Leningrad begins and lasts 17 months. Japan attacks Pearl Harbor, Hawaii. The United States enters the war.

- **1941–1942** Japan seizes the Philippines, Burma, Singapore, the Dutch East Indies, and French Indochina. Japan continues to press southward toward Australia.

- **1942** Battle of Midway in the Pacific. The United States regains naval superiority in the Pacific.

- **1942–1943** Battle of Stalingrad. German troops are forced to surrender after thousands have been killed. This battle marks a turning point in the East and allows Russian soldiers to begin to move west.

- **1943** In North Africa, Allied troops defeat Axis armies for control of the Mediterranean Sea and the Suez Canal.

- **June 6, 1944** Allied invasions of Normandy, France, across the English Channel. This was the largest such invasion in history, involving over 150,000 soldiers.

- **1944–1945** Bitter fighting in the Pacific (for example at Leyte, Iwo Jima, and Okinawa) costs thousands of American lives.

- **December 1944** Battle of the Bulge. A surprisingly strong response by German troops slows the movement of Allied forces eastward to Germany.

- **April 12, 1945** Franklin Roosevelt dies unexpectedly from a cerebral hemorrhage.

- **April 1945** Allied troops from the East and West meet at the Elbe River in Germany. Hitler commits suicide.

- **May 8, 1945** The end of war in Europe, celebrated as V-E Day (Victory in Europe).

- **August 6, 1945** The United States drops an atomic bomb on the Japanese city of Hiroshima.

- **August 9, 1945** The United States drops an atomic bomb on the Japanese city of Nagasaki.

- **August 14, 1945** Hirohito announces Japan's defeat to the Japanese people.

- **September 2, 1945** Japan formally surrenders.

ANALYZING DOCUMENTS

Examine the chart above. Then answer the following questions.

- What was the significance of the Battle of Midway?
- Which ended first, the war in Europe or the war in the Pacific?

Wartime Diplomacy

During the war, leaders of the Allied nations met in a series of conferences to discuss wartime strategies and plans for the postwar world. Key meetings are described below.

ATLANTIC CHARTER MEETING, 1941 Roosevelt and Churchill met on battleships in the North Atlantic to agree on certain principles for building a lasting peace and establishing free governments in the world. The document containing these agreements was called the Atlantic Charter.

CASABLANCA, 1943 Roosevelt met with Churchill to plan "victory on all fronts." They used the term "unconditional surrender" to describe the anticipated victory.

CAIRO, 1943 Roosevelt, Churchill, and Chiang Kai-shek of China planned the Normandy invasion.

World War II in the Pacific

TEHRAN CONFERENCE, 1943 Roosevelt and Churchill met with Stalin to discuss war strategy and plans for the postwar world.

YALTA, 1945 Roosevelt, Churchill, and Stalin outlined the division of postwar Germany into spheres of influence and planned for the trials of war criminals. The Soviet Union promised to enter the war against Japan.

POTSDAM, 1945 Allied leaders (with Truman now replacing Roosevelt) warned Japan to surrender to prevent utter destruction.

The Atomic Bomb
In an effort to bring the war to a speedy conclusion and to prevent further destruction and loss of life, Allied leaders decided to embark on an atomic research project.

THE MANHATTAN PROJECT In the spring of 1943, a group of scientists from the United States, Canada, Britain, and other European

READING STRATEGY

Analyzing Cause and Effect
At Yalta, Roosevelt, Churchill, and Stalin agreed to split Germany into four zones, each under the control of one of the major Allies. Stalin promised to allow elections in the nations his army liberated from the Germans in Eastern Europe. Stalin did not fulfill this promise.

- How did the agreements at Yalta set the stage for the problems that later arose during the Cold War?

countries began work on the top-secret atomic research program known as the **Manhattan Project.** The research was done primarily at Los Alamos, New Mexico, under the direction of Dr. Robert Oppenheimer. Many of the scientists involved in the projects were refugees from Hitler's Germany. By July 1945, the first atomic bomb was tested in New Mexico. The success of this project left the United States in the position of determining the ultimate use of the new weapon.

THE BOMBINGS OF HIROSHIMA AND NAGASAKI Within days after the first atomic test, Allied leaders warned Japan to surrender or face "prompt and utter destruction." Since no surrender occurred, President Truman made the decision to drop atomic bombs on the Japanese cities of Hiroshima and Nagasaki. The bombs killed more than 100,000 Japanese instantly, and thousands more died later from radiation sickness. For a time after World War II, the United States held a monopoly on atomic weapons. The world had entered the atomic age.

JAPAN SURRENDERS Within days of the devastating bombings of Hiroshima and Nagasaki, Japan formally surrendered, and World War II came to an end. Following Japan's surrender, the United States occupied Japan under the leadership of General Douglas MacArthur. A new constitutional monarchy went into effect introducing democratic reforms to Japan. Emperor Hirohito retained his throne, but only as a figurehead.

TURNING POINT

Several alternatives were considered before dropping the atomic bombs on Hiroshima and Nagasaki, Japan. The final decision rested with President Truman who made the decision to use the bombs to end the war as quickly as possible and thereby save American lives.

- Why might the dropping of the atomic bombs be considered a turning point in American history?

ANALYZING DOCUMENTS

Study the chart at right then answer the following question.

- Which country had the greatest number of military casualties during World War II?

Casualties in World War II

	Military Dead	Military Wounded	Civilian Dead
Britain	373,000	475,000	93,000
France	213,000	400,000	108,000
Soviet Union	11,000,000	14,102,000	7,000,000
United States	292,000	671,000	*
Germany	3,500,000	5,000,000	780,000
Italy	242,000	66,000	153,000
Japan	1,300,000	4,000,000	672,000

All figures are estimates
* Very small number of civilian dead

THE HOLOCAUST

When Adolf Hitler rose to power in Germany, he did so by finding a scapegoat, someone to blame for Germany's problems after World War I. By appealing to anti-Semitism, feelings of hatred against Jewish people, Hitler encouraged the Germans to turn viciously on all Jewish citizens.

The "Final Solution"

Early in his rise to power, Hitler had seized Jewish property, homes, and businesses and barred Jews from many jobs. At the Wannsee Conference of 1942, the Nazis set as a primary goal the total extermination, or genocide, of all Jews under their domination. This effort was to be kept secret from the German people and from the rest of the world. Hitler's plan to eliminate the Jews was known to the Nazis as the **Final Solution.**

The Horror of Concentration Camps

In the 1930s, the Nazis began to build concentration camps to isolate Jews and other groups from society and provide slave labor for industry. As Hitler's conquest of Europe continued, the camps became factories of death. More than six million Jews were killed in the camps as were another four million people—dissenters, Gypsies, homosexuals, the mentally and physically handicapped, Protestant ministers, and Catholic priests. Today, concentration camp names such as Auschwitz, Treblinka, and Dachau stand as memorials to the incredible human suffering and death of this time, a period now called the **Holocaust.**

The United States and other nations failed to take strong action to rescue Jews from Nazi Germany before World War II. In 1939, the *St. Louis,* a passenger ship carrying more than 900 Jewish refugees, left Europe for Cuba, but when they arrived, most of the refugees were denied permission to land there. The refugees were also denied permission to enter the United States, and the ship was forced to return to Europe. Most of the ship's passengers eventually were killed in the Holocaust.

After war broke out, the Allies still failed to speak out forcefully against the treatment of Jews or to make direct attempts to stop the genocide. Only toward the end of the war did the United States create the War Refugee Board to provide aid for Holocaust survivors.

War Crimes Trials

A final chapter to the Holocaust occurred in Nuremberg, Germany, in 1945 and 1946. At that time an international military court tried 24 high-level Nazis for atrocities committed during World War II. By finding former Nazis guilty of "crimes against humanity," a precedent was established that soldiers, officers, and national leaders could be held responsible for such brutal actions. Escaped Nazis who were found after the end of the war—even decades later—were also brought to trial for war-related crimes.

KEY THEMES AND CONCEPTS

Individuals, Groups, Institutions

During the Holocaust, individuals were singled out for persecution because of their membership in a group. Institutions were developed and individuals were put in place within those institutions to carry out the atrocities of the Holocaust. Genocide is the deliberate murder of an entire people.

List two other examples of genocide in the twentieth century.

1.

2.

READING STRATEGY

What important legal precedent was set at the Nuremberg trials?

Among the most infamous Nazis who were tried and convicted was Adolf Eichmann. He was captured in Argentina in 1960 and tried in Israel for the torture and deaths of millions of Jews. Eichmann was convicted of crimes against humanity and was hanged in 1962. Klaus Barbie, known as the "Butcher of Lyon" (France), was also apprehended and tried in 1987 for his wartime brutality to Jews.

War crime trials also occurred in Japan. These trials led to the execution of former premier Tojo and six other war leaders. About 4,000 other Japanese war criminals were also convicted and received less severe sentences.

⚷ **KEY THEMES AND CONCEPTS**

Economic Systems
Between 1939 and 1945 federal spending increased from $9.4 billion to $95.2 billion. The government financed about 41 percent of the war costs by increasing taxes. The rest of the money needed was borrowed from banks, private investors, and the public. Such deficit spending—government spending of borrowed money—turned the depressed economy of the 1930s around almost overnight. It also created a huge national debt.

AMERICAN PATRIOTISM DURING WORLD WAR II

After the United States entered the war, the nation moved to full-scale wartime production and mobilization of the armed forces. Americans rallied behind the war effort.

With the exception of the attack on Pearl Harbor and battles on several Pacific islands, World War II was not fought on American soil. Nonetheless, Americans were constantly preparing for attack. America's coastal areas and large cities held blackout drills. Americans were encouraged to support the war effort by rationing food, gasoline, and other necessities and luxuries. Government campaigns encouraged Americans to have "meatless Tuesdays," and many Americans planted "victory gardens" of their own to increase the food supply. Hollywood entertainers made special presentations to encourage citizens to buy war bonds to help the government finance the war.

The Role of American Women

World War II brought dramatic changes to the lives of American women in the military and in the civilian workforce.

IN THE MILITARY By the end of the war, more than 200,000 women had joined the military services. Although women served in separate units from men, such as the Women's Army Corps (WAC), women performed a variety of vital military duties. They operated radios and repaired planes and vehicles. They also were assigned, along with men, to clerical duties.

IN THE CIVILIAN WORKFORCE As millions of men joined the military, new employment opportunities opened up to women. Women who had been employed before the war eagerly applied for better-paying jobs, and many women who had worked inside the home now entered the paid workforce. Many women took jobs that had once been open to men only. More than five million women eventually worked in factories devoted to wartime production, although their pay never came close to equaling men's pay of the time. One song about a woman named **Rosie the Riveter** became popular during the war years because it captured the sense of duty and patriotism felt by millions of women. The term "Rosie the Riveter" became a slang term for all women who worked in wartime factories.

RESULTING CHANGE Women's wartime work resulted in important changes in employment and lifestyle, even after the war. Before the war, most employed American women were young and unmarried. During the war, large numbers of married women and mothers who had never worked outside the home before took jobs. This trend continued after the war. Although many women willingly returned to their homes and the roles of wife and mother at the end of the war, thousands more enjoyed the challenge of paid employment, as well as an improved standard of living.

The entry of so many women into the paid workforce during World War II marked the beginning of a long-term trend, as women continued to enter the workforce in greater numbers throughout the rest of the century. New issues became important. For example, child care became an important issue during the war years, and it remains an important one today.

African Americans

The experiences of African Americans during the war years provided the foundation of the civil rights movement of the 1950s and 1960s.

IN THE MILITARY Nearly one million African American men and women served in the military during World War II. Military units were segregated, and initially, African American soldiers were limited to support roles. As the war went on, these soldiers soon saw combat, where many distinguished themselves.

AT HOME In the 1940s, many southern African Americans began moving to northern cities in search of economic opportunity and freedom from discrimination. However, they met discrimination in the North as well, as white workers and homeowners feared the movement of African Americans into their workplaces and neighborhoods. Race riots broke out in Detroit and New York City in the summer of 1943. Membership in civil rights organizations began to grow as African Americans struggled against discrimination.

African Americans experienced gains during the war years. Politically, their migration north had made them a significant voting bloc in urban areas. Economically, new jobs in war industries brought many African Americans the chance to earn more than they ever had before. Although these gains were made, African Americans were still experiencing widespread discrimination and inequalities in salaries in the workplace. The black press urged that the struggle for freedom be fought on two fronts—overseas and at home as well.

 PREPARING FOR THE EXAM

What trend emerged following World War II in regard to women's participation in the labor force?

READING STRATEGY

Predicting Content
How might the experiences of African Americans during World War II have contributed to the rise of the civil rights movement during the 1950s?

Japanese Americans

Thousands of Japanese Americans faced hardship and economic losses after the attack on Pearl Harbor.

IMMIGRATION TO AMERICA Immigrants from Japan began arriving in the United States shortly after the Civil War. These immigrants settled mainly on the west coast of the United States. By 1941, thousands of Americans of Japanese descent, called **Nisei,** had been born in the United States and were American citizens. Thousands of them had never been to Japan, and many had no desire to go there.

WARTIME RELOCATION AUTHORITY (WRA) After the Japanese attack on Pearl Harbor, many Americans feared that Japanese Americans presented a threat to national security. Anti-Japanese sentiment grew, and in 1942 President Roosevelt issued Executive Order 9066, establishing military zones for the imprisonment of Japanese Americans. More than 100,000 people of Japanese descent were forced to leave their homes and move to **WRA camps,** hastily constructed military-style barracks ringed with barbed wire and guarded by troops. This discrimination was focused entirely on Japanese Americans; no such action was taken against citizens or residents of German or Italian descent.

PREPARING FOR THE EXAM

"It is a fact that the Japanese navy has been reconnoitering [investigating] the Pacific Coast. . . . It is [a] fact that communication takes place between the enemy at sea and enemy agents on land."

• Would the writer of this excerpt have supported the Supreme Court's decision in *Korematsu* v. *United States?*

KOREMATSU V. UNITED STATES In the 1944 landmark case *Korematsu* v. *United States,* the Supreme Court upheld the forced evacuation as a reasonable wartime emergency measure. However, no acts of Japanese-American sabotage or treason were ever identified, and thousands of Nisei fought honorably in the war. Almost 50 years after World War II, the United States government admitted that the wartime relocation program had been unjust. In 1988, Congress voted to pay $20,000 to each of the approximately 60,000 surviving Americans who had been interned. The first payments were made in 1990, and the government also issued a formal apology.

NISEI SOLDIERS Despite the injustices endured by Japanese Americans, thousands proved their loyalty by serving in the U.S. armed forces, primarily in Europe. The 442nd Regimental Combat Team, made up entirely of Japanese Americans, won more medals for bravery than any other unit of its size in the war.

DEMOBILIZATION

During the war, American factories, geared up for wartime production, had helped the nation recover from the Great Depression. Now the challenge was to convert from a wartime to a peacetime society. The United States underwent a period of demobilization, or the movement from a military to a civilian status. The United States armed forces reduced from 12 million members to 1.5 million. Factories that had made planes and tanks now began producing consumer goods. It also meant ensuring that the nation would not slip back into depression.

During President Truman's administration, legislation was passed to deal with different issues raised by demobilization.

SERVICEMEN'S READJUSTMENT ACT Also known as the GI Bill of Rights, this act authorized billions of dollars to pay for veterans' benefits, such as college education, medical treatment, unemployment insurance, and home and business loans. The GI Bill made it possible for more people to attend college and buy homes than ever before.

EMPLOYMENT ACT OF 1946 This act made full employment a national goal and set up a Council of Economic Advisors to guide the President on economic matters.

AN END TO PRICE CONTROLS Wartime legislation had put controls on the prices of most goods. In 1946, the government moved to end most such controls. However, the end of controls coupled with a tax cut caused a rapid increase in inflation. For example, food prices soared 25 percent in just two years.

THE TAFT-HARTLEY ACT Workers' wages could not keep up with inflation after the war. Major strikes were held as unions pushed for higher wages. Anti-union feelings grew and led Congress to pass the Taft-Hartley Act over Truman's veto. The act
- Provided an 80-day "cooling-off" period through which the President could delay a strike that threatened national welfare
- Barred the closed shop, under which workers had to belong to a union before being hired
- Allowed states to pass "right-to-work laws," which said workers could take jobs and not have to join a union
- Banned union contributions to political campaigns
- Required union leaders to swear they were not communists

National Security Concerns

Truman also moved to help the nation meet postwar international concerns. The National Security Act of 1947 created the National Military Establishment, which later became the Department of Defense. The act also created the Central Intelligence Agency to oversee intelligence gathering activities. As commander in chief, Truman also issued an executive order banning discrimination in the armed forces.

The Baby Boom

In addition to problems caused by converting to a peacetime economy, the nation also had to cope with the largest population explosion in its history. The economic hardships of the Great Depression that had encouraged smaller families were gone. Families grew larger once more. This "baby boom" brought with it the expansion of many public services, especially schools. You will learn more about the long-term effects of the baby boom in the next unit.

PREPARING FOR THE EXAM

Truman's legislative program aimed at promoting full employment, a higher minimum wage, greater unemployment compensation for workers without jobs, housing assistance, and other items was known as the Fair Deal, a play of words on Franklin Roosevelt's New Deal.

PREPARING FOR THE EXAM

The Taft-Hartley Act of 1947 was a setback for organized labor. It gave the President the power to delay (through court injunction) any strike that took place within an industry that the President deemed important to the nation's health or safety.

? **KEY THEMES AND**
⌐ **CONCEPTS**

Change
How did the prosperity of
the 1940s and 1950s
influence the nation's population growth rate?

The Election of 1948

Many voters had become dissatisfied with Truman's presidency
because of inflation, strikes, Truman's actions on civil rights, and the
developing cold war. Polls predicted that the Republican candidate,
Governor Thomas Dewey of New York, would defeat Truman easily
in the 1948 presidential election. Yet Truman pulled off one of the
greatest upsets in American political history by winning reelection.
He then attempted to build on this victory by proposing a program
called the Fair Deal that aimed to extend reforms started under FDR's
New Deal.

SECTION 2

Peace with Problems, 1945–1960

SECTION OVERVIEW

The end of World War II brought the desire to prevent such devastation from ever happening again. The United Nations was established to help nations find peaceful solutions to conflicts. Meanwhile, the uneasy wartime alliance between the United States and the Soviet Union dissolved as the Cold War took hold. As communism spread through the efforts of the Soviet Union and later China, the United States worked to strengthen its influence in Western Europe and Asia by providing economic aid and building strategic alliances. A growing anxiety about the spread of communism led the United States to become more deeply involved in global affairs, while also fearing a communist influence at home.

KEY THEMES AND CONCEPTS

As you review this section, take special note of the following key themes and concepts:

Change Why did the United States and the Soviet Union change from being allies in World War II to enemies during the Cold War?

Foreign Policy How did the United States use economic aid to build its influence in Europe and Asia?

Constitutional Principles How did the fear of communism lead to the violations of some people's civil rights in the United States?

KEY PEOPLE

Eleanor Roosevelt

George C. Marshall

Mao Zedong

Chiang Kai-shek

Douglas MacArthur

Alger Hiss

Joseph McCarthy

Ethel and Julius Rosenberg

★ THE BIG IDEA

The post-World War II hostilities between the United States and the Soviet Union are together known as the Cold War.

The Cold War

- lasted from about 1946 to 1991.

- was brought about by competition between the United States and the Soviet Union for power and influence in the world.

- consisted of political and economic conflict and military tensions throughout the globe.

KEY TERMS

containment
"iron curtain"
Truman Doctrine
Marshall Plan
Cold War
NATO
Warsaw Pact
38th parallel
HUAC

The United States emerged from World War II as the world's greatest military power. Compared to other nations, it had suffered relatively little physical destruction. For a short time, the United States held a monopoly on the ability to use nuclear power. After World War II, the United States was aware of its strength as a nation and its responsibility to preserve world peace.

THE UNITED NATIONS

American foreign policy changed dramatically as a result of World War II. Even before the conclusion of the war, the United States began planning for an international peacekeeping organization. Plans were made at the Yalta Conference for a United Nations Conference to be held in San Francisco in April 1945. The Soviet Union, under the leadership of Joseph Stalin, agreed to participate in planning the new organization which would be known as the United Nations. The United States Senate approved the United Nations Charter by a vote of 82 to 2.

Organization of the United Nations

The structure of the United Nations (UN) includes a General Assembly of all its members and a Security Council of 15 members. The Security Council consists of 10 rotating member nations and five permanent members. (The original permanent members were the United States, Great Britain, the Soviet Union, China, and France. After the breakup of the Soviet Union, the Russian Federation became a permanent member.)

The General Assembly serves as a forum for world leaders to speak on a variety of concerns. Although the UN has become militarily involved in a number of world crises, most of its members would agree that its greatest accomplishments have been in fighting hunger and disease and in promoting education. The headquarters of the United Nations is in New York City.

READING STRATEGY

Organizing Information
Who are the five permanent members of the United Nations Security Council?

1.

2.

3.

4.

5.

ANALYZING DOCUMENTS

Review the timeline below then answer the following questions.

• How long did the Korean War last?

• In what year was NATO formed?

The United States and the World, 1945–1954

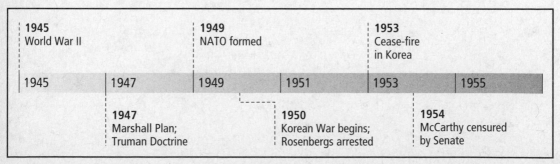

1945 World War II		1949 NATO formed		1953 Cease-fire in Korea	
1945	1947	1949	1951	1953	1955
	1947 Marshall Plan; Truman Doctrine		1950 Korean War begins; Rosenbergs arrested	1954 McCarthy censured by Senate	

The United Nations

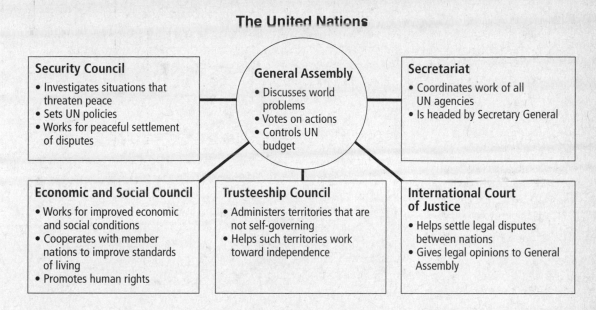

Security Council
- Investigates situations that threaten peace
- Sets UN policies
- Works for peaceful settlement of disputes

General Assembly
- Discusses world problems
- Votes on actions
- Controls UN budget

Secretariat
- Coordinates work of all UN agencies
- Is headed by Secretary General

Economic and Social Council
- Works for improved economic and social conditions
- Cooperates with member nations to improve standards of living
- Promotes human rights

Trusteeship Council
- Administers territories that are not self-governing
- Helps such territories work toward independence

International Court of Justice
- Helps settle legal disputes between nations
- Gives legal opinions to General Assembly

UNIVERSAL DECLARATION OF HUMAN RIGHTS In 1946, President Truman appointed former first lady Eleanor Roosevelt as a United Nations delegate, the only woman in the American delegation. The committee that Eleanor Roosevelt led authored the Universal Declaration of Human Rights, a proclamation that is still part of the guiding philosophy of the UN today. In the postwar years, people all over the world were especially eager to have an international organization succeed at defining human rights for all people.

CONTAINMENT AS A FOREIGN POLICY

American foreign policy after World War II was influenced by two factors: the willingness of the United States to become involved in international peacekeeping efforts and its determination to prevent the spread of communism.

Growing Distrust of the Soviet Union

In 1939, Germany and the Soviet Union had signed a nonaggression treaty, but after Germany violated the pact, the Soviet Union sought a new alliance to protect itself from Germany. The United States then allied with the Soviet Union throughout World War II. Although they were allies, American and Soviet leaders did not fully trust one another. After the war, it became apparent that the only common goal shared by the United States and the Soviet Union was the defeat of the Axis powers.

After World War II, the Soviet Union was viewed as a grave threat to the security of the noncommunist world. In defeating Nazi

ANALYZING DOCUMENTS

Study the chart above then answer the following questions.

- Which branch of the United Nations would help two countries resolve a legal dispute?

- Which branch sets UN policies?

ANALYZING DOCUMENTS

Examine the cartoon at right, then answer the following questions.

- Why is Communism represented by a vulture?
- What is the vulture carrying?
- Why is the U.S. Congress represented by a doctor?
- Where are the doctor and the vulture going?
- What does the caption mean?

In one or two sentences, write a summary of the idea this cartoon is conveying.

READING STRATEGY

Reinforcing Main Ideas
Containment of communism to the areas where it already existed was a central tenant of American foreign policy during the Cold War.

- How did communism spread to Eastern Europe?
- What had Stalin promised at Yalta in regards to Eastern Europe?

GEOGRAPHY IN HISTORY

Stalin wanted control of the Dardanelles, a narrow strait in Turkey, because it would give Soviet ports on the Black Sea access to the Mediterranean.

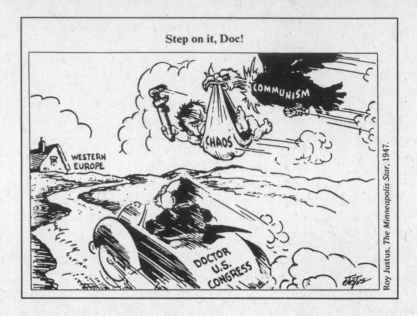

Step on it, Doc!

Roy Justus, *The Minneapolis Star,* 1947.

Germany, the Soviets had moved troops into the nations of Eastern Europe. After the war, the Soviet Union actively supported communist governments in those nations.

The United States, which had emerged as a superpower nation, took on the task of limiting communist expansion—a policy known as **containment**. The goal of containment was to confine communism to the area in which it already existed—the Soviet Union and the Eastern European nations. American presidential power increased during this time period as the United States sought to carry out this policy.

Following are key foreign policy developments related to the containment of communism immediately after World War II.

Churchill's "Iron Curtain" Speech

In his 1946 speech at Westminster College in Fulton, Missouri, Prime Minister Winston Churchill of Great Britain cautioned the world about the threat of communist expansion. He warned that "from Stettin in the Baltic to Trieste in the Adriatic, an iron curtain has descended across the Continent." Churchill's phrase **"iron curtain"** drew a clear picture of the postwar world. There had come to be recognizable division between the free Western Europe and the communist Eastern Europe.

The Truman Doctrine

Before World War II, Britain had been a powerful force in the Mediterranean. The tremendous losses and expense of World War II, however, weakened Britain's influence there. The Soviet Union, which had long been striving for access to the Mediterranean Sea by way of the Turkish straits, sought to extend its influence in the area.

The Soviets supported communist rebels in their attempt to topple the government of Greece. This led the United States to try to contain the spread of communism in the Mediterranean region. On March 12, 1947, President Truman asked Congress for $400 million in aid to Turkey and Greece. He called on the United States to support free people in resisting control by armed minorities or outside pressures. Truman believed that the failure of the United States to act at this time would endanger both the nation and the free world.

Congress approved Truman's request. By 1950, more than $660 million had been spent in aid to Turkey and Greece. This policy of economic and military aid became known as the **Truman Doctrine.** It represents a major step in the evolution of American foreign policy further away from isolationism and neutrality.

The Marshall Plan

World War II left much of Europe in ruins. Major cities and industrial centers were destroyed. Survivors of the war struggled to find food, shelter, and clothing. Dissatisfaction with such conditions grew rapidly. In many war-torn countries, the Communist party seemed to offer solutions to such problems.

To prevent the spread of communist influence in Europe, General George C. Marshall, secretary of state under President Truman, announced a new economic-aid program called the **Marshall Plan.** In a speech delivered on June 5, 1947, Marshall announced that the United States was against "hunger, poverty, desperation, and chaos." Between 1948 and 1952, about $13 billion in economic aid was allocated by the Republican-dominated Congress for the rebuilding of Europe under the Marshall Plan. The largest amount went to Britain, France, Italy, and West Germany.

This aid enabled Western Europe to begin consumer production once more and to build prosperous economies. Both Western Europe and the United States felt that with stabilized and improving economies, communist expansion would be halted.

The Beginning of the Cold War: Germany 1948–1949

At the end of World War II, Germany was divided into four zones of occupation controlled by Great Britain, France, the Soviet Union, and the United States. Berlin, the capital of Germany, was located in the Russian sector. However, the city was divided into four sections, each controlled by one of the four Allies. Disagreements during this period of occupation marked the beginning of the **Cold War,** a period of tension between the United States and the Soviet Union from the end of World War II to 1990.

THE BERLIN BLOCKADE The United States, France, and Great Britain cooperated in governing the western sectors of Germany.

ANALYZING DOCUMENTS

"In these circumstances, it is clear that the main element of any United States policy toward the Soviet Union must be that of a long-term, patient but firm and vigilant containment of Russian expansive tendencies."

—American diplomat George Kennan, July 1947

• In what ways were the Truman Doctrine and the Marshall Plan examples of "long-term, patient but firm and vigilant" containment of communism?

READING STRATEGY

Reading for Evidence
How were the Truman Doctrine and the Marshall Plan related?

**READING
STRATEGY**

Organizing Information
Who controlled the four
zones of occupation in
Germany following World
War II?

1.

2.

3.

4.

- In which zone was the
capital Berlin located?

- Which zones were
combined to form West
Germany?

- How did the Soviets
attempt to take control of
Berlin?

**KEY THEMES AND
CONCEPTS**

Foreign Policy
NATO represented the
principle of mutual military
assistance or collective
security. By joining NATO
the United States dropped
its opposition to military
treaties with Europe for the
first time since the Monroe
Doctrine. As a member of
NATO the United States
became actively involved in
European affairs.

Unable to reach agreement with the Soviet Union over the eventual
unification of Germany, the three western powers decided to unify
their zones without the Soviet zone. In 1949, the Federal Republic of
Germany, commonly known as West Germany was established. The
Soviets opposed the establishment of this separate government. On
June 24, 1948, the Soviets cut off all access to West Berlin by blockad-
ing the roads leading to the city, all of which had to go through the
Soviet-controlled sector of Germany. The Soviets hoped that the
blockade would force the western powers out of Berlin.

THE BERLIN AIRLIFT The United States, Great Britain, and France
would not back down. Recognizing that West Berlin could not get supplies by road anymore, the western powers began an airlift of food,
clothing, coal, medicine, and other necessities to the city. Almost a
year later, on May 12, 1949, the Soviets recognized their defeat in the
area and ended the blockade. Shortly afterward, the Soviets announced
the formation of the German Democratic Republic, commonly known
as East Germany. In 1955, West Germany was given full sovereignty.
The West had learned once again that although World War II was over,
its struggle against aggressor nations was not.

Point Four Program
The United States recognized that the Soviet Union's expansionist
aims were targeted not only at Europe but at developing nations of the
world as well. In 1950, Congress approved President Truman's Point
Four Program, which provided nearly $400 million for technical
development programs in Latin America, Asia, and Africa. The Point
Four Program was designed to modernize and strengthen the
economies of developing nations and thereby discourage the growth of
communism.

The North Atlantic Treaty Organization
The United States and other Western European nations also fought the
spread of communism by forming alliances. In April 1949, the United
States and 11 other western nations signed a collective security
agreement called the North Atlantic Treaty. This agreement bound the
participating nations to act together for their common defense.
Members pledged that an attack on any one of them would be
considered an attack on all of them. Defense arrangements were
coordinated through the North Atlantic Treaty Organization (**NATO**).
The Soviets later formed an opposing alliance with seven Eastern
European nations under the **Warsaw Pact.**

In 1949, President Truman announced that the Soviet Union had
successfully exploded an atomic bomb. Fearing the power that this
gave the Soviets, the United States worked to strengthen its influence
in the world by committing several billion dollars in assistance to
countries in Western Europe and elsewhere.

The Cold War in Europe

European Cooperation

In order to rebuild and strengthen their economies after the war, Western European nations made ever-increasing efforts at economic cooperation. In 1951, the European Coal and Steel Community formed to enable six European nations to set prices and regulate the coal and steel industries. By 1957, the scope of economic cooperation had broadened to include efforts to improve transportation and eliminate tariff barriers within Europe. Those same six nations signed a treaty in 1957 to form the European Economic Community (EEC), also known as the Common Market. As economic cooperation continued to broaden, this organization later transformed into the European Union (EU) that exists today.

The European Union has experienced many changes in recent years. The European Parliament, the legislative branch of the EU, now has the power to approve or reject the EU's budget. In 1999, eleven member states began using a common currency called the euro. The EU continues to grapple with such key issues as increasing employment opportunities for citizens in all member nations. The EU today has 15 member states and is preparing for the admission of new members from eastern and southern Europe.

ANALYZING DOCUMENTS

After losing more than 20 million people during the war and suffering widespread destruction, the Soviet Union was determined to rebuild in ways that would protect its own interests. One way was to establish satellite nations, countries subject to Soviet domination, on the western borders of the Soviet Union.

- How does this map illustrate the Soviet Union's desire to protect itself from non-communist rivals?

CONTAINMENT IN ASIA

During World War II, the United States had been an ally of China and an enemy of Japan. After World War II, the United States reversed its political alliances in Asia. With its new constitutional democracy, Japan became an American ally. Meanwhile a communist takeover in China made the United States increasingly suspicious of and hostile to that nation.

READING STRATEGY

Analyzing Cause and Effect

How might the victory of the Communists in the Chinese civil war in 1949 have contributed to United States involvement in the Korean War in 1950?

Communist Victory in China

In the 1930s, China had plunged into civil war. Mao Zedong, leader of the communist forces in China, sought to defeat the nationalist regime of Chiang Kai-shek. In 1949, the communist forces defeated the nationalists and renamed the now communist-led country the People's Republic of China. Chiang Kai-shek and the nationalists fled to the island of Taiwan.

The United States was alarmed by this development, because it feared that communism would spread beyond China. Because the United States had overseen the initial rebuilding of postwar Japan and had helped put a new constitutional democracy in place, it did not want to see communism spread to Japan. Support for Japan was now seen as a way of offsetting communist China's influence in Asia.

READING STRATEGY

Organizing Information

- Who fought on the side of communist North Korea during the Korean War?

- Who fought on the side of anticommunist South Korea during the Korean War?

The Korean War

During World War II, Korea had been occupied by Japan. At the end of the war, Korea was divided along the **38th parallel,** or line of latitude. The northern zone was under the influence of the Soviet Union, and the southern zone was controlled by the United States. By 1948, the southern zone had elected an anticommunist government headed by Syngman Rhee and was now called the Republic of Korea. In the northern zone, now named the Democratic People's Republic of Korea, a communist government ruled.

FIGHTING BEGINS North Korea invaded South Korea in 1950 in an attempt to unify the country. President Truman responded to this invasion by committing American troops to major involvement in the Korean conflict.

MacARTHUR IN COMMAND General Douglas MacArthur, a World War II hero, was sent to command the United States military in Korea. Troops from the United States, along with small numbers of soldiers from other UN member nations, were soon involved in battles as fierce as those of World War II. A particularly devastating loss came at the Yalu River, when Chinese forces entered the conflict and pushed UN troops south. By the middle of 1951, the war had reached a stalemate. Fighting continued, but neither side was able to advance successfully.

Disagreement over the objectives and military strategies of the Korean War caused a major conflict between President Truman and

General MacArthur. Although Truman was a civilian, the Constitution makes the President the commander in chief of the armed forces. When General MacArthur disagreed with Truman publicly about the conduct of the war, the President recalled him to the United States and dismissed him from command.

HOSTILITIES END Although truce talks began in June 1951, no resolution was reached before the American presidential election of 1952. During that campaign the Republican candidate, World War II hero Dwight D. Eisenhower, promised that if he were elected President he would go to Korea to aid in the peace negotiations. Eisenhower won the election and did keep his campaign promise, but a truce or cease-fire was not officially signed until July 27, 1953.

The war in Korea lasted for more than three years and cost more than $15 billion. Approximately 34,000 Americans and one million Koreans and Chinese died in the conflict.

NEW DIRECTIONS The policy of containment took a different course with American involvement in the Korean conflict. Early containment efforts focused primarily on economic aid programs. With the Korean War, the United States now showed its willingness to undertake military action to contain communism if it was necessary. American experiences in Korea were a warning of future global confrontations between democratic and communist opponents.

THE COLD WAR AT HOME

Even as the United States defended democratic freedoms worldwide, sometimes those same freedoms were in danger at home. The spreading of communism to China and the apparent growing strength of the Soviet Union led some Americans to fear that communism could spread to the United States. This fear led some Americans to take actions that violated the civil rights of others.

Many Americans charged that communist agents were trying to subvert, or destroy, the American political system. Other Americans responded that the actions of anticommunists were more subversive of American values and more dangerous to the nation.

Looking for Communists
The fear of communism in the United States had its roots in the period before World War II. Anticommunist activity began in the 1930s.

HUAC In 1938, the House Un-American Activities Committee (**HUAC**) was formed as a temporary investigative unit to look into communist activity in the United States. HUAC operated for more than 30 years. Its well-publicized probe of the movie industry in the 1940s and 1950s led to the blacklisting, or cutting off from employment, of many actors, writers, and directors.

KEY THEMES AND CONCEPTS
Civic Values
The Korean War caused enormous frustration at home. When the truce was signed in 1953, Korea remained divided at almost exactly the same place as before the war, near the 38th parallel. Americans wondered why more than 54,000 of their soldiers had been killed and 113,000 wounded for such limited results. Some Americans wondered if their government was serious about stopping communism.

KEY THEMES AND CONCEPTS
Foreign Policy
In what way did the Korean War mark a change in the United States' policy of containment?

READING
STRATEGY

Reinforcing Main Ideas

Americans' fears of communism resulted from the fact that Communists were openly hostile to American beliefs and values such as capitalism, private ownership of land and business, and First Amendment freedoms.

• What other foreign and domestic events contributed to Americans' fears of the spread of communism?

J. Edgar Hoover, director of the Federal Bureau of Investigation, often aided HUAC investigations. Critics argued that Hoover conducted anticommunist activities that often violated the civil rights of Americans.

THE SMITH ACT In 1940, Congress passed the Smith Act, which made it illegal for anyone to advocate "overthrowing . . . any government in the United States by force" or to "affiliate" with groups that called for such action.

In the 1951 landmark case of *Dennis* v. *United States,* the Supreme Court upheld the Smith Act. Eugene Dennis, general secretary of the Communist Party in the United States, and 10 others were convicted of advocating the violent overthrow of the government.

Two court decisions in 1957 weakened the intent of the Smith Act. In *Watkins* v. *United States,* the court ruled the HUAC could not punish witnesses who refused to cooperate with its investigations. In *Yates* v. *United States,* the court ruled that the Smith Act applied only to those who teach or advocate direct "action" to overthrow government, not to those who merely advocate it in principle.

THE LOYALTY PROGRAM In 1947, President Truman fueled anticommunist feelings by ordering a Loyalty Review Board to conduct security checks on thousands of government employees. Those whose loyalty was considered doubtful were dismissed.

In the early 1950s, Robert Oppenheimer, who had led the research to develop the atomic bomb, voiced his opposition to building the new, more destructive hydrogen bomb. This action and his past association with others whose loyalty was being questioned led to a government hearing about his own loyalty. He was determined to be a "loyal citizen," but his security clearance was removed, and he was barred from future government research.

PREPARING FOR
THE EXAM

What was the outcome of the Alger Hiss case and what was its significance?

THE HISS CASE The Alger Hiss case led many Americans to believe that there was a reason to fear that there were communists in the government. In 1948, Alger Hiss, a former adviser to President Roosevelt, was charged with having been a Communist spy during the 1930s. Whittaker Chambers, a former Communist party member, made these charges, which Hiss denied. A congressional committee investigated them.

A young Republican committee member from California, Richard Nixon, believed that Hiss was guilty. Nixon's pursuit of the case and Hiss's eventual conviction on perjury charges made Nixon a national figure. The conviction also added weight to Republican charges that Roosevelt and Truman had not been alert enough to the dangers of communism.

McCarthyism

Against this political background, Senator Joseph McCarthy of Wisconsin began his own hunt for communists. In 1950, McCarthy charged he had a list of State Department employees known to be communists. Over the next four years, McCarthy went on to charge that many other people and government agencies had been corrupted by communism.

McCarthy made bold accusations without any evidence. This tactic became known as "McCarthyism." He ruined the reputations of many people he carelessly accused of being communists. Meanwhile, the Rosenberg case and congressional legislation helped win public support for McCarthy's actions.

THE ROSENBERG CASE   In 1950, Ethel and Julius Rosenberg and Morton Sobell were charged with giving atomic secrets to the Soviets during World War II. After a highly controversial trial, they were convicted of espionage. The Rosenbergs were sentenced to death and Sobell to prison. The Rosenbergs were executed in 1953.

CONGRESSIONAL LEGISLATION   In the same year the Rosenbergs were arrested, Congress passed the McCarran Internal Security Act. The law aimed at limiting the actions of anyone the government considered a threat to United States security. The McCarran-Walter Act of 1952 restricted the immigration of persons from communist-dominated nations in Asia and southern and central Europe. President Truman vetoed the bill, but Congress passed it over his veto.

McCARTHY'S FALL   In 1954, McCarthy charged that even the army was full of communists. He held televised investigations into these charges. For the first time, millions of Americans saw McCarthy's bullying tactics for themselves. His public support quickly faded, and in December 1954 the Senate censured, or denounced, him for "conduct unbecoming a member." The fall of McCarthy ended the red scare of the 1950s, although anticommunist attitudes lingered as the Cold War continued to drag on.

KEY THEMES AND CONCEPTS

Constitutional Principles

Although many people knew that Senator McCarthy's claims were exaggerated at best, he was still able to gain power and ruin the lives of many people.

• How did McCarthy contribute to the suppression of free speech and open, honest debate?

 PREPARING FOR THE EXAM

McCarthyism during the 1950s had many similarities to the Red Scare following World War I.

• How were the actions of Attorney General A. Mitchell Palmer and McCarthy similar?

Questions for Regents Practice

For online Questions for Regents Practice,
visit the Prentice Hall Web site at www.phschool.com.

MULTIPLE CHOICE

Directions

Review the Test-Taking Strategies section of this book. Then answer the following questions, drawn from actual Regents examinations. Each question is followed by four choices. Read each question carefully. Decide which choice is the correct answer. Then on a separate piece of paper, mark your answer for each question.

1 United States senators who opposed the Treaty of Versailles objected mainly to
   1 United States membership in the League of Nations
   2 payment of reparations by Germany to the Allied nations
   3 the transfer of Germany's colonial possessions to the League of Nations
   4 the creation of new and independent nations in Eastern Europe

2 A major reason for the United States neutrality in the 1930s was the nation's
   1 belief in the domino theory
   2 disillusionment resulting from World War I
   3 strong approval of political conditions in Europe
   4 military and naval superiority

3 At the outbreak of both World War I and World War II in Europe, public opinion in the United States generally favored
   1 remaining neutral
   2 entering the war on the side of the Allies
   3 invading Europe in order to acquire territory
   4 settling the conflict through an international peace organization

4 Isolationism as a foreign policy is more difficult to achieve in the 20th century than in prior times mainly because
   1 the increase in the world's population has forced people to live more closely together
   2 there are more sovereign nations today than in the past
   3 modern technology had made nations more interdependent
   4 public opinion on issues is more easily disregarded

5 The appeasement policy followed by Western European leaders in the late 1930s was based primarily on the belief that war could be avoided by
   1 satisfying Hitler's desire for territorial expansion
   2 encouraging communist expansion into Nazi Germany
   3 limiting the development of Germany's armed forces
   4 appealing to the League of Nations for international cooperation

6 Which event led directly to United States entry into World War II?

1 invasion of Poland by Germany and Russia

2 attack on France by Italy

3 sinking of the *Lusitania* by Germany

4 attack on Pearl Harbor by Japan

Base your answer to question 7 on the announcement below and on your knowledge of social studies.

> **WESTERN DEFENSE COMMAND AND FOURTH ARMY WARTIME CIVIL CONTROL ADMINISTRATION**
>
> **Presidio of San Francisco, California**
> **April 1, 1942**
>
> **INSTRUCTIONS TO ALL PERSONS OF**
>
> # JAPANESE
>
> **ANCESTRY**
>
> **Living in the Following Area:**
>
> All that portion of the City and County of San Francisco, State of California, lying generally west of the north-south line established by Junipero Serra Boulevard, Worcester Avenue, and Nineteenth Avenue and lying generally north of the east-west line established by California Street, to the intersection of Market Street, and thence on Market Street to San Francisco Bay.
>
> All Japanese persons, both alien and non-alien, will be evacuated from the above designated area by 12:00 o'clock noon Tuesday, April 7, 1942.

7 During World War II, the action required by this announcement was based largely on

1 racial prejudice

2 a labor shortage

3 the needs for skilled workers in defense industries

4 a desire to protect Japanese Americans from military attack

8 The rulings of the Supreme Court in *Scott* v. *Sandford* (1857), *Plessy* v. *Ferguson* (1896), and *Korematsu* v. *United States* (1944) all demonstrate that the Supreme Court has

1 continued to extend voting rights to minorities

2 protected itself from internal dissent

3 sometimes failed to protect the rights of minorities

4 often imposed restrictions on free speech during wartime

9 An important effect of World War II on United States foreign policy was a

1 refusal to become involved in world affairs

2 smaller role for the President in foreign policy and national security issues

3 stronger commitment to collective security and world leadership

4 willingness to intervene only when the national economy is involved

10 After World War II, the United States was better able than its allies to adjust its economy from wartime to peacetime because the United States

1 possessed nuclear weapons

2 raised tariffs on imports

3 had collected its war debts from the Allies

4 had suffered no widespread wartime destruction

11 What was a major effect of World War II on women and minorities in the United States?

1 They were drafted into the military.

2 They had new opportunities in the workforce.

3 They received equal voting rights for the first time.

4 They were granted equal pay for equal work.

Base your answers to questions 12 and 13 on the speakers' conversation below and on your knowledge of social studies.

Speaker A: "We must provide arms to the legitimate governments of Greece and Turkey if they are to defeat Soviet-sponsored subversion."

Speaker B: "The first priority is to help rebuild the postwar economies of European countries so that democratic governments can survive."

Speaker C: "Our main goal is to create a system of collective security agreements to deal with any military threats."

Speaker D: "We must continue to build both our nuclear and our conventional arsenals if we are to have any hope of world peace."

12 The central concern of all the speakers is
   1 the containment of communism
   2 the defeat of the Axis Powers in World War II
   3 a ban on the proliferation of nuclear weapons
   4 the support of United Nations peace-keeping efforts

13 These speakers' statements would most likely have been made during the Presidential administration of
   1 Franklin D. Roosevelt
   2 Harry S Truman
   3 John F. Kennedy
   4 Richard M. Nixon

14 **"Wilson Order Controls on U.S. Industry to Fight War Against Germany"**

   "FDR OK's Destroyer Deal with England to Fight Sub Threat"

   "Truman Orders Airlift of Supplies to Berlin"

   Which generalization about governmental power in the United States is supported by these headlines?
   1 Important Presidential decisions usually follow the results of public opinion polls.
   2 Presidential actions during international crises have increased executive power.
   3 Foreign policy is ultimately determined by Congress's power to allocate funds.
   4 Presidential power to act in wartime cannot be exercised without bipartisan support.

15 The Truman Doctrine and the Eisenhower Doctrine were United States foreign policies concerning
   1 the international balance of payments
   2 the containment of communism
   3 worldwide environmental pollution
   4 nuclear disarmament

16 The North Atlantic Treaty Organization (NATO) and the Truman Doctrine were attempts to carry out a United States foreign policy of
   1 brinkmanship
   2 containment
   3 appeasement
   4 neutrality

17 After World War II, relations between the Soviet Union and the United States were marked by
1 conflicts where the superpowers supported opposing sides, but did not confront each other directly
2 refusal to negotiate on any issues
3 slow by steady decreases in military forces and armaments
4 reliance on international peace organizations to resolve disputes

18 The Red Scare and McCarthyism were similar in that both
1 advocated the development of the arts and sciences
2 supported United States foreign aid programs
3 encouraged nativist ideas
4 promoted economic development

19 The NATO alliance, Truman Doctrine, and Marshall Plan were all attempts to
1 contain the spread of communism
2 give military assistance to China
3 defend United Nations peacekeeping forces
4 bring peace to the Middle East

20 During the 1950s, Senator Joseph McCarthy held congressional hearings to expose suspected
1 Nazis
2 members of organized crime
3 terrorists
4 communists

21 The Cold War developed after World War II as a result of
1 a decrease in arms production
2 the collapse of the United Nations
3 Japan's new economic growth
4 tension between the superpowers

22 The need for an international peacekeeping organization after World War II resulted in the development of the
1 Red Cross
2 League of Nations
3 United Nations
4 Alliance for Progress

23 "We Americans live in a world we can no longer dominate, but from which we cannot isolate ourselves." The author of this quotation is saying that the United States should
1 become less dependent on foreign nations
2 realize that it is no longer a world power
3 recognize important changes in international relations
4 increase its economic and military strength

24 What was a major goal of United States foreign policy in Europe after 1945?
1 development of nuclear weapons for World War II Allies of the United States
2 liberation of nations under the control of the Soviet Union
3 military support for nationalist movements within individual European nations
4 promotion of international cooperation through political and economic agreements

25 In its dependence upon members to enforce human rights declarations, the United Nations most closely resembles the
1 Soviet Union under Josef Stalin.
2 United States under the federal Constitution.
3 United States under the Articles of Confederation.
4 Japanese government before World War II.

THEMATIC ESSAY

In developing your answers to the essay, be sure to keep these general definitions in mind:

(a) <u>discuss</u> means "to make observations about something using facts, reasoning, and argument; to present in some detail"

(b) <u>describe</u> means "to illustrate something in words or to tell about it"

(c) <u>evaluate</u> means "to examine and judge the significance, worth, or condition of; to determine the value of"

Directions

Write a well-organized essay that includes an introduction, several paragraphs addressing the task below, and a conclusion.

Theme: Foreign Policy

The primary aim of a nation's foreign policy is the self-interest of that nation. Throughout United States history, certain foreign policy actions have led to debate over whether they were in the national interest.

Task

Identify three different foreign policies that have been followed by the United States. Discuss a specific application of that policy by the United States. Include in your discussion one reason the United States applied that policy and one result of the application of that policy.

Suggestions

You may use any example from your study of United States foreign policy actions during the twentieth century. Some suggestions you might wish to consider include: isolationism, containment, formation of military alliances, reliance upon international alliances, nonrecognition.

You are *not* limited to these suggestions.

Guidelines

In your essay be sure to:

- Address all aspects of the *Task*
- Analyze, evaluate, or compare and/or contrast issues and events whenever possible
- Fully support the theme of the essay with relevant facts, examples, and details
- Write a well-developed essay that consistently demonstrates a logical and clear plan of organization
- Introduce the theme by establishing a framework that is beyond a simple restatement of the *Task*
- Conclude your essay with a strong summation of the theme

DOCUMENT-BASED ESSAY

For online Document-Based Essays,
visit the Prentice Hall Web site at www.phschool.com.

This task is designed to test your ability to work with historical documents and is based on the accompanying documents (1–7). Some of the documents have been edited for the purposes of this question. As you analyze the documents, take into account both the source of each document and any point of view that may be presented in the document.

Directions

This document-based question consists of two parts: Part A and Part B. In Part A, you are to read each document and answer the question or questions that follow the document. In Part B, you are to write an essay based on the information in the documents and your knowledge of United States history.

Historical Context

World events after 1939 drew the United States into greater international involvement. These events forced the United States to abandon its isolationist foreign policy in favor of more active global involvement.

Task

Using information from the documents and your knowledge of United States history and government, answer the questions that follow each document in Part A. Your answers to the questions will help you write the Part B essay in which you be asked to:

Discuss how the need for military security and the protection of democratic ideals have shaped American foreign policy since 1939.

PART A: SHORT ANSWER

DOCUMENT #1

> *"Yesterday, December 7, 1941, a date which will live in infamy, the United States of America was suddenly and deliberately attacked by naval and air forces of the Empire of Japan.*
>
> *"The attack yesterday on the Hawaiian Islands has caused severe damage to American naval and military forces. Very many American lives have been lost. In addition, American ships have been reported torpedoed on the high seas between San Francisco and Honolulu.*
>
> *"As Commander in Chief of the Army and Navy I have directed that all measures be taken for our defense. . . . I believe I interpret the will of the Congress and of the people when I assert that we will not only defend ourselves to the uttermost but will make very certain that this form of treachery shall never endanger us again.*
>
> *"I ask that the Congress declare that since the unprovoked and dastardly attack by Japan on Sunday, December 7, a state of war has existed between the United States and the Japanese Empire."*
>
> **—Franklin D. Roosevelt, "Address to Congress," December 8, 1941**

1 Why did President Roosevelt believe that the attack on Pearl Harbor justified the United States officially declaring war on Japan?

_____

_____

_____

_____

DOCUMENT #2

2 This cartoon represents Roosevelt, Stalin, and Churchill at the Yalta Conference. What does their activity in this cartoon say about their accomplishments at Yalta?

_____

_____

_____

DOCUMENT #3

> "[The Soviet Union] cannot be easily defeated or discouraged by a single victory on the part of its opponents . . . but only by intelligent long-range policies . . . no less steady in their purpose . . . than those of the Soviet Union itself. In these circumstances, it is clear that the main element of any United States policy toward the Soviet Union must be that of a long-term, patient but firm and vigilant containment of Russian expansive tendencies."
>
> **—Foreign service officer George Kennan, July 1947**

3 What foreign policy position did Kennan believe the United States should take toward the Soviet Union?

_____

_____

_____

DOCUMENT #4

> *"The Parties agree that an armed attack against one or more of them in Europe or North America shall be considered an attack against them all and consequently they agree that, if such an armed attack occurs, each of them, in exercise of the right of individual or collective self-defense. . . will assist the Party or Parties so attacked by taking . . . such action as it deems necessary, including the use of armed force, to restore and maintain the security of the North Atlantic area."*
>
> **—The North Atlantic Treaty, April 4, 1949**

4   How did joining NATO demonstrate the long-term commitment of the United States to international involvement?

_____

_____

_____

_____

DOCUMENT #5

> *"I believe that it must be the policy of the United States to support free peoples who are resisting attempted subjugation [takeover] by armed minorities or by outside pressures. . . . I believe that our help should be primarily through economic and financial aid which is essential to economic stability and orderly political processes. . . .*
>
> *"I therefore ask the Congress to provide authority for assistance to Greece and Turkey in the amount of $400,000,000. . . .*
>
> *"The free peoples of the world look to us for support in maintaining their freedoms. If we falter in our leadership, we may endanger the peace of the world-and we shall surely endanger the welfare of our own nation. Great responsibilities have been placed upon us by the swift movement of events. I am confident that the Congress will face these responsibilities squarely."*
>
> **—President Harry S Truman, *Address Before a Joint Session of Congress*, March 12, 1947**

5   Based on this quote, why did President Truman believe that the United States should help Greece and Turkey in their fight against a communist takeover?

_____

_____

_____

DOCUMENT #6
Berlin Airlift Statistics, 1948–1949

	Flights	Cargo (short tons)			
		Total	Food	Coal	Other
USA	189,963	1,783,573	296,319	1,421,119	66,135
UK	87,841	541,937	240,386	164,911	136,640
France	424	896	unknown	unknown	unknown
Total	278,228	2,326,406			

6 How does the chart above demonstrate the commitment that the United States made to prevent the Soviet Union from crippling West Berlin in the blockade of 1948–1949?

_____

_____

_____

_____

_____

DOCUMENT #7

"Our purpose in the Persian Gulf remains constant: to drive Iraq out of Kuwait, to restore Kuwait's legitimate government, and to ensure the stability and security of this critical region. Let me make clear what I mean by the region's stability and security. . . . We seek a Persian Gulf where conflict is no longer the rule, where the strong are neither tempted nor able to intimidate the weak.

"Most Americans know instinctively why we are in the Gulf. They know we had to stop [Iraqi leader] Saddam [Hussein] now, not later. . . . They know we must make sure that control of the world's oil resources does not fall into his hands, only to finance further aggression. They know that we need to build a new, enduring peace, based not on arms races and confrontation but on shared principles and the rule of law."

—President George Bush, State of the Union Address, January 29, 1991

7 According to this quote, why did President Bush believe that American involvement in the Persian Gulf War was necessary?

_____

_____

_____

_____

_____

_____

PART B: ESSAY

Directions
Using information from the documents provided, and your knowledge of United States history, write a well-organized essay that includes an introduction, several paragraphs, and a conclusion.

Historical Context
World events after 1939 drew the United States into greater international involvement. These events forced the United States to abandon its isolationist foreign policy in favor of more active global involvement.

Task
Using information from the documents and your knowledge of United States history and government, write an essay in which you

Discuss how the need for military security and the protection of democratic ideals have shaped American foreign policy since 1939.

Guidelines
When writing your essay, be sure to
- Address all aspects of the *Task* by accurately analyzing and interpreting at least <u>four</u> documents
- Incorporate information from the documents in the body of the essay
- Incorporate relevant outside information throughout the essay
- Richly support the theme with relevant facts, examples, and details
- Write a well-developed essay that consistently demonstrates a logical and clean plan of organization
- Introduce the theme by establishing a framework that is beyond a simple restatement of the *Task* or *Historical Context* and conclude the essay with a summation of the theme.

UNIT 7

The World in Uncertain Times, 1950–the Present

UNIT OVERVIEW

The foreign policies that began after World War II continued to shape America's response to events abroad for decades. The policy of containment, begun under President Truman, eventually led the United States into its longest war, one that caused deep splits within American society.

During the period from the 1950s to the present, life changed at home for Americans. An expanding civil rights movement, a major constitutional crisis, new technologies, and a changing economic picture are some of the highlights of these years.

Some key questions to help you focus on this time period include:

- How did the foreign policy concerns of the United States become more global in scope?
- What were the goals and the achievements of the civil rights movement?
- How did the war in Vietnam affect American society?
- How did relations of the United States with the Soviet Union change under Presidents Reagan and Bush?
- What are some of the major challenges that the nation will face in years to come?

1

Containment Abroad and Agreement at Home

SECTION OVERVIEW

During the 1950s, the Cold War intensified and spread to new locations around the world. Meanwhile, the new economic prosperity allowed many Americans to enjoy greater wealth and leisure than their parents had. At the same time, the civil rights movement intensified as African Americans demanded justice and equality.

KEY THEMES AND CONCEPTS

As you review this section, take special note of the following key themes and concepts:

Foreign Policy How did tensions between the United States and the Soviet Union increase and decrease during Eisenhower's presidency?

Citizenship How did African Americans begin to organize the civil rights movement?

Economic Systems Who benefited from the "Eisenhower prosperity," and who did not?

KEY PEOPLE

Dwight D. Eisenhower
Nikita Khrushchev
Fidel Castro
Jackie Robinson
Rosa Parks
Martin Luther King, Jr.

KEY SUPREME COURT CASE

Brown v. *Board of Education of Topeka, Kansas*

★ THE BIG IDEA

Foreign policy, especially the Cold War, influenced events in the 1950s. During this period

- President Eisenhower attempted to limit communism.

- policies toward Asia, the Middle East , and Latin America took shape.

- the economy of the United States improved.

- African Americans renewed their struggle for civil rights.

⚷ KEY TERMS

balance of power
brinkmanship
arms race
Sputnik
domino theory
Eisenhower doctrine
suburbanization
civil rights movement

THE COLD WAR CONTINUES

The United States emerged from World War II as the strongest nation in the world. It controlled the atomic bomb, and its economy was undamaged by the destruction of war. The Soviet Union, however, quickly became America's chief rival. By 1949, it too had the atomic bomb. It had also taken control of most of the nations of Eastern Europe and was seeking to extend its influence elsewhere.

The Cold War, 1950–1960

| 1950 Korean War begins | 1953 Korean War ends | 1956 Suez crisis begins; Hungarian revolt | 1960 U2 shot down over USSR |

| 1950 | 1952 | 1954 | 1956 | 1958 | 1960 |

| 1952 Dwight D. Eisenhower elected President | 1955 Summit conference in Geneva | 1959 Castro wins power in Cuba |

ANALYZING DOCUMENTS

Examine the timeline, then answer the following questions.

- Did the Korean War begin before or after Eisenhower became President?

- Which events on the timeline took place in Europe?

President Harry S Truman began the policy of containment after the war in an attempt to limit the spread of communism. As the United States and the Soviet Union—the two world superpowers—attempted to maintain a **balance of power,** a cold war developed.

Eisenhower's Foreign Policy

As President, Dwight D. Eisenhower continued Truman's basic policy of containment. However, he and his secretary of state John Foster Dulles introduced some new ideas.

MASSIVE RETALIATION Eisenhower worried that defense spending would bankrupt the nation. Yet he feared that the Soviets might see cutbacks in military spending as a sign of weakness.

Eisenhower and Dulles instead devised a "new look" for the nation's defense. The United States would rely more heavily on air power and nuclear weapons than on ground troops. Dulles announced a policy of massive retaliation. This meant that the United States would consider the use of nuclear weapons to halt aggression if it believed the nation's interests were threatened.

Dulles further stated that the nation must be ready to go "to the brink of war" in order to preserve world peace. This policy of **brinkmanship** greatly increased world tensions during the 1950s.

THE ARMS RACE The United States and the Soviet Union began an **arms race,** stockpiling nuclear and nonnuclear weapons. The United States exploded a hydrogen bomb in 1952, and the Soviets tested one a year later. Both nations rushed to develop missiles capable of carrying nuclear weapons. The balance of power became a balance of terror.

In 1953, Eisenhower announced the Atoms for Peace Plan at the United Nations. The plan called for United Nations supervision of a world search to find peaceful uses for nuclear technology. The Soviet Union refused to participate.

In 1957, the Soviets launched a satellite, **Sputnik,** into orbit around the earth. The arms race then became a space race as the United States rushed to launch its own satellites, some for military purposes.

Foreign Policy in Asia
Asia became a major area of concern for United States foreign policy. The communist victory in China in 1949 raised fears of further communist expansion. The war in Korea, even though it ended in what was basically a draw in 1953, added to these fears.

THE DOMINO THEORY As communists took control of the governments of China and, later, some nations of Southeast Asia, American worries about Communist expansion increased. Eisenhower stated that the United States must resist further aggression in the region and explained what came to be known as the **domino theory.** The nations of Asia, he said, were like a row of dominoes standing on end. If one fell to communism, the rest were sure to follow.

SEATO One way to resist aggression, Dulles claimed, was through alliances. To mirror the formation of NATO in Europe, Dulles in 1954 pushed for the creation of the Southeast Asia Treaty Organization (SEATO). Its original members—Pakistan, Thailand, the Philippines, Australia, New Zealand, Great Britain, and the United States— pledged to meet any "common danger" from communist aggression.

Foreign Policy in the Middle East
The Middle East was the scene of several outbreaks of trouble during the Eisenhower administration.

IRAN In 1954, the prime minister of Iran tried to nationalize that country's foreign-owned oil industry. The United States, through the Central Intelligence Agency, secretly arranged the overthrow of the prime minister's government and the restoration of the shah to the throne of Iran. This action helped secure America's supply of oil at the time but caused problems for the nation in years to come.

EGYPT Gamal Abdel Nasser, president of Egypt, had counted on economic support from the Soviet Union and the United States to build a huge dam at Aswan on the Nile River. Nasser's friendliness to the Soviet Union led the United States to withdraw its support. Nasser

♀ KEY THEMES AND
⬥ CONCEPTS
Interdependence
In 1954, the Central Intelligence Agency tried to overthrow the government of Iran and restore the country's former ruler, the shah. Why?

GEOGRAPHY
IN HISTORY

Nasser's seizure of the Suez Canal sparked a crisis that involved Great Britain, France, and Israel. Why was the Suez Canal so important to these nations?

PREPARING FOR THE EXAM

On the examination, you will need to understand United States foreign policy during the 1950s in the Middle East.

What is the Eisenhower Doctrine? List two countries to which it is applied.

1.

2.

then nationalized the Suez Canal, which was run by a British and French company. He planned to use revenues from the canal to pay for the dam.

Great Britain and France, joined by Israel, sent troops to seize the canal. Fearing that fighting would spread through the region, both the United States and the Soviet Union supported a United Nations resolution condemning the attack. Britain, France, and Israel withdrew, and the canal remained under Egyptian control.

THE EISENHOWER DOCTRINE Troubles in the Middle East led Congress to adopt what became known as the **Eisenhower Doctrine** in 1957. The United States pledged to help any Middle Eastern nation resist communist aggression.

LEBANON In 1958, the Eisenhower Doctrine was tested when the governments of Lebanon and Jordan asked for help. The United States sent marines to Lebanon, and Great Britain sent troops to Jordan to help restore political calm in those nations.

Foreign Policy in Latin America

Troubles also flared up closer to home during Eisenhower's time in office. Three instances are especially notable.

GUATEMALA The CIA staged a successful covert operation in Guatemala in 1954. It arranged a revolt that toppled a government considered to be too friendly to communists.

NIXON'S TOUR In 1958, Vice President Richard Nixon went on a goodwill tour of Latin America. In Peru and Venezuela, however, angry mobs surrounded his limousine, throwing rocks and eggs at it. This event revealed the strong anti-American feelings that had built up in Latin America in response to repeated interventions in the region by the United States.

READING STRATEGY

Analyzing Cause and Effect
Why did the policies of Fidel Castro anger the Eisenhower administration?

CUBA In 1956, Fidel Castro began a revolt against the government of Cuban dictator Fulgencio Batista. When the revolt ended with Castro's victory in 1959, the United States quickly recognized the new government.

Castro, however, soon adopted policies that angered the Eisenhower administration. He limited civil liberties and imprisoned political opponents. He also nationalized key industries and turned to the Soviet Union for aid.

Large numbers of Cubans fled Castro's rule, with many settling in southern Florida. Some worked actively to end Castro's rule. Meanwhile, they became one more immigrant group that contributed to the richness of the American multicultural experience.

Changing Relations with the Soviet Union

Tensions between the United States and the Soviet Union rose and fell during Eisenhower's time in office.

NEW SOVIET LEADERSHIP Josef Stalin, leader of the Soviet Union since the 1920s, died in 1953. In time, Nikita Khrushchev took over as the head of the Soviet government. This change marked a temporary easing of Cold War tensions as the Soviets began to focus more on improving conditions within their nation.

PEACEFUL COEXISTENCE Relations between the superpowers gradually improved. In 1955, the leaders of the United States, the Soviet Union, Great Britain, and France held the first summit meeting since World War II in Geneva, Switzerland. The superpower leaders began talks on disarmament that, in time, led to a suspension of nuclear testing.

POLAND AND HUNGARY In 1956, riots by Polish workers won concessions from the Communist Polish government. Inspired by this, students and workers in Hungary began demonstrations that fall that ended with the Soviet Union sending tanks and troops to bring that nation firmly back under Communist control. The suppression of the Hungarian revolt cooled relations between the United States and the Soviet Union.

CAMP DAVID Relations improved again by 1959. Khrushchev visited the United States, and he and Eisenhower held lengthy talks at Camp David, the presidential retreat near Washington, D.C. The spirit of goodwill that grew at these talks encouraged the leaders to announce another summit meeting in Paris in 1960.

THE U-2 INCIDENT The Paris summit proved a disaster. Shortly before it opened, the Soviet military shot down an American U-2 aircraft deep in Soviet territory. The pilot admitted that he had been spying on Soviet military bases.

Eisenhower said that he had approved the U-2 flights and promised to suspend them. Khrushchev denounced the United States and demanded an apology. Eisenhower refused, and the summit collapsed before it really started.

In summary, Eisenhower's foreign policy was primarily a continuation of Truman's containment policy. Many of the events of the 1950s can be compared to kettles ready to boil over in the 1960s. In later years, the Eisenhower administration was criticized by some as not being aware enough of the struggles of developing nations and of their desires to end colonial rule.

AN IMPROVING ECONOMY AT HOME

When Dwight Eisenhower became President in 1953, he was the first Republican President since 1933—the year Herbert Hoover left office during one of the worst years of the Great Depression. Since that time, Democrats Franklin D. Roosevelt and Harry S Truman had called for

KEY THEMES AND CONCEPTS
Foreign Policy
Relations between the United States and the Soviet Union changed several times during the 1950s. Following the death of Soviet leader Joseph Stalin in 1953, the new Soviet leader Nikita Khrushchev focused more on improving conditions within his nation. This eased cold war tensions.

• What event rekindled the Cold War in 1956?

TURNING POINT

Why is the U-2 incident considered a turning point in U.S.-Soviet relations?

KEY THEMES AND CONCEPTS

Presidential Decisions and Actions

President Eisenhower believed that what was good for business benefited the United States as a whole. He attempted to limit the federal government's power but expanded several social programs, including Social Security.

- Why did farm conditions present a problem for Eisenhower?

- How did Congress resolve the problem?

New Deal and New Society policies that had vastly increased both the federal government's spending and its role in society.

Eisenhower's Economic Policies

Eisenhower had a deep dislike for strong centralized government. In addition, he generally believed policies that were good for big business were good for the nation as a whole.

EISENHOWER'S DOMESTIC POLICIES Eisenhower attempted to cut back on the federal government's size and power. He reduced spending for defense and foreign aid.

Eisenhower did recognize that many social programs begun under the New Deal were very popular. He extended some of these and, in some cases, started new programs. The Social Security program was expanded to include seven million more people, and a new cabinet post, the Department of Health, Education, and Welfare, was created.

THE FARM PROBLEM Conditions on the nation's farms pulled Eisenhower between his desire to cut government spending and his wish to extend some social programs. Farm production had been increasing while prices for agricultural products had been declining.

Farmers had been receiving payments from the federal government to make up for changes in market conditions. Eisenhower's secretary of agriculture wanted to be able to cut such payments. Farmers protested, and in 1956, Congress approved a new program that paid farmers for not planting crops. Both types of payments are called subsidies, or direct payments by a government to private individuals.

"Eisenhower Prosperity" and Consumer Spending

Despite the problems noted above, the American people commonly prospered during the 1950s. There were several reasons for this.
- During World War II, Americans had worked hard and generally earned good wages. Because of rationing and shortages, however, they could usually only spend their money on basic necessities.
- By war's end, Americans had accumulated huge amounts of capital—wealth in the form of money or property. They were ready to spend this capital on consumer goods.
- By the 1950s, wartime price controls were over, and factories had converted from the production of military supplies to the production of consumer goods.

NEW HOMES The postwar years saw the start of a "baby boom." The growth in family size, the accumulation of capital, and the availability of government loans to veterans brought a rapid increase in home building.

SUBURBS Much new home building was done in areas surrounding major cities (urban areas). These areas are called suburbs. The suburbs

ANALYZING DOCUMENTS

Examine the advertisement at left, then answer the questions.

- What product is the advertisement promoting?

- Who is the advertisement targeting? What clues lead you to this conclusion?

- What does this advertisement suggest about the U.S. economy at the time?

- How is this advertisement similar to ads you see today? How is it different?

READING STRATEGY

Reinforcing Main Ideas
How did the growth of suburbs contribute to the decline of many cities?

offered limited jobs and services for their residents, most of whom worked in the cities. The suburbs grew rapidly. Levittown, New York, for example, became a symbol of **suburbanization,** with some 17,000 tract houses built in four years. By the 1960s, almost a third of all Americans lived in suburbs.

The growth of suburbs contributed to the decline of many cities. As people moved out of cities to suburbs, fewer taxpayers remained to help pay for essential services. At the same time, a greater concentration of poorer people in the cities increased the demand for many social services.

AUTOMOBILES Cars made the growth of suburbs possible, and suburbs increased the demand for cars. Since public transportation systems grew more slowly than suburbs, people in suburbs relied increasingly on their cars. Increased demand for automobiles benefited many areas of the nation's economy. Factories turned out the steel, glass, and rubber that went into new cars. Refineries also produced oil and gas that powered them.

The federal government stepped into the transportation picture with passage of the Federal Highway Act of 1956. This provided funding for what became a 44,000-mile network of interstate highways.

READING STRATEGY

Formulating Questions
The increase in demand for cars benefited many industries, such as the steel and oil industries. Increased automobile ownership also made it possible for people to live in suburbs without public transportation, because the government provided funding for an extensive highway network.

- What were some of the negative consequences of this increased reliance on cars?

**GEOGRAPHY
IN HISTORY**

In which areas of the United States did the population grow most quickly during in the 1950s? Give examples of three states that experienced rapid growth.

1.

2.

3.

**ANALYZING
DOCUMENTS**

Examine the bar graph at right. Between which two years did the number of homes with television sets increase most dramatically?

A NATION ON THE MOVE Americans moved from central cities to suburbs. They also moved to new areas of the country. Many people moved from the industrialized but decaying cities of the Northeast and Midwest and from the farms of the Midwest to the Sun Belt. This was the name given to the states of the South and West—including Florida, Texas, Arizona, and California—that experienced a faster than average population growth beginning in the postwar years.

The sun and warm climate of these states enticed both retirees and businesses that wished to relocate. As this region grew, it attracted more industry and prompted both population and job loss in what came to be called the Rust Belt. This region included the states of the Northeast (including New York and Massachusetts) and Midwest (including Ohio and Michigan).

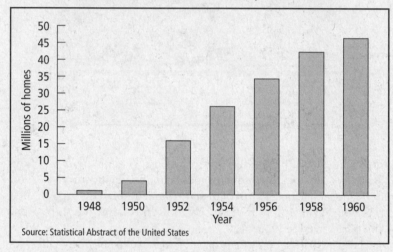

Homes with Television Sets, 1948–1960

Source: Statistical Abstract of the United States

TELEVISION After limited broadcasting in 1939, national broadcasting began in 1946. Television became the leading form of popular entertainment, and its growth, both as a source of amusement and a tool for learning, has continued to the present day.

A RENEWED STRUGGLE FOR CIVIL RIGHTS

Since the period of Reconstruction after the Civil War, African Americans faced discrimination, especially in southern states. Jim Crow laws limited the freedoms of African Americans. For generations, white southerners continued to maintain economic, social, and political control over the South.

Beginnings of Change

Until well into the twentieth century, much of the South was segregated, or separated by race. Although such segregation was less apparent in the North, African Americans were generally restricted to poorer neighborhoods and lower-paying jobs. Although African Americans fought for change, until the 1950s their gains were limited.

Not until 1947, for example, were African Americans permitted to play on major league baseball teams in this country. In that year, Jackie Robinson joined the Brooklyn Dodgers. This was one sign that public attitudes on segregation were beginning to change.

TRUMAN'S POLICIES ON CIVIL RIGHTS President Truman appointed a presidential commission on civil rights in 1946. Based on its report, Truman called for the establishment of a fair employment practices commission. Congress, however, failed to act on the idea.

Using his powers as commander in chief, Truman issued an executive order banning segregation in the armed forces. He also strengthened the Justice Department's civil rights division, which aided blacks who challenged segregation in the courts.

TURNING POINT

Why is it considered a turning point in the struggle for civil rights when Jackie Robinson joined the Brooklyn Dodgers?

READING STRATEGY

Organizing Information
The struggle to secure African American civil rights required the efforts of countless dedicated activists, organizers, and political leaders. What are two changes that President Truman made that had an impact on civil rights?

1.

2.

Civil Rights Milestones

1947: Jackie Robinson becomes first African American to play in major league baseball.

1948: Truman orders end to segregation in armed forces.

1954: Supreme Court issues *Brown v. Board of Education* ruling, stating that segregated schools are unconstitutional.

1955-1956: Montgomery bus boycott protests segregation on city buses; Supreme Court rules bus segregation unconstitutional.

1957: Eisenhower uses National Guard to enforce desegregation of schools in Little Rock, Arkansas.

Civil Rights and the Courts

In the 1950s, the Supreme Court made several important decisions concerning the civil rights of African Americans.

THE WARREN COURT In 1953, a vacancy occurred on the Supreme Court. President Eisenhower then appointed Earl Warren, former governor of California, as chief justice. Warren presided over the Supreme Court until 1969. During that period, the Court reached a number of decisions that deeply affected many areas of American life. Among the most far-reaching of the Warren Court's decisions were those dealing with civil rights for African Americans.

KEY THEMES AND CONCEPTS

Constitutional Principles
Brown v. *Board of Education of Topeka, Kansas* (1954) established that facilities separated by race were unequal. The decision reversed *Plessy* v. *Ferguson* (1896) and made integration of schools possible.

- How did the governor of Arkansas respond to *Brown* v. *Board of Education of Topeka, Kansas*?

BROWN V. *BOARD OF EDUCATION* Only a year after he became chief justice, Warren presided over the court as it reached a landmark decision in *Brown* v. *Board of Education of Topeka, Kansas.* Linda Brown, a young African American student, requested the right to attend a local all-white school in her Topeka neighborhood, rather than attend an all-black school that was further away.

The 1896 *Plessy* v. *Ferguson* decision had held that separate but equal public facilities were legal. Schools were such public facilities, and Brown was refused admittance to the all-white school.

The National Association for the Advancement of Colored People (NAACP) joined the case and appealed it all the way to the Supreme Court. In a unanimous decision, the Court reversed its ruling in *Plessy* v. *Ferguson* and held that in the field of public education, "the doctrine of separate but equal has no place."

LITTLE ROCK Although the Brown case opened the door for desegregation, integration did not follow immediately. Many Americans were shocked by the decision. In the South, whites began campaigns of "massive resistance" to public school desegregation.

Although the Supreme Court had ordered that school integration go forward "with all deliberate speed," many school systems openly defied the ruling. In 1957, the governor of Arkansas ordered the state's National Guard to prevent nine African American students from attending Central High School in Little Rock.

President Eisenhower was reluctant to step in, but the governor's defiance was a direct challenge to the Constitution. Eisenhower placed the Arkansas National Guard under federal control and then used it to enforce integration. At the end of the school year, the governor continued his defiance by ordering all city high schools closed for the following year. The tactic failed, however, and in 1959 the first racially integrated class graduated from Central High School.

African American Activism

Public facilities of all kinds were segregated in the South—schools, movie theaters, lunch counters, drinking fountains, restrooms, buses, and trains. Rather than wait for court rulings to end segregation, in the 1950s African Americans began to organize a **civil rights movement.**

THE MONTGOMERY BUS BOYCOTT In Montgomery, Alabama, in 1955, an African American seamstress named Rosa Parks refused to give up her seat to a white man and move to the back of the bus, as was required by law. She was arrested for violating the law, and her action inspired a boycott of the city's buses.

Martin Luther King, Jr., a young Baptist minister, emerged as a leader of the protest. King had studied the nonviolent methods of Mohandas Gandhi and Henry David Thoreau. His dynamic speaking style drew the attention and support of large numbers of people.

Major Civil Rights Protests, 1954–1965

Year	Event	Outcome
1954	*Brown* v. *Board of Education*	Supreme Court ruled that separate educational facilities for whites and African Americans are inherently unequal.
1955–1956	Montgomery Bus Boycott	Alabama bus company was forced to desegregate its buses. Martin Luther King, Jr., emerged as an important civil rights leader.
1961	Freedom Rides	Interstate Commerce Commission banned segregation in interstate transportation.
1963	James Meredith sues University of Mississippi for admission	Supreme Court upheld Meredith's right to enter the all-white institution.
1963	Protest marches in Birmingham, Alabama	Violence against peaceful demonstrators shocked the nation. Under pressure, Birmingham desegregated public facilities.
1963	March on Washington	More than 200,000 people demonstrated in an impressive display of support for civil rights.
1965	Selma March (Alabama)	State troopers attacked marchers. President Johnson used federal force to protect route from Selma to Montgomery and thousands joined march.

ANALYZING DOCUMENTS

The table at left outlines some of the major civil rights protests from 1954 to 1965.

• Which protest led to the rise of Dr. Martin Luther King, Jr., as an important civil rights leader?

• Which three key protests occurred in Alabama?

KEY THEMES AND CONCEPTS

Individuals, Groups, Institutions

African Americans began to take direct action to end segregation following *Brown* v. *Board of Education.* Boycotts of schools, lunch counters, and buses, for example, began.

• How did the actions of Rosa Parks and Martin Luther King, Jr., change attitudes toward segregation?

The boycott lasted 381 days. In the end, the Supreme Court ruled that segregation of public buses was illegal. Although Parks had not planned her action that day, her stand against injustice led the way for others.

Civil Rights Legislation

Congress also made some moves to ensure civil rights for African Americans. In August 1957, it passed the first civil rights act since Reconstruction. The bill created a permanent commission for civil rights and increased federal efforts to ensure blacks the right to vote. Another bill in 1960 further strengthened voting rights.

Although these bills had only limited effectiveness, they did mark the beginning of change. Martin Luther King, Jr., once remarked that it was impossible to legislate what was in a person's heart, but that laws can restrain the heartless.

THE BIG IDEA

The 1960s were a tumultuous era in American society. During this period

- the struggle for civil rights continued.

- the women's rights movement organized.

- other groups, including Native Americans, struggled for equality.

- New Frontier and Great Society programs expanded upon the New Deal of the 1930s.

- the Cold War affected foreign policy in Latin America.

KEY TERMS

civil disobedience
Civil Rights Act of 1964
Voting Rights Act of 1965
Equal Rights Amendment
affirmative action
United Farm Workers
American Indian Movement
mainstreaming
Americans with Disabilities
 Act of 1990
New Frontier
Great Society
Cuban missile crisis
Berlin Wall

SECTION OVERVIEW

In the early 1960s, the continuing pressure of African American civil rights groups, plus growing public sympathy, forced the passage of new legislation. Women, Latino Americans, Native Americans, and disabled Americans adapted civil rights tactics to achieve their own goals of equality. Meanwhile, the cold war tensions between the United States and the Soviet Union continued, as the two nations came into conflict in Germany and Cuba.

KEY THEMES AND CONCEPTS

As you review this section, take special note of the following key themes and concepts:

Citizenship How did the African American civil rights movement inspire others to struggle to achieve greater equality?

Government How did Presidents Kennedy and Johnson continue and expand upon traditions from the New Deal of the 1930s?

Foreign Policy How did the antagonism between the United States and the Soviet Union bring the two nations to the brink of war?

KEY PEOPLE

James Meredith
Medgar Evers
Lyndon B. Johnson
Malcolm X
Cesar Chavez

KEY SUPREME COURT CASES

Heart of Atlanta Motel v. *United States*
Roe v. *Wade*
Regents of the University of California v. *Bakke*

The Sixties

1961 Peace Corps created; Bay of Pigs invasion

1963 President Kennedy assassinated

1965 Medicaid, Medicare, Voting Rights acts passed

1968 Martin Luther King, Jr., assassinated; Richard M. Nixon elected President

1960 | 1962 | 1964 | 1966 | 1968 | 1970

1962 Cuban missile crisis

1964 Civil Rights Act passed; Johnson elected President

1967 War between Israel and Egypt

THE STRUGGLE FOR CIVIL RIGHTS CONTINUES

During the 1960s, the struggle of African Americans to win equality before the law grew more intense. In their fight, African Americans were seeking to overcome a heritage of racism that had been a part of American thought and tradition for more than 300 years.

By the 1960s, however, many African Americans were working together for the common goal of justice and equality. The successes they gained would deeply affect many parts of American society.

African Americans Organize

African Americans formed a number of different groups that used a variety of approaches in the attempt to achieve justice and equality. In the early 1960s, many groups followed the nonviolent methods introduced by Dr. Martin Luther King, Jr., and the Southern Christian Leadership Conference (SCLC), an organization of clergy who shifted the leadership of the civil rights movement to the South.

Many civil rights activists used a form of protest called **civil disobedience.** This means the deliberate breaking of a law to show a belief that the law is unjust. For example, they attempted to use segregated facilities at interstate train stations and bus depots. Usually they were arrested for such acts; often they were beaten.

JAMES MEREDITH The push to integrate education continued. In 1962, James Meredith, an African American Air Force veteran, made headlines when he tried to enroll at the all-white University of Mississippi. The governor of the state personally tried to stop Meredith from enrolling. Riots broke out, and federal marshals and the National Guard were called up. Although he had to overcome continued harassment, Meredith did finally enter and eventually graduate from the university.

Election of 1960

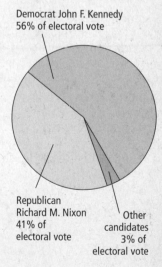

Democrat John F. Kennedy 56% of electoral vote

Republican Richard M. Nixon 41% of electoral vote

Other candidates 3% of electoral vote

"Perhaps it is easy for those who have never felt the stinging dark of segregation to say, 'Wait.' But when you have seen vicious mobs lynch your mothers and fathers at will and drown your sisters and brothers at whim; . . . when you see the vast majority of your twenty million Negro brothers smothering in an airtight cage of poverty in the midst of an affluent society; when you suddenly find your tongue twisted . . . as you seek to explain to your six-year-old daughter why she can't go to the public amusement park . . . and see tears welling up in her eyes when she is told that Funtown is closed to colored children, . . . then you will understand why we find it difficult to wait."
—Dr. Martin Luther King, Jr.,
"Letter from a Birmingham
Jail" (1963)

• How does King justify the immediate need for direct action to end discrimination?

Major African American Organizations

Organization	Date of Founding	Background
National Association for the Advancement of Colored People (NAACP)	1909	Organized by black and white progressives; W. E. B. Du Bois an early leader; favored court challenges to segregation; appealed primarily to the professional and college-educated.
Black Muslims	1931	Founded as a black separatist religious group; became the voice of black nationalism in the 1960s; Muhammed Ali converted in 1965; Malcolm X, a leading spokesperson, was assassinated in 1965.
Congress of Racial Equality (CORE)	1942	Became best known for the "freedom rides" of the 1960s, efforts to desegregate interstate transportation.
Southern Christian Leadership Conference (SCLC)	1957	Founded by Martin Luther King, Jr., to encourage nonviolent passive resistance; organized black Christian churches.
Student Nonviolent Coordinating Committee (SNCC)	1960	In early days, used nonviolent civil disobedience in sit-ins and boycotts; later supported the idea of "black power" put forward by Stokely Carmichael.

GREENSBORO Practicing civil disobedience, demonstrators protested such discrimination as segregated lunch counters and buses. Sit-ins at lunch counters—the 1960s version of fast-food restaurants—began at Greensboro, North Carolina, in 1960. There a group of African Americans sat at a "whites only" lunch counter and refused to leave until served. As such protests became popular, some sympathetic whites often joined the sit-ins.

BIRMINGHAM In 1963, Dr. Martin Luther King, Jr., and the SCLC began a campaign to bring integration to Birmingham, Alabama, which many considered to be the most segregated city in the South. At a protest march, police used dogs and fire hoses to break up the marchers and arrested more than 2,000 people. One of those jailed was King, who then wrote his famous "Letter from a Birmingham Jail," in which he defended his methods of nonviolent civil disobedience and restated the need for direct action to end segregation.

Television cameras had brought the scenes of violence in Birmingham to people across the country. This helped build support for the growing civil rights movement. In Birmingham, the protests eventually resulted in the desegregation of city facilities.

MEDGAR EVERS White reaction to African American protests sometimes turned deadly. Medgar Evers, field secretary of the NAACP, had been working to desegregate Jackson, Mississippi. In June 1963, Evers was murdered by a sniper outside his home.

UNIVERSITY OF ALABAMA Also in June 1963, Governor George Wallace of Alabama vowed to stop two African American students from registering at the state university. Pressure from President Kennedy and the later arrival of the National Guard forced Wallace to back down. The two students enrolled peacefully.

THE MARCH ON WASHINGTON The growing civil rights movement moved President Kennedy to deliver a televised speech to the nation in June 1963 on the need to guarantee the civil rights of African Americans. This marked the first speech by a President specifically on this issue. Eight days later, he sent the most comprehensive civil rights bill in the nation's history to Congress.

Civil rights groups organized a huge march on Washington, D.C., in August 1963, to show support for the bill. At the march, Dr. Martin Luther King, Jr., delivered his famous "I have a dream" speech to a crowd of more than 200,000 participants. In the speech, he eloquently expressed his hopes for a unified America.

Not all Americans shared King's dream, however. Just a few weeks after the March on Washington, white terrorists bombed an African American church in Birmingham, killing four young girls.

JOHNSON AND THE CIVIL RIGHTS ACT After the assassination of John F. Kennedy in November 1963, the new President, Lyndon Johnson, recognized the urgency of pushing forward with civil rights legislation. Johnson worked tirelessly for the passage of the bill, and in July 1964, he signed the **Civil Rights Act of 1964,** the most sweeping civil rights law in American history. The bill called for

- protection of voting rights for all Americans.
- opening of public facilities (restaurants, hotels, stores, restrooms) to people of all races.
- a commission to protect equal job opportunities for all Americans.

Passage of the Civil Rights Act came just months after ratification of the Twenty-fourth Amendment to the Constitution, which abolished the poll tax in federal elections. A poll tax was a fee that had to be paid before a person could vote. The poll tax had prevented poorer Americans—including many African Americans—from exercising their legal right to vote.

The Civil Rights Act of 1964 outlawed race discrimination in public accommodations, including motels that refused rooms to African Americans. In the landmark Supreme Court case *Heart of Atlanta Motel* v. *United States* (1964), racial segregation of private facilities engaged in interstate commerce was found unconstitutional.

TURNING POINT

Why is the Civil Rights Act of 1964 considered a turning point in the struggle for civil rights?

THE VOTING RIGHTS ACT OF 1965 Many southern states continued to resist civil rights legislation and Supreme Court rulings. Southern resistance to civil rights laws angered Johnson. He proposed new legislation, which was passed as the **Voting Rights Act of 1965.** This bill

- put an end to literacy tests—tests of a person's ability to read and write that had often been misused to bar African American voters.
- authorized federal examiners to register voters in areas suspected of denying African Americans the right to vote.
- directed the attorney general of the United States to take legal action against states that continued to use poll taxes in state elections.

CHANGES IN THE CIVIL RIGHTS MOVEMENT The summer of 1964 was known as "Freedom Summer" for its many demonstrations, protests, voter registration drives, and the March on Washington. Freedom Summer and the passage of the Voting Rights Act a year later marked highpoints of the civil rights movement.

By the mid-1960s, some civil rights activists became frustrated that the new legislation had not improved conditions enough. Some demanded "Black Power," stressing that African Americans should take total control of the political and economic aspects of their lives. Some advocated the use of violence. Meanwhile, more moderate leaders continued to call for nonviolent methods of protest. These splits weakened the effectiveness of the civil rights movement.

A new, more militant leader, Malcolm X, began to attract a following from African Americans who were frustrated by the pace of the civil rights movement. Malcolm X spoke against integration, instead promoting black nationalism, a belief in the separate identity and racial unity of the African American community. A member of the separatist group Nation of Islam until 1964, Malcolm X broke with that group to form his own religious organization, called Muslim Mosque, Inc. After a pilgrimage to the Muslim holy city of Mecca in Saudi Arabia, during which he saw millions of Muslims of all races worshipping peacefully together, he changed his views about integration and began to work toward a more unified civil rights movement. He had made enemies, though, and in February 1965, he was assassinated at a New York City rally.

In 1964 and 1965, frustration at the discrimination in housing, education, and employment boiled over into riots in New York City, Rochester, and the Watts neighborhood of Los Angeles. In Watts alone, 34 people were killed, and more than a thousand were injured.

The federal government set up the Kerner Commission to investigate the cause of the rioting. It concluded that the riots were a result of the anger that had been building in many of America's inner cities.

ASSASSINATIONS Dr. Martin Luther King, Jr., had been awarded the Nobel Peace Prize in 1964 "for the furtherance of brotherhood among men." He remained a leading speaker for African American rights, even as splits developed in the civil rights movement.

As a supporter of the underprivileged and the needy, King went to Memphis, Tennessee, in April 1968 to back a sanitation workers' strike. There he was shot and killed by a white assassin. The death of the leading spokesperson for nonviolence set off new rounds of rioting in American cities.

Just two months after King's death, Senator Robert F. Kennedy, brother of the late President and now a presidential candidate committed to civil rights, was assassinated. The shock of these deaths and the increasing urban violence made the goals of King and the Kennedys seem far off to many Americans.

THE WOMEN'S RIGHTS MOVEMENT

Like African Americans, women had long been denied equal rights in the United States. The successes of the African American civil rights movement in the 1960s highlighted the need for organized action by women to achieve similar goals.

Past Successes, New Goals

The women's rights movement was not just a product of the 1960s. The struggle for equality had been a long one. Some of the key events in the struggle are listed below.

1848 The Seneca Falls Convention marked the beginning of the organized women's rights movement in this nation.

1868 Passage of the Fifteenth Amendment granted the vote to African American men but not to any women. Susan B. Anthony arranged to have a women's suffrage amendment introduced in Congress. It was defeated there, but Anthony and others continued the fight.

1920 Ratification of the Nineteenth Amendment gave women the right to vote.

1940s Thousands of women took jobs in war-related industries.

By the 1960s, women had exercised the right to vote for 40 years, yet women still had not achieved equal status with men economically and socially. Women's groups renewed demands for a variety of goals including more job opportunities, equality of pay with men, and an end to discrimination based on sex.

Presidents Kennedy and Johnson appointed no women to major posts in their administrations. Yet in those years, fundamental changes occurred.

• More and more women entered fields that men had traditionally dominated, such as law, medicine, engineering, and the sciences.

• In 1963, Betty Friedan wrote *The Feminine Mystique,* a book arguing that society had forced American women out of the job market and

ANALYZING DOCUMENTS

According to the line graph below, between which years did the number of women working outside the home first exceed 50 percent?

Women Working Outside the Home, 1955–1990

Source: *Statistical Abstract of the United States*

back into the home after World War II. She said that not all women were content with the role of homemaker and that more job opportunities should be open to women.

- Title VII of the Civil Rights Act of 1964 barred job discrimination on the basis of sex as well as race.
- The National Organization for Women (NOW) formed in 1966 to push for legislation guaranteeing equality for women.
- Congress approved the **Equal Rights Amendment** (ERA) in 1972 and sent it to the states for ratification. The amendment stated "equality of rights under the law shall not be denied or abridged by the United States or any state on account of sex."
- The Equal Opportunity Act of 1972 required employers to pay equal wages for equal work.
- Title IX of the Educational Amendments Act of 1972 gave female college athletes the right to the same financial support as male athletes.

Median Incomes of Men and Women, 1950–1975

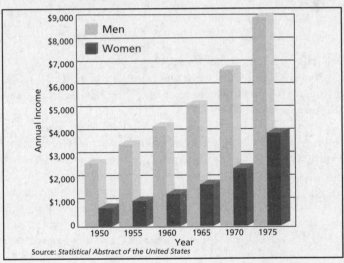

Source: *Statistical Abstract of the United States*

In the landmark case of *Roe* v. *Wade* (1973), the Supreme Court ruled that a woman's right to terminate a pregnancy is constitutionally protected. Laws making abortion a crime were overturned because they violated a woman's right to privacy; the Supreme Court held that the states could only limit abortion after the first six months of pregnancy. Challenges to the decision in *Roe* v. *Wade* continued for decades afterward.

AFFIRMATIVE ACTION Some of the laws guaranteeing equal opportunities for women, African Americans, and other minority groups called for **affirmative action.** This meant taking positive steps to eliminate the effects of past discrimination in hiring. In practice, it often meant giving preference to members of such groups when hiring workers or accepting applicants to schools. These affirmative action programs were begun during the Johnson administration of the 1960s.

Adapted from The New Yorker

"Founding Fathers? How come no Founding Mothers?"

WOMEN'S RIGHTS VOCABULARY The term *feminism* refers to the belief that women should have the same economic, social, and political rights as men. The women's rights movement is sometimes called the feminist movement.

The term *sexism* refers to beliefs or practices that discriminate against a person on the basis of sex. The women's movement directed its efforts at removing sexist terminology, practices, and literature from American business and education.

The term *glass ceiling* was used to describe a mid-level position to which women might be promoted in many jobs but which allowed women to see upper-level, better-paying positions that were held by men and were not open to women. This type of unspoken discrimination occurred in all types of employment and can still be found today.

Setbacks for the Women's Rights Movement

Not all Americans supported the women's rights movement. Some argued that women already had equal rights. Others claimed that those goals undermined "traditional" values. In 1971, President Nixon vetoed a bill that would have provided for a national system of day care for the children of working mothers. His reason for vetoing the bill was that he believed that the family rather than the government should be responsible for the care of children.

Critics also charged that affirmative action programs were a kind of reverse discrimination, in which white males lost chances at jobs to less-qualified women and members of minority groups. In 1979, the Supreme Court ruled in *Regents of the University of California* v. *Bakke* that the school used racial quotas when deciding

ANALYZING DOCUMENTS

Examine the cartoon at left, which features a painting by John Trumbull that shows the signing of the Declaration of Independence.

• What criticism about this painting are the two characters giving?

READING STRATEGY

Formulating Questions
Why might some women support the women's rights movement of the 1960s, while other might oppose it?

PREPARING FOR THE EXAM

Why did the proposed Equal Rights Amendment cause controversy?

ANALYZING DOCUMENTS

According to the graphic organizer below, how did Latinos gain political strength at a national level in the 1960s?

on applicants to medical school. This meant that Allan Bakke was rejected admission to the medical school in favor of less-qualified applicants. The Court ruled that Bakke had been denied equal protection under the Fourteenth Amendment. It nevertheless found that other affirmative action programs may be constitutional.

The proposed ERA generated tremendous controversy. Opponents claimed that the women's rights movement had led to rising divorce rates, increasing numbers of abortions, and the growing acceptance and recognition of homosexuality—all threats to traditional values, said critics. Ratification of the ERA, they argued, would cause still more problems for American society. By the 1982 deadline, the ERA was three states short of ratification and thus was defeated.

In the late 1980s and 1990s, women's groups began to demand legal protection against physical and mental abuse directed toward both women and children. Lawsuits began to occur to protest sexual harassment, especially in the workplace.

OTHER GROUPS STRUGGLE FOR THEIR RIGHTS

In addition to the African American and women's civil rights movements, Latinos, Native Americans, and disabled Americans fought for equality and justice.

Latino Victories in the 1960s

Latinos began to organize against discrimination in the 1960s.

Latinos

Latinos—people whose family origins are in the Spanish-speaking nations of Latin America—have often been denied equal opportunities in employment, education, and housing. The largest group of Latinos is Mexican Americans, often known as Chicanos.

By the early 1960s, large numbers of Chicanos were employed as farm workers, often migrants. They faced problems of discrimination, poor pay, and hazardous working conditions. In 1962, a Chicano named Cesar Chavez emerged as a labor leader, starting a union for migrant farm workers, a union that became the **United Farm Workers.** Chavez's work was especially helpful to grape and lettuce pickers in their struggle for higher wages and better working conditions.

Chavez, like Dr. Martin Luther King, Jr., believed in nonviolent methods. Chavez continued to serve as spokesperson for farm workers until his death in 1993. He helped raise the self-esteem of the nation's growing Latino population by making their contributions to the American economy and culture more visible.

Native Americans

In the twentieth century, some conditions for Native Americans had improved. They were granted full citizenship in 1924, and Franklin Roosevelt's Indian New Deal of the 1930s had changed earlier government policies and aimed to rebuild tribes and promote tribal cultures. As the circumstances of the Native Americans improved, their population began to increase.

Nevertheless, conditions remained poor for many Native Americans. The per capita income of Native Americans was well below the poverty level. Rates of alcoholism and suicide were the highest of any ethnic group in the United States. Unemployment rates were far higher than the national average, and the high-school dropout rate was near 50 percent.

NATIVE AMERICANS ORGANIZE In the early 1950s, Congress had enacted legislation to lessen government control over reservations, but this led to the loss of property by many Native Americans and forced some onto welfare. During the Johnson administration, the government tried to improve conditions by starting new programs to raise the standard of housing and to provide medical facilities, educational institutions, and vocational training.

Native Americans began demanding greater responsibility in making decisions that affected their lives. Native Americans took inspiration from the African American civil rights movement. They began to call for "Red Power" and formed the **American Indian Movement** (AIM) to further their goals.

In 1969, a group of militant Native Americans seized Alcatraz Island in San Francisco Bay with the demand that it be turned into an Indian cultural center. In 1972, members of AIM occupied the Bureau of Indian Affairs in Washington, D. C., demanding rights and property they said were guaranteed to them under earlier treaties. In 1973, AIM members occupied the reservation village of Wounded Knee, South Dakota, site

READING STRATEGY

Organizing Information
Latinos also faced problems of discrimination. What are two ways that they fought for equal rights?

1.

2.

 KEY THEMES AND CONCEPTS

Government
How did the federal government change its policies toward Native Americans in the early 1900s? What were the effects of these changes?

PREPARING FOR THE EXAM
• What problems did Native Americans face in the 1960s and 1970s?

• How did they draw attention to their plight?

of the last battle in the Indian wars of the 1800s. The takeover lasted two months, with the militants demanding changes in policies toward Native Americans.

Although these actions did not always achieve Native Americans' goals, the agitation did draw attention to their problems. Throughout the 1970s, court decisions tried to remedy earlier treaty violations. By 1989, Native Americans had been awarded more than $80 million as compensation for lost land.

In addition, government policies changed again. The Indian Self-Determination and Education Assistance Act of 1975 gave Native Americans more control over reservations. Also, the post of Assistant Secretary of the Interior for Indian Affairs was created in 1975 to protect Native American interests.

NEW YORK STATE AND NATIVE AMERICANS Some major court cases involving Native American rights have taken place in New York State. For example, in *County of Oneida* v. *Oneida Indian Nation of New York State* (1985), the Supreme Court ruled that Native Americans had a right to sue to enforce their original land rights. The Court further stated that New York's purchase of 872 acres from the Oneida Indians in 1795 was illegal, because it was neither witnessed by federal agents nor approved by Congress. Both these steps were required under the federal Indian Trade and Non-Intercourse Act of 1793. Such court decisions have encouraged other Native American groups in New York State and across the nation to sue for return of lost lands.

More recent controversies have arisen in northern New York regarding the St. Regis Indian Reservation, or Akwesasne Mohawk Reservation as it is also known. Violence erupted on the 14,000-acre reservation, which stretches into southern Canada, in the spring of 1990. At issue was gambling on the reservation. The incident involved questions of which Native American group controlled reservation policy as well as the role New York State has in dealing with the reservation.

Disabled Americans

Americans with disabilities have endured a long struggle to gain their full rights in American society. In the nation's early years, care of the handicapped was usually left to their families, often resulting in the neglect or abuse of the disabled. Reformers began to work for change in the early 1800s. For example, in Massachusetts, Dorothea Dix led a campaign to improve conditions for mentally ill people, resulting in the founding of more than 30 state institutions to care for them.

Educational opportunities for hearing-impaired students were gradually widened. Gallaudet College in Washington, D.C., was founded in 1857, and today that institution is internationally recognized for its educational programs for hearing-impaired students. In the late 1980s, its students successfully demonstrated to win appointment of a hearing-impaired person as president of the college. In New York

---

ⵕ KEY THEMES AND CONCEPTS

Constitutional Principles
The Supreme Court case *County of Oneida* v. *Oneida Indian Nation of New York State* (1985) established that Native American tribes had the right to sue state governments to reclaim their tribal lands.

- Why is *County of Oneida* v. *Oneida Indian Nation of New York State* important in the struggle for Native American equality?

READING STRATEGY

Reinforcing Main Ideas
How has the view of people with handicaps changed from the nation's early years to today?

State, the National Technical Institute for the Deaf at the Rochester Institute of Technology is another school for the hearing impaired whose programs have won wide recognition. The school provides deaf students with college training in technical and scientific fields.

Educational opportunities were also widened for visually-impaired students. In 1829, the Perkins School for the Blind opened in Boston and quickly became a model for schools elsewhere. Although such schools still exist and serve important functions, many visually-impaired students today attend regular schools under a practice called **mainstreaming.** The idea behind mainstreaming is to bring handicapped students out of the isolation of special schools and into the "mainstream" of student life.

NEW PROGRAMS FOR PEOPLE WITH DISABILITIES The federal government has been especially active in setting out new programs and policies for people with disabilities.

- President Kennedy established the Presidential Commission on Mental Retardation to study and highlight the problems of the mentally handicapped individuals in American society.
- President Kennedy also backed the establishment of the Special Olympics to provide both a showcase and encouragement for athletes with handicapping conditions.
- The Rehabilitation Act of 1973, Section 504, barred discrimination against people with disabilities in any programs, activities, and facilities that were supported by federal funds.
- The Education for All Handicapped Children Act of 1975 ensured a free, appropriate education for children with disabilities, including special education and related services.
- The **Americans with Disabilities Act of 1990** prohibited discrimination in employment, public accommodation, transportation, state and local government services, and telecommunications. Benefits of the act included greater accessibility to public buildings and transportation for people who use wheelchairs and the availability of electronic devices to allow hearing-impaired people to use telephones and enjoy movies.

Activism by disabled veterans, especially from the Vietnam War, drew increased attention to the needs of people with disabilities. Celebrities have also taken up the cause of working for increased congressional funding of medical research. Some examples include Elizabeth Taylor for AIDS research, Christopher Reeve for spinal cord injuries research, and Michael J. Fox for Parkinson's disease.

Schools began to mainstream students with disabilities into regular classrooms. Students who previously might have attended special schools with other students with similar disabilities have begun to attend regular public schools in a major attempt at deinstitutionalization. These efforts are known as programs of inclusion.

⚲ KEY THEMES AND CONCEPTS

Diversity
What is the purpose behind the practice of mainstreaming?

READING STRATEGY

Analyzing Cause and Effect
How did the Americans With Disabilities Act (1990) change the lives of people with handicaps?

**PREPARING FOR
THE EXAM**

On the examination, you
will need to understand the
major domestic programs of
the 1960s.

In the space below, give
two provisions of President
Kennedy's "New Frontier"
program and the reasons
for these provisions.

1.

2.

**PREPARING FOR
THE EXAM**

On the examination, you
will need to understand
major U.S. domestic policy.

In the space below, give
three provisions of
President Johnson's "Great
Society" program and the
reasons for these provisions.

1.

2.

3.

THE NEW FRONTIER AND THE GREAT SOCIETY

Not all legislation on domestic issues during the 1960s concerned civil rights. Kennedy's programs, known as the **New Frontier,** and Johnson's, known as the **Great Society,** continued and expanded upon traditions begun during Franklin Roosevelt's New Deal of the 1930s.

Kennedy

- *The space program* Following the successful launch of a Soviet cosmonaut in 1961, the first man in space, President Kennedy committed the nation to a space program with the goal of landing a person on the moon by the end of the 1960s. In July 1969, six years after Kennedy's death, that goal was met when astronaut Neil Armstrong stepped onto the moon's surface. The effort had cost some $25.4 billion.
- *The Peace Corps* This program sent thousands of American volunteers to developing nations where they trained local people in technical, educational, and health programs. The Peace Corps program was intended to offset the growth of communism in such nations. The program is still in existence.

Johnson

- *The VISTA program* The Volunteers in Service to America (VISTA) program was meant as a domestic Peace Corps, aiding poor citizens in rural and impoverished areas.
- *The Office of Economic Opportunity* Set up in 1964, this was the directing agency in President Johnson's War on Poverty. Its branches included Project Head Start (to provide education for preschoolers from low-income families), Project Upward Bound (to assist high-school students from low-income families to attend college), and the Job Corps (to provide vocational training for high-school dropouts).
- *The Elementary and Secondary Education Act* This 1965 measure provided more than $1 billion in federal aid to education, with the greatest share going to school districts with large numbers of students from low-income families. Sections of the bill required that schools accepting the money be integrated.
- *Medicare* Amendments to the Social Security Act provided health insurance and some types of health care to those over the age of 65. A Medicaid program provided states with funds to help the needy who were not covered by Medicare.
- *Department of Housing and Urban Development* This cabinet post was meant to oversee federal efforts to improve housing and aid economic development of cities. Its first head, Robert C. Weaver, was the first African American to hold a cabinet post.

FOREIGN POLICY IN THE 1960S

United States foreign policy under Kennedy and Johnson continued Truman's cold war policy of containment of communism. In Section 3, you will review how this policy led the nation into the **Vietnam War.** In this section, you will see how cold war concerns affected other aspects of the United States foreign policy in the 1960s.

A History of Involvement

As you remember, the United States has been deeply involved in the affairs of Latin America since early in its history. Latin American nations often resented such intervention, and United States policies have left a legacy of anger and hostility.

Some of the key events in United States-Latin American relations are listed on the next page. For additional discussion of these events, see Unit 3, Section 2.

Key Developments in United States— Latin American Relations

The Monroe Doctrine	In 1823, President Monroe warned the nations of Europe not to interfere with the nations of the Western Hemisphere, thus assuming the role of protector of the Western Hemisphere. However, this policy earned the United States a negative image in much of Latin America.
Spanish-American War (1898)	Victory in a war with Spain brought the United States an overseas empire. It also increased the nation's role in Latin America by giving it possession of Puerto Rico and much control over the government of Cuba.
Panama Canal (1901–1914)	The United States gained control over land where it wanted to build a canal by interfering in the internal affairs of Colombia. As a result, the United States made many enemies in Latin America.
Roosevelt Corollary (1904)	Under this addition to the Monroe Doctrine, President Theodore Roosevelt claimed the United States had the right to intervene in the affairs of Latin American nations guilty of "chronic wrongdoing."
"Dollar Diplomacy" (early 1900s)	This term describe President Taft's plan of increasing U.S. influence in Latin America through economic investment backed by military force.
"Good Neighbor" Policy (1933)	This was President Franklin Roosevelt's effort to improve relations with Latin America by stressing increased cooperation.

KEY THEMES AND CONCEPTS

Examine the table at left, then answer these questions.

- Which event resulted in the United States becoming an imperial nation?
- Which development was intended to improve relations with Latin American nations?

Foreign Policy

In the 1960s, the United States had an uneasy relationship with many Latin American nations. While Presidents Kennedy and Johnson supported the cold war policies begun under President Truman, Kennedy hoped to warm ties with Latin American through the Alliance for Progress. However, economic development funds from this program tended to support repressive, anticommunist governments.

- Why was the Bay of Pigs invasion of Cuba considered a failure?

TURNING POINT

Why is the Cuban missile crisis of 1962 considered a turning point in U.S.-Soviet relations?

Kennedy and Latin America

Some of President Kennedy's most significant foreign policy decisions involved Latin America.

THE ALLIANCE FOR PROGRESS Kennedy hoped to improve relations with Latin America and stop the spread of communism there through the Alliance for Progress, which pledged $20 billion to help economic development in the region. However, funds often went to aid repressive governments simply because they were anticommunist.

THE BAY OF PIGS After President Kennedy took office, he approved a CIA plan to overthrow Fidel Castro, the communist leader of Cuba. The plan called for Cuban exiles—supplied with U.S. arms, material, and training—to invade Cuba and set off a popular uprising against Castro. The invasion took place on April 17, 1961, at a location called the Bay of Pigs, about 90 miles from Havana. No uprising followed, and Castro's troops quickly crushed the invading forces, to the embarrassment of Kennedy and the United States government.

THE CUBAN MISSILE CRISIS Fearing another U.S. invasion attempt, Castro agreed to a Soviet plan to base nuclear missiles aimed at the United States in Cuba. Kennedy learned of the plan while the bases were under construction. On October 22, 1962, he announced a naval blockade of Cuba and demanded that the Soviets withdraw the missiles. The **Cuban missile crisis** brought the United States and the Soviet Union to the brink of war, but the Soviets backed down and withdrew their missiles.

Kennedy had clearly demonstrated that the United States would not tolerate a Soviet presence in the Western Hemisphere just 90 miles from its shores. By doing so, Kennedy also helped the nation recover some of the prestige it had lost in the failed Bay of Pigs invasion.

U.S. - Soviet Tensions, 1961–1963

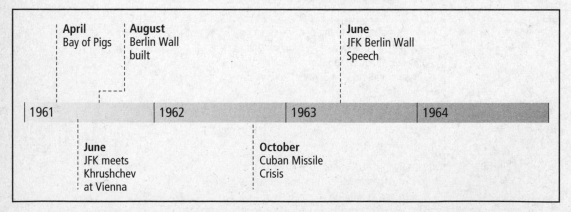

In 1963, the United States, Soviet Union, and Great Britain signed a nuclear test ban treaty in which they agreed not to test nuclear weapons in the air, in outer space, or under the sea. Underground testing was permitted.

Kennedy and Berlin

Since World War II, the division of Germany into a Communist East Germany and a democratic West Germany had added to cold war tensions. President Kennedy and Soviet Premier Nikita Khrushchev met in Austria in June 1961 to discuss relations between the United States and the Soviet Union. Khrushchev thought that the Bay of Pigs disaster revealed American weakness, and he tried to threaten Kennedy into removing NATO troops from Europe. Instead, Kennedy increased U.S. military and financial commitment to West Germany.

Response to the American moves came in August 1961, when the East German government built a wall between East and West Berlin. The **Berlin Wall** was meant to stop the flood of East Germans escaping to freedom in the West and quickly became a symbol of tyranny. In June 1963, Kennedy visited West Berlin, renewing the American commitment to defend that city and Western Europe. In a famous speech, he said that he and all people who wanted freedom were citizens of Berlin.

The Berlin Wall stood as a strong cold war symbol until 1989. In that year, political change sweeping through Eastern Europe led East Germany to tear down the wall. By October 1990, the rapid political changes in the region had led to the reunification of the two Germanys as a single nation for the first time since the end of World War II.

IMPACT OF KENNEDY'S DEATH Kennedy's energetic voice for world democracy and his multilingual wife, Jacqueline, helped to make friends for the United States in many areas of the world. His tragic and unexpected assassination in November 1963 caused an outpouring of grief from around the world as dozens of foreign heads of state came hurriedly to Washington, D.C., for Kennedy's funeral.

ANALYZING DOCUMENTS

Examine the timeline on page 316, then answer these questions.

• How many years passed between the fall of the Berlin Wall and the reunification of Germany?

• Which event occurred first: the meeting between President Kennedy and Soviet Premier Khrushchev, or the building of the Berlin Wall?

SECTION 3 Limits of Power

SECTION OVERVIEW

The fear of communist expansion led the United States to become increasingly involved in Southeast Asia. This involvement led to the Vietnam War—the longest war in United States history. As the war dragged on, American support began to erode. The combination of negative public opinion and the inability of the military to achieve clear-cut victory led to a gradual withdrawal from the war. Meanwhile, great social and cultural changes were taking place in many parts of American society.

KEY THEMES AND CONCEPTS

As you review this section, take special note of the following key themes and concepts:

Foreign Policy Why did the United States become involved in Vietnam?

Presidential Decisions and Actions How did the decisions made by Presidents Johnson and Nixon affect how the Vietnam War was conducted?

Change What social and cultural changes developed in the 1960s?

Constitutional Principles How did Congress limit the power of the President in wartime?

KEY PEOPLE

Lyndon B. Johnson
Richard Nixon
Henry Kissinger

Fear of communist expansion led the United States to become deeply involved in Southeast Asia. Review the chart below to learn about the growing involvement of the United States in this region.

Unrest in Asia, 1945–1960

Date	Event
September 1945	World War II ends in Asia; Ho Chi Minh, a member of the Communist party since 1920, proclaims the Democratic Republic of Vietnam.
1946–1949	France, which had controlled Vietnam since the nineteeth century, appoints a "puppet leader" named Bao Dai, who is ineffective against the power of Ho Chi Minh.
1949	Mao Zedong declares the (Communist) People's Republic of China; recognizes the Vietnamese government of Ho Chi Minh in 1950.
1950–1953	United States fights the Korean War and provides the French with financial aid in their struggle to hang onto Vietnam.
1953–1954	President Eisenhower debates how far the United States should go in backing the French.
1954	The forces of Ho Chi Minh defeat the French at Dienbienphu; Geneva Accords divide Vietnam at the 17th parallel; North and South Vietnam agree to hold elections in 1956 to reunite the country; the United States joins with seven Asian and European nations in the Southeast Asia Treaty Organization (SEATO), an anticommunist pact which extends protection to Vietnam.
1955	United States under Eisenhower increases aid to South Vietnam.
1956	South Vietnamese President Ngo Dinh Diem, fearing the popularity of Ho Chi Minh, refuses to hold elections scheduled under the Geneva Accords.
1960	Ho Chi Minh recognizes the Vietcong, Communist guerrillas in South Vietnam, as the National Liberation Front (NLF) of Vietnam; President Kennedy sends Vice President Johnson to study the crisis in Vietnam.

KENNEDY AND VIETNAM

President Kennedy shared Eisenhower's belief in the domino theory. He, therefore, continued to support the Diem regime. By 1963, the number of United States "advisers" in South Vietnam totaled about 17,000. That year, 489 Americans died in the fighting in Vietnam.

Debate Over Involvement

American advisers urged Diem to adopt reforms to broaden his support. Diem, however, brutally suppressed all opponents and ruled as a dictator. On November 2, 1963, the South Vietnamese military overthrew Diem, with the knowledge and approval of the United States. Around the same time, the White House announced that it intended to withdraw all United States military personnel from

GEOGRAPHY IN HISTORY

Laos shares a long border with North Vietnam. During the Vietnam War, the dense jungle terrain made it difficult for U.S. and South Vietnamese forces to cut off the supply lines that ran between Laos and North Vietnam.

- How might this role as supplier have an impact on Laos later in the war?

⚲ KEY THEMES AND CONCEPTS

Presidential Decisions and Actions

Without a formal declaration of war by Congress, Presidents Eisenhower, Kennedy, and Johnson all sent U.S. military forces to Vietnam.

- What authorized these Presidents to take these actions?

Vietnam, 1968

Vietnam by 1965. Kennedy was unable to keep this promise, because he was assassinated in 1963.

JOHNSON AND ESCALATION

Under the Constitution, only Congress can declare war. However, by 1964, three Presidents—Eisenhower, Kennedy, and Johnson—had sent United States aid and troops into Vietnam. Each did so by acting as the commander in chief of the nation's military forces.

The Tonkin Gulf Resolution

On August 4, 1964, President Johnson escalated the war dramatically. He announced on television that American destroyers had been the victim of an unprovoked attack by North Vietnamese gun boats. (It later appeared that the ships might have been protecting South Vietnamese boats headed into North Vietnamese waters.) The next day, Johnson asked Congress for the authority to order air strikes against North Vietnam. With only two dissenting votes, Congress passed the **Gulf of Tonkin Resolution.** The resolution empowered "the President, as commander in chief, to take all necessary measures to repel any armed attack against the forces of the United States and to prevent further aggression." Johnson used the resolution to justify expansion of the war. By April 1965, U.S. planes regularly bombed North Vietnam.

A GUERRILLA WAR At first, United States military leaders expected that the nation's superior technology would guarantee victory. However, they soon found themselves bogged down in a guerrilla war fought in the jungles of Southeast Asia. The enemy did not wear uniforms, and no clear battlefront emerged. Thousands of Vietnamese casualties occurred each month as the United States dropped more bombs on Vietnam, an area about twice the size of New York State, than it had used on Nazi Germany during the heaviest months of fighting during World War II.

REASONS FOR WAR The massive commitment in Vietnam raised questions in the minds of many Americans about why the United States got involved in Vietnam and why it stayed there. The administration argued that the United States was involved in Vietnam to prevent the fall of Vietnam to communism, to stop the rise of aggressor governments, and to protect the nation's position as a superpower and defender of democracy. However, as the war dragged on, many Americans began to question these motives.

Resistance to the War

By late 1965, an antiwar movement had begun to take shape in the United States.

HAWKS AND DOVES In Congress, there were differences of opinion concerning the war. Some stood solidly behind the President and argued in favor of victory at any cost. These members were known as **hawks.** Those who favored immediate withdrawal and an end to the war were known as **doves.**

STUDENT PROTESTS College campuses became centers of political protest against the war. Students organized a new form of protest called teach-ins, or meetings in which speakers, usually promoting unconditional American withdrawal from Vietnam, held study sessions and rallies. The strongest antiwar group in the 1960s was Students for a Democratic Society (SDS), founded in 1960. SDS was antiestablishment, or against big business and government. It led demonstrations, sit-ins, draft-card burnings, and protests against universities with "pro-establishment" regulations.

By 1969, the organization had collapsed into a number of splinter groups. However, SDS's legacy of protest against authority remained a strong force into the 1970s.

KEY THEMES AND CONCEPTS

Foreign Policy

In 1964, Congress passed the Gulf of Tonkin Resolution. The resolution, which empowered the President to "repel an armed attack against the forces of the United States," was used to escalate U.S. bombings in North Vietnam.

• What obstacles did U.S. troops fighting in Vietnam face?

PREPARING FOR THE EXAM

On the examination, you will need to have a thorough understanding of U.S. foreign policy.

List three reasons President Johnson's administration used to justify U.S. involvement in Vietnam.

1.

2.

3.

♀ KEY THEMES AND
⚘ CONCEPTS

Reform Movements
College campuses became centers of the antiwar movement in the United States. Students organized teach-ins and other protests aimed at getting the Johnson administration to end U.S. involvement in Vietnam. Protest marches featuring people of all ages took place in major cities.

- In what different ways did young people respond to the draft?

PROTEST MARCHES People of all ages joined in protest marches against the war. The first huge march took place in Washington, D.C., in 1965. In 1967, some 300,000 Americans marched in New York City. That same year, another 50,000 tried to shut down the Pentagon.

DRAFT RESISTERS By 1968, about 10,000 draft resisters, people unwilling to serve in the military after being drafted, had fled the country for Canada. The nation's youth became increasingly divided as some chose to fight for the United States in Vietnam, while others sought deferments to go to college. A large number of minorities, who could not afford the cost of college, responded to the draft and went to Vietnam. The attitude of American youth became increasingly hostile toward the Johnson administration and all war-related issues.

THE 1960S—POLITICAL AND SOCIAL UPHEAVAL

Some political analysts who studied the events of 1968 believed the nation had survived one of the biggest tests to its political institutions since the Civil War. The 1960s had been shaped by two movements: the civil rights movement and the antiwar movement. The political turmoil of the decade helped produce great social upheaval, especially among the nation's youth.

Cultural Changes

Some young people became disillusioned with traditional American values. For the first time in United States history, thousands of Americans flaunted the use of illegal drugs, often popularized in rock music.

Many young Americans referred to themselves as hippies or flower children. They claimed to be searching for a freer, simpler way of life. Communal living attracted thousands of youths who adopted lifestyles foreign to older Americans. Some spoke of a generation gap between youth and people over 30.

The civil rights movement and the Vietnam War also divided Americans. The assassinations of Robert Kennedy and Dr. Martin Luther King, Jr., heightened emotions.

NIXON AND VIETNAM

By 1969, President Nixon faced a national crisis. The Vietnam War had turned into the nation's most costly war. American support for the war was at an all-time low.

Winding Down the War

Nixon did not bring an end to the war right away. In fact, for a time, he widened American military activities, attacking North Vietnamese supply routes out of Laos and Cambodia.

Key Events of 1968

Month	Event
January	• North Vietnam launches the Tet (New Year's) offensive, using Soviet-made jets and weapons for the first time.
March	• Eugene McCarthy, a peace candidate and leading "dove," wins the Democratic presidential primary in New Hampshire. • Robert Kennedy announces his candidacy for the presidency. • President Johnson announces that he will not seek reelection and that he will devote the remainder of his term to trying to end the war.
April	• American forces in Vietnam reach 549,000; combat deaths climb to 22,951. • North Vietnam announces its willingness to enter into peace talks. • An assassin claims the life of Dr. Martin Luther King, Jr.
May	• Preliminary peace talks with the North Vietnamese begin, but serious negotiations do not take place for several years.
June	• An assassin claims the life of Robert Kennedy shortly after his victory in the California Democratic presidential primary.
August	• The Democratic National Convention nominates Hubert Humphrey amid the worst political rioting and demonstrations any convention has ever experienced; Humphrey (Johnson's Vice President) inherits a divided party and seeks election in a divided nation. • The Republican National Convention nominates Richard Nixon, whose only serious challenger is Ronald Reagan. • The American Independent party nominates Governor George Wallace of Alabama, showing that a third party could attract white-backlash voters who opposed the civil rights movement.
November	• Nixon wins the 1968 election with 43.4% of the popular vote; Humphrey claims 42.7%; Wallace takes 13.5%.

VIETNAMIZATION Nixon called for **Vietnamization** of the war, or a takeover of the ground fighting by Vietnamese soldiers. Both Kennedy and Johnson had favored this approach, but neither had been able to make it work. While Nixon promoted Vietnamization, he also bombed neighboring Cambodia, which he claimed served as a base for North Vietnamese guerrillas.

The bombings triggered a large student protest at Kent State University in Ohio. By the time the National Guard broke up the demonstration, four students lay dead and nine others wounded. More

♀ KEY THEMES AND ⚷ CONCEPTS

Presidential Decisions and Actions
What impact did President Nixon's decision to bomb Cambodia have on student protests?

and more Americans were questioning the role of the United States in Vietnam, yet President Nixon increased bombing raids on North Vietnam throughout 1970.

PEACE WITH HONOR Henry Kissinger, Nixon's chief foreign policy adviser, met in Paris with North Vietnamese officials seeking an end to the war. For several years, negotiations remained deadlocked. Finally, on January 15, 1973, Nixon announced that "peace with honor" had been reached and that a cease-fire would soon take effect.

The War Powers Act

Passed over President Nixon's veto in 1973, the War Powers Act gave Congress more power in dealing with international conflicts.

- The President can send troops overseas, but must inform Congress within 48 hours.

- Troops may not stay overseas more than 60 days without approval of Congress.

- Congress has the power to force the President to bring the troops home.

READING STRATEGY

Problem Solving
Why do you think Congress passed the War Powers Act over President Nixon's veto?

The War Powers Act

In November 1973, Congress passed the War Powers Act over Nixon's veto. This law helped reverse the precedent set by the Gulf of Tonkin Resolution, which gave the President sweeping powers in Vietnam. The **War Powers Act** included the following provisions:

- The President had to notify Congress within 48 hours of sending troops into a foreign country. At that time, the President would have to give Congress a full accounting of the decision.
- The President had to bring the troops home within 60 days unless both houses voted for them to stay.

Vietnam and Limits on United States Power

When the United States finally withdrew from Vietnam, the North Vietnamese overran South Vietnam. For two years, the United States poured billions of dollars of aid into South Vietnam. However, on April 30, 1975, the government in Saigon collapsed. Bitterness over the war still persisted. When the President asked for funds to evacuate the South Vietnamese who had helped the United States, Congress refused. In the end, some 100,000 people fled the country.

The United States had tried for 20 years to guarantee freedom to the people of South Vietnam. However, the United States ultimately could not count its efforts as a success. In the conflict, some 58,000 Americans died, and another 300,000 were wounded. The United States spent over $150 billion on the war effort. Not only did Vietnam fall to communism, but so did its neighbors Cambodia (Kampuchea) and Laos. Throughout the late 1970s and 1980s, the United States sought to understand the Vietnam experience. It was the subject of films, books, and national monuments such as the Vietnam Veterans Memorial in Washington, D.C.

Conclusions Drawn from U.S. Involvement in Vietnam

The following is a list of conclusions drawn from the Vietnam War era.

- The American political system acts in response to a variety of public pressures.
- Modern war technology is not always powerful enough if an opponent is armed with a determined spirit of nationalism.
- Successful military efforts require a well-prepared and supportive public. (Compare, for example, the differing experiences in Vietnam and World War II.)
- The United States was committed to a foreign policy that supported the global nature of United States involvement in foreign affairs.

PREPARING FOR THE EXAM

For the examination, it will be important to understand the *significance* of historical events, not just the dates of and participants in those events.

- Overall, was the Vietnam War a success or a failure? Why?

- What enduring lessons were learned from the war?

- How has the Vietnam War continued to be remembered in American society?

★ THE BIG IDEA
Beginning in the early 1970s, conservatism replaced liberalism in American politics. During this period

- President Nixon opened diplomatic relations with China and shaped a policy of détente toward the Soviet Union.

- President Ford pardoned President Nixon following his resignation over the Watergate affair.

- President Reagan supported a domestic program of New Federalism during the 1980s that was begun by President Nixon.

- the end of the Cold War led to the dissolution of the Soviet Union.

- President Clinton promoted many ambitious domestic programs during the 1990s.

⚷ KEY TERMS

détente
Watergate affair
stagflation
Camp David Accords
supply-side economics
"Star Wars"
Iran-Contra affair
Persian Gulf War
NAFTA
European Union

SECTION OVERVIEW

After the upheaval of the 1960s, Richard Nixon tried to take the nation into a new direction, but the Watergate affair led to his resignation. His successors, Gerald Ford and Jimmy Carter, struggled with lingering economic troubles. In the 1980s, conservatives Ronald Reagan and George Bush came to power. After the cold war ended, the United States struggled to determine its new role in international relations.

KEY THEMES AND CONCEPTS

As you review this section, take special note of the following key themes and concepts:

Presidential Decisions and Actions How did President Nixon shape a new policy toward China and the Soviet Union?

Economic Systems How did economic problems of the 1970s present unique challenges to the Nixon, Ford, and Carter administrations?

Change How did the international role of the United States change after the end of the cold war?

KEY PEOPLE

Mao Zedong	Jimmy Carter	George Bush
Warren Burger	Ronald Reagan	Bill Clinton
Gerald Ford	Mikhail Gorbachev	George W. Bush

KEY SUPREME COURT CASES

Engel v. *Vitale* (1962)
Gideon v. *Wainwright* (1963)
Escobedo v. *Illinois* (1964)
Miranda v. *Arizona* (1966)
Tinker v. *Des Moines Community School District* (1969)
New York Times v. *United States* (1971)
Roe v. *Wade* (1973)

An Era of Conservatism, 1972–1990

1972
Nixon visits
China, USSR

1974
Nixon
resigns

1978
Camp David
Accords

1983
U.S. invades
Grenada

1990
Operation Desert
Shield; Germany
reunited

| 1970 | 1975 | 1980 | 1985 | 1990 |

1973
Watergate
investigation
begins

1977
Panama
Canal
Treaties

1979
Iran seizes
U.S. hostages

1987
Iran-Contra
Hearings begin

FROM COLD WAR TO DETENTE

Although Nixon's main foreign policy objective was ending the Vietnam War, he had other foreign policy interests as well.

Nixon Doctrine

In 1969, Nixon announced what became known as the Nixon Doctrine. This doctrine stated that the United States would no longer provide direct military protection in Asia. Even though the Vietnam War was not yet concluded, Nixon promised Americans that there would be no more Vietnams for the United States.

A New Policy Toward China

Nixon also adopted a new foreign policy towards China. The United States had not had diplomatic relations with the People's Republic since the 1949 Communist revolution.

PRESIDENTIAL VISIT In 1971, Nixon stunned Americans by announcing that he had accepted an invitation to visit China. On February 21, 1972, Nixon arrived in China. National Security Adviser Henry Kissinger accompanied the President on his peace mission.

OPENING THE DOOR After more than 20 years of hostility, Nixon and Chinese leaders Mao Zedong and Premier Zhou Enlai agreed to open the door to normal diplomatic relations. Nixon's visit cleared the way for economic and cultural exchanges. American manufacturers, for example, now had a new market for their products. By following a policy toward China that was separate from the Soviet Union, Nixon underscored the splits that had occurred within communism.

A New Policy Toward the Soviet Union

Nixon balanced his openness with China by looking for ways to ease tensions with the Soviet Union, China's communist rival.

DÉTENTE Nixon and Kissinger shaped a policy called **détente.** The

TURNING POINT

Why is President Nixon's visit to China considered a turning point in U.S. foreign policy?

KEY THEMES AND CONCEPTS
Foreign Policy
As secretary of state, Henry Kissinger favored the political philosophy of *Realpolitik*. In your own words, how would you define *Realpolitik?*

ANALYZING DOCUMENTS

Based on the graphic organizer at right and your knowledge of social studies, would you characterize Nixon as a conservative or a liberal President? Provide two reasons to justify your answer.

1.

2.

goal of détente was to bring about a warming in the cold war. In contrast to President Truman's policy of containment, President Nixon's policy of détente was designed to prevent open conflict.

During the Nixon administration, the foreign policy of the United States was shaped by *Realpolitik,* a political philosophy favored by Kissinger. The meaning of *Realpolitik* is power politics. Therefore, in its dealings with China and the Soviet Union, the United States made its decisions based on what it needed to maintain its own strength— regardless of world opinion.

Nixon underscored his willingness to pursue détente by visiting the Soviet Union in May 1972. He was the first President since World War II to make such a journey.

SALT While in Moscow, Nixon opened what became known as the Strategic Arms Limitations Talks (SALT). These talks led to a 1972 agreement called the SALT Agreement. The agreement set limits on the number of defensive missile sites and strategic offensive missiles each nation would keep.

Nixon's Domestic Policies

Nixon's Policies

- Try to slow inflation
- Decrease support for Great Society social programs
- Strengthen law and order, discourage protests
- Move slowly on civil rights, appoint conservative justices to Supreme Court

NIXON'S DOMESTIC POLICIES

Nixon was mainly interested in foreign affairs. He knew that he faced a Congress controlled by a Democratic majority. Because of the system of checks and balances, Nixon realized that it would be almost impossible to push Republican policies through Congress. Therefore, he limited his domestic policy goals.

Nixon's Domestic Initiatives

In 1970, the Occupational Safety and Health Administration (OSHA) was created to ensure safe and healthful working conditions for all working Americans. OSHA assists states in providing research, information, education, and training in the field of occupational safety and health.

The Environmental Protection Agency (EPA), established in 1970, coordinated federal programs to combat pollution and protect the environment.

The Clean Air Act of 1970 was a major comprehensive federal law addressing topics related to air pollution. It was amended in 1977 to set new goals since many parts of the country did not meet the standards set by the 1970 act, it was amended again in 1990 to address problems such as acid rain, ground level ozone, stratospheric ozone depletion, and air toxins.

On July 12, 1973, President Nixon united several existing federal drug agencies into the Drug Enforcement Administration (DEA), which enforced federal drug laws and conducted investigations of illegal drugs overseas.

In 1974, the Energy Reorganization Act created the Nuclear Regulatory Commission to regulate the nuclear power industry and the Energy Research and Development Administration to manage the nuclear weapon, nuclear reactor, and energy development programs of the federal government. In 1977, under President Carter, the Department of Energy was established. Today, the department ensures energy security and safety.

New Federalism

Like Eisenhower, Nixon wanted to reduce the role of the federal government and turn over more activities to the states. Nixon called this policy the New Federalism. He criticized Johnson's Great Society as too costly and tried to reduce involvement of the federal government in social welfare programs. To achieve this goal, Nixon instituted revenue sharing, a policy in which the federal government gave part of its income to the states to spend on social welfare as they saw fit.

Curbing Inflation

The Vietnam War had helped trigger inflation, which was one of Nixon's biggest domestic problems. During the 1968 election, Nixon had promised to end inflation and balance the budget. By the time he took office, prices were rising faster than they had in 20 years. Unemployment was rising too. At the same time, the nation's gross national product (GNP) was declining. To bring the economy under control, Nixon implemented a 90-day wage-price freeze in August 1971. He was the first President to impose mandatory wage-price controls in peacetime.

Nixon, Civil Rights, and the Supreme Court

Each President hopes to influence the decisions of the Supreme Court through the appointment of justices. However, the appointees do not

PREPARING FOR THE EXAM

• What did Nixon intend to accomplish with his policy of New Federalism?

• To what previous presidential policy was he reacting?

Constitutional Principles

- Did these landmark Supreme Court cases provide more protection for individual rights or less protection?

- What effects did *Gideon* v. *Wainwright, Escobedo* v. *Illinois,* and *Miranda* v. *Arizona* have on people who were accused of a crime?

Science and Technology
Why was it significant that an American was the first person to set foot on the moon?

Change

- How did passage of the 26th Amendment affect the number of voters in the United States?

- Would you say that this amendment made the United States more democratic or less democratic?

always rule as a President might expect. For example, President Eisenhower regretted his appointment of Earl Warren to the Supreme Court, because Warren made many liberal decisions that opposed Eisenhower's conservative political views.

NIXON APPOINTEES In 1969, Warren retired, and Nixon appointed Warren Burger as chief justice. During his administration, Nixon also had the opportunity to appoint three other justices. Nixon's appointees were all strict constructionists, believing that Congress and the President have only those powers specifically given to them by the Constitution. The "Nixon Court," however, did not overturn many of the liberal rulings of the 1960s, as Nixon had expected.

OTHER DOMESTIC EVENTS UNDER NIXON

Advances in the space program, an increase in the electorate, and additional rights movements occurred in the 1970s.

The Space Program
In 1969, American astronaut Neil Armstrong became the first person to walk on the moon. The triumph of seeing Armstrong plant a United States flag on the moon's surface marked a bright spot in an otherwise troubled decade.

The Twenty-sixth Amendment
In 1971, the Twenty-sixth Amendment to the Constitution was ratified. This amendment extended the vote to people ages 18 and older. By lowering the voting age from 21 to 18, this amendment added almost 12 million new voters to the American electorate.

Women's Rights Movement
In the 1970s, more and more women enrolled in schools of law, medicine, engineering, and business, fields that had been traditionally reserved for men. However, full-time working women in 1971 were paid only 59 percent as much as men. Many of them also did not hold positions equal to their talents. As you read in Section 2, the Equal Rights Amendment failed to win ratification.

Consumer Rights Movement

A strong consumer rights movement also developed in the early 1970s to address abuses by major American industries. The movement was led by Ralph Nader, a young Washington lawyer who organized a protest in the 1960s against the automotive industry. Nader attracted a number of young volunteers, known as "Nader's Raiders," to his cause. They championed environmental and consumer protection.

THE WATERGATE AFFAIR

In 1972, the Republicans nominated Nixon for reelection. The Democrats selected George McGovern. Nixon claimed credit for bringing down inflation and scoring foreign policy triumphs abroad. He swept to victory, carrying the largest popular majority in United States history. Yet less than two years later, Nixon resigned from office.

- **What happened** An illegal break-in to wiretap phones in the Democratic Party headquarters with electronic surveillance equipment
- **Where** Watergate Towers, an apartment complex in Washington, D.C.
- **When** June 17, 1972
- **Who** The Committee to Reelect the President, acting with the knowledge of several high-level Nixon advisers
- **Why** To secure information to undermine the Democratic campaign against Nixon

The Cover-Up

Police captured the "burglars," who carried evidence linking them to the White House. Nixon did not know about the plan until after it happened. However, he then ordered a cover-up, which was a crime under federal law.

THE INVESTIGATION Reporters from the *Washington Post* probed into the case, now known as the **Watergate affair,** but their reports did not hinder Nixon's reelection. Then in 1973, the Senate set up a committee to look into "illegal, improper, or unethical activities" in the 1972 election. For more than a year, the Senate committee came closer and closer to implicating the President.

KEY THEMES AND CONCEPTS

Reform Movements
The consumer rights movement of the 1960s, led by Ralph Nader, achieved important reforms, such as improved safety features in U.S.-built automobiles.

- What earlier movement in American history championed the cause of improving products available to the American people?

READING STRATEGY

Reinforcing Main Ideas
The Watergate affair was a serious scandal that brought down a President.

- What was the reason behind the Watergate break-in?
- What was Nixon's role?
- How did Nixon's involvement in the Watergate affair lead to his resignation?
- How did the Watergate affair prove that the system of checks and balances works?

RESIGNATION OF AGNEW While the Watergate hearings were under way, the Justice Department charged Vice President Spiro Agnew with income tax evasion. Agnew resigned, and Nixon appointed Gerald R. Ford, the minority leader in the House of Representatives, as Vice President.

THE TAPES In mid-1973, the Senate committee learned that the White House had kept tape recordings of key conversations between Nixon and his top aides. Nixon refused to turn over the tapes. During the summer, the committee opened the hearings to television. The televised proceedings had the appeal of a soap opera as millions of Americans watched.

NIXON RESIGNATION The situation ended when the Supreme Court ordered Nixon to surrender the tapes in its ruling in *United States* v. *Richard Nixon.* Based on evidence in the tapes, the House Judiciary Committee began voting on articles of impeachment against the President. To avoid impeachment, Nixon resigned on August 9, 1974, becoming the first President to do so. On noon of that day, Gerald Ford took the oath of office.

Gerald Ford became the first nonelected President. To fill the office of Vice President, Ford named Nelson Rockefeller, the former governor of New York. From 1974 until 1977, the United States had both a President and Vice President who had not been elected to their offices but had been appointed. Such a situation had not occurred before and has not occurred since.

Significance of Watergate
Although Nixon was never charged with any specific crimes, President Ford pardoned him. Ford hoped to end what he called "our long national nightmare." Many of Nixon's advisers, however, were found guilty of crimes and sentenced to prison. The incident showed, as Ford put it, that "the Constitution works." The system of checks and balances had stopped Nixon from placing the presidency above the law.

TURNING POINT

Why is the Watergate affair considered a turning point in U.S. history?

THE FORD ADMINISTRATION

Many people called Nixon's administration the "Imperial Presidency" because of his disregard of the Constitution. Ford tried to rebuild the image of the President. However, the Watergate affair had disillusioned many Americans.

Ford's Domestic Policies

From the start, Ford faced a number of domestic problems.

- *Nixon's Pardon* Many Americans questioned Ford's decision to pardon Nixon when so many of his advisers stood trial, were convicted, and were jailed.
- *Amnesty Plan* Ford stirred bitter debate when he offered amnesty to thousands of young men who avoided military service in Vietnam by violating draft laws, fleeing the country, or deserting the military.
- *Inflation* In 1973, the Organization of Petroleum Exporting Countries (OPEC) placed an oil embargo on the United States for its support of Israel. The price of oil and gasoline more than doubled, setting off a new round of inflation. Temporary rationing of gasoline and federal incentives to research energy alternatives helped ease shortages. Even so, Americans remained highly dependent on foreign oil. Inflation topped 10 percent, and the nation entered into its worst recession since World War II.

KEY THEMES AND CONCEPTS

Presidential Decisions and Actions

Following a Senate investigation into the Watergate affair, President Nixon resigned on August 9, 1974. Vice President Gerald Ford became the first non-elected President in U.S. history. Although President Nixon was never charged with any crime, President Ford issued a pardon to him.

- Why do you think President Ford pardoned President Nixon?

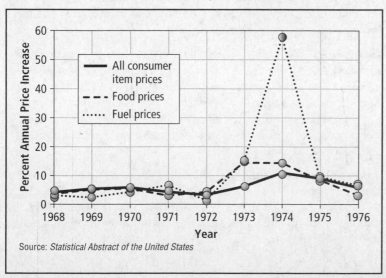

Rate of Inflation, 1968–1976

Source: *Statistical Abstract of the United States*

ANALYZING DOCUMENTS

Based on the chart at left and your knowledge of social studies, answer the following questions.

- What happened to fuel prices in 1973 and 1974?
- What caused the change in fuel prices in those years?
- How might the change in fuel prices and in all consumer item prices be related?

Ford's Foreign Policies

Henry Kissinger continued working with the Ford administration. Kissinger helped

- negotiate a cease-fire agreement between Egypt and Israel, thus ending the 1973 Yom Kippur War and OPEC oil embargo
- continue the policy of détente with the Soviet Union, including the sale of tons of grain to the Soviets and a hookup of Soviet and American space capsules
- oversee the end of the Vietnam War, including the withdrawal of the last American personnel from Saigon in 1975

The Election of 1976

The nation's bicentennial (200th anniversary) in 1976 gave the Ford presidency a boost. However, it was not enough to help Ford completely shake off his negative association with the Nixon years. He lost a close election to the Democratic candidate, James (Jimmy) Earl Carter, former governor of Georgia.

THE CARTER ADMINISTRATION

Jimmy Carter won the 1976 election, in part, because of his appeal to the American sense of honesty and integrity. He stated a desire to return to basic American "down home" values. He wanted to prove that an "outsider" could make government more responsive to the people. However, Carter's unfamiliarity with Washington politics proved a disadvantage. First Lady Rosalynn Carter became his most trusted adviser.

Carter's Domestic Policies

Carter's presidency was made more difficult by changes that had taken place within Congress because of Watergate. Newly elected members tended to question every executive act.

"STAGFLATION" Carter ran into the same economic woes as Ford—inflation coupled with rising unemployment. The problems were worsened by many welfare programs that increased the cost of government. With the economy apparently stalled in place, economists coined a new term, **stagflation,** to describe the situation. (The term referred to the stagnation of the economy and simultaneous inflation of prices.)

ENERGY PROBLEM As the world's leading industrial power, the United States was also the world's leading consumer of energy. By the late 1970s, the nation had to import more than 40 percent of its oil. OPEC kept prices high, and American dollars flowed out of the country, worsening the trade deficit—the situation in which a nation buys more foreign goods than it exports abroad.

Election of 1976

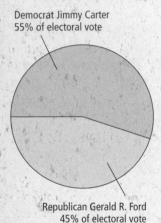

Democrat Jimmy Carter
55% of electoral vote

Republican Gerald R. Ford
45% of electoral vote

⚷ KEY THEMES AND CONCEPTS

Presidential Decisions and Actions

As you know from your study of United States history, all events are influenced by decisions, actions, and outcomes of earlier times.

- How was Carter's presidency influenced by the shadow of Nixon's presidency?

CORPORATE BAILOUTS Some American corporations were hard hit by stagflation and the decline in purchasing power at home. Foreign imports undersold some American goods, especially automobiles. The Chrysler Corporation and Lockheed Aircraft faced possible bankruptcy. Fearing the effect of massive layoffs on the economy, the federal government authorized huge loans to both corporations to keep them in business.

ENVIRONMENTAL PROBLEMS Acid rain, created by toxic air pollution, continued to threaten forests, lakes, and wildlife in the United States. President Nixon had taken steps to end harmful industrial pollution by creating the Environmental Protection Agency. Carter supported environmental programs as well, but inflation and energy shortages prevented him from undertaking ambitious programs to protect the environment. Coal polluted the air, but the nation needed coal to offset oil shortages. The nation needed to clean up the air, but emission devices for cars and factories pushed up prices.

NUCLEAR ENERGY Carter supported nuclear energy as an alternative to coal and oil. However, in 1979, an accident occurred at the Three Mile Island nuclear plant near Harrisburg, Pennsylvania. Although the problem was brought under control, the incident highlighted the hazards of the nuclear power industry, which by the late 1970s supplied about 4 percent of the nation's energy.

Carter's Foreign Policy
During his presidency, Carter faced a number of foreign-policy challenges.

HELSINKI ACCORDS In 1975, the United States and other nations signed the Helsinki Accords, promising to respect basic human rights. Carter believed that the United States should withhold aid from nations that violated human rights.

CAMP DAVID ACCORDS In 1977, Egyptian President Anwar el-Sadat surprised the world by visiting Israeli Prime Minister Menachem Begin. President Carter seized the opportunity for bringing peace to the Middle East by inviting the two leaders to Camp David, the President's retreat in Maryland. There, Sadat and Begin hammered out the terms for a peace treaty known as the **Camp David Accords.** The two leaders signed the treaty in 1979. Other Arab nations, however, still refused to recognize Israel.

PANAMA CANAL TREATIES In 1977, President Carter signed two treaties promising to turn over control of the Panama Canal to Panama in 1999. The treaties aroused bitter debate, but the Senate narrowly ratified them in 1978.

KEY THEMES AND CONCEPTS

Environment
In the 1970s, the United States faced a number of environmental problems.

- What steps did Nixon and Carter take to resolve some of these problems?

- Do any of these problems persist today? If so, which ones?

PREPARING FOR THE EXAM

What reasons led the American people to elect Ronald Reagan as President in 1980?

Election of 1980

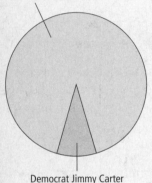

Republican Ronald Reagan 91% of electoral vote

Democrat Jimmy Carter 9% of electoral vote

KEY THEMES AND CONCEPTS

Presidential Decisions and Actions

President Reagan supported the policy of New Federalism that had been begun by President Nixon. New Federalism turned over government control of some social programs to the states. As part of New Federalism, Reagan also supported tax cuts for businesses, a balanced federal budget, and increased spending for national defense.

• Why do you think President Reagan supported New Federalism?

PROBLEMS WITH DÉTENTE In June 1979, Carter met with Soviet leader Leonid Brezhnev to negotiate the SALT II Treaty. However, a Soviet invasion of Afghanistan later that year ended détente. Carter cut off grain shipments to the Soviet Union and boycotted the 1980 summer Olympic games held in Moscow. Carter's tough line spurred debate at home.

HOSTAGE CRISIS The biggest foreign policy crisis for Carter came in Iran. In 1979, a revolution led by Islamic fundamentalists toppled the pro-American shah, Reza Pahlavi. The shah, suffering from terminal cancer, requested treatment in the United States, and Carter agreed. Islamic rebels struck back by seizing the United States embassy in Teheran and holding more than 50 Americans hostage.

The 1980 Election

During the 1980 presidential campaign, Carter was haunted by the continuing hostage crisis, persistent energy shortages, and lingering inflation. The conservative Republican candidate, former California governor Ronald Reagan, promised Americans a "new beginning" and a restoration of confidence at home and abroad. Reagan swept to victory, and on the day of his inauguration, Iran released the hostages after more than a year of captivity.

REAGAN AND THE CHALLENGES OF THE 1980s

A former actor, Reagan appealed to many Americans with his references to the "good old days" and his patriotic speeches. He used his prepared speeches to promote a conservative approach to government and the economy. He targeted inflation as his top priority and argued that big government was the cause of inflation. "In the present crisis," said Reagan, "government is not the solution to our problem; government is the problem."

Reagan's First-Term Domestic Policies

During his first term in office, Reagan supported a domestic program backed by both Eisenhower and Nixon. Like his Republican predecessors, he supported New Federalism, a policy that turned over federal control of some social welfare programs to the states.

SUPPLY-SIDE ECONOMICS Reagan called for cuts in taxes on businesses and individuals, especially those with large incomes. Reagan believed that they would reinvest in more businesses. These businesses would hire more workers and increase the supply of goods and services. Reagan argued that **supply-side economics** would end inflation without increasing the national debt. His ideas later became known as Reaganomics.

BALANCED BUDGET Reagan tried to balance the budget by reducing many social welfare programs. He also made sharp cuts in the Environmental Protection Agency. Despite such efforts, however, the national debt climbed throughout Reagan's presidency.

"STAR WARS" Reagan felt national security rested on defense and made every effort to fight off cuts in the military budget. He pushed for increased spending on missiles, ships, and bombers. He also asked for funding for the Strategic Defense Initiative (SDI), a massive satellite shield designed to intercept and destroy incoming Soviet missiles. SDI became popularly known as **"Star Wars."**

FARM AID In the 1980s, farmers experienced their worst economic problems since the Great Depression. A worldwide recession made it impossible for farmers to sell their surpluses—and to repay their loans. The Reagan administration responded by paying farmers not to plant millions of acres of land to reduce the supply and raise prices. However, prices did not rise, and the national debt grew.

IMMIGRATION In an effort to cut down on the number of undocumented workers living in the United States, Congress passed the 1986 Immigration Reform and Control Act, which forbade employers from hiring illegal immigrants. This new legislation did not solve the problem of the thousands of people who enter the United States illegally every year. These immigrants often work in sweatshop type factories, live in substandard housing, and are paid very low wages.

Origin of Immigrants, 1982–1995

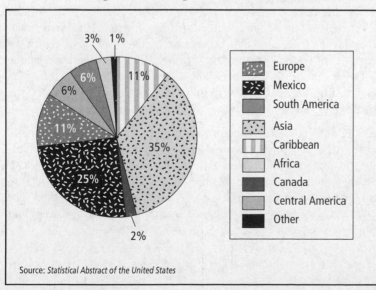

Legend:
- Europe
- Mexico
- South America
- Asia
- Caribbean
- Africa
- Canada
- Central America
- Other

Source: *Statistical Abstract of the United States*

ANALYZING DOCUMENTS

Use the graph at left and your knowledge of social studies to answer the following questions.

- From 1982 to 1995, where did the largest group of immigrants to the United States come from?

- How is this different than the origin of most immigrants in the 19th century?

Reagan's First-Term Foreign Policy

Reagan adopted a tough stand toward communism, describing the Soviet Union as an "evil empire."

QUESTIONING DÉTENTE Reagan's attitude hardened toward communism in December 1981, when the Polish government cracked down on Solidarity, an independent labor party. Reagan called for economic sanctions to force the communist-backed government to end martial law. A renewal of détente did not take place until Reagan's second term.

READING STRATEGY

Analyzing Cause And Effect
What factors contributed to United States military interventions in El Salvador, Nicaragua, and Grenada?

INTERVENTION IN CENTRAL AMERICA Reagan believed that unstable economic conditions opened the door to communism. He asked for aid to Latin American groups fighting communist takeovers and approved limited military intervention in some nations.

- *El Salvador* Reagan sent arms and military advisers to El Salvador to back anticommunist forces in a civil war. He also pressured the government to hold democratic elections.
- *Nicaragua* In 1979, Marxist guerrillas called the Sandinistas overthrew anticommunist dictator Anastasio Somoza. Because the Sandinistas accepted aid from Cuba and the Soviet Union, Reagan approved aid to the contras, rebels seeking to oust the Sandinistas. Actions by the CIA to help the contras angered Congress, and it cut off aid to the contras in 1987.
- *Grenada* In October, 1983, a rebellion in the Caribbean island nation of Grenada raised fears that it might become a communist base in the Caribbean. To prevent such a possibility, Reagan ordered a surprise United States invasion.

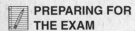 **PREPARING FOR THE EXAM**

Terrorism is random acts of violence that promote a political cause. Terrorist acts raised global concern during the 1980s.

- Why do you think terrorists bombed an American marine barracks in Lebanon in 1983?
- What effect did this bombing have on Reagan's policy in Lebanon?

TURMOIL IN THE MIDDLE EAST Religious conflicts in the Middle East increased tensions in an already unstable region. An international peacekeeping force went into Lebanon to try to end bloody fighting between Christians and Muslims. In October 1983, U.S. marines became the target of terrorists when a bomb-laden truck drove into their barracks, killing more than 300 people. In 1984, Reagan admitted the peacekeeping effort had failed and withdrew American troops.

TERRORISM Global concern was raised by an increase in terrorism, random acts of violence to promote a political cause. In some countries, Islamic fundamentalists engaged in terrorism as part of a jihad, or a struggle to protect the Islamic faith. Charges of terrorism were also leveled against the Soviets in September, 1983, when they shot down a South Korean airliner that strayed into their air space, killing some 269 innocent people.

The Election of 1984

In the presidential election of 1984, Walter Mondale won the Democratic nomination over several contenders including Jesse Jackson, an influential African American minister. Mondale selected Representative Geraldine Ferraro as his running mate. Reagan campaigned for reelection, with George Bush as his running mate. Reagan won the election and became the first President since Eisenhower to serve two full terms in office.

Reagan's Second-Term Domestic Policy

Reagan, nicknamed the Great Communicator by some journalists, used his charm and persuasive talents to convince many Americans to support a plan aimed at creating a balanced budget by the early 1990s.

Reagan and his supporters promised to make deep cuts in federal programs. Only a few select programs, such as Social Security and defense, were to be spared. Reagan also called for simplification of tax laws and tax cuts for about 60 percent of Americans. Some people charged that the cuts favored the rich. In fact, by the late 1980s, wealth was more unevenly distributed than at any time since the end of World War II.

TRADE IMBALANCE Despite drastic actions by the federal government, the national debt climbed. This was due, in part, to a huge trade imbalance, a situation in which a nation imports more goods than it exports. At the start of Reagan's second term, the trade deficit approached $150 billion.

Reagan's Second-Term Foreign Policy

Reagan redirected his foreign policy to meet changes taking place in the Soviet Union. However, an issue that arose out of the United States dealings in the Middle East and Latin America took up much of his attention.

THE IRAN-CONTRA AFFAIR In 1986, the American public learned that several top presidential aides had sold weapons to Iran in exchange for Iranian help in freeing American hostages held in Lebanon. The money from the sale of arms was then channeled to Nicaragua to support the contras.

Reagan had vowed never to bargain with terrorists or kidnappers. Also, Congress had banned aid to the contras. A congressional committee cleared the President of any wrongdoing in the Iran-Contra affair and concluded that the actions had been illegally undertaken at the direction of Colonel Oliver North and members of the CIA.

Election of 1984

Republican Ronald Reagan 98% of electoral vote

Democrat Walter Mondale 2% of electoral vote

**PREPARING FOR
THE EXAM**

How did Soviet leader
Mikhail Gorbachev work to
improve relations with the
United States?

RENEWAL OF DÉTENTE In 1985, Mikhail Gorbachev became the new charismatic leader of the Soviet Union. Gorbachev criticized Reagan's policy of "Star Wars" and called for a renewal of détente.

Gorbachev helped further relations by announcing his new policies of *glasnost* and *perestroika*. Glasnost called for greater openness, including increased political freedom in the Soviet Union and Eastern Europe. Perestroika allowed a measure of free enterprise to improve economic conditions within the Soviet Union.

ARMS REDUCTIONS In 1987, the United States and Soviet Union reached an agreement to eliminate short-range and medium-range land-based missiles.

TROUBLES ELSEWHERE Troubles over other foreign policy issues were not so easily resolved. These included

- *Continuing terrorism* Terrorists continued to claim some American lives. In 1985, for example, Palestinian terrorists killed an American passenger aboard the Italian cruise ship, the *Achille Lauro*. In 1988, a bomb destroyed a Pan Am jet over Scotland.
- *Battling the drug trade* First Lady Nancy Reagan launched an antidrug campaign with the slogan, "Just say no!"
- *Ending apartheid* Many people demanded that Americans divest, or get rid of, investments in South Africa to protest that nation's policy of apartheid, or strict racial segregation and discrimination. In 1986, Congress overrode Reagan's veto and imposed strict economic sanctions against South Africa until it ended apartheid.

**KEY THEMES AND
CONCEPTS**

Economic Systems
How did Americans protest
South Africa's policy of
apartheid?

The 1988 Election

In 1988, George Bush won the Republican nomination for President. He surprised the nation by choosing a little-known Indiana senator, Dan Quayle, as his running mate. Within the Democratic party, a primary battle shaped up between Jesse Jackson and Michael Dukakis, son of a Greek immigrant and governor of Massachusetts. Dukakis eventually won the nomination and selected Texas Senator Lloyd Bentsen as his running mate. In November, voters chose Bush to be the next President.

THE GEORGE H. W. BUSH ADMINISTRATION

The biggest issues of the Bush years were the budget, events abroad, and the economy.

Domestic Events

Bush inherited several of Reagan's problems from the late 1980s.

ECONOMIC TROUBLES During the election campaign, Bush had promised voters no new taxes. However, as the budget deficit mounted,

Bush was forced to break this promise in 1990. By 1992, an economic recession caused increased layoffs and rising unemployment.

SAVINGS AND LOAN SCANDAL In 1990, the misuse of funds by savings and loan institutions surfaced. American taxpayers would pay hundreds of billions of dollars to bail out the savings and loan industry.

SUPREME COURT APPOINTMENTS President Bush appointed two new justices to the Supreme Court: David Souter in 1990 and Clarence Thomas in 1991. Thomas was confirmed by the Senate after very controversial hearings in which he was charged with sexual harassment by Anita Hill, a former employee.

URBAN VIOLENCE In 1992, riots erupted in parts of Los Angeles after four white Los Angeles police officers were found innocent in the beating of African American motorist Rodney King.

Events Abroad

During Bush's presidency, the Cold War came to an end, but the United States entered military conflicts in Panama and the Persian Gulf.

END OF THE COLD WAR In November 1989, the world watched in amazement as Germans tore down the Berlin Wall—a symbolic reminder of the division between the communist and democratic worlds. Throughout the winter of 1989, communist governments in Eastern Europe crumbled. In 1990, Gorbachev received the Nobel Peace Prize for relaxing control over former Soviet satellites. In October of that year, East and West Germany were formally reunited. A failed coup by hardline communist leaders in 1991 led to the dissolution of the Soviet Union and the 1992 formation of a Commonwealth of Independent States.

ANALYZING DOCUMENTS

Use the graph below to answer these questions.

- How much did the federal budget deficit increase during the Bush administration?

- Did the greatest deficit occur during Reagan's or Bush's presidency?

Federal Budget Deficit, 1980–1992

Source: *Statistical Abstract of the United States*

The End of the Cold War

Causes	Results
• Anticommunist movements gain force in Eastern Europe • Soviet leader Mikhail Gorbachev encourages Eastern European leaders to adopt more open policies	• Reform leaders come to power after free elections in Poland and Czechoslovakia • New governments take charge in Bulgaria, Hungary, Romania, and Albania • Berlin Wall falls, East and West Germany are reunified • Soviet Union breaks apart

TURNING POINT

Why is the end of the Cold War in 1989 considered a turning point in history?

INVASION OF PANAMA As President, Bush continued Reagan's war on drugs. He ordered United States troops into Panama to capture General Manuel Noriega, the dictator of Panama, and return him to the United States to face drug charges. In 1992, Noriega was sentenced to serve 40 years in federal prison.

PERSIAN GULF WAR In August 1990, Iraqi leader Saddam Hussein invaded the oil-rich nation of Kuwait. Bush responded by sending United States troops into Saudi Arabia, with the agreement of Saudi leaders. The United Nations condemned Iraq's actions and approved economic sanctions against Iraq. The UN also authorized a joint military buildup in Saudi Arabia, called Operation Desert Shield.

Operation Desert Shield became Operation Desert Storm in January 1991 when the United States with a troop force of over 500,000 (the largest American military commitment since Vietnam) and Allied troops from a number of other nations began a total air assault on Iraq. By the end of February, Bush ordered a cease-fire, and Iraq accepted all UN demands to end the **Persian Gulf War.** More than 300 Allied lives were lost, but the Iraqi death toll was estimated at 100,000.

BOSNIA AND THE BALKANS The end of the Bush administration was marked by the outbreak of violence in the Balkans. In 1991, Slovenia and Croatia declared their independence from Yugoslavia, and fighting broke out throughout the area. Millions became refugees during the fighting. Bosnian Serbs, led by Slobodan Milosevic, carried out ethnic cleansing, or genocidal warfare, killing thousands of innocent civilians.

The 1992 Election

In the 1992 presidential election, George Bush ran as the Republican candidate with Dan Quayle as his running mate. The Democrats selected Arkansas governor Bill Clinton as their candidate, with Al Gore as his running mate. An independent challenger, Texas billionaire Ross Perot, also entered the race. The major issues of the campaign concerned the state of the American economy. In the election, Clinton made Bosnia an issue and promised to take strong action there.

Clinton carried 32 states with a total of 370 electoral votes. Although Perot did not earn any electoral votes, he received over 19 million popular votes. Women, African Americans, and Latino Americans were elected to Congress in record high numbers in 1992.

Election of 1992

Democrat Bill Clinton 43% of popular vote

Independent Ross Perot 19% of popular vote

Republican George Bush 38% of popular vote

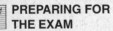

PREPARING FOR THE EXAM

Was Bill Clinton's victory in the 1992 Presidential election decisive? Why or why not?

THE APPROACH TO THE NEW MILLENIUM

THE CLINTON ADMINISTRATION

Domestic Issues

HEALTH-CARE REFORM In 1993, Clinton presented to Congress a health-care reform plan that would ensure health insurance for all Americans. Critics of the plan complained it was too expensive, complex and would limit choice in health care. In 1994, Congress rejected Clinton's plan.

SOCIAL SECURITY It became clear that the Social Security program, begun during the Great Depression, would run into trouble because of changing demographics. The number of recipients is increasing rapidly due to longer life spans and the aging baby boomer generation. Several plans to fund Social Security have been considered, but no plan has been agreed upon.

SUPREME COURT APPOINTEES Clinton's nominations of Ruth Bader Ginsburg and Stephen Breyer made him the first Democratic President in 26 years to name a Supreme Court justice.

THE 1994 CONGRESSIONAL ELECTIONS In 1994, Republicans took majority control of Congress for the first time in 40 years.

THE 1996 AND 1998 ELECTIONS At the end of 1995, disagreements between Republicans and Clinton over the budget led to a shutdown of the federal government. During the 1996 presidential campaign, Clinton focused public attention on the Republicans' role in the shutdown. He also adopted several Republican issues by signing welfare reform into law and supporting a balanced budget. Clinton easily won re-election. Republicans maintained their congressional majority after both elections, but Democrats gained five House seats in 1998.

SCANDAL AND IMPEACHMENT Many of President Clinton's activities were the subject of investigations, including the Whitewater affair, which accused him and his wife Hillary Rodham Clinton of involvement with an illegal real estate scheme in Arkansas. The Clintons were never formally charged.

In 1998, a special prosecutor accused President Clinton of several offenses, including lying under oath about his relationship with a White House intern. On December 19, 1998, the House impeached President Clinton on charges of perjury and obstruction of justice. The Senate acquitted the President two months later.

KEY THEMES AND CONCEPTS

Government
How did the 1994 Congressional elections shift the balance of power in Congress?

ANALYZING DOCUMENTS

Examine the cartoon below, then answer the questions.

- What does the book represent?

- What does the black spot stand for?

- What is the meaning of the title of the cartoon?

- What is the opinion that this cartoon is trying to convey?

ECONOMIC PROSPERITY In the 1990s, the United States enjoyed the longest period of economic growth in its history.

Foreign Issues

Developments in other nations also presented challenges.

THE MIDDLE EAST The Arab-Israeli conflict has long focused attention on the Middle East. Since 1948, Arabs and Israelis have waged four wars. In 1993, the Palestine Liberation Organization and Israel agreed to a measure of Palestinian self-government. However, incidents of violence slowed the peace process.

THE FORMER YUGOSLAVIA Tensions between ethnic groups in the former Yugoslavia led to war in Bosnia in the early 1990s. The United States helped win an agreement between the two sides in 1995 and President Clinton sent troops to enforce the plan. In 1998, violence erupted in Kosovo, where Serbian forces massacred ethnic Albanian civilians. A brief bombing campaign by NATO forced the Serbs to withdraw. Many Serbian leaders then were arrested for war crimes and put on trial.

NATO EXPANSION In March 1999, NATO welcomed the Czech Republic, Hungary, and Poland as new members.

SOUTH AFRICA In 1994, Nelson Mandela, the long-time leader of the campaign against apartheid, became his nation's first democratically elected president.

GLOBAL ECONOMY In 1992, the United States, Canada, and Mexico signed the North American Free Trade Agreement (NAFTA) in an effort to break down trade barriers among the three nations. American trade in Europe continued to be strong, despite the formation of the **European Union,** a trade organization designed to break down trade barriers within Europe.

THE 2000 ELECTION

In the 2000 presidential election, Texas Governor George W. Bush ran as the Republican candidate against the Democrat, Vice President Al Gore. In one of the closest presidential races in history, Florida emerged as the key state. The Florida vote was so close, a recount of ballots was ordered by law. The election ended when the Supreme Court ruled to discontinue the recounts. Although Gore won the popular vote, Bush won the electoral vote. The election marked the first time the Supreme Court intervened in a presidential election.

♀ KEY THEMES AND CONCEPTS

Presidential Decisions and Actions

In the early 1990s, war erupted in the Balkans as the former Yugoslavia fell into a bitter civil war.

- How did President Clinton handle tensions between ethnic groups in the former Yugoslavia in the 1990s?

- What gave Clinton the authority to take this action?

♀ KEY THEMES AND CONCEPTS

Economic Systems

By the 1990s, the economies of many nations had become more interdependent.

- Name two organizations or agreements designed to improve trade among member nations.

- To which of these does the United States belong?

THE GEORGE W. BUSH (43) ADMINISTRATION

Early in his presidency, Bush focused on a few central issues:

Domestic Issues

CUTTING TAXES Bush gained congressional approval of a tax cut. Most taxpayers received rebates of $300, which Bush argued would jumpstart the faltering economy. 2004 has experienced minor spurts of economic growth and continuing higher than normal rates of unemployment.

EDUCATIONAL REFORM On January 8, 2002 President Bush signed into law a major educational reform bill called No Child Left Behind. The plan called for increased student and teacher account- ability and targets funds for improving schools. Critics have said that it does not accomplish what it needs to do to improve American education.

SOCIAL SECURITY President Bush has decided to make Social Security Reform a primary agenda for himself and his administra- tion while his opponents claim that the System can be adjusted in more minor ways, with less financial risk. The President's plan to allow younger workers to chose private accounts for a portion of their Social Security system has drawn wide praise and equally strong criticism.

ELECTION 2004 In November 2004, George W. Bush, the Republican incumbent won a very close race against challenger, Massachusetts Senator and Vietnam War veteran, John Kerry. The pop- ular vote was Bush, 62,040,606 (51%) to Kerry's 59,028,109 (48%). The state of Ohio ultimately gave the President the needed Electoral votes to win, 286 to 252.

Vice President Dick Cheney continued for a second term. Dr. Condoleeza Rice, former National Security Advisor, became the first African American woman to hold the position of Secretary of State. Within the first few months of being appointed Secretary of State Rice made important trips to Europe, the Middle East and parts of Asia.

Foreign Issues

SEPTEMBER 11, 2001 AND RESULTING EVENTS Bush focused largely on foreign policy after the September 11, 2001 attacks on the World Trade Center in New York City and the Pentagon in Washington, D.C. Bush called the attacks "acts of war" and committed the country to a campaign against terrorists. American forces attacked military sites and terrorists training camps in Afghanistan. Bush urged Americans not to "expect one battle but a lengthy campaign unlike any other we have ever seen."

THE MIDDLE EAST Problems between the Israelis and Palestinians continue with repeated incidents of suicide bombers and cross border attacks by both sides. Attempts have been made by the United States to develop compromise solutions but episodes of violence delay peace keeping efforts.

In November 2004, Yasir Arafat the leader of the Palestine Liberation Organization and recipient of the Nobel Peace Prize died at 75 after an almost 50 year struggle to gain a permanent homeland for the Palestinian people.

KEY THEMES AND CONCEPTS

Presidential Decisions and Actions

How have President Bush's actions during the War in Iraq demonstrated his use of Presidential power?

WAR IN IRAQ In late 2002 and early 2003, the Bush Administration warned Saddam Hussein to eliminate Iraq's weapons of mass destruction (WMD). Hussein claimed not to have any WMD. The United Nations sent an inspection team, which reported little success finding these weapons. The United States worked to gain United Nations support for an invasion of Iraq. Failing to gain this support, a small number of countries led by the United States and Great Britain attacked Iraq in March 2003. More than 200,000 American troops were sent to the area. For the first time the United States military allowed reporters to be "embedded" with the troops. Bush declared an official end to the war on May 1, 2003.

In July 2003 both sons of Saddam Hussein were killed in a shootout by U.S. forces in Mosul, Iraq. Hussein himself continued to escape capture until December 2003. An Iraqi Governing Council was established during 2003 with the goal of allowing Iraq to be an independent, democratic nation when the United States military completes its transfer of political powers. American casualities continue to rise as the military meets with pockets of resistance. President Bush has defended the War on the grounds that a brutal dictator has been removed, that Hussein had terrorist links and that he was hiding Weapons of Mass Destruction. Given the rising human and financial costs to the United States and the failure to find WMD, critics have questioned the Bush Administration's activites in Iraq and it's long term plan for that country.

During 2004 President Bush and Secretary of Defense Donald Rumsfeld had to answer serious questions about the treatment of Iraqi prisoners when reports of abuse by American troops was disclosed. Some of the responsible soldiers have been found guilty and sentenced to prison terms themselves. In January 2005 with American and

Coalition Forces support the new Iraqi government held its first democratic elections under extremely tight security. Insurgents who oppose the new government and the American presence in Iraq continue to cause violent attacks on both military and civilians in Baghdad and elsewhere. By the spring of 2005, over 140,000 American troops continued to serve in Iraq with a goal of training Iraqis soldiers to eventually be able to replace the Americans. Over 1500 American servicemen and women have been killed in Iraq and thousands more have been seriously wounded.

OTHER WORLD AREAS The Bush Administration remained concerned with North Korea's development and possible use of nuclear power, but has been careful not to aggravate what could become an increasingly volatile area of the world. The President also made his first trips to Europe and Africa in 2003 to promote the United States as a caring member of the world community.

SECTION 5

Towards a Postindustrial Society: Living in a Global Age

⭐ **THE BIG IDEA**
Since the end of World War II, the rapid pace of change has turned the world into a "global village." Today

- technology and growing corporations have helped to increase job growth.

- most people have longer life expectancies, despite diseases such as AIDS.

- population growth and environmental concerns challenge the United States as well as other countries.

🔑 **KEY TERMS**
alternative energy sources
Internet
multinational corporations
Earth Day

SECTION OVERVIEW

The United States began as a nation of farmers. Today it is one of the leading economic and political powers in the world. Because of the advanced technology of the postindustrial age, the world has become what some call a "global village." Because of increased interdependence, major events in one part of the world have an impact upon the rest of the world.

KEY THEMES AND CONCEPTS

As you review this section, take special note of the following key themes and concepts:

Change What effects did technological change have on American society?

Places and Regions How did the United States play a unique role in helping resolve conflicts in other regions of the world?

Environment How are concerns about the environment being addressed by activist groups?

Interdependence How has the emergence of a global economy strengthened the interdependence of nations?

RAPID PACE OF CHANGE

Every generation since the Civil War has experienced the effects of the Industrial Revolution. However, the pace of technological change has picked up dramatically since World War II. Today, the United States is moving into a postindustrial age. That is, the American economy no longer rests on the development of new factories and heavy industries, such as the production of steel or coal. Instead, because of technological changes, service-related industries now occupy a larger sector of the economy.

Technology—What Is It?

Technology is the application of scientific knowledge to commerce and industry. To appreciate the effect of technological change, think of the following situations out of the past.

- George Washington, the nation's first President, never called a member of Congress on the telephone, never rode in a limousine, and never saw his photograph in a newspaper.
- Abraham Lincoln, President during the Civil War, never called generals on the telephone and never listened to battle reports on the radio.
- Franklin Roosevelt, President during World War II, never had a speech transmitted by satellite to Europe and never watched a program on television.
- John F. Kennedy, President in the early 1960s, never wrote a speech on a computer and never ate a snack heated up in a microwave.
- All recent Presidents have supported the American space program, but none has yet traveled into space. It is difficult even to imagine the changes that await future Presidents.

The Post-World War II Era

Since the end of World War II, a number of forces have had a great impact upon the economy and upon the lifestyles of Americans.

SCARCE ENERGY SOURCES Scarce oil supplies have led scientists to research **alternative energy sources,** such as solar power. Nuclear power is being used in some parts of the world. However, the hazards associated with nuclear energy, such as the storage of nuclear waste, have created controversy. The accident at a nuclear power plant at Chernobyl, Ukraine, in 1986 has increased debate even more.

USE OF NEW MATERIALS Inventions since World War II have replaced wood and steel in many jobs with synthetics, such as plastic. In some cases, these new materials are lighter and more durable than traditional materials.

SPREAD OF COMPUTERS The prevalent use of computers in American homes and businesses since the 1980s has revolutionized record keeping and the storage of information. Advocates of computers praise their ability to process and store large volumes of information. Critics charge that computers have increased the chances for the invasion of privacy as people access private records without permission, particularly as **Internet** use becomes increasingly widespread.

SECURITY CONCERNS The global increase in acts of terrorism, especially the attacks on the Pentagon and the World Trade towers, made some Americans fear that they were not safe. In response, the government took a number of measures. Airport security was tightened, as was security at bridges, tunnels, nuclear power plants, courthouses, and other vulnerable places. The Patriot Act of 2001 gave sweeping new powers to government agencies. To coordinate federal government efforts, President Bush created a new Cabinet-level department, Homeland Security. Its job was to coordinate the efforts of more than 40 federal agencies fighting terror. These agencies include the CIA, FBI, and the National Guard.

KEY THEMES AND CONCEPTS

Change

The United States faced a rapid pace of change during the Industrial Revolution, but that pace increased dramatically after World War II.

- How did the American economy change after World War II?

 PREPARING FOR THE EXAM

How has the United States economy been influenced by each of the following since the end of World War II?

- new energy sources
- new job opportunities
- computers

In 2002 President Bush and Congress created the independent, bipartisan National Commission on Terrorist Attacks on the United States. After extensive hearings by the Commission it released in the summer of 2004 a detailed public report. One of its major recommendations was to unify the United States Intelligence community under the leadership of a new National Intelligence Director. President Bush named John Negroponte, U.S. Ambassador to Iraq to this position in February 2005. The Commission made a number of other recommendations to improve the security of the United States.

GROWTH OF MULTINATIONAL CORPORATIONS Since the 1800s, the organization of American businesses has changed from single ownership and partnerships to corporations. In the post-World War II period, many corporations have become **multinational corporations,** or businesses with bases of operation in many nations.

INCREASED JOB OPPORTUNITIES The greatest increases in jobs in the early 2000s promise to be in the service fields. The largest declines will occur in agricultural employment. Technological advances have made it possible for fewer farmers to produce more food, which will continue to reduce the need for agricultural labor.

NEW LIFESTYLES AND LONGER LIFE SPANS American attitudes toward family size and divorce have changed since the 1950s. Average family size has declined. After years of expansion, many school districts throughout the nation, including New York's, experienced declining school enrollments in the 1980s. Divorce rates first rose and then remained constant. This created the largest number of single-parent households in the nation's history. At the same time, health-care improvements resulting from new technologies, such as laser surgery and organ transplants, have increased average life spans. This has increased the number of older Americans, who in recent years have organized to protect their rights and improve their lives.

EXPANSION OF PUBLIC EDUCATION Access to free public education has helped many Americans improve their standard of living. As individuals complete higher levels of education, they have the chance to secure better-paying jobs and more desirable housing. Thus, education helps further social mobility.

INCREASINGLY DIVERSE POPULATION If current trends continue, it is projected that the population of the United States will grow increasingly diverse over the next half century. More of the newest immigrants to the United States come from Asian and Latin American countries, compared with earlier waves of immigration that came from Europe.

DEALING WITH THE AIDS CRISIS Since the 1980s, medical researchers have gathered more information about AIDS, or Acquired Immune Deficiency Syndrome. Even so, AIDS has spread through some sectors of the American population at an alarming rate. Without a known

⚲ KEY THEMES AND CONCEPTS

Change

Changes in technology frequently have an impact on the availability of certain jobs. For example, early telephones did not have a dial or push buttons to make a phone call directly. Instead, a caller would have to place a call through an operator, who made the phone connections at a switchboard. Once technology improved and direct dialing became commonly available, the need for telephone operators decreased.

- In the 1990s and early 2000s, what impact did technological improvements have on agricultural job opportunities?

📝 PREPARING FOR THE EXAM

How have Americans' lifestyles been influenced by each of the following since the end of World War II?

- average family size
- longer life spans
- expansion of public education

The Changing Ethnic Composition of the United States

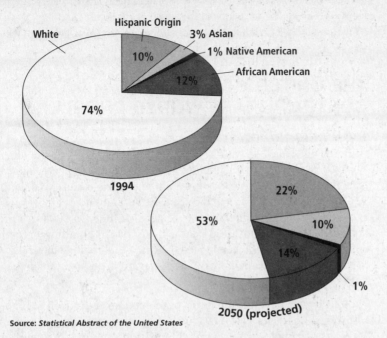

White — 74%
Hispanic Origin — 10%
3% Asian
1% Native American
African American — 12%

1994

53%
22%
10%
14%
1%

2050 (projected)

Source: *Statistical Abstract of the United States*

ANALYZING DOCUMENTS

Use the chart at left to answer the following questions.

- Between 1994 and 2050, which group of Americans is expected to grow most rapidly?

- Which group of Americans is expected to be a smaller proportion of the U.S. population?

- Which group is expected to remain the same proportion of the overall population?

cure, scientists and public health officials have tried to increase public awareness and prevention of the disease. Many critics have condemned the federal government for not acting faster to find a cure for AIDS.

HELPING THE HOMELESS Not everyone enjoyed the prosperity of the post-World War II years. President Johnson's Great Society programs in the 1960s tried to reduce poverty in the United States. However, cuts in social programs during the 1980s caused a significant rise in the number of Americans living below the poverty line. Local communities and private charitable organizations tried to provide relief, but the issue of homelessness has remained a troubling issue.

GUN CONTROL The issue of gun control became hotly debated in the late 1990s. Urban violence, as well as a number of highly publicized school shootings, caused millions of Americans to reconsider attitudes toward and the availability of guns in this nation. In May 2000, thousands of American mothers marched in the Million Mom March in Washington, D.C., to focus attention on the need to curb gun violence.

The National Rifle Association continues to be one of the strongest lobbyist groups and remains very vocal about the rights of gun owners. This topic will continue to be a controversial one for years to come.

RIGHT TO LIFE ISSUES The United States continues to be a very divided society on the topics of abortion and the right to life/the right to die. In March 2005 President Bush and the Congress took unprecedented actions by involving themselves in the case of Terri Schiavo. She was a terminally ill Florida woman whose right to die had been debated in the Florida courts for many years. Ultimately the decisions of the Florida courts were upheld. This allowed her husband to authorize the removal of a feeding tube which led to her death after a fourteen year period in which she had been medically determined to be in a persistent vegetative state.

THE UNITED STATES AND CONTEMPORARY WORLD PROBLEMS

International Terrorism

Although the attack on New York and Washington, D.C., on September 11, 2001, was aimed at one nation, it mobilized government leaders all over the world. The attacks showed how terrorism has expanded its global reach and has affected the security and stability of all nations.

As the War in Iraq fueled anti Western attitudes in 2004, terrorist activities caused almost 200 deaths in a railroad bombing in Spain. Other areas of the world heightened their efforts at limiting the ability of terrorist groups to share information, money, weapons and personnel.

Population Growth

Although most developed nations have experienced a decline in their birthrates, the developing nations have an overpopulation problem. Millions of people suffer from malnutrition, living only a marginal existence. Foreign aid from the United States has become of vital economic importance in combating world hunger.

Environmental Concerns

Because of increased interdependence, an environmental problem in one nation frequently raises global concerns. An example includes the destruction of the Brazilian tropical rain forests.

ENVIRONMENTAL ACTIVISTS A number of groups have organized to reduce and clean up pollution on the land, in the water, and in the air. Other activist groups work to save endangered species of animals.

Recycling efforts have been organized to reuse paper, glass, plastic, and aluminum. Community organizers are opposing plans to convert vacant lands into dumpsites. Communities are studying the effects of industrial pollution on the groundwater that people drink. In response to public pressure, the federal government has enacted laws requiring automobile manufacturers to put antipollution devices on their cars. Since the first **Earth Day** celebration in 1970, the American people, along with the rest of the world, have begun to realize their obligation to protect the environment for future generations.

NATURAL DISASTERS In December 2006 a tsunami, a giant destructive wave, caused upwards of 200,00 deaths and left as many as 5,000,000 homeless in parts of South East Asia, the Indian subcontinent and East Africa. It was the worst natural disaster in modern history and the international community joined together in a massive

KEY THEMES AND CONCEPTS

Interdependence
The concept of a global community means that the United States can not isolate itself from problems in other countries. Population growth in developing nations and environmental concerns in nations with essential ecosystems are two issues that affect the entire world.

- Why should the destruction of tropical rain forests be a concern to people in other nations, including the United States?

READING STRATEGY

Organizing Information
List three ways that environmental activists have raised public awareness about environmental issues.

1.

2.

3.

Foreign Policy After the Cold War

United States Foreign Policy

- Offered $2.5 billion aid package to Russia to help nation move toward democracy and capitalism.
- Tried unsuccessfully to control violence and civil war in Somalia and other African nations.
- Helped Irish and British leaders negotiate a peace agreement.
- U.S. leads small group of coalition nations in War in Iraq, 2003–5
- Sent troops to Bosnia as part of United Nations peacekeeping effort.
- Tried to help Israeli and Palestinian leaders negotiate a peace treaty.
- Troops to Afghanistan and Iraq in followup to terrorist attacks of September 11, 2001.

outpouring of financial aid. President Bush committed the United States to $350 million in aid and millions more were donated by Americans directly to private relief agencies. The President also requested his father, former President George H.W. Bush and former President Bill Clinton to work together to draw attention to the extent of disaster damage in the stricken areas, to visit the area and to solicit private funds to help in the immediate and long term needs of the people of the area.

Emerging Power Relationships

In the decades after World War II, a variety of power relationships emerged among nations. These relationships are broad categories, and there are exceptions to each.

- *East vs. West* During the cold war, tensions arose between the Soviet-dominated nations of Eastern Europe and the democratic nations of Western Europe and the United States. After the cold war, the relationship shifted from one based on ideology (or belief), to one based on economics and politics, as many of the nations of Eastern Europe began to enjoy some of the benefits of democracy and capitalism.
- *North vs. South* This relationship expressed the difference in power between the wealthier, industrialized nations of North America and Europe and many of the poorer, less industrialized nations of Africa, Asia, and Latin America.
- *Developed vs. developing (or haves vs. have-nots)* As the industrialized (or developed) nations continued to make great strides ahead because of improvements in technology, agriculture, and medicine, the gap widened between these developed countries and the developing nations that still lacked many basic amenities. Basic economic differences can be expected to cause problems in the decades ahead as developing nations struggle to raise their standards of living while resisting dependence upon the developed nations.

READING STRATEGY

Problem Solving
Why do you think the gap between rich and poor nations is widening?

Questions for Regents Practice

For online Questions for Regents Practice,
visit the Prentice Hall Web site at www.phschool.com.

MULTIPLE CHOICE

Directions

Review the Test-Taking Strategies section of this book. Then answer the following questions, drawn from actual Regents examinations. Each question is followed by four choices. Read each question carefully. Decide which choice is the correct answer. Then on a separate piece of paper, mark your answer for each question.

1   The quotations below are from two United States Supreme Court decisions.

I. "Separation of the races does not place a badge of inferiority upon one group over another, thus it is not a violation of the 14th amendment." (1896)

II. "To separate [children in grade school and high school] from others of similar age and qualifications solely because of their race generates a feeling of inferiority as to their status . . . that may affect their hearts and minds in a way unlikely ever to be un-done." (1954)

The difference in opinion between these two rulings best shows
1 a change in judicial philosophy and public attitudes
2 the persistent efforts of the major political parties to increase equal opportunity
3 a recognition that democracy depends on economic equality for all citizens
4 the refusal of the Supreme Court to deal with controversial issues

2   The successful launching of *Sputnik* by the Soviet Union in 1957 signaled the beginning of
1 American fears that the Soviets had achieved technological superiority
2 the Cold War with the United States
3 Soviet aggression in Afghanistan and China
4 disarmament discussions between the superpowers

3   Which development contributed most to the expansion of suburbs since the 1950s?
1 construction of interstate highways
2 invention of the computer
3 completion of transcontinental railroads
4 development of jet aircraft

4   When President Dwight D. Eisenhower sent federal troops to Little Rock, Arkansas, during the 1957 school integration crisis, he was exercising his constitutional power as
1 chief legislator
2 commander in chief
3 chief diplomat
4 head of state

5 Which is a valid conclusion based on
   United States involvement in the Korean
   War?
   1 The policy of containment was applied in
      Asia as well as in Europe.
   2 United Nations economic sanctions are
      more effective than military action.
   3 The American people will support United
      States participation in any war, whether
      declared or undeclared.
   4 United States cooperation with a wartime
      ally ends when the war ends.

6 What was the significance of the use of federal marshals to protect African American
   students in Little Rock, Arkansas, in 1957?
   1 It was the first time martial law had been
      declared in the United States.
   2 It led to federal takeover of many
      southern public schools.
   3 It strengthened control of education by
      state governments.
   4 It showed that the federal government
      would enforce court decisions on
      integration.

7 "We conclude that in the field of public
   education the doctrine of 'separate but
   equal' has no place. Separate educational
   facilities are inherently unequal."

   This quotation expresses the Supreme Court
   decision in the case of
   1 Plessy v. Ferguson
   2 Engel v. Vitale
   3 Tinker v. Des Moines Independent
      Community School District
   4 Brown v. Board of Education of Topeka,
      Kansas

8 The Supreme Court under Chief Justice Earl
   Warren had a major impact on the United
   States in that this Court
   1 became involved in foreign affairs by
      reviewing the constitutionality of treaties
   2 weakened the judiciary by refusing to
      deal with controversial issues
   3 supported the idea that states could
      nullify acts of Congress
   4 followed a policy of judicial activism,
      leading to broad changes in American
      society

9 Segregation in public schools was declared
   unconstitutional because it violated the
   1 reserved powers provision
   2 due process of law provision
   3 principle of equal protection under
      the law
   4 principle of a clear and present danger

10 Base your answer to question 10 on the
    song below and on your knowledge of
    social studies.

    "It isn't nice to block the doorway,
    It isn't nice to go to jail,
    There are nicer ways to do it,
    But the nice ways always fail,
    It isn't nice, it isn't nice,
    You told us once, you told us twice,
    But if that's freedom's price, we
       don't mind."

    —Malvina Reynolds, "It Isn't Nice"

    This song from the 1960s is most likely
    referring to the movement to
    1 liberalize immigration laws
    2 expand civil rights
    3 allow women to serve in combat roles
       in the military
    4 grant voting rights to 18-year-old citizens

11 "There are two types of laws: There are *just* laws and there are *unjust* laws. I would be the first to advocate obeying just laws. One has not only a legal but a moral responsibility to obey just laws. Conversely, one has a moral responsibility to disobey unjust laws."

—Martin Luther King, Jr.

This statement is a justification of the concept of
1 cultural pluralism
2 ethnic assimilation
3 reverse discrimination
4 civil disobedience

12 The women's movement was strengthened in the 1960s chiefly because
1 women became increasingly dissatisfied with their status and their roles in society
2 women were angered by the failure of the voters to elect them to Congress
3 job discrimination against women and minorities was eliminated
4 the radical liberation movements of the 1950s had failed

13 "And so my fellow Americans—ask not what you country can do for you—ask what you can do for your country."

When President John F. Kennedy made this statement, he was encouraging the American people to develop
1 a personal commitment to work for national ideals
2 an awareness of environmental hazards
3 a concern for national defense
4 an appreciation for the contributions of immigrants to American society

14 Which statement about the Cuban missile crisis (1962) is most accurate?
1 The crisis showed that the United States and the Soviet Union could agree on total disarmament.
2 The crisis brought the two major world powers very close to war.
3 The United States wanted to establish missile sites in Cuban territory.
4 The communist government in Cuba was overthrown.

15 President Lyndon B. Johnson's Great Society was an effort to solve the problem of
1 poverty
2 drug trafficking
3 overpopulation
4 illegal immigration

16 One similarity between the actions of President Franklin D. Roosevelt and Lyndon B. Johnson is that both
1 led the United States to victory in war
2 expanded the role of government in citizens' lives
3 vetoed legislation on the issue of rights for minorities
4 achieved a balanced federal budget during their terms in office

17 **"Four Students Killed at Kent State University"**

"Gulf of Tonkin Resolution Passed"

"Radical Protesters Disrupt Democratic Convention in Chicago"

These headlines relate to which even in United States history?
1 Civil War
2 World War II
3 Vietnam War
4 Persian Gulf War

18 During the Vietnam War, serious questions were raised in the United States concerning the
1 authority of the Supreme Court in regard to national security
2 extent of the President's powers as commander in chief
3 loyalty of United States military leaders
4 role of the North Atlantic Treaty Organization (NATO) in international peacekeeping

19 A major long-term effect of the Vietnam War has been
1 an end to communist governments in Asia
2 a change in United States foreign policy from containment to imperialism
3 a reluctance to commit United States troops for extended military action abroad
4 a continued boycott of trade with Asia

20 The outcome of the Watergate scandal reinforced the principle that
1 national security takes precedence over freedom of the press
2 the power of executive privilege is greater than the rule of law
3 the law applies equally to all citizens, including government officials
4 impeached government officials are immune from criminal prosecution

21 The Camp David accords promoted by President Jimmy Carter were significant because they represented
1 the first peace agreement between Israel and an Arab nation
2 the establishment of a worldwide human rights policy
3 a lasting arms-reduction treaty
4 the end of the Vietnam War

22 The "trickle down" economic theory of President Herbert Hoover and the "supply side" economic policies under President Ronald Reagan were based on the idea that
1 balanced budgets are essential to economic success
2 the federal government needs to assume more responsibility for solving economic problems
3 economic growth depends on making increased amounts of capital available to businesses
4 economic stability is the responsibility of federal monetary agencies

23 The North American Free Trade Agreement (NAFTA) between the United States, Mexico, and Canada is meant to
1 increase commerce and eliminate tariffs
2 encourage lower labor costs
3 raise environmental standards
4 allow citizens to move freely from one nation to another

24 **"Clinton Offers Economic Aid to Russia"**
"U.S. Sends Peacekeeping Troops to Bosnia"
"U.S. Airlifts Food and Medicine to Somalia"

These headlines illustrate that United States foreign policy during the 1990s stressed
1 containment
2 collective security
3 global involvement
4 neutrality

25 How does the present-day United States economy differ from the nation's economy of 1900?
1 Immigrants are no longer a source of labor.
2 Today's government plays a less active role in the economy.
3 The United States is less dependent on oil imports.
4 The growth of service industries is greater today.

THEMATIC ESSAY

In developing your answers to the essay, be sure to keep these general definitions in mind:

(a) <u>discuss</u> means "to make observations about something using facts, reasoning, and argument; to present in some detail"

(b) <u>describe</u> means "to illustrate something in words or to tell about it"

(c) <u>evaluate</u> means "to examine and judge the significance, worth, or condition of; to determine the value of"

Directions

Write a well-organized essay that includes an introduction, several paragraphs addressing the task below, and a conclusion.

Theme: Technological Change

Many aspects of United States society have been greatly affected by technological changes.

Task

Identify three aspects of United States society that have been affected by technological change since the beginning of the twentieth century. Explain how that aspect was affected by a specific technological change. Discuss the extent to which the impact of the change was positive or negative.

Suggestions

You may use any example from your study of the United States in the twentieth century. Some suggestions you might wish to consider include: environment, politics, agriculture, urbanization, individual rights, or cultural pluralism.

You are *not* limited to these suggestions.

Guidelines

In your essay be sure to:

- Address all aspects of the *Task*
- Analyze, evaluate, or compare and/or contrast issues and events whenever possible
- Fully support the theme of the essay with relevant facts, examples, and details
- Write a well-developed essay that consistently demonstrates a logical and clear plan of organization
- Introduce the theme by establishing a framework that is beyond a simple restatement of the *Task*
- Conclude your essay with a strong summation of the theme

DOCUMENT-BASED ESSAY

For online Document-Based Essays,
visit the Prentice Hall Web site at www.phschool.com.

This task is designed to test your ability to work with historical documents and is based on the accompanying documents (1–6). Some of the documents have been edited for the purposes of this question. As you analyze the documents, take into account both the source of each document and any point of view that may be presented in the document.

Directions

This document-based question consists of two parts: Part A and Part B. In Part A, you are to read each document and answer the question or questions that follow the document. In Part B, you are to write an essay based on the information in the documents and your knowledge of United States history.

Historical Context

The Preamble to the United States Constitution reads: "We the people of the United States, in order to form a more perfect union, establish justice, insure domestic tranquility, provide for the common defense, promote the general welfare, and secure the blessings of liberty to ourselves and our posterity, do ordain and establish this Constitution for the United States."

Task

Using the information from the documents and your knowledge of American history and geography, write an essay in which you discuss whether the America government, since 1950, has achieved the goals established for our nation in the preamble to the Constitution of the United States.

PART A: SHORT ANSWER

DOCUMENT #1

> *"I have a dream that one day this nation will rise up and live out the true meaning of its creed, 'We hold these truths to be self-evident, that all men are created equal.' I have a dream that one day on the red hills of Georgia, sons of former slaves and the sons of former slave owners will be able to sit down together at the table of brotherhood. . . . I have a dream that my four little children will one day live in a nation where they will not be judged by the color of their skin, but by the content of their character. . . . When we allow freedom to ring, when we let it ring from every village and every hamlet, from every state and every city, we will be able to speed up that day when all of God's children, black men and white men, Jews and Gentiles, Protestants and Catholics, will be able to join hands and sing in the words of the old Negro spiritual: 'Free at last. Free at last. Thank God Almighty, we are free at last.'"*
>
> **—Martin Luther King, Jr., "I Have a Dream" speech, 1963**

1 What does Dr. King's dream suggest about the United States government's success in achieving "the blessings of liberty" for all Americans?

_____

_____

_____

_____

DOCUMENT #2

> *"One thing became clear: that in the black movement I had been fighting for someone else's oppression, and now there was a way that I could fight for my own freedom, and I was going to be much stronger than I ever was."*
>
> **—Cathy Cade, women's rights activist**

2 What experience motivated Cathy Cade to work for the delivery of the "blessings of liberty" to women?

_____

_____

_____

_____

DOCUMENT #3
Selected Great Society Legislation, 1964-1966

Legislation	Purpose
Economic Opportunity Act, 1964	Created to combat causes of poverty, such as illiteracy and unemployment
Volunteers in Service to America (VISTA), 1964	Sent volunteers to help people in poor communities and set up community action programs to give the poor a voice in defining local housing, health, and education policies
Medicare, 1965	Provided hospital and low-cost medical insurance for most Americans aged 65 and older
Medicaid, 1965	Provided low-cost health insurance for low-income Americans of any age who could not afford private health insurance
Elementary and Secondary Education Act of 1965	Provided education aid to states based on the number of children from low-income households
Department of Housing and Urban Development (HUD), 1965	Established to oversee the nation's housing needs and to develop and rehabilitate urban communities. HUD also provided money for rent subsidies and low-income housing.
Water Quality Act, 1965 Clean Water Restoration Act, 1965	Established water and air quality standards and provided funding for environmental research
National Traffic and Motor Vehicle Safety Act, 1966	Established safety standards for all vehicles to protect consumers.

3 How did Lyndon Johnson's Great Society "promote the general welfare"?

_____

_____

_____

_____

DOCUMENT #4

4 What opinion does this cartoon express about how the American government should "provide for the common defense"?

_____

_____

_____

_____

DOCUMENT #5

> *"Nixon acts as if the kids had it coming. But shooting into a crowd of students, that is violence. They say it could happen again if the [National] Guard is threatened. They consider stones threat enough to kill children. I think the violence comes from the government."*
>
> **—Mother of Jeffrey Glenn Miller,**
> **a student killed at Kent State University, quoted in *Life* magazine, May 15, 1970**

5 What opinion did this speaker have about the actions of the National Guard at Kent State University?

_____

_____

_____

_____

6 Who did this speaker blame for the events at Kent State?

_____

_____

_____

_____

DOCUMENT #6

> *"He told me they didn't fire those shots to scare the students off. He told me they fired those shots because they knew the students were coming after them, coming for their guns. People are calling my husband a murderer; my husband is not a murderer. He was afraid."*
>
> **—Wife of a member of the National Guard, quoted in *Newsweek* magazine, May 18, 1970**

7 What opinion did this speaker have about the actions of the National Guard at Kent State University?

_____

_____

_____

PART B: ESSAY

Directions

Using information from the documents provided, and your knowledge of United States history, write a well-organized essay that includes an introduction, several paragraphs, and a conclusion.

Historical Context

The Preamble to the United States Constitution reads: "We the people of the United States, in order to form a more perfect union, establish justice, insure domestic tranquility, provide for the common defense, promote the general welfare, and secure the blessings of liberty to ourselves and our posterity, do ordain and establish this Constitution for the United States."

Task

Using the information from the documents and your knowledge of American history and geography, write an essay in which you discuss whether the America government, since 1950, has achieved the goals established for our nation in the preamble to the Constitution of the United States.

Guidelines

When writing your essay, be sure to

- Address all aspects of the *Task* by accurately analyzing and interpreting at least <u>four</u> documents
- Incorporate information from the documents in the body of the essay
- Incorporate relevant outside information throughout the essay
- Richly support the theme with relevant facts, examples, and details
- Write a well-developed essay that consistently demonstrates a logical and clean plan of organization
- Introduce the theme by establishing a framework that is beyond a simple restatement of the *Task* or *Historical Context* and conclude the essay with a summation of the theme.

Important People in
United States History and Government

The following list highlights the key people other than Presidents who are included in the New York State Core Curriculum for United States History and Government and therefore may be tested on the Regents Examinations. They represent the pluralism that is America.

Ansel Adams	• Photographer whose natural landscapes of the West are also a statement about the importance of the preservation of the wilderness
Samuel Adams	• Bostonian American Revolutionary War leader, political organizer, and journalist who helped to organize the Sons of Liberty and the Massachusetts Committee of Correspondence • Associated with the Boston Massacre and the Boston Tea Party • Member of the Continental Congress and signer of the Declaration of Independence
Jane Addams	• Progressive Era reformer in the social settlement house movement • Founder of Hull House, a Chicago settlement house • Cofounder and first president of Women's International League for Peace and Freedom • Corecipient of the Nobel Peace Prize (1931) • Involved in organizing of the NAACP
Susan B. Anthony	• Women's rights leader from 1851 until her death in 1906 • Most active for women's suffrage, but also worked for women's property rights and rights of married women
Yasir Arafat	• Palestinian leader involved in efforts to negotiate peace in the Middle East during President Clinton's administration • Led Palestinians during a number of violent clashes with Israel
Osama bin Laden	• Leader of the al-Qaeda terrorist network • Directed the September 11, 2001, attacks against the World Trade Center and the Pentagon
John Brown	• Extreme abolitionist who believed in use of violence to promote his cause • Became nationally known after his antislavery group killed proslavery settlers at the Pottawatomie Creek Massacre • His raid against a federal arsenal at Harper's Ferry led to his trial and execution. • Considered a martyr by some antislavery groups and was immortalized by Ralph Waldo Emerson in *John Brown's Body*
William Jennings Bryan	• Unsuccessful Democratic presidential candidate in 1896 and 1900 • Populist who supported farmers and free silver • Orator, religious fundamentalist (Scopes Trial), and anti-imperialist

John C. Calhoun	• Outspoken southern leader and advocate of states' rights • Favored nullification and the extension of slavery into the territories • Vice President under Presidents John Quincy Adams and Andrew Jackson; resigned over nullification issue • Secretary of state under President Tyler; successfully pressed for Texas annexation; opposed Mexican War and California statehood
Andrew Carnegie	• Industrialist and philanthropist who built Carnegie Steel Company, later part of U.S. Steel • In an article, *The Gospel of Wealth* (1889) he defended Social Darwinism, but also stated that the rich had a duty to help the poor, and improve society in areas they deemed important.
Rachel Carson	• Writer, scientist, and environmentalist whose book, *Silent Spring* (1962), identified the hazards of agricultural pesticides • Inspired the environmental movement and legislation
Willa Cather	• Pulitzer Prize winning writer of stories and novels about the struggle and the strength of the pioneers settling the frontier • Best known for *O Pioneers!* (1913), *My Antonia* (1918), *One of Ours* (1922), and *Death Comes to the Archbishop* (1927)
Cesar Chavez	• Latino leader of California farm workers from 1962 until his death in 1993 • Organized the United Farm Workers (UFW) to help migrant farm workers gain better pay and working conditions
Winston Churchill	• Prime minister of Great Britain during World War II
Father Charles Coughlin	• Roman Catholic priest who used his weekly radio program to attack President Franklin D. Roosevelt and his New Deal programs • Lost popularity because of his pro-fascist, anti-Semitic views; ordered by the Roman Catholic Church in 1942 to stop his political actions
Eugene V. Debs	• Union organizer and Socialist presidential candidate in every election from the 1890s until World War I
Dorothea Dix	• Nineteenth-century social reformer who revolutionized mental health reform; Superintendent of U.S. Army nurses in Civil War
Stephen Douglas	• Illinois Senator whose Kansas-Nebraska Act included his idea of popular sovereignty, which increased sectional tensions. • Lincoln-Douglas debates (1858) made Lincoln nationally known. • Candidate of northern faction of Democratic party in 1860 election
Frederick Douglass	• Former slave, abolitionist, lecturer, active in Underground Railroad • Supported Women's Suffrage, attended Seneca Falls Convention
W.E.B. Du Bois	• African American civil rights leader, historian, writer, sociologist • Cofounder of Niagara Movement and of NAACP • Influenced Harlem Renaissance by publishing African Americans in *The Crisis*. • Opposed Marcus Garvey's "back to Africa" movement and disagreed with Booker T. Washington by pressing for civil and political, not just economic equality for African Americans

John Foster Dulles	• Secretary of state under President Dwight Eisenhower • Made famous the concept of brinkmanship, a foreign policy that brought the United States just to the brink of war
Adolf Eichmann	• Nazi war criminal captured in Argentina after World War II, then tried and executed in Israel for the deaths of millions of Jews during World War II
Duke Ellington	• Songwriter, band leader, jazz composer, pianist, and a leading figure of the Harlem Renaissance • Helped popularize American music around the world • Famous songs include "Take the A Train," "Mood Indigo," and "Don't Get Around Much Anymore."
Medgar Evers	• African American activist and NAACP field secretary • Murdered in Mississippi in 1963 by a sniper outside his house
F. Scott Fitzgerald	• Novelist whose works reflect climate of the "roaring twenties" • Novels include *The Great Gatsby,* and *Tender Is the Night.*
Henry Ford	• Industrialist who headed Ford Motor Company • His innovative production methods reduced the cost of producing cars, making it possible for the average person to own an automobile.
Benjamin Franklin	• Philadelphia statesman, diplomat, scientist, writer in revolutionary period • Drafted the 1754 Albany Plan of Union • Member of Second Continental Congress; served on committee to write the Declaration of Independence, which he signed • Helped persuade France to sign the 1778 Treaty of Alliance against England and helped negotiate the Treaty of Paris of 1783, ending American Revolution • Influential Pennsylvania delegate to the Constitutional Convention
Sigmund Freud	• Austrian psychiatrist who developed psychoanalysis • Theories emphasized the importance of sexual freedom; influenced attitudes of the 1920s.
Betty Friedan	• Women's rights activist whose book, *The Feminine Mystique* (1963), encouraged women to find their own identity outside marriage • Helped found National Organization for Women (1966) and National Women's Political Caucus (1971)
Marcus Garvey	• African American nationalist leader who advocated pride and self-help as a means of empowerment • Founder of the Universal Negro Improvement Association, a nationalist and separatist group that wanted a separate black economy and urged African Americans to emigrate to Africa • Ideas influenced the 1960s Black Power movement
Samuel Gompers	• Organizer and president of American Federation of Labor, a craft union for skilled workers; stressed issues such as wages and hours

Alexander Hamilton	• New York delegate at Constitutional Convention who worked for a strong central government • Wrote 51 of *The Federalist Papers* supporting ratifying the Constitution • First secretary of the treasury; promoted national economic development
William Randolph Hearst	• Newspaper publisher whose yellow journalism style helped create public pressure for the Spanish-American War
Ernest Hemingway	• Novelist whose writings expressed conflict and concern created by changing American values • 1954 Nobel Prize for Literature winner
Patrick Henry	• Leader in the American Revolution in Virginia • As a member of Virginia House of Burgesses, introduced resolutions opposing the Stamp Act • Member of Continental Congress; supporter of independence • Opposed Constitution because of belief that it gave too much power to the federal government • Led movement for addition of the Bill of Rights to the Constitution
Alger Hiss	• Former State Department official investigated as a possible Communist spy by the House Un-American Activities Committee (HUAC) • Prosecution by Richard Nixon which made Nixon a national figure when Hiss was convicted of perjury in 1950
Langston Hughes	• Poet, playwright, and novelist who wrote about the African American experience, especially that of the poor and working class • A leading figure of the Harlem Renaissance
Saddam Hussein	• Long-time, ruthless Iraqi dictator • Invaded Kuwait causing Persian Gulf War in 1991; removed from power by U.S. during Iraq War in 2003
Chiang Kai-shek	• Leader of the Chinese Nationalists in civil war; when defeated by Mao Zedong in 1949 left China and established a government in Taiwan
Robert Kennedy	• Attorney general (1961–1963) and brother of President John F. Kennedy • Assassinated in June 1968
Martin Luther King, Jr.	• Civil rights leader who advocated civil disobedience and nonviolent demonstrations as methods for achieving change • Founded Southern Christian Leadership Conference in 1957 • Led bus boycott in Montgomery, Alabama • Led march from Selma to Montgomery for voting rights • Gave "I Have a Dream" speech in Washington, D.C. • Won Nobel Peace Prize • Assassinated in 1968

Henry Kissinger	• Secretary of state under Presidents Nixon and Ford • Deeply involved in foreign policy in Vietnam, China, the Soviet Union, and the Middle East • Advised Presidents Reagan, Bush, and Clinton
Robert La Follette	• Governor of Wisconsin whose program, the "Wisconsin Idea," became the model for progressive reform • Served as United States senator and Progressive leader • Ran for President as the Progressive party candidate in 1924
Meriwether Lewis and William Clark	• Explorers who led the 1804–1806 expedition to survey lands included in the Louisiana Purchase • Documented the land, plants, animals, and other natural resources from Missouri to Oregon in maps, diaries, and drawings
Sinclair Lewis	• Novelist whose work *Main Street* attacked middle class values • First American to win Nobel Prize for Literature (1930)
John Locke	• British Enlightenment writer whose ideas influenced the Declaration of Independence, state constitutions, and the United States Constitution • Believed that people are born free with certain natural rights, including the rights to life, liberty, and property
Henry Cabot Lodge	• Massachusetts Republican senator whose support of American imperialism and of a powerful navy strongly influenced Theodore Roosevelt • As chairman of Senate Foreign Relations Committee and Senate Majority leader, led successful fight against ratification of the Treaty of Versailles and entry of the United States into the League of Nations • Served as a U.S. representative to Washington Conference
Huey Long	• Populist governor of Louisiana and U.S. senator • Proposed that income and inheritance taxes on the wealthy be used to give each American a $2,500 income, a car, and a college education • Planned to challenge FDR for President, but was assassinated in 1935
Douglas MacArthur	• Led U.S. troops in the Pacific in World War II • Commander of U.S. occupation forces in Japan after World War II • Relieved of command by Truman after publicly disagreeing with him about the conduct of the Korean War
Malcolm X	• Leader of the 1960s Black Power movement • Assassinated in 1965
Horace Mann	• Nineteenth century educator, lawyer, and public official whose support helped create tax-based, nonsectarian public schools free to all children as well as better teacher-training institutions
George C. Marshall	• Army chief of staff during World War II and secretary of state under President Truman promoted the Marshall Plan, which assisted the economic recovery of Europe after World War II

John Marshall	• Chief justice of the United States (1801–1835) • Established prestige of the Supreme Court and strengthened power of federal government in cases such as *Marbury* v. *Madison, McCulloch* v. *Maryland,* and *Gibbons* v. *Ogden.* • First stated the right of judicial review in *Marbury* v. *Madison* (1803).
Cotton Mather	• New England Puritan associated with the concept of the Puritan work ethic (meaning that hard work is its own reward) and an appreciation of thrift and industry • Supported the Salem witch trials
Joseph R. McCarthy	• Republican Senator of the late 1940s and early 1950s who led a campaign to root out suspected Communists in American life • The term *McCarthyism* came to be associated with an era of government investigation of the private lives of many in public service and in the entertainment industry.
Baron de Montesquieu	• French Enlightenment philosopher who admired the British system of republican government • Influence is seen in separation of powers and in the checks and balances provisions in the Constitution.
John Muir	• Naturalist, conservationist, and writer; influenced President Theodore Roosevelt to protect more land; founded the Sierra Club
Ralph Nader	• Consumer rights crusader; wrote *Unsafe at Any Speed* (1965) to expose the lack of safety standards for cars • Third party presidential candidate (1996, 2000, 2004)
Frank Norris	• Naturalist writer whose 1901 novel, *The Octopus,* told of the struggle between the railroad and California wheat growers
Robert Oppenheimer	• Physicist who led the American effort to build the first atomic bomb
Thomas Paine	• English-born writer and political philosopher whose influential pamphlet *Common Sense* (1776) pressed for independence from Great Britain
Rosa Parks	• African American civil rights activist whose 1955 refusal to give up her seat to a white person led to the Montgomery, Alabama, bus boycott and helped launch the civil rights movement.
Frances Perkins	• Social reformer and political leader • Named secretary of labor under President Franklin D. Roosevelt in 1933, becoming the first woman to serve in a cabinet position
H. Ross Perot	• Third-party candidate and billionaire businessman who challenged George Bush and Bill Clinton for the presidency in 1992 with new ideas about balancing the federal budget and about other economic issues
Matthew Perry	• Led 1853–1854 naval mission to open Japan to world trade and negotiated U.S. trading rights with Japan (Treaty of Kanagawa)

Gifford Pinchot	• Conservationist and politician who led the Division of Forestry of the Department of Agriculture under President Theodore Roosevelt • Dismissed by Taft after attacking the Secretary of the Interior for removing from federal protection about a million acres of land
Joseph Pulitzer	• Publisher of the *New York Journal,* whose "yellow journalism" in a circulation war with William Randolph Hearst helped provoke the Spanish-American War
al-Qaeda	• International terrorist network founded by Osama bin Laden in 1980s whose goal is to establish governments based on Islamic law and without Western influence • Responsible for terrorist training camps, 9/11/01 attack on the World Trade Center and many attacks and threats all over the world
Yitzhak Rabin	• Prime minister of Israel who signed a peace agreement with PLO leader Yasir Arafat in 1993 as a result of President Clinton's efforts • Assassinated in 1995
Jacob Riis	• Journalist, photographer, and social reformer of the Progressive Era • Used writings and photographs to show the need for better housing for the poor, such as in his 1890 book *How the Other Half Lives*
Jackie Robinson	• Professional baseball player • Became the first African American to play in major league baseball when he joined the Brooklyn Dodgers in 1947
John D. Rockefeller	• Industrialist and philanthropist • Founder of the Standard Oil Company
Nelson A. Rockefeller	• Former governor of New York who was appointed Vice President by President Gerald Ford in 1974 • Only nonelected Vice President to serve with a nonelected President
Eleanor Roosevelt	• Political activist and First Lady • Early and long-time activist for rights for African Americans and women during the New Deal as First Lady and as political activist on her own • Played a key role in creation of United Nations Declaration on Human Rights (1948) and heading the UN Commission on Human Rights (1961) • Chaired the Presidential Commission on the Status of Women during the Kennedy Administration
Julius and Ethel Rosenberg	• Convicted and executed for treason in 1953 during the era of McCarthyism; innocence is still debated
Jean-Jacques Rousseau	• French Enlightenment philosopher • Influenced the Declaration of Independence with his arguments in support of government by the consent of the governed
Sacajawea	• Native American guide for part of the Lewis and Clark expedition • Honored in 2000 with her image on a dollar coin

Nicola Sacco and Bartolomeo Vanzetti	• Italian immigrants and anarchists executed for armed robbery and murder at the height of the antiradical, anti-immigrant feelings of the 1920s • Cleared by the Massachusetts governor in 1977, some 50 years later
Margaret Sanger	• Pioneering advocate of birth control • Organized first American birth control conference in 1921 • Founder of a birth-control lobbying group that became Planned Parenthood in 1942
Upton Sinclair	• Muckraking journalist of the Progressive Era • Influenced the passage of the 1906 Meat Inspection Act with his novel *The Jungle,* which deals with the exploitation of the poor and the factory conditions that led to contaminated meat
Adam Smith	• In *The Wealth of Nations* (1776), this Scottish political economist rejected mercantilism and advocated a free enterprise system, the basis of modern capitalism. • He argued for free trade, the division of labor, competition, individual freedom, supply and demand, and *laissez-faire* as necessary for a sound economy.
Alfred E. Smith	• Reform governor of New York and first Catholic to run for President • Lost to Hoover in the 1928 election, largely because voters did not want a Catholic President and because Smith favored repeal of the Eighteenth Amendment • Right-wing conservative Democrat who helped organized American Liberty League (1934) and opposed New Deal
Bessie Smith	• Harlem Renaissance blues singer known as the "Empress of the Blues" • Recorded with prominent jazz musicians, such as Louis Armstrong and Benny Goodman
Elizabeth Cady Stanton	• Leading crusader for women's rights; also for abolition and temperance • Began women's rights movement with Seneca Falls Convention in New York in 1848; wrote Declaration of Sentiments (1848) • With Susan B. Anthony, cofounded the National Woman Suffrage Association and coedited *Revolution,* a women's rights journal
Lincoln Steffens	• Muckraking journalist, editor, and reformer; wrote about corruption in government and business in his 1906 novel, *The Shame of the Cities*
John Steinbeck	• Author whose novels often deal with problems of the working class during the Great Depression • *The Grapes of Wrath* (Pulitzer Prize, 1939) describes the effect of the drought that created the Dust Bowl on a group of farmers forced to leave Oklahoma and work as migrant laborers in California.
Harriet Beecher Stowe	• Writer whose emotional, controversial, and best selling novel, *Uncle Tom's Cabin* (1850), focused attention on slavery and contributed to the start of the Civil War

Ida Tarbell	• Muckraking journalist whose *History of Standard Oil Company* exposed Rockefeller's unfair and often ruthless business practices.
Norman Thomas	• Political leader, minister, pacifist who ran six times as Socialist party candidate for President • Supporter of moderate social reforms, strongly anticommunist • Helped organize the American Civil Liberties Union and urged nuclear disarmament
Dr. Francis Townsend	• Opponent of the New Deal who promoted a financially impossible plan to provide government pensions for the elderly
Mark Twain	• Author and humorist of the late nineteenth and early twentieth centuries, famous, in part, for his homespun stories about life along the Mississippi River • Mark Twain was the pen name of Samuel L. Clemens.
Voltaire	• French Enlightenment philosopher who praised British institutions and rights and influenced framers of the Constitution • Wrote against religious intolerance and persecution
Earl Warren	• Chief justice of the Supreme Court (1953–1969) • Landmark cases such as *Brown* v. *Board of Education* and *Miranda* v. *Arizona* marked his tenure.
Booker T. Washington	• African American educator, author, and leader • Founded Tuskegee Institute (1881) and wrote *Up from Slavery* (1901) • Urged vocational education and self-improvement rather than confrontation as the way for African Americans to gain racial equality
Ida Wells-Barnett	• African American journalist, suffragist, and reformer • Launched a national crusade against lynching in the 1890s • Cofounder of the NAACP and of the National Association of Colored Women
Edith Wharton	• 1920s novelist who expressed concern about old versus new values in books such as *The Age of Innocence* (1921)
Mao Zedong	• Leader of the communist Chinese government from 1949 until 1976 • Met with President Nixon on Nixon's historic trip to China in 1972
John Peter Zenger	• German immigrant, printer and journalist • Tried for criminal libel for criticizing New York governor in his paper; jury found him not guilty on the grounds that he had printed the truth. • His case was an early step in establishing freedom of the press.

Landmark Supreme Court Cases

Every Supreme Court case deals with important constitutional principles. Some cases have had such an enduring impact on United States history and government that they require greater examination. The lasting significance and central constitutional principles of 32 landmark Supreme Court cases are outlined briefly in this section. For more information about the meaning of the constitutional principles, review Unit 2, Section 1, Part 4.

Year	Name of Case	Constitutional Principle	Why Decision is Important
1803	*Marbury* v. *Madison*	• Separation of Powers: Checks and Balances • The Judiciary	• Established the Supreme Court's right of *judicial review*—the right to determine the constitutionality of laws • Strengthened the judiciary in relation to other branches of government
1819	*McCulloch* v. *Maryland*	• Federalism: Federal Supremacy • National Power: *Necessary and Proper Clause* • The Judiciary	• Said no state could tax a federally chartered bank because the power to tax involves the power to destroy. • Supported the use of the elastic clause to expand federal power • Ruling established the principle of national supremacy—that the Constitution and federal laws overrule state laws when the two conflict • Expanded national power by supporting use of necessary and proper clause to carry out constitutional powers.
1824	*Gibbons* v. *Ogden*	• Federalism: Federal Supremacy • Property rights and economic policy: Interstate Commerce state • The Judiciary	• States may regulate only what is solely intrastate commerce (within a state) • Congress has power to regulate interstate commerce, including commerce that involved intrastate-interstate activity. • Ruling established the basis of congressional regulation of interstate commerce
1832	*Worcester* v. *Georgia*	• Federalism • National power • Separation of powers • Equality	• The Constitution gives the federal, not state governments, exclusive jurisdiction over Indian nations. • Treaties between the United States government and Indian nations are the Supreme Law of the Land; • Therefore, Georgia laws taking jurisdiction of Cherokee people and land were void • President Andrew Jackson defied the ruling and the national policy of Indian Removal followed.

Year	Name of Case	Constitutional Principle	Why Decision is Important
1857	*Dred Scott* v. *Sanford*	• The Judiciary • Equality • Civil Liberties	• Ruled that African-Americans were not citizens. (Overturned by 14th Amendment) • Declared that slaves were property of owners • As property, protected by 5th amendment, slaves could be taken anywhere; therefore, Missouri Compromise was unconstitutional
1883	*Civil Rights Cases*	• Equality • National power: Congress • Rights of Ethnic & Racial Groups: 13th and 14th Amendments	• Declared 1875 Civil Rights Act unconstitutional. • 14th amendment prohibited states from discrimination, not individual actions in the private sector such as in theaters, hotels, restaurants • Private discrimination was not a violation of the 13th amendment prohibition against slavery and involuntary servitude
1886	*Wabash, St. Louis & Pacific RR* v. *Illinois*	• Property rights/ economic policy: Interstate Commerce • National power • Federalism	• Invalidated state law setting railroad rates on that part of an interstate trip within state borders • By declaring it a federal power to regulate rates and by limiting state regulations, Court strengthened Constitution's interstate commerce clause. • Ruling paved way for creation in 1887 of Interstate Commerce Commission.
1895	*United States* v. *E.C. Knight Co.*	• National power	• While federal government did have the right to regulate some parts of economy, states, under 10th amendment, could regulate intrastate economic activities such as manufacturing • Refineries were manufacturing operations, not commerce; therefore, the Sherman Anti-Trust Act could not be applied to American Sugar Refining Co. although company controlled 90% of sugar processing in the nation.
1895	*In Re Debs*	• National Power: Commerce Clause	• Ruled that federal government under commerce clause of Constitution had right to halt 1894 Pullman strike • Said strike hurt general welfare of nation by disrupting commerce and mail delivery

Year	Name of Case	Constitutional Principle	Why Decision is Important
1896	*Plessy* v. *Ferguson*	• Equality • Rights of Ethnic/ Racial groups: *colored* races	• Upheld Louisiana law providing for equal but separate accommodations for white and colored races • Said law did not conflict with 13th or 14th amendments, nor with interstate commerce • 14th amendment was not intended to enforce what court called social equality • Provided legal justification for separate but equal segregation policy until overturned in 1954 by Brown v Board of Education
1904	*Northern Securities Co.* v. *United States*	• National Power: Anti-Trust, Commerce Clause • Property rights/ Economic policy	• Federal suit brought as part of Theodore Roosevelt's trust-busting using Sherman Antitrust Act. • Court ruled that the Northern Securities Company was formed only to eliminate competition and ordered it to be dissolved • Congress under commerce clause had authority to eliminate competition.
1905	*Lochner* v. *New York*	• Property rights and economic policy • Civil Liberties: 14th Amendment	• Ruled that a New York law limiting bakers to 10-contract hour days and 60-hour weeks in order to protect public health was unconstitutional. It violated the right and liberty of an individual to contract • New York law went beyond legitimate police powers of a state
1908	*Muller* v. *Oregon*	• Civil Liberties: 14th Amendment • Federalism: 10th v. 14th Amendments • Equality • Rights of women	• Upheld an Oregon law that limited women to a 10-hour work day in laundries or factories in order to protect women's health • Cited the physical differences between men and women when ruling that need to protect women's health outweighed the liberty to make a contract that was upheld in Lochner
1919	*Schenck* v. *United States*	• Civil Liberties: Limited in wartime • Freedom of Speech	• Established limits on free speech; right is not absolute but dependent on circumstances, i.e. person is not protected if falsely shouts fire in a crowded theatre • In this case saw defendants' actions as a clear and present danger to security of the nation in wartime.

Year	Name of Case	Constitutional Principle	Why Decision is Important
1935	*Schechter Poultry Corporation* v. *United States*	• Separation of powers • Property Rights/ Economic Policy	• Placed limits on the ability of Congress to delegate legislative powers to President • By narrowly defining interstate commerce also restricted congressional powers to regulate commerce • Declared the New Deal's National Industrial Act unconstitutional
1944	*Korematsu* v. *United States*	• Civil liberties: Equal Protection • Presidential Power in Wartime • Rights of ethnic/ racial groups	• Upheld the power of the president in wartime to limit a group's civil liberties. • Ruled that forcible relocation of Japanese Americans to Wartime Relocation Agency Camps during World War II was legal
1954	*Brown* v. *Board of Education*	• Equality: Equal Protection • Federalism • Rights of ethnic/ racial groups	• In this school segregation case, Court overturned Plessy v Ferguson separate but equal doctrine • Ruled that separate educational facilities are inherently (inseparably) unequal and violate the 14th amendment's equal protection clause
1957	*Watkins* v. *United States*	• Criminal Procedures: Due Process • National Power: Congressional Investigations • Civil Liberties	• Congressional investigations must spell out their legislative purpose and jurisdiction investigations • The Bill of Rights is applicable to congressional investigations • Watkins was within his rights to refuse to testify to matters beyond scope of House Committee on Un-American Activities
1961	*Mapp* v. *Ohio*	• Criminal Procedures: 4th Amendment • Civil Liberties: 14th Amendment	• Ruled that 4th and 14th Amendments protected citizen from illegal searches • Applied exclusionary rule to state courts, i.e. evidence obtained unconstitutionally—in this case without a search warrant—could not be used in federal or state courts
1962	*Baker* v. *Carr*	• Avenues of Representation: Voting Rights; Equal Protection • Federalism	• Court has jurisdiction over apportionment of seats in state legislatures • Overrepresentation of rural voters and under representation of urban voters was a violation of 14th amendment's equal protection clause • Ruling led to other court cases that established one person-one vote concept.

Year	Name of Case	Constitutional Principle	Why Decision is Important
1962	*Engel* v. *Vitale*	• Civil Liberties: Establishment Clause, 1st and 14th Amendments	• Reciting of an official prayer in the schools violated the 1st amendment's establishment of religion clause, which was applied to the states by the 14th amendment • Although students were not required to say the non-denominational prayer, its recitation in class put them under pressure
1963	*Gideon* v. *Wainwright*	• Civil Liberties • Criminal Procedures: 6th and 14th Amendments	• Ruled unanimously that the 6th amendment right to an attorney, which was applied to the states by the 14th amendment, required that a state provide lawyers for poor people accused of felony crimes, not just capital crimes
1964	*Heart of Atlanta Motel* v. *United States*	• National Power: Commerce Clause • Civil Liberties: Equal Protection Clause	• Upheld constitutionality of 1964 Civil Rights Act's use of Congressional interstate commerce powers to prohibit discrimination in private facilities whose operations affect interstate commerce
1966	*Miranda* v. *Arizona*	• Criminal Procedures: Due Process • Civil Liberties: Equal Protection	• Established the requirement prior to questioning to inform those accused of crimes that they have the right to remain silent, the right to a lawyer, and that what they say can be used against them in court • Evidence obtained without this warning may not be used in court under the exclusionary rule
1969	*Tinker* v. *Des Moines Independent Community School District*	• Civil Liberties: 1st Amendment • Student Rights/Safe School Environment	• While recognizing the authority of schools to prescribe and control conduct in the schools, the court ruled that neither students or teachers shed their constitutional rights to freedom of speech or expression at the schoolhouse gate • Symbolic, silent expression of opinion in absence of any disorder (wearing of black armbands to protest Vietnam War) is protected under the 1st amendment
1971	*New York Times Co.* v. *United States*	• Civil Liberties: Freedom of the Press • National Power	• Court narrowly upheld first amendment right to Freedom of the Press • Ruled that government had not met the heavy burden of prior restraint i.e. not made a strong enough case to stop publication of The Pentagon Papers on the grounds that national security would be hurt

Year	Name of Case	Constitutional Principle	Why Decision is Important
1973	*Roe* v. *Wade*	• Civil Liberties: Right to Privacy • Rights of Women	• Declared state laws making abortions illegal to be unconstitutional while stating certain limits and conditions • Basis of decision was right to privacy, citing primarily the due process clause of 14th amendment
1974	*United States* v. *Nixon*	• Separation of powers: Due Process	• By 8-0 vote, Court ruled that Nixon had to turn over the Watergate Tapes to the Special Prosecutor • No president was above the law; executive privilege (confidentiality) was not absolute • Separation of powers does not protect a president from judicial review of executive privilege, nor from the needs of the judicial process
1985	*New Jersey* v. *T.L.O.*	• Civil Liberties: 4th Amendment • Student Rights v. Safe School Environment	• Affirmed that 4th amendment prohibition on unreasonable searches and seizures applied to school officials • But, necessity of maintaining discipline allowed for searches when there are reasonable grounds that the law or school rules have been broken compared to police requirement of probable cause
1990	*Cruzan* v. *Director, Missouri Department of Health*	• Civil Liberties: Due Process	• Ruled that under due process clause, a competent person has the right to refuse life-sustaining treatment • Evidence of the wishes of an incompetent person must be clear and convincing; evidence not presented in this case • Cruzan's parents then gathered what Missouri Court agreed was clear and convincing evidence and the life support system was removed
1992	*Planned Parenthood of Southeastern Pennsylvania et al.*v. *Casey*	• Civil Liberties • Rights of Women	• Upheld Roe decision • Determined that Pennsylvania law with provisions such as 24 hour waiting period and parental consent to a minor's abortion did not create undue burden or substantial obstacles to abortion • Struck down requirement of husband notification
1995	*Vernonia School District* v. *Acton*	• Civil Liberties: 4th Amendment • Student Rights v. Safe School Environment	• Ruled that a school's practice of testing athletes randomly for drug use did not violate their rights under 4th and 14th amendments • Cited schools need to maintain student safety and fulfill its educational mission

Presidents of the United States

George Washington (1732–1799) *Years in office:* 1789–1797 No political party *Elected from:* Virginia *Vice Pres.:* John Adams	• Commanded the Continental army during the American Revolution • President of the Constitutional Convention • Set precedents that were followed by other Presidents, such as forming a cabinet • Strengthened new government through support of Hamilton's financial policies and use of force against the Whiskey Rebellion • Kept peace through Proclamation of Neutrality and Jay Treaty • Set basis of U.S. foreign policy in his Farewell Address
John Adams (1735–1826) *Years in office:* 1797–1801 Federalist *Elected from:* Massachusetts *Vice Pres.:* Thomas Jefferson	• American Revolution leader who protested Stamp Act • Helped draft Declaration of Independence • President during times of war in Europe • Alien and Sedition Acts contributed to his unpopularity and the fall of his party.
Thomas Jefferson (1743–1826) *Years in office:* 1801–1809 Democratic-Republican *Elected from:* Virginia *Vice Pres.:* Aaron Burr, George Clinton	• Major author of the Declaration of Independence • Opposed Federalists • Favored limited, decentralized government • Opposed Hamilton's financial plan and Alien and Sedition Acts • Approved the Louisiana Purchase from France, which doubled the size of the nation
James Madison (1751–1836) *Years in office:* 1809–1817 Democratic-Republican *Elected from:* Virginia *Vice Pres.:* George Clinton, Elbridge Gerry	• Called the Father of the Constitution • One author of the Virginia Plan; his journals provide a record of events at the Constitutional Convention. • Wrote 29 of the Federalist Papers • Proposed the Bill of Rights to Congress • Lost popularity over lack of leadership in War of 1812
James Monroe (1758–1831) *Years in office:* 1817–1825 National Republican *Elected from:* Virginia *Vice Pres.:* Daniel Tompkins	• Established U.S. foreign policy in the Western Hemisphere with the Monroe Doctrine • Settled boundaries with Canada (1818) • Acquired Florida (1819)
John Quincy Adams (1767–1848) *Years in office:* 1825–1829 National Republican *Elected from:* Massachusetts *Vice Pres.:* John Calhoun	• Elected President after election was decided in the House of Representatives • Secretary of state to James Monroe • After leaving office as President, served in House of Representatives; only President to have done so

Andrew Jackson (1767–1845) *Years in office:* 1829–1837 Democrat *Elected from:* Tennessee *Vice Pres.:* John Calhoun, Martin Van Buren	• Hero of Battle of New Orleans (War of 1812) • Opposed Calhoun and nullification • Vetoed rechartering of Second National Bank • Supported Native American removal policy • Associated with mass politics and nominating conventions • Used spoils system
Martin Van Buren (1782–1862) *Years in office:* 1837–1841 Democrat *Elected from:* New York *Vice Pres.:* Richard Johnson	• First New Yorker to become President • Served as Vice President to Jackson • Opposed Texas annexation • Presidency weakened by economic crisis of the Panic of 1837
William Henry Harrison (1774–1841) *Years in office:* 1841 Whig *Elected from:* Ohio *Vice Pres.:* John Tyler	• While governor of Indiana Territory, led military actions against Native Americans in the Battle of Tippecanoe (1811) • Elected as first Whig candidate on the slogan "Tippecanoe and Tyler Too" • First President to die in office; served only one month
John Tyler (1790–1862) *Years in office:* 1841–1845 Whig *Elected from:* Virginia *Vice Pres.:* none	• Became President after the death of Harrison • Texas annexed largely because of his influence
James K. Polk (1795–1849) *Years in office:* 1845–1849 Democrat *Elected from:* Tennessee *Vice Pres.:* George Dallas	• Supporter of manifest destiny • Influenced acquisition of Oregon Country and Mexican Cession
Zachary Taylor (1784–1850) *Years in office:* 1849–1850 Whig *Elected from:* Louisiana *Vice Pres.:* Millard Fillmore	• West Point graduate and military hero of Mexican War, known as Old Rough and Ready • Supported Compromise of 1850 • Died in office
Millard Fillmore (1800–1874) *Years in office:* 1850–1853 Whig *Elected from:* New York *Vice Pres.:* none	• New Yorker by birth, became President on death of Taylor • Supported and signed Compromise of 1850 • Supported Fugitive Slave Law • Candidate for the Know-Nothings
Franklin Pierce (1804–1869) *Years in office:* 1853–1857 Democrat *Elected from:* New Hampshire *Vice Pres.:* William King	• New Englander who supported Kansas-Nebraska Act • Gadsden Purchase ratified during his presidency • Trade treaty with Japan became effective during his administration, due to the efforts of Commodore Perry

James Buchanan (1791–1868) *Years in office:* 1857–1861 Democrat *Elected from:* Pennsylvania *Vice Pres.:* John Breckinridge	• In office when *Dred Scott* decision and John Brown's raid occurred • Took no action in response to the secession of South Carolina and other southern states
Abraham Lincoln (1809–1865) *Years in office:* 1861–1865 Republican *Elected from:* Illinois *Vice Pres.:* Hannibal Hamlin, Andrew Johnson	• Became nationally known as result of Lincoln-Douglas debates in 1858 • First Republican to be elected President • Used war powers of the presidency during Civil War to achieve his goal of preserving the nation • Gave Gettsyburg Address; issued Emancipation Proclamation • Assassinated before he could act on his plans of reconstruction
Andrew Johnson (1808–1875) *Years in office:* 1865–1869 Republican *Elected from:* Tennessee *Vice Pres.:* none	• Impeached by House after bitter disagreements with Congress over Reconstruction; acquitted by a single vote • 13th and 14th Amendments ratified during his presidency
Ulysses S. Grant (1822–1885) *Years in office:* 1869–1877 Republican *Elected from:* Illinois *Vice Pres.:* Schuyler Colfax, Henry Wilson	• Civil War military leader who served as supreme commander of the Union army • Transcontinental railroad completed and 15th Amendment ratified during his presidency • Crédit Mobilier and the Whiskey Ring scandals marred his presidency.
Rutherford B. Hayes (1822–1893) *Years in office:* 1877–1881 Republican *Elected from:* Ohio *Vice Pres.:* William Wheeler	• Election decided through compromise, preventing a constitutional crisis after a dispute over electoral votes • Federal troops removed from the South, marking the end of Reconstruction
James A. Garfield (1831–1881) *Years in office:* 1881 Republican *Elected from:* Ohio *Vice Pres.:* Chester A. Arthur	• Assassinated after four months in office
Chester A. Arthur (1830–1886) *Years in office:* 1881–1885 Republican *Elected from:* New York *Vice Pres.:* none	• Vetoed Chinese Exclusion Act (1882) • Supported Pendleton Act (1883), which enacted civil service reform

Grover Cleveland (1837–1908) *Years in office:* 1885–1889; 1893–1897 Democrat *Elected from:* New York *Vice Pres.:* Thomas Hendricks, Adlai Stevenson	• Expanded the civil service • Only President to serve two nonconsecutive terms • Served as governor of New York
Benjamin Harrison (1833–1901) *Years in office:* 1889–1893 Republican *Elected from:* Indiana *Vice Pres.:* Levi Morton	• Elected President with most electoral but not popular votes • Supported Sherman Antitrust Act
William McKinley (1843–1901) *Years in office:* 1897–1901 Republican *Elected from:* Ohio *Vice Pres.:* Garret Hobart, Theodore Roosevelt	• President during a period of expansionism marked by Spanish-American War • A high tariff and the Gold Standard Act passed during his administration • Assassinated in 1901
Theodore Roosevelt (1858–1919) *Years in office:* 1901–1909 Republican *Elected from:* New York *Vice Pres.:* Charles Fairbanks	• Progressive governor of New York (1899–1900) • Presidential programs called the Square Deal • Known as a trustbuster, conservationist, reformer, and nationalist • Used the power of presidency to regulate economic affairs of the nation and to expand its role in Asia and Caribbean • Issued the Roosevelt Corollary to the Monroe Doctrine
William Howard Taft (1857–1903) *Years in office:* 1909–1913 Republican *Elected from:* Ohio *Vice Pres.:* James Sherman	• Policy of "dollar diplomacy" gave diplomatic and military support to U.S. business investment in Latin America • Continued Progressive Era policies of business regulation, but his tariff and conservation policies, which were conservative, split the party
Woodrow Wilson (1856–1924) *Years in office:* 1913–1921 Democrat *Elected from:* New Jersey *Vice Pres.:* Thomas Marshall	• Progressive Era President whose program was known as New Freedom • Reform regulation included Clayton Antitrust Act, Federal Reserve System, Federal Trade Commission Act, and Underwood Tariff Act (which lowered rates) • Led the nation during World War I • Supported the Treaty of Versailles and League of Nations, which the Senate failed to approve
Warren G. Harding (1865–1923) *Years in office:* 1921–1923 Republican *Elected from:* Ohio *Vice Pres.:* Calvin Coolidge	• Led nation into Roaring Twenties on a call for "normalcy" • Administration known for corruption and scandals, including the Teapot Dome Scandal • Opened Washington Conference on Naval Disarmament in 1921, although he opposed internationalism

Calvin Coolidge (1872–1933) *Years in office:* 1923–1929 Republican *Elected from:* Massachusetts *Vice Pres.:* Charles Dawes	• Presidency marked by conservative, laissez-faire attitudes toward business • Presided over "Coolidge prosperity"
Herbert Hoover (1874–1964) *Years in office:* 1929–1933 Republican *Elected from:* New York *Vice Pres.:* Charles Curtis	• Used government resources against the Great Depression without success • Supported loans through Reconstruction Finance Corporation • Opposed direct relief • Used federal troops against the World War I veterans' "Bonus Army"
Franklin D. Roosevelt (1882–1945) *Years in office:* 1933–1945 Democrat *Elected from:* New York *Vice Pres.:* John Garner, Henry Wallace, Harry S Truman	• New Deal policies and leadership in World War II increased the power of the federal government • Tried to expand number of Supreme Court justices when the Court opposed New Deal programs • Pushed for social welfare legislation, such as the Social Security Act • New Deal programs criticized as both inadequate and too extreme • Urged cooperation in Western Hemisphere under the Good Neighbor Policy • Supported Japanese American internment during World War II • Only President to serve more than two terms
Harry S Truman (1884–1972) *Years in office:* 1945–1953 Democrat *Elected from:* Missouri *Vice Pres.:* Alben Barkley	• Made decision to drop two atomic bombs on Japan in 1945 to end World War II • Began the policy of containment of communism with the Truman Doctrine • Supported economic recovery in Europe through the Marshall Plan • Continued the New Deal philosophy with his Fair Deal • Entered into the Korean War during his presidency
Dwight D. Eisenhower (1890–1969) *Years in office:* 1953–1961 Republican *Elected from:* New York *Vice Pres.:* Richard M. Nixon	• Allied commander of forces in Europe during World War II • Issued Eisenhower Doctrine • Approved Saint Lawrence Seaway and 1956 Federal Highway Act • Sent troops to Little Rock to support school desegregation • In office when Alaska and Hawaii became 49th and 50th states
John F. Kennedy (1917–1963) *Years in office:* 1961–1963 Democrat *Elected from:* Massachusetts *Vice Pres.:* Lyndon B. Johnson	• Promoted the New Frontier program (which centered on containment), the Peace Corps, and the Alliance for Progress • Successfully resolved the Cuban missile crisis • Assassinated in 1963
Lyndon B. Johnson (1908–1973) *Years in office:* 1963–1969 Democrat *Elected from:* Texas *Vice Pres.:* Hubert Humphrey	• Promoted antipoverty programs and civil rights through his Great Society program • Used the Gulf of Tonkin Resolution to expand the Vietnam War • Division over his war policy led to his decision not to seek reelection. • President during a period of active civil rights movements for African Americans and women

Richard M. Nixon (1913–1994) *Years in office:* 1969–1974 Republican *Elected from:* New York *Vice Pres.:* Spiro Agnew, Gerald R. Ford	• "Vietnamization" policy and increased bombing followed by a 1973 cease-fire in Vietnam • Relaxed relations with USSR and the People's Republic of China • Resigned as President because of Watergate affair
Gerald R. Ford (1913–) *Years in office:* 1974–1977 Republican *Elected from:* Michigan *Vice Pres.:* Nelson Rockefeller	• Only President not to be elected by the American public; appointed as Vice President under Nixon and succeeded to the presidency after Nixon's resignation • Pardoned Nixon
Jimmy Carter (1924–) *Years in office:* 1977–1981 Democrat *Elected from:* Georgia *Vice Pres.:* Walter Mondale	• Domestic problems included inflation and oil shortages • Supported international human rights and Panama Canal treaties • Opposed the Soviet invasion of Afghanistan • Greatest success was the Camp David Accords, which led to peace between Egypt and Israel
Ronald Reagan (1911–2004) *Years in office:* 1981–1989 Republican *Elected from:* California *Vice Pres.:* George H.W. Bush	• Took a conservative viewpoint on social issues, such as abortion and prayer in school • Based his supply-side economic policy (or "Reaganomics") on the belief that government can destroy individual initiative • Presidency marked by huge trade and federal budget deficits • Arms control agreement signed with the USSR in 1985, 1986, and 1987 • Foreign policy aimed at keeping communism out of Latin America • Popularity damaged and foreign policy weakened by Iran-Contra scandal
George H.W. Bush (1924–) *Years in office:* 1989–1993 Republican *Elected from:* Texas *Vice Pres.:* J. Danforth Quayle	• Inherited the budget deficits, savings and loan scandals, and legacy of Iran-Contra Affair from the Reagan administration • In office when cold war ended, and Communist governments in Eastern Europe and Soviet Union fell • Led the United States in the Persian Gulf War against Iraq
William (Bill) Clinton (1946–) *Years in office:* 1993–2000 Democrat *Elected from:* Arkansas *Vice Pres.:* Albert Gore, Jr.	• Domestic policies centered on health care and social security reform, as well as economic issues, such as reduction of the national deficit • Secured approval of NAFTA (North American Free Trade Agreement) • Participated in air war against Iraq and Serbia • Impeached by the House of Representatives in 1998 on charges of perjury and obstruction of justice, but acquitted by the Senate
George W. Bush (1946–) *Years in office:* 2001– Republican *Elected from:* Texas *Vice Pres.:* Dick Cheney	• Took office after a close election in which a dispute over ballot recounts in Florida was ended by the Supreme Court in *Bush* v. *Gore*. • Conservative President whose early proposals included a tax cut, education reform, new energy policies, and a missile defense plan. • Declared war on international terrorism and ordered U.S. forces into Afghanistan to defeat Taliban and al Qaeda extremists. • Led the United States into a War against Iraq to end the dictatorship of Sadam Hussein and to eliminate weapons of mass destruction

Regents Examination—June 2005

This section contains the Regents Examination in United States History and Government that was given in New York State in June 2005.

Circle your answers to Part I on this exam and write your answers to the thematic essay and document-based essay questions on separate sheets of paper. Be sure to refer to the test-taking strategies in the front of this book as you prepare to answer the test questions.

Part I

Answer all questions in this part.

Directions (1–50): For each statement or question, write on the separate answer sheet the *number* of the word or expression that, of those given, best completes the statement or answers the question.

Base your answer to question 1 on the series of maps below and on your knowledge of social studies.

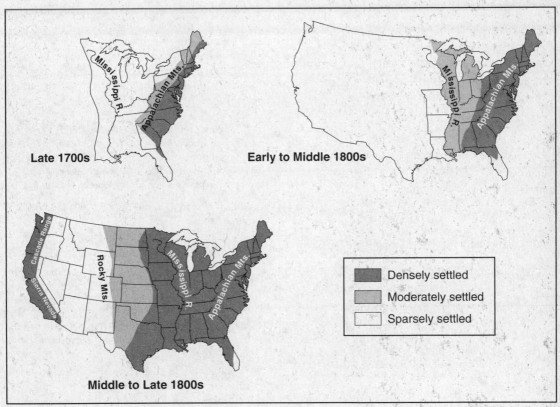

Source: *Atlas of Our Country*, NYSTROM (adapted)

1 What is the best title for this series of maps?

   (1) Industrialization of the United States

   (2) Sectional Conflicts in the United States

   (3) Transportation Revolution in the United States

   (4) Shifting Frontier of the United States

2 Which statement is most accurate about the movement for independence in the thirteen colonies?

(1) The independence movement began soon after the founding of the Plymouth Colony.
(2) Protests against British colonial policies gradually led to demands for independence.
(3) The King of England required the colonists to become economically self-sufficient.
(4) The movement for independence was equally strong in all of the colonies.

3 According to the Declaration of Independence, the fundamental purpose of government is to

(1) protect people's natural rights
(2) equalize opportunities for all citizens
(3) provide for the defense of the nation
(4) establish a system of free public education

4 To address the weaknesses of the Articles of Confederation, delegates at the Constitutional Convention agreed to

(1) eliminate the slave trade
(2) increase the powers of the central government
(3) decrease the number of states
(4) allow states to set tariff rates

5 During the Constitutional Convention of 1787, the major disagreement between the large and small states occurred over the issue of

(1) continuation of slavery
(2) guaranteeing States rights
(3) representation in Congress
(4) control of interstate commerce

6 ". . . it is the opinion of this committee that a national government ought to be established consisting of a Supreme Legislature, Judiciary, and Executive. . . ."

— Resolution submitted by Edmund Randolph, delegate to the Constitutional Convention, 1787

In adopting this resolution, the framers of the Constitution showed their belief in the idea of

(1) judicial review
(2) an elastic clause
(3) States rights
(4) separation of powers

7 The requirement to conduct a census was included in the United States Constitution to

(1) control the numbers of immigrants
(2) determine income tax rates
(3) determine the number of members from each state in the House of Representatives
(4) record the birth and death rates of the population

8 Which role of the president is considered part of the unwritten constitution?

(1) nominating federal judges
(2) signing or vetoing legislation
(3) acting as the leader of his political party
(4) serving as commander in chief of the armed forces

9 ". . . Now, one of the most essential branches of English liberty is the freedom of one's house. A man's house is his castle; and whilst he is quiet, he is as well guarded as a prince in his castle. . . ."

James Otis, *Against the Writs of Assistance*, 1761

Which provision in the Bill of Rights includes this same belief?

(1) right to a fair trial
(2) protection against unreasonable search and seizure
(3) guarantee against double jeopardy
(4) prohibition of cruel and unusual punishment

10 Which proposal was included in Secretary of the Treasury Alexander Hamilton's financial plans in the 1790s?

(1) incentives to encourage agricultural expansion
(2) creation of a national bank
(3) direct taxes on the states to support government operations
(4) free trade with other nations

11 President George Washington's principal reason for issuing the Proclamation of Neutrality (1793) was to

(1) repay France for help in the Revolutionary War
(2) protect United States interests in the Caribbean area
(3) safeguard the newly won independence
(4) punish the British for failing to withdraw from American territory

12 The Supreme Court decision in *Marbury* v. *Madison* (1803) was important because it

(1) established the principle of judicial review
(2) led to the reelection of President Thomas Jefferson
(3) showed that the states were stronger than the federal government
(4) proved that the legislative branch was the most powerful branch of government

13 During the first half of the 19th century, the construction of canals and roads led to the

(1) expansion of trade between midwestern farmers and eastern merchants
(2) growth of plantation agriculture in Texas and New Mexico
(3) severe economic decline of the South
(4) bankruptcy of several railroad companies in the Mississippi Valley

14 Which term did Americans use in the 1840s to describe the idea that the United States should possess the entire continent?

(1) containment
(2) globalization
(3) Manifest Destiny
(4) popular sovereignty

15 During the 1840s, abolitionists opposed annexation of new western territory because they

(1) feared the admission of new slave states
(2) wanted to limit the power of the national government
(3) were concerned with the legal rights of Native American Indians
(4) supported an isolationist foreign policy

16 In the ten years following the Civil War, a large numbers of former slaves earned a living by becoming

(1) conductors on the Underground Railroad
(2) workers in Northern factories
(3) sharecroppers on Southern farms
(4) gold miners in California

17 During the late 1800s, the defenders of Social Darwinism would most likely have supported

(1) labor unions
(2) progressive income taxes
(3) laissez-faire capitalism
(4) environmental conservation

Base your answers to questions 18 and 19 on the passage below and on your knowledge of social studies.

". . . This, then, is held to be the duty of the man of Wealth: First, to set an example of modest, unostentatious living, shunning display or extravagance; to provide moderately for the legitimate wants of those dependent upon him; and after doing so to consider all surplus revenues which come to him simply as trust funds, which he is called upon to administer, and strictly bound as a matter of duty to administer in the manner which, in his judgment, is best calculated to produce the most beneficial results for the community— . . ."

— Andrew Carnegie, "Wealth," *North American Review*, June 1889

18 According to this passage, the responsibility of the wealthy is to

(1) invest in future industry to increase wealth
(2) share their excess wealth with the community
(3) maintain a lifestyle consistent with their wealth
(4) influence government to assist all people

19 Andrew Carnegie carried out the ideas expressed in this statement by

(1) funding numerous libraries and educational institutions
(2) serving many years in the federal government
(3) investing his fortune in several new industries
(4) promoting programs to benefit the wealthy

20 The Interstate Commerce Act and the Sherman Antitrust Act were attempts by Congress to

(1) regulate the activities of big business
(2) protect consumers against unsafe products
(3) impose government regulations on agricultural production
(4) bring transportation activities under government ownership

Base your answers to questions 21 and 22 on the cartoon below and on your knowledge of social studies.

ONE SEES HIS FINISH UNLESS GOOD GOVERNMENT RETAKES THE SHIP.

Source: George B. Luks, *The Verdict*, June 5, 1899 (adapted)

21 What is the main idea of the cartoon?

(1) Government policies have created a recession.

(2) Americans support the activities of trusts.

(3) Good government has saved the country from trusts.

(4) Trusts are a threat to the nation.

22 Which group would most likely have favored government action to address the issue shown in the cartoon?

(1) bankers   (3) industrialists

(2) unions   (4) railroad owners

23 A goal of President Theodore Roosevelt's Big Stick policy and President William Howard Taft's Dollar Diplomacy policy toward Latin America was to

(1) join Western Hemisphere nations in a military alliance

(2) protect American economic and political interests

(3) encourage foreign nations to establish colonies

(4) raise Latin America's standard of living

24 A major reason the United States entered World War I was to

(1) gain additional colonial possessions

(2) react to the bombing of Pearl Harbor

(3) safeguard freedom of the seas for United States ships

(4) honor prewar commitments to its military allies

25 Which factor contributed most to the growth of nativist attitudes in the United States in the years immediately following World War I?

(1) the establishment of national Prohibition
(2) a decline of organized religions
(3) the increase in the number of settlement houses
(4) the large numbers of immigrants from southern and eastern Europe

26 What was a principle reason for rapid economic growth in the United States during the 1920s?

(1) prosperity of American agriculture
(2) increase of American imports
(3) development of many new consumer goods
(4) increased spending on defense

27 What was one factor that led to the Great Depression?

(1) government limitations on the amount of money in circulation
(2) high wages paid by employers
(3) increases in the tax rate for corporations
(4) excessive speculation in the stock market

28 Much of the domestic legislation of the New Deal period was based on the idea that the federal government should

(1) favor big business over labor and farming
(2) assume some responsibility for the welfare of people
(3) own and operate the major industries of the country
(4) require local communities to be responsible for social welfare programs

29 Which wartime policy toward Japanese Americans was upheld by the Supreme Court in its 1944 ruling in *Korematsu* v. *United States*?

(1) deportation to Japan
(2) mandatory military service
(3) denial of voting rights
(4) confinement in internment camps

Base your answers to questions 30 and 31 on the cartoon below and on your knowledge of social studies.

Source: Fred O. Seibel, *Richmond Times-Dispatch*, January 8, 1937

30 What is the main idea of this cartoon?

(1) The legislative branch disagreed with the executive branch during the presidency of Franklin D. Roosevelt.
(2) President Franklin D. Roosevelt wanted the Supreme Court to support his programs.
(3) Justices of the Supreme Court were not asked for their opinion about New Deal programs.
(4) The three branches of government agreed on the correct response to the Great Depression.

31 President Roosevelt responded to the situation illustrated in the cartoon by

(1) calling for repeal of many New Deal programs
(2) demanding popular election of members of the judicial branch
(3) asking voters to elect more Democrats to Congress
(4) proposing to increase the number of justices on the Supreme Court

32 The goal of President Harry Truman's Fair Deal was to

(1) continue reforms begun during Franklin D. Roosevelt's presidency

(2) decrease government spending on social welfare programs

(3) reduce taxes on large corporations and wealthy individuals

(4) restore domestic policies that existed in the 1920s

33 A controversial issue that resulted from World War II was the

(1) future role of the League of Nations

(2) morality of nuclear warfare

(3) commitment of troops without congressional approval

(4) civilian control of the military

34 McCarthyism in the early 1950s resulted from

(1) new commitments to civil rights for African Americans

(2) opposition to the Marshall Plan

(3) charges that Communists had infiltrated the United States government

(4) increased public support for labor unions

35 What was a major outcome of the Korean War (1950–1953)?

(1) Korea continued to be a divided nation.

(2) North Korea became an ally of the United States.

(3) South Korea became a communist nation.

(4) Control of Korea was turned over to the United Nations.

36 ". . . Let every nation know, whether it wishes us well or ill, that we shall pay any price, bear any burden, meet any hardship, support any friend, oppose any foe to assure the survival and the success of liberty. . . ."

— President John F. Kennedy, Inaugural Address, 1961

This statement by President Kennedy suggests a continued commitment to the foreign policy of

(1) isolationism   (3) containment

(2) appeasement   (4) imperialism

37 The Supreme Court decisions in *Gideon* v. *Wainwright* (1963) and *Miranda* v. *Arizona* (1966) have been criticized because these rulings

(1) expanded the rights of the accused

(2) granted more powers to federal judges

(3) lengthened prison sentences for the guilty

(4) reinstated the use of capital punishment

Base your answer to question 38 on the table below and on your knowledge of social studies.

Federal Debt, 1970–1998
(billions of dollars)

Year	Debt
1970	$ 380.9
1975	$ 541.9
1980	$ 909.0
1982	$1,137.3
1984	$1,564.6
1986	$2,120.5
1988	$2,601.1
1990	$3,206.3
1992	$4,001.8
1994	$4,643.3
1996	$5,181.5
1998	$5,478.2

Source: *Historical Tables, Budget of the United States Government,* Fiscal Year 2005 (adapted)

38 Which practice of the federal government has contributed most to the situation shown in the table?

(1) taking steps to reduce growth of the gross domestic product

(2) raising taxes to try to reduce inflation

(3) spending more money than is received in revenues

(4) lowering taxes during election years

39 The Supreme Court decision in *Roe* v. *Wade* (1973) was based on the constitutional principle of

(1) protection of property rights

(2) freedom of speech

(3) right to privacy

(4) freedom of religion

Base your answer to question 40 on the cartoon below and on your knowledge of social studies.

Source: Walt Handelsman, *The Times-Picayune* (adapted)

40 The point of view expressed in this cartoon is that

    (1) President and Mrs. Clinton have made Chicago their new home

    (2) President Clinton supports adoption over abortion

    (3) Republican issues should not be part of the Democratic National Convention

    (4) Democrats sometimes support traditionally Republican issues

---

41 President Richard Nixon's policy of détente is best characterized by his

    (1) decision to dismantle the nuclear weapons arsenal of the United States

    (2) attempt to reduce tensions with the Soviet Union

    (3) order to bomb Cambodia

    (4) support for membership in the United Nations for communist countries

42 The War Powers Act of 1973 was passed by Congress as a response to the

    (1) spread of nuclear weapons during the Cold War

    (2) invasion of Kuwait by Iraq

    (3) threat of communism in the Middle East

    (4) United States involvement in the Vietnam War

43 "I believe that our young people [18–20 years old] possess a great social conscience, are perplexed by the injustices which exist in the world and are anxious to rectify [correct] these ills."

    — Senator Jennings Randolph, 1971,
    The New York Times

Those who favor this point of view would likely have supported

    (1) a constitutional amendment extending voting rights

    (2) a presidential decision to raise speed limits

    (3) a Supreme Court ruling to reverse desegregation

    (4) a law passed by Congress to increase Social Security benefits

Base your answer to question 44 on the tables below and on your knowledge of social studies.

United States Trends in Farming, 1910 – 1960

Table A		Table B	
Number of Farms		Number of People in Agriculture	
1910	6,406,000	1910	11,770,000
1920	6,518,000	1920	10,790,000
1930	6,546,000*	1930	10,560,000
1940	6,350,000*	1940	9,575,000
1950	5,648,000*	1950	7,870,000
1960	3,963,000*	1960	5,970,000
*Includes Alaska and Hawaii			

Source: United States Census Bureau (adapted)

44 Which situation is associated with the trends in agriculture shown in these tables?

(1) Farm foreclosures decreased.
(2) Farm size was substantially reduced.
(3) Farm output declined.
(4) Farmers became a smaller percentage of the labor force.

45 The Supreme Court decisions in *New York Times Co. v. United States* (1971) and *United States* v. *Nixon* (1974) reinforced the principle that the president of the United States

(1) has unlimited use of the veto power
(2) is protected from unfair media criticism
(3) may not be convicted of a crime
(4) is not above the law

46 The beginning of the collapse of communism in Eastern Europe is most closely associated with the

(1) fall of the Berlin Wall
(2) admission of Warsaw Pact nations to the North Atlantic Treaty Organization (NATO)
(3) intervention of the North Atlantic Treaty Organization (NATO) in Yugoslavia
(4) formation of the European Union

47 Which development led to the other three?

(1) growth of tenements and slums
(2) shift from a rural to an urban lifestyle
(3) rapid industrial growth
(4) widespread use of child labor

48 The dispute over counting Florida voter ballots in the presidential election of 2000 was settled by

(1) an order of the governor of Florida
(2) an agreement between the candidates
(3) a vote of the United States Senate
(4) a United States Supreme Court decision

49 As the average age of the nation's population increases, there will be a need to

(1) create more child care facilities
(2) address the financing of Medicare
(3) increase the number of public schools
(4) reform immigration laws

50 Reducing interest rates to stimulate economic growth is a function of the

(1) Department of Commerce
(2) Federal Reserve System
(3) Federal Deposit Insurance Corporation
(4) Securities and Exchange Commission

Answers to the essay questions are to be written in the separate essay booklet.

In developing your answer to Part II, be sure to keep these general definitions in mind:

(a) <u>discuss</u> means "to make observations about something using facts, reasoning, and argument; to present in some detail"

(b) <u>describe</u> means "to illustrate something in words or tell about it"

(c) <u>evaluate</u> means to "examine and judge the significance, worth, or condition of; to determine the value of"

Part II

THEMATIC ESSAY QUESTION

Directions: Write a well-organized essay that includes an introduction, several paragraphs addressing the task below, and a conclusion.

Theme: Reform Movements in the United States

> Reform movements are intended to improve different aspects of American life. Through the actions of individuals, organizations, or the government, the goals of these reform movements have been achieved, but with varying degrees of success.

Task:

> Identify *two* reform movements that have had an impact on American life and for *each*
> - Discuss *one* major goal of the movement
> - Describe *one* action taken by an individual, an organization, or the government in an attempt to achieve this goal
> - Evaluate the extent to which this goal was achieved

You may use any reform movement from your study of United States history. Some suggestions you might wish to consider include the abolitionist movement, woman's suffrage movement, temperance movement, Progressive movement, civil rights movement, women's rights movement, and environmental movement.

You are *not* limited to these suggestions.

Guidelines:

In your essay, be sure to:
- Develop all aspects of the task
- Support the theme with relevant facts, examples, and details
- Use a logical and clear plan of organization, including an introduction and a conclusion that are beyond a restatement of the theme

NAME _____ SCHOOL _____

In developing your answer to Part III, be sure to keep this general definition in mind:

> <u>discuss</u> means "to make observations about something using facts, reasoning, and argument; to present in some detail"

Part III

DOCUMENT-BASED QUESTION

This question is based on the accompanying documents. It is designed to test your ability to work with historical documents. Some of the documents have been edited for the purposes of the question. As you analyze the documents, take into account the source of each document and any point of view that may be presented in the document.

Historical Context:

> After World War I, events in Europe caused the United States to review its foreign policy. This review led to controversies between those who supported a return to isolationism and those who wanted to see the United States take a more active role in world affairs.

Task: Using information from the documents and your knowledge of United States history, answer the questions that follow each document in Part A. Your answers to the questions will help you write the Part B essay in which you will be asked to

> • Discuss United States foreign policy toward Europe prior to World War II. In your discussion, include the arguments used by those who *supported* isolationism *and* those who were *opposed* to it.

Part A
Short-Answer Questions

Directions: Analyze the documents and answer the short-answer questions that follow each document in the space provided.

Document 1

> . . . No people came to believe more emphatically than the Americans that the Great War [World War I] was an unalloyed [absolute] tragedy, an unpardonably costly mistake never to be repeated. More than fifty thousand American doughboys [soldiers] had perished fighting on the western front, and to what avail? So far from being redeemed by American intervention, Europe swiftly slid back into its historic vices of authoritarianism and armed rivalry, while America slid back into its historic attitude of isolationism. Isolationism may have been most pronounced in the landlocked Midwest, but Americans of both sexes, of all ages, religions, and political persuasions, from all ethnic groups and all regions, shared in the postwar years a feeling of apathy toward Europe, not to mention the rest of the wretchedly quarrelsome world, that bordered on disgust. "Let us turn our eyes inward," declared Pennsylvania's liberal Democratic governor George Earle in 1935. "If the world is to become a wilderness of waste, hatred, and bitterness, let us all the more earnestly protect and preserve our own oasis of liberty." . . .

Source: David M. Kennedy, *Freedom from Fear*, Oxford University Press, 1999

1 Based on this document, state *one* reason many Americans wanted to return to a policy of isolationism after World War I. [1]

_____

_____

Score ☐

Document 2

> . . . It seems to be unfortunately true that the epidemic of world lawlessness is spreading.
>
> When an epidemic of physical disease starts to spread, the community approves and joins in a quarantine of the patients in order to protect the health of the community against the spread of the disease.
>
> It is my determination to pursue a policy of peace. It is my determination to adopt every practicable measure to avoid involvement in war. It ought to be inconceivable that in this modern era, and in the face of experience, any nation could be so foolish and ruthless as to run the risk of plunging the whole world into war by invading and violating, in contravention [violation] of solemn treaties, the territory of other nations that have done them no real harm and are too weak to protect themselves adequately. Yet the peace of the world and the welfare and security of every nation, including our own, is today being threatened by that very thing. . . .
>
> War is a contagion [virus], whether it be declared or undeclared. It can engulf states and peoples remote from the original scene of hostilities. We are determined to keep out of war, yet we cannot insure ourselves against the disastrous effects of war and the dangers of involvement. We are adopting such measures as will minimize our risk of involvement, but we cannot have complete protection in a world of disorder in which confidence and security have broken down. . . .

Source: President Franklin D. Roosevelt, Quarantine Speech, October 5, 1937

2 According to this document, what was President Franklin D. Roosevelt's viewpoint about United States involvement in war? [1]

_____

_____

Score ☐

Document 3

In this speech, Senator Robert A. Taft agrees with President Franklin D. Roosevelt's policy concerning the war in Europe.

> . . . Secondly, it has been widely argued that we should enter the war to defend democracy against dictatorship. The President himself, less than a year ago, suggested that it was our duty to defend religion, democracy, and good faith throughout the world, although he proposed methods short of war. I question the whole theory that our entrance into war will preserve democracy. The purpose of the World War [I] was to save democracy, but the actual result destroyed more democracies and set up more dictatorships than the world had seen for many days. We might go in to save England and France and find that, when the war ended, their governments were Communist and Fascist. Nothing is so destructive of forms of government as war. . . .
>
>   The arguments for war are unsound and will almost certainly remain so. The horrors of modern war are so great, its futility is so evident, its effect on democracy and prosperity and happiness so destructive, that almost any alternative is to be desired. . . .

Source: Senator Robert A. Taft, speech in Minneapolis, September 6, 1939

3 Based on this document, state **one** reason Senator Taft was opposed to the United States entering the war in Europe.   [1]

_____

_____

Score

Document 4

This cartoon is a view of United States foreign policy from the perspective of a British cartoonist in 1940.

"So this is isolation."

Source: David Low, *Evening Standard*, July 4, 1940

4 According to this cartoon, what is threatening the United States policy of isolationism? [1]

_____

_____

Score ☐

Document 5

> In the spring of 1940 opinion polls indicated, as they had for some time, that two thirds of the American public believed it was more important to keep out of war than to aid Britain; by September less than half of the American public held this view; and by January 1941 70 per cent were prepared to aid Britain at the risk of war. The German victory in the West, climaxed by the fall of France in June 1940, brought about a change in American public opinion and in public policy which the nation's most influential political leader of the twentieth century [President Franklin D. Roosevelt] had tried but failed to bring about since at least 1937. By every index [opinion poll], a substantial majority of Americans came at last to the view that the avoidance of British defeat was sufficiently in the American interest to justify the risk of war. On the basis of that shift in public opinion the presidential campaign of 1940 was fought and the groundwork laid for Lend-Lease and accelerated rearmament. . . .

Source: W. W. Rostow, *The United States in the World Arena*, Harper & Brothers, 1960

5a According to this document, how did public opinion change between the spring of 1940 and January 1941? [1]

_____

_____

Score ☐

b Based on this document, identify **one** event that caused public opinion to change during this time period. [1]

_____

_____

Score ☐

Document 6

> . . . The lend-lease-give program is the New Deal's triple A foreign policy; it will plow under every fourth American boy.
>
> Never before have the American people been asked or compelled to give so bounteously [much] and so completely of their tax dollars to any foreign nation. Never before has the Congress of the United States been asked by any President to violate international law. Never before has this Nation resorted to duplicity [deception] in the conduct of its foreign affairs. Never before has the United States given to one man the power to strip this Nation of its defenses. Never before has a Congress coldly and flatly been asked to abdicate.
>
> If the American people want a dictatorship—if they want a totalitarian form of government and if they want war—this bill should be steam-rollered through Congress, as is the wont [desire] of President Roosevelt.
>
> Approval of this legislation [Lend-Lease bill] means war, open and complete warfare. I, therefore, ask the American people before they supinely [passively] accept it, Was the last World War worth while? . . .

Source: Senator Burton K. Wheeler, speech in Congress, January 21, 1941

6 Based on this document, state *one* reason Senator Wheeler was opposed to the Lend-Lease bill. [1]

_____

_____

Score ☐

Document 7

> . . . War is not inevitable for this country. Such a claim is defeatism in the true sense. No one can make us fight abroad unless we ourselves are willing to do so. No one will attempt to fight us here if we arm ourselves as a great nation should be armed. Over a hundred million people in this nation are opposed to entering the war. If the principles of democracy mean anything at all, that is reason enough for us to stay out. If we are forced into a war against the wishes of an overwhelming majority of our people, we will have proved democracy such a failure at home that there will be little use fighting for it abroad. . . .

Source: Charles Lindbergh, speech at a rally of the America First Committee, April 23, 1941

7 Based on this document, state **one** reason Charles Lindbergh believed that the United States should stay out of the war. [1]

_____

_____

Score ☐

Document 8

> . . . It has been said, times without number, that if Hitler cannot cross the English Channel he cannot cross three thousand miles of sea. But there is only one reason why he has not crossed the English Channel. That is because forty-five million determined Britons in a heroic resistance have converted their island into an armed base from which proceeds a steady stream of sea and air power. As Secretary Hull has said: "It is not the water that bars the way. It is the resolute determination of British arms. Were the control of the seas by Britain lost, the Atlantic would no longer be an obstacle — rather, it would become a broad highway for a conqueror moving westward."
>
> That conqueror does not need to attempt at once an invasion of continental United States in order to place this country in deadly danger. We shall be in deadly danger the moment British sea power fails; the moment the eastern gates of the Atlantic are open to the aggressor; the moment we are compelled to divide our one-ocean Navy between two oceans simultaneously. . . .

Source: *The New York Times*, "Let Us Face the Truth," editorial, April 30, 1941

8   According to this editorial excerpt, what is *one* reason Americans should oppose the United States policy of isolationism?   [1]

_____

_____

Score [ ]

Part B

Essay

Directions: Write a well-organized essay that includes an introduction, several paragraphs, and a conclusion. Use evidence from *at least **five*** documents in your essay. Support your response with relevant facts, examples, and details. Include additional outside information.

Historical Context:

After World War I, events in Europe caused the United States to review its foreign policy. This review led to controversies between those who supported a return to isolationism and those who wanted to see the United States take a more active role in world affairs.

Task: Using information from the documents and your knowledge of United States history, write an essay in which you

> • Discuss United States foreign policy toward Europe prior to World War II. In your discussion, include the arguments used by those who *supported* isolationism **and** those who were *opposed* to it.

Guidelines:

In your essay, be sure to:
• Develop all aspects of the task
• Incorporate information from *at least **five*** documents
• Incorporate relevant outside information
• Support the theme with relevant facts, examples, and details
• Use a logical and clear plan of organization, including an introduction and a conclusion that are beyond a restatement of the theme

Regents Examination—January 2005

This section contains the Regents Examination in United States History and Government that was given in New York State in January 2005.

Circle your answers to Part I on this exam and write your answers to the thematic essay and document-based essay questions on separate sheets of paper. Be sure to refer to the test-taking strategies in the front of this book as you prepare to answer the test questions.

Part I

Answer all questions in this part.

Directions (1–50): For each statement or question, write on the separate answer sheet the *number* of the word or expression that, of those given, best completes the statement or answers the question.

1 Because of fertile land and a long growing season, plantations in the thirteen colonies developed in

(1) New England
(2) the Middle Atlantic region
(3) the South
(4) the upper Mississippi River valley

Base your answer to question 2 on the map below and on your knowledge of social studies.

Source: *U.S. History: Preparing for the Advanced Placement Examination*, AMSCO (adapted)

2 What would be the best title for this map?

(1) British Domination of the Americas
(2) Colonial Trade Routes
(3) Spanish Colonies in the New World
(4) The United States in 1750

Base your answer to question 3 on the quotation below and on your knowledge of social studies.

. . . I challenge the warmest advocate [supporter] for reconciliation, to shew [show], a single advantage that this continent can reap [gain], by being connected with Great Britain. I repeat the challenge, not a single advantage is derived [acquired]. Our corn will fetch its price in any market in Europe, and our imported goods must be paid for, buy them where we will. . . .

— Thomas Paine, *Common Sense*, 1776

3 This speaker is most likely opposed to

(1) mercantilism
(2) capitalism
(3) direct democracy
(4) representative government

4 A major argument for American independence found in the Declaration of Independence was that the British

(1) stopped participating in the slave trade
(2) refused to sell products to Americans
(3) deprived Americans of their natural rights
(4) censored American representatives in Parliament

5 The Preamble of the United States Constitution states the purposes of government and is based on the belief that

(1) the states have ultimate authority
(2) members of Congress should be appointed
(3) Supreme Court Justices should be elected
(4) the people are sovereign

Base your answers to questions 6 and 7 on the statements below and on your knowledge of social studies.

Speaker A: We want a strong national government to provide order and protect the rights of the people.

Speaker B: We want a weak national government so that it will not threaten the rights of the people or the powers of the states.

Speaker C: We want to add a bill of rights to the Constitution to protect the people against abuses of power.

Speaker D: A bill of rights is unnecessary because the new government's powers are limited by the Constitution.

6 A common theme in the statements is a concern about

(1) excessive state power
(2) the Land Ordinance of 1785
(3) the rights of the individual
(4) creation of the Articles of Confederation

7 These statements represent points of view that differ between

(1) pro-independence Patriots and pro-British Tories
(2) leaders of the North and the West
(3) supporters of Congress and the president
(4) Federalists and Antifederalists

8 How did President George Washington react to the conflict between France and England in 1793?

(1) He used the opportunity to begin the war for American independence.
(2) He declared the neutrality of the United States.
(3) He aided the French because they had supported the American Revolution.
(4) He negotiated a peace settlement between the warring nations.

9 The framers of the United States Constitution included the concepts of federalism, checks and balances, and separation of powers in the document because they

(1) feared a government with unlimited power
(2) favored the poor over the rich
(3) wanted to increase the powers of the states
(4) hoped to expand the democratic process

10 The power of judicial review allows the Supreme Court to

(1) repeal amendments to the Constitution
(2) determine the constitutionality of a law
(3) break tie votes in the electoral college
(4) impeach the president and other high-level officials

11 The development of political parties and of the committee system used in Congress illustrates the application of

(1) constitutional amendments
(2) federal legislation
(3) the unwritten constitution
(4) Supreme Court decisions

12 A loose interpretation of the Constitution was applied when

(1) George Washington appointed John Jay to the Supreme Court
(2) John Adams signed the Alien and Sedition Acts
(3) Thomas Jefferson purchased the Louisiana Territory
(4) James Monroe delivered his State of the Union message

13 One reason James Madison and Thomas Jefferson objected to Alexander Hamilton's financial policies was that they believed

(1) the establishment of a national bank was unconstitutional
(2) a laissez-faire policy would not help the country's economy
(3) the government should encourage industrial development
(4) high tariffs were needed to protect America's economic interests

14 As a result of President Andrew Jackson's policies, Native American Indians were

(1) relocated to reservations in Mexico
(2) forcibly removed to areas west of the Mississippi River
(3) gradually allowed to return to their ancestral lands
(4) given United States citizenship

15 The Missouri Compromise (1820), the Compromise of 1850, and the Kansas-Nebraska Act (1854) were all efforts to

(1) end fighting between midwestern farmers and Native American Indians
(2) encourage manufacturing in the West
(3) increase the number of people who voted in presidential elections
(4) settle disputes over the spread of slavery to the western territories

16 The institution of slavery was formally abolished in the United States by the

(1) Compromise of 1850
(2) Emancipation Proclamation of 1863
(3) creation of the Freedmen's Bureau in 1865
(4) ratification of the 13th amendment in 1865

17 In an outline, which main topic would include the other three?

(1) Erie Canal
(2) 19th-Century Internal Improvements
(3) Transcontinental Railroad
(4) National Road

18 Which leader founded a vocational training institution in the late 1800s to improve economic opportunities for African Americans?

(1) George Washington Carver
(2) Frederick Douglass
(3) W. E. B. Du Bois
(4) Booker T. Washington

19 In the last half of the 1800s, which development led to the other three?

(1) expansion of the middle class
(2) growth of industrialization
(3) formation of trusts
(4) creation of labor unions

20 The "new immigrants" to the United States between 1890 and 1915 came primarily from

(1) southern and eastern Europe
(2) northern and western Europe
(3) East Asia
(4) Latin America

21 Both the Interstate Commerce Act and the Sherman Antitrust Act were

(1) inspired by the effectiveness of earlier state laws
(2) designed to protect business from foreign competition
(3) declared unconstitutional by the Supreme Court in the late 1800s
(4) passed by the federal government to regulate big business

22 Why was there increased interest in building a canal across Central America in the late 1800s?

(1) The United States had acquired colonies in the Pacific region.
(2) Tariffs on Chinese and Japanese products had ended.
(3) The main source of immigration had shifted from northern Europe to southern Europe.
(4) Transcontinental railroads had not yet been completed.

23 Much of the economic growth of the 1920s was based on

(1) increased trade with other nations
(2) the production of new consumer goods
(3) rising prices of agricultural products
(4) the rapid development of the West

24 Langston Hughes and Duke Ellington are noted for their contributions to the cultural movement of the 1920s known as the

(1) Gospel of Wealth
(2) Lost Generation
(3) Harlem Renaissance
(4) Gilded Age

Base your answer to question 25 on the graph below and on your knowledge of social studies.

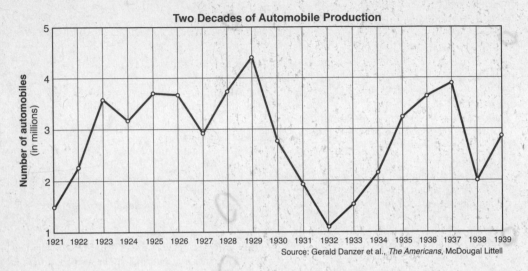

Two Decades of Automobile Production

Source: Gerald Danzer et al., *The Americans*, McDougal Littell

25 Which conclusion is best supported by the information on the graph?

(1) The level of automobile production remained constant.

(2) The average American family found the automobile too expensive to purchase.

(3) By 1929, most of the automobiles in the world were produced in the United States.

(4) Changes in economic conditions led to changes in automobile production.

---

26 The failure of national Prohibition led to a public awareness that

(1) crime rates decline when the sale of alcoholic beverages is banned

(2) economic prosperity encourages social conformity

(3) unpopular laws are difficult to enforce

(4) geographic conditions affect law enforcement

27 A lasting effect of the New Deal has been a belief that government should

(1) own the principal means of producing goods and services

(2) allow natural market forces to determine economic conditions

(3) maintain a balanced federal budget during hard economic times

(4) assume responsibility for the well-being of its citizens

28 ". . . The American people are sick and tired of being afraid to speak their minds lest they be politically smeared as 'Communists' or 'Fascists' by their opponents. Freedom of speech is not what it used to be in America. It has been so abused by some that it is not exercised by others. The American people are sick and tired of seeing innocent people smeared and guilty people whitewashed. But there have been enough proved cases to cause nationwide distrust and strong suspicion that there may be something to the unproved, sensational accusations. . . ."

— Senator Margaret Chase Smith,
United States Senate, June 1, 1950

When Senator Smith spoke these words, she was reacting to

(1) the Yellow Peril

(2) McCarthyism

(3) the Eisenhower Doctrine

(4) Progressivism

Base your answers to questions 29 and 30 on the cartoon below and on your knowledge of social studies.

Source: *PM*, May 15, 1941 (adapted)

Ho Hum! No Chance of Contagion.

29 In the cartoon, most of the "diseases" refer to the

(1) military dictatorships of the 1930s
(2) Allied powers of World War II
(3) nations banned from the United Nations after World War II
(4) Communist bloc countries in the Cold War

30 Which action is most closely associated with the situation shown in the cartoon?

(1) signing of the Atlantic Charter
(2) passage of the Neutrality Acts of 1935–1937
(3) first fireside chat of Franklin D. Roosevelt
(4) declaration of war on Japan

31 Which foreign policy decision by President Harry Truman is an example of the policy of containment?

(1) relieving General MacArthur of his Korean command
(2) recognizing the new nation of Israel
(3) supporting the trials of war criminals in Germany and Japan
(4) providing military aid to Greece and Turkey

32 Before ratification of the 22nd amendment in 1951, most presidents served no more than two terms because of

(1) a federal law
(2) a Supreme Court decision
(3) the elastic clause
(4) custom and tradition

33 Which constitutional principle was tested in the cases of *Plessy* v. *Ferguson* and *Brown* v. *Board of Education of Topeka*?

(1) separation of powers
(2) popular sovereignty
(3) equal protection of the law
(4) separation of church and state

34 ". . . My fellow citizens of the world: ask not what America will do for you, but what together we can do for the freedom of man. . . ."
— John F. Kennedy, Inaugural Address, 1961

To implement the idea expressed in this statement, President Kennedy supported the

(1) creation of the Marshall Plan
(2) formation of the Peace Corps
(3) removal of United States troops from Korea
(4) establishment of the South East Asia Treaty Organization

Base your answer to question 35 on the cartoon below and on your knowledge of social studies.

Declined with Thanks
The Antis—"Here take a dose of this anti-fat and get thin again!"
Uncle Sam—"No, Sonny! I never did take any of that stuff, and I'm too old to begin."

Source: J. S. Pugh, *Puck*, September 5, 1900 (adapted)

35 Which foreign policy is the main issue of this cartoon?

   (1) containment   (3) internationalism

   (2) imperialism   (4) neutrality

---

36 The police enter an individual's home without invitation or a warrant and seize evidence to be used against the individual.

Which Supreme Court decision may be used to rule this evidence inadmissible in court?

(1) *Baker* v. *Carr*
(2) *Gideon* v. *Wainwright*
(3) *Mapp* v. *Ohio*
(4) *Roe* v. *Wade*

37 The war in Vietnam led Congress to pass the War Powers Act of 1973 in order to

(1) affirm United States support for the United Nations
(2) strengthen the policy of détente
(3) increase United States participation in international peacekeeping operations
(4) assert the role of Congress in the commitment of troops overseas

38 The ratification of the 26th amendment, which lowered the voting age to 18, was a result of the

(1) participation of the United States in the Vietnam War
(2) fear of McCarthyism
(3) reaction to the launching of Sputnik by the Soviet Union
(4) reporting of the Watergate scandal

39 The decisions of the United States Supreme Court in *Tinker* v. *Des Moines* and *New York Times Co.* v. *United States* were based on interpretations of the

(1) meaning of a republican form of government
(2) powers delegated specifically to Congress
(3) president's right to executive privilege
(4) rights guaranteed by the 1st amendment

Base your answer to question 40 on the cartoon below and on your knowledge of social studies.

Source: Joe Heller, *Utica Observer-Dispatch*, March 27, 2001 (adapted)

40 According to the cartoonist, the United States has

(1) an ethnically diverse population
(2) an overly restrictive immigration policy
(3) a national requirement that high school students learn foreign languages
(4) a census report printed in languages that are spoken in the United States

41 One responsibility of the Federal Reserve System is to

(1) balance the federal budget
(2) raise or lower income taxes
(3) control the supply of money
(4) regulate the stock market

Base your answers to questions 42 and 43 on the table below and on your knowledge of social studies.

Participation in High School Sports

School Year	Boys	Girls
1971–72	3,666,917	294,015
2003–04	4,038,253	2,865,299

Source: National Federation of State High School Associations (adapted)

42 The data included in the table suggest that since 1971

(1) boys are losing interest in participating in sports
(2) participation in sports by boys and girls is nearly equal
(3) girls' participation in sports equals that of boys
(4) girls' participation in sports is increasing at a faster rate than that of boys

43 Which development contributed most to the changes shown in the table?

(1) passage of the Civil Rights Act of 1964
(2) inclusion of Title IX in the Education Amendments of 1972
(3) the beginning of Head Start programs in the 1960s
(4) increase in the number of nonpublic schools since the 1970s

Base your answer to question 44 on the cartoon below and on your knowledge of social studies.

"But we're not just talking about buying a car— we're talking about confronting this country's trade deficit with Japan."

Source: Mort Gerberg in *Macroeconomics, Principles and Policy*, Dryden Press (adapted)

44 The cartoonist is trying to encourage American consumers to consider that

(1) the United States buys more from Japan than Japan buys from the United States
(2) cars produced in the United States are often inferior to foreign-made automobiles
(3) single purchases of automobiles do not have an impact on calculating foreign trade balances
(4) automobile dealerships in the United States should offer more incentives for purchasing American-made cars

45 Since 1980, most new jobs in the United States have been in

(1) education
(2) heavy industry
(3) service industries
(4) civil service

46 President George Washington in his Farewell Address, President James Monroe in the Monroe Doctrine, and the opponents of the League of Nations all wanted the United States to

(1) avoid European conflicts
(2) avoid trade with foreign nations
(3) refuse diplomatic recognition of non-democratic nations
(4) reduce foreign influence by establishing immigration quotas

Base your answer to question 47 on the cartoon below and on your knowledge of social studies.

Source: Mike Luckovich, *The Atlanta Constitution*

47 In this cartoon, what is the main concern of the cartoonist?

(1) The technology needed to run the federal government is too expensive.
(2) Consumers should be protected from false advertising in the media.
(3) Technology makes it easier to influence legislators.
(4) The government is unable to safeguard the privacy of Internet users.

48 How were the presidential elections of 1876 and 2000 similar?

(1) The winner of the popular vote lost the electoral vote.
(2) Third-party candidates did not affect the outcome.
(3) The outcome of the election was decided by Congress.
(4) The winner was decided by the Supreme Court.

Base your answers to questions 49 and 50 on the graph below and on your knowledge of social studies.

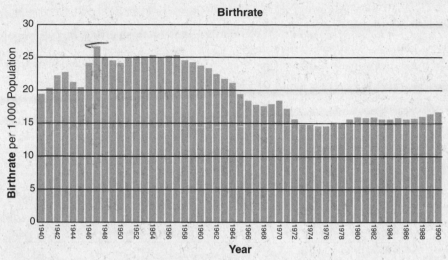

Birthrate

Source: U.S. Census Bureau, *Statistical Abstract of the United States* (adapted)

49 Which situation can be inferred from the population trend shown on the graph?

(1) In the 1980s, more new schools were needed than in the early 1960s.

(2) In the 1970s, there was increased migration to the northeast.

(3) In the 1980s, the number of baby boomers was recognized as a threat to the future of Social Security benefits.

(4) In the 1990s, death rates increased.

50 Information on the graph shows that the birthrate peaked in

(1) 1940   (3) 1957

(2) 1947   (4) 1970

Answers to the essay questions are to be written in the separate essay booklet.

In developing your answer to Part II, be sure to keep these general definitions in mind:

(a) <u>discuss</u> means "to make observations about something using facts, reasoning, and argument; to present in some detail"

(b) <u>evaluate</u> means "examine and judge the significance, worth, or condition of; to determine the value of"

Part II

THEMATIC ESSAY QUESTION

Directions: Write a well-organized essay that includes an introduction, several paragraphs addressing the task below, and a conclusion.

Theme: Foreign Policy

> Since 1900, United States foreign policy actions have often been based on national self-interest. These actions have had immediate and long-term results.

Task:

> Identify *two* important United States foreign policy actions **since 1900** and for *each*
> - Discuss the historical circumstances surrounding the action
> - Discuss *one* immediate **or** *one* long-term result of the action
> - Evaluate the extent to which the action promoted the nation's self-interest

You may use any important foreign policy action since 1900 from your study of United States history. Some suggestions you might wish to consider include Theodore Roosevelt's Corollary to the Monroe Doctrine (1904), Woodrow Wilson's Fourteen Points (1918), the Lend-Lease Act (1941), the Marshall Plan (1947), the blockade of Cuba (1962), the Strategic Arms Limitation Talks (SALT) agreements (1972), and the Persian Gulf War (1991).

You are *not* limited to these suggestions.

Guidelines:

In your essay, be sure to:
- Develop all aspects of the task
- Support the theme with relevant facts, examples, and details
- Use a logical and clear plan of organization, including an introduction and a conclusion that are beyond a restatement of the theme

NAME _____ SCHOOL _____

In developing your answer to Part III, be sure to keep this general definition in mind:

> <u>discuss</u> means "to make observations about something using facts, reasoning, and arguments; to present in some detail"

Part III

DOCUMENT-BASED QUESTION

This question is based on the accompanying documents. This question is designed to test your ability to work with historical documents. Some of the documents have been edited for the purposes of the question. As you analyze the documents, take into account the source of each document and any point of view that may be presented in the document.

Historical Context:

> During the late 1800s and early 1900s, Progressive reformers worked to improve American society. Their goals included **protecting consumers**, **regulating child labor**, **improving working conditions**, and **expanding democracy**.

Task: Using information from the documents and your knowledge of United States history, answer the questions that follow each document in Part A. Your answers to the questions will help you write the Part B essay in which you will be asked to

> Choose **three** goals mentioned in the historical context and for **each**
> * Discuss the conditions that led Progressive reformers to address the goal
> * Discuss the extent to which the goal was achieved

Part A

Short-Answer Questions

Directions: Analyze the documents and answer the short-answer questions that follow each document in the space provided.

Document 1

> . . . There were the men in the pickle rooms, for instance, where old Antanas had gotten his death; scarce a one of these that had not some spot of horror on his person. Let a man so much as scrape his finger pushing a truck in the pickle rooms, and he might have a sore that would put him out of the world [lead to his death]; all the joints in his fingers might be eaten by the acid, one by one. Of the butchers and floorsmen, the beef boners and trimmers, and all those who used knives, you could scarcely find a person who had the use of his thumb; time and time again the base of it had been slashed, till it was a mere lump of flesh against which the man pressed the knife to hold it. The hands of these men would be criss-crossed with cuts, until you could no longer pretend to count them or to trace them. They would have no nails,—they had worn them off pulling hides; their knuckles were swollen so that their fingers spread out like a fan. There were men who worked in the cooking rooms, in the midst of steam and sickening odors, by artificial light; in these rooms the germs of tuberculosis might live for two years, but the supply was renewed every hour. There were the beef luggers, who carried two-hundred-pound quarters into the refrigerator cars, a fearful kind of work, that began at four o'clock in the morning, and that wore out the most powerful men in a few years. . . .

Source: Upton Sinclair, *The Jungle*, 1906

1 Based on this document, state *two* effects of poor working conditions in this factory. [2]

(1) _____

_____

Score [ ]

(2) _____

_____

Score [ ]

Document 2

> . . . In just one week a scandalized public had snapped up some 25,000 copies of *The Jungle*. Almost all of those readers missed the socialist message. Sinclair had hoped to draw their attention to "the conditions under which toilers [workers] get their bread." The public had responded instead to the disclosures about corrupt federal meat inspectors, unsanitary slaughter houses, tubercular cattle, and the packers' unscrupulous [unethical] business practices.
>
> One of the most outraged readers was President Theodore Roosevelt. Few politicians have ever been as well-informed as TR, who devoured books at over 1,500 words per minute, published works of history, and corresponded regularly with leading business, academic, and public figures. Roosevelt recognized immediately that the public would expect government at some level—local, state, or federal—to clean up the meat industry. He invited Sinclair for a talk at the White House, and though he dismissed the writer's "pathetic belief" in socialism, he promised that "the specific evils you point out shall, if their existence be proved, and if I have the power, be eradicated [eliminated]."
>
> Roosevelt kept his promise. With the help of allies in Congress, he quickly brought out a new bill, along with the proverbial [well-known] big stick. Only four months later, on June 30, he signed into law a Meat Inspection Act that banned the packers from using any unhealthy dyes, chemical preservatives, or adulterants. The bill provided $3 million toward a new, tougher inspection system, where government inspectors could be on hand day or night to condemn animals unfit for human consumption. Senator Albert Beveridge of Indiana, Roosevelt's progressive ally in Congress, gave the president credit for the new bill. "It is chiefly to him that we owe the fact that we will get as excellent a bill as we will have," he told reporters. Once again, Americans could put canned meats and sausages on the dinner table and eat happily ever after. Or so it would seem. . . .

Source: James Davidson and Mark Lytle, *After the Fact: The Art of Historical Detection*, Alfred A. Knopf

2 According to this document, what action did President Theodore Roosevelt take to keep his promise to Upton Sinclair? [1]

_____

Score ☐

Document 3a

> ... During the same winter three boys from a Hull-House club were injured at one machine in a neighboring factory for lack of a guard which would have cost but a few dollars. When the injury of one of these boys resulted in his death, we felt quite sure that the owners of the factory would share our horror and remorse, and that they would do everything possible to prevent the recurrence of such a tragedy. To our surprise they did nothing whatever, and I made my first acquaintance then with those pathetic documents signed by the parents of working children, that they will make no claim for damages resulting from "carelessness."
>
> The visits we made in the neighborhood constantly discovered women sewing upon sweatshop work, and often they were assisted by incredibly small children. I remember a little girl of four who pulled out basting threads hour after hour, sitting on a stool at the feet of her Bohemian mother, a little bunch of human misery. But even for that there was no legal redress [remedy], for the only child-labor law in Illinois, with any provision for enforcement, had been secured [achieved] by the coal miners' unions, and was confined to children employed in mines. . . .
>
> There was at that time no statistical information on Chicago industrial conditions, and Mrs. Florence Kelley, an early resident of Hull-House, suggested to the Illinois State Bureau of Labor that they investigate the sweating system [sweatshops] in Chicago with its attendant [use of] child labor. The head of the Bureau adopted this suggestion and engaged Mrs. Kelley to make the investigation. When the report was presented to the Illinois Legislature, a special committee was appointed to look into the Chicago conditions. I well recall that on the Sunday the members of this commission came to dine at Hull-House, our hopes ran high, and we believed that at last some of the worst ills under which our neighbors were suffering would be brought to an end. . . .

Source: Jane Addams, *Twenty Years at Hull-House with Autobiographical Notes*, MacMillan, 1912

3a Based on this document, identify *one* social problem Jane Addams wanted to reform. [1]

_____

_____

Score ☐

Document 3b

First Factory Law of Illinois

FACTORIES AND WORKSHOPS

. . . 4. Children under 14 years of age prohibited from being employed in any manufacturing establishment, factory or work shop in the state. Register of children under 16 years shall be kept. The employment of children between ages of 14 and 16 years prohibited unless an affidavit by the parent or guardian shall first be filed in which shall be stated the age date and place of birth. Certificates of physical health may be demanded by the inspectors. . . .

Source: "Factories and Workshops," *Laws of the State of Illinois*, Thirty-Eighth General Assembly, 1893

b Based on this document, state *one* provision of the Illinois factory law. [1]

_____

_____

Score ☐

Document 4

State Actions Affecting Working Conditions	
1911	Recommendations of Illinois Commission on Occupational Disease (1909) result in Illinois Occupational Disease Act (ventilation, sanitation, fumes, temperature)
1911	Wisconsin becomes first state to pass workman's compensation legislation
1911	Wisconsin legislature limits hours of labor for women and children
1911–1915	Recommendations of New York State Factory Investigating Commission result in dozens of new laws creating healthier and safer factory working conditions during New York's "golden era in remedial factory legislation"
1912	New York State Factory Investigating Commission requires automatic sprinklers for all floors above seventh floor of buildings; broadens regulation and inspection of workplace safety (fire escapes, safe gas jets, fireproof receptacles, escape routes, fire drills)
1912	Massachusetts passes first state minimum wage law
1913	Oregon law requires payment of overtime for workers in mills or factories (over ten hours a day)

4 Based on this document, identify *two* examples of how a state action resulted in the improvement of working conditions. [2]

(1) _____

_____

Score ☐

(2) _____

_____

Score ☐

Document 5

Source: United States Bureau of the Census
(adapted)

5 Based on this graph, how did the use of child labor change between 1900 and 1920? [1]

_____

_____

Score [ ]

Document 6a

Bosses of the Senate

Source: Joseph J. Keppler, *Puck*, 1889 (adapted)

Document 6b

> . . . The Senate of the United States shall be composed of two Senators from each State, elected by the people thereof, for six years; and each Senator shall have one vote. The electors in each State shall have the qualifications requisite for electors of the most numerous branch of the State legislatures. . . .

— 17th Amendment, Section 1, 1913

6   State *one* way the 17th amendment addressed the concern expressed in the cartoon.   [1]

_____

_____

Score ☐

Document 7

> . . . Indeed, the growth of fundamental democracy in this country is astonishing. Thirty years ago the secret ballot was regarded as a passing craze by professional politicians. Twenty years ago it was a vital issue in nearly every American state. To-day the secret ballot is universal in American politics. Ten years ago the direct primary was the subject of an academic discussion in the University of Michigan by a young man named La Follette of Wisconsin. Now it is in active operation in over two-thirds of our American states, and over half of the American people use the direct primary as a weapon of self-government. Five years ago the recall was a piece of freak legislation in Oregon. To-day more American citizens are living under laws giving them the power of recall than were living under the secret ballot when [President] Garfield came to the White House, and many times more people have the power to recall certain public officers to-day than had the advantages of the direct primary form of party nominations when [President] Theodore Roosevelt came to Washington. The referendum is only five years behind the primary. Prophecy with these facts before one becomes something more than a rash guess. [With these facts in mind, predicting the future becomes something more than rash guessing.] . . .

Source: William Allen White, *The Old Order Changeth*, Macmillan, 1910

7 According to William Allen White, what were **two** reforms the Progressives supported to expand democracy? [2]

(1) _____

_____

Score ▢

(2) _____

_____

Score ▢

Document 8

. . . Women compose one-half of the human race. In the last forty years, women in gradually increasing numbers have been compelled to leave the home and enter the factory and work-shop. Over seven million women are so employed and the remainder of the sex are employed largely in domestic services. A full half of the work of the world is done by women. A careful study of the matter has demonstrated the vital fact that these working women receive a smaller wage for equal work than men do and that the smaller wage and harder conditions imposed on the woman worker are due to the lack of the ballot. . . .

The great doctrine of the American Republic that *"all governments derive their just powers from the consent of the governed,"* justifies the plea of one-half of the people, the women, to exercise the suffrage. The doctrine of the American Revolutionary War that taxation without representation is unendurable [intolerable], justifies women in exercising the suffrage. One great advantage, however, of the suffrage is in raising women to a position of greater honor and dignity so that the children of the land shall show and feel greater reverence and honor for their mothers, and that the mothers may teach the elementary principles of good government while they are teaching them good manners, morality and religion. . . .

Source: Senator Robert Owen, Speech, 1910

8 Based on this document, state *two* reasons for giving women the right to vote.   [2]

(1) _____

_____

Score ☐

(2) _____

_____

Score ☐

Part B

Essay

Directions: Write a well-organized essay that includes an introduction, several paragraphs, and a conclusion. Use evidence from at least *five* documents in the body of the essay. Support your response with relevant facts, examples, and details. Include additional outside information.

Historical Context:

> During the late 1800s and early 1900s, Progressive reformers worked to improve American society. Their goals included **protecting consumers**, **regulating child labor**, **improving working conditions**, and **expanding democracy**.

Task: Using information from the documents and your knowledge of United States history, write an essay in which you

> Choose *three* goals mentioned in the historical context and for *each*
> • Discuss the conditions that led Progressive reformers to address the goal
> • Discuss the extent to which the goal was achieved

Guidelines:

In your essay, be sure to:
• Develop all aspects of the task
• Incorporate information from *at least five* documents
• Incorporate relevant outside information
• Support the theme with relevant facts, examples, and details
• Use a logical and clear plan of organization, including an introduction and conclusion that are beyond a restatement of the theme

Regents Examination—August 2004

This section contains the Regents Examination in United States History and Government that was given in New York State in August 2004.

Circle your answers to Part I on this exam and write your answers to the thematic essay and document-based essay questions on separate sheets of paper. Be sure to refer to the test-taking strategies in the front of this book as you prepare to answer the test questions.

Part I

Answer all questions in this part.

Directions (1–50): For each statement or question, write on the separate answer sheet the *number* of the word or expression that, of those given, best completes the statement or answers the question.

1 In its economic relationship with its North American colonies, Great Britain followed the principles of 18th-century mercantilism by

(1) outlawing the African slave trade

(2) limiting the colonies' trade with other nations

(3) encouraging the development of manufacturing in the colonies

(4) establishing laws against business monopolies

2 The principles of government that Thomas Jefferson included in the Declaration of Independence were most influenced by

(1) John Locke's social contract theory

(2) Adam Smith's ideas of free enterprise

(3) Louis XIV's belief in divine right

(4) William Penn's views on religious toleration

3 The necessary and proper clause, the amendment process, and the unwritten constitution are evidence that our constitutional system of government provides for

(1) popular sovereignty

(2) equal representation

(3) flexibility

(4) ratification

4 What economic change resulted from the transportation revolution before the Civil War?

(1) The Northeast became better connected to the western section of the country.

(2) Trade between the United States and Europe was sharply reduced.

(3) The system of slavery on southern plantations began to disappear.

(4) The federal government began to regulate new businesses.

5 In 1788 and 1789, a major controversy between the Federalists and the Antifederalists focused on

(1) expansion of slavery into the territories

(2) the wisdom of creating a two-house legislature

(3) division of power among different levels of government

(4) the issue of allowing women the right to vote

6 Antifederalist objections to the ratification of the Constitution led to the

(1) addition of a Bill of Rights

(2) seven-year delay in the ratification of the Constitution

(3) rewriting of major parts of the Constitution

(4) elimination of states' rights

7 In 1853, Commodore Matthew Perry's visit to Japan was important to the United States because it

(1) ended the United States policy of neutrality
(2) opened new trading opportunities in Asia
(3) began a military alliance between the two nations
(4) acquired cheap labor for America's factories

8 As the Civil War began, President Abraham Lincoln stated that his primary goal was to

(1) end slavery
(2) set new national boundaries
(3) increase congressional powers
(4) preserve the Union

9 The Civil War affected the northern economy by

(1) causing a severe depression
(2) increasing unemployment rates
(3) decreasing demand for agricultural products
(4) stimulating industrialization

10 During the 19th century, New York was one of the most powerful states in the nation because it

(1) became the financial and industrial center of the nation
(2) led the nation in achieving political reforms
(3) produced more presidents than any other state
(4) offered more civil liberties than any other state

11 During the late 19th century, which practices were used by employers against workers?

(1) boycotts and lockouts
(2) picketing and walkouts
(3) blacklists and yellow-dog contracts
(4) mass rallies and sit-down strikes

12 The term *robber baron* was used to criticize the

(1) tactics of big-business leaders
(2) corruption of government officials
(3) dishonesty of carpetbaggers
(4) unskilled labor of illegal immigrants

13 What major trend related to population occurred during the industrialization boom of the late 1800s?

(1) Immigration decreased.
(2) Suburbanization decreased.
(3) Urbanization increased.
(4) Migration to rural areas increased.

14 The Gentlemen's Agreement, literacy tests, and the quota system were all attempts by Congress to restrict

(1) immigration
(2) property ownership
(3) voting rights
(4) access to public education

15 One result of the Spanish-American War of 1898 was that the United States was

(1) recognized as a world power
(2) committed to isolationism
(3) drawn into World War II
(4) forced into an economic depression

16 During the Progressive Era, muckrakers published articles and novels primarily to

(1) advance their own political careers
(2) make Americans aware of problems in society
(3) help the federal government become more efficient
(4) provide entertainment for readers

17 During his reelection campaign in 1916, President Woodrow Wilson used the slogan, "He kept us out of war." In April of 1917, Wilson asked Congress to declare war on Germany. What helped bring about this change?

(1) Bolshevik forces increased their strength in Germany and Italy.
(2) Britain was invaded by nations of the Central Powers.
(3) Russia signed a treaty of alliance with the Central Powers.
(4) Germany resumed unrestricted submarine warfare.

18 In the 1930s, shantytowns, often called "Hoovervilles," sprang up across the United States because of President Herbert Hoover's

(1) support for federal programs to provide jobs for the unemployed
(2) refusal to provide direct federal aid to the homeless
(3) efforts to help the residents return to their farms
(4) emergency relief program to provide food to the poor

19 Supporters of a graduated national income tax argued that it was the fairest type of tax because the

(1) rate of taxation was the same for all persons
(2) rate of taxation increased as incomes rose
(3) income tax provided the most revenue for the government
(4) income tax replaced state and local government taxes

20 Henry Ford produced a more affordable car primarily because his company

(1) paid workers lower wages than its competitors paid
(2) used foreign-made parts
(3) developed a less expensive method of production
(4) offered a variety of options to buyers

21 Which pair of events illustrates an accurate cause-and-effect relationship?

(1) Sacco and Vanzetti trial → ratification of the woman suffrage amendment
(2) rebirth of the KKK → formation of the Populist Party
(3) Red Scare → demand for limits on immigration
(4) high food prices → start of the Great Depression

22 Which situation helped cause the stock market crash of 1929?

(1) excessive speculation and buying on margin
(2) unwillingness of people to invest in new industries
(3) increased government spending
(4) too much government regulation of business

23 The Neutrality Acts passed by Congress in the mid-1930s were efforts to

(1) avoid mistakes that led the country into World War I

(2) create jobs for the unemployed in the military defense industry

(3) support the League of Nations efforts to stop wars in Africa and Asia

(4) help the democratic nations of Europe against Hitler and Mussolini

Base your answer to question 24 on the cartoon below and on your knowledge of social studies.

A Wise Economist Asks a Question

Source: *Chicago Tribune*, August 19, 1931
(adapted)

24 Which factor contributed most to the situation shown in the cartoon?

(1) low tariff rates

(2) shortages of consumer goods

(3) nonregulation of banks

(4) creation of a national bank

---

25 The decision of the Supreme Court in *Korematsu v. United States* (1944) upheld the power of the president during wartime to

(1) ban terrorists from entering the country

(2) limit a group's civil liberties

(3) stop mistreatment of resident legal aliens

(4) deport persons who work for enemy nations

26 Why was the United States called the "arsenal of democracy" in 1940?

(1) The leaders in the democratic nations of Europe were educated in the United States.

(2) Most of the battles to defend worldwide democracy took place on American soil.

(3) The United States supervised elections in European nations before the war.

(4) The United States provided much of the weaponry needed to fight the Axis powers.

27 Shortly after entering World War II, the United States began the Manhattan Project to

(1) work on the development of an atomic bomb

(2) increase economic production to meet wartime demands

(3) defend New York City against a nuclear attack

(4) recruit men for the military services

28 The experiences of African Americans serving in the military forces during World War II influenced their postwar decision to

(1) renew support for the principle of separate but equal

(2) join the armed forces in record numbers

(3) increase efforts to end racial discrimination

(4) move back to the rural south

29 The main foreign policy objective of the Marshall Plan (1948–1952) was to

(1) stop communist aggression in Korea

(2) fight poverty in Latin America

(3) rebuild the economies of European nations

(4) provide jobs for unemployed Americans

30 During the Korean War, President Harry Truman removed General Douglas MacArthur from command because MacArthur

(1) called for an immediate end to the war

(2) refused to serve under the United Nations

(3) lacked the experience to provide wartime leadership

(4) threatened the constitutional principle of civilian control of the military

Base your answer to question 31 on the cartoon below and on your knowledge of social studies.

No Pushover

U.S.

RUSSIA

BERLIN

Fred O. Seibel. Richmond Times-Dispatch.

FRED O. SEIBEL

Source: Fred O. Seibel, *Richmond Times-Dispatch*

31 The United States carried out the idea expressed in this late 1940s cartoon by

(1) forming a military alliance with Russia
(2) airlifting supplies to West Berlin
(3) accepting Russian authority over West Berlin
(4) agreeing to turn over control of Berlin to the United Nations

32 What was a result of the takeover of Cuba by Fidel Castro?

(1) Relations between the Soviet Union and Cuba worsened.
(2) Many Cuban Americans returned to their homeland.
(3) Trade between the United States and Cuba increased.
(4) Many people fled from Cuba to the United States.

Base your answer to question 33 on the passage below and on your knowledge of social studies.

". . . I was disappointed not to see what is inside Central High School. I don't understand why the governor [of Arkansas] sent grown-up soldiers to keep us out. I don't know if I should go back. But Grandma is right, if I don't go back, they will think they have won. They will think they can use soldiers to frighten us, and we'll always have to obey them. They'll always be in charge if I don't go back to Central and make the integration happen. . . ."

— Melba Beals, *Warriors Don't Cry*,
an African American student, 1957

33 President Dwight D. Eisenhower reacted to the situation described in this passage by

(1) forcing the governor of Arkansas to resign
(2) allowing the people of Arkansas to resolve the problem
(3) asking the Supreme Court to speed up racial integration
(4) sending federal troops to enforce integration

34 In 1965, Congress established Medicare to

(1) provide health care to the elderly
(2) assist foreign nations with their health problems
(3) grant scholarships to medical students
(4) establish universal health care

35 The Supreme Court decisions in *Mapp* v. *Ohio*, *Gideon* v. *Wainright*, and *Miranda* v. *Arizona* all expanded

(1) integration of public facilities
(2) rights of the accused
(3) presidential powers
(4) equality in the workplace

36 The main purpose of the War Powers Act of 1973 was to

(1) expand the power of Congress to declare war
(2) limit the president's ability to send troops into combat abroad
(3) allow people to vote on the issue of United States commitments overseas
(4) end the Vietnam War on favorable terms

37 In the Supreme Court cases *New Jersey* v. *T.L.O.* and *Tinker* v. *Des Moines School District*, the Court ruled that

(1) individual student rights are more important than a safe school environment
(2) students can be expelled from school without a hearing
(3) civil liberties can be both protected and limited in schools
(4) the Bill of Rights does not apply to minors

38 In the United States, regional differences in economic development are primarily due to

(1) settlement patterns of immigrant groups
(2) pressure from various religious groups
(3) state and federal election laws
(4) geographic factors in various parts of the nation

Base your answer to question 39 on the chart below and on your knowledge of social studies.

United States Budget, 1940–1990
Percentage Spent on Defense

1940 — 18%
1950 — 32%
1960 — 52%
1990 — 24%

Source: *Historical Tables*, Budget of the United States Government, Fiscal Year 1997 (adapted)

39 The changes shown on the chart most clearly reflect the

(1) effects of the Cold War
(2) influence of the business cycle
(3) failure of United States military policy
(4) reverses in political party control of Congress

40 In the United States, support for the passage and expansion of the North American Free Trade Agreement (NAFTA) has been strongest among

(1) labor unions
(2) environmentalists
(3) big business
(4) farmers

Base your answer to question 41 on the cartoon below and on your knowledge of social studies.

IT'S TIME TO RECLAIM AMERICA FROM ILLEGAL IMMIGRANTS!

I'LL HELP YOU PACK.

Source: Steve Kelley, San Diego *Union-Tribune*

41 What Native American Indian viewpoint does the cartoonist support?

(1) Illegal immigrants should not be allowed to settle on Native American Indian reservations.
(2) European settlers took Native American Indian land.
(3) Government efforts to restrict immigration should be supported.
(4) Native American Indians support government efforts to stop illegal immigration.

42 A major goal of the Republican Party since the 1980s has been to

(1) increase welfare benefits
(2) increase the size of the federal workforce
(3) reduce defense spending
(4) cut federal taxes

43 During the next 30 years, what will be the most likely impact of the baby boom that followed World War II?

(1) More money will be spent on national defense.

(2) The cost of health care will decrease.

(3) Social Security will have to provide for increasing numbers of retired people.

(4) The elderly will be the smallest segment of the population.

44 The Articles of Confederation and the theory of nullification were both attempts to

(1) strengthen the national government

(2) form new political parties

(3) protect states' rights

(4) strengthen the presidency

45 Which pair of circumstances represents an accurate cause-and-effect relationship?

(1) more jobs in factories → migration of African Americans from the South to northern cities

(2) establishment of Jim Crow laws → beginning of Reconstruction

(3) Dred Scott decision → passage of the Fugitive Slave Law

(4) closing of the frontier → completion of the transcontinental railroad

46 In a United States history textbook, the terms *bread and butter unionism*, *Gospel of Wealth*, and *mechanization* would most likely be found in a chapter entitled

(1) Reconstruction (1865–1877)

(2) Industrialization (1870–1900)

(3) Imperialism (1898–1905)

(4) The Roaring Twenties (1920–1929)

47 **"Soviets Create Iron Curtain in Eastern Europe"**
"Mao Zedong Leads Successful Revolution in China"
"North Korean Invasion of South Korea Leads to War"

Which development is reflected in these headlines?

(1) the post–World War II expansion of communism

(2) the beginning of détente between the Soviet Union and the United States

(3) the return to an isolationist foreign policy

(4) the beginning of pro-democracy movements during the Cold War

48 Presidents Franklin D. Roosevelt and Lyndon B. Johnson supported domestic policies that

(1) favored only one region of the nation

(2) attempted to increase the wealth of the rich

(3) led to tax cuts for all Americans

(4) provided direct help to those in need

49 The change in the nation's attitude toward membership in the League of Nations and membership in the United Nations shows the contrast between

(1) neutrality and containment

(2) appeasement and internationalism

(3) isolationism and involvement

(4) interventionism and détente

50 Which topic has been the focus of four different amendments to the United States Constitution?

(1) voting rights

(2) term limits on federal officeholders

(3) the electoral college

(4) prohibition of alcoholic beverages

Answers to the essay questions are to be written in the separate essay booklet.

In developing your answer to Part II, be sure to keep these general definitions in mind:

(a) <u>describe</u> means "to illustrate something in words or tell about it"

(b) <u>discuss</u> means "to make observations about something using facts, reasoning, and argument; to present in some detail"

(c) <u>evaluate</u> means "to examine and judge the significance, worth or condition of; to determine the value of"

Part II

THEMATIC ESSAY QUESTION

Directions: Write a well-organized essay that includes an introduction, several paragraphs addressing the task below, and a conclusion.

Theme: Reform Movements

> Reform movements have been an important part of United States history.

Task:

> Identify *two* reform movements in the United States since 1800 and for *each* reform movement
> * Describe the historical circumstances that led to the need for reform
> * State *one* goal of the movement and discuss *two* actions taken by the government, a group, or an individual in support of this goal
> * Evaluate the extent to which the reform movement has made an impact on the United States

You may use any reform movement in the United States from 1800 to the present. Some suggestions you might wish to consider include the abolitionist movement, Populist movement, Progressive movement, women's rights movement, civil rights movement, and the labor movement.

You are *not* limited to these suggestions.

Guidelines:

In your essay, be sure to
* Address all aspects of the *Task*
* Support the theme with relevant facts, examples, and details
* Use a logical and clear plan of organization
* Introduce the theme by establishing a framework that is beyond a simple restatement of the *Task* and conclude with a summation of the theme

NAME _____ SCHOOL _____

In developing your answers to Part III, be sure to keep these general definitions in mind:

(a) <u>describe</u> means "to illustrate something in words or tell about it"

(b) <u>discuss</u> means "to make observations about something using facts, reasoning, and argument; to present in some detail"

Part III

DOCUMENT-BASED QUESTION

This question is based on the accompanying documents (1–8). The question is designed to test your ability to work with historical documents. Some of the documents have been edited for the purpose of this question. As you analyze the documents, take into account the source of each document and any point of view that may be presented in the document.

Historical Context:

During the 1800s, the federal government promoted westward expansion in a variety of ways. This expansion changed the shape and character of the country.

Task: Using information from the documents and your knowledge of United States history, answer the questions that follow each document in Part A. Your answers to the questions will help write the Part B essay in which you will be asked to

- Describe the actions taken by the federal government that led to westward expansion during the 1800s
- Discuss the impact of westward expansion on the United States

Part A

Short-Answer Questions

Directions: Analyze the documents and answer the short-answer questions that follow each document in the space provided.

Document 1

Territorial Growth of the United States (1783–1853)

Source: *Historical Maps On File*, Revised Edition, Facts On File, Inc., 2003 (adapted)

1   Based on the map, state *two* methods used by the United States government to acquire new territory. [2]

(1)_____

_____

Score ☐

(2)_____

_____

Score ☐

Document 2

> An act to provide for an exchange of lands with the Indians residing in any of the states or territories, and for their removal west of the river Mississippi.
>
> Be it enacted by the Senate and House of Representatives of the United States of America, in Congress assembled, That it shall and may be lawful for the President of the United States to cause so much of any territory belonging to the United States, west of the river Mississippi, not included in any state or organized territory, and to which the Indian title has been extinguished [revoked], as he [the president] may judge necessary, to be divided into a suitable number of districts, for the reception of such tribes or nations of Indians as may choose to exchange the lands where they now reside, and remove there; and to cause each of said districts to be so described by natural or artificial marks, as to be easily distinguished from every other. . . .

— Indian Removal Act of 1830

2 Based on this document, state *one* way that the Indian Removal Act of 1830 would affect many Native American Indians. [1]

_____

_____

Score [ ]

Document 3

> . . . Instead of this, however, we have been exerting [putting forth] our best efforts to propitiate [gain] her [Mexico's] good will. Upon the pretext that Texas, a nation as independent as herself, thought proper to unite its destinies with our own, she has affected to believe that we have severed [removed] her rightful territory, and in official proclamations and manifestoes has repeatedly threatened to make war upon us for the purpose of reconquering Texas. In the meantime we have tried every effort at reconciliation [restoring harmony]. The cup of forbearance [tolerance] had been exhausted even before the recent information from the frontier of the Del Norte [Mexican-American border]. But now, after reiterated [repeated] menaces, Mexico has passed the boundary of the United States, has invaded our territory and shed American blood upon the American soil. She has proclaimed that hostilities have commenced [begun], and that the two nations are now at war. . . .

— President James K. Polk, Message to Congress, May 11, 1846

3   Based on this passage, state *one* reason President Polk asked Congress to declare war on Mexico.   [1]

_____

_____

Score ☐

Document 4

> . . . Regarding it as a war [Mexican War] to strengthen the "Slave Power," we are conducted to a natural conclusion, that it is virtually, and in its consequences, a war against the free States of the Union. Conquest and robbery are attempted in order to obtain a political control at home; and distant battles are fought, less with a special view of subjugating [conquering] Mexico, than with the design of overcoming the power of the free States, under the constitution. The lives of Mexicans are sacrificed in this cause; and a domestic question, which should be reserved for bloodless debate in our own country, is transferred to fields of battle in a foreign land. . . .

— Resolution passed by the Massachusetts Legislature opposing the Mexican War;
Massachusetts House Documents, 1847

4   According to this resolution, what was *one* reason the Massachusetts legislature opposed the Mexican War?   [1]

_____

_____

Score ☐

Document 5

Stephen Douglas replied to Abraham Lincoln's question about the Kansas-Nebraska Act in a speech given at Freeport, Illinois. This reply occurred during the second debate in the political contest for the United States Senate seat from Illinois in 1858.

> . . . The next question propounded [put forward] to me by Mr. Lincoln is, can the people of a Territory in any lawful way, against the wishes of any citizen of the United States, exclude slavery from their limits prior to the formation of a State Constitution? I answer emphatically, as Mr. Lincoln has heard me answer a hundred times from every stump [platform] in Illinois, that in my opinion the people of a Territory can, by lawful means, exclude slavery from their limits prior to the formation of a State Constitution. Mr. Lincoln knew that I had answered that question over and over again. He heard me argue the Nebraska bill [Kansas-Nebraska Act] on that principle all over the State in 1854, in 1855, and in 1856, and he has no excuse for pretending to be in doubt as to my position on that question. It matters not what way the Supreme Court may hereafter decide as to the abstract question whether slavery may or may not go into a Territory under the Constitution, the people have the lawful means to introduce it or exclude it as they please, for the reason that slavery cannot exist a day or an hour anywhere, unless it is supported by local police regulations. Those police regulations can only be established by the local legislature, and if the people are opposed to slavery they will elect representatives to that body who will by unfriendly legislation effectually prevent the introduction of it into their midst. If, on the contrary, they are for it, their legislation will favor its extension. Hence, no matter what the decision of the Supreme Court may be on that abstract question, still the right of the people to make a slave Territory or a free Territory is perfect and complete under the Nebraska bill. I hope Mr. Lincoln deems my answer satisfactory on that point. . . .

Source: Stephen Douglas, Freeport Doctrine, 1858

5 According to this document, how did the Kansas-Nebraska Act attempt to resolve the issue of slavery in the territories? [1]

_____

_____

Score ☐

Document 6

. . . With the secession of Southern states from the Union and therefore removal of the slavery issue, finally, in 1862, the Homestead Act was passed and signed into law. The new law established a three-fold homestead acquisition process: filing an application, improving the land, and filing for deed of title. Any U.S. citizen, or intended citizen, who had never borne arms against the U.S. Government could file an application, improving the land and lay claim to 160 acres of surveyed Government land. For the next 5 years, the homesteader had to live on the land and improve it by building a 12-by-14 dwelling and growing crops. After 5 years, the homesteader could file for his patent (or deed of title) by submitting proof of residency and the required improvements to a local land office.

Local land offices forwarded the paperwork to the General Land Office in Washington, DC, along with a final certificate of eligibility. The case file was examined, and valid claims were granted patent to the land free and clear, except for a small registration fee. Title could also be acquired after a 6-month residency and trivial improvements, provided the claimant paid the government $1.25 per acre. After the Civil War, Union soldiers could deduct the time they served from the residency requirements. . . .

— National Archives and Records Administration, *Teaching with Documents: The Homestead Act of 1862*

6 According to this document, how did the Homestead Act encourage the settlement of the West? [1]

_____

_____

Score ☐

Document 7

> . . . Sec.2. *And be it further enacted,* That the right of way through the public lands be, and the same is hereby, granted to said company [The Union Pacific Railroad Company] for the construction of said railroad and telegraph line; and the right, power, and authority is hereby given to said company to take from the public lands adjacent to the line of said road, earth, stone, timber, and other materials for the construction thereof; said right of way is granted to said railroad to the extent of two hundred feet in width on each side of said railroad where it may pass over the public lands, including all necessary grounds for stations, buildings, workshops, and depots, machine shops, switches, side tracks, turn-tables, and water stations. The United States shall extinguish as rapidly as may be, the Indian titles to all lands falling under the operation of this act and required for the said right of way and grants hereinafter made.
>
> Sec.3. *And be it further enacted,* That there be, and is hereby, granted to the said company, for the purpose of aiding in the construction of said railroad and telegraph line, and to secure the safe and speedy transportation of the mails, troops, munitions of war, and public stores thereon, every alternate section of public land, designated by odd numbers, to the amount of five alternate sections per mile on each side of said railroad, on the line thereof, and within the limits of ten miles on each side of said road, not sold, reserved, or otherwise disposed of by the United States, and to which a preëmption or homestead claim may not have attached, at the time the line of said road is definitely fixed: *Provided,* That all mineral lands shall be excepted from the operation of this act; but where the same shall contain timber, the timber thereon is hereby granted to said company. And all such lands, so granted by this section, which shall not be sold or disposed of by said company within three years after the entire road shall have been completed, shall be subject to settlement and preëmption, like other lands, at a price not exceeding one dollar and twenty-five cents per acre, to be paid to said company. . . .

— The Pacific Railroad Act, July 1, 1862

7a According to this document, what did the federal government give the Union Pacific Railroad Company to help them construct the railroad and the telegraph line?   [1]

_____

_____

Score ☐

b According to this document, how did the Pacific Railroad Act help the United States expand westward?   [1]

_____

_____

Score ☐

Document 8

"... The white man, who possesses this whole vast country from sea to sea, who roams over it at pleasure, and lives where he likes, cannot know the cramp we feel in this little spot, with the underlying remembrance of the fact, which you know as well as we, that every foot of what you proudly call America, not very long ago belonged to the red man. The Great Spirit gave it to us. There was room enough for all his many tribes, and all were happy in their freedom. But the white man had, in ways we know not of, learned some things we had not learned; among them, how to make superior tools and terrible weapons, better for war than bows and arrows; and there seemed no end to the hordes [huge numbers] of men that followed them from other lands beyond the sea.

"And so, at last, our fathers were steadily driven out, or killed, and we, their sons, but sorry remnants of tribes once mighty, are cornered in little spots of the earth all ours of right— cornered like guilty prisoners, and watched by men with guns, who are more than anxious to kill us off.

"Nor is this all. The white man's government promised that if we, the Shoshones, would be content with the little patch allowed us, it would keep us well supplied with everything necessary to comfortable living, and would see that no white man should cross our borders for our game, or for anything that is ours. *But it has not kept its word!* The white man kills our game, captures our furs, and sometimes feeds his herds upon our meadows. And your great and mighty government – Oh sir, I hesitate, for I cannot tell the half! It does not protect us in our rights. It leaves us without the promised seed, without tools for cultivating the land, without implements [tools] for harvesting our crops, without breeding animals better than ours, without the food we still lack, after all we can do, without the many comforts we cannot produce, without the schools we so much need for our children. . . ."

— Chief Washakie of the Shoshone tribe from a speech to Governor John W. Hoyt of the Wyoming Territory, 1878

8 According to this document, what were *two* criticisms that Chief Washakie had against the white man and/or the federal government? [2]

(1) _____

_____

Score ☐

(2) _____

_____

Score ☐

Part B

Essay

Directions: Write a well-organized essay that includes an introduction, several paragraphs, and a conclusion. Use evidence from at least *five* documents in your essay. Support your response with relevant facts, examples, and details. Include additional outside information.

Historical Context:

During the 1800s, the federal government promoted westward expansion in a variety of ways. This expansion changed the shape and character of the country.

Task: Using information from the documents and your knowledge of United States history, write an essay in which you

- Describe the actions taken by the federal government that led to westward expansion during the 1800s
- Discuss the impact of westward expansion on the United States

Guidelines:

In your essay, be sure to

- Address all aspects of the task by accurately analyzing and interpreting at least *five* documents
- Incorporate information from the documents in the body of the essay
- Incorporate relevant outside information
- Support the theme with relevant facts, examples, and details
- Use a logical and clear plan of organization
- Introduce the theme by establishing a framework that is beyond a simple restatement of the *Task* or *Historical Context* and conclude with a summation of the theme

Regents Examination—June 2004

This section contains the Regents Examination in United States History and Government that was given in New York State in June 2004.

Circle your answers to Part I on this exam and write your answers to the thematic essay and document-based essay questions on separate sheets of paper. Be sure to refer to the test-taking strategies in the front of this book as you prepare to answer the test questions.

Part I

Answer all questions in this part.

Directions (1–50): For each statement or question, write on the separate answer sheet the *number* of the word or expression that, of those given, best completes the statement or answers the question.

1 In writing the *Declaration of Independence*, Thomas Jefferson was influenced most by John Locke's idea of

(1) due process of law
(2) natural rights
(3) the rights of the accused
(4) the right to privacy

2 During the Constitutional Convention of 1787, the plans for Congress proposed by delegates from New Jersey and Virginia differed mainly over the issue of

(1) life terms of office or short terms of office
(2) appointed legislators or elected legislators
(3) equal state representation or proportionate state representation
(4) power to check other branches or power limited to lawmaking

3 Which governmental action illustrates the system of checks and balances?

(1) a senator helping a governor solve a state problem
(2) the president negotiating a trade agreement with foreign diplomats
(3) the Senate ratifying a peace treaty
(4) Congress raising taxes to pay for federal programs

4 A major criticism of the electoral college system has been that

(1) party loyalty is weakened after a presidential election
(2) electors frequently fail to vote for a candidate
(3) members of the electoral college are appointed for life terms
(4) a president may be elected without receiving the majority of the popular vote

5 Which feature must a nation have to be considered a democracy?

(1) a strong president
(2) citizen participation in government
(3) elected judges to conduct trials
(4) a set of laws

6 The Supreme Court has the power to

(1) control the federal budget
(2) vote to end a tie in the Senate
(3) approve presidential appointments
(4) interpret the Constitution

7 Conflicts between Jeffersonians and Hamiltonians during President George Washington's first administration led directly to the

(1) end of the Era of Good Feelings
(2) decision to replace the Articles of Confederation
(3) addition of the elastic clause to the Constitution
(4) start of the first political parties

8 The term *Manifest Destiny* was first used to support

(1) independence from Great Britain
(2) westward expansion to the Pacific Ocean
(3) efforts to stop secession of Southern states
(4) laws restricting labor union activity

9 Which region of the United States was most directly affected by the passage of the Homestead Act?

(1) Atlantic Coast
(2) Rocky Mountains
(3) Appalachian Mountains
(4) Great Plains

Base your answer to question 10 on the poster below and on your knowledge of social studies.

CAUTION!!

COLORED PEOPLE
OF BOSTON, ONE & ALL,

You are hereby respectfully CAUTIONED and advised, to avoid conversing with the

Watchmen and Police Officers of Boston,

For since the recent ORDER OF THE MAYOR & ALDERMEN, they are empowered to act as

KIDNAPPERS
AND
Slave Catchers,

And they have already been actually employed in KIDNAPPING, CATCHING, AND KEEPING SLAVES. Therefore, if you value your LIBERTY, and the *Welfare of the Fugitives* among you, *Shun* them in every possible manner, as so many *HOUNDS* on the track of the most unfortunate of your race.

Keep a Sharp Look Out for KIDNAPPERS, and have TOP EYE open.

APRIL 24, 1851.

Source: Library of Congress, *The American Time Capsule: Three Centuries of Broadsides and other Printed Ephemera*

10 This poster from the 1850s appeared in response to the
(1) passage of the fugitive slave law
(2) start of the Civil War
(3) issuance of the Emancipation Proclamation
(4) enactment of the 13th Amendment

11 In the mid-1800s, the growth of the populations of California and the western territories was mainly a result of the
(1) discovery of gold and silver
(2) opening of the Panama Canal
(3) migration of freedmen after the Civil War
(4) secession of the Southern states

12 In the late 1800s, the Granger movement tried to improve conditions for farmers by
(1) lowering the rate of inflation
(2) strengthening the gold standard
(3) forcing railroads to lower their rates
(4) making labor unions stronger

13 The passage of the Dawes Act in 1887 was primarily an attempt by the United States government to
(1) limit the power of the Bureau of Indian Affairs
(2) return eastern land to Native American Indian tribes
(3) encourage Native American Indians to give up their traditional cultures
(4) hire Native American Indians as military scouts

14 In the late 1800s, supporters of laissez-faire capitalism claimed that government regulation of business would be
(1) essential to protect the rights of consumers
(2) necessary to provide jobs for the unemployed
(3) useful in competing with foreign nations
(4) harmful to economic growth

15 Why did the United States follow a policy of open immigration during much of the 1800s?
(1) Many United States citizens wanted to live abroad.
(2) The United States had a shortage of labor.
(3) Prosperous conditions in Europe resulted in fewer immigrants coming to the United States.
(4) Immigrants provided United States industry with investment capital.

16 An important result of the Spanish-American War of 1898 was that the United States
(1) acquired territories in Africa
(2) became a world power with an overseas empire
(3) improved its relations with Germany
(4) lost interest in Latin American affairs

Base your answer to question 17 on the cartoon below and on your knowledge of social studies.

Source: Herman Viola, *Why We Remember: United States History*, Addison–Wesley (adapted)

17 Which economic concept is best illustrated by the cartoon?

(1) supply and demand   (3) monopoly
(2) mercantilism   (4) trade

18 Mark Twain labeled the late 1800s in the United States the "Gilded Age" to describe the

(1) end of the practice of slavery
(2) absence of international conflicts
(3) extremes of wealth and poverty
(4) achievements of the labor movement

19 One idea that both Booker T. Washington and W. E. B. Du Bois supported is that

(1) African Americans should have increased civil rights
(2) vocational training was the best approach to education
(3) immigration was responsible for racial segregation
(4) Jim Crow laws were needed to help African Americans

20 During the late 1800s and early 1900s, where did most of the immigrants to the United States settle?

(1) urban centers of the Northeast
(2) plantations of the New South
(3) mining areas of the Far West
(4) farming regions of the Great Plains

21 Which reform idea was a common goal of the Populists and the Progressives?

(1) restoration of the nation's cities
(2) expansion of opportunities for immigrants
(3) improvement in the status of African Americans
(4) greater control of government by the people

22 Jane Addams and Jacob Riis were most notable for their efforts to

(1) treat the wounded in World War I
(2) stop the spread of diseases in Latin America
(3) legalize birth control for women
(4) aid the urban poor

23 The Federal Reserve System was created to

(1) maintain a national petroleum supply
(2) provide military support for the armed forces
(3) protect consumers from fraud
(4) manage the nation's supply of currency and interest rates

24 One goal for a lasting peace that President Woodrow Wilson included in his Fourteen Points was

(1) establishing a League of Nations
(2) maintaining a permanent military force in Europe
(3) returning the United States to a policy of isolationism
(4) blaming Germany for causing World War I

25 Which event of the 1920s symbolized a conflict over cultural values?

(1) election of Herbert Hoover
(2) transatlantic flight of Charles Lindbergh
(3) Scopes trial
(4) stock market crash

Base your answers to questions 26 and 27 on the chart below and on your knowledge of social studies.

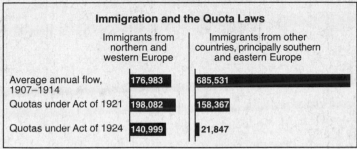

Immigration and the Quota Laws

	Immigrants from northern and western Europe	Immigrants from other countries, principally southern and eastern Europe
Average annual flow, 1907–1914	176,983	685,531
Quotas under Act of 1921	198,082	158,367
Quotas under Act of 1924	140,999	21,847

Source: Thomas A. Bailey et al., *The American Pageant*, D.C. Heath and Co., 1998 (adapted)

26 The data in the chart support the idea that the immigration laws of 1921 and 1924 were primarily designed to

(1) stop illegal entry into the country
(2) admit skilled workers
(3) encourage immigration from southern Europe
(4) reduce immigration from specific regions

27 The United States adopted the immigration policies shown in the chart mainly because of

(1) pressures from nativists and labor unions
(2) hardships caused by the Great Depression
(3) prejudices generated during World War II
(4) threats from other nations to stop migration to the United States

28 The "clear and present danger" doctrine stated by the Supreme Court in the case of *Schenck* v. *United States* (1919) had an important impact on the Bill of Rights because it

(1) limited the powers of the president
(2) placed limits on freedom of speech
(3) clarified standards for a fair trial
(4) expanded the rights of persons accused of crimes

29 Which group of Americans generally failed to experience the economic prosperity of the 1920s?

(1) farmers   (3) consumers
(2) retailers   (4) manufacturers

30 A primary objective of United States foreign policy during the 1930s was to

(1) avoid involvement in Asian and European conflicts
(2) protect business interests in Africa through direct intervention
(3) strengthen international peacekeeping organizations
(4) acquire overseas land as colonies

31 Which statement best illustrates a basic idea of President Franklin D. Roosevelt's New Deal?

(1) Communism provides the only real solution to economic problems.
(2) Unemployed workers should rely on the states rather than on the federal government for help.
(3) The United States reached its economic peak in the 1920s and is now a declining industrial power.
(4) The economy sometimes needs public money to encourage business activity.

32 Which action by President Franklin D. Roosevelt challenged the principle of checks and balances?

(1) frequently vetoing New Deal legislation
(2) trying to increase the number of justices on the Supreme Court
(3) taking over the Senate's treaty ratification power
(4) desegregating defense industries

Base your answer to question 33 on the maps below and on your knowledge of social studies.

The Korean War

| June 25, 1950 | Sept. 14, 1950 | Nov. 25, 1950 | July 27, 1953 |

Source: Thomas A. Bailey et al., *The American Pageant: A History of the Republic,* Houghton Mifflin Company, 1998
(adapted)

33 Which generalization about the Korean War is supported by information on the maps?

(1) The war began when South Korea attacked North Korea.
(2) General MacArthur launched an invasion from China early in the war.
(3) Neither side experienced a major military victory during the war.
(4) At the end of the war, Korea remained a divided nation.

34 During World War II, many Japanese Americans living on the West Coast were relocated to detention centers primarily because they

(1) were known spies for Japan
(2) were seen as a security threat
(3) refused to serve in the United States military
(4) expressed their support for Italy and Germany

35 To help pay for World War II, the United States government relied heavily on the

(1) money borrowed from foreign governments
(2) sale of war bonds
(3) sale of United States manufactured goods to neutral nations
(4) printing of additional paper money

36 The primary goal of the United States foreign policy of containment was to

(1) return to noninvolvement in world affairs
(2) stop communist influence from spreading
(3) gain territories in Africa and Latin America
(4) overthrow existing dictatorships

37 The GI Bill affected American society after World War II by

(1) eliminating child labor
(2) expanding voting rights
(3) increasing spending on space exploration
(4) extending educational and housing opportunities

Base your answer to question 38 on the passage below and on your knowledge of social studies.

". . . In a sense we've come to our nation's capital to cash a check. When the architects of our republic wrote the magnificent words of the Constitution and the Declaration of Independence, they were signing a promissory note to which every American was to fall heir. This note was a promise that all men, yes, black men as well as white men, would be guaranteed the 'unalienable Rights of Life, Liberty, and the pursuit of Happiness.' It is obvious today that America has defaulted on this promissory note insofar as her citizens of color are concerned. Instead of honoring this sacred obligation, America has given the Negro people a bad check, a check which has come back marked 'insufficient funds.' ". . .

— Martin Luther King, Jr., August 28, 1963

38 The focus of this passage from Dr. King's speech was his belief that

(1) equal rights for all were guaranteed by the founders of this nation
(2) Americans had become blind to racial differences
(3) violence was often necessary for the protection of civil liberties
(4) civil rights for African Americans would always be a dream

---

39 As a result of the Supreme Court ruling in *Miranda* v. *Arizona* (1966), a person accused of a crime is entitled to

(1) a speedy trial
(2) reasonable bail
(3) a reading of his or her rights at the time of arrest
(4) protection against cruel or unusual punishment

40 A major goal of President Lyndon B. Johnson's Great Society was to

(1) provide government aid to business
(2) end poverty in the United States
(3) conserve natural resources
(4) stop emigration from Latin America

41 In 1991, one of the reasons President George H. W. Bush committed United States troops to the Persian Gulf War was to

(1) maintain the flow of trade through the Suez Canal
(2) fulfill military obligations as a member of the North American Free Trade Agreement (NAFTA)
(3) contain the spread of communism in the Middle East
(4) assure the flow of Middle East oil to the United States and its allies

42 The program that promotes preference in hiring for African Americans and other minorities to correct past injustices is known as

(1) Title IX   (3) affirmative action
(2) open admissions   (4) Head Start

43 Which Supreme Court case is correctly paired with the constitutional issue it addressed?

(1) *Gibbons* v. *Ogden* — interstate commerce
(2) *Dred Scott* v. *Sanford* — executive privilege
(3) *Gideon* v. *Wainwright* — voting rights
(4) *Roe* v. *Wade* — rights of the accused

44 One similarity between the actions of Samuel Gompers and Cesar Chavez is that both leaders

(1) organized workers to strive for better conditions
(2) relied on the use of force to gain minority rights
(3) advocated federal regulation of railroad rates
(4) worked to improve consumer product safety

45 Which heading would be most appropriate for the partial outline below?

I. _____

   A. Wages lagging behind the cost of living
   B. Overproduction of consumer goods
   C. Excessive buying on credit

(1) Mercantilist Economic Theory
(2) Features of a Bull Stock Market
(3) Monopolistic Business Practices
(4) Causes of the Great Depression

Base your answers to questions 46 and 47 on the speakers' statements below and on your knowledge of social studies.

Speaker A: "The current situation has necessitated that more women enter the workforce."

Speaker B: "My family will have to get along without sugar and flour this week."

Speaker C: "I say we should continue to support our president, even if a president has never been elected to four terms before now."

Speaker D: "I support the government in everything it has to do, to be sure we are safe from fascism here at home."

46 These speakers would have made these statements during

(1) World War I   (3) the Korean War
(2) World War II   (4) the Vietnam War

47 Which situation is *Speaker B* describing?

(1) destruction of crops during wartime
(2) need for importation of food products
(3) food rationing to support a war effort
(4) limitation of agricultural production through farm subsidies

48 "The right of citizens of the United States to vote shall not be denied or abridged by the United States or by any State on account of sex. . . ."

— 19th Amendment, *United States Constitution*

Which group of women worked for the passage of this amendment?

(1) Harriet Tubman, Jane Addams, and Dorothea Dix
(2) Susan B. Anthony, Carrie Chapman Catt, and Elizabeth Cady Stanton
(3) Madeline Albright, Geraldine Ferraro, and Sandra Day O'Connor
(4) Clara Barton, Amelia Earhart, and Eleanor Roosevelt

49 Which foreign policy agreement had the most direct influence on the Middle East?

(1) Kellogg-Briand Pact
(2) Yalta Conference declaration
(3) SALT I Treaty
(4) Camp David Accords

50 The domino theory was used to justify United States involvement in the

(1) War on Poverty   (3) Bosnian crisis
(2) Berlin airlift   (4) Vietnam War

Answers to the essay questions are to be written in the separate essay booklet.

In developing your answer to Part II, be sure to keep these general definitions in mind:

(a) <u>discuss</u> means "to make observations about something using facts, reasoning, and argument; to present in some detail"

(b) <u>describe</u> means "to illustrate something in words or tell about it"

Part II

THEMATIC ESSAY QUESTION

Directions: Write a well-organized essay that includes an introduction, several paragraphs addressing the task below, and a conclusion.

Theme: Geography and United States Government Actions

> Geographic factors often influence United States government actions, both foreign and domestic. Some of these factors include location, physical environment, movement of people, climate, and resources.

Task:

> Identify *two* actions taken by the United States government that were influenced by geographic factors, and for *each* action:
> • Discuss the historical circumstances that resulted in the government action
> • Discuss the influence of a geographic factor on the action
> • Describe the impact of the government action on the United States

From your study of United States history, you may use any federal government action that was influenced by geography. Some suggestions you might wish to consider include the Louisiana Purchase (1803), issuance of the Monroe Doctrine (1823), passage of the Homestead Act (1862), decision to build the transcontinental railroad (1860s), acquisition of the Philippines (1898), decision to build the Panama Canal (early 1900s), and passage of the Interstate Highway Act (1956).

You are *not* limited to these suggestions.

Guidelines:

In your essay, be sure to
• Address all aspects of the *Task*
• Support the theme with relevant facts, examples, and details
• Use a logical and clear plan of organization
• Introduce the theme by establishing a framework that is beyond a simple restatement of the *Task* and conclude with a summation of the *Theme*

NAME _____ SCHOOL _____

In developing your answer to Part III, be sure to keep this general definition in mind:

<u>discuss</u> means "to make observations about something using facts, reasoning, and argument; to present in some detail"

Part III

DOCUMENT-BASED QUESTION

This question is based on the accompanying documents (1–8). The question is designed to test your ability to work with historical documents. Some of the documents have been edited for the purposes of the question. As you analyze the documents, take into account both the source of each document and any point of view that may be presented in the document.

Historical Context:

The Civil War and the period of Reconstruction brought great social, political, and economic changes to American society. The effects of these changes continued into the 20th century.

Task: Using information from the documents and your knowledge of United States history, answer the questions that follow each document in Part A. Your answers to the questions will help you write the Part B essay in which you will be asked to

> • Identify and discuss *one* social, *one* political, **AND** *one* economic change in American society that occurred as a result of the Civil War or the period of Reconstruction

Part A

Short-Answer Questions

Directions: Analyze the documents and answer the short-answer questions that follow each document in the space provided.

Document 1

> . . . All persons born or naturalized in the United States, and subject to the jurisdiction thereof, are citizens of the United States and of the State wherein they reside. No State shall make or enforce any law which shall abridge the privileges or immunities of citizens of the United States; nor shall any State deprive any person of life, liberty, or property, without due process of law; nor deny to any person within its jurisdiction the equal protection of the laws. . . .

— 14th Amendment, Section 1, 1868

1a How does the 14th Amendment define citizenship? [1]

_____

_____

Score ☐

b During Reconstruction, how was the 14th Amendment intended to help formerly enslaved persons? [1]

_____

_____

Score ☐

Document 2

> . . . History does not furnish an example of emancipation under conditions less friendly to the
> emancipated class than this American example. Liberty came to the freedmen of the United
> States not in mercy, but in wrath [anger], not by moral choice but by military necessity, not by
> the generous action of the people among whom they were to live, and whose good-will was
> essential to the success of the measure, but by strangers, foreigners, invaders, trespassers, aliens,
> and enemies. The very manner of their emancipation invited to the heads of the freedmen the
> bitterest hostility of race and class. They were hated because they had been slaves, hated
> because they were now free, and hated because of those who had freed them. Nothing was to
> have been expected other than what has happened, and he is a poor student of the human heart
> who does not see that the old master class would naturally employ every power and means in
> their reach to make the great measure of emancipation unsuccessful and utterly odious [hateful].
> It was born in the tempest and whirlwind [turmoil] of war, and has lived in a storm of violence
> and blood. When the Hebrews were emancipated, they were told to take spoil [goods or
> property] from the Egyptians. When the serfs of Russia were emancipated [in 1861], they were
> given three acres of ground upon which they could live and make a living. But not so when our
> slaves were emancipated. They were sent away empty-handed, without money, without friends,
> and without a foot of land to stand upon. Old and young, sick and well, were turned loose to the
> open sky, naked to their enemies. The old slave quarter that had before sheltered them and the
> fields that had yielded them corn were now denied them. The old master class, in its wrath, said,
> "Clear out! The Yankees have freed you, now let them feed and shelter you! . . ."

Source: Frederick Douglass, *Life and Times of Frederick Douglass*, Park Publishing Co., 1881

2 According to this document, what did Frederick Douglass identify as a problem with the way the
United States government emancipated the slaves? [1]

_____

_____

_____

Score ☐

Document 3

> . . . We believe you are not familiar with the description of the Ku Klux Klans riding nightly over the country, going from county to county, and in the county towns, spreading terror wherever they go by robbing, whipping, ravishing, and killing our people without provocation [reason], compelling [forcing] colored people to break the ice and bathe in the chilly waters of the Kentucky river.
>
> The [state] legislature has adjourned. They refused to enact any laws to suppress [stop] Ku-Klux disorder. We regard them [the Ku-Kluxers] as now being licensed to continue their dark and bloody deeds under cover of the dark night. They refuse to allow us to testify in the state courts where a white man is concerned. We find their deeds are perpetrated [carried out] only upon colored men and white Republicans. We also find that for our services to the government and our race we have become the special object of hatred and persecution at the hands of the Democratic Party. Our people are driven from their homes in great numbers, having no redress [relief from distress] only [except] the United States court, which is in many cases unable to reach them.
>
> We would state that we have been law-abiding citizens, pay our taxes, and in many parts of the state our people have been driven from the polls, refused the right to vote. Many have been slaughtered while attempting to vote. We ask, how long is this state of things to last? . . .

— Petition to the United States Congress, March 25, 1871, Miscellaneous Documents of the United States Senate, 42nd Congress, 1st Session, 1871

3a Based on this document, identify *one* way the Ku Klux Klan terrorized African Americans. [1]

_____

Score ☐

b According to this document, how did the actions of the Ku Klux Klan affect African Americans' participation in the political process? [1]

_____

Score ☐

Document 4

Barrow Plantation
1860

Barrow Property
1880

■ Houses of tenant farmers who were
former slaves of Barrow Family

Sources: *Scribner's Monthly*, "A Georgia Plantation," April 1881 and
Graebner and Richards, *The American Record*, McGraw Hill, 2001 (adapted)

4   According to these illustrations, how did the economic role of African Americans change between
1860 and 1880?   [1]

_____

_____

Score ☐

Document 5

. . . When we come to the New Industrial South the change is marvellous, and so vast and various that I scarcely know where to begin in a short paper that cannot go much into details. Instead of a South devoted to agriculture and politics, we find a South wide-awake to business, excited and even astonished at the development of its own immense resources in metals, marbles, coal, timber, fertilizers, eagerly laying lines of communication, rapidly opening mines, building furnaces, foundries [workplace where melted metal is poured into molds], and all sorts of shops for utilizing the native riches. It is like the discovery of a new world. When the Northerner finds great foundries in Virginia using only (with slight exceptions) the products of Virginia iron and coal mines; when he finds Alabama and Tennessee making iron so good and so cheap that it finds ready market in Pennsylvania; and foundries multiplying near the great furnaces for supplying Northern markets; when he finds cotton-mills running to full capacity on grades of cheap cottons universally in demand throughout the South and Southwest; when he finds small industries, such as paper-box factories and wooden bucket and tub factories, sending all they can make into the North and widely over the West; when he sees the loads of most beautiful marbles shipped North; when he learns that some of the largest and most important engines and mill machinery were made in Southern shops; when he finds in Richmond a "pole locomotive," made to run on logs laid end to end, and drag out from Michigan forests and Southern swamps lumber hitherto inaccessible; when he sees worn out highlands in Georgia and Carolina bear more cotton than ever before by help of a fertilizer the base of which is the cotton seed itself (worth more as a fertilizer than it was before the oil was extracted from it); when he sees a multitude of small shops giving employment to men, women, and children who never had any work of that sort to do before; and when he sees Roanoke iron cast in Richmond into car irons, and returned to a car factory in Roanoke which last year sold three hundred cars to the New York and New England Railroad—he begins to open his eyes. The South is manufacturing a great variety of things needed in the house, on the farm, and in the shops, for home consumption, and already sends to the North and West several manufactured products. With iron, coal, timber contiguous [adjoining] and easily obtained, the amount sent out is certain to increase as the labor becomes more skillful. The most striking industrial development today is in iron, coal, lumber, and marbles; the more encouraging for the self-sustaining life of the Southern people is the multiplication of small industries in nearly every city I visited. . . .

Source: Charles Dudley Warner, "The South Revisited," *Harper's New Monthly Magazine* (March 1887)

5   According to this passage, what was **one** economic change that had occurred in the South by 1887? [1]

Score

Document 6

A Public Fountain in North Carolina, 1950

— Photograph by Elliott Erwitt

Source: Steve Kasher, *The Civil Rights Movement: A Photographic History, 1954–68*, Abbeville Press

6   What does this photograph show about the treatment of African Americans in the South after Reconstruction?   [1]

_____

_____

Score ☐

Document 7

> . . . Since 1868 there has been a steady and persistent determination to eliminate us from the politics of the Southern States. We are not to be eliminated. Suffrage is a federal guaranty and not a privilege to be conferred [given] or withheld by the States. We contend for the principle of manhood suffrage as the most effective safeguard of citizenship. A disfranchised citizen [one who is deprived of the right to vote] is a pariah [outcast] in the body politic. We are not opposed to legitimate restriction of the suffrage, but we insist that restrictions shall apply alike to all citizens of all States. We are willing to accept an educational or property qualification, or both; and we contend that retroactive legislation depriving citizens of the suffrage rights is a hardship which should be speedily passed upon by the courts. We insist that neither of these was intended or is conserved [protected] by the new constitutions of Mississippi, South Carolina or Louisiana. Their framers intended and did disfranchise a majority of their citizenship [deprived them of the right to vote] because of "race and color" and "previous condition," and we therefore call upon the Congress to reduce the representation of those States in the Congress as provided and made mandatory by Section 2 of Article XIV of the Constitution. We call upon Afro-Americans everywhere to resist by all lawful means the determination to deprive them of their suffrage rights. If it is necessary to accomplish this vital purpose to divide their vote in a given State we advise that they divide it. The shibboleth [custom] of party must give way to the shibboleth of self-preservation. . . .

— Afro-American Council public statement, 1898
Source: Francis L. Broderick and August Meier, *Negro Protest Thought in the Twentieth Century*, Bobbs-Merrill Company

7   What political problem is being described in this passage? [1]

_____

_____

Score ☐

Document 8

We hold these truths to be self-evident: that all men are created equal.

Parade in New York City sponsored by the NAACP in 1917

Source: Robert Divine et al., *America Past and Present,* Addison Wesley (adapted)

8   What was the general goal of the marchers shown in this photograph?   [1]

_____

_____

Score [ ]

Part B

Essay

Directions: Write a well-organized essay that includes an introduction, several paragraphs, and a conclusion. Use evidence from at least *five* documents in your essay. Support your response with relevant facts, examples, and details. Include additional outside information.

Historical Context:

The Civil War and the period of Reconstruction brought great social, political, and economic changes to American society. The effects of these changes continued into the 20th century.

Task: Using information from the documents and your knowledge of United States history, write an essay in which you

---

• Identify and discuss *one* social, *one* political, **AND** *one* economic change in American society that occurred as a result of the Civil War or the period of Reconstruction

---

Guidelines:

In your essay, be sure to
• Address all aspects of the *Task* by accurately analyzing and interpreting at least *five* documents
• Incorporate information from the documents in the body of the essay
• Incorporate relevant outside information
• Support the theme with relevant facts, examples, and details
• Use a logical and clear plan of organization
• Introduce the theme by establishing a framework that is beyond a simple restatement of the *Task* or *Historical Context* and conclude with a summation of the theme

Regents Examination—January 2004

This section contains the Regents Examination in United States History and Government that was given in New York State in January 2004.

Circle your answers to Part I on this exam and write your answers to the thematic essay and document-based essay questions on separate sheets of paper. Be sure to refer to the test-taking strategies in the front of this book as you prepare to answer the test questions.

Part I

Answer all questions in this part.

Directions (1–50): For each statement or question, write on the separate answer sheet the *number* of the word or expression that, of those given, best completes the statement or answers the question.

1 Which heading best completes the partial outline below?

> I. _____
>
> A. Committees of Correspondence
> B. Nonimportation Agreements
> C. Boston Tea Party
> D. First Continental Congress

(1) Protests Against Slavery in the American Colonies
(2) British Parliamentary Actions to Punish Colonial Americans
(3) Colonial Responses to British Mercantile Policies
(4) Colonial Attempts to End the British Policy of Salutary Neglect

2 **"New Congress to Have Two Houses"**
"Slaves to Count as Three-Fifths of a Person"
"President to be Chosen by Electoral Vote"

Which conclusion about the Constitutional Convention is best supported by these headlines?

(1) The framers of the Constitution were able to compromise on important issues.
(2) States that were small in area would lose power in the new Constitution.
(3) States with large populations controlled the outcome of the convention.
(4) The president and Congress would have equal power under the new constitution.

3 Which power is shared by the federal government and the New York State government?

(1) enacting immigration laws
(2) levying taxes
(3) granting patents and copyrights
(4) issuing passports

4 The unwritten constitution is best defined as the

(1) amendments to the United States Constitution
(2) powers that the Constitution reserves for the states
(3) powers that the Constitution denies to Congress and to the states
(4) practices of the government that are based on custom and tradition

5 "The Congress shall have Power . . . To make all Laws which shall be necessary and proper for carrying into Execution the foregoing Powers, and all other Powers vested [granted] by this Constitution in the Government of the United States, or in any Department or Officer thereof. . . ."

This section of the United States Constitution was frequently used during the 20th century to

(1) expand federal control of interstate commerce
(2) reduce the number of federal courts
(3) overturn decisions of the electoral college
(4) impeach the president

6 New York State and the United States have republican forms of government because both have

(1) a bill of rights
(2) a written constitution
(3) an elected legislature
(4) three branches of government

7 In the case of *Marbury* v. *Madison* (1803), the Supreme Court increased its power by

(1) establishing the practice of judicial review
(2) upholding the presidential appointment power
(3) expanding the meaning of individual liberties
(4) declaring the principle of states' rights unconstitutional

8 One similarity in the foreign policies of Presidents George Washington, Thomas Jefferson, and James Monroe was that they

(1) favored France over England
(2) promoted colonial expansion
(3) came to the defense of Latin American nations
(4) sought to avoid involvement in European political struggles

9 The Declaration of Sentiments from the Seneca Falls Convention of 1848 proclaimed that

(1) the abolition of slavery was necessary
(2) all men and women are created equal
(3) California should be admitted as a free state
(4) the sale of alcoholic beverages should be illegal

10 One way that "Bleeding Kansas," the Dred Scott decision, and John Brown's raid on Harper's Ferry had a similar effect on the United States was that these events

(1) ended conflict over slavery in the territories
(2) eased tensions between the North and the South
(3) contributed to the formation of the Whig Party
(4) made sectional compromise more difficult

11 The Homestead Act of 1862 helped the development of the West by

(1) providing free land to settlers
(2) granting land for construction of trans-continental railroads
(3) allowing slavery to spread to the territories
(4) placing Native American Indians on reservations

12 Between 1880 and 1900, most immigrants coming to the United States settled in the cities along the east coast because

(1) many factory jobs were available in the East
(2) little farmland remained to be settled in the Midwest
(3) most immigrants came from the cities of Europe
(4) city laws afforded special rights and protections for immigrants

Base your answers to questions 13 and 14 on the speakers' statements below and on your knowledge of social studies.

Speaker A: "When demand ran high, and markets were scarce, he showed little mercy, broke his contracts for delivery and raised prices."

Speaker B: "The man of wealth must hold his fortune 'in trust' for the community and use it for philanthropic and charitable purposes."

Speaker C: "It is cruel to slander the rich because they have been successful. They have gone into great enterprises that have enriched the nation and the nation has enriched them."

Speaker D: "The fruits of the toil of millions are boldly stolen to build up colossal fortunes for the few, unprecedented in the history of mankind."

13 Which two speakers would most likely label late 19th-century industrialists as *robber barons*?

(1) *A* and *B*
(2) *A* and *D*
(3) *B* and *C*
(4) *C* and *D*

14 The most valid conclusion that can be drawn from the different viewpoints of these speakers is that industrialists of the late 19th century

(1) benefited and harmed society
(2) treated their workers fairly
(3) used illegal means to gain wealth
(4) generally opposed the free-enterprise economic system

15 In *Plessy* v. *Ferguson* (1896), the Supreme Court ruled that

(1) states may not secede from the Union
(2) racial segregation was constitutional
(3) slaves are property and may not be taken from their owners
(4) all western territories should be open to slavery

Base your answers to questions 16 and 17 on the cartoon below and on your knowledge of social studies.

Source: Lewis Paul Todd and Merle Curti, *Rise of the American Nation*, Harcourt Brace Jovanovich (adapted)

16 What is the main idea of this cartoon from the 1800s?

(1) Labor is gaining power over big business.
(2) Most Americans support the labor movement.
(3) Business has advantages over labor.
(4) Government should support the expansion of railroads.

17 The American Federation of Labor responded to the situation shown in the cartoon by

(1) organizing skilled workers into unions
(2) encouraging open immigration
(3) forming worker-owned businesses
(4) creating a single union of workers and farmers

---

18 The Sherman Antitrust Act and the Clayton Antitrust Act were passed in an effort to

(1) promote the formation of new trusts
(2) maintain competition in business
(3) increase business investment
(4) limit the activities of foreign corporations

19 Between the 1890s and the start of World War I, the United States expanded its access to overseas markets and raw materials through the policy of

(1) containment
(2) imperialism
(3) isolationism
(4) neutrality

Base your answer to question 20 on the table below and on your knowledge of social studies.

Progressive Era Legislation

Date	Legislation	Purpose
1905	United States Forest Service established	Manage the nation's water and timber resources
1906	Meat Inspection Act	Regulate meat processing to ensure clean conditions
1906	Pure Food and Drug Act	Outlaw dishonest labeling of food and drugs
1913	Department of Labor established	Promote the interests of working people

20 The common purpose of these legislative acts was to

(1) protect the nation's natural resources
(2) improve conditions for recent immigrants to the United States
(3) advance the growth of big business
(4) promote the general welfare of the American public

21 The success of the Populist Party of the 1890s can best be measured by which development?

(1) The party replaced one of the two major parties.
(2) The party gained support among business leaders.
(3) Two of the party's candidates were elected to the presidency.
(4) Several of the party's proposed reforms were made into laws.

22 The Open Door policy of 1899 was originally adopted so that the United States could

(1) restrict Chinese immigration
(2) stop Japan from colonizing China
(3) gain equal trading rights in China
(4) encourage the development of democracy in China

23 During the Progressive Era, Jane Addams responded to urban conditions by working to establish

(1) settlement houses that provided assistance to the poor
(2) newspapers that helped to inform Americans about slum conditions
(3) laws that restricted certain immigrant groups
(4) free public schools located in inner-city neighborhoods

24 During World War I, many American women helped gain support for the suffrage movement by

(1) protesting against the war
(2) joining the military service
(3) lobbying for child-care facilities
(4) working in wartime industries

25 Following World War I, the United States Senate refused to ratify the Treaty of Versailles primarily because the treaty

(1) failed to include most of President Wilson's Fourteen Points

(2) did not punish Germany for starting the war

(3) contained provisions that might lead the United States into foreign conflicts

(4) made no provision for reduction of military weapons

26 The migration of African Americans to the North during and following World War I was mainly a result of the

(1) success of military desegregation

(2) efforts of the civil rights movement

(3) availability of new factory jobs

(4) impact of affirmative action programs

27 During the 1920s, controversies concerning the Scopes trial, national Prohibition, and the behavior of "flappers" were all signs of disagreement over

(1) the return to normalcy

(2) traditional values and changing lifestyles

(3) causes of the Great Depression

(4) the benefits of new technology

28 A major goal of the immigration acts of the 1920s was to

(1) allow unlimited immigration from Southeast Asia

(2) assure equal numbers of immigrants from all nations

(3) favor wealthy and well-educated immigrants

(4) use quotas to limit immigration from southern and eastern Europe

29 Which conditions are most characteristic of an economic depression?

(1) high unemployment and overproduction

(2) large business investments and low taxes

(3) too much money in circulation and high stock prices

(4) high employment and increased real estate investments

30 The New Deal tried to solve many problems of the Great Depression by

(1) providing federal aid to many sectors of the economy

(2) reducing taxes on big business to stimulate job creation

(3) lowering federal spending to maintain a balanced budget

(4) decreasing foreign competition by raising tariffs

31 President Franklin D. Roosevelt tried to pack the United States Supreme Court, but Congress did not support him. This situation is an example of

(1) Congress undermining the separation of powers

(2) the president using the unwritten constitution

(3) the use of the system of checks and balances

(4) how federalism was preserved by one branch of government

32 In the 1930s, Congress attempted to avoid the situations that led to United States involvement in World War I by

(1) enacting a peacetime draft law

(2) passing a series of neutrality acts

(3) authorizing the deportation of American Communist Party members

(4) relocating Japanese Americans to internment camps

33 During World War II, the federal government used rationing to

(1) hold down prices of military weapons

(2) increase educational benefits for veterans

(3) increase imports of scarce products

(4) provide more resources for the military

34 What was the main purpose of the GI Bill passed by Congress shortly before the end of World War II?

(1) to offer low-interest loans to the defense industry

(2) to provide economic aid to veterans

(3) to contain the spread of international communism

(4) to expand career opportunities in the military

Base your answer to question 35 on the photograph below and on your knowledge of social studies.

Source: Loomis Dean, *Life*

35 What does this photograph indicate about the United States in the 1950s?

(1) Extraordinary steps were taken to hide atomic weapons.

(2) The nation had become the only nuclear superpower.

(3) Much fear was created by the Cold War.

(4) Only government officials would be safe in a nuclear attack.

36 The rapid growth in personal income in the decade after World War II contributed to

(1) a decrease in the birthrate

(2) a major economic depression

(3) expansion of the middle class

(4) shortages in the supply of luxury goods

Base your answer to question 37 on the cartoon below and on your knowledge of social studies.

"Wonder why we're not keeping pace?"

Source: Herblock, *The Washington Post* (adapted)

37 Which event of the 1950s most likely led to the publication of this cartoon?

(1) Russia put cosmonauts on the Moon.

(2) The Soviet Union launched the *Sputnik* satellite.

(3) The United States was defeated in the Vietnam War.

(4) American students scored low on tests in math and science.

38 What was one outcome of the Cuban missile crisis in 1962?

(1) Cuba became a communist nation.

(2) The United States seized military control of Cuba.

(3) The Soviet Union withdrew its nuclear missiles from Cuba.

(4) Fidel Castro met with President John F. Kennedy.

39 The policy of détente was used by President Richard Nixon in an effort to

(1) decrease tensions between the Soviet Union and the United States
(2) improve relations with Latin America
(3) promote democratic government in China
(4) create stronger ties with Western Europe

40 ". . . Our decision about energy will test the character of the American people and the ability of the President and the Congress to govern. This difficult effort will be the 'moral equivalent of war'— except that we will be uniting our efforts to build and not destroy. . . ."

— President Jimmy Carter
Address to the Nation, April 18, 1977

President Carter put these ideas into practice by

(1) halting construction of nuclear power plants
(2) increasing imports of foreign oil
(3) urging the development of alternative fuel sources
(4) imposing a price freeze on all petroleum products

Base your answer to question 41 on the cartoon below and on your knowledge of social studies.

"Whoever wins will have a mandate to keep the seat warm for the next four years."

Source: Bruce Beattie, Daytona Beach News-Journal, (adapted)

41 This cartoon from the disputed presidential election of 2000 suggests that the winner might

(1) lack strong popular support for his programs
(2) easily win reelection in 2004
(3) succeed in fulfilling his campaign promises
(4) be unable to claim victory in the electoral college

42 "Clinton Offers Economic Aid to Russia"
"U.S. Sends Peacekeeping Troops to Bosnia"
"U.S. Airlifts Food and Medicine to Somalia"

These headlines illustrate that United States foreign policy during the 1990s stressed

(1) containment
(2) collective security
(3) global involvement
(4) neutrality

Base your answer to question 43 on the graph below and on your knowledge of social studies.

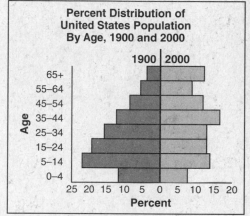

Percent Distribution of United States Population By Age, 1900 and 2000

Source: United States Census Bureau (adapted)

43 The changes shown in the graph support the recent concerns of Americans about the

(1) future of Social Security and Medicare
(2) return to an agrarian society
(3) surplus of health care workers
(4) shortage of schools and colleges

44 The Federal Reserve System has an impact on economic conditions in the United States by

(1) regulating the amount of money in circulation
(2) providing direct loans to farmers and small businesses
(3) enforcing strict antitrust laws
(4) controlling imports from other nations

Base your answers to questions 45 and 46 on the graph below and on your knowledge of social studies.

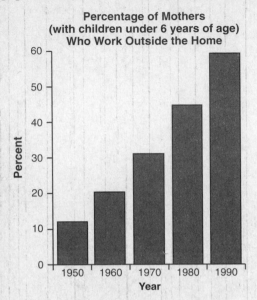

**Percentage of Mothers
(with children under 6 years of age)
Who Work Outside the Home**

Source: *1996 Green Book*, U.S. Department of Labor, Bureau of Labor Statistics (adapted)

45 Which statement is most clearly supported by the information in the graph?

(1) More children were under age 6 in 1990 than in 1950.
(2) Since 1990, women have made up more than half of the workforce.
(3) The gap between male and female incomes has declined.
(4) Fewer women are staying home to raise their young children.

46 A candidate for public office would likely conclude from a study of this graph that the public would favor increased government support for

(1) additional foreign aid
(2) health care facilities
(3) child day-care centers
(4) colleges and universities

47 William Lloyd Garrison, Harriet Tubman, and Harriet Beecher Stowe are best known for their efforts to

(1) create free public schools
(2) begin the temperance movement
(3) expand the rights of women
(4) oppose the practice of slavery

48 Which heading best completes the partial outline below?

I. _____

A. Open Door policy
B. Panamanian Revolt (1903)
C. Roosevelt Corollary
D. Truman Doctrine

(1) American Domestic Programs
(2) Cold War Events
(3) United States Interventionism
(4) Efforts at Isolationism

49 Rachel Carson and Ralph Nader are similar to the muckrakers of the Progressive Era because they have

(1) advocated a total change in the structure of government
(2) attempted to expose societal problems
(3) failed to influence public opinion
(4) supported anti-American activities

50 In which war was Manifest Destiny used to justify United States government actions?

(1) Revolutionary War
(2) Mexican War
(3) Civil War
(4) Vietnam War

Answers to the essay questions are to be written in the separate essay booklet.

In developing your answer to Part II, be sure to keep this general definition in mind:

(a) <u>discuss</u> means "to make observations about something using facts, reasoning, and argument; to present in some detail"

Part II

THEMATIC ESSAY QUESTION

Directions: Write a well-organized essay that includes an introduction, several paragraphs addressing the task below, and a conclusion.

Theme: Constitutional Change

> Amendments to the United States Constitution have changed our government and our society.

Task:

> Identify *two* amendments to the United States Constitution and for *each*:
> - Discuss the historical circumstances that led to the adoption of the amendment
> - Discuss how the amendment changed the United States government and/or American society

You may use any constitutional amendment from your study of United States history. Some suggestions you might wish to consider include the 1st Amendment — personal freedoms (1791), 15th amendment — right to vote (1870), 16th Amendment — income tax (1913), 17th Amendment — election of senators (1913), 18th Amendment — Prohibition (1919), 19th Amendment — suffrage (1920), or 22nd Amendment — term limits (1951).

You are *not* limited to these suggestions.

Guidelines:

In your essay, be sure to
- Address all aspects of the *Task*.
- Support the theme with relevant facts, examples, and details.
- Use a logical and clear plan of organization.
- Include an introduction and a conclusion that are beyond a simple restatement of the *Theme*.

NAME _____ SCHOOL_____

In developing your answer to Part III, be sure to keep these general definitions in mind:

  (a) <u>discuss</u> means "to make observations about something using facts, reasoning, and argument; to present in some detail"

  (b) <u>evaluate</u> means "to examine and judge the significance, worth, or condition of; to determine the value of"

Part III

DOCUMENT-BASED QUESTION

This question is based on the accompanying documents (1–8). The question is designed to test your ability to work with historical documents. Some of the documents have been edited for the purposes of the question. As you analyze the documents, take into account the source of each document and any point of view that may be presented in the document.

Historical Context:

> Although Americans place a high value on education, access to formal education has not always been available to all. Since colonial times, educational opportunities have been extended to more and more people in the United States.

Task: Using information from the documents and your knowledge of United States history, answer the questions that follow each document in Part A. Your answers to the questions will help you write the Part B essay in which you will be asked to:

  • Discuss the efforts made by individuals and the government (federal, state, or local) to extend educational opportunities in American society
  • Evaluate the extent to which these efforts were successful

Part A

Short-Answer Questions

Directions: Analyze the documents and answer the short-answer questions that follow each document in the space provided.

Document 1

The Land Ordinance of 1785 provided for the orderly survey and sale of public lands in the Northwest Territory. The grid below shows the numbering of sections of land for sale in a township.

The Land Ordinance of 1785
One township (6 miles square)

Land sold in Section 16 supported public schools.

Source: Thomas A. Bailey et al., *The American Pageant*, Houghton Mifflin (adapted)

1 According to this grid, how did the Land Ordinance of 1785 encourage education in the Northwest Territory? [1]

_____

Score ☐

Document 2

. . . The inquiry to which these remarks have conducted us is this: what is offered by the plan of female education here proposed, which may teach or preserve among females of wealthy families that purity of manners which is allowed to be so essential to national prosperity, and so necessary to the existence of a republican government?

[1] Females, by having their understandings cultivated, their reasoning powers developed and strengthened, may be expected to act more from the dictates of reason and less from those of fashion and caprice [unpredictability].

[2] With minds thus strengthened they would be taught systems of morality, enforced by the sanctions of religion; and they might be expected to acquire juster and more enlarged views of their duty, and stronger and higher motives to its performance.

[3] This plan of education offers all that can be done to preserve female youth from a contempt of useful labor. The pupils would become accustomed to it in conjunction with the high objects of literature and the elegant pursuits of the fine arts; and it is to be hoped that, both from habit and association, they might in future life regard it as respectable. . . .

Source: Emma Willard,
"An Address to the Public, Particularly the Members of the Legislature of New York,
Proposing a Plan for Improving Female Education," 1819

2 Based on this passage, state *one* reason Emma Willard believed females would benefit from education. [1]

_____

Score [ ]

Document 3

> . . . Education, then, beyond all other devices of human origin, is the great equalizer of the
> conditions of men—the balance-wheel of the social machinery. I do not here mean that it so
> elevates the moral nature as to make men disdain and abhor the oppression of their fellowmen.
> This idea pertains to another of its attributes. But I mean that it gives each man the
> independence and the means, by which he can resist the selfishness of other men. It does better
> than to disarm the poor of their hostility towards the rich; it prevents being poor. Agrarianism
> [movement to improve the economic status of farmers] is the revenge of poverty against wealth.
> The wanton destruction of the property of others, — the burning of hay-ricks and corn-ricks, the
> demolition of machinery, because it supersedes hand-labor, the sprinkling of vitriol [caustic
> substances] on rich dresses, — is only agrarianism run mad. Education prevents both the
> revenge and the madness. On the other hand, a fellow-feeling for one's class or caste is the
> common instinct of hearts not wholly sunk in selfish regards for person, or for family. The spread
> of education, by enlarging the cultivated class or caste, will open a wider area over which the
> social feelings will expand; and, if this education should be universal and complete, it would do
> more than all things else to obliterate factitious distinctions in society. . . .

— Horace Mann, *12th Annual Report of the Secretary of the Massachusetts Board of Education*, 1848
Source: Lawrence Cremin, ed., *The Republic and the School: Horace Mann on the Education of Free Men*,
Columbia University

3 Based on this passage, identify *two* reasons Horace Mann believed public education benefits American
society. [2]

(1)_____

Score ☐

(2)_____

Score ☐

Document 4

Source: Andrew Cayton et al., *America: Pathways to the Present*,
Prentice Hall (adapted)

4*a* According to this photograph, what action did the federal government take to encourage educational opportunities for African Americans in the period after the Civil War? [1]

_____

Score ☐

> Our school begun—in spite of threatenings from the whites and the consequent fear of the blacks—with twenty-seven pupils, four only of whom could read, even the simplest words. At the end of six weeks, we have enrolled eighty-five names, with but fifteen unable to read. In seven years teaching at the North, I have not seen a parallel to their appetite for learning, and their active progress. Whether this zeal will abate with time, is yet a question. I have little fear that it may. Meanwhile it is well to "work while the day lasts." Their spirit now may be estimated somewhat, when I tell you that three walk a distance of four miles, each morning, to return after the five-hours session. Several come three miles, and quite a number from two and two-and-a-half miles. . . .

— Mary S. Battey, schoolteacher, Andersonville, Georgia, 1866
Source: Gerda Lerner, *The Female Experience: An American Documentary*, Bobbs-Merrill Company

b According to this passage, how were African-American students in the South affected by educational opportunities in 1866? [1]

_____

_____

Score ☐

Document 5

India Harris Simmons came to Kansas from Ohio to join her homesteading parents and was soon appointed as the first schoolteacher of the Prairie Range district of northwest Kearny County.

> . . . The nondescript supply of books which each pupil had brought from whatever state was 'back home' to him was placed on the bench by his side. Slates, which had to take the place of both blackboard and tablets, were of all sizes and descriptions, from Jimmy's tiny one with the red felt covered frame and pencil tied to it with a string, to Mary's big double one with the wide home-made frames fastened together with strong hinges and cut deep with initials and hearts. She had found it packed away among grandfather's books which he had used away back in Ohio. There were histories from Illinois, spellers and writing books from Iowa, readers from St. Louis city schools, and even some old blue-backed spellers, with their five-syllabled puzzlers.
>
> From this motley array the teacher made the assignments and arranged the classifications, depending entirely upon her own judgment. The pupils had been without school privileges long enough to be glad to have an opportunity to study, and their rapid progress showed they came, for the most part, from intelligent families. True, there was not a suspension globe for explaining mathematical geography, but an apple and a ball did very well. There was no case of the latest wall maps on rollers, but the large ones in the books answered the purpose when care was taken to hold them correctly. . . .

— India Harris Simmons (1888)
Source: Joanna Stratton, *Pioneer Women: Voices from the Kansas Frontier*, Simon and Schuster

5 Based on this document, state *two* ways that India Harris Simmons used the materials available to her to teach the children in her school. [2]

(1)_____

_____

Score [ ]

(2)_____

_____

Score [ ]

Document 6

GRANITE CITY
AMERICANIZATION SCHOOLS

Monday
and
Thursday
Evenings
7:30 p. m.

Underwood & Underwood

These two men are brothers, one is an American Citizen and the other has just come to this country with their old mother. See the difference in the way they dress and look. America is a great country. In America everybody has a chance. Everybody who comes to America from the old country ought to learn the American language and become an American citizen. If the people that come to America do not become Americans, this country will soon be like the old country.

Beginning
Monday,
September
the 27th,
1920

SCHOOLS:

HIGH SCHOOL, 20TH AND D STREETS
LINCOLN PLACE, 917 PACIFIC AVENUE

LIBERTY SCHOOL, 20TH AND O STREETS
MADISON SCHOOL, 1322 MADISON AVENUE

Keep America Great.   Become an American Citizen   **Learn The Language.**

Press Record Publishing Co. ◄► 1834 D St., Granite City, Ill

—file 27671/44, Americanization files, Records of the Immigration and Naturalization Service, Record Group 85
Source: *Teaching With Documents: Using Primary Sources From the National Archives,*
National Archives Trust Fund Board (adapted)

6 According to this poster, what advantage would immigrants gain by attending an Americanization school? [1]

_____

_____

Score ☐

Document 7

STATE OF EDUCATION
BLACK AND WHITE

. . . On average, Southern states spent half as much educating a black child as they spent educating a white. Investment in white school plants [buildings] was four times higher, white teachers' salaries 30 percent higher.

Seventeen segregating states spent $42 million busing white children — less than $1 million on blacks.

Median years of schooling in segregating states and Washington, D.C.: whites — 8.4; blacks — 5.1. The percent of whites finishing school was four times that of blacks.

Segregating states spent $86 million on white colleges, $5 million on black ones. There was 1 accredited medical school for blacks, 29 for whites; 1 accredited black school for pharmacology, 40 for whites; 1 law school for blacks, 40 for whites. There was no engineering school for blacks, 36 for whites.

In 1946, an estimated one quarter of the entire black population was functionally illiterate. . . .

Source: Harold Evans et al., *The American Century*, Alfred A. Knopf (adapted)

7 Based on this document, state *two* ways that "separate but equal" was not equal when it came to education in the segregated states before 1954. [2]

(1)_____

Score [ ]

(2)_____

Score [ ]

Document 8

... Segregation of white and colored children in public schools has a detrimental effect upon the colored children. The impact is greater when it has the sanction of the law, for the policy of separating the races is usually interpreted as denoting the inferiority of the negro group. A sense of inferiority affects the motivation of a child to learn. Segregation with the sanction of law, therefore, has a tendency to [retard] the educational and mental development of negro children and to deprive them of some of the benefits they would receive in a racial[ly] integrated school system.

Whatever may have been the extent of psychological knowledge at the time of *Plessy* v. *Ferguson*, this finding is amply supported by modern authority. Any language in *Plessy* v. *Ferguson* contrary to this finding is rejected.

We conclude that, in the field of public education, the doctrine of "separate but equal" has no place. Separate educational facilities are inherently unequal. Therefore, we hold that the plaintiffs and others similarly situated for whom the actions have been brought are, by reason of the segregation complained of, deprived of the equal protection of the laws guaranteed by the Fourteenth Amendment. This disposition makes unnecessary any discussion whether such segregation also violates the Due Process Clause of the Fourteenth Amendment . . . .

— Chief Justice Earl Warren, Opinion of the Court, *Brown v. Board of Education of Topeka* (1954)

8 According to this document, what was the Supreme Court's ruling regarding the "separate but equal" doctrine as it applied to public schools? [1]

_____

_____

Score ☐

Part B

Essay

Directions: Write a well-organized essay that includes an introduction, several paragraphs, and a conclusion. Use evidence from at least *five* documents in the body of the essay. Support your response with relevant facts, examples, and details. Include additional outside information.

Historical Context:

Although Americans place a high value on education, access to formal education has not always been available to all. Since colonial times, educational opportunities have been extended to more and more people in the United States.

Task: Using information from the documents and your knowledge of United States history, write an essay in which you:

- Discuss the efforts made by individuals and the government (federal, state, or local) to extend educational opportunities in American society
- Evaluate the extent to which these efforts were successful

Guidelines:

In your essay, be sure to
- Address all aspects of the *Task* by accurately analyzing and interpreting at least *five* documents
- Incorporate information from the documents in the body of the essay
- Incorporate relevant outside information
- Support the theme with relevant facts, examples, and details
- Use a logical and clear plan of organization
- Include an introduction and a conclusion that are beyond a simple restatement of the *Historical Context*

Regents Examination—August 2003

This section contains the Regents Examination in United States History and Government that was given in New York State in August 2003.

Circle your answers to Part I on this exam and write your answers to the thematic essay and document-based essay questions on separate sheets of paper. Be sure to refer to the test-taking strategies in the front of this book as you prepare to answer the test questions.

Great Plains

- Dry (dust bowl)
- Buffalo : Plain Indians
- Homstead Act / Railroads

Mayflower Compact - agree to be governed

House of Burgesses - representative democracy

Const. Text
    Bill of Rights
    Federalist & anti-federalist papers
    James Madison's Note

Govt powers - Sep of Powers
           - No king

water
- farming
- transportation
- trade

Zenger
- NY time vs. us } Freedom of pres

Missouri compromise ME - Free
                       MO - Slaves
divide territories < Free / Slave
maintain balance in senate

Delegated Powers : In the const
Implied : Elastic Clause &
           &(Necessary & proper)

Enlightenment : People should be RULE!
- government is the people
- government limited by natural rts

Part I   1-20

Answer all questions in this part.

Directions (1–50): For each statement or question, write on the separate answer sheet the *number* of the word or expression that, of those given, best completes the statement or answers the question.

1 In the 1800s, the Great Plains region of the United States was characterized primarily by

(1) exceptionally high amounts of annual rainfall
(2) heavily wooded forests covering most of the area
(3) an extensive system of navigable rivers
(4) vast expanses of native grasses

2 In the early 1800's, the need for a water route to help farmers ship their products to market was one reason for the

(1) Gadsden Purchase
(2) Louisiana Purchase
(3) Mexican Cession
(4) Missouri Compromise

3 The Mayflower Compact and the House of Burgesses were important to the development of democracy in colonial America because they

(1) expanded freedom of religion
(2) promoted self-government
(3) protected private ownership of property
(4) granted voting rights to all white males

4 The main criticism of the Articles of Confederation was that they failed to

(1) allow for the admission of new states
(2) limit the powers of the president
(3) provide adequate powers for the central government
(4) prevent the development of military rule

5 Which information on the writing of the Constitution is considered a primary source?

(1) a newspaper editorial written in 1887
(2) an encyclopedia article on the Constitution
(3) the book, *An Economic Interpretation of the Constitution*, by Charles Beard
(4) notes from the Constitutional Convention taken by James Madison

6 To avoid having too much power concentrated in one branch of government, the framers of the Constitution established

(1) a bicameral national legislature
(2) division of power among different levels of government
(3) the system of two political parties
(4) the system of checks and balances

7 Congress established a minimum wage for workers and regulations on radio broadcasts by combining its delegated power to regulate interstate commerce with the

(1) sanctity of contract clause
(2) due process clause
(3) elastic clause
(4) writ of habeas corpus clause

8 Which concept found in the United States Constitution was a belief held by the social contract philosophers of the Enlightenment period?

(1) presidential cabinet
(2) judicial review
(3) limited monarchy
(4) sovereignty of the people

9 Court decisions in the trial of John Peter Zenger (1735) and the case of *New York Times Co. v. United States* (1971) strengthened

(1) freedom of religion
(2) freedom of the press
(3) due process rights
(4) the right to counsel

Base your answer to question 10 on the map below and on your knowledge of social studies.

The Presidential Election of 1860

Source: James West Davidson et al., *The American Nation*, Prentice Hall (adapted)

10 The election results shown on this map most clearly reflect the influence of

(1) nationalist motives
(2) sectional differences
(3) political stability
(4) ethnic conflicts

11 As Secretary of the Treasury, Alexander Hamilton was most noted for

(1) devising a plan to pay off the nation's debts
(2) beginning a system to tax exports
(3) arranging necessary loans from European nations
(4) raising revenue from the sale of western lands

Hamilton: Financial Plan — payoff
Strong Federal govt

12 On what grounds would strict constructionists of the United States Constitution have questioned the purchase of the Louisiana Territory?

(1) It violated the guarantee of states' rights.
(2) The president was not specifically given the power to purchase new land.
(3) Congress was opposed to expansion west of the Mississippi River.
(4) The Constitution applied only to the original thirteen states.

13 President Andrew Jackson claimed that use of the spoils system increased democracy in the federal government because it

(1) removed property-holding qualifications for voting
(2) limited the role of the electoral college in presidential elections
(3) allowed larger numbers of citizens to hold office
(4) used nominating conventions to pick political party candidates

14 Both the Missouri Compromise of 1820 and the Compromise of 1850 settled conflicts between the North and the South over

(1) admission of states to the Union
(2) Supreme Court decisions
(3) presidential election results
(4) voting rights

Base your answer to question 15 on the information below and on your knowledge of social studies.

> *To the Honorable Senate and House of Representatives in Congress Assembled,*
>
> *We the undersigned, citizens of the United States, but deprived of some of the privileges and immunities of citizens among which, is the right to vote, beg leave to submit the following resolution:*
>
> *Resolved; that we the officers and members of the National Woman Suffrage Association, in convention assembled, respectfully ask Congress to enact appropriate legislation during its present session to protect women citizens in the several states of this Union, in their right to vote.*
>
> — Susan B. Anthony, Matilda Joslyn Gage, and Elizabeth Cady Stanton (1873)

Source: National Archives and Records Administration

15 This resolution illustrates the constitutional right to

(1) petition for redress of grievances
(2) protection against unreasonable search and seizure
(3) a speedy and public trial
(4) freedom of religion

16 What was a major result of the Civil War?

(1) States now had the right to secede from the Union.
(2) Congress passed an amendment to provide for the direct election of senators.
(3) The power of the central government was strengthened.
(4) The judiciary became the dominant branch of the federal government.

17 Which statement describes a result of the Industrial Revolution in the United States?

(1) Farm production decreased.
(2) Slavery in the South increased.
(3) The population of the cities decreased.
(4) Immigration to the United States increased.

18 In the late 19th century, the federal government aided the growth of transcontinental railroads by

(1) legalizing rate rebates for large shippers
(2) providing free land for laying railroad tracks
(3) requiring standard-gauge tracks on all interstate lines
(4) forcing small lines to consolidate into large systems

19 The Populist movement was most interested in improving conditions for

(1) farmers
(2) business leaders
(3) African Americans
(4) Native American Indians

20 What was the main benefit that labor unions of the late 19th century gained for their members?

(1) job security
(2) improved wages and hours
(3) paid vacations
(4) health insurance

21 During the late 1800s, business leaders formed trusts mainly to

(1) reduce prices
(2) eliminate competition
(3) improve worker productivity
(4) establish overseas factories

Base your answer to question 22 on the cartoon below and on your knowledge of social studies.

Source: Herman Viola, *Why We Remember: United States History*, Scott Foresman–Addison Wesley Publishing Co. (adapted)

22 What is the main idea of this cartoon?

(1) The Standard Oil Company was a harmful monopoly.
(2) The best way to develop major industries was to form proprietorships.
(3) Government regulations were strangling the Standard Oil Company.
(4) Foreign competition in the oil industry was hurting American companies.

23 In the late 1800s, the theory of laissez-faire capitalism was used by many industrialists to

(1) petition the government for assistance during times of financial crisis
(2) oppose colonial expansion in Africa and Asia
(3) argue against government regulation of business practices
(4) defend limits on the number of immigrants allowed to work in factories

24 During the late 1800s, a major reason labor unions had difficulty achieving their goals was that

(1) government supported business over labor
(2) industrialization created better working conditions
(3) there was a shortage of new workers
(4) businesses promoted labor officials to management positions

Base your answers to questions 25 and 26 on the quotation below and on your knowledge of social studies.

". . . Whether they will or no, Americans must now begin to look outward. The growing production of the country demands it. An increasing volume of public sentiment demands it. . . ."

— Alfred T. Mahan, *The Atlantic Monthly,* December 1890

25 This statement encouraged popular support among Americans for

(1) isolationism   (3) neutrality
(2) protectionism   (4) imperialism

26 Supporters of Mahan's ideas most likely favored a foreign policy that would

(1) limit the military arms race
(2) acquire foreign markets
(3) abandon the Monroe Doctrine
(4) establish an international peace organization

27 Which president was known as a trustbuster?

(1) George Washington
(2) Calvin Coolidge
(3) Theodore Roosevelt
(4) Dwight Eisenhower

28 President Woodrow Wilson supported creation of the Federal Reserve System in 1913 to

 (1) balance the federal budget
 (2) regulate the amount of money in circulation
 (3) serve as a source of loans for farmers
 (4) solve the financial problems of the Great Depression

Base your answer to question 29 on the graph below and on your knowledge of social studies.

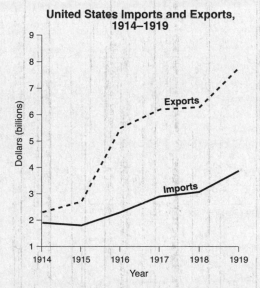

United States Imports and Exports, 1914–1919

Source: United States Bureau of the Census (adapted)

29 Data from this graph support the conclusion that World War I

 (1) caused the United States trade deficit to increase
 (2) cost the United States many billions of dollars
 (3) was a significant benefit to the American economy
 (4) created an unfavorable balance of trade

30 In the case *Schenck v. United States* (1919), the United States Supreme Court settled the issue of limits on individual freedoms during wartime by establishing the

 (1) clear and present danger test
 (2) states' rights principle
 (3) separate but equal doctrine
 (4) popular sovereignty principle

31 Many senators who opposed United States membership in the League of Nations argued that joining the League would

 (1) involve the nation in future military conflicts
 (2) reduce freedom of the seas
 (3) end the country's free-trade policy
 (4) endanger the nation's military preparedness

32 The economic boom of the 1920s was primarily caused by the

 (1) new economic policies of the League of Nations
 (2) development of new consumer goods industries
 (3) advent of advertising on radio
 (4) elimination of barriers to international trade

33 During most of the 1920s, which group experienced the most severe economic problems?

 (1) owners of small family farms
 (2) workers in the automobile industry
 (3) bankers in urban centers
 (4) entertainers in the field of radio

34 New Deal programs such as the Civilian Conservation Corps (CCC) and the Works Progress Administration (WPA) were primarily intended to help

 (1) farmers
 (2) homeowners
 (3) businesses
 (4) unemployed workers

35 Passage of the Neutrality Acts of 1935 and 1937 indicated that the United States desired to

 (1) isolate itself from conflicts in Europe and Asia
 (2) form alliances to stop the aggression of dictators
 (3) expand trade outside the Western Hemisphere
 (4) support the policies of the League of Nations

Base your answer to question 36 on the map below and on your knowledge of social studies.

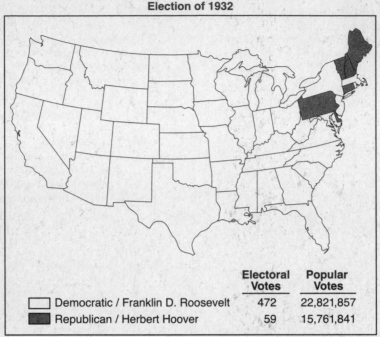

Election of 1932

	Electoral Votes	Popular Votes
☐ Democratic / Franklin D. Roosevelt	472	22,821,857
■ Republican / Herbert Hoover	59	15,761,841

Source: http://www.archives.gov/federalregister/electoralcollege/votes (adapted)

36 What was the most likely cause of the election results shown on the map?

(1) Most voters blamed President Herbert Hoover for the Great Depression.
(2) It is difficult to defeat an incumbent president.
(3) Franklin D. Roosevelt had more business experience than Herbert Hoover.
(4) Republican Party popularity had been declining for several elections.

37 Congress refused to enact President Franklin D. Roosevelt's court-packing plan because the plan

(1) threatened to upset the constitutional system of checks and balances
(2) entrusted too much power to the judicial branch
(3) called for an increase in income taxes
(4) required passage of a constitutional amendment

38 Which federal policy was enacted during World War II and justified as a wartime necessity?

(1) a ban on German-language books
(2) internment of Japanese Americans
(3) exclusion of Chinese immigrants
(4) adoption of the quota system of immigration

39 In 1944, Congress enacted the GI Bill of Rights in order to

(1) provide economic aid to veterans
(2) reduce military expenditures
(3) ban racial segregation in the armed forces
(4) create government jobs for returning soldiers

Base your answer to question 40 on the poster below and on your knowledge of social studies.

KEEP THESE HANDS OFF!

BUY the New VICTORY BONDS

Source: G. K. Odell, National Archives and Records Administration

40 During World War II, this poster was used primarily to

(1) contain the spread of communism
(2) create jobs for the unemployed
(3) gain financial support for the war
(4) convince women to fill vacant factory jobs

41 Since the 1950s, the term *McCarthyism* has been applied to events that are related to

(1) the basic rights of citizens to own and carry guns
(2) the violent activities of international terrorists
(3) reckless accusations unsupported by evidence
(4) questionable methods used to finance political campaigns

Base your answers to questions 42 and 43 on the speakers' statements below and on your knowledge of social studies.

Speaker A: "We have to take care of our own problems. If we get too involved in the world's affairs, we'll get dragged into conflicts that have nothing to do with our own security."

Speaker B: "This world is different now. Two oceans can no longer protect us. We have to take a leading role in order to stop problems before they harm our economic and security interests. We need collective security, and we have to help our allies to be economically strong."

Speaker C: "Perhaps if we had taken an active part in international peacekeeping organizations in the past, we wouldn't have to take on the superpower role that we face now. Now we must get more involved and meet our international obligations."

Speaker D: "The arms makers and the bankers got us involved in war. The Europeans are only interested in gaining territory. Let them solve their own problems."

42 Which speakers reflect the foreign policy beliefs of the Truman administration after World War II?

(1) A and B   (3) B and C
(2) A and D   (4) C and D

43 The statements of Speakers *A* and *D* express support for the policy of

(1) containment   (3) internationalism
(2) imperialism   (4) isolationism

44 In 1957, the Eisenhower Doctrine expanded the principles of the Truman Doctrine by extending Middle East military assistance in order to

(1) offset communist influence in the region
(2) combat anti-American terrorist threats
(3) force the Organization of Petroleum Exporting Countries (OPEC) to end its oil embargo
(4) defend Israel against Arab invasions

45 The immediate impact of the 1957 launch of *Sputnik I* was that it

(1) forced the United States to find new sources of fuel
(2) focused attention on the need to regulate the uses of outer space
(3) heightened the space race as a form of Cold War competition
(4) ended the period of peaceful coexistence between the United States and the Soviet Union

46 President John F. Kennedy supported the 1961 Bay of Pigs invasion of Cuba as an effort to

(1) remove a communist dictator from power
(2) stop the flow of illegal drugs to the United States
(3) support Fidel Castro's efforts for reform
(4) rescue hostages held by Cuban freedom fighters

47 Supreme Court decisions in *Mapp* v. *Ohio*, *Gideon* v. *Wainwright,* and *Miranda* v. *Arizona* affected individual liberties by

(1) eliminating the poll tax as a voting requirement
(2) preventing the use of organized prayer in public schools
(3) requiring equal pay for men and women performing the same job
(4) expanding the constitutional rights of people accused of crimes

48 *The Feminine Mystique* by Betty Friedan was an influential book in the 1960s because it

(1) helped strengthen family values
(2) led directly to the defeat of the Equal Rights Amendment
(3) energized a new women's rights movement
(4) reinforced the importance of women's traditional roles

49 The trial of Sacco and Vanzetti in the 1920s was similar to the trial of the Rosenbergs in the 1950s in that both trials were accompanied by

(1) nativist fears of foreign influence in the United States
(2) concern that the United States would sink into a depression
(3) public reactions against organized crime
(4) a grassroots movement to gain equal rights for minorities

50 Which United States foreign policy action resulted from the close geographic relationship between the United States and Latin America?

(1) Monroe Doctrine   (3) Marshall Plan
(2) Truman Doctrine   (4) Open Door policy

Answers to the essay questions are to be written in the separate essay booklet.

In developing your answer to Part II, be sure to keep these general definitions in mind:

(a) <u>discuss</u> means "to make observations about something using facts, reasoning, and argument; to present in some detail"
(b) <u>evaluate</u> means "to examine and judge the significance, worth, or condition of; to determine the value of"

Part II

THEMATIC ESSAY QUESTION

Directions: Write a well-organized essay that includes an introduction, several paragraphs addressing the task below, and a conclusion.

Theme: Foreign Policy

> During the course of its history, the United States has taken foreign policy actions that have been consistent with the national interest.

Task:

> Identify *two* events in United States history that demonstrate how the United States has promoted the national interest by taking foreign policy actions and for *each* event:
>
> • Discuss the historical circumstances that led the United States to take that action
> • Evaluate the success or failure of that foreign policy action in promoting the national interest of the United States

You may use any events from your study of United States history. Some suggestions you might wish to consider include President George Washington's Proclamation of Neutrality (1793), congressional declaration of war against Mexico (1846), acquisition of the rights to build the Panama Canal (1901), United States entry into World War I (1917), implementation of the Marshall Plan (1947), United States entry into the Korean War (1950), escalation of the Vietnam War beginning in 1964, and President Jimmy Carter's efforts to negotiate the Camp David Accords (1978).

You are *not* limited to these suggestions.

Guidelines:

In your essay, be sure to:
• Address all aspects of the *Task*
• Support the theme with relevant facts, examples, and details
• Use a logical and clear plan of organization
• Introduce the theme by establishing a framework that is beyond a simple restatement of the *Task* and conclude with a summation of the theme

NAME_____   SCHOOL_____

In developing your answer to Part III, be sure to keep these general definitions in mind:

(a) <u>discuss</u> means "to make observations about something using facts, reasoning, and argument; to present in some detail"
(b) <u>describe</u> means "to illustrate something in words or tell about it"

Part III

DOCUMENT-BASED QUESTION

This question is based on the accompanying documents (1–6). The question is designed to test your ability to work with historical documents. Some of the documents have been edited for the purposes of the question. As you analyze the documents, take into account the source of each document and any point of view that may be presented in the document.

Historical Context:

> Since 1900, African Americans and women have had difficulty achieving their civil rights. The government, groups, and individuals have taken actions to help African Americans and women achieve their civil rights.

Task: Using information from the documents and your knowledge of United States history, answer the questions that follow each document in Part A. Your answers to the questions will help you write the Part B essay in which you will be asked to:

> - Discuss problems experienced by African Americans and problems experienced by women in achieving their civil rights since 1900
> - For *each* problem, describe *one* action taken by the government, a group, or an individual in an attempt to help African Americans and women achieve their civil rights

Part A

Short-Answer Questions

Directions: Analyze the documents and answer the short-answer questions that follow each document in the space provided.

Document 1

Adoption of Voting Restrictions in Southern States 1889–1908					
Year	Poll Tax	Literacy Test	Property Test	Grandfather Clause	Other*
1889	FL				TN, FL
1890	MS, TN	MS			MS
1891					AR
1892	AR				
1893					AL
1894					SC, VA
1895	SC	SC			SC
1896					
1897					LA
1898	LA	LA	LA	LA	
1899					NC
1900	NC	NC	NC	NC	
1901	AL	AL	AL	AL	
1902	VA, TX	VA	VA		VA
1903					
1904					
1905					
1906					
1907					
1908		GA	GA	GA	GA

KEY

Alabama	AL
Arkansas	AR
Florida	FL
Georgia	GA
Louisiana	LA
Mississippi	MS
North Carolina	NC
South Carolina	SC
Tennessee	TN
Texas	TX
Virginia	VA

*Registration, multiple-box, secret ballot, understanding clause.

Source: *The American Record: Images of the Nation's Past, Volume Two,*
edited by William Graebner and Leonard Richards (adapted)

1 Based on this chart, state **two** methods used by southern states to deny the vote to African Americans.   [2]

(1) _____

Score ▢

(2) _____

Score ▢

Document 2

> . . . The great doctrine of the American Republic that "all governments derive their just powers from the consent of the governed" justifies the plea of one-half of the people, the women, to exercise the suffrage. The doctrine of the American Revolutionary War that taxation without representation is unendurable justifies women in exercising the suffrage.

— Oklahoma Senator Robert L. Owen, 1910

2 What problem is described in this quotation?   [1]

_____

_____

Score ☐

Document 3

WHO SHARES THE COST OF WAR?

Who face death in order to give life to men?   **WOMEN.**

Who love and work to rear the sons who then are killed in battle?   **WOMEN.**

Who plant fields and harvest crops when all the able-bodied men are called to war?   **WOMEN.**

Who keep shops and schools and work in factories while men are in the trenches?   **WOMEN.**

Who nurse the wounded, feed the sick, support the helpless, brave all danger?   **WOMEN.**

Who see their homes destroyed by shell and fire, their little ones made destitute, their daughters outraged?   **WOMEN.**

Who are sent adrift, alone, no food, no hope, no shelter for the unborn child?   **WOMEN.**

Who must suffer agony for every soldier killed?   **WOMEN.**

Who are called upon to make sacrifices to pay the terrible tax of war?   **WOMEN.**

Who dares say that war is not their business? In the name of Justice and Civilization give women a voice in Government and in the councils that make or prevent war.

VOTE for the WOMAN SUFFRAGE AMENDMENT IN NOVEMBER

PENNSYLVANIA WOMAN SUFFRAGE ASSOCIATION
Headquarters: 201-5 Arcade Building, Harrisburg

N. W. S. Publishing Co., Inc.

Source: Library of Congress, Rare Book and Special Collections Division, (adapted)

3 According to this poster, what were *two* reasons that people should vote in favor of the 19th Amendment supporting women's suffrage?   [2]

(1) _____

Score ▢

(2) _____

Score ▢

Document 4

The major sections [titles] of the Civil Rights Act of 1964 included these provisions:

(1) Title I banned the use of different voter registration standards for blacks and whites.

(2) Title II prohibited discrimination in public accommodations, such as motels, restaurants, gas stations, theaters, and sports arenas.

(3) Title VI allowed the withholding of federal funds from public or private programs that practice discrimination.

(4) Title VII banned discrimination on the basis of race, sex, religion, or national origin by employers and unions.

(5) Title VII also created the Equal Employment Opportunity Commission (EEOC) to investigate charges of job discrimination.

4 Based on this document, state *two* provisions of the Civil Rights Act of 1964 that attempted to end discrimination for African Americans and women.   [2]

(1) _____

Score [ ]

(2) _____

Score [ ]

Document 5

> . . . I ask the Congress under the power clearly granted by the 15th amendment to enact legislation [Voting Rights Bill] which would:
>
> 1. Strike down restrictions to voting in all elections—Federal, State, and local—which have been used to deny Negroes the right to vote.
>
> 2. Establish in all States and counties where the right to vote has been denied on account of race a simple standard of voter registration which will make it impossible to thwart the 15th amendment.
>
> 3. Prohibit the use of new tests and devices wherever they may be used for discriminatory purposes.
>
> 4. Provide adequate power to insure, if necessary, that Federal officials can perform functions essential to the right to vote whenever State officials deny that right. . . .

— President Lyndon B. Johnson, Message to the House of Representatives, March 15, 1965
Source: *Congressional Record*

5 According to this passage, what was the main purpose of the Voting Rights Bill? [1]

_____

_____

Score ☐

Document 6

... Until the Equal Pay Act of 1963, only the state of Wyoming had passed an equal pay law for employees of the state government. The federal act provided equal pay for men and women in jobs requiring equal skill, responsibility, and effort. Although to help insure passage it excluded business and professional women, as well as almost two-thirds of working women, especially low-paid women in agriculture and domestic service from its provisions, the Equal Pay Act represented the first significant step toward ending wage discrimination for women workers. In 1963 full-time, year-round female workers were earning on average 63 percent less than male workers. By 1971 the disparity had dropped to 57 percent; and by the twenty-fifth anniversary of the act in 1998, the gap had closed to under 25 percent. Because there is an imprecision in determining what constitutes equal skill, responsibility, and effort, enforcement of the Equal Pay Act has proven difficult, and the disparity of wages between men and women has not yet been corrected. However, feminists and equal rights advocates have achieved success in court cases that consider comparable worth in job descriptions and wages, and women have won numerous lawsuits in the 1980s and 1990s, particularly in city and state jobs in which qualifications and requirements are more precisely quantified. The Equal Pay Act of 1963 has, despite slow gains, helped change attitudes and employment practices that in some cases have ended and in others mitigated [relieved] wage discrimination. . . .

Source: Deborah G. Felder, *A Century of Women: The Most Influential Events In Twentieth-Century Women's History,* Birch Lane Press

6 According to this author, how did the Equal Pay Act affect women workers?   [1]

_____

_____

Score [ ]

Part B

Essay

Directions: Write a well-organized essay that includes an introduction, several paragraphs, and a conclusion. Use evidence from at least *four* documents in the body of the essay. Support your response with relevant facts, examples, and details. Include additional outside information.

Historical Context:

Since 1900, African Americans and women have had difficulty achieving their civil rights. The government, groups, and individuals have taken actions to help African Americans and women achieve their civil rights.

Task: Using information from the documents and your knowledge of United States history, write an essay in which you:

> - Discuss problems experienced by African Americans and problems experienced by women in achieving their civil rights since 1900
> - For *each* problem, describe *one* action taken by the government, a group, or an individual in an attempt to help African Americans and women achieve their civil rights

Guidelines:

In your essay, be sure to:

- Address all aspects of the *Task* by accurately analyzing and interpreting at least *four* documents
- Incorporate information from the documents in the body of the essay
- Incorporate relevant outside information
- Support the theme with relevant facts, examples, and details
- Use a logical and clear plan of organization
- Introduce the theme by establishing a framework that is beyond a simple restatement of the *Task* or *Historical Context* and conclude with a summation of the theme

Glossary

abolitionist: a person seeking the legal end of slavery

affirmative action: steps taken to increase the representation of women and minorities, especially in jobs and higher education

AFL/CIO: influential labor union consisting of a merger between the American Federation of Labor and the Congress of Industrial Organizations in 1955

agrarian protest: demands by farmers for improvements in areas affecting agriculture, especially in the late 1800s

alien: a citizen of a foreign country

alliance: a group of nations mutually allied by treaty

Allies: the World War I alliance of Great Britain, France, Russia, and later the United States; also the World War II alliance of Great Britain, the United States, the Soviet Union, and other nations

al-Qaeda: world terrorist organization responsible for September 11, 2001 attacks on the World Trade Center and the Pentagon, led by Osama bin Laden

amendment: a change in or addition to a legal document, motion, bylaw, law, or constitution

American system: a plan offered by Henry Clay for internal improvements

annex: to attach new territory to an existing area, such as a country

Antifederalist: a person opposed to the Constitution during the ratification debate of 1787

anti-Semitism: prejudice against Jews

antitrust: opposed to practices and agreements that restrict trade, such as monopolies, price-fixing, and trusts

appeasement: the policy of giving in to an aggressor's demands in order to keep the peace

appellate jurisdiction: the authority of a court to review the decisions of inferior (lower) courts

Articles of Confederation: the first American constitution

assassination: the murder of a public figure

assembly line: a method of production in which automobiles or other items being manufactured move past workers and machines and are assembled piece by piece until completed

assimilation: the process of becoming part of another culture

assumption plan: the taking over of state debts by the federal government after the American Revolution

atomic age: a term used to describe period begun by the explosion of the first atomic bomb in 1945

baby boom: the rapid growth in the population of the United States between 1945 and 1964

balance of power: distribution of political and economic power that prevents any one nation from becoming too strong

balance of terror: a balance of power achieved when opposing sides possess nuclear weapons

balance of trade: the difference in value between a nation's imports and its exports

bankruptcy: a court action to release a person or corporation from unpaid debts

belligerents: nations fighting a war, usually after a declaration of war

bicameral legislature: a lawmaking body composed of two houses

big business: corporations or monopolies seen as having too much control over a society and its economy

bill: a proposal presented to a legislative body for possible enactment as law

Bill of Rights: the first 10 amendments to the U.S. Constitution, dealing mostly with civil rights

bipartisan: supported by two political parties

Black Codes: laws passed, especially by southern states after the Civil War, to control the actions and limit the rights of African Americans

blacklist: a list, circulated among employers, of people who will not be hired because of their views, beliefs, or actions

blitzkrieg: a sudden invasion or "lightning war," first practiced by Germany in World War II

blockade: the shutting off of a port to keep people or supplies from moving in or out

blue-collar worker: someone who holds and industrial or factory job

boycott: an organized refusal to buy or use a product or service, or to deal with a company or group of companies, as a protest or as a means to force them to take some action

brinkmanship: the policy of being willing to go "to the brink" of war to preserve peace

bureaucracy: a collective term for all of the workers who run the agencies that do the everyday business of government

cabinet: the group of officials who head government departments and advise the President

capitalism: the economic system based on private initiative, competition, profit, and the private ownership of the means of producing goods and services

carpetbagger: pejorative name for a Northerner who went to the South during Reconstruction

checks and balances: the system set up by the U.S. Constitution in which each branch of the federal government has the power to limit the actions of the other branches

citizen: a person who by birth or naturalization owes loyalty to, and receives the protection of, a nation's government

citizenship: the duties, rights, and privileges of a citizen

civil disobedience: nonviolent protest against unjust laws

civil liberties: certain rights guaranteed to all citizens of a nation

civil rights: rights guaranteed to citizens by the U.S. Constitution and laws of the nation

civil service: government jobs for which appointments and promotions are now based on merit rather than on political patronage

closed shop: a workplace in which employees must be labor union members in order to be hired

coalition: an alliance of political groups

Cold War: the state of tension between the United States and the Soviet Union after World War II

collective bargaining: the process by which a union negotiates with management for a contract

collective security: a system in which member nations agree to take joint action to meet any threat or breach of international peace

colonialism: the practice under which a nation takes control of other lands for its economic, military, or other use

colony: a settlement of people in a distant land who are ruled by a government of their native land

commerce clause: Article I, Section 8, Clause 3 of the U.S. Constitution, which gives Congress the power to regulate trade

committee system: method under which members of the legislative branch form into smaller groups to facilitate such business as considering proposed legislation and holding investigations

communism: the economic system based on the collective ownership of property and the means of production, with all individuals expected to contribute to society according to their abilities and to receive from it according to their needs

compromise: the resolution of conflict in which concessions are made by all parties to achieve a common goal

concentration camp: a place where political opponents or other "enemies" of a nation are forcibly confined, especially those established by Nazi Germany before and during World War II

concurrent powers: powers shared by the national and state governments

confederation: an alliance of independent states

conference committee: a temporary joint committee of both houses of a legislature, created to reconcile differences between the two houses' version of a bill

conglomerate: a corporation that owns many different, unrelated businesses

Congress: the legislative, or lawmaking, branch of the United States government, made up of the Senate and the House of Representatives

consent of the governed: principle that says people are the source of the powers of government

conservation: the careful use or preserving of natural resources

conspicuous consumption: public enjoyment of costly possessions done in such a way as to emphasize the fact that one can afford such possessions

constitution: body of fundamental law, setting out the basic principles, structures, processes, and functions of a government and placing limits on its actions; (Cap.) the supreme law of the United States

constitutional: permissible under the Constitution

Constitutional Convention: formal meeting of state delegates in Philadelphia in 1787 at which the Constitution was written

consumer: person who spends money on goods and services

consumer goods: goods produced for use by individuals as opposed to use by businesses

consumerism: the practice of protecting consumers by publicizing defective and unsafe products or misleading business practices

consumer protection: measures to shield buyers of goods and services from unsafe products and unfair or illegal sales practices

containment: the U.S. policy after World War II of trying to keep the Soviet Union from expanding its area of influence and dominance

corporation: business owned by many investors that raises money by selling stocks or shares to those investors

court packing: Franklin Roosevelt's 1937 plan to add justices to the Supreme Court

credit: delayed payment for goods or services

creditor nation: a nation that is owed money by other nations

cultural diversity: many cultures existing in the same society

cultural pluralism: the idea that different cultures can exist side by side in the same society, all contributing to the society without losing their identities

culture: the way of life of a given people

custom: a habit or practice so established that it has the force of law

debtor nation: a nation that owes money to another nation or nations

Declaration of Independence: the 1776 document that stated Britain's North American colonies had become free and independent of the parent country

deficit: the amount by which money spent is greater than money received

deficit spending: government practice of spending more money than it takes in from taxes and other revenues

delegated powers: powers given by the Constitution to the national government and denied to state governments

demagogue: a person who gains political power by rousing the passions of the people

demobilization: the process by which a nation reconverts to peacetime status after a war or the threat of war

democracy: system of government in which supreme authority rests with the people, either directly or through elected representatives

Democratic party: one of the modern political parties, descended from Jefferson's Democratic-Republican party; also one of the oldest continuous political parties in the world

Democratic-Republican party: one of the first political parties in the United States, led by Jefferson and other leaders who were opposed to the Federalists; also known as Jeffersonian Republicans

demography: the study of populations through statistics

depression: a long and severe decline in economic activity

détente: the easing of tension between nations

dictatorship: form of government in which the power to govern is held by one person or a small group

direct democracy: system of government in which the people participate directly in decision making through the voting process

direct election of senators: system put into practice under the Seventeenth Amendment whereby the voters rather than the state legislatures elect members of the U.S. Senate

disarmament: reduction of a nation's armed forces or weapons of war

discrimination: policy or attitude that denies rights to people based on race, religion, sex, or other characteristics

disestablishment: depriving a state church of official support from the government, or never allowing a state church to be founded

diversity: variety

divestiture: a refusal to hold stock in companies that have operations in South Africa

division of powers: basic principle of federalism; the constitutional provisions by which governmental powers are divided between the national and the state governments

dollar diplomacy: President Taft's policy of encouraging United States investment in Latin America

domestic policy: everything a nation's government says and does in relation to internal matters

domino theory: the idea, prevalent during the Vietnam War, that if one Asian nation became Communist, neighboring nations would as well

due process of law: constitutional guarantee that government will not deprive any person of life, liberty, or property by any unfair, arbitrary, or unreasonable action

economic: pertaining to production, distribution, and use of wealth

economic nationalism: policies focused on improving the economy of one's own nation

economic programs: any policies set forward by a government that relate to the workings of its economy

elastic clause: Article I, Section 8, Clause 18 of the Constitution, which is the basis for the implied powers of Congress

electoral college: an assembly elected by the voters that meets every four years to formally elect the President of the United States

electoral vote: the results of the voting by the electoral college

electorate: all the persons entitled to vote in a given election

emancipation: the act of setting a person or people free

Emancipation Proclamation: the Presidential decree, effective January 1, 1863, that freed slaves in Confederate-held territory

empathy: the process of sharing and understanding the feelings or thoughts of another person

English Bill of Rights: the 1689 agreement between Parliament and William and Mary which established that representative government and the rule of law outweighed the power of any monarch

Enlightenment: Eighteenth-century movement that emphasized science and reason as key to improving society

entrepreneur: a person who organizes, operates, and assumes the risks of a business enterprise

environment: natural surroundings and all the things that make them up

equal protection under the law: a right guaranteed to American citizens under the Fourteenth Amendment

espionage: spying

ethnic group: people of foreign birth or descent living in another country

European Economic Community: organization, also known as the Common Market, formed in 1957 to ease trade and travel among member European nations

European Union: the economic organization of European nations designed to increase the economic power of Europe in the world economy

excise tax: taxes levied on the production, transportation, sale, or consumption of goods or services

executive branch: part of a government that carries out its laws

executive power: the powers of the head of an executive branch of government to carry out the laws

executive privilege: the right claimed by Presidents to withhold information from the legislative or judicial branches

expansionism: desire to enlarge the territory owned or controlled by one's nation

expatriate: a person who gives up her or his homeland to live in another country

expressed powers: those delegated powers of the national government that are given to it in so many words by the Constitution

farm output: total value of products produced by a nation's farms

fascism: political philosophy that calls for glorification of the state, a single party system with a strong ruler, and aggressive nationalism

federal government: the central or national government

federalism: a system of government in which authority is divided between national and state governments; the belief in or advocacy of such a system

Federalist: supporter of the Constitution in the ratification debate of 1787, favored a strong national government

Federalist Party: one of the first political parties in the United States, organized by those who favored the ratification of the Constitution

Federal Reserve System: the nation's central banking system, established in 1913; a system of 12 regional banks overseen by a central board

feminist movement: the struggle of women for equality

First Amendment: Bill of Rights' guarantee of freedom of religion, speech, press, assembly, and petition

fiscal policy: policies relating to a nation's finances

flapper: nickname for a young woman in the 1920s who declared her independence from traditional rules

foreign policy: the actions and stands that every nation takes in every aspect of its relationships with other countries; everything a nation's government says and does in world affairs

Fourteen Points: President Woodrow Wilson's proposal in 1918 for a postwar European peace

Fourteenth Amendment: "due process" amendment that gave African Americans the right to vote and extended Bill of Rights protections to citizens of the states

free enterprise: an economic system based on private ownership, individual enterprise, and competition

freedom of speech: the right of freedom of expression guaranteed to Americans by the First Amendment

frontier: the border of a country; as defined by the U.S. Bureau of the Census, the edge of settlement beyond which the land was occupied by two or fewer people per square mile

frontier thesis: idea set forth by historian Frederick Jackson Turner that the nation's frontier regions shaped its character and institutions

Fugitive Slave Law: part of the Compromise of 1850, the Fugitive Slave Law required all citizens to help catch runaway slaves.

fundamentalist: one who believes that the Bible is the literal word of God

General Agreement on Tariffs and Trade (GATT): international agreement on reducing tariffs and expanding world trade

genocide: the systematic destruction of a race of people

Gentlemen's Agreement: informal agreement between the United States and Japan in 1907 to limit Japanese immigration to this country

Gettysburg Address: famous speech by President Abraham Lincoln on the meaning of the Civil War, given in November 1863 at the dedication of a national cemetery on the site of the Battle of Gettysburg

ghetto: area in which many members of some minority group live, to which they are restricted by economic pressure or social discrimination

Gilded Age: term used to describe the period from 1865 to 1900

glasnost: a period of "openness" in relations between the United States and the Soviet Union that began in the late 1980s

global interdependence: the idea that the nations of the world must rely on each other in many different ways, including trade, transportation, and communication

Glorious Revolution: the bloodless revolution in 1689 in which the English Parliament overthrew James II and replaced him with William and Mary

gold standard: a system in which a nation's currency is based on the value of gold

Good Neighbor Policy: Franklin D. Roosevelt's policy toward Latin America intended to strengthen relations with the nations of that region

government: that complex of offices, personnel, and processes by which a state is ruled, and by which its public policies are made and enforced

grandfather clause: laws passed in some southern states giving the right to vote only to people who had that right on January 1, 1867, and their descendants; intended to keep blacks from voting

Grangers, The: organization of farmers founded for social reasons in 1867, which later campaigned for state regulation of railroads and other reforms

grass-roots support: political backing from ordinary citizens, especially from rural areas

Great Compromise: the plan for a two-house legislature adopted at the Constitutional Convention in 1787 that settled differences between large and small states over representation in Congress

Great Depression: period of economic hard times from 1929 to 1941

Great Migration: migration of English settlers to the Massachusetts Bay Colony beginning in the 1630s

Great Society: the name given to President Johnson's domestic program in the 1960s

gross national product (GNP): the total value of all the goods and services produced in a nation in a year

guerrilla warfare: fighting by stealth and with small bands, which make surprise raids against stronger forces

hemisphere: half of the earth's surface

holding company: a company that gains control of other companies by buying their stock

Holocaust: name given to Nazi Germany's persecution of Jews before and during World War II; in this time, more than 6 million Jews died

Homestead Act: 1862 law that offered 160 acres of western land to settlers

House of Representatives: lower house of the U.S. Congress in which states are represented according to the size of their populations

humanitarian: one who is concerned with the welfare of all people

human rights: basic rights that should belong to all people including freedom of speech, religion, and the press

immigration: the movement of people from other countries into a country

immigration laws: laws controlling the movement of people into a country

immigration quota: limit on immigration allowing only a certain number of people to move into a country during a specified period

impeachment: the process by which the House of Representatives makes an accusation of wrongdoing against the President or other high federal officials

imperialism: policy by which one country takes control of another either directly or through economic or political dominance

implied powers: those delegated powers of the national government implied by (inferred from) the expressed powers; those powers "necessary and proper" to carry out the expressed powers

income tax: a tax levied on individual and corporate income

incumbent: person currently occupying a political office at the time of a new election

indemnities: money paid by a losing nation to a winning nation after a war

independence: freedom from the control, influence, or support of other people or nations

Indian Removal Policy: under President Andrew Jackson, the policy of moving all Native Americans to lands west of the Mississippi River in the 1830s

individual rights: basic rights that belong to each person

industrialization: process by which a nation begins to develop large industries

inflation: an economic condition in which prices rise substantially over a significant period of time

injunction: a court order prohibiting a given action; used frequently against workers in nineteenth-century labor-management disputes

interdependence: a condition in which parties are reliant on each other

internal affairs: public or business matters within the boundaries of a country

internal improvements: roads, bridges, canals, and other similar projects funded by the national government

internationalism: the belief, held by some Americans in the 1930s, that the United States should aid the victims of international aggression

international law: the norms of behavior generally agreed to and followed by the nations of the world in their dealings with each other

internment camps: places of confinement, especially in wartime

interstate commerce: trade among the states

intervention: interference by one nation in the affairs of another

intrastate commerce: trade within the borders of a state

Iron Curtain: the line between Soviet-dominated Eastern Europe and the West, so-called because the Soviets and their satellite nations prevented the free passage of people, information, and ideas across their borders

isolationism: a policy of avoiding alliances and other types of involvement in the affairs of other nations

isthmus: a narrow strip or neck of land running from one larger land area to another

Japanese-American relocation: policy under which Americans of Japanese ancestry were confined during World War II

Jim Crow laws: laws in the Southern states in the nineteenth and twentieth centuries that forced the segregation of the races

jingoism: aggressive nationalism

joint resolution: legislative measure which must be passed by both houses and approved by the chief executive to become effective; similar to a bill, with the force of law, and often used for unusual or temporary circumstances

judicial activism: broad interpretation of the Constitution leading to court-directed change

judicial branch: part of the government that decides if laws are carried out fairly

judicial restraint: narrow interpretation of the Constitution

judicial review: power of the Supreme Court to determine the constitutionality of acts of the legislative and executive branches of the government

judiciary: judicial branch of a government, its system of courts

jurisdiction: power of a court to hear (to try and decide) a case

jury: a group of people who hear evidence in a legal case and give a decision based on that evidence

justice: fairness; trial and judgment according to established process of the law

Know-Nothing party: common name for the American party, a nativist political organization formed in 1849

Korean War: conflict over the future of the Korean peninsula, fought between 1950 and 1953 and ending in a stalemate

Ku Klux Klan: secret society first formed in the South during Reconstruction to ensure white supremacy over blacks; reformed in the 1920s to express opposition to Jews, Catholics, Bolsheviks, and others considered "un-American"

labor union: workers organized as a group to seek higher wages, improve working conditions, and obtain other benefits

laissez-faire: noninterference; has come to mean a policy by which the government minimizes its regulation of industry and the economy

landslide election: an election in which a victorious candidate gathers an overwhelming percentage of the total votes cast

law: rule recognized by a nation, state, or community as binding on its members

League of Nations: association of nations to protect the independence of member nations, proposed by President Wilson in his Fourteen Points and formed after World War I

legislative branch: the lawmaking agencies of a government

legislature: group of people with the power of making laws for a nation or state

less developed nations: nations that have not fully industrialized, usually Third World nations

lifespan: the lifetime of an individual

limited government: basic principle of the American system of government; belief that government is not all-powerful, and may only do those things the people have given it the power to do

Lincoln-Douglas debates: the series of political debates between Stephen Douglas and Abraham Lincoln during the Senate campaign of 1858, which catapulted Lincoln to the national spotlight

literacy: the ability to read and write

literacy test: test of a potential voter's ability to read and write; once used in several states to prevent blacks and other minorities from voting; now outlawed

lobby: to attempt to influence legislation; also, groups that attempt to do so

lockout: during a labor dispute, the closing of a business (by locking the gates) to keep employees from entering

loose interpretation: a belief that the provisions of the Constitution, especially those granting power to the government, are to be construed in broad terms

Louisiana Purchase: purchase by the United States of the Louisiana Territory from France in 1803

lynch: to execute someone illegally, by hanging, burning, or other means

majority: at least one more than half (e.g., over 50 percent of the votes in an election)

Manhattan Project: secret American program during World War II to develop an atomic bomb

Manifest Destiny: a belief held in the first half of the nineteenth century that the United States had a mission to expand its borders to incorporate all land between the Atlantic and Pacific oceans

margin: a small part of the total price of a stock purchase deposited with a broker at the time of purchase with the promise to pay the full sum at a later date

Marshall Court: the Supreme Court during the tenure of John Marshall as chief justice, in which key decisions were made that strengthened the federal government's role in the nation's economic business

mass circulation: reaching a very large audience

mass production: rapid manufacture of large numbers of a product

Mayflower Compact: agreement signed by Pilgrims before landing at Plymouth

McCarthyism: the use of indiscriminate and unfounded accusations and sensationalist investigative methods to suppress political opponents portrayed as subversive; term taken from the name of Senator Joseph McCarthy, who carried out such practices

melting pot theory: the idea that different immigrant groups in the United States will lose their old identities and that a new American identity will emerge from the blending of cultures

mercantilism: economic theory that a nation's strength came from building up its gold supplies and expanding its trade

merger: a combining of two or more companies into a larger company

Mexican Cession: lands turned over to the United States after the Mexican War in what is now the states of California, Nevada, Utah, and parts of Wyoming, Colorado, Arizona, and New Mexico

Mexican War: conflict between the United States and Mexico from 1846 to 1848, ending with a victory for the United States

militarism: policy of building up strong military forces to prepare for war

minimum wage: the lowest wage that can be paid to certain workers as set by national or state law

minority: less than half

minority group: group within a nation that differs from most of the population in race, religion, national origin, etc.

minor party: one of the less widely supported political parties in a governmental system

missionary: one who attempts to spread the religious ideas of a faith in a foreign land

mobilization: a call-up of military forces, usually in preparation for war

monarchy: government headed by a single ruler, usually a king or queen

monetary policy: actions and positions taken by a government in regard to its system of money

monopoly: dominance in or control of a market for certain goods or services by a single company or combination of companies

Monroe Doctrine: policy statement of President James Monroe in 1823 warning nations of western Europe not to interfere with the newly independent nations of Latin America

moral diplomacy: a term describing President Woodrow Wilson's approach to foreign policy, which emphasized the use of negotiation and arbitration rather than force to settle international disputes

Mormons: members of the Church of Jesus Christ of Latter-day Saints; in the 1840s, thousands moved to Utah seeking freedom from religious persecution

muckraker: early twentieth-century American journalist who tried to improve society by exposing political corruption, health hazards, and other social problems

multilateral action: joint action taken by three or more nations

municipal government: the government of a city, town, or village

National Association for the Advancement of Colored People (NAACP): an organization founded in 1909 to fight for the rights of African Americans

national bank: bank chartered by the federal government

national government: in the United States, the federal government

nationalism: pride in or devotion to one's country

National Organization for Women (NOW): founded in 1966 to work for equal rights for women

national self interest: aim of all foreign policy

nativism: a belief in the superiority of the way of life of one's home country; in the United States, this was often associated with a desire to limit immigration

North Atlantic Treaty Organization (NATO): an alliance formed for mutual defense in 1949 under the North Atlantic Treaty, and now made up of 15 nations stretching from Canada to Turkey

naturalization: the process by which a citizen of one country becomes a citizen of another

natural rights: rights that all people are entitled to from birth

Nazism: belief in the policies of Adolf Hitler

necessary and proper clause: another name for the elastic clause, which is the basis of the implied powers of Congress

negotiation: talking over an issue by two or more parties with the aim of reaching a mutually agreeable settlement

neutrality: the policy of not taking sides in a dispute or a war

New Deal: name given to the programs of President Franklin D. Roosevelt

New Federalism: name given to the attempt to lessen the federal government role in its dealings with states during the presidencies of Nixon and Reagan

New Freedom: name given to the programs of President Woodrow Wilson

New Frontier: name given to the programs of President John F. Kennedy

New Nationalism: plan under which Theodore Roosevelt ran for President in 1912

nominating convention: political gathering at which a party names candidates for office

noninvolvement: policy of taking no side in international disputes, neutrality

nonrecognition: refusal to establish formal diplomatic relations with the new government of a nation

normalcy: President Warren G. Harding's term for the return to peace after World War I

North American Free Trade Agreement (NAFTA): agreement calling for the removal of trade restrictions between the United States, Canada, and Mexico

nuclear freeze: a halt in the manufacture and deployment of nuclear weapons

nuclear power: energy produced from a controlled atomic reaction

nuclear waste: the byproducts of the production of nuclear power

nullification: a state's refusal to recognize a federal law

Nuremberg Trials: post-World War II trials in which German government and military figures were tried for crimes committed during the war

Open Door Policy: policy toward China set out by Secretary of State John Hay allowing any nation to trade in any other nation's sphere of influence

original jurisdiction: the court in which a case is heard firsthand

overproduction: a condition that exists when the supply of a product exceeds the demand for that product

pacifist: a person who is opposed to war and refuses to fight under any circumstances

pardon: a release from the punishment or legal consequences of a crime granted by a President or governor

parliament: the legislature of Great Britain

patent and copyright laws: laws giving rights to inventions, literary, musical, and artistic works to their creators

patriotism: love and support of one's nation

peaceful coexistence: phrase describing the aim of U.S.–Soviet relations during a time of improved relations between those nations in the 1950s

per capita income: income per person

perestroika: the restructuring of the Soviet Union's economy under Mikhail Gorbachev that began a move toward free enterprise

plantation: large estate farmed by many workers

political party: organized group that seeks to control government through the winning of elections and the holding of public office

political system: the way a nation is governed

poll tax: a tax that must be paid before one can vote, often used in Southern states to discourage or prevent blacks from voting and now banned in national elections by the Twenty-fourth Amendment

pool: method of ending competition used by railroads in the late 1800s in which they divided up business in given areas and fixed prices

popular sovereignty: basic principle of the American system of government that the people are the only source of any and all governmental power

popular vote: votes cast by the people for the electors representing candidates in presidential elections

Populist movement: political movement begun by farmers and members of labor unions in the late 1800s seeking to limit the power of big businesses and grant greater say in the governmental process to individuals

power: control, authority, right

preamble: an introduction to a speech or piece of writing

prejudice: unfavorable opinion about people who are of different religion, race, or nationality

President: the chief executive of a modern republic, especially of the United States

primary: election held before a general election in which voters choose their party's candidates for office

Progressive era: the period of 1900–1920 that saw the greatest action by Progressive reformers

Progressive movement: reform movement that worked to correct abuses in American society

Prohibition: the period 1920–1933 when the making and sale of liquor was illegal in the United States

propaganda: spreading of ideas or beliefs that help a particular cause and hurt an opposing cause

protectionism: belief in policies that favor the protection of domestically produced goods

protective tariff: tax on imports designed to discourage their sale and to favor the development of domestic industry

protectorate: a country under the protection and partial control of a stronger country

public opinion: those attitudes held by a significant number of persons on matters of government and politics; expressed group attitudes

purchasing power: the ability to buy goods and services; the value of what money could buy at one time compared to what the same amount could buy at another time

racial equality: a condition in which people are treated in the same manner by law and society regardless of their race

racism: belief that one race is superior to another

Radical Republicans: group of Republicans in Congress who wanted to protect the rights of freedmen in the South and keep rich Southern planters from regaining political power

ratification: formal approval, final consent to the effectiveness of a constitution, constitutional amendment, or treaty

raw materials: natural substances before processing that will in some way increase their value or usefulness

recession: a decline in economic activity usually shorter and less severe than a depression

Reconstruction: the period 1867–1877 when the federal government or local republican governments ruled the Southern states that had seceded

recovery: a restoring to a normal condition; one of the aims of FDR's New Deal

Red Scare: term used to describe periods in the 1920s and 1950s when American fear and suspicion of communism was at its height

reform: change for the better; one of the goals of FDR's New Deal

regulatory agencies: parts of the federal bureaucracy charged with overseeing different aspects of the nation's economy

religious freedom: the ability to worship as one chooses, guaranteed in this nation by the First Amendment

reparations: payments for losses a nation has suffered during a war

representation: condition of being acted and spoken for in government

representative government: system of government in which voters elect representatives to make laws for them

republic: nation in which voters choose representatives to govern them

Republican party: one of the modern political parties, founded in 1854 in opposition to slavery

reservation: limited area set aside for Native Americans by the U.S. government

reserved powers: those powers held by the state in the American federal system

revenue: income

robber baron: terms used to describe large-scale entrepreneurs of the late 1800s

Roosevelt Corollary: expansion of the Monroe Doctrine announced by President Theodore Roosevelt in 1904 that claimed the United States had the right to intervene in Latin America to preserve law and order

rural: in or of the country

salad bowl theory: idea that people of different backgrounds can exist side by side in the United States, maintaining their identities while still contributing to the overall society

salutary neglect: manner in which England governed the American colonies in the late 1600s and early 1700s, marked by weak enforcement of laws regulating colonial trade

scalawag: white Southerner who supported Radical Republicans during Reconstruction

scarcity: too small a supply

secession: the act of formally withdrawing from membership in a group or organization; in the United States, the withdrawing of 11 southern states from the Union in 1861

sectionalism: strong sense of loyalty to a state or section instead of to the whole country

sedition: an attempt to incite a rebellion against a national government

segregation: separation of people of different races

Selective Service: the military draft name first used during World War I

self-determination: right of national groups to their own territories and their own forms of government

Senate: upper house of the U.S. Congress in which each state has two members

separate but equal: principle upheld in *Plessy* v. *Ferguson* (1896) in which the Supreme Court ruled that segregation of public facilities was legal

separation of church and state: principle set out in the First Amendment that the government shall take no actions to establish or interfere with the practice of religion

separation of powers: the principle that gives the powers of making, enforcing, and interpreting laws to separate legislative, executive, and judicial branches of government

settlement house: a private center providing social services for the poor in a needy neighborhood

sharecropper: farmer who works land owned by another and gives the landowner part of the harvest

sitdown strike: work stoppage in which employees refuse to leave the workplace and occupy it in an attempt to force their employer to come to terms

slavery: condition in which one person is the property of another; banned in this country by the Thirteenth Amendment

social contract theory: the idea that people agreed to give up some rights and powers to a government that would provide for their safety and well-being

Social Darwinism: the belief that the evolutionary idea of "survival of the fittest" applied to societies and businesses

socialism: economic and political system based on the public ownership of the means by which goods and services are produced, distributed, and exchanged

social reform: efforts to better conditions within a society

social security: programs of the federal government to provide economic assistance to the disabled, unemployed, poor, and aged

social welfare: programs to promote public well-being

sovereignty: absolute power of a state within its own territory

soviet: elected assembly in the Soviet Union; (Cap.) pertaining to the Soviet Union

speculator: person who invests in a risky business venture in hopes of making a large profit

spoils system: system or practice of giving appointed offices as rewards from the successful party in an election; name for the patronage system under President Andrew Jackson

Square Deal: name given to programs of President Theodore Roosevelt

stagflation: an economic condition characterized by both inflation and recession

states rights: idea that individual states had the right to limit the power of the federal government

stereotype: a fixed, oversimplified idea about a person or group

stock market: place where shares in corporations are traded

strict interpretation: a literal reading of the Constitution holding that the federal government has only those powers explicitly delegated to it in the Constitution

suburbs: smaller towns surrounding large cities

suffragists: people who campaigned for women's right to vote

summit meetings: conferences of the heads of two or more nations

supply-side economics: the theory that the government can best stimulate the economy by cutting taxes and encouraging investment in business

supremacy clause: Article VI, Section 2 of the Constitution, which makes that document and federal laws and treaties the "supreme law of the land"

Supreme Court: the highest federal court and the final interpreter of the Constitution

surplus goods: extra goods

tariff: tax placed on goods brought into a country

technology: the complete body of ways a society provides itself with material objects

temperance: movement: campaign against the sale or drinking of alcohol

tenant farming: system of farming in which a farmer rents land to farm from a landowner

territorial integrity: condition in which a nation's borders are guaranteed against disturbance by other nations

territory: a political division of the United States before it becomes a state; a large area of land

terrorism: the use of violence, intimidation, and coercion to achieve an end, to gain publicity for a cause, or to disrupt the normal functioning of society

Tet Offensive: 1968 attack by Viet Cong and North Vietnamese forces throughout South Vietnam; a turning point in the Vietnam War

Third World: during the Cold war, nations in the modern world that professed not to be allied with the Soviet Union and its allies or the United States and its allies, especially the developing nations of Asia, Africa, and Latin America

three branches of government: the division of the powers of government into legislative, executive, and judicial functions

three-fifths compromise: compromise reached at the Constitutional Convention of 1787 whereby three-fifths of a state's slave population would be figured into the state's total population

totalitarian: form of government in which the power to rule embraces all matters of human concern

tradition: the handling down of beliefs, customs, and practices from generation to generation

Trail of Tears: the forced movement of Cherokee in 1838–1839 to land west of the Mississippi River

transcontinental railroad: railway extending from coast to coast, completed in 1869

treaty: a formal agreement concluded between two or more countries

Treaty of Versailles: treaty marking the end of World War I that the U.S. Senate refused to ratify

Triple Alliance: name of the alliance of Germany, Austria-Hungry, and Italy before World War I

Triple Entente: name of the alliance of Great Britain, France, and Russia before World War I

trust: group of corporations run by a single board of directors

trustbuster: person who wanted to break up some or all trusts

two-party system: political system in which the candidates of only two major parties have a reasonable chance of winning elections

unconstitutional: not permitted by the constitution of a nation

unilateral action: an action taken by one nation only

unitary government: form of government in which all of the powers are held in a single agency

universal suffrage: the right to vote is extended to all adults

urban: in or of the city

urbanization: process by which more of a nation's population becomes concentrated in its cities

venture capital: money invested in a new corporation or other business enterprise

veto: chief executive's power to reject a bill passed by a legislature

Vietnam War: nation's longest war, fought in Southeast Asia from the late 1950s to 1973

void: without legal force or effect

War of 1812: war between the United States and Great Britain

War Powers Act: law passed in 1973 requiring the President to seek congressional approval if troops are sent into action for longer than 60 days

Weapons of mass destruction: WMD, devices used for large scale and total destruction, i.e. nuclear bombs, nerve gas, chemical warfare.

Whig party: one of the first political parties, standing for the limitation of executive power and the defense of liberty; by the 1850s had declined in power

white-collar worker: someone holding a job in business or in a profession

women's rights movement: the struggle of women for equality

work ethic: a belief that hard work is a virtuous end in itself

World War I: conflict between Allied Powers and Central Powers from 1914 to 1918

World War II: conflict between Allied and Axis nations from 1939 to 1945

yellow journalism: sensational style of reporting used by some newspapers in the late 1800s

yellow peril: derogatory term implying that Asian peoples threatened the ways of life of white Americans

Index

U.S. Regents Tues June 20 per. 9
12 noon sm 232

Possible Essays

① Constitution- foundations/compromises

② Federalism

③ Bill of Rights

④ Foreign Policy

⑤ Impact of Civil war/reconst.

⑥ Gilded Age- monopolies

⑦ Reform Movements- 1840's- 1850's Progressive Era

⑧ Civil rights/women's rights

⑨ Depression

⑩ New Deal

⑪ cold war/containment